The Color Encyclopedia *of*
HOSTAS

The Color Encyclopedia of
HOSTAS

The Color Encyclopedia of
HOSTAS

DIANA GRENFELL

&

MICHAEL SHADRACK

Foreword by
His Royal Highness The Prince of Wales

TIMBER PRESS
Portland · Cambridge

Published in 2004 by

Timber Press, Inc.   Timber Press
The Haseltine Building   2 Station Road
133 S.W. Second Avenue, Suite 450   Swavesey
Portland, Oregon 97204-3527, U.S.A.   Cambridge CB4 5QJ, U.K.

Designed by Susan Applegate
Printed in China

Library of Congress Cataloging-in-Publication Data

Grenfell, Diana.
    The color encyclopedia of hostas / Diana Grenfell and Michael
Shadrack; foreword by HRH The Prince of Wales.
       p. cm.
Includes bibliographical references (p.   ).
ISBN 0-88192-618-3 (hardcover)
    1. Hosta. I. Shadrack, Michael. II. Title.
SB413.H73 G73 2004
635.9'3432–dc22

                                              2003015698

A catalog record for this book is also available from the British Library.

For Roger,
without whose help and forbearance
this book could never have been written.

DIANA GRENFELL

To Kathy, my future.

MICHAEL SHADRACK

CONTENTS

FOREWORD
by
HIS ROYAL HIGHNESS THE PRINCE OF WALES

Hostas have been one of my favourite plants for a long time and even more so when, at Highgrove, I discovered they did well and were not too badly plagued by slugs. The time came when I thought that growing them as collections in several carefully chosen sites would make more impact than having individual hostas or small plantings of hostas scattered all over the garden. I was also mindful of my role as Patron of the N.C.C.P.G....

As the Stumpery was taking shape in the mind's eye, I could immediately envisage the potential of planting substantial groupings of a variety of different, huge-leafed hostas to contrast with the tough, spiny-leafed butcher's broom, and to act as a foil for the delicate tracery of the groups of ferns which would form the remainder of the planting plan. The Stumpery, a revival of the eighteenth century Picaresque movement, was planned as an enclosed glade and designed by Julian and Isabel Bannerman.

As these plantings matured, I began to see the possibilities and benefits of extending the Stumpery into the adjacent Woodland Garden which was about to undergo a long overdue revitalization programme.

It was suggested to me during the planning stage of this new Woodland Garden that I might apply for National Plant Collection status for my ever-increasing collection of very large-leafed hostas. This exciting prospect focused my mind still further on the genus which, although now among the most popular perennials both in the United Kingdom and the United States, has come a very long way from its humble far-eastern origins.

Different categories of National Plant Collections of Hosta already exist, but having the space at Highgrove and the support of a talented and enthusiastic gardening team, I felt that I, too, could play my part by helping to amass a comprehensive collection. In this way both the newest varieties can be assessed for their garden value and I can also help to conserve some almost forgotten varieties, raised and introduced by early pioneers of the genus, which must be saved from disappearing from our gardens. I need hardly say that I am indebted to Diana Grenfell for all the expert advice and help she has given with this particular garden project.

As Patron of the National Council for the Conservation of Plants and Gardens, I warmly welcome the publication of such a comprehensive book written by a leading expert on the genus and illustrated with superb photographs, which cannot but tempt all gardeners who are attracted by exotic, luxuriant-leafed perennials to learn more about this supremely attractive foliage plant.

PREFACE
& ACKNOWLEDGEMENTS

Hostas have moved on since my first book was published in 1990. During the research stage for that book, in addition to my own observations, I waded through all the learned publications available, sifted through the records of various societies, spent days in libraries and museums, wrote numerous letters and made endless telephone calls. Now one only has to switch on the computer to find this information at the touch of a button, and communication is almost instantaneous.

Before the 1990s hosta enthusiasts were thirsting for knowledge and were less discerning—or less critical—about the available hostas, rarely discarding any which were considered less than perfect. Now, thanks to the expeditions being undertaken by more and more collectors, breeders and nursery owners who study hostas in the wild in Japan, Korea and China, we know more about the habitats and conditions in which the species live and so are better able to grow them more successfully in our gardens. We are also learning from scientific research which hostas should no longer be considered species—and that the input of taxonomists on hostas is still in its infancy.

What is most exciting to the gardener is that hostas are now, and have been for several years, the number one perennial plant in the United States. There are, and always were, excellent reasons for this being so. First and foremost is the sheer sumptuousness of their leaves: they outshine the leaves of every other foliage plant in the garden. There is also the diversity of the size, shape and color of the leaves, the ease of cultivation and the quick response to a gar-

dener's care and attention. They have given shade gardening the recognition and cachet it deserves, especially in hot climates, where cool shaded areas are prized over sunny borders. All these qualities have earned hostas their place as the supreme shade plant. Moreover, small and large nurseries as well as tissue-culture laboratories are springing up everywhere, making a huge and ever-increasing range of hostas available to the gardening public.

I have chosen to list the hostas described in this book according to leaf color and type of variegation rather than alphabetically. An alphabetical listing would be an easier and a more obvious way to tackle a book on colorful flowers, but I am suggesting that the leaves of *Hosta* have such a special appeal that the descriptions deserve to be arranged in a directory. I hope this directory will enable readers to make more finely tuned hosta selections for their gardens as they consider how different-colored leaves perform in various garden situations and locations. The final chapter of the directory covers those hostas that experience tells us are mainly for connoisseurs, and I provide explanations in that chapter.

For a number of years I have been aware of a gap in the market for a hosta book that has an illustration accompanying each hosta featured. I am grateful to my constructive and patient editor, Anna Mumford, Timber Press's commissioning editor in the United Kingdom, for offering me the opportunity to write the comprehensively illustrated book I had always hoped to write one day.

Hostas can look ravishing in pictures but only someone

who knows them well and understands their garden value and cultural needs can fully capture their qualities. Over the years at hosta conventions and meetings on both sides of the Atlantic, I have been aware, while taking notes, of Mike Shadrack busy with his camera. The results of his work bore fruit when he won the Hostas and Their Companions section at the American Hosta Society's annual Hosta in Focus Photographic Weekend in 1997. His pictures feature regularly in the American Hosta Society's journals and, more recently, in the gardening press and hosta specialist nursery catalogues. Mike was undoubtedly the obvious person to collaborate with me on this project, and it has been a joy to work with such a professional and good-humored colleague.

Many people have helped me in the preparation of this book and I am grateful to them all, but I should like to single out Dr. Warren Pollock for his valuable contribution by vetting the text for American hosta growers.

The number of books on hostas now published has made researching them considerably easier. Nevertheless, a book of this complexity could not have been written without the help of hosta enthusiasts who have freely shared with me their knowledge and experience, much of it garnered over many years. I extend my thanks, in alphabetical order, to Michelle and Tony Avent, Dr. Gwen Black, Ann and Roger Bowden, Sandra Bond, Leila Bradfield, Chris Brickell, Mary Chastain, Donald Church, Oscar and Peter Cross, Ian Crystal, Una Dunnett, Clarence Falstad, Joyce and Marco Fransen, Roger Grounds, Kathy Guest, Dr. Joe Halinar, Hans Hansen, Jack Hirsch, Jay Hislop, David Howard, Bob Kuk, Gary Lindheimer, Ran Lydell, Bill Meyer, Lu and Dan Nelson, Peg and Ray Prag, Charles Purtymun, Jean and Peter Ruh, Tim Saville, W. George Schmid, Jim Schwarz, Barry Sligh, Nancy and Bob Solberg, Alex Summers, Susan and Alan Tower, The Virginia Tech Entomology Department, Shirley and Van Wade, Kevin Walek, Mary Walters, Jerry Webb and Dr. James Wilkins.

DIANA GRENFELL

I WOULD LIKE TO THANK the countless hosta people in England, Holland, France, Canada and the United States who have allowed me to photograph their plants over the years. Special thanks are due to Van and Shirley Wade, Dr. Ed Elslager, Marco and Joyce Fransen, W. George Schmid, Ann and Roger Bowden, Bob Kuk, Sandra Bond, Peter and Jean Ruh, Margo and Udo Dargatz, Dr. Gwen Black and Dick and Jane Ward. They all allowed me unfettered access to their large hosta collections and gave so freely of their knowledge and advice.

MIKE SHADRACK

CHAPTER ONE

HOSTAS *in the* WILD

HOSTAS ARE NATIVES OF THE FAR EAST, with their center of distribution being Japan. Outlying species occur in China and Korea. Hostas are thought to have evolved from lilylike ancestors that migrated from east-central China by two different routes that recombined some time later to produce the hostas we know today. One group went by a northerly route through southeastern Russia and thence southward into Hokkaido and Honshu. The more primitive group, ancestors of the present-day *Hosta plantaginea*, migrated via a more southerly route through southern Manchuria into the Korean peninsula and from thence to southern Japan. In the aeons it took them to migrate, the two populations became substantially differentiated, though not sufficiently so in their reproductive organs to prevent cross-pollination. The Japanese mainland, with its great diversity of physical and climatological habitats, encouraged further differentiation, although only those populations that were physically isolated have remained distinct. Plainly, most wild populations have been interbreeding for many centuries, whereas those that were geographically isolated have now been largely brought together by the intervention of man.

The wild species of *Hosta* are typically clump-forming perennial plants, most of which have broadly or narrowly heart-shaped leaves and clusters of lilylike flowers carried on upright stems just above the foliage mound. Typically, the wild species grow on forest margins or in open glades in woodlands, and it is from these that most garden varieties have been derived. A number of lesser-known species have adapted to growing in quite different habitats. *Hosta hypoleuca*, for example, can grow in dense shade, enveloped in thick mist, but equally well clinging to near-vertical, sun-baked volcanic cliffs in which it produces just one large leaf, the back of which is covered in fine white power that protects it from the sun's heat that is reflected off bare rocks. At the other extreme, the grassy-leaved *H. longissima* grows in damp, cloud-shrouded meadows at high altitudes where its thin leaves are shaded in summer by taller miscanthus grasses. A few diminutive species, such as *H. venusta,* with leaves no bigger than a thumbnail, grow as epiphytes on mossy tree trunks, while *H. alismifolia* forms extensive colonies in wet sphagnum bogs and *H. kiyosumiensis* perches on rocks or mossy tree roots at the edges of streams, trailing its roots in the water.

All the wild species of *Hosta* and the cultivated varieties too are reliably hardy. They require winter chilling to less than 40°F (4.4°C) for several weeks to achieve proper dormancy. The underground parts can remain unharmed even when the ground around them is frozen solid for long periods.

Most of the wild species grow in areas of dense shade with much higher rainfall than is typical in areas where they are most widely cultivated. On the main islands of Japan, the average annual precipitation is 62 ³⁄₁₆ in. (1555 mm), a figure that in America can only be matched or bettered by the Pacific Northwest, with 61 to 81 ⁵⁄₁₆ in. (1524 to 2032 mm), in Europe only by Scotland, with 50 ¹³⁄₁₆ to 61 in. (1270 to 1524 mm) and by the west coast of New Zealand, with 81 5/16 in. (2032 mm). By comparison, the Northeastern and Midwestern states of America receive only 20 5/16 to 40 5/8 in. (508 to 1016 mm) of rain, the same as most of Europe, including England, and southeastern Australia.

While a few *Hosta* species, typically those with thin leaves, naturally grow in marshy or boggy conditions, and a few in habitats where they are periodically or regularly submerged, the majority grow in moisture-retentive but free-draining soils or other media. The conditions favored by hostas are generally those with high relative humidity, especially in summer, when humidity can reach 75 to 80 percent. Inclement weather is not uncommon in the wild habitats of hostas. In addition to frosts and snowfalls, ice and hail storms also occur, as well as severe tropical storms. These events devastate the top growth of the hostas but seldom damage their roots so that in time the hostas recover.

The long-tubed flowers of *Hosta plantaginea*.

CHAPTER TWO

HOSTAS *in the* WEST

History

Long before hostas reached the West they were selected for their ornamental value and cultivated in Japan and possibly in China and Korea for literally hundreds of years. The first Westerner ever to knowingly see a hosta, and certainly the first to draw and describe one, was Engelbert Kaempfer (1651–1715), a medical doctor with the Dutch East India Company stationed on Deshima, an artificial island in Nagasaki harbor. He was never allowed to visit the mainland, Japan still being fiercely hostile to foreigners, but he made reasonably accurate drawings of two hostas, one of which was later identified as *Hosta* 'Lancifolia'. The first hosta to actually reach the West was *H. plantaginea*, seed of which was sent to the Jardin des Plantes in Paris by the French consul in Macao sometime between 1784 and 1789. With its large, pure white flowers and exotic fragrance it was soon being grown by the thousands in public gardens throughout France, from whence it was distributed to the rest of Europe. A second Chinese species, *H. ventricosa*, followed soon after, and was first cultivated in a private botanic garden in London.

It was not until forty years later that hostas from Japan started reaching the West. The person responsible for their arrival was Philipp von Siebold (1791–1866), another botanizing medical doctor with the Dutch East India Company. His first shipment arrived in Europe in 1829, and more shipments followed. The hostas, as well as other plants, were grown on in Siebold's nursery in Ghent and later dispersed to botanic and other gardens across Europe,

some varieties eventually reaching America. Other notable plant hunters followed, such as Robert Fortune (1813–1880), and the collecting of hostas in their wild habitats goes on to this day, although it is now strictly controlled by international agreements. In 1985 an expedition mounted by the U.S. National Arboretum in Washington, D.C., under the auspices of the Friends of the Arboretum and led by Barry Yinger, introduced two species not previously known in the West, and an expedition by members of the American Hosta Society (AHS) in 1995 introduced other, previously unknown varieties. In 1997 Tony Avent, Dan Hinkley, Darrell Probst and Bleddyn and Sue Wynn-Jones undertook an expedition to South Korea, where several new forms of *Hosta* were collected. Both George Schmid and Mark Zilis, in preparation for the publication of their superb books, have also studied hosta species in their native habitats, which has greatly added to our knowledge. In Japan itself, new species and varieties are still being discovered, and there are probably more to be found in China and Korea.

The first major shipment of hostas to reach America directly from Japan was organized by Thomas Hogg Jr. The son of a London nurseryman of the same name who had migrated to America, Thomas was made a United States marshal by President Lincoln, who sent him to Japan in 1862. While there he bought hostas, especially variegated ones, from street markets and it is likely that these hostas were included in the consignments of plants he sent back to the family nursery in Manhattan.

The bell-shaped flowers of *Hosta ventricosa*.

especially temple gardens, and that the plants were in fact garden varieties, having been selected and maintained in cultivation by gardeners. This has led to problems in their naming and in the way their names are expressed. For example, *Hosta decorata* was so named when it was thought to be a species, even though it has white-margined leaves, and the species name was expressed in italics to denote its specific status. Now that it is known to be a garden variety, its second name is usually written in Roman type, inside single quotation marks, as in 'Decorata', to show that it is a cultivated variety. However, taxonomists seem unable to agree about this plant's status. The variegated form of *Hosta* 'Decorata' is sometimes known as *H. decorata* var. *decorata*, while the wild, green-leaved version is known as *H. decorata* f. *normalis*. Such terminological confusion may be unnecessary since the plants are plainly cultivated varieties.

Classification

Hostas are monocotyledonous plants (meaning they produce one seed leaf, not two) and were for a long time placed in the family Liliaceae. This placement was not satisfactory since Liliaceae was a huge family embracing an extraordinarily varied selection of disparate plants. Under a new system of classifying the monocotyledons that was originally devised by R. M. T. Dahlgren, H. T. Clifford and P. F. Yeo in 1985 and adopted by the Royal Botanic Gardens, Kew, in 1987, hostas are now placed in their own family, Hostaceae. This classification is generally accepted today.

The name *Hosta* was first applied to this genus in 1812. It honors the Austrian botanist Nicholas Thomas Host (1761–1834), who wrote a flora of Austria. The name was supplanted for some years, however, by the name *Funkia*, which honors Heinrich Christian Funk, a botanist of whom little is now known. The term *Funkia* will be found in books by Gertrude Jekyll, William Robinson and their contemporaries, and it is still used as a vernacular name for hostas in many parts of Europe. However, the correct naming of plants is now governed by two international codes, the *International Code of Nomenclature for Cultivated Plants* and the *International Code of Botanical Nomenclature*, and under these codes, *Hosta* has been determined as the correct name for this genus.

When hostas first reached the West, botanists generally assumed that they were all species, even though many of them were variegated. It turns out that some of these hostas had been found by the early collectors not in the wild (where they were seldom allowed to go) but in gardens,

Botany

Hostas are frost-hardy perennial herbs that arise from short, sometimes rhizomatous, white, fleshy roots. The leaves, which are stalked and varied in size from small to large, rise directly from the rootstock and form rounded or spreading mounds. The flowers are large by botanical standards, tubular, flared and funnel- or spider-shaped, usually with six spreading lobes called tepals They vary in color from white to deep purple and are presented in a raceme at the top of a usually unbranched scape. The reproductive organs at the heart of each flower consist of six stamens (the male organs) that rest on the tube of the flower and protrude from it, their tips upturned like an eyelash, and of a stigma, a style and an ovary (the female organs). If fertilized, the ovary will swell into an elongated, many-chambered capsule, and seed will mature in about six weeks. Plants start into growth as the ground warms in the spring, withering away at the onset of winter, perennating as roots with dormant buds.

The shape of a hosta is primarily determined by its root type. Those hostas with compact root systems produce rounded mounds of foliage, whereas those with running rootstocks produce spreading colonies of foliage.

LEAVES

The leaves of hostas arise directly from the crown, the fibrous collar that connects the above-ground parts to the below-ground parts. They are made up of two parts, the petiole (stalk) and the blade, and the two are usually clearly differentiated. However, in a few species and cultivars, such

The emerging shoots of *Hosta* 'El Capitan'.

The spider-shaped flowers of *Hosta laevigata*.

The expanding shoots of *Hosta* 'El Capitan'.

The funnel-shaped flowers of *Hosta* 'Yellow Splash'.

as *Hosta longissima*, the two are confluent. The size and shape of both can be diagnostic.

The petioles are never quite flat but are, in varying degrees, U- or V-shaped. The color of the petiole is normally the color of the blade, possibly in a paler tone, and any variegation is carried down into the petiole. Some species, in particular *Hosta longipes* and *H. pycnophylla*, have distinctly red- or purple-dotted petioles. This trait was originally passed on automatically to many hybrids and considered of no particular significance. Among the first hybrids to be prized for this characteristic was *H.* 'Regal Rhubarb'. Now breeders are making crosses to create even brighter red petioles (*H.* 'Emeralds and Rubies' and *H.* 'Fire Island' are two examples), and in the latest hybrids, such as *H.* 'One Man's Treasure', the red dots are visible well into the base of the leaf blade.

Most hostas pass through both juvenile and adult phases producing both juvenile and adult leaves, and these usually differ in shape. For the purposes of this book, an adult (mature) hosta (one which produces adult leaves) is one that has completed its sixth growing season after root division. Many hostas also produce summer leaves that are different from their vernal leaves. In the directory section of this book, the leaves described are adult leaves unless otherwise stated.

The leaves of hostas are classified in various ways, by size, shape, leaf blade, venation, substance, finish and color.

The leaves of hostas fall into one of the six **SIZE** categories determined by the American Hosta Society. They are as follows:

Class 1 (Giant)	144 sq. in. (900 cm²) and larger
Class 2 (Large)	81–144 sq. in. (530–900 cm²)
Class 3 (Medium)	25–81 sq. in. (160–530 cm²)
Class 4 (Small)	6–25 sq. in. (36–160 cm²)
Class 5 (Miniature)	2–6 sq. in. (13–36 cm²)
Class 6 (Dwarf)	2 sq. in. (13 cm²) or less

Leaf **SHAPE** is described in terms of leaf length to width ratios:

Oval	2:1 or 3:2
Broadly oval	6:5
Round	1:1
Elliptical	3:1
Lance-shaped	6:1

Definitions of the shapes of hosta leaves and the possible variations on tip and base shapes may seem very exact, but in practice the leaves in any one clump of hosta may vary considerably and fall between definitions. The base of the leaf or lobes may be:

heart-shaped (cordate): having two equal, rounded lobes on each side of the petiole where the petiole joins the leaf blade. On round leaves, the lobes will be conspicuously overlapping or folded.
truncate: where the leaf appears to have been cut straight across.
wedge-shaped (cuneate): with the leaf's sides straight but converging.
attenuate: with the sides of the leaf curved and converging.

The tip of the leaf may be:

mucronate: coming abruptly to a sharp point, as in *H.* 'Tokudama'.
cuspidate: tapering gradually to a sharp point, as in *H. montana*.

Hosta 'Fire Island', petioles.

Hosta 'Emeralds and Rubies'

acute: coming straight to a sharp point, as in *H.* 'Lancifolia'.
obtuse: rounded with a vestigial point, as in *H.* 'Decorata'.

The margins of hostas are usually entire; that is they are rarely toothed, cut or lobed. Occasionally there may be very slight serrations. Margins may also be flat, undulate, rippled or evenly and deeply rippled, which, in hosta parlance, is known as "piecrusted."

The midrib is lighter in color than the blade, often colorless, and can appear to pierce the blade, particularly in glaucous, self-colored leaves.

The **LEAF BLADE** may be level, undulate or twisted and can be shallowly or deeply cupped, as in *Hosta* 'Abiqua Drinking Gourd'. The surface may also be smooth, as in *H.*

'Gay Blade', dimpled, as in *H*. 'Blue Wedgwood', seersuck-ered, as in *H*. 'Midas Touch', puckered, as in *H*. 'Millenium', or furrowed, as in *H. montana*. Although the veins may give a ridged effect, the finish of the blade's upper surface can be matt, as in *H*. 'Gold Standard', satiny, as in *H*. 'Fragrant Bouquet', shiny, as in *H*. 'Bubba', or glaucous, as in *H. sieboldiana* 'Elegans'.

The **VEINS** on hosta leaves are arranged in a form called campylodrome, which means the veins that enter the leaf at its base curve outward as the leaf widens and inward as the leaf narrows toward the tip. The veins can appear deeply impressed when seen from above and prominently raised when seen from below.

The leaves of hostas, that is, the area between the veins, may be thick or thin, and this is known as their **SUBSTANCE**. It is sometimes incorrectly called their texture. The greater the substance, the stiffer and more rigid are the leaves.

The leaves are always smooth (glabrous), that is without hairs or roughness. They may be matt or shiny, but most have an in-between **FINISH** known as satiny.

The leaves of the wild species of hostas are normally green, though variegated sports do occasionally occur. **COLOR** in the leaves arises from pigments carried in bodies called plastids, the dominant plastids throughout the plant kingdom being green ones called chloroplasts. Different colors are the result of other pigments carried in other chloroplasts, but since all chloroplasts are very similar, it takes only a minute change or error in replication for chloroplasts to slip from one color to another. This slippage seems to happen more frequently with hostas than with other plants.

The growing tip or meristem of a plant is always essentially the same, but different parts of the plant develop from different parts of the growing tip. Hosta leaves are made up of three layers, known as L1, L2 and L3. L1 is the outer layer or epidermis, and it is particularly important in the formation of leaf margins. If colored plastids occur in this layer, the leaf will have a colored margin. L2 is the middle layer of the leaf, and if colored plastids arise here they will produce a colored center to the leaf. Perhaps surprisingly, plastids can move from one layer of a leaf to another. Colored plastids originating in L2 can move to L1, and this is what happens when a streaked hosta turns into a hosta with a marginal variegation. Plastids can lose their coloring as easily as they become colored, which is what happens when a variegated hosta leaf sports to a single color. All variegation is thus more or less unstable, though marginal variegations are usually more stable than central variegations.

FLOWERS

The flowers of hostas are borne in racemes at the tops of **SCAPES** (stems) which arise directly from the rootstock or crown at the base of the leaf mound. The scapes themselves are usually round and solid, rarely hollow, as in *Hosta minor*, occasionally ridged, as in *H. minor* and *H. venusta*, and usually simple and rarely branched, as in *H. tibae*. They may be upright or may lean, and can be straight or curved. In the following descriptions, the measurement given for scapes refers to the length, not the height.

The individual flowers are held away from the scape by short stems known as **PEDICELS**. These may hold the flower away from the scape at a right angle or may allow the flower to droop. The pedicels emerge from bracts on the scape, which are known as flower bracts. In some species and cultivars, these flower bracts are so small they can scarcely be seen with the naked eye, while in others they are so large that they may be taken for true leaves, as in *H. kikutii*. Most flower bracts fall between these extremes. They typically wither once flowering is over.

Some hostas have a second type of bract on the flower scape, and these are known as foliaceous or **LEAFY BRACTS**. They are also called inflorescent leaves. Leafy bracts can always be distinguished from flower bracts because they occur only on the lower part of the scape beneath the flowers. The largest leafy bracts occur toward the base of the scape, and the bracts are usually outward-facing, rarely small and stem-clasping. In several species and varieties, these bracts can be showy, and if the true leaves are variegated, the bracts will be similarly variegated, as in *H*. 'Undulata'.

The raceme or flower cluster may be dense, as in *Hosta* 'Blue Moon', or sparse, as in *H. sparsa*. The flowers are usually disposed to one side of the scape, called secund, an exception being *H*. 'Koryu', in which the flowers are disposed all around the scape, called whorled. The flowers of hostas each last only a day. They are bisexual, the female organs consisting of an ovary (with three cavities) at the base of the flower from which arises a long, tubular style at the tip of which is a three-lobed stigma that receives pollen in season. These are surrounded by the male organs consisting of six stamens, at the tips of which are the anthers, which produce pollen. The style is usually longer than the stamens, but both usually protrude from the mouth of the flower. All are surrounded by and contained within the flower (perianth), which consists of a narrow tube followed by a flaring section composed of six lobes. Three of these lobes are exterior lobes (which is actually the calyx), and three are interior lobes (the corolla), but they are scarcely differentiated and are called tepals or, more commonly, lobes or petals. In outline, the flowers of hostas may be funnel-shaped (infundibuliform), bell-shaped (campanulate) or spider-shaped (arachnoid), though the latter are basically funnel-shaped but with narrow, widely separated lobes. Many flowers fall between these two extremes, and most cultivars have more or less flaring flowers. In one species, *H. clausa*, for example, and its varieties, the flowers remain closed and then fall away from the pedicel.

Pollination occurs when the pollen of one plant reaches the stigma of another (mechanisms exist to prevent self-pollination). The pollination of hostas is chiefly carried out by insects. After a grain of pollen lands on a stigma, it grows a pollen tube down through the hollow style to the ovary, carrying the male gametes with it. Once the tube reaches the ovary, it discharges the gametes and fertilization takes place.

Hosta flowers vary in color within a limited spectrum. Typically, most are described in terms of lavender, but they can vary from white through to deep purple, often with stripes of a deeper tone. The amount of red in the coloration will determine whether the flower color is perceived as leaning more toward blue or mauve.

SEED

If fertilized, the ovaries of hostas swell into oval, many-chambered pods that are usually the same color as the leaves

The opening buds in a dense cluster, *Hosta* 'Deep Blue Sea'.

(and often variegated if the leaves are variegated). The pods ripen about six weeks after fertilization. On opening they reveal three chambers, and in each chamber, there are two rows of flat, oval seeds that are shiny and black if fertile or pale beige or white if infertile. A few varieties produce pods that do not contain seeds or they produce no pods at all, in which case the scapes wither after flowering. Both are usually denoted as sterile varieties. Fertile seed usually germinates quickly and easily.

CHAPTER THREE

The CULTIVATION *of* HOSTAS

THE ART OF GROWING GOOD HOSTAS lies in understanding their needs and in providing them. In broad terms, hostas need a fertile soil that is moist but well drained, a measure of protection against the heat of the sun and shelter from strong winds. However, they vary greatly in their individual requirements, and fine-tuning is needed to get the best from a wide range of hostas.

General Considerations of Climate

Hostas are hardy perennial plants well adapted to cultivation throughout the temperate world and, to a lesser degree, in some subtropical regions. They are reliably frost tolerant to about 28°F (−2°C). They can tolerate summer temperatures as high as 100°F (38°C), and somewhat higher for short times. Heat dormancy occurs above temperatures of 95°F (35°C). All hostas require a measure of winter chilling to below 40°F (4.4°C) for several weeks as part of their annual cycle of growth and rest.

Since hostas in the wild receive far higher rainfall than they are likely to receive in cultivation in the West, that amount needs to be supplemented to raise it to about 1 in. (25 mm) per week while the hostas are in active growth. Hostas are also very drought tolerant, but when they are under stress from drought, their leaves will wither and burn. They are also tolerant of temporary flooding but will not stand long periods of inundation when dormant.

Soil

Hostas are tolerant of a wide range of soil types but grow best in a rich, friable loam with a pH of about 6. They are less happy on shallow soils over chalk. Varieties with green in their leaves tend to exhibit the typical symptoms of chlorosis: the areas between the veins turn yellow or yellowish while the veins remain green; blue-leaved varieties assume a muddy tinge.

Large hostas, such as *Hosta sieboldiana*, grow well on heavy clay soils that are rich in plant nutrients, but they take time to become established. They will establish more quickly and grow better if the ground is thoroughly prepared before planting. Given that the roots of a hosta spread out below ground to the edge of the leaf mound or beyond and that a mature specimen of *H. sieboldiana* or *H. montana* can be 6 to 8 ft. (180 to 240 cm) across, one should prepare a planting hole 6 to 8 ft. across. Preparing the soil means incorporating lavish quantities of coarse grit and organic materials to a depth of at least one spit (the depth of a spade's blade) and in equal amounts by volume. Since clay soils tend to revert to clay over time, it is important to maintain the gains made by the incorporation of these materials by continuing to use them as a mulch in succeeding years.

The problems posed by sandy soils are quite different, though the remedy is much the same. Sandy soils are poor

Hosta montana f. *macrophylla*

largely because they are free draining, meaning that nutrients quickly get washed through them. Hostas in such soils rapidly develop large root systems that go in search of water and nutrients, though the plant's top-growth is often sparse. To grow good hostas on sandy soils, it is essential to add large amounts of organic matter and to mulch with similar materials in succeeding years. The hostas may also need regular feeding with packaged organic materials, such as pelleted chicken manure or animal manure, proprietary fertilizers or a foliar feed.

Small and miniature hostas have quite different soil requirements from the larger ones and may not thrive in competition with the larger ones. Their prime requirement is for a free-draining but moisture-retentive growing medium, and this is most readily created by adding plenty of grit to the soil and then mulching it with finely chopped peat, leaf-mold or a similar material. Coarse materials should not be used as they may smother the hosta. Collections of small and miniature hostas are probably best grown in gravel gardens or in raised beds filled with spe-

cially prepared soil. The beds can be created using peat blocks, decaying tree trunks or branches, brick or stone or railroad ties or sleepers.

Sun and Shade

Hostas are widely thought of as shade-tolerant or even shade-loving plants but this is only part of the story. While shade seems essential for the protection of the large expanses of hosta leaves, more sun is required to produce good flowers. Many hostas will grow in a great deal more sunlight than the conditions in which they are normally planted, provided they receive sufficient moisture at the roots.

Shade is created whenever something intervenes between the sun and some third object. But shade is more than merely the absence of direct sunlight. The presence of shade modifies the climate in the shaded area, making it generally cooler and more humid, while at the same time moderating the extremes of diurnal and seasonal temperature

Hosta 'Lakeside Black Satin' needs a site in full shade to produce its exceptionally dark green leaves.

fluctuations, making the air more humid and enabling the soil to retain a more constant level of moisture.

Most hostas in cultivation do need to be grown in more or less shaded conditions, but this is partly because they seldom receive the amount of moisture at their roots that they really need. However, there are notable exceptions. *Hosta plantaginea* and its hybrids can be grown in full sun in most regions; indeed, in the United Kingdom it will not flower unless grown in the sun. For most hostas, a balance has to be struck between the amount of moisture available and the amount of sun reaching the leaves. The more moisture at the roots, the more sun the leaves will tolerate. In an experiment conducted by the author, *H.* 'Francee' was grown for several years in a pot standing up to its crown in a pond in sunlight all day long without so much as a scorched margin. In normal soils, the same hosta has to be grown in dappled shade to prevent leaf burn.

Shade can vary considerably in its quality or intensity. The sort of shade cast by thin, high cloud is quite different from that cast by the canopy of dense, evergreen trees, by a brick wall or a solid fence. In general, hostas need good light such as the kind they would receive at the foot of a north wall (in the Northern Hemisphere) where they are shaded from direct sunlight yet receive good light from the open skies above. Light, dappled shade cast by a high tree canopy is also ideal. Hostas will not flourish in dense shade and should never be planted in parts of the garden that are too shaded for anything else to grow. Using a felt bag coated with a copper solution will help to ameliorate competition from tree roots.

As a generalization, hostas with blue-green leaves suc-

ceed best in shaded places, as do hostas with white variegation, whether central or marginal. Hostas with green, chartreuse or yellow leaves will take more sun provided that there is adequate moisture at the roots. Most hostas multiply best in sun because this gives them the maximum opportunity to photosynthesize, which is why hosta nursery people often grow them in rows in fields. Their leaves may be scorched and deformed with such exposure, but they soon recover once in cultivation.

CREATING AND REDUCING SHADE

Shade is most naturally created by planting trees, although trees tend to go on growing beyond their desired size and have roots that may compete directly with the hosta roots. The choice of tree is important. Beeches (*Fagus*), birches (*Betula*), cherries (*Prunus*), large maples (*Acer*) and willows (*Salix*) have roots that run just below the soil's surface and are best avoided. Cherries, poplars (*Populus*) and wingnuts (*Pterocarya*) produce undesirable quantities of suckers. Some cherries and willows have roots that make an impenetrable mat, and it is hopeless to try to grow hostas near them. Gum trees (*Eucalyptus*) and shagbark hickories (*Carya ovata*) shed their bark in unsightly strips that can damage hostas as they fall. Lime trees (*Tilia*) attract aphids that drip honeydew on all beneath them. Oak trees (*Quercus*), by contrast, put their roots down deeply, well below those of the hostas, as do many genera of small, ornamental trees. Some suitable ornamental trees include the service trees (*Amelanchier*), the Japanese maples (*Acer palmatum* and its forms), the pagoda tree or honey locust (*Cercidiphyllum japonicum*), the silver bells tree (*Halesia monticola* var. *vestita*), apples and crabs (*Malus*), the black tupelo (*Nyssa sylvatica*), *Sorbus*, *Gleditsia*, *Liquidambar*, *Halesia*, *Stuartia*, *Styrax* and several magnolias, including *Magnolia salicifolia*, *M.* ×*proctoriana* and *M.* ×*loebneri* forms (such as the fragrant, white-flowered *M.* ×*loebneri* 'Merrill' and the pink *M.* ×*loebneri* 'Leonard Messel') as well as *M. sprengeri* and its hybrids (such as *M. sprengeri* 'Spectrum' and *M. sprengeri* 'Star Wars').

Many large shrubs that ultimately form small, multi-stemmed trees can cast enough shade for a small collection of hostas, or indeed a collection of small hostas. Among the best of these are the various witch hazels (*Hamamelis*), the taller, winter-flowering viburnums, the hazel (*Corylus*) in its color-leaved forms and photinias, such as *Photinia* 'Birmingham' and *P.* 'Red Robin' with their new, red leaves.

If shade is too dense for hostas to flourish, whole trees may have to be removed, but all that is generally needed is to remove the lower branches, so raising the canopy. A raised canopy will allow light and air in.

ARTIFICIAL SHADE

One way to beat the problems of ever-increasing shade cast by trees and their constantly invading roots is to use an artificial structure such as a pergola or a shade house (also known as a lath house). Shade houses look roughly like greenhouses but are usually constructed of stout uprights linked by less bulky tie-bars to which are attached roofing laths. In the Northern Hemisphere, lath houses should be oriented so that the ridge runs east-west, and the laths themselves run north-south. This alignment of the laths ensures that as the sun appears to move across the sky, the shadows cast by the laths move across the hostas at a steady rate. If the laths were aligned east-west, the movement of the shadows would be much less and the amount of sun reaching the hostas might be enough to damage the leaves. If 2 in. (5 cm) laths are used, then the spacing between them should be 2⅜ to 2¾ in. (6 to 7 cm), but this spacing can be varied along the length of the house, so allowing for hostas that like deeper shade to be grown at one end, and those that prefer more sun at the other.

Pergolas may seem in many ways an ideal compromise between living trees and artificial structures since, once covered in climbing plants, they can take on a fairly natural appearance. The problem, as is the case with trees, is that many climbers have greedy roots. *Fallopia baldschuanica*, for example, has roots that spread far and wide, while many honeysuckles (*Lonicera*) make dense mats of roots in which little else will grow. Moreover, many climbers soon cast too dense a shade, but if they are cut back, they will cast insufficient shade. It can be difficult to get the balance right.

What to Look for When Buying Hostas

The two factors which contribute most to the success of hostas are the buying of a good plant in the first place and the proper preparation of the ground.

The most important things to look for when buying a hosta are healthy leaves and healthy roots. The leaves, if they are present, should be turgid, of good color and not discolored; they should also not show signs of any physical damage. The roots too should be plump and white, and they should be plentiful enough to bind the soil without filling the pot or encircling the bottom of the pot. If the soil falls away from the roots, the plant has not been in the pot long enough to establish itself, and if the roots fill too much of the pot, it has probably been in the pot too long.

Reject any hosta that has poor, mainly brown roots or that has any sign of damage to the roots. Particular care should be taken when buying tissue-cultured plants, as these are not always properly weaned.

Planting

As a general rule, hostas can be planted at any time when the soil is open and workable. Clearly this varies with local climatic conditions.

WHEN TO PLANT

In a mild, maritime climate, planting can be undertaken at almost any time of year from mild spells in the depths of winter to damp periods in high summer, but in harsher continental climates, the planting season may be more limited. In North Carolina the planting season is usually early May and late August. Planting at these times enables the hostas to establish themselves before both the heat and droughts of summer and the frosts of winter. The best time to plant hostas is when they are actively making new roots. This is not when they are creating the first flush of new leaves but a little later, when the first leaves have hardened off but before the second flush of leaves has started. Some hostas also make a second burst of root growth in late summer once the hottest weather is past. The important thing is to plant hostas at least six weeks before the date of the first killing frost. This gives them time to settle in while the ground is still warm, and it gives the ground time to firm up before the frosts. If planting is left any later, the likely air gaps in the soil will allow the frost to penetrate directly to the roots of the hostas.

PREPARING THE GROUND

The most important single factor in the success of any plant is the thorough prior preparation of the ground. No amount of watering and feeding after planting will make up for poor soil preparation. The ideal soil for hostas is one that is easily worked, is rich in plant foods and that retains moisture while draining well. Most garden soils can be improved by adding organic matter such as peat or coir, finely chopped bark, farmyard manure or good garden compost. Coarse grit should also be added to clays and other heavy soils. The goal of adding all this organic matter to the soil is to produce humus, which is a colloidal black or brown substance that can hold water and bind with the particles of clay soil, making it more open. The organic materials themselves are not humus, and their very coarseness helps create spaces in the soil through which roots can penetrate. However, the bacteria that convert organic matter to humus exhaust much of the available nitrogen in the process, thereby depriving the hostas of vital nitrogen. This means that whenever organic matter is added to the soil, some nitrogen fertilizer should also be applied.

If only a single hosta is to be planted, then a single hole should be dug that is proportional in size to the expected size of the hosta. For large hostas, the hole should be a minimum of 3 ft. (90 cm) in diameter, possibly as much as 5 ft. (150 cm), but since hostas are not deep rooting, the hole need be no more than 18 in. (45 cm) deep. However, it is important to loosen the soil at the bottom of the hole. The hole should then be back-filled with alternating 2¾ in. (7 cm) layers of soil and organic matter. Each layer that is added should be thoroughly mixed with the previous layers and then well firmed with the feet.

Where a larger number of hostas is to be planted, it is simpler to prepare the whole area, either by double-digging or with a mechanical tiller (rotovator). The tiller should be set to its maximum depth and the ground turned over. Any roots or large rocks thrown up in the process should be removed. The area should then be covered with 2¾ to 4 in. (6 to 10 cm) of organic matter and a scattering of balanced, general purpose fertilizer, then tilled again. On all except sandy or gravelly soils, about 1 in. (2.5 cm) of coarse grit or pea-shingle should then be spread over the area, and this too should be tilled into the ground. The planting area or the individual holes should be left to settle for several weeks before planting begins.

HOW TO PLANT

At planting time, dig a hole large enough to take all the hosta roots, well spread out, not bent or folded. Then make a small mound in the middle of the hole so that the crown of the hosta can rest on that with the roots running downhill. The roots of the hosta should be teased out and spread over the sides of the mound. This is particularly important with pot-grown hostas whose roots may be very congested. Then return the soil to the hole, firming it with hands or feet. Finally, water the hosta thoroughly. The soil around the hosta should be mulched to keep the roots cool and prevent water loss through its surface.

Watering

Hostas being natives of areas of high rainfall have therefore evolved a metabolism that demands plenty of water at the roots, a trait they have brought with them into cultivation and passed on to the modern hybrids grown in gardens. Leaves that are deprived of sufficient precipitation will wilt and turn yellow, and if the situation persists, the plants may die back to their overwintering buds. Although they may start into growth again once there is sufficient moisture in the soil, the leaves will be much smaller than before. Thus, for hostas to thrive, it is essential to ensure a sufficient and regular supply of water during the growing season.

While it may seem self-evident that the best way to water plants is by whatever means most nearly resembles rainfall, this is certainly not the case with hostas. Overhead artificial watering can lead to water lying on the leaves, which can in turn cause them to rot, become the focus of fungal infections and attract slugs and snails. Overhead watering of blue-leaved hostas can severely damage the glaucous bloom, since the individual water droplets hitting the leaves actually erode the waxy coating. Even fine mist sprays, which do not cause actual physical damage, can leave unsightly chalky or other discolorations.

Lightly sprinkling hostas using overhead irrigation is also harmful because such a practice only dampens the surface of the soil, resulting in roots that turn upward toward the surface to get what little water is available instead of in deep, life-sustaining roots. The hostas thus become extraordinarily vulnerable in times of drought.

Water is best applied directly to the roots of hostas, beneath the leaves, using a watering can without a rose, a watering wand attached to a hose, or a hose that is left trickling slowly for several hours. Seep hoses are an excellent means of applying water in the right place and can be looped around clumps of hostas, though the girth of the loop must be increased every year. Watering is best done in the early morning to give hostas maximum benefit. Watering in the evening and at night tends to encourage slugs and snails.

The same watering principles apply to hostas in containers. These will need to be watered at least every two to three days from the time the leaves emerge in spring until they die down in the autumn. Very large hostas, especially those growing in sun or in a droughty place, will need as much as 3 gallons (12 liters) of water every day, while hostas of average size will need at least 1 gallon (4.5 liters) a day.

Feeding and Mulching

Hostas only achieve their sumptuous potential if, in addition to adequate supplies of water, they also receive plenty of nourishment from the soil. They are generally considered gross feeders and will respond well to liberal though not excessive applications of manures and fertilizers.

In this age of green awareness, organic feeds such a farmyard manure, garden compost or leaf-mold are much advocated. However, excellent though they are as mulches and as contributors to soil humus levels, their nutritional value varies from batch to batch and is always unbalanced and often negligible. Generally, it is more useful to use artificial fertilizers whose nutritional values are known. These fertilizers may come in the form of granules, pellets or powder; some are liquid feeds that are applied either to the roots or the foliage.

Ideally, hostas should be lightly mulched in spring and autumn and fed in spring and early summer, and this applies both to hostas in the ground and hostas in containers. Any heavy fertilization after mid-summer will promote soft, sappy growth that will be enjoyed by slugs and snails.

The purposes of mulching are firstly to keep the roots cool, secondly to reduce water evaporation through the surface of the soil and thirdly to continue to add humus to the soil. The materials used for mulching tend to vary from area to area, largely depending on local availability and cost. Generally, farmyard manure, peat, coir, cocoa shells, garden compost, shredded bark, crushed corncobs, pine needles, seaweed, salt hay and similar organic materials are suitable. Organic materials eventually decompose and contribute to the humus level in the soil, but inorganic mulches such as stones or gravel are sometimes used, as are plastic or woven materials that suppress weeds.

Where hostas have been planted singly, the mulch should be applied in a ring around the hosta, and care should be taken not to bury the crown itself as this might cause it to rot in the winter. The mulch should be spread up to or beyond the circumference of the leaf mound. However, while most hostas are frost hardy throughout the temperate world, it is sometimes expedient to cover the crowns lightly with straw, dry fern fronds or salt hay to prevent heaving in alternating spells of cold and warmth. The mulch should not be too thick; a depth of no more than 1 in. (2.5 cm) for large hostas and 3/16 in. (5 mm) for small hostas is usually sufficient. The spread of the mulch should be slightly greater than the anticipated spread of the leaf mound.

Where hostas are planted together in large groups, the mulch should be spread over the whole area, again without covering the crowns. The petioles should not be covered as this can be a cause of fungal diseases, especially Southern stem blight. Mulches that are laid too thickly will create an ideal nesting site for voles and other rodents. Undecayed organic matter, such as fresh lawn mowings and fresh vegetable waste from the house, should be composted before being used in the garden.

Hosta 'Blue Mouse Ears' surrounded by a mulch of small stones.

Growing in Containers

The first essential when growing hostas in containers is to make sure that the containers are large enough to take the roots with room to spare for two or three years of development. The containers should have large enough holes in the bottom to ensure good drainage, but the holes themselves should be covered with crocks (pieces of broken terracotta pots or roof tiles), wire screening or porous matting so that the growing mix does not slip through them. In general, medium to large and very large hostas are best grown in a soil-based growing mix, though medium and small or miniature hostas do better in soilless potting mixes with coarse grit added. If large and very large hostas are grown in soilless mixes, special care must be taken not to let the mix dry out as it is difficult to then rewet, a particular problem for large-leafed hostas that metabolize huge quantities of water daily.

As a result of so much watering, any nutrients in the soil are soon leached out and will need to be replaced. With very large hostas, it is a good idea to put a layer of organic manure such as farmyard manure over the crocks before adding the potting mix and then to mix some organic manure in with the growing mix. Some growing mixes contain fertilizer, but it is usually designed to last for only a few weeks. Several-month controlled-release fertilizer granules or pellets should then be scattered on the growing mix under the plant's leaves, but this should not be done more than once or twice in the growing season, and never after mid-summer. An alternative is a weekly, dilute foliar feed, but again this should not be used after mid-summer.

Any healthy hosta will outgrow its pot sooner or later. It will then need to be moved on to a larger container or split and put back in the same pot but in fresh growing mix. If

Hosta 'Cat's Eyes' in a container.

this is not done, the leaves of the hostas will diminish in size and may become misshapen.

While most hostas are suitable for cultivation in containers, hostas of the Elegans Group, the Golden Medallion Group and the Tokudama Group are usually less successful in containers because they develop a fibrous core at the crown, which impedes their development if they are kept in containers for more than two or three years. On the other hand, hostas of the Fortunei Group, with their finer root system, remain in good condition in containers for longer than average.

Propagation

Hostas can be readily increased by seed or division, but the only way to be certain that the newly propagated hosta will be an exact replica of its parent is to divide it.

DIVISION

The easiest way to increase a large hosta from a well-established clump is to take a slice out of it rather as one would take a slice from a circular cake, using a sharp spade. The slice, once removed, can then be broken down or cut into smaller pieces. For smaller hostas a knife is usually all that is required. Whatever instrument is used should be dipped in a fungicidal solution before and after use, and the cut surfaces of the hostas should also be dusted with a fungicidal powder. The newly separated pieces can then be potted up or planted out to grow on. The hole left by the removal of the original slice should be filled with good garden soil, and after a season or so, the clump will look as though it has never been disturbed.

Alternatively, the whole clump can be dug out of the ground and split by using two forks back-to-back as levers to tease the clump into two or more parts. Once the clumps are out of the ground they can be split down to individual buds or fans of leaves using a sharp knife or saw. Some hostas with a tough, dense and almost woody crown such as *Hosta sieboldiana* must be split with a sharp knife or saw, but other hostas with looser, more diffuse root systems such as *H. sieboldii* can simply be shaken or pulled apart. The roots of most hostas lie somewhere between these extremes.

The number of new plants that can be obtained from an established clump is limited to the number of buds or fans in that clump. The main buds of hostas are normally cone-shaped and mauve or violet (sometimes they are dark brown or almost black), but careful examination of the white rootstock just below the bud will usually reveal a number of much smaller, latent buds. If the main bud is damaged or destroyed, some of these latent buds may start into growth and make new fans of leaves after several weeks. The simplest way of provoking these latent side buds into growth is to trample on the emerging crowns and destroy the shoots as soon as they poke up through the earth in the spring. Alternatively, hostas can be "mown," which involves cutting the leaves off about 3/16 to 3/8 in. (5 to 10 mm) above the ground. Mowing, which is a more certain method of provoking growth than trampling, can be done twice in any one growing season.

A further technique, which can be useful with rare or particularly slow-growing hostas, is known as the "Ross method" after its American inventor, Henry Ross. The earth is scraped away from around the hosta revealing its rootstock. A knife is inserted into a fan of leaves at the point where the leaves emerge from the rootstock and then pushed down through the roots into the soil. The knife is removed and inserted into the same fan of leaves but at right angles to the original insertion, then again pushed down through the roots into the earth. This method of dividing each fan into four without taking the hosta out of the earth can be repeated for every fan of leaves. The soil should be returned around the roots and the plant left to grow on. Some leaves will turn yellow and blotchy over the following weeks, but the plant will soon return to its usual, healthy self. Many nursery people employ a further technique of growing hostas for division in full sunlight since they grow faster that way.

Hostas are usually divided in spring just as the shoots are coming through the surface of the soil, but this is more a counsel of convenience than of perfection: it is easy to see what one is trying to separate when no leaves are in the way. Some people prefer to divide in July or August when the plants are in full leaf because it gives the cut surfaces time to heal and the young plantlets time to make new roots while the soil or growing medium is still warm and before the winter chill sets in. If hostas are divided in high summer their leaves should be cut off to within ³⁄₁₆ to ³⁄₈ in. (5 to 10 mm) of the crown. They will then produce new leaves.

The typical reason for wanting to divide a hosta is simply to increase it, but one might also want to divide a hosta because it has produced a sport. A sport is a part of a plant that is different in character from the original plant, as for example when a stem with double flowers or variegated leaves appears on an otherwise unvariegated plant. It is usually wise to wait until the sport has appeared in more than one season, and then, rather than removing the piece that has sported, remove the parts of the plant that have not sported. Ultimately, the piece that has sported can be lifted and divided, then potted up or grown on.

TISSUE CULTURE

Tissue culture propagation, also known as micropropagation, is merely a form of division. Cells are usually taken from meristematic tissue, for hostas most often a shoot tip, and grown on in a sterile jelly in a test tube under sterile conditions in a laboratory. Temperature, lighting and feeding are manipulated to persuade these cells to grow on into tiny plantlets which, once weaned and further grown on, will exactly resemble the parent plant. Once the cells are established in test tubes, they can be divided again and again, making it possible to produce huge numbers of the same plant far more quickly than by conventional means. A small proportion of the plants produced in this way sometimes fail to conform to the character of the parent plant, and these are usually rogued out and destroyed. Sometimes a plantlet departs from the required true-to-type uniformity in a way that actually makes it more attractive than the original plant. Such sports are then themselves grown on and in due course may be named and tissue cultured. *Hosta* 'June' arose in this way, as have a great many of the new varieties of hosta now coming on the market.

SEED

Most hostas produce abundant seed, and if the seed heads are left standing through the fall for their decorative winter effect, seedlings will likely appear. Hostas are promiscuous, and it is most unlikely that any seedling will have more than a passing resemblance to the seed or pod parent, nor any particular merit of their own. Few will be worthy of space in the garden unless they are the results of crosses deliberately made in pursuit of clear breeding objectives. So high

have hosta breeders raised expectations that only the very best seedlings are now good enough. The only hosta that will come true from seed is *Hosta ventricosa*, which is apomictic.

Not all hostas produce fertile seed, however, and not all seed in any one pod is necessarily fertile. Pods should be picked as soon as they start to open and placed in clearly labeled paper (not plastic) bags. If the pods are picked too soon the immature seeds are likely to rot, but if picked too late, they may already have been shed. Seed should be allowed to fall in the bag and then carefully winnowed. This involves tipping the seeds from the paper bag onto a sheet of white paper so that they can be clearly seen. The husks, any infertile seeds and other debris should be removed because any non-seed matter that remains with the seeds is likely to rot or become infected once sown, which could cause the loss of an entire batch of seed. Seed can either be sown to overwinter and germinate in the spring or stored for spring sowing. Stored seed should be placed in a suitable envelope and clearly labeled, not only with the name of the hosta or the cross, but also with the year. The envelope should be placed in an airtight tin that is stored in a refrigerator until it is needed. Seed normally remains fully viable for six months, though viability varies from variety to variety. The seed of large-flowered, fragrant hostas seems to be much less viable than that of other varieties and should be sown within a month of ripening. The viability of the seed of all other hostas will start to decline after six months, even if it has been stored properly.

Since hosta seeds are fully frost hardy they can be sown out of doors at any time of the year. Other problems, however, may prevent their successful germination. If periods of frost alternate with periods of milder weather, heaving of the soil or growing mix could expose the seeds to the elements, and they may then be eaten by vermin or become desiccated. Sowing seeds in frames or under glass allows for greater control over such hazards. Once the seed has germinated, the seedlings should be kept shaded and watered until they are large enough to prick out into individual pots. Eventually they should be lined out in beds or planted where they are to grow in the garden. Many professional growers grow their hostas on under artificial lights since this enhances their photosynthetic rate.

HYBRIDIZING

The purpose of hybridizing hostas is to try to raise new hostas that seem, if only in the eyes of the breeder, to be an improvement on other hostas. Breeders should be clear in their own minds about what improvement or improvements they are seeking so that they can select the most suitable parents and also have a yardstick by which to judge whether the objective has been achieved.

Crossing plants is a simple matter of transferring the pollen from the anthers of the pollen parent to the stigma of the pod parent. The real skill, however, lies firstly in preventing the pod parent from being pollinated beforehand by unwanted insects, and secondly in getting the timing right. The usual practice is to use a razor blade to slit the bud of the pod parent open before it opens naturally and then to cut away the petals, sepals and male reproductive organs to prevent self-pollination. Since hostas can only be pollinated by visiting insects and the insects have no platform on which to land, pollination by insects cannot now take place.

The transfer of pollen to the pod parent is most simply done by brushing the anther (using the filament as a handle) across the tip of the stigma. Some breeders prefer to transfer the pollen using a small, camel-hair paintbrush, but if the brush is used more that once there is always the danger that pollen from a previous cross may remain on the brush, even when the brush is sterilized in methylated spirits and air-dried. Whatever means is used, timing is critical. Ripe pollen has a dry, dustlike texture: if it is sticky it has lost its potency. The tip of the stigma becomes sticky and slightly swollen when it is receptive, but once moisture (like a drop of dew) appears at the tip, the moment has been missed. The most successful matings generally take place in the middle of the morning, particularly if the same flower is pollinated two or three times during the morning.

While most hostas may be crossed with relative ease, *Hosta plantaginea* and most of its fragrant derivatives are notoriously difficult to cross. This may be partly because *H. plantaginea* is a nocturnally opening species and is not therefore sexually receptive at the same time as other hostas. Some breeders have found that crosses made at 4 P.M. the day before the flower opens are more successful than those made the following morning. Some growers find that putting pollen of *H. plantaginea* around the rim of the stigma and the pollen of the desired pollen parent on the tip of the stigma is more successful than just the pollen parent's own. Each cross should be clearly labeled, the label carrying the name of both parents and stating clearly which is the pod parent. The label should also state the date on which the cross was made.

Hosta 'Cinnamon Sticks', with its red-spotted petioles, is useful as either a pod or pollen parent for introducing red features into leaves, petioles and scapes.

Seed usually takes six to eight weeks to ripen. Once sown it generally germinates quickly, within two to six weeks. Seed that is not sown out of doors as soon as it is gathered can be stored in an air-tight tin in a refrigerator through the winter and then sown indoors or out as spring begins. Raising seedlings indoors allows the grower greater control over pests and diseases. Seedlings should be grown on for two or even three years before even the most elementary evaluation is made, and at that stage all worthless seedlings should be discarded. Worthless seedlings will not improve with time and should be ruthlessly trashed. Even highly successful breeders find that, in general, less than 5 percent of seedlings are worth keeping at this stage. A higher proportion of seedlings should be kept if the hostas are being bred for their flowers since the first flowers are seldom typical. When breeding for foliage, breeders should retain the best seedlings until they produce mature leaves, which may take as long as seven years.

If after all this effort you succeed in producing a seemingly worthwhile hosta, you may want to name it, but it is worth remembering that more than four thousand named hostas already exist, of which some two thousand have been registered. To be worth naming, a hosta needs to be really special. If it is to be registered with the International Cultivar Registration Authority for *Hosta*, that authority will require it to be distinct from all other hostas, to be uniform and stable in its characteristics and to maintain those characteristics when propagated.

CHAPTER FOUR

GARDENING *with* HOSTAS

HOSTAS ARE, IN THE MAIN, EASY, ADAPTABLE garden plants, and the range available is now so diverse that hostas can be grown in most gardens and in a wide variety of garden habitats. But any plant as bold or as brightly colored as the hosta—or at least most of them—draws the eye very strongly. It is therefore often helpful to look at their placing in the garden through the eyes of a garden designer who can see the overall picture rather than through the eyes of a hostaphile who is forever comparing the merits or defects of different varieties. Even the eyes of an ecologist are not helpful because ecologists will try to fit the hosta to its habitat rather than consider the aesthetics of its placement.

Considerations of Design

Gardens replete with little else but hostas are for collectors and breeders, and there is nothing wrong with that. But for most gardeners, hostas gain by being set in the context of other plants and in a strong garden framework. Essentially, design is about manipulating space, keeping a balance between voids and solids, voids being open spaces like lawns, grass or water, solids being big, bulky things like trees, shrubs (including hedges) or buildings. Gardens are most enjoyable to be in when the voids predominate.

The first principle of planting is not to mix like with like but to contrast like with unlike. Most hostas have solid leaves with entire margins, so plants with many-fingered leaves, such as *Helleborus orientalis*, dicentras with their finely divided leaves and ferns with their lacy fronds afford a contrast, as do many sedges with their linear leaves. In his book on botanical Latin, William Stearn (1996) lists no less than 138 different leaf shapes, not to mention 27 variations on the leaf tip and 12 on the base of the leaf, with a further nine on the form of the margin and 10 on the ways the leaf may be cut or divided. The diversity is there for those who have the desire to seek it out.

The size of the leaf also matters. Large leaves look larger when grown next to small leaves, which makes the small leaves look smaller too. Next to *Gunnera manicata*, the leaves of even the largest hostas look quite small, though the leaves of *Helxine soleirolia* (now *Soleirolia soleirolii*) are minute when compared with the leaves of even tiny hostas such as *Hosta venusta*. Texture matters too. Further interesting associations are created by contrasting plants with shiny leaves with those that have matt or furry leaves. Hosta leaves offer a number of interesting leaf surfaces, from the lustrously oily H. 'Bubba' to the almost rough-to-the-touch H. 'Rhino'. Some have raised, fused areas, such as H. 'Koryu' or H. 'Praying Hands', while others such as H. 'Azure Snow' and H. 'Winfield Blue' have leaves that look like frosted icing.

The same principle of contrasting size and texture applies to hostas that are grown in both the sun or shade, though many of the most suitable companions for sun-loving hostas are monocotyledons such as agapanthus, crocosmias and grasses, which tends to limit the range of foliage to strap-shaped or linear leaves. The most suitable compan-

An island bed of hostas.

A luxuriant planting of hostas and other exotics at Glen Chantry
near Colchester in Essex, England.

Hosta 'Golden Sunburst' and *H.* 'Shade Fanfare' in a rocky setting at Hillside Gardens.

An exhibit of small and miniature hostas.

Hosta 'Daybreak' in the foreground of a lush planting of hostas
and other foliage in Gil Jones's garden.

ions for shade-loving hostas are dicotyledons, and these generally have a far wider range of leaf forms. While the leaves of shade-loving plants are often large or finely divided (the better to catch what little sunlight reaches them), the internal economy of sun-loving plants is quite different. Their leaves are often small, often pungent and sometimes covered in a layer of fine, silvery hairs. While most hostas will flower better in the sun than in shade, one hosta, *Hosta plantaginea*, is better adapted through evolution to growing in the sun than other hostas and in cooler climates its leaves can become yellow and etiolated if it is grown in shade all day.

HOSTAS IN WOODLAND

Hostas have always been considered shade-loving plants, though shade-tolerant is a more accurate term since they are plants of woodland and forest margins, rather than of the dark, deep heart of the forest. Most hostas, particularly the larger sorts, grow best in light, open woodland with high, filtered shade and shelter from desiccating winds. Their natural companions will be native oaks (*Quercus*) and pines (*Pinus*), together with exotics such as larch (*Larix*) and spruce (*Picea*) and an understory of lace-cap hydrangeas, rhododendrons, azaleas and butchers broom. Beneath the feet of the ground-level story of larger ferns

(*Woodwardia fimbriata*, *Dryopteris goldiana*, *D. ludoviciana*) would be a scattering of Solomon's seal (*Polygonatum*), *Smilacina racemosa* and *Disporum sessile*, as well as ground-covering ivies and early spring bulbs. Generally, large groups of hostas with muted, solid colors, mid-green or gray-blue leaves blend better into a landscape of natural woodland, public parks and the wilder areas of large country estates than hostas of brighter hues. *Hosta* 'Blue Angel' for example, may eventually achieve a spread of at least 9 ft. (270 cm) across and will look majestic under a stand of oaks, with smaller hostas (such as drifts of *H. sieboldii* or *H.* 'Decorata') weaving around groups of low-growing ferns on the woodland floor. More formal public parks and open spaces tend to use hostas as ribbon planting or as edging in the foreground and varieties like *H.* 'Bold Edger' or *H.* 'Resonance' as ground cover, which can also help prevent soil erosion on steep banks or slopes.

Woodland glades in suburban or small country gardens, where the trees are often ornamental rather than native, are much better suited to the more sophisticated and colorful hostas. Plant associations here are likely to be more thoughtful, with color contrasts or echoes involving foliage, bark and stem. Such associations can be just as effective as flower power, though on a more subtle level.

Hosta 'Niagara Falls'

Hosta 'Green Piecrust'

THE MIXED BORDER

The mixed border has largely taken over from the traditional herbaceous border, mainly because it needs less maintenance. If thoughtfully planted it gives at least three seasons of enjoyment, starting with early spring bulbs and ending with the dying embers of late autumn foliage. It also ensures that in regions where it is impossible to garden (where it is too cold, for example) for several months of winter, there is an outline of shrubs and trees, albeit a fairly stark one, to look at from the house.

Provided there is shade for part of the day, preferably after midday, hostas will associate well with a wide variety of small ornamental trees, shrubs, roses, traditional cottage garden flowers and bulbs in a harmonious arrangement. The hostas in such a setting can be used for either their foliage or their flowers; some can be used for both. Preeminent among hostas grown for their flowers are *Hosta* 'Royal Standard', whose leaves look good for the whole season and whose fragrant white flowers provide a long, mid- to late summer display; *H.* 'Tall Boy' with its towering spires of mauve-blue flowers; and the much smaller *H. clausa* f. *normalis* with its dense heads of vivid purple flowers. Hostas with colored or variegated foliage can be used to draw the eye to a flowering group or to reinforce the coloring of a flower group.

Hosta 'Halcyon' at the RHS Garden, Wisley.

Hosta 'Sun Power', *H.* 'Fortunei Aureomarginata' and *H.* 'Fringe Benefit' with a background of ancient stone walls at the Old Kennels, Nunwick, near Hadrian's Wall in Northumberland, England.

HOSTAS IN CONTAINERS

The increasing popularity of growing hostas in pots is partly because the leaf mound of most hostas is the perfect complement to a typical pot and partly because it is easier to prevent leaf damage by slugs and snails when the hosta is being grown in a container.

Generally it is the largest hostas that look best in pots but, as always, where several pots are grouped together, it is important to vary the size of the hostas as well as their leaf shape and coloring or variegation, especially if all the pots contain hostas. This is slightly less important if the hostas are already being grown in a setting of quite different plants, which might be the case near a house with a foundation planting largely of shrubs. Similarly, varied associations might be less important if hostas are growing among other sorts of potted plants such as yuccas, agaves, dasylirions, phormiums and even opuntias in sun, or ferns, carices, aspidistras and rhododendrons in shade.

While the first choice of hostas to grow in pots and other containers may be the large and medium-sized varieties, small and even minute hostas can be very successfully cultivated in pots, sinks and troughs. However, these small and tiny hostas will need quite different conditions and growing mixes. On the whole, very small hostas are best grown on in pots in a sharply draining growing mix until they have formed substantial clumps before they are set out in the garden. They should never be divided down into very small segments since larger divisions grow away better, especially in pots, and there is less time to wait before the hosta is mature enough to enjoy.

HOSTAS AT THE WATERSIDE

While it is true that certain hostas do grow in the wild in water meadows and in other very wet conditions, they are mostly smaller species and scarcely what one would choose to grow in the rampant vegetation that normally surrounds a pond or, to a lesser degree, a stream. Whether by nature or nurture, most of us tend to expect the vegetation around water to grow larger and be more vigorous than vegetation in drier ground. Medium-sized, large and even giant hostas are very much in keeping with this expectation and may indeed have even more sumptuous leaves than many genuinely riverine plants. They are certainly bold enough to compete with waterside irises, ferns, ligularias, rodgersias and the other familiar denizens of damp garden habitats.

A problem is that relatively few gardens have natural

A trough planting of tiny hostas at Hosta Choice Nursery and
Gardens in Ontario, Canada.

Reflections on water. *Hosta* 'Albomarginata' at Longstock Water
Garden near Stockbridge in Hampshire, England.

Hostas among other waterside plants at Cambridge Botanic Garden, Cambridge, England.

ponds or streams. The water in most gardens is held in place by concrete, butyl or some other artificial material so that there is no natural transitional zone of dampness between the water and the dry land. But this does not mean that waterside hostas cannot be grown; it simply means that a little more trouble has to be taken to meet their cultural needs.

The simplest way to overcome the problem of dry soil outside the pond is to enrich the soil with copious quantities of organic matter and to water it with a seep hose (which is a leaky hose) hidden under mulch. Alternatively, the ground can be dug out and a liner placed in the depression as though for a pond but with a few holes in the liner that is then backfilled with earth, the objective being to im-

pede drainage, not prevent it altogether. Either method creates conditions in which hostas and moisture-loving plants will thrive. Artificial ponds are usually sited in full sun, so it may also be necessary to plant a tree or two to cast light, filtered shade over the hostas. Avoid willows whose roots form impenetrable mats.

There is little in the literature about growing hostas directly in water, but the author's own early experiments show that *Hosta longissima*, *H.* 'Francee' and *H.* 'Undulata' and its several forms will succeed. Presumably, *H. kiyosumiensis* and its forms would also succeed if their pots were stood in water with the crown above water level throughout the summer.

CHAPTER FIVE

PESTS, DISEASES & OTHER THREATS *to* HOSTAS

THE THREE BEST DEFENSES AGAINST the pests and diseases that can trouble hostas are to grow healthy, vigorous plants, to study the needs of each particular hosta so as to grow it in optimum conditions and to be vigilant in checking for the presence of pests and diseases so that they can be dealt with using a minimum of chemicals.

Slugs and Snails

Slugs and snails are notorious for being the most troublesome pests of hostas. Both are classified in phylum Mollusca, class Gastropoda, and are known collectively as mollusks, but several different genera are involved.

Slugs remain active throughout the whole year and can feed whenever the temperature rises above 41°F (5°C). Snails, by contrast, become inactive at the onset of cold weather and take shelter for the winter, typically in flowerpots, in logs or against walls. They seal their shells onto a hard surface with mucilage that dries to become hard, in effect gluing the shell to a chosen surface. There are some 25 species of slugs in the United Kingdom and more in the United States, but only 5 species eat leaf foliage, the rest being carnivores that eat other slugs or worms. The real enemies of hostas are the little black and brown slugs that eat both shoots and roots.

Although slugs and snails are hermaphrodite they still need to pair up to breed. Breeding usually occurs in spring or autumn when the weather is mild and moist. Small white or creamy spherical eggs up to ⅕₀ in. (2 mm) long are laid in batches of up to 50 in cavities in the soil. These eggs hatch into tiny versions of their parents and take about three years to reach maturity. When young they are susceptible to death through desiccation if the soil dries out and also to being eaten by song thrushes, hedgehogs, snakes, frogs and toads, shrews and slowworms. Some beetles, such as ground (carabid) beetles and rove (staphylinid) beetles feed on them, as do some insects including glowworms and sciomyzid fly larvae.

HUMAN INTERVENTION

The most effective way of reducing slug and snail populations in most gardens is to go out at night with a light and collect these pests in a container that is suitable for destruction. They are particularly easy to find when the garden is wet after rain or when there is a heavy dew. Unless you have done this nighttime collecting, you may well be unaware of the sheer size of the mollusk population in your garden.

The most widely used poisons for controlling slugs and snails are metaldehyde and methiocarb slug pellets. (A Certified Applicator's Permit is required for purchase of methiocarb in the United States.) Recently introduced in the United States are small pellets containing 1% iron phosphate. Slug baits are most effective when applied around the garden on mild evenings, particularly in warm weather in early spring. Slugs are inactive in very hot and very dry weather, so there is little point in using the pellets then.

Baits with iron phosphate reportedly can be used around domestic animals and wildlife, but metaldehyde and methiocarb pellets can be fatal to cats, dogs and prowling wildlife. However, it is unlikely that cats or dogs will find pellets that are concealed under a roofing slate or tile propped up on a stone, placed in the angle between the earth and a wall or a fence or laid across the gutter between lawn and border. Moreover, using slates or tiles in this way creates the cool, damp conditions that slugs and snails find most attractive, thereby ensuring they find the pellets. Some slug pellets are blue, which is a difficult color for birds to see, thus making it unlikely that they will eat the pellets. Also, some baits have a very bitter chemical added, making it highly unlikely they will be ingested by children, domestic animals and wildlife.

Another chemical, one that is far less toxic to pets than metaldehyde and methiocarb, is aluminum sulfate. It comes in the form of crystals that can be scattered on the surface of the soil around the hostas. It acts as a contact poison and is particularly effective among germinating hosta seeds.

A number of other substances are also poisonous to slugs and snails. Among these are salt, borax, ammonia and caffeine. These act as contact poisons and are most effective when applied directly onto the slug or snail and their eggs instead of when scattered on the soil. Applying a 10% solution of household ammonia to the crown and nearby area when shoots first emerge in the spring can be an effective preventive. There are some reports of used coffee grounds being effective when applied to the soil around hostas.

An alternative to using poisons in deterring slugs and snails is the use of barriers since mollusks avoid surfaces that are sharp, hairy or very absorbent. Several substances are used, most of which are commonly occurring. Among those that deter because of their sharpness are sand, coarse grit, sharp cinders, wood ashes, diatomaceous earth, broken eggshells and crushed oyster and scallop shells. Many proprietary products such as porous volcanic rock (which is marketed in England, Europe and Australia as Mollbar) are also suitable. Other types of barriers, such as continuous strips or tapes of copper or aluminum placed around the hostas, cause a chemical reaction which makes the mollusks overproduce mucilage resulting in their desiccation. Although they are effective as deterrents they are expensive and suffer the same shortcomings as other types of barriers. The hosta leaves arch over the barrier and then touch the ground, thereby affording slugs and snails a bridge over the barrier.

Where hostas are growing in containers, slugs and snails can be deterred to some extent if the containers are raised off the ground on small feet and if a band of petroleum jelly or fruit-tree grease is placed around the outside of the container, since slugs and snails will not be able to motor across it. Penetrating oils (one proprietary product is WD-40) act as deterrents if they are sprayed on the outsides of containers. Copper tape tied round the outside of pots will also deter slugs and snails.

A third way of dealing with slugs and snails is through biological controls. Biological control through a pathogenic nematode, *Phasmarhabditis hermaphrodita*, has been available for some years but is not equally successful in all gardens. The nematodes are most effective when applied in spring and are more effective on light sandy soils than on heavy clay soils.

An additional measure of control over slugs and snails can be achieved by understanding their needs and then denying them. This means removing dead and dying leaves and not allowing a litter of decaying vegetation to build up in the garden. Hosta leaves should be removed as soon as they start to turn yellow or show signs of decay. Ideally, one should be just as vigilant with the leaves of other plants in the garden. The slug and snail problem is, unfortunately, exacerbated by the fact that hostas seem to grow best in soils rich in organic matter, which is usually supplied in the form of mulches (vegetable matter in one form or another) or as animal manure. Both types of organic matter provide ideal breeding grounds for slugs and snails.

Controlling these pests is also helped if other sorts of garden rubbish are kept to a minimum. Bricks or planks of wood, for example, that are left lying around the garden provide ideal breeding sites. The continual cultivation of the soil's surface can also keep slugs and snail populations down by exposing their eggs to the air, thereby destroying them.

Another method of limiting the number of snails and slugs is by making use of plant associations. The foliage of hostas is attractive to slugs and snails at all times, and the more hostas one grows, the more one seems to attract slugs and snails. However, not all plants are equally attractive since some have a texture or chemical content that slugs and snails dislike. Hairy-leaved plants are often left well alone. Where hostas are mixed among such plants, the levels of damage to the hostas may be considerably lessened. The following is a list of plants that, while not immune to damage from slugs and snails, tend to survive unscathed in most gardens.

Acanthus mollis
Achillea filipendulina
Agapanthus hybrids and cultivars
Alchemilla mollis
Anemone hupehensis and A. ×hybrida
Antirrhinum majus
Aquilegia species
Armeria species
Aster amellus, A. ×frikartii and A.
    novae-angliae
Astilbe ×arendsii
Astrantia major
Bergenia
Centaurea dealbata and C. montana
Corydalis lutea
Cynara cardunculus
Dicentra spectabilis
Digitalis purpurea

Eryngium species
Euphorbia species
Foeniculum vulgare
Fuchsia cultivars
Gaillardia aristata
Geranium species
Geum chiloense
Liatris spicata
Lysimachia punctata
Myosotis species
Nepeta ×fassenii
Papaver nudicaule
Papaver orientale
Pelargonium
Phlox paniculata
Physostegia virginiana
Polemonium foliosissimum
Polygonatum species

Potentilla hybrids and cultivars
Pulmonaria species
Rudbeckia fulgida
Salvia ×superba
Saxifraga ×urbium
Scabiosa caucasica
Sedum spectabile
Sempervivum species
Sisyrinchium species
Solidago species
Stachys macrantha
Tanacetum coccineum
Thalictrum aquilegiifolium
Tradescantia virginiana
Tropaeolum species
Verbascum species
ferns and ornamental grasses

Hosta 'Island Charm' surrounded by ferns.

Vine Weevils

Vine weevils (*Otiorhynchus sulcatus*), sometimes called black vine weevils to distinguish them from clay-colored weevils, are highly damaging to hostas both in the larval and adult stages, though the larvae do most damage. These are fat, creamy white, C-shaped, legless grubs about ⅜ in. (1 cm) long that have tiny heads of a malicious shade of burnt sienna. They feed on the roots of hostas and many other plants, especially when the plants are growing in pots. They sometimes destroy all the roots, thereby causing the leaves to turn yellow and the plant to wilt and usually die. The adult weevils are quite distinct in their waisted shape and are dull black, minutely speckled with tiny tufts of yellow hairs. They have roughened wing-cases beneath which are no wings. They feed at night, hiding by day in the basal leaves of low-growing plants and under stones and suchlike.

Vine weevils are often more of a problem in pots than in the open ground, especially if the pots are in tunnels or under glass and if the plants are growing in a soilless growing mix and have not been repotted for over a year. They can also be a considerable problem in damp or ill-drained ground. Once vine weevils become established they can be difficult to eradicate completely. However, there is a biological control that is effective under most conditions, and there are several other lines of defense.

HUMAN INTERVENTION

Although hostas are sometimes decimated by vine weevil, there are other plants that vine weevils prefer both as hosts for their grubs and as food for the adults. Among these are adiantums, begonias, bergenias, cyclamen, primulas, saxifrages and sedums. Some nursery people place pots of one or other of these plants at the entrance to their tunnels in the hope that the vine weevils will go to them rather than to the hostas.

Adult vine weevils can also be trapped, especially under glass or in tunnels, by placing rolls of corrugated paper, old sacking or canvas on or near the ground to provide daytime refuge for the weevils. These materials should be inspected daily and shaken out over a clean surface where the weevils can be spotted and destroyed. The adults can also be seen quite easily by torchlight after dark, picked off the plants and destroyed.

Plants in pots that are yellowing or wilting should be tipped out of their pots and the remaining roots, if any, washed off under running water and then repotted in fresh growing mix. The original soil should be burned or otherwise sterilized before being reused or put on the garden.

Vine weevils once were controlled by highly toxic organochlorine insecticides. However, these chemicals are very persistent in the soil, found their way into the food chain and also killed beneficial insects. They are now banned and no effective alternatives have been found. Acephate, ranked among the best insecticide available to home gardeners, is only somewhat effective. Treatment with acephate requires application in springtime, and a second and third application later on to help control emerging adults.

The best mitigation for vine weevils is to kill the larvae, that is, their grubs. The chemical imidacloprid, which kills these and several other grubs on contact, is now available in nurseries and garden centers. In the United Kingdom it can be found as a packet specifically marketed for vine weevil control. In the United States and some other countries, home gardeners wanting to use imidacloprid for vine weevil control will need to purchase this chemical as an insecticide for the white grubs of Japanese beetles in lawns and gardens. It is available as both a granule and liquid, and is easily spread or sprayed onto hosta beds as well as containers. It is best to apply imidacloprid to the soil in advance of when larvae will be feeding. Some nurseries use a potting compost containing imidacloprid or other grub-killing chemicals already mixed into it.

A parasitic nematode, *Heterorhabditis megidis*, provides the most effective control of vine weevil. It is usually bought by mail order and is applied in the same way as the nematode for the control of slugs.

Foliar Nematodes

Foliar nematodes (*Aphelenchoides fragariae* and *Ditylenchus dipsaci*), which can cause severe damage to hostas, were virtually unknown in the United States until about 1991, apparently having been brought into the country on imported plants. The nematodes are spread by splashing water. They overwinter in the crowns of hostas, migrating in the spring to the leaf blade, where they feed and multiply between the veins, causing the characteristic interveinal browning of the leaves. However, this browning is often not apparent until mid- or late summer.

Removing affected foliage may limit the infestation but will not be a complete remedy. Mildly infested plants can be ridded of the nematode and its eggs by soaking individual divisions in water held at a temperature of 120°F (49°C) for 15 to 20 minutes, after which they should be potted up and grown on in isolation from other hostas for at least six months.

According to a nematologist at Ohio State University, significant success was reported following applications of trichlorfon (as Dylox 80 powder) and ethoprop, and moderate success with applications of oxamyl (a restricted pesticide), diazinon (now banned from U.S. markets), trichlorfon (as Dylox 6.2 granular), a proprietary hydrogen dioxide (also called hydrogen peroxide) solution and insecticidal soap. No product available to the home gardener completely eradicates this problem.

Leaf Spotting and Petiole Rot

Necrotic spots appear on the leaves of hostas for various reasons. Spots can appear in late spring if early spring was particularly cold and damp. These appear as minute brown spots with a tiny pinhole in the middle. Damage can usually be averted by ensuring good frost drainage. Once damaged, the leaves cannot be made whole again, though unsightly leaves can be cut off. With warmer weather, new leaves should come through normally.

Leaf spotting can also be caused by the fungi *Alternaria*, *Phyllostricta* and *Colletotrichum omnivorum*. Further damage can be prevented by two or three sprays of thiophanate-methyl or thiram fungicide at two-week intervals. However, the careless use of garden chemicals can also cause leaf spotting.

A number of fungi and bacteria can cause petiole blight and crown rot in hostas. Southern stem blight or rot, also called petiole rot, caused by the fungi *Sclerotium rolfsii* and *S. rolfsii* var. *delphinii*, seems to be the most common of these infestations. This was first observed in the southern states but appears to be traveling northwards as summers get longer and hotter and is more prevalent in times of high humidity. Seldom occurring before June, its identifying characteristics are spherical balls—hard, white then brown and about the size of mustard seeds—where the petioles meet the crown, as well as white cottony mycelium masses in the areas. The affected leaves usually have fallen over and easily detach if pulled gently. The plant should be dug up, all soil removed and all affected parts scraped away with a sharp knife and burned. It should then be soaked in a 3-percent solution of hydrogen peroxide or 10-percent solution of household bleach for up to two hours. (Use the same treatment for hostas growing in pots.) The hostas should then be isolated at least until the end of the season, and no hostas should be planted where the infection occurred.

Fungicides that are both preventive and curative are azoxystrobin, kresoxim-methyl and trifloxystrobin, which are strobilurins, and flutolanil, a benzamide. Flutolanil is listed specifically for control of *Sclerotium rolfsii*. Several applications will be required. A soil drench, such as bleach solution or pentachloronitrobenzene (PCNB), is sometimes helpful.

Crown rot is a term for the rotting disease that primarily affects the crowns of hostas, usually in early season. The hosta's crown is soft, mushy or deteriorated. Affected tissue is usually light brown or reddish. Frequently an unpleasant rotting odor is noted. The roots in this area may also be affected. Crown rot is caused by bacterial and fungal (but not *Sclerotium rolfsii*) organisms believed to enter through some kind of plant damage. Corrective action is similar to that for stem blight: dig up the plant and trim away all rotted tissue; soak in bleach solution; and plant in fresh soil. A preventative and curative fungicide is thiophanate-methyl; several applications may be required. A bleach solution or PCNB as a soil disinfectant is often applied.

Fungal infestations are sometimes caused by too many applications of high-nitrogen fertilizer and by overly dense mulches packed tightly around the hosta clump since these prevent the movement of air or sufficient drainage of the soil. Dense mulches should be avoided.

In the southern United States, where humidity is very high, *Fusarium oxysporum* and *Verticillium albo-atrum* are the causes of progressive yellowing of the outer to the inner leaves of a hosta clump. Fungicides can be used as prophylactics, but they need to be applied regularly and frequently.

Viral Infections

Viral infections are more likely to infect hostas that are in poor health or have been damaged by insects. It is much more difficult to contain the spread of a virus in large collections of a single genus, where it quickly spreads from plant to plant. Single plants found to be infected can be easily isolated and treated, or they can be burned if too badly infected to save. Prevention is better than cure, so it is always prudent when dividing hostas to dip the knife in alcohol or a bleach solution before making the cut, and again afterwards.

The most common viral infections affecting hostas are Hosta Virus X (HVX), tobacco rattle virus and tomato ring spot virus. HVX can be identified by a procedure developed at the University of Minnesota. The Arabic mosaic virus, which produces chlorotic leaves with some stunting,

Virus infecting the leaves of *Hosta* 'Gold Standard'.

Hosta plantaginea 'Aphrodite'. The intensely fragrant, nocturnal, waxy, long-tubed flowers are attractive to deer.

may also affect hostas. Sometimes what appears to be a viral infection in the form of stunted or deformed leaves is actually drought damage, and the mosaic patterning is often mistaken for a mottled sport.

Cutworms

Many species of cutworms exist. They are up to 1⅛ in. (3 cm) long, are soft bodied and smooth and curl up tightly when disturbed. They can be dull gray, brown or black and may be striped or spotted. They are night feeding and can cut off plants either at or below the soil surface. Some cutworms feed on the leaves or buds of hostas, while others feed on the roots. They are particularly destructive early in the season.

These pests can be prevented from causing damage without an insecticide being used. A stiff, 2¾ in. (7 cm) cardboard collar should be placed around the plant stem. The collar should extend about 1 in. (2.5 cm) into the soil and protrude 2 in. (5 cm) above the soil, clearing the stem by about ⅜ in. (1 cm). A newly patented, reusable cutworm shield can be purchased to protect the stems.

If damage is to the leaf surface, shine a torch on the leaves at night while these pests are feeding and squash them as they fall. *Bacillus thuringiensis* will kill cutworms and is safe to use. If cultural control fails, a proprietary insecticide should be applied.

Fungus Gnats

Fungus gnats (families Fungivoridae and Sciaridae) are black with long, thin wings. They are very small, usually less than 1⁄50 in. (2 mm) in length, although some species

may reach ¼ in. (6 mm). They are not a problem as adults, but in the larval stage they feed on the roots and can cripple and topple hosta seedlings.

Fungus gnats can be controlled indoors with pyrethrin as a surface drench, backed up by yellow sticky cards 2¾ × 4 in. (7 × 10 cm) cut in 1 in. (2.5 cm) strips and placed horizontally at soil level. These cards actually catch the emerging adult before it can fly and lay eggs.

Disulfoton systemic granules can be spread on the surface of the soil or, after the planting tray has been half-filled with soil, it can be spread in a layer and then covered with the remaining soil. Seed would then be sown. Watering activates the granules, creating a vapor that could escape into the room if used on top of the soil.

Deer

Of all the four-legged creatures that have a taste for hostas, deer are by far the most voracious and can be a considerable problem in the country in certain regions of both Europe and the United States. Their depredations can start in the spring, when they often chew hostas right down to the ground and then continue through the growing season, eating almost any part of a hosta. They are most attracted to hostas with fragrant flowers, especially *Hosta plantaginea* and its hybrids. A number of folk cures for deer exist, including hair (preferably human), urine (preferably human), lion and tiger dung (obtainable from some zoos), scarecrows, various shiny things such as CD discs suspended from strings so that they move in the wind, pepper sprays and large dogs. The traditional wisdom is that barriers are only effective when they are over 8 ft. (240 cm) tall. Where space permits, a sequence of lower barriers is effective, especially if they are too close together for the deer to gather themselves to spring over the next one.

Rodents

Mice, rats, gray squirrels, rabbits and voles can all wreak havoc in a bed of hostas. Most merely chew the foliage, making clumps unsightly, but voles actually devour the roots and can thus do a vast amount of damage. They often move into polytunnels and greenhouses for warmth during the winter. Since the plants are dormant and not under a gardener's constant observation (as they would be when in leaf), rodents can do plenty of harm before their presence is noticed. Vigilance, therefore, is essential. Various traps and baits are available for the control of these creatures, and a measure of control can be attained with chlorophacinone formulated as paraffinized pellets. This chemical is on re-stricted sale, and in some states requires an applicator's li-cense.

Climatic and Other Damage

Sudden late frosts in some regions can cause unsightly damage to the newly emerged leaves of some hostas. *Hosta montana* 'Aureomarginata', *H.* 'Lancifolia' and *H. plan-taginea* and its forms are particularly vulnerable.

Damage can often be averted by planting hostas in places where there is good frost drainage. A plastic bucket that is placed over the emerging hosta leaves in early evening and then removed in the morning can also prevent damage. If the damaged leaves are cut off, the new leaves will be un-scathed unless further frosts occur. Repeated damage over the years will reduce the size and vigor of the hostas.

Spring burn is mainly a problem with those forms of *Hosta sieboldiana* that have yellow in their leaves and is the result of a combination of conditions. It occurs in spring when the leaves are growing rapidly, when night tempera-tures drop down close to freezing and if the leaves are then exposed to direct sunlight or strong winds. The yellow parts of the leaves are desiccated and they turn orange-brown and look as though they have developed rust. Oddly, the blue areas of the leaves do not seem to be affec-

ted, nor do the white-margined or white-centered forms of *H. sieboldiana*.

The problem of spring burn is largely solved by planting susceptible varieties out of the wind and where they will not be in direct sunlight in the early mornings. In Britain, where the climate is both cooler than in much of the United States, this kind of damage is seldom seen.

Melting out is a phenomenon usually seen only in hostas with white centers to their leaves. The center of the white area turns brown and desiccates, eventually decaying and leaving one or several holes at the center of the brown area. In some varieties, the damage can reduce the leaf blade to brown, white and green shreds. It used to be thought that the problem was caused by growing susceptible plants in too much sun, but the problem can occur with hostas growing in positions where direct sunlight never reaches them. The problem is less likely to occur in plants growing in moist soils and bright light.

Leaf-scorch or sunburn is revealed when large sections of the leaves turn light yellow and then become crisp and brown. The problem is simply the result of hostas being grown in too much sun. It often occurs in gardens where shade for the hostas is created by trees, but either the hostas leaf-up early or the trees are late into leaf.

Center-clump dieback, also called centering out, though unsightly in the garden, is not a disease but merely a con-sequence of the natural development of a hosta clump. Like most perennial plants, hostas usually grow from the center outward in an ever-expanding ring. The center of the clump, being the oldest part, suffers senescence, exhausts the soil beneath it and gets deprived of light by the more vigorous leaves of younger parts of the clump around it. In a sense there is no cure. The worry when this happens to hostas in the garden is that the moribund parts of the plant will develop a pernicious rot that might destroy the rest of the clump, though in fact this seldom happens. All that can be done is to dig up and divide the plant, replanting it in another part of the garden, but you will have a smaller plant in subsequent years. The soil where the plant was growing should be enriched with organic matter and fer-tilizer, and if no rot has occurred, another hosta can be planted there.

CHAPTER SIX

HOSTAS *with* GREEN LEAVES

HOSTAS WITH PLAIN GREEN LEAVES must have very special qualities nowadays to capture the interest of modern hosta growers. In the 1950s and 1960s, very few variegated hostas were available, and there were virtually none with golden yellow leaves and only a few with a central variegation. Any and all hosta introductions were eagerly welcomed and quickly disseminated. Nowadays our expectations are much higher, and if a green-leaved hosta is to rank on the popularity polls, it must be in the class of *Hosta* 'Devon Green', *H.* 'Lakeside Looking Glass', or *H.* 'Niagara Falls'; that is it must have an unusual surface texture, an interesting leaf shape or plant habit or an exceptional characteristic such as heavy racemes of flower, an intensely white back, outstanding red petioles and scapes, or carry genes that make it a good breeding plant.

Many older hostas have been omitted from this list as they have long been superseded by more attractive garden varieties. Such hostas will now usually only be found growing in National Plant Collections or as part of special species or early hybrid collections so that their unique genetic characteristics do not disappear forever.

Hosta 'Abiqua Miniature' (Walden-West 1988)

DWARF

Origin: Unknown.

Clump Size & Habit: 7½ in. wide × 3⅛ in. high (19 × 8 cm). A dense mound.

Description: Leaf blade: 1½ × ⅜ in. (4 × 1 cm); of average substance, bright green, matt above and glossy whitish green below, slightly dimpled; edge slightly undulate, folded, oval to heart-shaped with an acute tip, tapered open to pinched lobes. Petiole: narrow, light green. Flower: funnel-shaped, pale lavender on an upright, leafy, light green, 7½ in. (19 cm) scape from mid- to late season; fertile.

Comments & Special Needs: Grow in two hours of morning sun in cooler climates, otherwise shade all day. Ideal for sinks or small containers. Of moderate increase.

Distinguishing Features: One of the smallest hostas. Reblooms.

Similar: *H. venusta.

Hosta aequinoctiiantha (Koidzumi ex Araki)

MEDIUM–LARGE

Origin: Central Honshu, Japan.

Clump Size & Habit: 36 in. wide × 18 in. high (90 × 45 cm). An open mound.

Description: Leaf blade: 9 × 4¾ in. (22 × 12 cm); thin, mid- to dark green, shiny above with a shiny whitish coating below, prominently marked veins; edge shallowly rippled, flat to slightly arching, oval with a thin, cuspidate tip, round to heart-shaped overlapping lobes. Petiole: mid-green with purple dotting which is more dense toward the crown. Flower: long, funnel- to bell-shaped, lavender on an oblique, purple-dotted, 10 to 18 in. (25 to 45 cm) scape in late summer to early autumn; fertile.

Comments & Special Needs: Emerges early in spring.

Distinguishing Features: Differs from *H. longipes* in that it blooms some three weeks later and has impressive white bracts subtending the flowers.

Hosta 'Abiqua Miniature'

Previous page: *Hosta* 'Hirao Splendor'

Hosta aequinoctiiantha

Hosta 'Apple Green'

Hosta 'Ballerina'

Similar: Some authorities consider *H. aequinoctiiantha* to be a smaller form of **H. longipes*; *H.* 'Iwa Soules' has thicker leaves and blooms somewhat earlier; *H. okomotoi* and *H. takiensis* are similar.

Hosta 'Apple Green' (K. Anderson 1982)

SMALL

Origin: *H. nakaiana* hybrid.

Clump Size & Habit: 20⅜ in. wide × 14 in. high (51 × 35 cm). A compact, symmetrical mound.

Description: Leaf blade: 4 × 2¾ in. (10 × 7 cm); of average substance, light green to chartreuse, matt above and thinly glaucous below, dimpled, ribbed veins when mature; edge flat, slightly cupped, widely oval with a cuspidate tip, heart-shaped overlapping lobes. Petiole: narrow, pale green. Flower: bell-shaped, pale lavender on an upright, bare, light green, 18 in. (45 cm) scape in mid-summer; fertile.

Comments & Special Needs: Site in dappled shade. Leaves will turn more yellow if exposed to strong sunlight. Increases rapidly.

Distinguishing Features: The flowers are widely spaced down the scape, almost reaching the leaf mound.

Hosta 'Ballerina' (R. Savory 1982)

MEDIUM

Origin: *H. venusta* hybrid.

Clump Size & Habit: 24 in. wide × 12 in. high (60 × 30 cm). An open mound.

Description: Leaf blade: 5⅛ × 2 in. (13 × 5 cm); of average substance, shiny, mid-green, slightly lighter near the veins, veins ribbed; edge rippled, arching, lightly twisted, widely oval to nearly round with a cuspidate tip, heart-shaped pinched lobes. Petiole: arching, pale green. Flower: bell-shaped, pendent, near white on a thin, upright, bare, green, 24 in. (60 cm) scape from mid- to late summer; fertile.

Comments & Special Needs: Site in light to moderate shade. A rapid increaser. Grow as a foreground specimen or in a rock or gravel garden.

Distinguishing Features: The leaves extend outward from the petioles.

Hosta 'Barney Fife' (Avent 1993)
MEDIUM

Origin: *H.* 'August Moon' × *H.* 'Tardiflora'.

Clump Size & Habit: 24 in. wide × 12 in. high (60 × 30 cm). A symmetrical mound.

Description: Leaf blade: 7⅛ × 2¾ in. (18 × 7 cm); thick, satiny, dark green with a blue cast, ribbed veins when mature, slightly dimpled; edge slightly rippled, widely oval with a cuspidate tip, round to heart-shaped open lobes. Petiole: dark green. Flower: tubular, lilac on an upright, leafy, gray-purple, 24⅜ in. (61 cm) scape in high summer; fertile.

Comments & Special Needs: Will tolerate some morning sun in cooler climates and dappled shade in the hottest regions. Reasonably pest resistant.

Distinguishing Features: Differs from *H.* 'Andy Taylor', which has near white flowers and more wedge-shaped leaves.

Similar: **H.* 'Andy Taylor' is a brother seedling.

Hosta 'Benny McRae' (Suggs 1989)
MEDIUM

Origin: *H. plantaginea* hybrid.

Clump Size & Habit: 30⅜ in. wide × 24⅜ in. high (76 × 61 cm). An unsymmetrical mound.

Description: Leaf blade: 11 × 4½ in. (28 × 11.5 cm); thin, glossy, light to mid-green; edge undulate, arching and somewhat pinched toward the recurved tip, narrowly oval, rounded to heart-shaped pinched lobes. Petiole: mid-green. Flowers: funnel-shaped, fragrant, lavender on an oblique, leafy, green 24⅜ in. (61 cm) scape from late summer to early autumn; fertility unknown.

Comments & Special Needs: Will tolerate several hours of morning sun even in hot climates provided there is plenty of moisture at the roots. Exposure to sun will turn the leaves a muted chartreuse.

Similar: **H.* 'Honeybells', which has wider leaves.

Hosta 'Betsy King' (F. Williams & AHS 1986)
MEDIUM

Origin: *H.* 'Decorata' × *H. sieboldii* hybrid.

Hosta 'Barney Fife'

Hosta 'Benny McRae'

Clump Size & Habit: 24⅜ in. wide × 16 in. high (61 × 40 cm). An upright mound.

Description: Leaf blade: 4¾ × 2⅜ in. (12 × 6 cm); of average substance, glossy, dark green, closely veined, some dimpling when mature; edge shallowly undulate, flat, oval with an obtuse tip, tapered, open to pinched lobes. Petiole: dark green. Flowers: widely flared rich purple, in abundance, on an upright, leafy, dark green 30 in. (75 cm) scape in late summer.

Comments & Special Needs: Site in light to moderate shade. The scape bracts are small.

Distinguishing Features: Rhizomatous root structure. Small leafy bracts and superb flowers.

Similar: *H.* 'Decorata Normalis', which has slightly smaller leaves.

Hosta 'Betty' (R. Benedict 1983)
SMALL

Origin: *H. nakaiana* × *H. ventricosa* hybrid.

Hosta 'Betsy King'

Hosta 'Betty'

Clump Size & Habit: 18 in. wide × 6 in. high (45 × 15 cm). A flattish open mound.

Description: Leaf blade: 4 × 2¾ in. (10 × 7 cm); of average substance, satiny, dark green with widely spaced veins; edge evenly piecrusted, slightly arching or cupped, triangular with a twisted tip, round pinched lobes. Petiole: narrow, arching, lighter green. Flower: flared, lavender on an upright, leafy, green, 10 in. (25 cm) scape in early summer; fertile.

Comments & Special Needs: Leaves of average substance. Light to medium shade. A delightful small accent hosta that would complement one with blue leaves and flat edges.

Similar: *H.* 'Elisabeth'.

Hosta 'Birchwood Elegance' (Shaw & AHS 1986)

GIANT

Origin: *H. sieboldiana* hybrid.

Clump Size & Habit: 65½ in. wide × 30 in. high (164 × 75 cm). A huge, impressive, rounded mound.

Description: Leaf blade: 16 × 15 in. (40 × 38 cm); thick, dark green, matt above and glaucous below, seersuckered and puckered; edge flat, shallowly undulate, widely oval to nearly round with a mucronate tip, heart-shaped, pinched to overlapping lobes. Petiole: stout, green. Flower: funnel-shaped, palest lavender to near white on an upright, leafy, glaucous green, 40 in. (100 cm) scape in mid-summer; fertile.

Comments & Special Needs: Leaves are darkest green if well fed and grown in full shade with moist soil. Grow as a

Hosta 'Birchwood Elegance'

Hosta 'Black Hills'

Hosta 'Bountiful'

massive specimen or in a woodland planting alongside, tall vigorous ferns.

Similar: *H.* 'Birchwood Green', which has smaller, more crinkled leaves.

Hosta 'Black Hills' (R. Savory 1983)

LARGE

Origin: *H.* 'Green Gold' hybrid.

Clump Size & Habit: 50¾ in. wide × 30 in. high (127 × 75 cm). An unruly mound.

Description: Leaf blade: 8⅜ × 7⅛ in. (21 × 18 cm); thick, very dark green with a blue-black cast, shiny above and thickly glaucous below, seersuckered and deeply puckered; edge almost flat, shallowly cupped, widely oval to nearly round with a mucronate tip, heart-shaped overlapping lobes. Petiole: lighter glaucous green, appearing to pierce the blade. Flower: widely funnel-shaped, lilac, from darker buds, on an upright, leafy, paler glaucous green, 40 in. (100 cm) scape in mid-summer; fertile.

Comments & Special Needs: Intense puckering or even distortion of the leaves appears only with maturity. Light to full shade. Pest resistant.

Similar: **H.* 'Birchwood Elegance'.

Hosta 'Bountiful' (Fisher 1971)

SMALL

Origin: *H. nakaiana* seedling.

Clump Size & Habit: 18 in. wide × 14 in. high (45 × 35 cm). An even, overlapping mound.

Description: Leaf blade: 6¾ × 2¾ in. (17 × 7 cm); of average substance, green with a gray cast, matt above and glaucous below, closely ribbed veins; edge widely undulate to kinked, arching with a cuspidate tip, lanceolate to wedge-shaped, heart-shaped folded lobes. Petiole: narrow,

pale gray-green. Flower: near bell-shaped, pale lavender in dense racemes, on a thin, upright, leafy, glaucous green, 22 in. (55 cm) scape in high summer; fertile.

Comments & Special Needs: Site in high, filtered to moderate shade. A rapid increaser. Plant at the edge of woodland.

Distinguishing Features: The leaves are narrower than those of *H.* 'Candy Hearts' to which it is otherwise similar.

Hosta 'Bridegroom' (H. Benedict & Gowen 1990)

SMALL–MEDIUM

Origin: Seedling from *H.* 'Holly's Honey' selfed.

Clump Size & Habit: 34 in. wide × 16 in. high (85 × 40 cm). Low mound with leaves held in an upward stance.

Description: Leaf blade: 5⅛ × 4 in. (13 × 10 cm); thin, smooth, glossy, dark olive-green, prominently marked veins; edge rippled, triangular, the side of the leaf sloping downward, the center and the twisted tip curving upward, heart-shaped open lobes. Petiole: narrow, dark green, pur-

Hosta 'Bridegroom'

Hosta 'Bubba'

ple dotted toward the crown. Flower: funnel-shaped, lavender on an upright, bare, green, 18 in. (45 cm) scape in late summer; sterile.

Comments & Special Needs: Site in light to moderate shade. Slow to moderate growth. Vulnerable to pests but worth the extra effort to preserve the leaves intact since this is one of the best of the newer green-leaved hostas.

Distinguishing Features: The leaves are uniquely curved upward, hence the name.

Similar: *H.* 'Stirfry'.

Hosta 'Bubba' (Avent 1998)

SMALL–MEDIUM

Origin: *H.* 'Sum and Substance' hybrid.

Clump Size & Habit: 24 in. wide × 12 in. high (60 × 30 cm). A dense mound.

Description: Leaf blade: 6⅜ × 4⅜ in. (16 × 11 cm); thick, olive-green, glossy above and satiny below, dimpled; edge flat, slightly folded, widely oval with a cuspidate to mucronate tip, rounded, pinched lobes. Petiole: short, lighter green, red dotted toward the crown. Flower: bell-shaped, pale lavender on an upright, green, 20 in. (50 cm) scape in late summer; sterile.

Comments & Special Needs: Site in bright light to moderate shade beside glaucous blue-leaved hostas to set off the exceptionally lustrous leaf surface. A moderate growth rate.

Hosta 'Candy Hearts' (Fisher & Ruh 1998)

MEDIUM

Origin: *H. nakaiana* hybrid.

Clump Size & Habit: 30 in. wide × 15 in. high (75 × 38 cm). A dense, spreading mound.

Description: Leaf blade: 4⅜ × 3½ in. (11 × 9 cm); of good substance, dark green with a gray cast, matt to satiny

Hosta 'Candy Hearts'

above and glaucous below, slightly dimpled when mature; edge slightly undulate, widely oval with a mucronate tip, heart-shaped overlapping lobes. Petiole: slightly arching, light green. Flower: tubular, opening from large ballooning buds on an upright or oblique, bare, gray-green, 25⅛ in. (63 cm) scape in mid-summer; fertile.

Comments & Special Needs: Site in dappled shade, where the leaves will retain their early, attractive blue-gray cast for longer into the summer. Good in pots and also excellent for mass landscaping in light woodland since it increases rapidly.

Similar: *H.* 'Happy Hearts'; *H.* 'Heartleaf', which is larger; *H.* 'Minnie Klopping', which has slightly grayer leaves; **H.* 'Pearl Lake'.

Sports: **H.* 'Amber Maiden'; **H.* 'Fair Maiden'; *H.* 'Heartsong'.

Hosta capitata, flowers.

Hosta 'Cinnamon Sticks'

Hosta capitata (Nakai)

SMALL–MEDIUM

Origin: Southern Korea and Shikoku Island, Japan.

Clump Size & Habit: 30 in. wide × 10 in. high (75 × 25 cm). A dense mound.

Description: Leaf blade: 4¾ × 3½ in. (12 × 9 cm); thin, mid-green, matt above and shiny below, closely ribbed veins; edge distinctly rippled, oval with a drooping cuspidate tip, round to heart-shaped, open to pinched lobes. Petiole: narrow, lighter green. Flower: narrowly funnel-shaped, purple with a white throat on a thin, arching, purplish green, 22 in. (55 cm) scape in mid-summer; fertile.

Comments & Special Needs: Site in light to moderate shade. Useful as a breeding plant for producing piecrust leaf edges and heavy racemes of purple flowers that cluster around the top of the scape.

Distinguishing Features: Scapes are noticeably ridged; flower buds are tightly ball-shaped.

Similar: *H. minor*; *H. nakaiana*.

Hosta 'Cinnamon Sticks' (Herold NR)

SMALL–MEDIUM

Origin: *H. longipes* 'Hypoglauca' × *H.* 'Maruba Iwa'.

Clump Size & Habit: 24 in. wide × 10 in. high (60 × 25 cm). A low, open mound.

Description: Leaf blade: 6 × 4⅜ in. (15 × 11 cm); thick, leathery, light green, matt above and thickly glaucous below, widely spaced veins; edge flat but kinked toward the overlapping lobes, heart-shaped to nearly round with a cuspidate tip. Petiole: wide, shallow, dotted claret-purple back and front. Flower: bell-shaped, lavender in dense clusters on a leaning, leafy, claret-purple dotted, 14 in. (35 cm) scape in late summer and early autumn; fertile.

Comments & Special Needs: Site in light to moderate shade. Lovely with *Heuchera* 'Cathedral Windows', whose pewter and burgundy marbling affords a fine contrast with the hosta's burgundy petioles. A useful breeding hosta, both pod and pollen fertile for introducing red features into leaves, petioles and scapes. Autumn temperatures in the North may not be high enough for the seeds to set.

Distinguishing Features: The red dotting continues from the petiole into the palm of the blade but less intensely than in *H.* 'One Man's Treasure'. The leafy scape bracts are also claret-purple.

Similar: *H.* 'Chopsticks' has rounder leaves with a heavy white back; *H.* 'One Man's Treasure', whose flowers and scapes are a deeper color and the purple dotting more intense.

Hosta clausa (Nakai)

MEDIUM

Origin: Korea.

Clump Size & Habit: 12 in. wide × 12 in. high (30 × 30 cm). A dense, rhizomatous mound.

Description: Leaf blade: 6 × 2 in. (15 × 5 cm); of average substance, shiny mid- to dark green, closely spaced veins; edge slightly undulate, narrowly oval to elliptic with an acute tip, tapered pinched lobes. Petiole: green, intensely red dotted. Flower: widely spaced purple buds that do not open, on an upright, leafy, green 30 in. (75 cm). scape in late summer; barely fertile.

Comments: Dimensions are usually much exceeded when grown in cultivation. A moisture-lover and best grown alongside river banks where it will soon colonize huge areas.

Distinguishing Features: The botanical variant, *H. clau-*

Hosta clausa

Hosta 'Collector's Choice'

sa f. *normalis*, has showy purple flowers that open normally.

Hosta 'Collector's Choice' (Janssen NR)

DWARF

Origin: *H. venusta* selection.

Clump Size & Habit: 20 in. wide × 5⅛ in. high (50 × 13 cm). A tight mound.

Description: Leaf blade: 1½ × ⅜–1 in. (4 × 1–2.5 cm); of average substance, smooth, mid-green with a blue cast, matt above and shiny below; edge slightly undulate, folded, oval to nearly heart-shaped with rounded open to pinched lobes. Petiole: narrow, pale green. Flower: see *H. venusta*.

Comments & Special Needs: Site in light to moderate shade to retain the slight blueness in the leaves for longer. Grow with other tiny hostas in a stone sink or ceramic container.

Similar: **H. venusta*; *H.* 'Tot Tot', whose green leaves have a slightly blue cast.

Hosta 'Crocodile Rock' (J. Wilkins 2000)

MEDIUM–LARGE

Origin: Unknown.

Clump Size & Habit: 30 in. wide × 18 in. high (75 × 45 cm). An upright mound.

Description: Leaf blade: 7⅛ × 4 in. (18 × 10 cm); thick, satiny light green, evenly seersuckered; edge flat with occasional kinks, flat to slightly undulate, spoon-shaped, with an acute tip, rounded to tapered open lobes. Petiole: narrow, arching, very pale green. Flower: Funnel-shaped, rich deep purple on an upright, bare, green, 30 in. (75 cm) scape in high summer; fertile, green seedpods.

Hosta 'Crocodile Rock'

Comments & Special Needs: Site in light to medium shade. Of moderate to rapid growth.

Distinguishing Features: Intensely seersuckered leaves have a pebbly texture resembling a crocodile's skin when mature.

Hosta 'Curls' (Fairway Enterprises 1990)

SMALL–MEDIUM

Origin: *H.* 'Tall Twister' × *H.* 'Circus Clown'.

Clump Size & Habit: 14 in. wide × 14 in. high (35 × 35 cm). An even, tiered mound.

Description: Leaf blade: 8⅜ × 4 in. (21 × 10 cm); of average substance, glossy, mid-green, closely ribbed veins; edge intensely rippled, arching with a slightly twisted cuspidate tip, widely lanceolate, tapered folded lobes. Petiole: narrow, green. Flower: funnel-shaped, purple-striped lavender on an upright, leafy, green, 28⅜ in. (71 cm) scape in late summer; fertility unknown.

Hosta 'Curls'

Hosta 'Cutting Edge'

Comments & Special Needs: Site in light to full shade.

Similar: *H. 'Betty', which has more heart-shaped, less pointed leaves.

Hosta 'Cutting Edge' (Gowen & Benedict 1999)

MEDIUM–LARGE

Origin: H. 'Salute' × H. pycnophylla.

Clump Size & Habit: 27⅛ in. wide × 22 in. high (68 × 55 cm). A dense, tiered mound.

Description: Leaf blade: 11½ × 6⅜ in. (29 × 16 cm); of good substance, mid-green with a blue cast, satiny above and distinctly glaucous below, closely spaced veins, dimpled when mature; edge heavily rippled, folded, slightly arching, oval graduating to a cuspidate tip, rounded to tapered open to pinched lobes. Petiole: pale, glaucous gray-green appearing to pierce the blade. Flower: funnel-shaped, pale lavender on an upright, bare, glaucous gray-green, 28 in. (70 cm) scape in high summer; fertility unknown.

Comments & Special Needs: Site in light to moderate shade. Reasonably pest resistant.

Distinguishing Features: The leaf edge sometimes furls upward revealing the distinctly thickly powdered white backs.

Hosta 'De Luxe Edition' (Walden-West & Hyslop 1999)

LARGE

Origin: Unknown.

Clump Size & Habit: 56 in. wide × 27⅛ in. high (140 × 68 cm). An upright mound.

Description: Leaf blade: 10¼ × 8⅜ in. (26 × 21 cm); thick, satiny to glossy dark olive-green, dimpled; edge almost flat, folded to slightly cupped, widely oval with a mu-

cronate tip, heart-shaped pinched to overlapping lobes. Petiole: very long, mid-green. Flower: funnel-shaped white on an upright, leafy, light green, 34 in. (85 cm) scape in high summer; fertile, green seedpods.

Comments & Special Needs: A background hosta for a wide border against a north wall or in light woodland. Of slow to average increase. Pest resistant.

Hosta 'Devon Discovery' (A. & R. Bowden NR)

LARGE

Origin: Unknown.

Clump Size & Habit: 60 in. wide × 36 in. high (150 × 90 cm). An arching, rippled mound.

Description: Leaf blade: 18 × 11 in. (45 × 28 cm); thick, matt light to mid-green, deeply furrowed veins; edge rippled to kinked, arching, folded, oval with a twisted, cuspidate tip, heart-shaped open to pinched lobes. Petiole: stout, light green. Flower: funnel-shaped, near white on a thin, upright, leafy, pale green, 45⅛ in. (113 cm) scape in midsummer; fertility unknown.

Comments & Special Needs: A shapely background plant for shaded gardens or light woodland. Pest resistant.

Similar: H. 'Green Acres', which has slightly less rippled and wider leaves.

Hosta 'Devon Green' (A. & R. Bowden NR)

MEDIUM

Origin: Sport of H. 'Halcyon'.

Clump Size & Habit: 36 in. wide × 18 in. high (90 × 45 cm). A dense, overlapping mound.

Description: Leaf blade: 7⅛ × 4 in. (18 × 10 cm); thick, smooth, glossy dark olive-green, closely veined; edge flat, widely oval with an acute tip, heart-shaped pinched lobes.

Hosta 'De Luxe Edition'

Hosta 'Devon Green'

Hosta 'Devon Discovery'

Petiole: purple-dotted, lighter olive-green, which appears to pierce the blade. Petiole: olive-green. Flower: see *H.* 'Halcyon'.

Comments & Special Needs: Site in light to moderate shade. A moderately rapid increaser. Lovely in a cream stone container. The best-selling, green-leaved hosta in Europe.

Distinguishing Features: Purple-dotted, dark green scapes.

Similar: *H.* 'Canadian Shield'; *H.* 'Peridot'; *H.* 'Valerie's Vanity'.

Hosta 'Donahue Piecrust' (Donahue & Ruh 1999)

LARGE–GIANT

Origin: *H. montana* hybrid.

Clump Size & Habit: 60 in. wide × 28 in. high (150 × 70 cm). A symmetrical mound.

Description: Leaf blade: 11½ × 7½ in. (29 × 19 cm); of good substance, mid- to dark green, satiny above and glaucous below, prominently veined; edge distinctly rippled which turns upward, slightly arching or convex, widely oval

with an often pinched, cuspidate tip, heart-shaped pinched lobes. Petiole: light green, appearing to pierce the blade. Flower: bell-shaped, near white from lavender buds on an upright to oblique, leafy, green, 27⅛ in. (68 cm) scape in mid-summer; fertile.

Comments & Special Needs: Site in moderate shade. Slow to increase and the spectacular piecrust edge takes several years to develop fully. The parent of earlier introductions with piecrust edges but not as popular nowadays.

Similar: *H.* 'Green Piecrust'; *H.* 'Green Ripples; *H.* 'Mesa Fringe'.

Hosta 'Dragon Wings' (Lefever 1996)

LARGE

Origin: *H. montana* × *H.* 'Fortunei'.

Clump Size & Habit: 60¾ in. wide × 24 in. high (152 × 60 cm). A semi-upright, flowing mound.

Description: Leaf blade: 18 × 10½ in. (45 × 27 cm); of average substance, satiny, mid- to dark green, prominently veined; edge evenly rippled, arching, broadly oval with a pinched, cuspidate tip, heart-shaped open lobes. Petiole:

Hosta 'Donahue Piecrust'

dark green. Flower: funnel-shaped, palest lavender on a leaning, leafy, green, 5 ft. (150 cm) scape in late summer; fertile.

Comments & Special Needs: Site in moderate shade. Of slow to moderate increase. Plant as a specimen so that the graceful leaves can be seen close up.

Distinguishing Features: Elegantly elongated pinched tip that causes the leaves to droop.

Hosta 'Edge of Night' (R. Savory 1988)

LARGE

Origin: *H.* 'Green Gold' × *H.* 'Halcyon'.

Clump Size & Habit: 49 in. wide × 24 in. high (122 × 60 cm). An unruly mound.

Description: Leaf blade: 9 × 8⅜ in. (22 × 21 cm); thick, dark olive to spinach-green with a blue cast, matt above and glaucous below, dimpled and puckered; edge flat, deeply cupped, nearly round with a mucronate tip, heart-shaped overlapping lobes. Petiole: glaucous, light olive-green. Flower: flared, lavender on an upright, leafy, green, 23⅛ in. (58 cm) scape in high summer; fertility unknown.

Comments & Special Needs: Site in light to moderate shade. Of slow to moderate increase. Pest resistant.

Similar: *H.* 'Black Hills'.

Hosta 'Edge of Night'

Hosta 'Dragon Wings'

Hosta 'Elatior'

Hosta 'Emeralds and Rubies'

Hosta 'Elatior' (Maekawa & Ruh 2002)

GIANT

Origin: Now considered a probable hybrid of *H. montana*.

Clump Size & Habit: 69½ in. wide × 31⅛ in. high (174 × 78 cm). An immense, semi-upright, wide-spreading mound.

Description: Leaf blade: 14 × 9½ in. (35 × 24 cm); thick, light to mid-green, shiny above and glossy below; prominent, widely spaced veins, barely puckered; edge shallowly undulate, broadly oval with a cuspidate tip, heart-shaped open lobes. Petiole: oblique, stout, light green. Flower: funnel-shaped, lavender, patterned near white on an upright, light green, 69 in. (172 cm) scape in late summer; fertile.

Comments & Special Needs: Site in light to moderate shade. A superb specimen for a woodland setting. Can suffer from stem blight.

Distinguishing Features: Has the tallest flower scape of any hosta: the scapes have small, near white bracts.

Similar: *H. fluctuans*; **H.* 'Green Sheen'; *H.* 'Green Wedge'.

Sports: *H.* 'Victory', which has widely, cream-margined leaves and is somewhat similar to **H.* 'Sagae'.

Hosta 'Emeralds and Rubies' (Dishon 1994)

SMALL

Origin: *H.* 'Emerald Carpet' hybrid.

Clump Size & Habit: 12 in. wide × 6 in. high (30 × 15 cm). An arching, upright, rhizomatous mound.

Description: Leaf blade: 3⅛ × 1 in. (8 × 2.5 cm); of average substance, mid-green, matt above and glossy below, widely spaced veins; edge slightly rippled, arching, lanceolate with an acute tip, tapered open lobes. Petiole: arching, bright red. Flower: tubular, purple-striped lavender on an upright, bare, dark red, 20 in. (50 cm) scape in mid-summer; fertile.

Comments & Special Needs: Site in light to moderate shade. Grow at eye level so as to appreciate the startlingly red petiole and scape. Of moderate increase.

Distinguishing Features: The red coloring in the petiole and scape is solid rather than dotted or streaked.

Hosta 'Fall Bouquet' (Aden 1986)

SMALL

Origin: Selected form of *H. longipes* 'Hypoglauca'.

Clump Size & Habit: 18 in. wide × 12 in. high (45 × 30 cm). A dome-shaped mound.

Description: Leaf blade: 5½ × 2¾ in. (14 × 7 cm), of average to good substance; satiny, mid- to dark green, smooth; edge flat to shallowly rippled, from lanceolate to widely oval with an a cuspidate tip, heart-shaped open lobes. Petiole: narrow, purple-tinted green. Flower: funnel-shaped, lavender in a dense raceme on an upright, bare, claret-colored, 16 in. (40 cm) scape in early autumn; sterile.

Comments & Special Needs: Will tolerate some sun everywhere except in the hottest climates. A thoroughly undervalued hosta considering its many attributes.

Distinguishing Features: Late season of flower combined with the claret petiole and scape.

Similar: **H.* 'Cinnamon Sticks', but the petiole and scape are less noticeably red.

Hosta 'Fall Bouquet'

Hosta 'Floradora'

Hosta 'Fall Emerald'

Hosta 'Fall Emerald' (Summers & Ruh 1997)

MEDIUM–LARGE

Origin: *H. sieboldiana* hybrid, probably with *H. montana*.

Clump Size & Habit: 43½ in. wide × 25⅛ in. high (109 × 63 cm). A tiered, upright mound.

Description: Leaf blade: 9½ × 8⅜ in. (24 × 21 cm); thick, dark green with a gray cast, satiny above and matt below, closely ribbed veins, seersuckered; edge distinctly rippled, slightly arching, widely oval with a cuspidate tip, heart-shaped overlapping lobes. Petiole: light green. Flower: funnel-shaped, white-striped lavender on an upright, leafy, light green, 35⅛ in. (88 cm) scape in mid- to high summer; fertility unknown, but an abundance of green seedpods.

Comments & Special Needs: Site in light to moderate shade. A rapid growth rate, probably inherited from its likely *H. montana* parent.

Distinguishing Features: Leaves hold their color until well into autumn, hence its name.

Similar: *H.* 'Fortunei Gigantea'.

Hosta 'Floradora' (Aden 1978)

MINIATURE

Origin: *H. nakaiana* × *H. longipes* hybrid.

Clump Size & Habit: 16 in. wide × 5⅛ in. high (40 × 13 cm). A dense, spreading mound.

Description: Leaf blade: 2 × 1 in. (5 × 2.5 cm); of average substance, green with a gray cast, matt above and glaucous below, slightly dimpled when mature; edge flat, triangular with a mucronate tip, flat to rounded open lobes. Petiole: narrow, pale gray-green. Flower: bell-shaped, purple on an upright, narrow, bare, gray-green, 12 in. (30 cm) scape in high summer; fertile.

Comments & Special Needs: Site in light to moderate shade. Increases rapidly, providing excellent ground cover with many scapes of densely clustered flowers.

Hosta 'Fried Green Tomatoes' (Solberg 1995)

MEDIUM

Origin: *H.* 'Guacamole' sport.

Clump Size & Habit: 18 in. wide × 10 in. high (45 × 25 cm). An open, semi-upright mound.

Description: Leaf blade: 8 × 6 in. (20 × 15 cm); of good substance, glossy olive-green, prominent widely spaced veins, slight dimpling when mature; edge flat with an occasional kink, slightly arching, widely oval with a mucronate tip, rounded open to pinched lobes. Petiole: pale olive-green. Flower: see *H.* 'Guacamole'.

Comments & Special Needs: Leaves will tolerate some

sun even in the hottest climates provided there is a plentiful supply of water. Large, fragrant, near white flowers are a bonus.

Similar: *H.* 'Fried Bananas', which has glossy, old-gold leaves.

Hosta 'Fried Green Tomatoes'

Hosta 'Frilly Puckers' (Fisher & AHS 1986)

LARGE–GIANT

Origin: *H. sieboldiana* hybrid.

Clump Size & Habit: 30 in. wide × 30 in. high (75 × 75 cm). A dome-shaped mound.

Description: Leaf blade: 12 × 8⅜ in. (30 × 21 cm); thick, dark olive-green, matt above and glaucous below, some seersuckering; edge distinctly but shallowly rippled, convex, widely oval to nearly round with a mucronate tip, heart-shaped overlapping lobes. Petiole: light olive-green. Flower: funnel-shaped, lavender on an upright, bare, green, 46¾ in. (117 cm) scape in early to mid-summer; fertile.

Comments & Special Needs: Use as a background border specimen or in light woodland. Pest resistant.

Distinguishing Features: Leaves vary considerably in shape and puckering is evident on mature plants. A most inappropriate name for a hosta whose chunky, downturned leaves more nearly resemblance a macho carapace than frilly underwear.

Hosta 'Frilly Puckers'

Hosta 'Garnet Prince'

Hosta 'Garnet Prince' (P. Banyai & Dishon 1991)

MEDIUM–LARGE

Origin: *H. nigrescens* hybrid.

Clump Size & Habit: 34 in. wide × 16 in. high (85 × 40 cm). An upright mound.

Description: Leaf blade: 7½ × 5⅛ in. (19 × 13 cm); very thick, leathery, satiny, dark olive-green, closely ribbed veins, slight dimpling; edge flat, arching, elliptic with an obtuse tip, tapered open lobes. Petiole: dark olive-green, stained dark cherry-red toward the base, on the underside the color extends from the crown to the leaf base. Flower: tubular, rich violet on an upright, bare, dark green, 50¼ in. (126 cm) scape from high summer until early autumn; fertility unknown; red seedpods.

Comments & Special Needs: Grow in light shade at eye level to best appreciate the color contrasts between the dark green leaves and red-black of the upright petiole.

Hosta 'Glacier Cascade' (Zilis & Cross 1999)

LARGE

Origin: *H. kikutii* × *H. hypoleuca*.

Clump Height & Habit: 36 in. wide × 26 in. high (90 × 65 cm). An upright, flowing mound.

Description: Leaf blade: 10½ × 4⅜ in. (27 × 11 cm); of average substance, light olive-green, matt above and thickly glaucous below, closely veined; edge widely and evenly rippled, slightly twisted to moderately wavy, lanceolate, elongated acute tip, tapered open lobes. Petiole: narrow olive-green. Flower: tubular, lavender-striped, near white, reflexed at the tip on a leaning, leafy, light green, 30 in. (75 cm) scape in mid-summer; fertile; green seedpods.

Comments & Special Needs: Site in light to moderate shade. Of moderate growth.

Hosta 'Glacier Cascade'

Hosta 'Grand Slam'

Distinguishing Features: Cascading leaves with distinctive white backs.

Hosta 'Grand Slam' (H. Benedict & Gowen 1990)

SMALL–MEDIUM

Origin: Selfed clone of *H. longipes* 'Latifolia'.

Clump Size & Habit: 26⅜ in. wide × 10 in. high (66 × 25 cm). A dome-shaped rippled mound.

Description: Leaf blade: 7⅛ × 6⅜ in. (18 × 16 cm); very leathery, dark olive-green, shiny above and thickly glaucous below, slightly dimpled; edge distinctly and evenly rippled, flat, heart-shaped with a cuspidate tip, heart-shaped overlapping lobes. Petiole: narrow, purple-tinted green. Flower:

funnel-shaped, rich violet on an upright, leafy, purple, 20⅜ in. (51 cm) scape in early to mid-autumn; fertile.

Comments & Special Needs: Good pollen parent for leaf substance and shape. Grow at eye level for best effect in light to moderate shade. Pest resistant.

Similar: *H. 'One Man's Treasure'.

Hosta 'Green Fountain' (Aden 1979)
MEDIUM–LARGE

Origin: H. 'Green Wedge' × H. longipes.

Clump Size & Habit: 56 in. wide × 16 in. high (140 × 40 cm). A cascading mound.

Description: Leaf blade: 12 × 3½ in. (30 × 9 cm); moderately thick, smooth, olive-green, shiny above and very glossy below, widely spaced prominent veins; edge heavily rippled, oblong to elliptic, pinched just above the recurved tip, tapered pinched lobes. Petiole: red-streaked green. Flower: large trusses of funnel-shaped lilac on a drooping, leafy, intensely red-streaked green, 50¾ in. (127 cm) scape in late summer; fertile.

Comments & Special Needs: Site in light to moderate shade all day. A very graceful hosta, best appreciated cascading down walls or from terracotta chimney pots, but also valuable for its showy late flowers.

Similar: *H. kikutii 'Caput Avis'.

Hosta 'Green Piecrust' (F. Williams & AHS 1986)
GIANT

Origin: Unknown.

Clump Size & Habit: 60 in. wide × 30 in. high (150 × 75 cm). A compact, dome-shaped mound.

Description: Leaf blade: 10 × 7½ in. (25 × 19 cm); thick, mid-green with a blue cast in spring, matt above and satiny below, closely ribbed veins, slightly dimpled; edge evenly and shallowly piecrusted, convex and drooping toward the somewhat twisted, exaggeratedly cuspidate tip, widely oval with heart-shaped pinched to overlapping lobes. Petiole: pale green, appearing to pierce the leaf blade. Flower: flared, pale lavender on an upright, leafy, green, 52¾ in. (132 cm) scape in mid-summer; fertile.

Comments & Special Needs: Site in light to moderate shade. Moderate to rapid growth rate. Good autumn color. Pest resistant.

Distinguishing Features: Has less noticeably piecrusted edges than some more modern hostas of this type but was a novelty when it was first introduced.

Similar: H. 'Birchwood Ruffled Queen', a hybrid of H. 'Green Piecrust', is similar but has a slightly less noticeable piecrust edge.

Hosta 'Green Fountain'

Hosta 'Green Piecrust'

Sports: H. 'Grey Piecrust' has gray-green leaves; H. 'Piecrust Promise' has a central variegation.

Hosta 'Green Sheen' (Aden 1978)
GIANT

Origin: H. 'Green Wedge' × H. 'Chartreuse Wedge'.

Clump Size & Habit: 48 in. wide × 36 in. high (120 × 90 cm). A dense mound.

Description: Leaf blade: 18 × 12 in. (45 × 30 cm); very thick, bright light green, a waxy sheen above and intensely glaucous below, furrowed veins; edge almost flat to slightly rippled, folded, oval to nearly round with a mucronate tip, heart-shaped pinched to overlapping lobes. Petiole: wide, pale green. Flower: bell-shaped, near white on an upright, bare, green, 60 in. (150 cm) scape from late summer to early autumn; fertile.

Comments & Special Needs: Sun tolerant in the North, but if grown in shade the leaf color will darken. Pest resistant.

Similar: H. 'Green Wedge'.

Hosta 'Green Sheen'

Hosta 'Heideturm' (Fischer NR)

MEDIUM–LARGE

Origin: Unknown.

Clump Size & Habit: 24 in. wide × 18 in. high (60 × 45 cm). A dense mound.

Description: Leaf blade: 9⅛ × 6⅜ in. (23 × 16 cm); of good substance, bright apple-green, matt above and satiny below, closely ribbed veins, dimpled to seersuckered; edge slightly rippled, undulate, widely oval and pinched toward the slightly cuspidate tip, open to pinched lobes. Petiole: light green. Flower: funnel-shaped, near white on an upright, leafy, sometimes branched, 73⅛ in. (183 cm) scape in mid- to high summer; fertility unknown.

Comments & Special Needs: Will tolerate full sun in cooler climates, especially if grown with moisture at its roots. The German name means 'Heath Tower'.

Distinguishing Features: The scapes, which occasionally branch, tower above the foliage mound making *H.* 'Heideturm' quite a distinct hosta.

Hosta 'Hirao Majesty' (Zilis NR)

GIANT

Origin: Seed sent from Dr. Hirao in Japan to a United States nursery. Named in 1993 by Mark Zilis.

Clump Size & Habit: 66 in. wide × 26 in. high (165 × 65 cm). A swirling mound.

Description: Leaf blade: 15 × 9⅛ in. (38 × 23 cm); thick, smooth, mid-green, shiny above and glossy below, widely spaced veins; edge widely rippled, undulate, arching or drooping and recurved at the cuspidate tip, widely oval, heart-shaped open lobes. Petiole: widely channeled. Flower: open funnel-shaped, pale lavender in dense clusters in a habit like those of *H. kikutii* on a leaning, leafy, two-tone,

Hosta 'Heideturm'

Hosta 'Hirao Majesty'

light green, 40 in. (100 cm) scape in high summer; occasionally fertile.

Comments & Special Needs: Light to medium shade; full shade in Southern gardens.

Distinguishing Features: Floppy, pinched leaf blades cascade downward as does the dense raceme of flowers on long scapes.

Similar: *H.* 'Colossal'; *H.* 'Hirao Supreme', which is also thought to be a tetraploid.

Hosta 'Hirao Splendor' (Hirao & Zilis & Ruh 1997)

SMALL

Origin: Seed sent from Dr. Hirao to a United States nursery.

Clump Size & Habit: 18 in. wide × 12 in. high (45 × 30 cm). A dense mound.

Description: Leaf blade: 5½ × 2 in. (14 × 5 cm); of average substance, light green, shiny above and satiny below, prominent close veining; edge flat to sometimes shallowly rippled, lanceolate with an acute tip, tapered open lobes. Petiole: green with red dots at the crown. Flower: funnel-shaped, purple-striped lavender on an upright, leafy, red-tinted dark green, 21½ in. (54 cm) scape in autumn; sterile.

Comments & Special Needs: Site in light to full shade. Slow to increase.

Hosta 'Holly's Honey' (Holly & AHS 1986)

LARGE

Origin: Unknown.

Clump Size & Habit: 40¾ in. wide × 23⅛ in. high (102 × 58 cm). A dense mound.

Description: Leaf blade: 9⅛ × 6⅜ in. (23 × 16 cm); thin, satiny dark green, widely spaced veins; edge evenly but shallowly rippled to piecrusted, widely oval, pinched at the drooping cuspidate tip, convex, heart-shaped pinched lobes. Petiole: dark green. Flower: bell-shaped, purple in high summer; fertile.

Comments & Special Needs: Site in moderately dense shade. Of moderate to rapid increase. Vulnerable to pests because of the thin-leaved *H. ventricosa* in its ancestry.

Distinguishing Features: Leaves are dome-shaped and puckered.

Similar: *H.* 'Holly's Dazzler' (*H.* 'Holly's Honey' selfed).

Hosta 'Honeybells' (Cummings & AHS 1986)

MEDIUM–LARGE

Origin: *H. plantaginea* × *H. sieboldii*.

Clump Size & Habit: 50¾ in. wide × 26⅜ in. high (127 × 66 cm). A lax mound.

Hosta 'Hirao Splendor'

Hosta 'Holly's Honey'

Description: Leaf blade: 10 × 6⅜ in. (25 × 16 cm); thinnish, olive-green, satiny to glossy above and shiny below, widely spaced veins; edge shallowly undulate, arching to drooping from the base, oval with an obtuse tip, rounded open to pinched lobes. Petiole: narrow, light olive-green. Flower: open funnel-shaped, slightly fragrant, palest lavender on an upright, leafy, green, 45⅛ in. (113 cm) scape from late summer to early autumn; fertile.

Comments & Special Needs: Now superseded as a garden specimen and mainly used for landscaping. Leaves are said to be attractive to deer. Tolerates full sun, which brings out the elusive fragrance of the flowers. Flowers open as the temperature rises, but the leaves will turn a sickly green unless they receive a plentiful supply of water.

Similar: *H.* 'Benny McRae'; *H.* 'Buckwheat Honey'; *H.* 'Royal Standard'; *H.* 'Savannah Emerald'; *H.* 'Sweet Marjorie'; *H.* 'Sweet Susan'.

Sports: *H.* 'Sugar and Cream'; *H.* 'Sweet Standard'.

Hosta 'Honeybells'

Hosta hypoleuca (Murata)

MEDIUM–LARGE

Origin: Aichi and Shizuoka Prefectures, Japan.

Clump Size & Habit: 45½ in. wide × 15 in. high (114 × 38 cm). A lax, open mound.

Description: Leaf blade: 13⅛ × 9⅛ in. (33 × 23 cm); thick, leathery, mid- to dark green, satiny above and thickly glaucous below, dimpled when mature, prominently veined; edge shallowly rippled, slightly arching, oval with a cuspidate tip, deeply heart-shaped, open to pinched lobes. Petiole: narrow, arched, red-dotted green. Flower: bell-shaped, purple-suffused white on an oblique to recumbent, leafy, purple-dotted, light green, 26 in. (65 cm) scape in late summer; fertile.

Comments & Special Needs: Sun tolerant but grows equally well in shade. *Hosta hypoleuca* changes its characteristics more than any other species when grown in cultivation. In the wild it is often found clinging to a rock face in full sun, where it has only one or two very large leaves; in the garden it forms a typical hosta clump, albeit retaining the white back that in the wild acts as protection from the heat reflected off rocks.

Hosta hypoleuca

Distinguishing Features: Extraordinarily thick, white pruinose coating on the underside of the leaf.

Similar: *H. pycnophylla*, which is more difficult to cultivate.

Sports: *H.* 'Maekawa'.

Hosta 'Invincible'

Hosta 'Jade Beauty'

Hosta 'Invincible' (Aden 1986)

MEDIUM–LARGE

Origin: Unknown.

Clump Size & Habit: 49 in. wide × 20 in. high (122 × 50 cm). A dense mound.

Description: Leaf blade: 8⅜ × 6⅜ in. (21 × 16 cm); leathery, glossy olive-green, widely spaced veins; edge distinctly rippled, folded, wedge-shaped with a cuspidate tip, heart-shaped open to folded lobes. Petiole: narrow, lightly red-dotted green. Flower: lightly fragrant, funnel-shaped, palest lavender on a leaning, very leafy, pale green, 25⅛ in. (63 cm) scape in late summer; fertile.

Comments & Special Needs: Emerges early. Best in morning sun but will tolerate sun all day in cooler climates if given plenty of water. Not as pest resistant as its name might suggest in spite of the excellent substance of the leaves. Nonetheless a superb hosta.

Distinguishing Features: Has been known to have multi-branched scapes in wet summers. Scapes are stained red where the leafy bracts are attached and immediately above the bracts. Occasionally produces hose-in-hose double flowers.

Similar: *H.* 'Polished Jade'; *H.* 'Rippled Honey'; **H.* 'Sweet Bo Peep'.

Sports: **H.* 'Devon Cloud'.

Hosta 'Jade Beauty' (Zilis & T & Z Nursery 1988)

MEDIUM–LARGE

Origin: Tissue-cultured sport of *H.* 'Francee'.

Clump Size & Habit: 40¾ in. wide × 22 in. high (102 × 55 cm). A dense mound.

Description: Leaf blade: 9⅛ × 6⅜ in. (23 × 16 cm); of average to good substance, rich dark green, matt above and glaucous below, dimpled to puckered when mature; edge almost flat, widely oval to almost round with a cuspidate tip, heart-shaped folded to overlapping lobes. Petiole: paler green. Flower: see *H.* 'Francee'.

Comments & Special Needs: Increases fairly rapidly. Best in light to full shade. Not just another sport to be named. A super green-leaved hosta in its own right, having all the attributes of its *H.* 'Fortunei' ancestry.

Similar: *H.* 'Fortunei Aoki'.

Hosta 'Jade Cascade' (Heims NR)

GIANT

Origin: *H. montana* f. *macrophylla* seedling.

Clump Size & Habit: 60 in. wide × 40 in. high (150 × 100 cm). Dramatically arching, open mound.

Description: Leaf blade: 21⅛ × 8⅜ in. (53 × 21 cm); of good substance, glossy, bright olive-green, slightly dimpled between the conspicuous veins; edge widely rippled, elongated lanceolate to oval with an acute tip, heart-shaped pinched lobes. Petiole: deeply channeled, green, up to 15 in. (38 cm) in length. Flower: funnel-shaped, pale lavender on a leaning, leafy, green, 42 in. (105 cm) scape from mid- to late summer; fertility unknown.

Comments & Special Needs: Grow in light to moderate shade. An ideal woodland hosta.

Distinguishing Features: Deeply furrowed veining. Individual flowers are widely spaced on scapes which are mahogany tinted below the distinct floral bracts.

Similar: **H.* 'Devon Discovery'.

Hosta 'Joseph' sporting to *H.* 'Josephine'

Hosta 'Jade Cascade'

Hosta kikutii

Hosta 'Joseph' (Kuk 1987)

MEDIUM

Origin: Sport of *H.* 'Josephine'.

Clump Size & Habit: 30 in. wide × 16 in. high (75 × 40 cm). An arching mound.

Description: Leaf blade: 6⅜ × 5½ in. (16 × 14 cm); thick, glossy, very dark olive-green, ribbed veins, some seersuckering; edge slightly rippled, convex, widely oval nearly round with a mucronate tip, heart-shaped open lobes. Petiole: narrow, light olive-green with maroon dots on the reverse. Flower: flared, lavender on an upright, leafy, maroon-dotted, 16¾ in. (42 cm) scape in late summer; fertility unknown.

Comments & Special Needs: Site in light to moderate shade. Slower growing than *H.* 'Josephine'.

Similar: **H.* 'Black Hills'; **H.* 'Lakeside Accolade'; **H.* 'Lakeside Black Satin'; **H.* 'Second Wind'; **H.* 'Spinach Patch'; **H. ventricosa*.

Hosta kikutii (Maekawa)

MEDIUM–LARGE

Origin: Honshu, Shikoku and Kyushu Islands, Japan.

Clump Size & Habit: 36 in. wide × 16 in. high (90 × 40 cm). A dense, fountainlike mound.

Description: Leaf blade: 11½ × 4⅜ in. (29 × 11 cm); of average substance, bright mid-green, shiny above and whitish and shiny below, closely spaced, deeply impressed veins; edge flattish, arching, elongated to oval with an acute tip, heart-shaped overlapping lobes. Petiole: narrow, lighter green. Flower: funnel-shaped, near white stained lavender, reflexing at the tip, on stiff, long pedicels with distinct silvery bracts clustered at the top of a conspicuously leaning, leafy, green, 24 in. (60 cm) scape in late summer; fertile.

Comments & Special Needs: Site in morning sun followed by dappled shade. The heavy, dense clusters of flowers, droop downward from the scape.

Similar: *H. kikutii* 'Caput Avis' has conspicuous, narrow veining on matt olive-green leaves, purplish brown dotting on leafy bracts and the flower buds have a fancied resemblance to a bird's beak; *H. kikutii* 'Yakushimensis' has longer, curled tips to the leaves and the petiole extends into the bright glossy green leaf making a delightful tonal contrast; *H. kikutii* 'Leuconota' (Schmid 1991) has leaves half the size of those of the species, the leaves and petiole emerging with a white pruinose coating, the upper surface of the leaf becoming green during the summer; *H. kikutii* 'Polyneuron' has strongly marked narrowly spaced veins giving a ribbed effect, matt, dark green leaves, paler green with a satin sheen below, and is very slow growing; *H. kikutii* 'Tosana', said by some authorities to be a separate species, is a good breeding plant for red petioles.

Sports: **H. kikutii* 'Kifukurin Hyuga'.

Hosta 'King Michael' (Krossa & Summers & Ruh 1992)

GIANT

Origin: *H. montana* f. *macrophylla* hybrid.

Clump Size & Habit: 47½ in. wide × 33½ in. high (119 × 84 cm). A huge, arching mound.

Description: Leaf blade: 12⅜ × 9⅛ in. (31 × 23 cm); thick, leathery, mid-green, satiny above and glossy and rough-textured below, deeply furrowed veins; edge rippled, arching, widely oval with a cuspidate tip, heart-shaped open lobes. Petiole: stout, light green. Flower: flared, white on an upright, bare, pale green, 75⅛ in. (188 cm) scape in early summer; fertile.

Hosta 'King Michael'

Hosta 'Komodo Dragon'

Comments & Special Needs: Site in light to medium shade. A superb background hosta for woodland gardens. Contrariwise, it makes the perfect single specimen in a paved courtyard.

Similar: *H.* 'Bee's Colossus'; *H.* 'Big Boy'; *H.* 'Colossal'; *H.* 'Green Acres'; *H.* 'King James'; *H.* 'Mikado', a sport from **H. montana* 'Aureomarginata'.

Hosta 'Komodo Dragon' (M. Seaver NR)

GIANT

Origin: Unknown.

Clump Size & Habit: 73⅛ in. wide × 28 in. high (183 × 70 cm). An open, almost vase-shaped mound.

Description: Leaf blade: 15 × 11 in. (38 × 28 cm), thick, blue-tinted dark green, matt above and glaucous below, distinct widely spaced veins, dimpled; edge conspicuously and evenly rippled, widely oval with a cuspidate tip on mature leaves, heart-shaped open lobes. Petiole: stout, blue-green. Flower: funnel-shaped, palest lavender on an upright, leafy, light green, 36 in. (90 cm) scape in mid-summer; fertility unknown.

Comments & Special Needs: Site in light to moderate shade. A rapid increaser. Pest resistant. An impressive specimen for the woodland garden.

Distinguishing Features: Attractive regular shallow piecrust edge on the leaves.

Similar: *H.* 'Big Sam'; *H.* 'Green Ripples'; *H.* 'Lakeside Ripples'; *H.* 'Sea Drift'.

Sports: *H.* 'Chinese Dragon' is a streaked form.

Hosta laevigata (Schmid)

SMALL

Origin: Islands off the coast of Korea.

Clump Size & Habit: 30¾ in. wide × 12 in. high (77 × 30 cm). A dense mound.

Description: Leaf blade: 8⅜ × 2⅜ in. (21 × 6 cm); thick, emerging chartreuse turning light green, matt above and satiny below, slightly dimpled; edge tightly ruffled, arching, narrowly lanceolate with an acute tip, tapered open lobes. Petiole: flat, light green. Flower: broad, spiderlike, purple on an upright, green, 36 in. (90 cm) scape in late summer to early autumn; fertile.

Comments & Special Needs: Closely related to *H. yingeri*. Good for hybridizing as it passes on the ruffled edges and spiderlike flowers. Site in light shade. Pest resistant. Winner of the 1996 Alex J. Summers Distinguished Merit Hosta Award.

Distinguishing Features: The flowers are spiderlike with very thin petals. The flower buds can produce over 30 blooms on one scape.

Hosta 'Lakeside Accolade' (Chastain 1988)

MEDIUM

Origin: Open-pollinated seedling of *H.* 'Little Aurora'.

Clump Size & Habit: 18 in. wide × 12 in. high (45 × 30 cm). A tight mound.

Description: Leaf blade: 9⅛ × 8 in. (23 × 20 cm) thick, leathery, dark spinach green, shiny above and thinly glaucous below, slightly dimpled, occasional puckering; edge almost flat, often cupped, nearly round with a mucronate tip, heart-shaped open lobes. Petiole: dark green. Flowers: pale lavender on an upright, bare scape up to 42 in. (105 cm) in late summer; fertile.

Comments & Special Needs: Can be considerably larger in optimum growing conditions. Shade all day. Pest resistant.

Hosta laevigata

Hosta 'Lakeside Accolade'

Hosta 'Lakeside Black Satin'

Hosta 'Lakeside Leprechaun'

Distinguishing Features: Leaf cupping and distinct tip distinguish it from other similar hostas.

Similar: *H. 'Joseph'; *H. 'Second Wind'; *H. 'Spinach Patch'.

Hosta 'Lakeside Black Satin' (Chastain 1993)

MEDIUM

Origin: *H. ventricosa* hybrid.

Clump Size & Habit: 40¾ in. wide × 18 in. high (102 × 45 cm). An open mound.

Description: Leaf blade: 9⅛ × 8⅜ in. (23 × 21 cm); thin, lustrous black-green, very glossy below, smooth, widely spaced veins; edge closely and evenly rippled, widely oval with a mucronate tip, heart-shaped open lobes. Petiole: dark green. Flower: widely spaced, bell-shaped, white-striped, deep purple on an upright, bare, dark green, 34¾ in. (87 cm) scape in mid-to late summer; fertility unknown.

Comments & Special Needs: Site in full shade all day. First of the "black-leaved hostas."

Distinguishing Features: Exceptionally dark green leaves with very widely spaced veins.

Similar: *H. 'Holly's Honey'; H. 'Lakeside Coal Miner' has nearer black, twisted leaves and smaller purple flowers; *H. ventricosa.

Sports: H. 'Stained Satin' has attractive, centrally margined leaves, but is not as vigorous as its parent.

Hosta 'Lakeside Leprechaun' (Chastain 1991)

MINIATURE

Origin: Sport of H. 'Little Aurora'.

Clump Size & Habit: 24 in. wide × 5⅛ in. high (60 × 13 cm). A compact mound.

Description: Leaf blade: 4 × 3½ in. (10 × 9 cm); thick,

chartreuse to bright rich green turning golden yellow by autumn, matt above and glaucous below, seersuckered; edge lightly rippled, cupped, widely oval to nearly round with a cuspidate tip, heart-shaped pinched lobes. Petiole: long, narrow, lighter green. Flower: see H. 'Little Aurora'.

Comments & Special Needs: Light shade all day. Pest resistant.

Similar: H. 'Cody'.

Hosta 'Lakeside Lollipop' (Chastain 1993)

SMALL

Origin: Unknown.

Clump Size & Habit: 16 in. wide × 8⅜ in. high (40 × 21 cm). A low, spreading mound.

Description: Leaf blade: 3½ × 2¾ in. (9 × 7 cm); thick, shiny dark green, seersuckered, prominently veined; edge flat, nearly round with a mucronate tip, rounded open lobes. Petiole: lighter green, appearing to pierce the blade. Flower: funnel-shaped, pure white on an upright, leafy, dark green, 16 in. (40 cm) scape in mid-summer; fertile.

Comments & Special Needs: Site in light to moderate shade. Slow to increase. Plant in the foreground of a border; ideal for a gravel garden.

Distinguishing Features: The almost perfectly round leaf blade and petiole form the shape of a lollipop.

Hosta 'Lakeside Looking Glass' (Chastain 1997)

MEDIUM

Origin: *H. yingeri* hybrid.

Clump Size & Habit: 12 in. wide × 10 in. high (30 × 25 cm). A fairly dense mound.

Description: Leaf blade: 8⅜ × 5½ in. (21 × 14 cm); thick, leathery dark green, shiny above and very glossy

Hosta 'Lakeside Lollipop'

Hosta 'Lakeside Neat Petite'

Hosta 'Lakeside Looking Glass'

below, widely spaced, light green veins, dimpled; edge rippled, arching, widely elliptic with an obtuse tip, rounded pinched lobes. Petiole: flattish blue-black. Flower: spider-shaped, bright purple on an arching, very leafy, light green, 12 in. (30 cm) scape in mid-summer; fertile, green seed-pods.

Comments & Special Needs: Light to full shade will keep the leaves a better color. Can be prone to late spring frost damage in colder climates. A rapid increaser.

Distinguishing Features: Very glossy, lustrous leaves. Green leafy bracts form toward the top of the flower scape, which is slightly purple dotted at base. The flower scape, when elongating, presents a star-burst of closely packed bracts, each one shielding an immature flower bud.

Similar: *H. laevigata*; H. yingeri 'Treasure Island'.

Hosta 'Lakeside Neat Petite' (Chastain 1991)

MINIATURE

Origin: *H. venusta* × *H.* 'Blue Cadet'.

Clump Size & Habit: 20 in. wide × 7⅛ in. high (50 × 18 cm). A tight mound.

Description: Leaf blade: 2¾ × 2 in. (7 × 5 cm); of average substance, mid-green with a slight blue cast, matt above and thinly glaucous below; edge flat with occasional wide undulations, slightly cupped, widely oval with a cuspidate tip, near heart-shaped pinched lobes. Petiole: short, mid-green. Flower: funnel-shaped, orchid to violet on a dark green, bare, upright, 12 in. (30 cm) scape in mid-summer; limited fertility.

Comments & Special Needs: Site in light to moderate shade. An excellent edging or foreground hosta and lovely in a container.

Distinguishing Features: Superb dense clusters of flowers disposed on the top 2 to 2¾ in. (5 to 7 cm) of the scape.

Similar: *H.* 'Peedee Elfin Bells'; *H.* 'Quilting Bee'.

Hosta 'Lancifolia' (Engler)

SMALL–MEDIUM

Origin: Origins in doubt, but it is often confused with *H. cathayana* and *H. sieboldii*.

Clump Size & Habit: 40¾ in. wide × 16 in. high (102 × 40 cm). A dense, spreading mound.

Description: Leaf blade: 7⅛ × 2⅜ in. (18 × 6 cm); thin, mid- to dark green, shiny above and glossy below; edge slightly undulate, elliptic to narrowly oval with an acute tip, tapered open to pinched lobes. Petiole: green, purple dotted toward the crown. Flower: narrowly bell-shaped, lavender, in a dense raceme on an upright, leafy, purple-

Hosta 'Lancifolia'

dotted, green, 20 in. (50 cm) scape in late summer; limited fertility.

Comments & Special Needs: Emerges early; the leaves may be damaged by spring frost. Vigorous and floriferous. Has been used for mass planting in both public and private gardens since its introduction to the United States in the 1800s. An excellent "beginner's hosta" and also lovely in large wooden containers.

Distinguishing Features: Differs from *H. cathayana* in its low level of fertility and is far better known.

Similar: *H. cathayana*.

Sports: *H.* 'Lancifolia Aurea' has chartreuse-yellow leaves.

Hosta 'Leather Sheen' (Zilis & Lohman 1988)

SMALL

Origin: *H.* 'Sum and Substance' × *H. venusta* seedling.

Clump Size & Habit: 48⅜ in. wide × 16¾ in. high (121 × 42 cm). A dense mound.

Description: Leaf blade: 7½ × 4⅜ in. (19 × 11 cm); thick, leathery, glossy very dark green, prominently veined, dimpled when mature; edge slightly undulate, blade flat,

Hosta 'Leather Sheen'

narrowly oval with an acute tip, tapered pinched lobes. Petiole: mid- to dark green. Flower: bell-shaped, pale lavender on an upright, bare, light green, 22¾ to 30 in. (57 to 75 cm) scape from mid- to late summer; barely fertile.

Comments & Special Needs: Site in morning sun in the North. Good growth rate. Somewhat pest resistant.

Hosta longipes 'Hypoglauca'

Distinguishing Features: Light green scape and buds make a contrast with the leaves that have a black cast.

Similar: *H. 'Tardiflora'; **H. tardiva*.

Hosta longipes (Franchet & Savatier)

SMALL–MEDIUM

Origin: Honshu Island, Japan.

Clump Size & Habit: 20 in. wide × 9½ in. high (50 × 24 cm). A rhizomatous mound.

Description: Leaf blade: 8 × 4¾ in. (20 × 12 cm); thick, leathery dark green, shiny above and glossy, lighter green below, deeply ribbed veins; edge almost flat, widely oval with a cuspidate tip, flat pinched to folded lobes. Petiole: almost horizontal, purple-dotted light green. Flower: near funnel-shaped, lavender on an oblique to horizontal, purple-dotted, green, 12 in. (30 cm) scape from late summer to early autumn; fertile.

Comments & Special Needs: Site in light shade. Average to fast growth rate. Very variable in the wild. Many botanical forms are much used in breeding.

Distinguishing Features: Nearly flat, overlapping mound of wide leaves.

Hosta longipes

Forms: *H. longipes* 'Hypoglauca' has longer, narrower leaves with an intensely glaucous underside, distinctly red-streaked petioles and is the parent of many hybrids to whom it has passed on this characteristic, including *H.* 'Brandywine' and *H.* 'Granddaddy Redlegs'. *Hosta longipes* 'Latifolia' has distinctly rippled edges and a long, pointed tip. Now considered to be synonymous with *H. rupifraga* by some authorities.

Hosta longipes 'Latifolia'

Hosta longissima

Hosta 'Bitsy Green'

Hosta longissima (Honda)

SMALL

Origin: Central and western Honshu, Shikoku, Kyushu, Japan.

Clump Size & Habit: 25⅛ in. wide × 9½ in. high (63 × 24 cm). A low, arching, dense mound.

Description: Leaf blade: 8 × 1 in. (20 × 2.5 cm); of av-erage substance, mid-green, matt above and shiny below, smooth; edge flat with the occasional kink, linear to lance-olate with an acute tip, graduating into the purple-dotted petiole. Flower: funnel-shaped purple on an upright, leafy, light green, 22 in. (55 cm) scape from early to late autumn; fertile.

Comments & Special Needs: Needs an abundance of

Hosta 'Manhattan'

Hosta 'Maraschino Cherry'

moisture at its roots. Shade all day. Can be grown in garden ponds successfully if the crown is kept above the water line.

Distinguishing Features: Strap-shaped leaves are among the narrowest in the genus.

Similar: *H.* 'Bitsy Green' a hybrid, is almost identical; *H. longissima* 'Brevifolia' has much narrower leaves; *H. clavata*, not usually grown in gardens, is slightly wider.

Hosta 'Manhattan' (Brincka & Petryszyn 1994)

MEDIUM–LARGE

Origin: *H.* 'Sea Frolic' hybrid.

Clump Size & Habit: 36 in. wide × 14 in. high (90 × 35 cm). A compact mound.

Description: Leaf blade: 11 × 8 in. (28 × 20 cm); thick, light gray-green turning darker green with bluish overtones, shiny above and matt below, intensely seersuckered and puckered; edge distinctly pie-crusted, arching toward the cuspidate tip, widely oval with heart-shaped pinched lobes. Petiole: stout, light green, appearing to pierce the blade. Flower: funnel-shaped, lavender from attractive bulging purple buds on an upright, leafy, blue-green to purple, 36 in. (90 cm) scape in early summer; fertile.

Comments & Special Needs: Grow in light to medium shade. Very slow to increase. An interesting hosta with almost too many good features.

Distinguishing Features: Intensely rippled edge to the deeply seersuckered surface texture of the leaf makes an unusual combination. The ball-like purple buds enclosed by purple bracts.

Similar: *H.* 'Niagara Falls' has similar pie-crusted edges but a smooth surface texture.

Hosta 'Maraschino Cherry' (Zilis & Solberg 1999)

MEDIUM

Origin: Sport of *H.* 'Cherry Berry'.

Clump Size & Habit: 36 in. wide × 16 in. high (90 × 40 cm). An upright mound.

Description: Leaf blade: 7⅛ × 2¾ in. (18 × 7 cm); thin, glossy dark green, ribbed veins when mature; edge flat to occasionally kinked, elliptic with an acute tip, tapered pinched lobes. Petiole: purple-dotted green. Flower: see *H.* 'Cherry Berry'.

Comments & Special Needs: Site in light to full shade. A rapid increaser. Vulnerable to pests.

Distinguishing Features: Remarkable dark red scapes towering above the leaf mound, followed by red seedpods, in contrast to the dark green leaves, make this a most unusual hosta.

Hosta minor (Nakai)

SMALL

Origin: Korea.

Clump Size & Habit: 22 in. wide × 8⅜ in. high (55 × 21 cm). A spreading mound.

Description: Leaf blade: 3½ × 2½ in. (9 × 6 cm); of average substance, mid- to dark green, matt above and shiny below; edge undulate, arching, slightly folded, oval with a curved tip, tapered open lobes. Petiole: narrow, purple-dotted green. Flower: funnel-shaped, widely disposed, light violet on an upright, thin, ridged, green, leafy, 18 to 24 in. (45 to 60 cm) scape in mid-summer; fertile.

Comments & Special Needs: Site in light to moderate shade. Superb trusses of flowers. Very variable in the wild

Hosta minor, flowers.

and often wrongly named in cultivation. Ideal for rock and sink gardens and other containers.

Distinguishing Features: Ridged, hollow scapes. Faint purple dotting at the scape base. The rebloom characteristic.

Similar: **H. capitata*; **H. nakaiana*; **H. venusta* is usually smaller.

Hosta 'Misty Morning' (Kuk's Forest 1986)

SMALL

Origin: *H. venusta* hybrid.

Clump Size & Habit: 18 in. wide × 4¾ in. high (45 × 12 cm). A low, shapely mound.

Description: Leaf blade: 4 × 3⅛ in. (10 × 8 cm); thick, vivid light green, satiny above and glaucous below, dimpled when mature, conspicuously veined toward the edge; edge flat, widely oval with a mucronate tip, heart-shaped open to pinched lobes. Petiole: light green. Flower: funnel-shaped, lavender on an upright, bare, pale green, 15 in. (38 cm) scape in mid-summer; fertility unknown.

Comments & Special Needs: Site in some morning sun except in the hottest climates followed by light shade. Pest resistant.

Hosta 'Misty Morning'

Distinguishing Features: Registered as a green-leaved hosta but it leans toward chartreuse and gold.

Hosta montana (Maekawa)

LARGE–GIANT

Origin: Populations spread widely throughout Japan.

Hosta montana, flowers.

Hosta 'Moongate Little Dipper'

Clump Size & Habit: 48⅜ in. wide × 24 in. high (121 × 60 cm). An upright mound.

Description: Leaf blade: 12 × 9⅛ in. (30 × 23 cm); thick, olive-green, satiny above and glossy below and rough to the touch, deeply furrowed veins, slightly dimpled when mature; edge shallowly undulate, arching, slightly folded, widely oval with a cuspidate tip, heart-shaped overlapping lobes. Petiole: stout, light green. Flower: funnel-shaped, suffused lavender to almost white on a leaning, leafy, 49 in. (122 cm) scape in mid-summer; fertile.

Comments & Special Needs: Site in light to moderate shade. Very variable in the wild. Usually much larger in cultivation. Emerges much later than its best-known sport, *H. montana* 'Aureomarginata'. Some morning sun in cooler climates, otherwise light to full shade. The parent of many large-leaved hybrids.

Distinguishing Features: Very long, dense racemes and numerous leafy bracts. Heavy production of pods weigh the scape down.

Similar: *H. montana* f. *macrophylla* has much wider leaves; *H. 'Elatior'.

Sports: *H.* 'Emma Foster', a gold-leaved form, is rarely grown because it is not vigorous.

Hosta 'Moongate Little Dipper' (Issacs & Solberg 1996)

SMALL–MEDIUM

Origin: *H.* 'Serendipity' × *H.* 'Blue Blazes'.

Clump Size & Habit: 18 in. wide × 12 in. high (45 × 30 cm). A low mound.

Description: Leaf blade: 4⅜ × 3½ in. (11 × 9 cm); thick, dark green with a slight blue cast, glossy above and matt below, dimpled to seersuckered; edge flat, deeply cupped,

Hosta nakaiana

nearly round with a mucronate tip, heart-shaped, pinched to overlapping lobes. Petiole green. Flower: tubular, lavender on a thin, upright to oblique, leafy, glaucous mauve, 15 in. (38 cm) scape in mid-summer; fertile.

Comments & Special Needs: Site in light to moderate shade. Slowish growth rate. Pest resistant. Plant to contrast its distinctively cupped leaves with hostas that have linear leaves.

Distinguishing Features: Small, deeply cupped green leaves. Quite similar to its *H.* 'Serendipity' parent.

Hosta nakaiana (Maekawa)

SMALL

Origin: Southern and central Korea; Saga, Nagasaki and Hyogo Prefectures, Japan.

Clump Size & Habit: 32 in. wide × 12 in. high (80 × 30 cm). A dense, overlapping, domed mound.

Description: Leaf blade: 3½ × 2⅜ in. (9 × 6 cm); thin, mid-green with a slight gray cast, matt above and satiny below, smooth, ribbed veins when mature; edge undulate, slightly folded, widely oval with a mucronate tip, heart-shaped pinched lobes. Petiole: narrow, green. Flower: funnel-shaped, purple with a white throat on an upright, ridged, leafy, pale green, 15 to 22¾ in. (38 to 57 cm) scape in mid- to high summer; fertile.

Comments & Special Needs: Site in light to moderate shade. A rapid increaser. Feed in spring and autumn.

Distinguishing Features: Very floriferous, producing abundant seed. Scapes are ridged.

Similar: *H. capitata*; *H. minor*.

Hosta 'Neat and Tidy' (Simpers 1980)

LARGE–GIANT

Origin: *H.* 'Golden Circles' hybrid.

Clump Size & Habit: 32 in. wide × 30 in. high (80 × 75 cm). An unruly mound.

Description: Leaf blade: 9⅛ × 8 in. (23 × 20 cm); thick, blue-tinted dark green, crumpled and puckered, matt to shiny above and glaucous below, conspicuously veined; edge slightly rippled, convex with the midrib grooved, occasionally cupped, near round with a mucronate tip, heart-shaped pinched lobes. Petiole: glaucous light green. Flower: bell-shaped, pale lavender on an upright, leafy, 36 in. (90 cm) scape in late summer; fertile.

Comments & Special Needs: Site in light to moderate shade. At its best as a young plant. Can achieve larger dimensions in optimum growing conditions.

Distinguishing Features: Crumpled, rather distorted leaves.

Similar: *H.* 'Black Hills', in which the leaf crumpling is less exaggerated.

Hosta 'Niagara Falls' (Brincka & Petryszyn 1991)

LARGE

Origin: *H. montana* f. *macrophylla* × *H.* 'Sea Drift'.

Clump Size & Habit: 30 in. wide × 20 in. high (75 × 50 cm). An open, spreading mound.

Description: Leaf blade: 15 × 9 in. (38 × 22 cm); thick, dark green, smooth, matt to glaucous above and shiny below, deeply impressed veins; edge with small, even ripples, arching, widely oblong to oval with a cuspidate tip, heart-shaped pinched lobes. Petiole: stout, pale green. Flower: flared, pale violet on a leaning, leafy, 48 in. (120 cm) scape; fertility unknown.

Comments & Special Needs: Dimensions are much lar-

Hosta 'Neat and Tidy'

ger in optimum growing conditions. Light to full shade all day.

Distinguishing Features: Glaucous bloom on the leaf surface assumes a waxy sheen later in the season. Piecrust edges are not present on young plants.

Similar: *H.* 'Hoosier Dome', which has more pronounced, inverted cupping on rounder leaves; *H.* 'Lakeside Ripples'.

Hosta 'One Man's Treasure' (H. Benedict & Solberg 1999)

MEDIUM

Origin: *H. longipes* 'Hypoglauca' hybrid.

Clump Size & Habit: 24 in. wide × 14 in. high (60 × 35 cm). An open, arching mound.

Description: Leaf blade: 6⅜ × 5½ in. (16 × 14 cm); thick, leathery, mid- to dark green, matt above and glossy below, widely spaced veins; edges undulate, widely oval with a twisted cuspidate tip, heart-shaped to flat open lobes. Petiole: shallow, olive-green, intensely burgundy dotted. Flower: bell-shaped, violet, white-striped inside on a stout, upright, leafy, deep burgundy-red, 20 to 24 in. (50 to 60 cm) scape in early autumn; fertile, purple seedpods.

Comments & Special Needs: Site in light to moderate shade. Plant with burgundy-veined *Mitella stylosa*, which also has burgundy leaf stems as an echo. An outstanding hosta; among the best of all hostas in flower. Excellent hybridizing potential for passing on its red petioles and even darker scapes. Moderate growth rate.

Distinguishing Features: Purple-black scapes, purple-stained flower bracts, deep violet pedicels and flower tubes, violet bell-shaped flowers; mahogany-purple dotting on both sides of the petiole, the dotting reaching well into the palm of the blade.

Hosta 'Niagara Falls'

Hosta 'One Man's Treasure'

Hosta 'Pearl Lake'

Similar: **H.* 'Cinnamon Sticks', whose flowers and scapes are a paler color; *H.* 'Granddaddy Redlegs', a sister seedling; *H.* 'Swizzle Sticks'.

Hosta **'Pearl Lake'** (Piedmont Gardens 1982)

MEDIUM

Origin: Unknown, thought to be a *H. nakaiana* hybrid.

Clump Size & Habit: 36 in. wide × 15 in. high (90 × 38 cm). A dense, dome-shaped mound.

Description: Leaf blade: 5⅛ × 4⅜ in. (13 × 11 cm); of average substance, mid- to dark green with a gray cast, matt to glaucous above and shiny below, slight dimpling; edge slightly undulate, slightly folded, heart-shaped with a mucronate tip, heart-shaped pinched to overlapping lobes. Petiole: narrow, green. Flower: bell-shaped, purple-striped pale lavender in a dense raceme on a narrow, upright, leafy, light green, 20 in. (50 cm) scape in early summer; fertile.

Comments & Special Needs: Grow in dappled shade. Vigorous, a rapid increaser. Ideal as ground cover or for woodland margins. Has never become a favorite in spite of being chosen as the Alex J. Summers Distinguished Merit Hosta Award in 1982.

Similar: *H. nakaiana*; *H. 'Candy Hearts'; H. 'Drummer Boy'; H. 'Happy Hearts'; H. 'Pastures New'; H. 'Saint Fiacre'; H. 'Twiggy'.

Sports: *H. 'Veronica Lake'.

Hosta 'Permanent Wave' (P. Banyai 1989)

MEDIUM

Origin: Unknown.

Clump Size & Habit: 32⅜ in. wide × 12 in. high (81 × 30 cm). A tiered, open mound.

Description: Leaf blade: 6 × 3½ in. (13 × 9 cm); of average substance, mid-green, matt above and satiny below, closely ribbed veins; edge closely rippled to piecrusted, arching, widely lanceolate with a cuspidate tip, tapered open to pinched lobes. Petiole: very light green, appearing to pierce the blade. Flower: widely spaced, small, tubular,

Hosta 'Permanent Wave'

pale lavender on an upright, green, 19⅛ in. (48 cm) scape in high summer; fertility unknown.

Comments & Special Needs: Site in light to moderate shade. Emerges early in the season. Lovely with ferns used to complement or contrast the distinctly rippled edges.

Distinguishing Features: An outstanding, graceful, cascading mound.

Hosta 'Placemat' (Soules 1991)

LARGE–GIANT

Origin: H. sieboldiana × H. 'Tokudama'.

Clump Size & Habit: 60 in. wide × 30 in. high (150 × 75 cm). A dense mound.

Description: Leaf blade: 12 × 11 in. (30 × 28 cm); thick, leathery, glossy dark green with overtones of blue, heavy puckering between the veins; edge slightly rippled, shallowly cupped or convex, nearly round with a mucronate tip, heart-shaped overlapping lobes. Petiole: stout, green. Flower: bell-shaped, near white on an upright, bare, glaucous green, 24 to 30 in. (60 to 75 cm) scape in early summer; fertile.

Comments & Special Needs: Site in light to moderate shade. Among the first to flower. Slow to increase. Pest resistant.

Distinguishing Features: Flowers are level with the top of the leaf mound.

Similar: *H. 'Blue Umbrellas', whose leaves are blue-green.

Hosta plantaginea (Ascherson)

LARGE

Origin: Southern China.

Clump Size & Habit: 60 in. wide × 24 in. high (150 × 60 cm). A dome-shaped mound.

Hosta 'Placemat'

Description: Leaf blade: 11 × 7⅛ in. (28 × 18 cm); thin, pale to mid-green, satiny above and glossy below, closely ribbed veins, slightly dimpled when mature; edge slightly rippled, arching, oval with cuspidate tip, heart-shaped pinched lobes. Petiole: mid-green. Flower: very long-tubed, widely funnel-shaped, exceedingly fragrant, white on an upright to oblique, leafy, chartreuse, 32 in. (80 cm) scape from late summer to autumn; fertile.

Comments & Special Needs: Leaves turn chartreuse in sun. Tolerates a half to three-quarters of a day's sun in the hottest, humid regions and full sun all day in other areas provided it is supplied with enough moisture. Leaves take several weeks to completely unfurl after the shoots first sprout. It passes on its sweet fragrance to many hybrids, but adequate moisture and heat are necessary to set seed. Feed and water throughout the growing season.

Hosta plantaginea

Hosta plantaginea 'Aphrodite', flower.

Hosta plantaginea 'Grandiflora', flowers.

Distinguishing Features: Intensely fragrant, nocturnal, waxy, long-tubed (up to 5⅛ in. or 13 cm) white flowers.

Similar: *H. 'Royal Standard'.

Sports: H. plantaginea 'Aphrodite' has extra petals, creating the effect of a double flower, and it needs a hot, humid climate for the flowers to open; in cooler climates the buds usually abort before flowering. Hosta plantaginea 'Venus' is a true double and a much more effective flower. Hosta plantaginea 'White Swan' is similar. Hosta plantaginea 'Ming Treasure' has margins that change from chartreuse to white. Hosta plantaginea 'Grandiflora' has laxer leaves and flowers with an even longer tube, and its sport H. plantaginea 'Chelsea Ore' has yellow leaves with a narrow, dark green margin and a notably weak constitution; it needs a hot, humid climate in which to thrive.

Hosta 'Potomac Pride' (Avent 1996)

LARGE

Origin: H. yingeri × H. 'Blue Umbrellas'.

Clump Size & Habit: 49 in. wide × 28 in. high (122 × 70 cm). A rounded, semi-upright mound.

Description: Leaf blade: 12 × 8⅜ in. (30 × 21 cm); thick, leathery, very dark green with a blue cast, glossy above and a powdery bloom below, crumpled and puckered, ribbed veins; edge almost flat to slightly rippled, mostly convex, widely oval, mucronate tip, rounded open to pinched lobes. Petiole: pale green, appearing to pierce the leaf blade. Flower: small, spider-shaped, lavender on an upright, leafy, pale green, 34 in. (85 cm) scape in mid- to late summer; fertile.

Comments & Special Needs: Performs equally well in cooler regions although southern-raised. Tolerates full sun for ½ to ¾ of the day. Vigorous, a rapid increaser. A superb hosta that just gets better with each succeeding season.

Similar: H. 'Flower Power', whose flowers extend down the scape and whose leaves are greener, more oval and more dimpled than seersuckered.

Hosta pulchella (Fujita)

DWARF–MINIATURE

Origin: Mount Ubatake, Kyushu Island, Japan.

Clump Size & Habit: 8 in. wide × 4 in. high (20 × 10 cm). An open mound.

Description: Leaf blade: 1½ × ¾ in. (4 × 2 cm); leathery, mid- to dark green, shiny above and shiny, pale green below, smooth; edge widely undulate, slightly arching, oval with a cuspidate tip, heart-shaped pinched lobes. Petiole: green, purpled dotted on the back, appearing to pierce the blade. Flower: funnel-shaped purple on an oblique, leafy, burgundy-stained green, 4¾ to 12 in. (12 to 30 cm) scape in early to mid-summer; fertile.

Comments & Special Needs: The parent of many popular small-leaved hostas. Ideal in sinks or small containers with other tiny hostas. Light shade all day.

Distinguishing Features: Blooms very early.

Similar: *H. gracillima; *H. 'Sugar Plum Fairy'.

Sports: *H. pulchella 'Kifukurin Ubatake' has creamy, yellow-margined leaves.

Hosta 'Purple Lady Finger' (Savory 1982)

MEDIUM

Origin: H. longissima × H. clausa.

Clump Size & Habit: 18 to 20⅜ in. × 15 in. (45 to 51 × 38 cm). A diffuse, upright mound.

Description: Leaf blade: 6¾ to 10 × ¾ in. (17 to 25 × 2

Hosta 'Potomac Pride'

Hosta pulchella

cm); of average substance, mid-to dark green, satiny above and shiny paler green below; edge very ruffled when young, the ruffles becoming shallower with maturity, linear to lanceolate with an obtuse tip, the lobes tapering into the flat, ruffle-edged, pale green petiole. Flower: potentially funnel-shaped, purple striped that remains closed on an upright or oblique, leafy, dark green, 16 to 18 in. (40 to 45 cm) scape from high summer until early autumn; fertility unknown.

Comments & Special Needs: Site in light to moderate shade. Attractive violet-purple flower buds are widely spaced along the raceme. Probably most effective when grown with ferns or plants other than hostas.

Distinguishing Features: Long-lasting flower buds elongate but do not open, a characteristic inherited from its *H. clausa* parent.

Similar: **H. longissima*.

Hosta 'Purple Lady Finger'

Hosta 'Purple Passion' (H. & D. Benedict NR)

SMALL

Origin: Unknown.

Clump Size & Habit: 18 in. wide × 10 in. high (45 × 25 cm). A dense mound.

Description: Leaf blade: 7½ × 2⅜ in. (19 × 6 cm); of average substance, mid-to dark green, satiny above and glossy paler green below, smooth, closely ribbed veins; edge distinctly rippled, arching, folded, narrowly oval with a cuspidate tip, tapered open lobes. Petiole: purple-dotted light green. Flower: funnel-shaped, deep purple on an upright or oblique, dark purple, leafy, 20 in. (50 cm) scape from mid- to late summer; fertile, purple-black seedpods.

Comments & Special Needs: Light shade all day. A good breeding plant with several characteristics worth passing on.

Distinguishing Features: Purple-black scapes, dark violet flowers and near black seedpods.

Hosta 'Quill' (Herold NR)

SMALL−MEDIUM

Origin: *H. pycnophylla* × *H. yingeri*.

Clump Size & Habit: 18 in. wide × 9 in. high (45 × 22 cm). A dense mound.

Description: Leaf blade: 6⅜ × 2 in. (16 × 5 cm); thick, green with a blue cast, matt above and thickly glaucous below, closely ribbed veins; edge widely rippled, arching, lanceolate with an acute tip, tapered open lobes. Petiole: light green, appearing to pierce the leaf blade. Flower: small, spiderlike, lavender on an upright, leafy, light green, 15 in. (38 cm) scape in mid- to high summer; fertile.

Comments & Special Needs: Tolerates at least half a day's sun in the North.

Hosta 'Purple Passion'

Hosta 'Quill'

Hosta 'Raspberry Sorbet'

Hosta 'Quilting Bee'

Similar: *H. 'Purple Passion', which is darker colored in all its parts.

Hosta 'Quilting Bee' (R. O'Harra 1999)

SMALL

Origin: Unknown.

Clump Size & Habit: 26⅜ in. wide × 9 in. high (66 × 22 cm). A low-growing, neat, dense mound.

Description: Leaf blade: 4 × 2¾ in. (10 × 7 cm); thick, dark olive-green, satiny above and matt below, dimpled to seersuckered; edge flat to slightly rippled, cupped or convex, widely oval to nearly round with a mucronate tip, heart-shaped open lobes. Petiole: flattish, light olive-green. Flower: near bell-shaped, striped lavender on an upright, bare, green, 18 in. (45 cm) scape in mid- to late summer; fertility unknown.

Comments & Special Needs: Moderate growth rate. Shade all day. Pest resistant.

Distinguishing Features: Scapes rise well above the leaf mound. A pleasing mound of attractively shaped leaves that have a quilted surface texture.

Hosta 'Raspberry Sorbet' (Lohman & Zilis 1999)

SMALL–MEDIUM

Origin: H. rupifraga × H. 'Shining Tot'.

Clump Size & Habit: 34⅜ in. wide × 12 in. high (86 × 30 cm). A rippling mound.

Description: Leaf blade: 6¾ × 3½ in. (17 × 9 cm), thick, dark green, very glossy above and shiny gray-white below; edge rippled, slightly arching, cupped at the base, widely lanceolate with a cuspidate tip, tapered open lobes. Petiole: bright red toward the crown. Flower: widely spaced, flared, purple-striped mauve on an upright, leafy, 20 in. (50 cm) scape that is bright red toward the raceme in late summer; fertile.

Comments & Special Needs: Site in light to moderate shade. A moderate to rapid increaser.

Distinguishing Features: Red scapes are an excellent contrast to the rich mauve flowers.

Similar: H. 'Red Neck Heaven', which is H. kikutii selfed.

Hosta 'Razzle Dazzle' (Kuk's Forest 1987)

SMALL

Origin: H. sieboldiana hybrid.

Clump Size & Habit: 12 in. wide × 6¾ in. high (30 × 17 cm). An overlapping mound.

Description: Leaf blade: 5½ × 3½ in. (14 × 9 cm); thick, lustrous olive-green, ribbed veins, slight dimpling when mature; edge rippled, folded or arching, oval with a cuspidate tip, tapered, open to pinched lobes. Petiole: narrow, maroon-dotted pale green. Flower: tubular, white on an

Hosta 'Razzle Dazzle'

Hosta rectifolia

upright, leafy, maroon-dotted, glaucous pale green, 15 in. (38 cm) scape in mid- to high summer; fertility unknown.

Comments & Special Needs: Site in light to moderate shade. Of moderate increase. Pest resistant. Grow at eye level to best appreciate the attractive red petioles.

Distinguishing Features: Leaves have a waxy edge.

Hosta rectifolia (Nakai)

MEDIUM

Origin: Northern Honshu and Hokkaido, Japan.

Clump Size & Habit: 32 in. wide × 14 in. high (80 × 35 cm). An upright mound.

Description: Leaf blade: 6⅜ × 2¾ in. (16 × 7 cm); thin, mid-green, matt above and glossy below, ribbed veins; edge slightly undulate, convex, elliptic to oval, pinched at the cuspidate tip, tapered pinched lobes. Petiole: green. Flower: widely funnel-shaped, purple-striped bright mauve from darker buds on a green scape up to 39½ in. (99 cm); fertile.

Comments & Special Needs: Site in some morning sun except in the hottest regions. A broad spectrum species with many attractive variegated forms not yet in commerce. The scapes are known to tower over 7 ft. (210 cm), a characteristic that could more often be exploited in hybridizing programs.

Distinguishing Features: Tall scapes of late-flowering blooms on a low foliage mound.

Similar: *H.* 'Decorata Normalis'; *H.* 'Tall Boy', a putative hybrid of *H. rectifolia* × *H. ventricosa*, has spectacularly tall scapes up to 70¾ in. (177 cm) in optimum growing conditions, with long racemes of lavender flowers in late summer.

Sports: *H. rectifolia* 'Chionea' is a white-margined form

Hosta 'Regal Rhubarb'

similar to *H.* 'Ginko Craig'; *H. rectifolia* 'Nakai' is a narrow-leaved, cream-margined form; *H.* 'White Triumphator' is a form grown for its superb white flowers.

Hosta 'Regal Rhubarb' (Sellers 1983)

LARGE

Origin: Thought to be of *H. nigrescens* ancestry.

Clump Size & Habit: 56 in. × 31⅛ in. high (140 × 78 cm). An open, upright to vase-shaped mound.

Description: Leaf blade: 7⅛ × 4 in. (18 × 10 cm), thick, mid- to dark green, matt to satiny above and thinly glaucous below, some dimpling, conspicuously veined; edge slightly undulate, flat nearer the tip, arching, oval with a cuspidate tip, tapered pinched lobes. Petiole: stout, scarlet-dotted dark green. Flower: funnel-shaped, purple from darker purple buds on an upright, bare, 48 in. (120 cm) scape that is burgundy-purple toward the crown in high summer; fertile.

Comments & Special Needs: Light to full shade all day. *Hosta* 'Regal Rhubarb' is one of the first hostas introduced on account of its burgundy-red petioles. A hosta that is still worth growing though many others now have this trait in a more pronounced form. Grow with the petioles at eye level for the most impact. Underplant with *Heuchera* 'Mint Chocolate', whose strong vein markings echo the color of the petioles.

Distinguishing Features: There can be noticeable red-dotting piercing the blade from the petiole.

Similar: *H.* 'Flower Power'; *H.* 'Tall Boy'.

Sports: *H.* 'Rhubarb Pie', a superb new introduction with red petioles and a distinctly pie-crusted leaf edge; the underside of the leaf has a white indumentum.

Hosta 'Rippled Honey' (H. R. Benedict NR)
MEDIUM

Origin: *H. plantaginea* × *H.* 'Holly's Honey'.

Clump Size & Habit: 36 in. wide × 20 in. high (90 × 50 cm). An open mound.

Description: Leaf blade: 12 × 3½ in. (30 × 9 cm); thick, smooth, light apple-green, glossy above and shiny below, closely ribbed veins; edge distinctly rippled, narrowly oval with a cuspidate tip, flat to tapered open lobes. Petiole: light green, appearing to pierce the leaf bade. Flower: widely flared, white to palest lavender depending on temperature, on an upright, leafy, pale green, 26 to 29⅛ in. (65 to 73 cm) scape in late summer; fertility unknown.

Comments & Special Needs: Morning sun in the hottest climates, three-quarters of a day's sun in cooler regions. A moderate to rapid increaser. Vulnerable to pest damage.

Similar: *H.* 'Invincible'.

Hosta 'Rippling Waves' (Nesmith & AHS 1986)
LARGE

Origin: *H.* 'Tokudama' × *H. sieboldiana*.

Clump Size & Habit: 74 in. wide × 22 in. high (185 × 55 cm). A rounded mound.

Description: Leaf blade: 12 × 9½ in. (30 × 24 cm); thick, dark green with a slight blue cast, matt above and glaucous below; heavily seersuckered, closely ribbed veins; edge shallowly undulate, sometimes cupped, sometimes oval and arching with the paler midrib clearly showing, sometimes convex and near round, twisted at the mucronate tip, heart-shaped, overlapping lobes. Petiole: stout, pale green. Flower: funnel-shaped, pale lavender on an upright, leafy, pale green, 32 in. (80 cm) scape at mid-summer; fertile.

Comments & Special Needs: Light to medium shade all day. Pest resistant. Plant as a specimen, where its unusual combination of leaf shapes can make a statement.

Distinguishing Features: Some leaves are nearly round while others veer toward widely lanceolate.

Hosta 'Rosedale Barnie' (Hadrava 1999)
MEDIUM

Origin: *H. ventricosa* × *H.* 'Invincible'.

Clump Size & Habit: 36 in. wide × 15 in. high (90 × 38 cm). An open mound.

Description: Leaf blade: 6⅜ × 5⅛ in. (16 × 13 cm); of average substance, dark green, matt above and slightly shiny below, slight dimpling; edge rippled, nearly round with a cuspidate tip, tapered open lobes. Petiole: dark green. Flower: long, bell-shaped, violet-striped pale lavender from deep violet buds in dense clusters on a stout, slightly leaning, leafy, green, 9½ to 16 in. (24 to 40 cm)

Hosta 'Rippled Honey'

Hosta 'Rippling Waves'

scape in a dense raceme in mid- to late summer; fertility unknown.

Comments & Special Needs: Site in light to moderate shade. Can reach 40 in. (100 cm) wide in optimum growing conditions but is slow-growing.

Distinguishing Features: An excellent display of flowers.

Hosta 'Royal Standard' (Grulleman & Wayside 1986)

LARGE

Origin: *H. plantaginea* × *H. sieboldii*.

Clump Size & Habit: 50¾ in. wide × 36 in. high (127 × 90 cm). A dense mound.

Description: Leaf blade: 9 × 5⅛ in. (22 × 13 cm); of average substance, bright green, satiny above and shiny below, slightly dimpled when mature; edge slightly undulate, slightly arching, oval with an acute tip, tapered open to pinched lobes. Petiole: light green. Flower: funnel-shaped, fragrant, white, from lavender-tinted buds on an upright to slightly oblique, leafy, pale green, 42 in. (105 cm) scape from late summer until autumn; fertile.

Comments & Special Needs: First hosta to receive a plant patent. Vigorous, fast growing. Morning sun in the hottest climates and three-quarters of a day's sun in cooler regions; water and feed copiously throughout the growing season. Leaves will turn chartreuse when exposed to full sunlight.

Distinguishing Features: Very fragrant, waxy, white flowers that are far more abundant than those of its *H. plantaginea* parent; will bloom well in cooler regions.

Similar: **H.* 'Honeybells'; **H.* 'Sweet Susan'.

Sports: **H.* 'Hoosier Harmony'; *H.* 'Prairieland Memories' with yellow leaves; *H.* 'Royal Accolade', which does not hold its central variegation for as long as *H.* 'Hoosier Harmony'.

Hosta rupifraga (Nakai)

MEDIUM

Origin: Hachijo Island, Japan.

Clump Size & Habit: 25⅛ in. wide × 8 to 9½ in. high (63 × 20 to 24 cm). A widely overlapping mound.

Hosta 'Royal Standard'

Hosta rupifraga

Hosta 'Rosedale Barnie'

Description: Leaf blade: 8 × 4¾ in. (20 × 12 cm); thick, mid-green, glossy above and waxy below, strongly marked veins, smooth; edge evenly rippled, flat, oval to heart-shaped with a cuspidate tip, heart-shaped open to pinched lobes. Petiole: green. Flower: bell-shaped, purple striped in a dense raceme on an oblique to arching, blue-green, 18 in. (45 cm) scape in autumn; fertile.

Comments & Special Needs: Site in light to moderate shade.

Distinguishing Features: Glossy, leathery leaves.

Similar: *H.* 'Maruba Iwa' has longer scapes; **H.* 'Rhapsody in Blue', which has leaves with a blue cast.

Hosta 'Saishu Jima' (Davidson & Summers NR)

SMALL

Origin: Unknown but probably a form of *H. sieboldii*.

Clump Size & Habit: 20 in. wide × 8⅜ in. high (50 × 21 cm). An upright mound.

Description: Leaf blade: 3½ × ⅜ in. (9 × 1 cm); of average substance, dark green, glossy above and shiny below, smooth; edge rippled when mature, arching, lanceolate with an acute tip, tapered open lobes. Petiole: green. Flower: bell-shaped, purple-striped lavender on an upright, bare, pale green, 6 to 12 in. (15 to 30 cm) scape from late summer to early autumn; fertile.

Comments & Special Needs: Site in light to moderate shade. Fast growing. Ideal for edging or for tubs and containers.

Distinguishing Features: Distinctly rippled edges, which take time to develop.

Similar: An unnamed variant of *H.* 'Saishu Jima', whose flowers remain closed, still very rare; *H.* 'Yakushima Mizu'.

Hosta 'Sea Monster' (M. Seaver 1978)

GIANT

Origin: *H.* 'Brookwood Blue' hybrid.

Clump Size & Habit: 50¾ in. wide × 28 in. high (127 × 70 cm). An unruly mound.

Description: Leaf blade: 16 × 12 in. (40 × 30 cm); very thick, bright green, seersuckered and puckered, matt to shiny above and glaucous below; edge flat to slightly rippled, shallowly cupped or convex, flat, widely oval to rounded with a mucronate tip, heart-shaped overlapping lobes. Petiole: deeply channeled, pale green, appearing to pierce the blade. Flower: bell-shaped, pale lavender striped white on an upright to leaning, bare, pale green, 30⅜ in. (76 cm) scape in mid-summer; fertile.

Comments & Special Needs: Much used as a parent in the Seaver hybridizing programs. Very slow to establish,

Hosta 'Saishu Jima'

Hosta 'Sea Monster'

taking up to seven years for the crumpled appearance of the leaves to reach their best. Shade all day. Pest resistant.

Similar: *H.* 'Birchwood Green'; **H.* 'Wrinkles and Crinkles', which is smaller.

Sports: *H.* 'Lochness Monster' has intensely seersuckered, yellow-margined leaves.

Hosta 'Sea Octopus' (M. Seaver 1881)

MINIATURE–SMALL

Origin: *H.* 'Sea Sprite' hybrid.

Clump Size & Habit: 12 to 16 in. high × 6¾ to 9 in. high (30 to 40 × 17 to 22 cm). An upright mound.

Description: Leaf blade: 4 × ¾ in. (10 × 2 cm); of average substance, olive-green, matt above and slightly shiny below, closely ribbed veins, slightly dimpled when mature; edge widely and evenly rippled, arching, lanceolate with an acute tip, tapered, pinched lobes. Petiole: narrow, pale olive-green. Flower: flared, purple-striped pale lavender

Hosta 'Sea Octopus'

Hosta 'Second Wind'

Hosta sieboldii 'Weihenstephan'

from a rich purple bud on an upright or oblique, leafy, pale green, 20 in. (50 cm) scape in late summer; fertile.

Comments & Special Needs: Site in light shade. Best set off with a huge, blue, round-leaved hosta.

Distinguishing Features: Excellent flower trusses are more of a bonus than the noticeably rippled leaves, though not remarkably rippled by today's standards. Popular when first introduced.

Similar: *H. laevigata; *H. 'Permanent Wave'.

Hosta 'Second Wind' (Kulpa 1991)

MEDIUM

Origin: Sport of H. 'Whirlwind'.

Clump Size & Habit: 22 in. wide × 11 in. high (55 × 28 cm). A dense mound.

Description: Leaf blade: 6⅜ × 4⅜ in. (16 × 11 cm); thick, leathery dark green, waxy to glossy above and thinly glaucous below, dimpled when mature, widely spaced veins; edge almost flat, widely oval with a mucronate tip, heart-shaped pinched lobes. Petiole: dark green. Flower: see H. 'Fortunei Hyacinthina' from which H. 'Whirlwind' mutated.

Comments & Special Needs: Site in light to moderate shade. Will easily exceed its registered dimensions. Among the best of the hostas with dark green leaves.

Similar: *H. 'Black Beauty'; H. 'Rosedale Spoons'.

Hosta sieboldii 'Alba' (Irving)

SMALL–MEDIUM

Origin: Sport of H. sieboldii, occasionally found in the wild in Japan.

Clump Size & Habit: 25⅛ in. wide × 11 in. high (63 × 28 cm). A dense, spreading mound.

Description: Leaf blade: 5½ × 2⅜ in. (14 × 6 cm); thin, mid- to dark green, matt above and satiny, paler green below, smooth; edge slightly undulate, slightly arching, widely elliptic with an acute tip, tapered open lobes. Petiole: pale green. Flower: widely flared, white on a thin, upright, leafy, pale green, 24 in. (60 cm) scape in late summer; fertile.

Comments & Special Needs: Good light to light shade all day. An excellent ground cover that is usually grown in gardens for its floral display rather than its leaves.

Similar: H. 'Snowflakes'; H. sieboldii 'Weihenstephan', which has even larger flowers.

Hosta 'Slick Willie' (Hadrava 1996)

MEDIUM

Origin: H. ventricosa × H. 'Invincible'.

Clump Size & Habit: 50¾ in. wide × 20 in. high (127 × 50 cm). An open mound.

Hosta 'Slick Willie'

Hosta 'Sparkling Burgundy'

Hosta 'Spinach Patch'

Description: Leaf blade: 8⅜ × 6⅜ in. (21 × 16 cm); of moderate substance, very glossy dark green with a black cast, well-marked veins; edges somewhat rippled when mature, slightly cupped or convex, broadly oval to almost round with a cuspidate tip, heart-shaped open to pinched lobes. Petiole: short, mid-green. Flower: funnel-shaped, pale lavender on an upright, leafy, pale green, 20 to 28 in. (50 to 70 cm) scape in mid- to late summer; sterile.

Comments & Special Needs: Light to moderate shade. Moderate growth rate. Outer leaves of the clump are the darkest green.

Distinguishing Feature: The oily appearance of the leaf surface, especially when splashed with raindrops, makes this an impressive and unusual hosta.

Similar: *H.* 'Lily Pad'.

Hosta 'Sparkling Burgundy' (Savory 1982)

MEDIUM

Origin: *H.* 'Ginko Craig' hybrid.

Clump Size & Habit: 36 in. wide × 18 in. high (90 × 45 cm). An upright mound.

Description: Leaf blade: 7½ × 4 in. (19 × 10 cm); thick, smooth, mid- to dark olive-green, glossy above and whitish satiny below, ribbed veins, slight dimpling; edge widely kinked, elliptic with an acute tip, flat to tapered lobes. Petiole: olive-green. Flower: widely flared, pale lilac from violet buds on an upright, leafy, dark red-purple, 22¾ in. (57 cm) scape in late summer; fertile.

Comments & Special Needs: Light to full shade. Pest resistant.

Distinguishing Features: Long racemes of flowers which are poised almost at right angles to the scape well above the leaf mound.

Similar: **H.* 'Maraschino Cherry'.

Sports: *H.* 'Obsession' has mid-green leaves margined with a near black, jagged border pattern.

Hosta 'Spinach Patch' (Vaughn NR)

LARGE

Origin: Unknown.

Clump Size & Habit: 50¾ in. wide × 22 in. high (127 × 55 cm). An open mound.

Description: Leaf blade: 11½ × 9 in. (29 × 22 cm); thick, dark spinach-green, matt above and glaucous below, heavily seersuckered and crumpled, ribbed veins; edge flat, convex, almost round, pinched at the mucronate tip, heart-shaped pinched to overlapping lobes. Petiole: flattish, pale olive-green, appearing to pierce the leaf blade. Flower: funnel-shaped, white on an upright, dark green, bare, 28⅜ to 32 in. (71 to 80 cm) scape in mid-summer; fertility unknown.

Hosta 'Strawberry Delight'

Hosta 'Sugar Plum Fairy'

Comments & Special Needs: Light to full shade. Grow as a specimen with plenty of space around it to display the unruly, twisted and puckered leaves.

Hosta '**Strawberry Delight**' (Sugita & Ruh 1998)
MEDIUM

Origin: *H. longipes* × *H. pycnophylla*.

Clump Size & Habit: 27⅛ in. wide × 15 in. high (68 × 38 cm). An open mound.

Description: Leaf blade: 8⅜ × 5⅛ in. (21 × 13 cm); of average substance, light to mid-green, glossy above and glaucous below, smooth, widely spaced veins; edge attractively rippled, flat, wedge-shaped with a distinctly cuspidate tip, flat pinched lobes. Petiole: purple-dotted light green. Flower: bell-shaped, purple-striped lavender on an upright, bare, pale green, 19⅛ to 22 in. (48 × 55 cm) scape in late summer; sterile.

Comments & Special Needs: Among the best of many recently introduced hybrids with rippled margins.

Similar: **H. ventricosa*, which has much darker green leaves.

Hosta '**Sugar Plum Fairy**' (Briggs Nursery 1987)
DWARF

Origin: Putative hybrid of *H. gracillima* × *H. venusta*.

Clump Size & Habit: 24 in. wide × 10 to 12 in. high (60 × 25 to 30 cm). A dense, unruly, arching mound.

Description: Leaf blade: 4 × ¾ in. (10 × 2 cm); of moderate substance, glossy olive-green; rippled edges, arching, folded, curved, lanceolate with an acute tip, tapered open lobes. Petiole: shallow, dark green. Flower: funnel-shaped, purple-striped pale lavender on an upright, leafy, green, 12 in. (30 cm) scape from late summer to early autumn; fertile.

Hosta 'Sweet Bo Peep'

Comments & Special Needs: Site in some morning sun. Increases rapidly and makes a good edging hosta; is also very suitable for small containers.

Distinguishing Features: In very strong sunlight, the leaves bleach to creamy green with the dark green veins making a marked contrast.

Similar: **H. gracillima*; **H.* 'Saishu Jima'.

Hosta '**Sweet Bo Peep**' (H. Benedict NR)
MEDIUM

Origin: *H.* 'Invincible' hybrid.

Clump Size & Habit: 40¾ in. wide × 16 in. high (102 × 40 cm). An open mound.

Description: Leaf blade: 6⅜ × 4⅜ in. (16 × 11 cm); thick, leathery, mid- to dark olive-green, glossy above and shiny below, smooth, widely ribbed veins; edge slightly rippled, slightly folded, oval with a mucronate tip, heart-shaped pinched lobes. Petiole: olive-green, red-stained to-

Hosta 'Sweet Susan'

Hosta 'Tardiflora Honey Glaze'

ward the crown. Flower: funnel-shaped, slightly fragrant, pale lavender on an upright or oblique, leafy, olive-green, 34 in. (85 cm) scape in late summer; fertility unknown.

Comments & Special Needs: Grow in morning sun except in the hottest climates.

Distinguishing Features: Differs from *H.* 'Invincible' in having smaller, rounder leaves.

Hosta 'Sweet Susan' (Williams 1986)
MEDIUM

Origin: *H. sieboldii* × *H. plantaginea*.

Clump Size & Habit: 30⅜ in. wide × 18 in. high (76 × 45 cm). A dense mound.

Description: Leaf blade: 9 × 4¾ in. (22 × 12 cm); of average substance, mid-green, shiny above and lustrous below, ribbed veins; edge flat to slightly rippled, arching, oval with an acute tip, round to heart-shaped pinched lobes. Petiole: stout, lighter green. Flower: funnel-shaped, fragrant lilac-lavender on an oblique, leafy, 25⅛ in. (63 cm) scape from high summer until the frosts; fertile.

Comments & Special Needs: Sun for at least half a day in the North; some morning sun in the South will produce the best flowers. Apply food and water in plentiful supplies. Increases rapidly.

Distinguishing Features: A long season of flower, the flowers being a much richer color in cooler climates. *Hosta* 'Sweet Susan' was one of the first hybrids with fragrant lavender flowers. It blooms slightly earlier than most, the flowers are a deeper lavender and it is a good parent

Similar: *H.* 'Sweet Marjorie'; *H.* 'Sweet Winifred' has fragrant white flowers.

Sports: *H.* 'Sweet Serenity' has creamy white margins.

Hosta 'Tardiflora' (Irving NR)
SMALL–MEDIUM

Origin: Once considered a species, now thought to be of Japanese garden origin.

Clump Size & Habit: 26 in. wide × 12 in. high (65 × 30 cm). A dense mound.

Description: Leaf blade: 6 × 3⅛ in. (15 × 8 cm); thick, leathery, smooth, dark olive-green, satiny above and glossy below; edge shallowly rippled, oval with an acute tip, rounded open lobes. Petiole: narrow, purple-streaked olive-green. Flower: narrowly funnel-shaped, lavender in a dense raceme on an upright, purple-streaked, 24 in. (60 cm) scape in autumn; fertile.

Comments & Special Needs: Site in good light to dappled shade. Most memorable for being the pod parent of the Tardiana Group, the well-known hybrids between *H.* 'Tardiflora' × *H. sieboldiana* 'Elegans' raised in the 1960s and 1970s. Autumn flowers make *H.* 'Tardiflora' a very valuable hosta. Grow with low-growing asters, autumn crocus and colchicums. Excellent for Southern gardens as it has a long life cycle. Pest resistant.

Distinguishing Features: Individual flowers are disposed all round the scape.

Sports: *H.* 'Tardiflora Honey Glaze', whose leaves have an overlay of honey-gold; *H.* 'National Velvet' has somewhat heart-shaped leaves with a velvety sheen.

Hosta tardiva (Nakai)
SMALL–MEDIUM

Origin: Shikoku and Kyushu Islands and the Kii Peninsula, Japan.

Clump Size & Habit: 32 in. wide × 16 in. high (80 × 40 cm). An irregular, arching mound.

Hosta 'Tardiflora'

Hosta tardiva

Description: Leaf blade: 6⅜ × 3⅛ in. (16 × 8 cm); very thin, bright olive-green, prominently veined, shiny above and glossy below; edge flat but with the occasional kink, arching, narrowly oval with an acute tip, tapered pinched lobes that are mostly hidden in the foliage mound. Petiole: purple-dotted green. Flower: bell- to funnel-shaped, rich

violet on an upright, bare, burgundy-dotted, 24 in. (60 cm) scapen autumn; fertility uncertain.

Comments & Special Needs: Not normally grown in gardens except by serious collectors.

Similar: *H. takahashii*, which is sometimes listed as a species; *H.* 'Southern Comfort', once incorrectly thought to be *H. tardiva*.

Hosta 'Teaspoon' (Nyikos 1998)

MINIATURE–SMALL

Origin: *H.* 'Birchwood Parky's Gold' × *H.* 'Golden Tiara'.

Clump Size & Habit: 21⅛ in. wide × 7½ in. high (53 × 19 cm). An upward-facing mound.

Description: Leaf blade: 3½ × 2¾ in. (9 × 7 cm); of average substance, bright mid-green, matt above and satiny below, dimpled when mature; edge irregularly serrated, cupped, folded, widely oval with a mucronate tip, heart-shaped open lobes. Petiole: long, narrow, pale green appearing to pierce the blade. Flower: tubular, pinkish on an upright, bare, pale green, 20 to 22 in. (50 to 55 cm) scape in mid-summer; fertile.

Hosta 'Teaspoon'

Hosta 'Temple Bells'

Hosta tibae

Comments & Special Needs: Moderate growth rate. Light to full shade.

Distinguishing Features: Leaves have a fancied resemblance to a teaspoon.

Similar: *H.* 'Cody'; **H.* 'Quilting Bee'.

Hosta 'Temple Bells' (P. Banyai 1992)

SMALL

Origin: Seedling of a green-leaved *H.* 'Beatrice'.

Clump Size & Habit: 32 in. wide × 14 in. high (80 × 35 cm). A compact mound.

Description: Leaf blade: 6⅜ × 3½ in. (16 × 9 cm); of average substance, satiny mid-green; edge slightly rippled, elliptic, acutely tipped, with tapered open lobes. Petiole: mid-green. Flower: widely bell-shaped, deep purple on an upright, bare, green, 18 in. (45 cm) scape in late summer; fertile.

Comments & Special Needs: Site in morning sun and good light in the North to maximize flowering potential.

Distinguishing Features: Grow this hosta for its profusion of rich purple drooping flowers rather than its undistinguished leaves. Lovely in early autumn with *Aster frikartii* 'Moench', *Liriope muscari* 'Majestic' and autumn crocus.

Hosta tibae (Maekawa 1984)

SMALL

Origin: Nagasaki, Kyushu, Japan.

Clump Size & Habit: 44¾ in. wide × 16 in. high (112 × 40 cm). A dense mound.

Description: Leaf blade: 8⅜ × 4¾ in. (21 × 12 cm); of average substance, mid-green, shiny above and glossy below, prominently veined, slightly dimpled when mature; edge lightly rippled, flat, sometimes kinked and pinched at

the acute tip, oval with heart-shaped pinched lobes. Petiole: burgundy-dotted, mid-green. Flower: funnel-shaped, white-striped purple disposed around the scape on an upright, leafy, 24 in. (60 cm) scape in early autumn; fertile.

Comments & Special Needs: Valuable for its late flowers. Light to full shade.

Distinguishing Features: Thin, multi-branched scapes, an unusual characteristic of *Hosta*.

Hosta tsushimensis

SMALL–MEDIUM

Origin: Tsushima Island in the Korean Strait.

Clump Size & Habit: 31⅛ in. wide × 12 in. high (78 × 30 cm). An upright mound.

Description: Leaf blade: 7½ × 3½ in. (19 × 9 cm); thin, smooth, mid-green, satiny above and glossy below, shallow, widely spaced veins; edge widely undulate, elliptic to oval with an acute tip, tapered open lobes. Petiole: intensely

Hosta tsushimensis

Hosta 'Undulata Erromena'

burgundy dotted. Flower: funnel-shaped pale lavender to near white with thin purple lines on an oblique, burgundy-dotted green, 26 to 30 in. (65 to 75 cm) scape in early autumn; fertile.

Comments & Special Needs: Not much grown in gardens. Light shade.

Distinguishing Features: Branching scapes with sparsely displayed flowers.

Hosta 'Undulata Erromena' (AHS 1987)

MEDIUM–LARGE

Origin: Green-leaved sport of *H.* 'Undulata'.

Clump Size & Habit: 47⅛ in. wide × 21⅛ in. high (118 × 53 cm). A lax mound.

Description: Leaf blade: 8⅜ × 4⅜ in. (21 × 11 cm); of average substance, mid- to dark green, satiny above and shiny, lighter green below, moderately prominent veins; edge slightly rippled, widely oval with a recurved acute tip, heart-shaped pinched lobes. Petiole: stout, lighter green. Flower: funnel-shaped, pale lavender on an upright, leafy, green, 47⅛ in. (118 cm) scape in early to mid-summer; marginally fertile.

Comments & Special Needs: Leaves are of average substance. Well suited to growing in large clumps along a wild riverbank since it will tolerate having its roots almost permanently wet; will consequently tolerate more sun than many other green-leaved hostas. Flower habit is poor since only a few flowers are open consecutively and the scape begins to decline before flowering is over.

Sports: *H.* 'Journeyman' is a larger and more vigorous selected form raised at the Savill Garden, Windsor Great Park, England; *H.* 'See Saw' has narrow, white-margined leaves.

Hosta ventricosa

Hosta ventricosa (Stearn)

LARGE

Origin: China and North Korea.

Clump Size & Habit: 50¾ in. wide × 22 in. high (127 × 55 cm). A symmetrical mound.

Description: Leaf blade: 9⅛ × 8⅜ in. (23 × 21 cm); thin, smooth, dark spinach-green, veins widely spaced becoming strongly ribbed when mature, shiny above and glossy below; edge evenly rippled to pie-crusted, slightly convex with a distinct mucronate tip, heart-shaped overlapping lobes. Petiole: deeply channeled, purple-dotted, shiny light green. Flower: bell-shaped, rich purple to violet on an upright then oblique, leafy, satiny, burgundy-dotted pale green, 32 to 38 in. (80 to 95 cm) scape in late summer and early autumn; fertile.

Comments & Special Needs: Naturally occurring tetraploid. The only hosta known to come true from seed. Seeds are produced without fertilization by a process known as *apomixis*. Can be used in breeding as a pollen plant, however, and is the parent of many piecrust-leaved introductions. The very thin leaves can scorch at the edges in the South, even if grown in full shade.

Flowers do not begin to open until the scape is fully extended.

Similar: *H.* 'Taffeta', which is a seedling of *H. ventricosa* 'Aureomarginata', has near black leaves.

Sports: **H. ventricosa* 'Aureomaculata'; **H. ventricosa* 'Aureomarginata'.

Hosta venusta (Maekawa)

DWARF

Origin: Quelpaert Island, Korea.

Clump Size & Habit: 10 in. wide × 2¾ in. high (25 × 7 cm). A dense, spreading mound.

Description: Leaf blade: 1⅛ × ⅜ to ¾ in. (3 × 1 to 2 cm); of average substance, smooth, mid- to dark green, matt above and shiny below; edge slightly undulate, folded, widely oval with an acute tip, rounded to flat open to pinched lobes. Petiole: narrow, lighter green, appearing to pierce the blade. Flower: attractive, widely funnel-shaped, rich purple with a near white throat on an oblique, bare, ridged, 14 in. (35 cm) scape in late summer; fertile.

Comments & Special Needs: Site in light to moderate shade. Leaves of average substance. A very variable species in leaf size and shape. Light to full shade. More suitable for small containers and rock gardens than a border, where it is likely to become swamped by larger plants. Increases rapidly.

Sports: *H.* 'Awesome' is a typical form of *H. venusta* but scaled down in size (it is about the same size as *H.* 'Uzo-No-Mai', which has no petioles and is virtually impossible to grow); *H.* 'Elsley Runner', a selection with more lance-shaped leaves, clumps up very quickly and is also good in pots; *H.* 'Thumb Nail' and *H.* 'Suzuki Thumbnail' are identical to *H. venusta*, differing only in the shade of lavender of the flowers.

Similar: *H.* 'Paradise Puppet', a seedling which has ridged scapes, *H.* 'Tiny Tears'.

Hosta 'Warwick Ballerina' (Jones NR)

MEDIUM–LARGE

Origin: Unknown.

Clump Size & Habit: 36 in. wide × 18 in. high (90 × 45 cm). An open, tiered mound.

Description: Leaf blade: 9 × 8⅜ in. (22 × 21 cm); of good substance, glossy, mid- to dark olive-green depending on light levels, widely space ribbed veins; edge frilly, convex, somewhat floppy, recurved mucronate tip, nearly round with heart-shaped overlapping lobes. Petiole: dark green. Flower: funnel-shaped, lavender on an upright, dark olive-green, 28 in. (70 cm) scape in mid-season; fertility unknown.

Comments & Special Needs: Light shade. Slow to increase.

Distinguishing Features: The almost umbrella-shaped, frilly-edged leaves, which have a swirling movement.

Hosta 'Wrinkles and Crinkles' (Englerth 1985)

MEDIUM

Origin: Unknown.

Clump Size & Habit: 40¾ in. wide × 15 in. high (102 × 38 cm). An unruly mound.

Description: Leaf blade: 10 × 5½ in. (25 × 14 cm); thick, green with a blue cast, shiny above and glaucous below, ribbed veins when mature, intensely seersuckered and puckered; edge flat, convex, nearly round with a mucronate

Hosta venusta

Hosta 'Warwick Ballerina'

tip, heart-shaped pinched lobes. Petiole: stout, dark green. Flower: funnel-shaped, near white on an upright, bare, glaucous green, 30 in. (75 cm) scape in mid-summer; fertility unknown.

Similar: *H.* 'Crumples', which has apple-green leaves and is a slightly smaller plant.

Hosta 'Yakushima Mizu' (Japan, Benedict NR)

MINIATURE

Origin: Yakushima Island, Japan.

Clump Size & Habit: 14 in. wide × 6⅜ in. high (35 × 16 cm). A flattish, open mound.

Description: Leaf blade: 2¾ × ¾ in. (7 × 2 cm); thin, mid- to shiny dark green; edge rippled, lanceolate with an acute tip, tapered open lobes. Petiole: pale green, appearing to pierce the leaf blade. Flower: funnel-shaped, lavender on an upright, bare, green, 10¼ in. (26 cm) scape in late summer; fertile.

Comments & Special Needs: Probably a form of *H. gracillima* (*fide* Schmid).

Distinguishing Features: Flowers are disposed sparsely on the scape.

Similar: *H.* 'Saishu Jima'.

Hosta yingeri (Jones)

SMALL–MEDIUM

Origin: Islands off the southwest coast of Korea.

Clump Size & Habit: 30 in. wide × 9⅛ in. high (75 × 23 cm). A compact mound.

Description: Leaf blade: 6⅜ × 3⅛ in. (16 × 8 cm); very thick, bright mid- to dark green, glossy above and glossy

Hosta 'Yakushima Mizu'

Hosta 'Wrinkles and Crinkles'

Hosta yingeri

Hosta 'Treasure Island'

below with a white coating, smooth to slightly dimpled when mature; edge slightly undulate, arching when mature, oval to wedge-shaped with an acute tip, rounded open to pinched lobes. Petiole: oblique, purple-dotted green, appearing to pierce the leaf blade to the tip. Flower: thin, spider-shaped, purple on an upright, leafy, green, 25⅛ in. (63 cm) scape from late summer to early autumn; fertile.

Comments & Special Needs: Site in good light to high, filtered shade except in cooler climates where it can tolerate morning sun. Moderate growth rate but can achieve dimensions of 36¾ × 18¾ in. (92 × 47 cm) in cultivation. Closely related to *H. laevigata*. A superb hosta for hybridizing as it passes on its very glossy leaves and spiderlike flowers, one of the best offspring being *H.* 'Sweet Tater Pie' having thick, oval leaves in varying shades of chartreuse to gold, topped with deep purple, spiderlike flowers. *Hosta* 'Harpoon' is an excellent but still rare, white-margined form. Moisture at the roots is essential. Pest resistant.

Distinguishing Features: Very thick, lustrous leaves and spiderlike flowers.

Similar: *H.* 'Lily Pad' is a seed selection from Korea with spidery flowers and shiny round leaves that have a blunt tip; *H.* 'Treasure Island' is a selected form; *H.* 'Crystal Chimes' has pure white spiderlike flowers.

CHAPTER SEVEN

HOSTAS *with* CHARTREUSE, YELLOW & GOLD LEAVES

THIS CATEGORY EMBRACES HOSTAS whose leaves range through shades of yellow from chartreuse to deep, rich gold. Yellowness in hostas is genetically determined, the relevant gene acting as a classical Mendelian inhibitor. It blocks or significantly slows down the production of chlorophyll or its precursors in the leaves, and this absence of chlorophyll makes the leaves appear yellow in varying degrees. The phenomena of lutescence and viridescence are also caused by this or related genes that are sensitive to temperature. With viridescence, rising temperatures slow down the activity of the inhibitor gene, so that increasingly more chlorophyll is produced as temperatures rise. With lutescence, on the other hand, the gene or genes become more and more inhibiting as temperatures rise so that less and less chlorophyll is produced.

The first yellow-leaved hostas came on the market in the late 1960s and were at once seized upon by hosta enthusiasts, but it was many years before they were generally available. However, they are now appearing on the market in ever-increasing numbers, not only because of their undoubted popularity but also because of the high yield of yellow seedlings.

Where possible I am stating which hostas are viridescent and which lutescent, and I hope this will be a useful guide as to where to place them in the garden. Lutescent hostas need more sunlight than viridescent hostas to bring out their coloring to its fullest. Lutescent hostas, especially the brightest lemon to golden yellows, will light up dark areas of the garden and will actually draw the eye to that spot. Do not overdo the use of yellow, however, as too many individual, yellow-leaved hostas scattered over a border among darker shades can produce a spotty, inharmonious effect and can appear agitating in an otherwise restful garden. Yellow hostas, if planted sensitively, will blend in well with hostas of other colors, especially blues, grays and those with gold margins. Those yellow leaves that are particularly sensitive to strong sunlight are at their most vulnerable early in the season when the leaves are expanding. Such hostas need temporary shade if they put on their leaves before the trees.

Hosta 'Abiqua Ariel' (Walden-West & Hyslop 1999)

SMALL–MEDIUM

Origin: *H.* 'Aspen Gold' × *H.* 'Golden Chimes' seedling.

Clump Size & Habit: 22 in. wide × 8⅜ in. high (55 × 21 cm). An upright, compact mound.

Description: Leaf blade: 7½ × 4¾ in. (19 × 12 cm); thick, pale grayish yellow, matt above and glaucous below, heavily seersuckered; edge almost flat, cupped, widely oval with a mucronate tip, heart-shaped open lobes. Petiole: dull chartreuse. Flower: bell-shaped, pink to near white in profusion on an upright, bare, grayish yellow, 10 to 15 in. (25 to 38 cm) scape in mid-summer; sterile.

Comments & Special Needs: Lutescent, but never as brilliant yellow as *H.* 'Aspen Gold' or *H.* 'Midas Touch'. Site in morning sun to bring out the color except in the South, then light shade. Pest resistant.

Distinguishing Features: Subtle grayish bloom distinguishes it from those with golden yellow leaves.

Hosta 'Abiqua Gold Shield' (Walden-West 1987)

LARGE

Origin: *H.* 'White Vision' hybrid.

Clump Size & Habit: 41½ in. wide × 15 to 15¾ in. high (104 × 38 to 39 cm). A spreading mound.

Description: Leaf blade: 11½ × 8⅜ in. (29 × 21 cm); thick, glaucous yellow with green undertones, heavily seer-suckered and puckered; edge slightly undulate, folded to cupped or convex, widely oval with a mucronate tip, heart-shaped pinched lobes. Petiole: pale chartreuse. Flower: bell-shaped, pale lavender to near white on an oblique to upright, leafy, glaucous, pale chartreuse, 22¾ in. (57 cm) scape in late summer; fertility unknown.

Comments & Special Needs: Site in morning sun, except in the South, to produce the best color. Slow to increase. Pest resistant.

Hosta 'Abiqua Ariel'

Previous page: *Hosta* 'Great Lakes Gold'

Hosta 'Abiqua Gold Shield'

Hosta 'Abiqua Recluse'

Distinguishing Features: Eventually becomes one of the largest of the pale chartreuse-yellow hostas.

Similar: *H. 'Abiqua Recluse', which is better known, has rounder leaves.

Hosta 'Abiqua Recluse' (Walden-West 1989)

MEDIUM–LARGE

Origin: *H*. 'White Vision' × *H*. 'Sum and Substance'.

Clump Size & Habit: 36 in. wide × 18 in. high (90 × 45 cm). An unruly mound.

Description: Leaf blade: 12¾ × 9⅛ in. (32 × 23 cm); thick, metallic golden yellow, shiny above and thinly glaucous below, lightly seersuckered, ribbed veins; edge almost flat, cupped or convex, oval with a mucronate tip, heart-shaped pinched to overlapping lobes. Petiole: pale chartreuse-yellow. Flower: widely funnel-shaped, palest lavender to near white on an upright, leafy, chartreuse, 20 in. (50 cm) scape in late summer; fertile.

Comments & Special Needs: Colors best in some sun, but grow in shade in afternoons in very hot climates. A slow to moderate increaser. Pest resistant.

Similar: *H. 'Abiqua Gold Shield'; *H. 'August Moon'; *H. 'City Lights'; *H. 'Radiance'; *H. 'White Vision'.

Sports: *H. 'Electrum Stater'; H. 'Wooden Nickel', which has yellow-margined green leaves.

Hosta 'Alice Gladden' (D. & J. Ward 1998)

MEDIUM–LARGE

Origin: *H*. 'White Vision' × *H. montana* f. *macrophylla*.

Clump Size & Habit: 60 in. wide × 24 in. high (150 × 60 cm). An open, arching mound when mature.

Hosta 'Alice Gladden'

Description: Leaf blade: 14 × 11 in. (35 × 28 cm); thick, golden yellow, shiny above and dull below, furrowed veining, dimpled; edge and blade shallowly undulate, oval with a cuspidate tip, heart-shaped open or pinched lobes. Petiole: stout, wide, chartreuse-yellow. Flower: funnel-shaped, near white on an upright, leafy, pale yellow, 26 in. (65 cm) scape in mid-summer; fertile, green seedpods.

Comments & Special Needs: Lutescent. Keeps its color better in light to moderate shade for half the day. Vigorous. Pest resistant. An arresting specimen or border plant needing space around it to set off its distinctive poise. Lovely when backed by shrubs with dark green leaves.

Similar: *H. 'Solar Flare'.

Hosta 'Amber Tiara' (Walters Gardens 1998)

SMALL

Origin: Tissue-cultured sport of *H.* 'Grand Tiara'.

Clump Size & Habit: 20 in. wide × 12 in. high (50 × 30 cm). A spreading mound.

Description: Leaf blade: 4⅜ × 3⅛ in. (11 × 8 cm); thick,

*Indicates plants fully described elsewhere in this book.

Hosta 'Amber Tiara'

Hosta 'Archangel'

matt, rich yellow turning chartreuse-yellow, widely spaced veins; edge randomly rippled, slightly twisted, oval with an obtuse tip, rounded pinched lobes. Petiole: narrow, chartreuse. Flower: see *H.* 'Golden Tiara'.

Comments & Special Needs: Viridescent. Site in morning sun in cooler climates. A rapid increaser. Probably a tetraploid, as is its parent. Slug resistant.

Distinguishing Features: Flashes of white or green can appear in the leaves.

Hosta 'Archangel' (Q & Z Nursery NR)

MEDIUM–LARGE

Origin: Sport of *H.* 'Halo', which becomes much larger than its registered dimensions.

Clump Size & Habit: 50¾ in. wide × 18 in. high (127 × 45 cm). A dense mound.

Description: Leaf blade: 10¼ × 8⅜ in. (26 × 21 cm); thick, soft chartreuse turning pale yellow, matt above and paler green and glaucous below, closely ribbed veins, dimpled; edge almost flat, slightly cupped, widely oval with a cuspidate tip, round to heart-shaped pinched lobes. Petiole: narrow, pale chartreuse. Flower: funnel-shaped, pale lavender on an oblique, bare, pale glaucous green, 22 in. (55 cm) scape in mid-summer; fertile.

Comments & Special Needs: Lutescent. Needs sun in all but the hottest regions to bring out the leaf color. Slow to increase. Pest resistant.

Distinguishing Features: Has paler leaves than the other yellow hostas.

Hosta 'Aspen Gold' (Grapes 1986)

MEDIUM–LARGE

Origin: Open-pollinated seedling of *H.* 'Golden Medallion'.

Hosta 'Aspen Gold'

Clump Size & Habit: 36 in. wide × 20 in. high (90 × 50 cm). A stiff, spreading mound.

Description: Leaf blade: 10 × 8⅜ in. (25 × 21 cm) thick, chartreuse to bright yellow, intensely seersuckered, matt above and glaucous pale yellow below; edge slightly undulate, deeply cupped, nearly round with a mucronate tip, heart-shaped pinched to overlapping lobes. Petiole: glaucous, pale yellow. Flower: funnel-shaped, palest lavender to near white on an upright, leafy, glaucous pale yellow, 21⅛ in. (53 cm) scape, barely overtopping the foliage in mid-summer; fertile.

Comments & Special Needs: Lutescent. Colors best in some sun and takes several weeks for the yellow to brighten. In cooler, shady gardens there will always be an underlying green tint. Slug resistant. Slow to increase. Grow as a specimen or accent among darker-leaved hostas or ferns, or with *Geranium pratense* 'Victor Reiter' as a complete contrast. Has received the attention it deserves only since the late 1990s.

Hosta 'August Moon'

Distinguishing Features: In mature specimens the leaves become so deeply cupped that the glaucous undersides offer a contrast with the golden yellow upper surfaces.

Similar: *H.* 'Lime Krinkles'; **H.* 'Midas Touch'; *H.* 'Sun Glow', **H.* 'Super Bowl'.

Sports: *H.* 'Hoosier Homecoming' is a narrow, white-margined sport; **H.* 'Millie's Memoirs'; *H.* 'On The Edge'; *H.* 'Tranquility'.

Hosta 'August Moon' (Langfelder & Summers & Ruh 1996)

MEDIUM–LARGE

Origin: Unknown.

Clump Size & Habit: 42 in. wide × 20 in. high (105 × 50 cm). A dense, somewhat unsymmetrical mound.

Description: Leaf blade: 9⅛ × 8 in. (23 × 20 cm); thick, matt, chartreuse, turning soft yellow then glowing golden yellow, seersuckered and puckered, strongly marked veins; edge slightly undulate, usually slightly convex, widely oval to nearly round with a cuspidate tip, heart-shaped open to pinched lobes. Petiole: chartreuse. Flower: large, bell-shaped, soft lavender to near white on an upright, leafy, glaucous grayish yellow, 32⅜ in. (81 cm) scape in high summer; fertile, greenish seedpods.

Comments & Special Needs: Lutescent. Vigorous, fast growing. Among the first yellow-leaved hostas introduced. Although considered a classic, it has never quite hit the headlines in spite of its many good qualities, such as its sun tolerance, but is better known for its many glamorous sports. Except in the Deep South, where it grows exceptionally well, it colors best in four to five hours of morning sun.

Distinguishing Features: Although similar in appearance to many yellow-leaved *H. sieboldiana* types, it flowers three weeks later and increases faster.

Sports: **H.* 'Abiqua Moonbeam'; **H.* 'Crystal Moon'; *H.* 'Gemini Moon' has wider margins; *H.* 'Indiana Knight' has chartreuse-margined green leaves; *H.* 'Indiana Moonshine' has pale, green-margined, muted yellow leaves; *H.* 'Jupiter' has gold-margined green leaves; *H.* 'Lunar Eclipse', an early sport, exhibits the "drawstring" effect; *H.* 'Lunar Magic'; **H.* 'Lunar Orbit'; *H.* 'Lunar Sea' has green-margined yellow leaves; **H.* 'September Sun'; *H.* 'September Surprise' has green-margined chartreuse leaves.

Hosta 'Aztec Treasure' <small>(Vaughn 1997)</small>

MEDIUM

Origin: *H.* 'Golden Waffles' × *H.* 'Rough Waters' seedling.

Clump Size & Habit: 25⅛ in. wide × 12 in. high (63 × 30 cm). A dome-shaped mound.

Hosta 'Aztec Treasure'

Description: Leaf blade: 6¾ × 5⅛ in. (17 × 13 cm); thick, vivid chartreuse to chartreuse-yellow, matt above and glaucous below, slightly dimpled, closely ribbed veins; edge almost flat to slightly rippled, mostly convex, widely oval to nearly round with a distinctly cuspidate tip, heart-shaped pinched to overlapping lobes. Petiole: chartreuse. Flower: bell-shaped, rich purple on an upright, bare, glaucous yellow, 25⅛ to 28 in. (63 to 70 cm) scape in high summer; fertile.

Comments & Special Needs: Sometimes takes several moves to different sites in the garden to get the right balance between sun and shade to enhance the latent golden yellow color. Slow to increase. Pest resistant.

Similar: *H.* 'Gold Pan'; **H.* 'Golden Waffles'; **H.* 'Tijuana Brass'.

Hosta 'Birchwood Parky's Gold' <small>(Shaw & AHS 1986)</small>

SMALL–MEDIUM

Origin: *H. nakaiana* hybrid.

Clump Size & Habit: 40¾ in. wide × 17⅜ in. high (102 × 43 cm). A dense, spreading mound.

Hosta 'Birchwood Parky's Gold'

Description: Leaf blade: 6 × 4¾ in. (15 × 12 cm); thin, smooth, chartreuse turning old-gold, matt above and thinly glaucous below; edge nearly flat to slightly undulate, widely oval to heart-shaped with a mucronate tip, heart-shaped open lobes. Petiole: narrow, chartreuse. Flower: funnel-shaped, lavender on an upright, bare, chartreuse, 36 in. (90 cm) scape in mid-summer; fertile.

Comments & Special Needs: Some morning sun in cooler climates, otherwise light to medium shade. Vigorous, a rapid increaser. Ideal for lighting up woodland areas. Grow with *H.* 'Blue Cadet' or *H.* 'Pearl Lake'.

Similar: *H.* 'Gold Cadet'; **H.* 'Gold Edger'.

Sports: **H.* 'Sweet Home Chicago'; *H.* 'Zuzu's Petals' has light green leaves and a wide yellow margin.

Hosta 'Bitsy Gold' (Savory 1985)

MINIATURE–SMALL

Origin: *H. longissima* hybrid.

Clump Size & Habit: 12 to 18 in. wide × 6 in. high (30 to 45 × 15 cm). A diffuse, spreading mound.

Description: Leaf blade: 4¾ × ¾ in. (12 × 2 cm); thin, chartreuse turning yellow, matt above and shiny below; edge slightly rippled, more rippled at the petiole, linear to lanceolate with an acute tip, decurrent with the petiole. Flower: small, funnel-shaped lavender on an upright, leafy, chartreuse, 14 in. (35 cm) scape in mid- to late summer; fertile.

Comments & Special Needs: Moisture is its main requirement. Will tolerate some morning sun in all but the Deep South. Can be grown in a pot plunged in a pond as long as the crown is above water level.

Similar: *H.* 'Bitsy Green' has green leaves; **H. longissima*.

Hosta 'Blackfoot' (Plater-Zyberk & Solberg 1994)

SMALL–MEDIUM

Origin: *H. sieboldii* 'Kabitan' hybrid.

Clump Size & Habit: 16 in. wide × 10 in. high (40 × 25 cm). A moderately dense, rhizomatous mound.

Description: Leaf blade: 6 × 4 in. (15 × 10 cm); of average substance, chartreuse turning yellow, matt above and satiny below, closely ribbed veins, slight dimpling when mature; edge flat, slightly arching, slightly convex, narrowly oval with an acute tip, rounded open to pinched lobes. Petiole: narrow, mahogany-brown. Flower: funnel-shaped, purple-veined lavender on an upright, bare, burgundy, 16 in. (40 cm) scape from high to late summer

Comments & Special Needs: Lutescent. Grow in good light rather than exposed to sunlight. Will perform best in hotter, humid climates.

Distinguishing Features: A colorful hosta with brown petioles, red scapes and purple flowers that makes a great contrast with the intensely yellow leaves.

Hosta 'Blond Elf' (Aden NR)

SMALL

Origin: Sport of *H.* 'Fresh'.

Clump Size & Habit: 24 in. wide × 8⅜ in. high (60 × 21 cm). A dense, dome-shaped mound.

Description: Leaf blade: 4⅜ × 2 in. (11 × 5 cm); thin, chartreuse to muted yellow-gold, matt above and shiny below, closely veined; edge widely rippled, oval with an acute tip, tapered open lobes. Petiole: narrow, chartreuse, appearing to pierce the blade. Flower: funnel-shaped, lavender on an upright, leafy, chartreuse, 14 in. (35 cm) scape in high to late summer; fertile.

Hosta 'Bitsy Gold'

Hosta 'Blackfoot'

Hosta 'Blond Elf'

Comments & Special Needs: Lutescent. Will tolerate morning sun, except in the South, in spite of its thin substance. A rapid increaser, useful as an edging hosta or at the front of the border.

Distinguishing Features: Color holds well into autumn.

Similar: *H.* 'Devon Gold'; *H.* 'Lemon Lime'.

Hosta 'Bright Glow' (Aden 1986)

MEDIUM

Origin: Unknown. Once thought, erroneously, to be a yellow-leaved seedling belonging to the Tardiana Group.

Clump Size & Habit: 16 in. wide × 12 in. high (40 × 30 cm). A symmetrical mound.

Description: Leaf blade: 6 × 4 in. (15 × 10 cm); thick, chartreuse-yellow turning rich golden yellow, matt above and glaucous below, closely veined, dimpled; edge flat but with a kink toward the lobes, flat, heart-shaped with a mucronate tip, flat open lobes. Petiole: narrow, chartreuse. Flower: funnel-shaped, white on an upright, bare, glaucous pale yellow, 16 in. (40 cm) scape in high summer; fertile.

Hosta 'Bright Glow'

Comments & Special Needs: Lutescent. Some exposure to sun will enhance the color. A moderate increaser. Pest resistant.

Similar: *H.* 'Bengee'; *H.* 'Golden Bullion'; *H.* 'Golden Medallion', which needs shade to prevent the edges scorching; *H.* 'Thai Brass'.

Hosta 'Centrefold'

Hosta 'Cheatin Heart'

Hosta 'Chesterland Gold'

Hosta 'Centrefold' (Kamp 1994)

LARGE

Origin: Unknown.

Clump Size & Habit: 46⅜ in. wide × 24 in. high (116 × 60 cm). A dense, unruly mound.

Description: Leaf blade: 10 × 9⅛ in. (25 × 23 cm); thick, satiny, chartreuse turning golden yellow, intensely seersuckered; edge slightly rippled, convex or slightly cupped, folded, widely oval with a cuspidate tip, heart-shaped overlapping lobes. Petiole: light green. Flower: flared, near white on an upright, bare green, 18 in. (45 cm) scape in mid- to high summer; fertility unknown.

Comments & Special Needs: Lutescent. Good light to dappled shade. A moderate increaser.

Distinguishing Features: Leaf blades markedly folded in center, hence its name.

Similar: *H. 'Aspen Gold'; *H. 'Golden Waffles'; *H. 'Midas Touch', which has rounder leaves.

Hosta 'Cheatin Heart' (Zumbar 1995)

MINIATURE

Origin: Seedling identified as H. "Subcrocea F" × H. 'Birchwood Gem'.

Clump Size & Habit: 18 in. wide × 8⅜ in. high (45 × 21 cm). A compact mound.

Description: Leaf blade: 2⅜ × 1⅛ in. (6 × 3 cm); thin, matt, chartreuse turning rich golden yellow, slightly dimpled, green veins; edge rippled, folded, oval with a cuspidate tip, heart-shaped to flat pinched lobes. Petiole: narrow, pale green. Flower: tubular, lavender on an upright, bare, yellow, 7½ to 10 in. (19 to 25 cm) scape from mid- to high summer; fertile.

Comments & Special Needs: Moderate growth rate.

Color can intensify to orange-gold in sunlight. Thought to have a diploid leaf edge and a tetraploid leaf center. Ideal for a rock garden with the dwarf variegated London pride *Saxifraga ×urbium* in its variegated form at its feet.

Similar: H. 'Heartbroken', a sport of H. 'Faithful Heart', whose golden yellow leaves are viridescent; H. 'Yellow Submarine'.

Sports: H. 'Faithful Heart' and H. 'Stolen Kiss' have green-margined yellow leaves; H. 'Illicit Affair' has yellow-margined green leaves.

Hosta 'Chesterland Gold' (Zilis & Ruh 1997)

MEDIUM

Origin: Tissue-cultured sport of H. 'Paul's Glory'.

Clump Size & Habit: 56 in. wide × 10 in. high (140 × 25 cm). A rounded mound.

Description: Leaf blade: 9⅛ × 7⅛ in. (23 × 18 cm); thick, emerging chartreuse, slowly turning brilliant yellow-gold, satiny above and matt below, seersuckered; edge flat to barely rippled, widely oval with a mucronate tip, markedly heart-shaped overlapping lobes. Petiole: olive-green. Flower: see *H.* 'Paul's Glory'.

Comments & Special Needs: Lutescent. Leaf turns a harsh orange-gold if exposed to direct sunlight and is better grown in light shade. Moderate growth rate. Pest resistant.

Similar: *H.* 'Gold Glory'.

Hosta 'Christmas Gold' (M. Seaver NR)

MEDIUM

Origin: Sport of *H.* 'Christmas Tree'.

Clump Size & Habit: 40¾ in. wide × 18 in. high (102 × 45 cm). An unruly mound.

Description: Leaf blade: 9⅛ × 8⅜ in. (23 × 21 cm); thick, emerging chartreuse, turning first lemon-yellow and finally golden yellow, holding its color into autumn, satiny above and glaucous below, intensely seersuckered, crumpled and puckered; edge almost flat, cupped or convex, widely oval to nearly round with a mucronate tip, heart-shaped overlapping lobes. Petiole: light green. Flower: funnel-shaped, near white on an upright, leafy, glaucous, gray-green turning mahogany purple, 22¾ in. (57 cm) scape in mid- to high summer; fertile.

Comments & Special Needs: Lutescent. Colors best in sun, which it will take all day except in the Deep South. Adequate moisture is essential to prevent leaf scorch. Slow to increase. Pest resistant.

Distinguishing Features: Mature leaves can be crumpled to the point of distortion. The mahogany-purple scape and deep purple seedpods.

Sports: *H.* 'Jason and Katie' has yellow-margined green leaves; *H.* 'Lucy Vitols'.

Hosta 'City Lights' (Aden 1978)

LARGE

Origin: *H.* 'White Vision' × *H.* 'Golden Prayers'.

Clump Size & Habit: 49 in. wide × 25⅛ in. high (122 × 63 cm). An open mound.

Description: Leaf blade: 9⅛ × 8⅜ in. (23 × 21 cm); thick, glaucous, emerging chartreuse turning a pale metallic yellow-gold, intensely seersuckered, strongly veined; edge almost flat, shallowly cupped or convex, widely oval with a mucronate tip, heart-shaped open lobes. Petiole: stout, very light green. Flower: open funnel-shaped, near white on an upright, bare, pale green, 31⅛ in. (78 cm) scape in mid-summer; fertile.

Comments & Special Needs: Lutescent. The glaucous bloom soon burns off the upper surface of the leaf leaving a satiny finish. Light to medium shade all day. Slow to increase. Pest resistant.

Similar: *H.* 'Golden Waffles'; *H.* 'Zounds', which has slightly darker golden yellow leaves.

Hosta 'Daybreak' (Aden 1986)

LARGE

Origin: Unknown.

Clump Size & Habit: 60 in. wide × 12 in. high (150 × 30 cm). A wide, low-spreading mound with the leaves poised horizontally.

Description: Leaf blade: 14 × 10¼ in. (35 × 26 cm); thick, chartreuse-yellow turning deep golden yellow, shiny above and thinly glaucous below, closely ribbed veins, some dimpling when mature; edge shallowly undulate, slightly convex, heart-shaped with a cuspidate tip, heart-shaped pinched lobes. Petiole: light chartreuse-yellow, appearing to pierce the blade. Flower: deep lavender-blue on a drooping, leafy, dark green, 34 in. (85 cm) scape in mid- to late summer; fertile.

Comments & Special Needs: Lutescent. Site in afternoon shade, particularly in hot climates. Among the best in this category. Pest and weather resistant. Will light up dark borders.

Distinguishing Features: Flowers are densely packed toward the tip of the scape. Leaf tip pinches and droops in maturity.

Similar: *H.* 'Alice Gladden'; *H.* 'Solar Flare', whose leaves are oval and more distinctly undulate.

Sports: *H.* 'Day's End', which has mid-green leaves with irregular golden yellow margins that widen considerably as the plant matures.

Hosta 'Christmas Gold'

Hosta 'Dee's Golden Jewel' (Walek 1996)

MEDIUM–LARGE

Origin: *H.* 'Royal Standard' × *H.* 'Galaxy'.

Clump Size & Habit: 18 in. wide × 24 in. high (45 × 60 cm). An upright, rhizomatous mound.

Description: Leaf blade: 6⅜ × 8⅜ in. (16 × 21 cm); very thick, chartreuse to golden yellow, matt above and glaucous below, ribbed veins, dimpled to seersuckered; edge rippled, folded or shallowly cupped, widely oval with a cuspidate tip, heart-shaped pinched lobes. Petiole: chartreuse. Flower: funnel-shaped, near white in a dense raceme on a slightly leaning, leafy, chartreuse, 30 in. (75 cm) scape in mid-summer; barely fertile.

Comments & Special Needs: Lutescent. Its sun tolerance, even in the South, and heavy substance more than compensate for its less than spectacular leaf color. Very slow growing.

Sports: *H.* 'Jewel of the Nile'.

Hosta 'City Lights'

Hosta 'Daybreak'

Hosta 'Dee's Golden Jewel'

Hosta 'Devon Gold'

Hosta 'Doubloons'

Hosta 'Devon Gold' (A. & R. Bowden NR)

MINIATURE

Origin: Unknown.

Clump Size & Habit: 6⅜ in. wide × 5⅛ in. high (16 × 13 cm). A neat mound.

Description: Leaf blade: 2½ × 1¼ in. (6 × 3 cm); thin, butter-yellow, matt above and shiny below, prominently veined; edge distinctly rippled, folded, widely lanceolate to narrowly oval with an acute tip, tapered open lobes. Petiole: long, pale yellow. Flower: funnel-shaped, purple on an upright, leafy, pale yellow, 9⅛ in. (23 cm) scape in late summer; fertile.

Comments & Special Needs: Lutescent. Shade essential. A rapid increaser.

Distinguishing Features: The long, drawn-out petiole in relation to the small leaf.

Similar: *H.* 'Blond Elf'; *H. sieboldii* 'Subcrocea'.

Hosta 'Doubloons' (Zumbar NR)

MEDIUM

Origin: Sport of *H.* 'Alvatine Taylor'.

Clump Size & Habit: 45½ in. wide × 20 in. high (114 × 50 cm). An open mound.

Description: Leaf blade: 10 × 7½ in. (25 × 19 cm); thick, chartreuse to golden yellow, satiny above and glossy below, dimpled; edge slightly undulate, slightly folded, oval with a cuspidate tip, heart-shaped pinched lobes. Petiole: narrow, chartreuse. Flower: see *H.* 'Alvatine Taylor'.

Comments & Special Needs: Lutescent. Slow growing but eventually forms a large clump. A good all-round performer, tolerating only morning sun. Edges do not scorch like many yellow-leaved hostas with a *H. sieboldiana* 'Elegans' background. Pest resistant.

Distinguishing Features: Bright golden leaf color has a metallic cast.

Hosta 'Drawn Butter'

Hosta 'Drawn Butter' (Belle Gardens 1994)

MEDIUM

Origin: *H.* 'Whoopie' hybrid.

Clump Size & Habit: 25⅛ in. wide × 16¾ in. high (63 × 42 cm). An open, semi-upright mound.

Description: Leaf blade: 5½ × 2⅜ in. (14 × 6 cm); thick, leaves greenish gold turning pale yellow then a rich deep gold, matt above and glaucous below, closely ribbed veins, dimpled when mature; edge rippled, flat to slightly undulate, oval with a mucronate tip, rounded pinched lobes. Petiole: chartreuse with purple dotting toward the crown. Flower: funnel-shaped, pale purple on an arching, leafy, maroon-dotted, 20 to 24 in. (50 to 60 cm) scape in late summer; fertile.

Comments & Special Needs: Lutescent. Best in dappled to medium shade, where it will light up darker leaved shrubs. Slow to increase. Pest resistant.

Hosta 'English Sunrise'

Hosta 'Eola Salad Bowl'

Hosta 'English Sunrise' (Zilis NR)

SMALL–MEDIUM

Origin: Tissue-cultured sport of *H*. 'June'.

Clump Size & Habit: 30 in. wide × 16 in. high (75 × 40 cm). An overlapping mound.

Description: Leaf blade: 5⅛ × 3½ in. (13 × 9 cm); thick, smooth, bright golden yellow softening to chartreuse-green by mid-summer but remaining bright in good light, matt above and glaucous below; edge slightly rippled, oval with a cuspidate tip, heart-shaped pinched lobes. Petiole: chartreuse. Flower: see *H*. 'Halcyon'.

Comments & Special Needs: Viridescent. The yellow centers of the leaves will remain yellow for longer if grown in morning sun. Like its parent, it needs careful placing in the garden to get the best from the available light.

Similar: *H*. 'Brazen Hussy'; *H*. 'May'.

Hosta 'Eola Salad Bowl' (Monrovia NR)

SMALL

Origin: Unknown.

Clump Size & Habit: 24 in. wide × 8⅜ in. high (60 × 21 cm). Upward and outward-facing leaves make a loose, un-ruly mound.

Description: Leaf blade: 4 × 2 in. (10 × 5 cm); thin, chartreuse to old-gold, matt above and shiny below, widely spaced veins; edge nicely rippled, slightly cupped or folded, elliptic to oval with a cuspidate tip, tapered or flat open lobes. Petiole: narrowly channeled chartreuse, appearing to pierce the blade. Flower: funnel-shaped, purple on an upright, leafy, light green, 14 in. (35 cm) scape in mid-summer; fertility unknown.

Comments & Special Needs: Lutescent. Needs good light in the morning to enhance the color, then light shade. Not suitable for containers but ideal for a raised bed with

Hosta 'Eternity'

other small hostas, such as *H*. 'Little Wonder' or *H*. 'Island Charm'. Deserves to be better known.

Distinguishing Features: Distinctly rippled margins on a small leaf that is not lanceolate.

Hosta 'Eternity' (J. & J. Wilkins 1995)

MEDIUM

Origin: *H*. 'William Lachman' hybrid.

Clump Size & Habit: 30 in. wide × 18 in. high (75 × 45 cm). A moderately dense, upright mound.

Description: Leaf blade: 8⅜ × 6⅜ in. (21 × 16 cm); thick, bright golden yellow turning green, glossy above and glaucous below, prominent, widely spaced veins, dimpled; edge with occasional kinks, slightly cupped, oval with a cuspidate tip, heart-shaped open to pinched lobes. Petiole: wide, chartreuse-green. Flower: funnel-shaped, near white to pure white on an upright, leafy, chartreuse, 20 to 24 in. (50 to 60 cm) scape in late summer; fertility unknown.

Comments & Special Needs: Viridescent. Moderate to rapid increaser making it very suitable for landscaping in areas with sun for half a day. Pest resistant.

Hosta 'Eye Catcher' (Goodwin 1996)

SMALL–MEDIUM

Origin: Unknown, open-pollinated seedling.

Clump Size & Habit: 24 in. wide × 12 in. high (60 × 30 cm). A rigid, low mound.

Description: Leaf blade: 4 × 2¾ in. (10 × 7 cm); thick, vivid golden yellow fading to chartreuse, matt above and glaucous below, prominently veined, intensely seersuckered and puckered; edge flat, cupped, near round with a mucronate tip, heart-shaped open to pinched lobes. Petiole: pale chartreuse appearing to pierce the leaf blade. Flower: funnel-shaped, pale lavender opening from dark chartreuse buds on an upright, leafy, thick, chartreuse, 18 in. (45 cm) scape.

Comments & Special Needs: Viridescent. Increases rapidly, often with a second flush of leaves. A brilliant golden yellow in spring, quite living up to its name, but equally attractive later on if grown in some morning sun followed by good light. Pest resistant. Among the very best of the small-leaved golden yellows and deserves to be better known.

Distinguishing Features: Resembles a golden yellow leaved H. 'Tokudama' but is much smaller. Margins remain a slightly deeper gold but there are hints of green in the depths of the seersuckering. The first few flowers are tucked into the base of the scape leaves, the opening blooms creating the impression of a Christmas tree; fertile, light green seedpods.

Similar: *H. 'Little Aurora', which is a paler shade of golden yellow; *H. 'Maui Buttercups', which is slightly larger.

Hosta 'Feather Boa' (O'Harra 1991)

SMALL

Origin: H. sieboldii 'Subcrocea' derivative.

Clump Size & Habit: 15 in. wide × 9⅛ in. high (38 × 23 cm). A dense mound.

Description: Leaf blade: 4 × 2 in. (10 × 5 cm); thin, bright pale yellow becoming chartreuse, matt above and shiny below; edge rippled to kinked, arching, elliptic with a cuspidate tip, tapered open lobes. Petiole: narrow, light yellow. Flower: bell-shaped, purple-striped lavender on a thin, upright, leafy, 16 in. (40 cm) scape in high summer; fertile.

Comments & Special Needs: Viridescent. Site in good light all day or morning sun to maintain the leaf color. A rapid increaser that needs plenty of moisture.

Similar: Virtually identical to *H. sieboldii 'Subcrocea'; H. 'Yellow Boa'.

Hosta 'Fire Island' (Brincka 1998)

MEDIUM

Origin: H. longipes 'Hypoglauca' × H. 'Crested Surf'.

Clump Size & Habit: 34 in. wide × 14 in. high (85 × 35 cm). A dense mound.

Description: Leaf blade: 6⅜ × 4⅜ in. (16 × 11 cm); of moderate substance, bright, pale acid-yellow turning chartreuse, shiny above and matt below, intensely seersuckered; edges distinctly rippled, widely oval with a cuspidate tip, flat to tapered pinched lobes. Petiole: intensely bright red-dotted and streaked, this color persisting throughout the

Hosta 'Eye Catcher'

Hosta 'Feather Boa'

season. Flower: funnel-shaped, lavender on an upright, leafy, chartreuse, 18 to 20 in. (45 to 50 cm) scape in late summer; fertile, green seedpods.

Comments & Special Needs: Viridescent. Site in shade all day. A rapid rate of growth. Most effective when grown at eye level.

Distinguishing Features: One of the only yellow-leaved hostas with red dotting on the leaf blade.

Similar: *H. longipes* 'Ogon Amagi'.

Hosta 'Fire Island'

Hosta 'Fort Knox' (J. & J. Wilkins 1989)

LARGE

Origin: *H.* 'Gold Regal' × *H.* 'Aspen Gold'.

Clump Size & Habit: 43½ in. wide × 24 in. high (109 × 60 cm). An upright mound.

Description: Leaf blade: 8⅜ × 5⅛ in. (21 × 13 cm); thick, chartreuse turning bright, clear yellow, satiny above and thinly glaucous below, seersuckered; edge flat to slightly kinked, folded, widely oval with a cuspidate tip, heart-shaped pinched lobes. Petiole: stout, chartreuse to olive-green. Flower: flaring, lavender on an upright, leafy, chartreuse-green, 30 in. (75 cm) scape in high to late summer; fertility unknown.

Comments & Special Needs: Lutescent. Can easily exceed its registered dimensions. Moderate growth rate. Will tolerate longer periods of full sun than the related *H.* 'Ultraviolet Light'. Pest resistant.

Distinguishing Features: Many large bracts are disposed around the raceme.

Similar: **H.* 'Ultraviolet Light', which is viridescent and flowers a few weeks earlier.

Hosta 'Fort Knox'

Hosta 'Fortunei Albopicta Aurea'

Hosta 'Fortunei Albopicta Aurea' (Hylander & AHS 1987)

MEDIUM

Origin: Natural sport of *H.* 'Fortunei Albopicta'.

Clump Size & Habit: 40¾ in. wide × 18 in. high (102 × 45 cm). A dense mound.

Description: Leaf blade: 8⅜ × 5⅛ in. (21 × 13 cm); of average substance, palest ivory-green to soft butter-yellow, netted with thin green veins, gradually turning green, matt above and glaucous below, dimpled when mature; edge slightly rippled, convex, widely oval with a cuspidate tip, heart-shaped overlapping lobes. Petiole: light chartreuse. Flower: see *H.* 'Fortunei Albopicta'.

Comments & Special Needs: Viridescent. A hosta for cooler climates, where the exquisite leaf color will be maintained for much longer. Site in light shade all day. Leaves are not suitable for flower arrangement as the petioles are too floppy. One of the first yellow-leaved hostas to be used for hybridizing but has now been superseded by the introduction of lutescent cultivars.

Similar: *H.* 'Gold Haze'; *H.* 'Gold Leaf'; **H.* 'Zitronenfalter'.

Hosta 'Fragrant Gold' (Aden 1982)

LARGE

Origin: *H.* 'Sum and Substance' hybrid.

Clump Size: 44¾ in. wide × 22 in. high (112 × 55 cm). A rounded mound.

Description: Leaf blade: 10 × 8⅜ in. (25 × 21 cm); thick, chartreuse-green slowly turning muted old-gold, prominently veined, dimpled; edge almost flat, convex, widely oval with a cuspidate tip, heart-shaped pinched lobes. Petiole: stout, chartreuse. Flower: widely flared funnel-shaped, slightly fragrant, pale lavender on an upright, bare, chartreuse, 34 in. (85 cm) scape in late summer; fertile.

Comments & Special Needs: Lutescent. Morning sun followed by dappled shade otherwise the leaves will not turn golden yellow. Pest resistant. Fragrance is only apparent in hot, humid climates.

Distinguishing Features: Midrib and veins remain green when the leaves turn golden yellow.

Similar: **H.* 'Fried Bananas', whose leaves are a clearer color.

Hosta 'Fragrant Gold'

Hosta 'Ga Ga'

Hosta 'Frosty Morn'

Hosta 'Frosty Morn' (W. & E. Lachman 1993)

SMALL–MEDIUM

Origin: *H. rupifraga* seedling.

Clump Size & Habit: 21⅛ in. wide × 9⅛ in. high (53 × 23 cm). Leaves are tightly furled in an upright manner. A dense mound.

Description: Leaf blade: 6⅜ × 6 in. (16 × 15 cm); thick, glaucous, chartreuse to old-gold, closely seersuckered, prominently veined; edge distinctly rippled, folded to slightly cupped, almost round with a cuspidate tip, heart-shaped open to pinched lobes. Petiole: wide, palest chartreuse, appearing to pierce the blade. Flower: funnel-shaped, pale lavender on an upright, bare, golden yellow, 15 to 20 in. (38 to 50 cm) scape in late summer; fertile.

Comments & Special Needs: Lutescent. Lovely when grown with *Geranium* 'Black Ice' in dappled to light shade. Pest resistant.

Distinguishing Features: Leaves have exceptionally white, powdery backs and a frosted appearance on the upper surface.

Hosta 'Ga Ga' (O'Harra NR)

MINIATURE

Origin: Unknown.

Clump Size & Habit: 12 in. wide × 6 in. high (30 × 15 cm). A diffuse mound.

Description: Leaf blade: 3⅛ × 1 in. (8 × 2.5 cm); thin, glossy, smooth, chartreuse turning bright golden yellow, widely spaced prominent veins; edge rippled, slightly arching, lanceolate with an acute tip, tapered open lobes. Petiole: flattish, chartreuse to yellow. Flower: tubular, purple (in bud) on an upright, leafy, yellow, 10 in. (25 cm) scape in late summer; fertility unknown.

Comments & Special Needs: Lutescent. Leaves widen to become elliptic on mature plants. Site in good light but not direct sunlight. Vivid leaf color and glossy surface will lighten up a shaded border. Still rare but deserves to be better known.

Distinguishing Features: Flowers remain closed.

Similar: *H. sieboldii* 'Subcrocea'.

Hosta 'Glory' (R. Savory 1985)

MEDIUM

Origin: *H.* 'August Moon' seedling.

Clump Size & Habit: 24 in. wide × 10½ in. high (60 × 27 cm). A rounded mound.

Description: Leaf blade: 5⅛ × 5⅛ in. (13 × 13 cm); thick, glaucous, chartreuse turning bright yellow, intensely seersuckered and puckered, ribbed veins; edge rippled, convex or cupped, almost round with a cuspidate tip, heart-

Hosta 'Glory'

Hosta 'Gold Drop'

shaped pinched or overlapping lobes. Petiole: chartreuse. Flower: bell-shaped, purple clustered together near the top on an upright, leafy, green, 19⅛ in. (48 cm) scape in mid-summer; fertile.

Comments & Special Needs: Lutescent. Rapid increaser that will easily exceed its registered dimensions.

Distinguishing Features: Differs from *H.* 'August Moon' in having more ripple-edged leaves and the midrib and veins remaining green.

Similar: *H.* 'August Moon'.

Sports: *H.* 'Old Glory' has a dark green margin.

Hosta 'Gold Drop' (Anderson 1977)

MINIATURE

Origin: *H. venusta* × *H.* 'August Moon'.

Clump Size & Habit: 18 in. wide × 5⅛ to 6⅜ in. high (45 × 13 to 16 cm). An unsymmetrical mound.

Description: Leaf blade: 2 × 1⅛ in. (5 × 3 cm); of moderate substance, smooth, chartreuse to muted golden yellow, matt above and thinly glaucous below, slightly dimpled when mature; edge almost flat, folded, oval to heart-shaped with a cuspidate tip, heart-shaped open to pinched lobes. Petiole: narrow, chartreuse. Flower: near bell-shaped, pale lavender, produced in abundance on a narrow, oblique to upright, leafy, chartreuse, 10 to 15 in. (25 to 38 cm) scape from mid- to late summer; fertile.

Comments & Special Needs: Lutescent. Easy to grow and will soon exceed its registered dimensions. Sun tolerant. A useful edging hosta. Has produced many sports and seedlings.

Similar: *H.* 'Midwest Magic'.

Sports: *H.* 'Crown Jewel', a poor performer and not recommended; **H.* 'Dew Drop'; *H.* 'Drip Drop' has char-

Hosta 'Gold Edger'

treuse-white margins; *H.* 'Gum Drop' has pale green-gray leaves'; *H.* 'Pooh Bear' has green-margined yellow leaves; *H.* 'Sun Drop' has superb yellow-margined, dark, blue-green leaves.

Hosta 'Gold Edger' (Aden 1978)

SMALL–MEDIUM

Origin: *H.* 'Blue Cadet' × *H.* 'Gold Cadet'.

Clump Size & Habit: 25⅛ in. wide × 9⅛ to 12 in. (63 × 23 to 30 cm). A dense, symmetrical mound.

Description: Leaf blade: 3½ × 2⅜ in. (9 × 6 cm); thick, muted golden yellow fading to chartreuse, matt to glaucous above and glaucous below, dimpled; edge sometimes kinked, cupped, widely oval with a mucronate tip, heart-shaped overlapping lobes. Petiole: narrow, chartreuse. Flower: bell-shaped, lavender on an oblique to upright, bare, chartreuse, 12 in. (30 cm) scape in late summer; fertile.

Hosta 'Golden Delight'

Comments & Special Needs: Viridescent. Usually exceeds registered dimensions. Leaf color is very dependent upon the quality of the light. Will tolerate full sun all day except in the South. The parent of several excellent sports. As its name implies, it is a popular edging hosta.

Distinguishing Features: Leaves are a slightly brighter color than those of *H*. 'Midwest Gold' and the leaf surface is more "pebbled" than *H*. 'Gold Drop'.

Similar: *H. 'Birchwood Parky's Gold'; *H. 'Gold Drop'; *H*. 'Midwest Gold'.

Sports: *H*. 'Gold Edger Supreme', with greenish gold leaves and a thin white margin, and *H*. 'Gold Edger Surprise', which has bluish green leaves narrowly margined white, are sports recommended for only the most avid collectors; *H. 'Hawkeye'; *H*. 'June Bug', which has green-margined leaves; *H. 'Olympic Edger'; *H*. 'Radiant Edger'; *H. 'Royal Tiara'; *H*. 'Timothy', which has green leaves with muted yellow margins.

Hosta 'Golden Delight' (Kuk 1994)

LARGE

Origin: Open-pollinated *H*. 'Wayside Blue'.

Clump Size & Habit: 49 in. wide × 27⅛ in. high (122 × 68 cm). A compact mound.

Description: Leaf blade: 10 × 9 in. (25 × 22 cm); thick, emerging blue turning chartreuse and finally golden yellow, matt above and glaucous below, intensely seersuckered, prominently veined; edge barely rippled, moderately cupped, nearly round with a micronate tip, heart-shaped overlapping lobes. Petiole: stout, glaucous chartreuse to yellow. Flower: bell-shaped, near white on an upright, bare, yellow, 20 in. (50 cm) scape in high summer; fertile.

Comments & Special Needs: Lutescent. Site in dappled to full shade since exposure to direct sunlight can cause the edges to scorch. Slow to increase but a strong grower. Pest resistant.

Similar: *H. 'Aspen Gold'; *H. 'Midas Touch'.

Hosta 'Golden Empress' (Kuk 1990)

SMALL–MEDIUM

Origin: *H*. 'Wayside Blue' seedling.

Clump Size & Habit: 18 in. wide × 10 in. high (45 × 25 cm). A compact mound.

Description: Leaf blade: 4⅜ × 3½ in. (11 × 9 cm); thick, glaucous bright chartreuse to light yellow-gold, seersuckered; edge slightly undulate, slightly folded, widely oval with a cuspidate tip, heart-shaped pinched lobes. Petiole: thin, chartreuse.

Hosta 'Golden Empress'

Flower: funnel-shaped, lavender on a thin, purple-tinted green, leafy, 18 in. (45 cm) scape in late summer; fertile.

Comments & Special Needs: Lutescent. Increases rapidly. Will tolerate sun in the North, which is unusual in a hosta of *H*. 'Tokudama' ancestry. Dappled to full shade is recommended in hotter regions.

Distinguishing Features: Leaf color is muted because of its heavy glaucous bloom. Flower scape towers above the leaf mound.

Hosta 'Golden Gate' (Brincka & Petryszyn 1994)

LARGE

Origin: *H*. 'Niagara Falls' × *H*. 'Blue Whirls'.

Clump Size & Habit: 52¾ in. wide × 26⅜ in. high (132 × 66 cm). A rounded mound.

Description: Leaf blade: 12 × 8 in. (30 × 20 cm); thick, emerging green turning yellow-gold and finally a rich, deep gold, glossy above and matt below, deeply ribbed veins, dimpled when mature; edge evenly rippled, slightly folded then arching toward the cuspidate tip, widely oval, heart-shaped pinched lobes. Petiole: chartreuse. Flower: funnel-shaped, palest lavender from darker buds on an upright or

Hosta 'Golden Gate'

oblique, leafy, dark green, 44⅜ in. (111 cm) scape in late summer; fertile.

Comments & Special Needs: Lutescent. Leaves remain chartreuse toward the petiole in the early season especially in deep shade. Will turn gold later even in full shade. Site in light shade. A moderate increaser. Pest resistant.

Hosta 'Golden Medallion'

Hosta 'Golden Prayers'

Distinguishing Features: Evenly rippled edges. Scapes are purple dotted toward the raceme.

Hosta 'Golden Medallion' (Eisel & AHS 1984)

MEDIUM

Origin: Group name embracing all yellow-leaved natural sports of *H*. 'Tokudama'.

Clump Size & Habit: 40¾ in. wide × 16 in. high (102 × 40 cm). A rounded mound.

Description: Leaf blade: 7⅛ × 6⅜ in. (18 × 16 cm); thick, glaucous chartreuse turning bright golden yellow, intensely seersuckered with some puckering; edge almost flat, shallowly cupped, nearly round with a mucronate tip, heart-shaped overlapping lobes. Petiole: chartreuse. Flower: see *H*. 'Tokudama'.

Comments & Special Needs: Lutescent. Among the first yellow-leaved hostas introduced. Needs plenty of moisture and should be sited in light to medium shade all day otherwise the edges can scorch. Slow to increase. Pest resistant. Now largely superseded by gold-leaved hostas, which do not scorch.

Distinguishing Features: Cupping is not as deep as it is in *H*. 'Aspen Gold' or *H*. 'Midas Touch'.

Similar: *H*. 'Golden Bullion', another group name embracing all naturally occurring gold-leaved sports of **H*. 'Tokudama Flavocircinalis', which have longer, narrower leaves.

Hosta 'Golden Prayers' (Aden 1976)

MEDIUM

Origin: Seedling of *H*. 'Golden Waffles'.

Clump Size & Habit: 16 to 18 in. wide × 9½ to 12 in. high (40 to 45 × 24 to 30 cm). An upright mound.

Description: Leaf blade: 8 × 6⅜ in. (20 × 16 cm); thick, glaucous, chartreuse turning golden yellow, intensely seersuckered, with occasional puckering; edge almost flat, deeply cupped or folded, widely oval with a mucronate tip, rounded pinched lobes. Petiole: chartreuse to yellow. Flower: funnel-shaped, near white on an upright, bare, yellow, 20 in. (50 cm) scape in mid-summer; fertility uncertain.

Comments & Special Needs: Lutescent. Needs shade all day otherwise the leaf edge can scorch. Slow to moderate growth. Pest resistant.

Distinguishing Features: Registration details are at variance with what is now thought to be the "true" *H*. 'Golden Prayers'. Has also been confused in the trade with **H*. 'Little Aurora'.

Similar: *H*. 'Golden Bullion'; **H*. 'Golden Medallion'; **H*. 'Golden Waffles'; **H*. 'King Tut'; *H*. 'Thai Brass'.

Hosta 'Golden Scepter' (Savory 1983)

SMALL

Origin: Natural sport of *H*. 'Golden Tiara'.

Clump Size & Habit: 18 in. wide × 12 in. high (45 × 30 cm). A spreading mound.

Description: Leaf blade: 4¾× 3¾ in. (12 × 9.5 cm); thin, chartreuse turning deep golden yellow, matt above and shiny below, slightly dimpled when mature; edge almost flat, widely oval to heart-shaped with a cuspidate tip, heart-shaped open to pinched lobes. Petiole: long, thin, pale green. Flower: see *H*. 'Golden 'Tiara'.

Comments & Special Needs: Lutescent. Dappled to full shade all day. Lovely when grown near dark-leaved rhododendrons and other shrubs with an open habit.

Distinguishing Features: Slower growing than its parent.

Similar: *H*. 'Sweet Tater Pie', which is a hybrid between *H*. 'Golden Scepter' and *H. yingeri*, having the burnished

Hosta 'Golden Scepter' (left) with *H.* 'Grand Tiara' (right)

Hosta 'Golden Sculpture'

golden leaf color of the former and the plant habit of the latter.

Sports: *H.* 'Emerald Tiara'; *H.* 'Platinum Tiara'.

Hosta 'Golden Sculpture' (Anderson 1982)

LARGE

Origin: *H. sieboldiana* 'Elegans' hybrid.

Clump Size & Habit: 50 in. wide × 26 in. high (125 × 65 cm). A vase-shaped mound.

Description: Leaf blade: 11 × 10 in. (28 × 25 cm); thick, sharp chartreuse-yellow fading to lighter yellow, thinly glaucous, evenly seersuckered; edge widely undulate, convex when mature, slightly arching at the cuspidate tip, widely oval, heart-shaped overlapping lobes. Petiole: chartreuse. Flower: funnel-shaped, near white in a dense raceme on an upright, leafy, green, 40¾ in. (102 cm) scape in mid-summer; fertile.

Comments & Special Needs: Lutescent. Grow in some morning sun in the North, otherwise in shade all day as the edges can scorch. Easily exceeds its registered dimensions although it is slow to increase; it is well worth the wait as it is a most impressive hosta. Pest resistant. Winner of the 1991 Alex J. Summers Distinguished Merit Hosta Award.

Distinguishing Features: Midrib and veins remain green.

Similar: *H.* 'Fort Knox'; *H.* 'High Noon'.

Sports: *H.* 'Garden Party', which has narrow green margins, is slow to increase.

Hosta 'Golden Spades' (Kuk's Forest 1986)

SMALL

Origin: Open-pollinated *H. sieboldii* 'Kabitan' seedling.

Clump Size & Habit: 20 in. wide × 7⅛ in. high (50 × 18 cm). A dense mound.

Hosta 'Golden Spades'

Description: Leaf blade: 4 × 2¾ in. (10 × 7 cm); thin, deep golden yellow fading to chartreuse-yellow, matt above and shiny below with green veining; edge widely undulate, slightly folded, wedge-shaped with a cuspidate tip, rounded open lobes. Petiole: narrow chartreuse. Flower: funnel-shaped, violet-striped palest mauve from mauve buds on a thin, upright, chartreuse, 16 in. (40 cm) scape from mid- to high summer; fertile.

Comments & Special Needs: Viridescent. Achieves the best leaf color in high, filtered shade, the color being brightest early in the season. Lovely with glossy, dark green hostas or with contrasting burgundy foliage such as that of *Berberis thunbergii* 'Nana' and *Coleus* 'Pineapple'.

Distinguishing Features: Leaves have a fancied resemblance to the outline of a spade.

Hosta 'Golden Spider'

Hosta 'Golden Teacup'

Hosta 'Golden Spider' (Harshbarger & Ruh 1987)

SMALL

Origin: Unknown.

Clump Size & Habit: 17⅜ in. wide × 11 in. high (43 × 28 cm). A dense, spreading mound.

Description: Leaf blade: 4⅜ × 3½ in. (11 × 9 cm); thick, bright chartreuse-yellow turning green, matt above and shiny below, closely ribbed veins, dimpled to seersuckered; edge flat, widely oval to nearly round with an acute tip, rounded overlapping lobes. Petiole: chartreuse. Flower: funnel-shaped, lilac on an oblique, leafy, chartreuse, 18 in. (45 cm) scape from mid- to high summer; fertile.

Comments & Special Needs: Viridescent. Site in bright light to light shade. A moderate to fast increaser.

Distinguishing Features: Foliage color and flowers are outstanding.

Similar: *H.* 'Gold Edger'.

Hosta 'Golden Teacup' (J. & J. Wilkins 1989)

SMALL

Origin: *H.* 'Aspen Gold' × *H.* 'Gold Regal'.

Clump Size & Habit: 18 in. wide × 12 in. high (45 × 30 cm). An upright mound.

Description: Leaf blade: 4¾ × 4⅜ in. (12 × 11 cm); thick, bright yellow turning chartreuse; matt above and glaucous below, intensely seersuckered; edge flat, folded to deeply cupped, widely oval to round, cuspidate tip, heart-shaped pinched to overlapping lobes. Petiole: narrow, chartreuse. Flower: flaring, white on an upright, bare, 12 in. (30 cm) scape from mid- to late summer; fertile.

Comments & Special Needs: Viridescent. Golden color remaining longer if grown in some morning sun. Slow but worth the wait as the leaves have an attractive shape and surface texture. Pest resistant.

Hosta 'Golden Waffles'

Similar: *H.* 'Eye Catcher'; *H.* 'Little Aurora', which has more closely spaced seersuckering; *H.* 'Maui Buttercups', which is less cupped and does not have a distinctive white flower.

Hosta 'Golden Waffles' (Aden 1976)

MEDIUM

Origin: *H.* "Aden 381" × *H.* "Aden 388."

Clump Size & Habit: 24 in. wide × 16 in. high (60 × 40 cm). A layered mound.

Description: Leaf blade: 9⅛ × 8⅜ in. (23 × 21 cm); very thick, chartreuse to bright gold depending on light levels, satiny above and thinly glaucous below, intensely seersuckered, strongly veined; edge shallowly rippled; convex to occasionally cupped, arching toward the mucronate tip, widely oval, heart-shaped overlapping lobes. Petiole: chartreuse. Flower: open funnel-shaped, purple-striped pale lavender borne in profusion on an oblique, bare, olive-green, 30 in. (75 cm) scape in high summer; fertile.

Comments & Special Needs: Lutescent. Will easily exceed its registered dimensions. One of the earlier golden leaved hybrids and now much used as a parent because it has heavy substance and is deeply seersuckered.

Hosta 'Gold Regal' (Aden 1974)

LARGE–GIANT

Origin: Unknown.

Clump Size & Habit: 50¾ in. wide × 36 in. high (127 × 90 cm). A semi-upright, dense mound of overlapping leaves.

Description: Leaf blade: 8⅜ to 11 × 7½ to 8⅜ in. (21 to 28 × 19 to 21 cm); thick, chartreuse to old-gold, matt above and thickly glaucous below, deeply impressed veins, dimpled; edge flat, slightly folded, widely oval with a cuspidate tip, tapered, pinched lobes. Petiole: stout, glaucous chartreuse appearing to pierce the blade. Flower: large, bell-shaped, grayish mauve on a stout, leafy, upright, glaucous green, 30 to 39⅛ in. (75 to 98 cm) scape in mid-summer; fertile.

Comments & Special Needs: Lutescent. Superb flowers are only one of this hosta's many attributes. Tolerant to long exposure to sun in most regions but morning sun only in the hottest climates. An excellent breeding plant. Pest resistant.

Distinguishing Features: Leaves will remain chartreuse if grown in shade all day.

Similar: H. 'Golden Torch', which is brighter and has a more vase-shaped habit; *H. 'Ultraviolet Light', a seedling, is similar in clump and leaf shape but the leaves are brighter gold and smaller.

Sports: *H. 'Alex Summers'; H. 'David Reath', which has yellow-margined, dark green leaves; H. 'Independence Day', has pale green leaves with muted yellow margins; H. 'Misty Regal' has green-margined, streaky chartreuse leaves; H. 'Rascal'.

Hosta 'Goldsmith' (Smith & Morss & BHHS 1988)

MEDIUM

Origin: H. 'Lancifolia' × H. sieboldii 'Kabitan'.

Clump Size & Habit: 40¾ in. wide × 18 in. high (102 × 45 cm). An arching mound.

Description: Leaf blade: 9⅛ × 4 in. (23 × 10 cm); of average substance, shiny, rich golden yellow fading to drab chartreuse, some dimpling when mature, strongly veined; edge slightly rippled, arching, widely lanceolate with an acute tip, heart-shaped open lobes. Petiole: chartreuse. Flower: funnel-shaped purple on an upright, leafy, olive-green, 25⅛ in. (63 cm) scape in late summer; fertile.

Comments & Special Needs: Viridescent, the leaves are a brilliant golden color, at their best in early summer. Good light or dappled shade. Requires plenty of moisture.

Similar: H. 'Golden Oriole'.

Hosta 'Good as Gold' (Aden NR)

MEDIUM

Origin: Sport of H. 'Gaiety'.

Clump Size & Habit: 24 in. wide × 14 in. high (60 × 35 cm). A slightly rhizomatous mound.

Description: Leaf blade: 6⅜ × 3⅛ in. (16 × 8 cm); thick, chartreuse turning yellow, matt above and glaucous below, seersuckered; edge slightly rippled, widely oval with a mucronate tip, heart-shaped pinched lobes. Petiole: chartreuse. Flower: funnel-shaped, orchid-lavender on an upright, leafy, chartreuse, 18 in. (45 cm) scape in mid-summer; fertile.

Comments & Special Needs: Lutescent. The all-yellow

Hosta 'Gold Regal'

Hosta 'Goldsmith'

sport of a streaked leaf parent. Some morning sun in the North. Pest resistant.

Hosta 'Gosan Gold Midget' (Schmid 1989)

DWARF

Origin: *H. venusta* × *H.* 'Golden Prayers'.

Clump Size & Habit: 5⅛ in. wide × 3⅛ in. high (13 × 8 cm). A tight mound.

Description: Leaf blade: 1⅜ × ⅜ to 1 in. (3.5 × 1 to 2.5 cm); of average substance, glossy yellow turning chartreuse, slightly dimpled when mature; edge flat, oval with an obtuse tip, tapered open lobes. Petiole: flattish, yellow turning chartreuse. Flower: flaring, lavender on an upright, bare, pale chartreuse, 6⅜ to 10 in. (16 to 25 cm) scape in high summer; fertile.

Comments & Special Needs: Viridescent; grow in some morning sun to maintain the leaf color. Among the very

few miniature gold-leaved hostas. Ideal for sinks and rock gardens.

Distinguishing Features: Scapes sometimes branch.

Hosta 'Granary Gold' (Smith & BHHS 1988)

MEDIUM

Origin: *H.* 'Fortunei Aurea' hybrid.

Clump Size & Habit: 50¾ in. wide × 20 in. high (127 × 50 cm). An open unsymmetrical mound.

Description: Leaf blade: 8⅜ × 5⅛ in. (21 × 13 cm); of average substance, bright golden yellow fading to drab chartreuse-green in high summer, matt above and glaucous below, some dimpling when mature, strongly marked veins; edge with occasional shallow ripples, widely oval with a cuspidate tip, heart-shaped pinched lobes. Petiole: narrow, chartreuse. Flower: funnel-shaped, lavender on an upright, leafy, chartreuse, 36 in. (90 cm) scape in mid-summer; fertility unknown.

Comments & Special Needs: Viridescent. Midrib and veins remain green. Best in cooler climates, where it can tolerate exposure to some morning sun to maintain the leaf color for longer. Moderate growth rate.

Distinguishing Features: Retains its golden yellow leaf color for much longer than *H.* 'Fortunei Aurea' and has more substantial substance.

Hosta 'Great Lakes Gold' (D. & J. Ward 2000)

LARGE

Origin: *H.* 'White Vision' × *H. montana* f. *macrophylla*.

Clump Size & Habit: 67⅛ in. wide × 22 in. high (168 × 55 cm). An open, tiered mound.

Description: Leaf blade: 12 × 10 in. (30 × 25 cm); of good substance, matt chartreuse turning golden yellow,

Hosta 'Good as Gold'

Hosta 'Gosan Gold Midget'

Hosta 'Granary Gold'

furrowed veins, some dimpling; edge distinctly and attractively rippled, arching toward the cuspidate tip, oval with deeply heart-shaped open to pinched lobes. Petiole: stout, yellow. Flower: funnel-shaped, pale lavender on an upright, leafy, green, 27⅛ to 29⅛ in. (68 to 73 cm) scape in early summer; fertile, green seedpods.

Comments & Special Needs: Lutescent. Needs morning sun (if there is plenty of moisture) everywhere except the hottest climates to maintain the leaf color. Pest resistant.

Distinguishing Features: One of very few large, golden yellow hostas having distinctly rippled edges.

Similar: *H. 'Jimmy Crack Corn' is slightly smaller.

Hosta 'Hadspen Samphire' (Smith & Eason & Ruh 1997)
SMALL–MEDIUM

Origin: *H. sieboldiana* 'Elegans' × *H. sieboldii* 'Kabitan'.

Clump Size & Habit: 40¾ in. wide × 18 in. high (102 × 45 cm). A dense, rippling mound.

Description: Leaf blade: 9⅛ × 4 in. (23 × 10 cm); thinnish, lustrous bright yellow with green undertones toward the base, fading to green, smooth; edges deeply rippled, acutely tipped, narrowly oval when mature, rounded to tapered lobes. Petiole: chartreuse. Flower: narrowly funnel-shaped, lavender on a thin, arching, leafy, shiny green, 20 in. (50 cm) scape in late summer; fertile, green seedpods.

Comments & Special Needs: Viridescent, but among the hostas with the brightest golden yellow leaves early in sum-

Hosta 'Great Lakes Gold'

Hosta 'Hadspen Samphire'

mer. Keeps its color best in high, filtered shade. Slow to establish.

Similar: *H.* 'Chiquita'.

Hosta 'Harvest Glow' (Walters Gardens 1988)

MEDIUM

Origin: Tissue-cultured sport of *H.* 'Moon Glow'.

Clump Size & Habit: 16 to 20 in. wide × 14 to 20 in. high (40 to 50 × 35 to 50 cm). A rounded mound.

Description: Leaf blade: 5½ to 6⅜ × 4 to 4⅜ in. (14 to 16 × 10 to 11 cm); thick, emerging chartreuse, slowly turning lemon-yellow then rich yellow, satiny above and glaucous below, seersuckered, strongly ribbed veins; edge slightly rippled, mostly convex, oval with a mucronate tip, heart-shaped pinched lobes. Petiole: olive-green to chartreuse. Flower: see *H.* 'August Moon'.

Comments & Special Needs: Lutescent. Good light to light shade all day. Slow to increase. Pest resistant. Does not suffer from the slight drawstring effect of its parent so the leaves look larger and flatter.

Hosta 'Heartache' (H. Benedict NR)

MEDIUM−LARGE

Origin: *H. ventricosa* seedling × *H.* 'Gold Regal'.

Clump Size & Habit: 42 in. wide × 20 in. high (105 × 50 cm). An unruly, rounded mound.

Description: Leaf blade: 9 × 8 in. (22 × 20 cm); of good substance, bright creamy yellow to golden yellow with chartreuse undertones appearing later in the summer, seersuckered and puckered, widely spaced veins; edge almost flat, convex or cupped, nearly round with a mucronate tip, heart-shaped pinched to overlapping lobes. Petiole: yellow. Flower: superb, funnel-shaped, rich purple-striped violet

on an upright, stout, leafy, chartreuse, 40 in. (100 cm) scape in late summer; fertility unknown but it develops an abundance of seedpods. Pest resistant.

Comments & Special Needs: Viridescent. A deservedly very popular hosta having a great color contrast between its yellow leaf and deep purple flower. Grow in good light or moderate shade.

Similar: *H.* 'Golden Friendship'.

Hosta 'High Noon' (M. Seaver NR)

LARGE

Origin: Unknown. Originally called *H.* 'Sea High Noon'.

Clump Size & Habit: 40¾ to 48 in. wide × 26 in. high (102 to 120 × 65 cm). An upright, open mound.

Description: Leaf blade: 14 × 9⅛ in. (35 × 23 cm); moderately thick, chartreuse to golden yellow, matt above and slightly glaucous below, seersuckered; edge shallowly un-

Hosta 'Heartache'

Hosta 'Harvest Glow'

Hosta 'High Noon'

dulate, cupped at the base then arching, widely oval with a cuspidate tip, heart-shaped folded lobes. Petiole: chartreuse. Flower: funnel-shaped, lavender on an upright, 32⅜ in. (81 cm) scape from mid- to late summer; fertile, very long seedpods.

Comments & Special Needs: Lutescent. Some morning sunlight will brighten the color and remove the early season chartreuse hue. Pest resistant.

Distinguishing Features: Leaves are more elegantly pointed than most hostas with similar characteristics.

Similar: *H. 'Fort Knox'; *H. 'Golden Sculpture'; *H. 'Rising Sun'.

Sport: H. 'Afternoon Delight', which has chartreuse- to yellow-margined green leaves.

Hosta 'Honey Moon' (Anderson 1982)

SMALL

Origin: H. venusta seedling × H. 'August Moon'.

Clump Size & Habit: 24 in. wide × 18 in. high (60 × 45 cm). A compact mound.

Description: Leaf blade: 5½ × 4¾ in. (14 × 12 cm); thick, satiny, chartreuse-yellow, dimpled, widely spaced prominent veins; edge flat, slightly cupped, heart-shaped with a mucronate tip, heart-shaped overlapping lobes. Petiole: chartreuse. Flower: funnel-shaped, lavender on an upright, leafy, chartreuse, 26 in. (65 cm) scape in mid- to high summer; fertile.

Comments & Special Needs: Will exceed its registered dimensions in most gardens. Some morning sun will intensify the color. Pest resistant.

Similar: *H. 'Gold Drop', which is smaller.

Hosta 'Jimmy Crack Corn' (Sawyer NR)

LARGE

Origin: H. 'Piedmont Gold' hybrid.

Clump Size & Habit: 44 in. wide × 24 in. high (110 × 60 cm). Leaves are held horizontally on an upright, open mound.

Description: Leaf blade: 8⅜ × 5⅛ in. (21 × 13 cm); of good substance, chartreuse to bright golden yellow, satiny above and thinly glaucous below, conspicuously furrowed veining, dimpled when mature; edges heavily rippled, slightly folded and arching, oval with a cuspidate tip, heart-shaped pinched lobes. Petiole: chartreuse. Flower: funnel-shaped, near white in dense clusters on an upright, leafy, chartreuse, 24 to 30 in. (60 × 75 cm) scape in early summer; fertile.

Comments & Special Needs: Lutescent. Grow in good light or dappled shade in the morning, then full shade. Pest resistant.

Distinguishing Features: The gracefully rippled edge is unusual on a hosta with golden yellow leaves of this size.

Hosta 'Kevin Kelley' (R. Goodwin 1996)

MEDIUM

Origin: H. 'Sum and Substance' hybrid.

Clump Size & Habit: 36 in. wide × 20 in. high (90 × 50 cm). An unruly, upright mound.

Description: Leaf blade: 6⅜ × 5⅛ in. (16 × 13 cm); of average substance, lime-yellow, glossy above and satiny below, ribbed veins, dimpled; edge slightly rippled, slightly convex, widely oval with a mucronate tip, heart-shaped pinched lobes. Petiole: light green. Flower: tubular, pale lavender on an upright or oblique, leafy, pale green, 12 to

Hosta 'Honey Moon'

Hosta 'Jimmy Crack Corn'

18 in. (30 to 45 cm) scape in late summer; fertile, green seedpods.

Comments & Special Needs: Site in good light to dappled shade. A rapid increaser. Pest resistant. Lovely with cream-margined hostas such as *H.* 'Bold Ribbons'.

Distinguishing Features: Unusual greenish yellow color and the conspicuously down-turned leaf edges.

Hosta 'Kevin Kelley' with *H.* 'Bold Ribbons'

Hosta 'King Tut' (Harshbarger 1881)

MEDIUM

Origin: *H.* 'Tokudama Aureonebulosa' hybrid.

Clump Size & Habit: 30 in. wide × 18¾ in. high (75 × 47 cm). A symmetrical mound.

Description: Leaf blade: 8 × 6⅜ in. (20 × 16 cm); thick, unfurls chartreuse slowly turning yellow, matt above and glaucous below, seersuckered; cupped, widely oval with a mucronate tip, heart-shaped open to pinched lobes. Petiole: chartreuse. Flower: narrowly funnel-shaped, lavender-striped near white on an upright, leafy, chartreuse, 34¾ in. (87 cm) scape in mid-summer; fertile.

Comments & Special Needs: Lutescent. Considered to be among the best of the golden yellow leaved Tokudama Group as it forms a shapely mound. Also notable for throwing good offspring. Pest resistant. Slow to establish.

Distinguishing Features: The flower scapes are tall for a hosta of this ancestry.

Similar: **H.* 'Golden Medallion'; *H.* 'Golden Nugget'; **H.* 'Golden Waffles'; *H.* 'Treasure'.

Sports: *H.* 'Mister Watson'; *H.* 'Tut Tut'.

Hosta 'King Tut'

Hosta 'Kiwi Gold Rush'

Hosta 'Lakeside San Kao'

Hosta 'Lemon Chiffon'

Hosta 'Kiwi Gold Rush' (Sligh 1999)

MEDIUM

Origin: Unknown.

Clump Size & Habit: 24 in. wide × 15 in. high (60 × 38 cm). An open mound.

Description: Leaf blade: 6⅜ × 5⅛ in. (16 × 13 cm); thick, matt chartreuse turning golden yellow, seersuckered and puckered, prominently ribbed veins; edge undulate, flat to arching, oval with a mucronate tip, rounded open to pinched lobes. Petiole: chartreuse. Flower: long, funnel-shaped, pale lavender on an upright, leafy, chartreuse, 25⅛ in. (63 cm) scape in mid-summer; fertile.

Comments & Special Needs: Lutescent. Makes an enchanting group grown in filtered to full shade with *Dicentra* 'Gold Bullion', *Filipendula* 'Aurea' and *Heuchera* 'Chocolate Ruffles'. Will also tolerate sun in cooler climates. Vigorous, a rapid increaser.

Hosta 'Lakeside San Kao' (Chastain 1995)

LARGE

Origin: *H.* 'Piedmont Gold' hybrid.

Clump Size & Habit: 46⅜ in. wide × 18 in. high (116 × 45 cm). An open mound.

Description: Leaf blade: 11½ × 8⅜ in. (29 × 21 cm); very thick, satiny, creamy chartreuse, strongly marked veins; edge rippled, slightly convex at the base and slightly arching toward the tip, widely oval with a cuspidate tip, heart-shaped pinched lobes. Petiole: chartreuse. Flower: long, tubular, lavender on a bare, arching, burgundy, 15 to 18¾ in. (38 to 47 cm) scape in mid-summer; fertile.

Comments & Special Needs: Lutescent. Leaves emerge lime-white becoming yellowish in mid- to late summer, then turning parchment. Morning sun or light shade all day except in the South. Pest resistant. A hosta with many assets.

Distinguishing Features: Bright green veins embedded in the contrasting cream leaves. The contrasting burgundy scapes are an additional embellishment.

Hosta 'Lemon Chiffon' (P. Banyai 1988)

MEDIUM–LARGE

Origin: *H. montana* hybrid.

Clump Size & Habit: 28⅜ in. wide × 24 in. high (71 × 60 cm). An open mound.

Description: Leaf blade: 11 to 12 × 7⅛ in. (28 to 30 × 18 cm); of good substance, matt chartreuse to creamy yellow, seersuckered, prominently and closely veined; edge rippled, slightly arching, widely oval with a mucronate tip, rounded open to pinched lobes. Petiole: olive-green. Flower: funnel-shaped, pale lavender on an upright or oblique, leafy, olive-green, 18 in. (45 cm) scape in mid-summer; fertile.

Hosta 'Lemon Lime'

Hosta 'Lime Piecrust'

Comments & Special Needs: Lutescent. Site in good light to dappled shade. Green veins stand out from the creamy yellow leaves. Fast growing. Deserves to be better known.

Distinguishing Features: The green midrib and veins contrast well with the creamy yellow leaves.

Similar: *H.* 'Lakeside San Kao', which has paler colored leaves.

Hosta 'Lemon Lime' (Savory 1988)

MINIATURE

Origin: *H. sieboldii* derivative.

Clump Size & Habit: 36 in. wide × 12 in. high (90 × 30 cm). A tight, dense mound.

Description: Leaf blade: 3½ × 1⅜ in. (9 × 3.5 cm); thin, chartreuse which turns yellow toward the edges, matt above and glossy whitish green below, prominently veined; edge rippled, folded, widely lanceolate with an acute tip, rounded to tapered open lobes. Petiole: narrow, green. Flower: funnel-shaped, deep, purple-striped rich violet from green buds on an upright, bare, green, 12 to 18 in. (30 to 45 cm) scape from mid-summer; fertile.

Comments & Special Needs: Three flushes of leaves may be produced each season. Some rebloom is possible in late summer if the first scapes are cut to the ground after flowering. Leaves remain chartreuse unless the hosta is grown in bright light. Not sun tolerant. Vigorous, a rapid increaser.

Distinguishing Features: Dense carpets of pointed leaves above which rise tall scapes.

Similar: *H.* 'Chartreuse Waves'; *H.* 'Feather Boa'; *H.* 'Hydon Sunset', which does not have purple-dotted petioles; *H.* 'Ogon Koba'.

Sports: *H.* 'Iced Lemon'; *H.* 'Lemon Delight'; *H.*

'Lemon Frost', which is as vigorous as its parent; *H.* 'Twist of Lime'.

Hosta 'Lime Piecrust' (W. & E. Lachman 1990)

MEDIUM–LARGE

Origin: *H.* 'Aspen Gold' hybrid × *H.* 'Aspen Gold' hybrid.

Clump Size & Habit: 60 in. wide × 25⅛ in. high (150 × 63 cm). An open mound.

Description: Leaf blade: 12 × 9⅛ in. (30 × 23 cm); thick, chartreuse to light yellow, matt above and glaucous below, prominently veined, dimpled when mature; edge attractively rippled, widely oval with a mucronate tip, heart-shaped open to pinched lobes. Petiole: narrow, pale green. Flower: flaring, palest lavender to near white on an upright, leafy, pale green, 26 in. (65 cm) scape in mid-summer; fertile.

Comments & Special Needs: Lutescent. Leaf color depends on the light level available. Slow to increase. Pest resistant.

Distinguishing Features: Distinctively rippled edges.

Similar: *H.* 'Jimmy Crack Corn'.

Hosta 'Limey Lisa' (Zumbar NR)

MINIATURE

Origin: Open-pollinated hybrid derived from *H.* 'Ogon Koba'.

Clump Size & Habit: 26 in. wide × 12 in. high (65 × 30 cm). A flattish, open mound.

Description: Leaf blade: 2¾ × 2 in. (7 × 5 cm); thick, green-chartreuse, matt to satiny above and glossy below, widely spaced veins, dimpled when mature; edge flat but kinked toward the open lobes, slightly cupped, round to

Hosta 'Limey Lisa'

Hosta 'Little Aurora'

spoon-shaped with a mucronate tip, heart-shaped open to pinched lobes. Petiole: long, flat, pale green. Flower: lavender in mid- to late summer; fertility unknown.

Comments & Special Needs: Viridescent. Fast growing. Ideal for sinks and containers. Needs good light but not direct sun except in cooler climates.

Distinguishing Features: Spoon-cupped tiny leaves that remain lime-green.

Hosta 'Little Aurora' (Aden 1978)

SMALL

Origin: Registered as *H.* 'Tokudama Aureonebulosa' × *H.* 'Golden Waffles', although there is now some disagreement about this.

Clump Size & Habit: 25⅛ in. wide × 10 in. (63 × 25 cm) high. A compact mound.

Description: Leaf blade: 4⅜ × 3½ in. (11 × 9 cm); thick, chartreuse turning rich gold with a metallic sheen, thinly glaucous below, seersuckered when mature, some puckering; edge almost flat, shallowly cupped, widely oval with a mucronate tip, heart-shaped overlapping lobes. Petiole: narrow, chartreuse. Flower: widely flared, pale lavender to near white on an upright to leaning, olive-green, 10 to 18 in. (25 to 45 cm) scape in mid-summer; fertile.

Comments & Special Needs: Lutescent. The best color is achieved in good light or light shade. Scape is often no higher than the top of the foliage mound and the flowers tend to nestle among the leaves. Although the dimensions given are an average size, it can become somewhat larger. Moderate to good growth rate but is more successful in Northern gardens. Pest resistant.

Distinguishing Features: Much confused in the trade with *H.* 'Golden Prayers', which is larger and produces up-

Hosta 'Little Black Scape'

right leaves in a praying position. The identity of many sports attributed to *H.* 'Little Aurora' is therefore in doubt.

Similar: **H.* 'Bright Glow', which is a deeper color; **H.* 'Vanilla Cream', which is a paler color.

Sports: **H.* 'Delia'; *H.* 'Goldbrook Grace'; *H.* 'Just So'; **H.* 'Lakeside Leprechaun'; **H.* 'Little Sunspot'; *H.* 'Not So'; **H.* 'Subtlety'; **H.* 'Sultana'; **H.* 'Tattoo'.

Hosta 'Little Black Scape' (Avent 1995)

MEDIUM

Origin: Open-pollinated seedling of *H.* 'Sum and Substance'.

Clump Size & Habit: 24 in. wide × 10 in. high (60 × 25 cm). A compact mound.

Description: Leaf blade: 5⅛ × 4⅜ in. (13 × 11 cm); of good substance, matt chartreuse-green turning golden yellow, dimpled, widely spaced veins; edge mainly flat but kinked toward the base, oval with an acute tip, tapered open lobes. Petiole: short, light green. Flower: funnel-shaped, lavender, from violet buds on an upright or oblique, occasionally leafy, glossy, darkest purple to black, 22 in. (55 cm) scape in mid-summer; not fertile in the South, unknown elsewhere.

Comments & Special Needs: Lutescent. Grow in morning sun to enhance the leaf and scape color. Plant with *Hemerocallis* 'Sir Blackstem' and *Ophiopogon planiscapus* 'Nigrescens' to create an eye-catching effect. Moderate growth rate.

Distinguishing Features: The contrasts among the chartreuse-yellow leaves, the dusky scapes and violet flower buds make *H.* 'Little Black Scape' one of the most distinct and unusual hostas.

Hosta 'Marilyn' (Zilis 1990)

SMALL–MEDIUM

Origin: *H.* 'Gold Drop' × *H.* 'Green Piecrust'.

Clump Size & Habit: 30 in. wide × 12 in. high (75 × 30 cm). A dense mound.

Description: Leaf blade: 8⅜ × 3½ in. (21 × 9 cm); of average to good substance, chartreuse soon turning golden yellow finally becoming bright gold by high summer, distinctly ribbed veins, slight dimpling; edge widely undulate and rolled under, heart-shaped with a cuspidate tip, tapered open to pinched lobes. Petiole: chartreuse to yellow. Flower: funnel-shaped, pale lavender on an upright, bare, chartreuse, 24 in. (60 cm) scape in high summer; fertility unknown.

Comments & Special Needs: Lutescent. Will easily exceed its registered dimensions and quickly makes a dense mound. In cooler climates, protect the early emerging leaves from late frosts; elsewhere morning sun enhances the leaf color. Leaves emerge early. A hosta with nice movement to its leaves.

Hosta 'Maui Buttercups' (W. Vaughn 1991)

SMALL

Origin: *H.* 'Frances Williams' × *H.* 'August Moon'.

Clump Size & Habit: 14 in. wide × 10 in. high (35 × 25 cm). A diffuse, upward-facing mound.

Description: Leaf blade: 5⅛ × 4 in. (13 × 10 cm); thick, chartreuse to bright yellow, shiny above and glaucous below, intensely seersuckered and puckered toward the tip; edge flat, deeply cupped to folded, nearly round with a mucronate tip, heart-shaped pinched to overlapping lobes. Petiole: wide, flattish chartreuse to yellow. Flower: flared to bell-shaped, green-tipped, palest lavender on an upright,

Hosta 'Marilyn'

Hosta 'Maui Buttercups'

sturdy, leafy, glaucous chartreuse, 18 in. (45 cm) scape in late summer; fertile.

Distinguishing Characteristics: A noticeable hyaline line around the leaf edge. Very large leafy bracts along the scape and around the raceme.

Comments & Special Needs: Lutescent. Will tolerate early morning sun followed by dappled shade in cooler climates, denser shade in the South. Slow to establish but eventually has a moderate growth rate. A superb small yellow-leaved hosta having great presence in the garden.

Similar: *H.* 'Eye Catcher'; *H.* 'Golden Teacup'; *H.* 'Little Aurora'.

Sports: *H.* 'Rainforest Sunrise' has dark green leaves with yellow margins. A much sought after hosta introduced at the turn of the 21st century.

Hosta 'Midas Touch'

Hosta 'Midas Touch' (Aden 1978)

MEDIUM

Origin: *H.* 'Gold Cup' × *H.* 'Golden Waffles'.

Clump Size & Habit: 40 in. wide × 20 in. high (100 × 50 cm). A dense mound.

Description: Leaf blade: 9 × 8 in. (22 × 20 cm); thick, emerging soft pale chartreuse slowly turning bright yellow, matt above and glaucous below, intensely seersuckered to deeply puckered; edge shallowly undulate, deeply cupped, nearly round with a mucronate tip, heart-shaped pinched lobes. Petiole: chartreuse to old-gold. Flower: a dense raceme of flared, pale lavender-striped near white from gray buds on a leafy, upright, pale green, 24 in. (60 cm) scape in early summer; fertility unknown.

Comments & Special Needs: Lutescent. Leaves will always have a green undertone, especially the midrib and veins if grown in shade, but will assume a brassy, metallic hue if exposed to strong sunlight for long periods. Slow to establish. Pest resistant.

Distinguishing Features: The very pebbled surface texture of the leaf and the deep cupping that causes exposure of the underside of the leaf.

Similar: **H.* 'Aspen Gold'; **H.* 'King Tut'; *H.* 'Lime Krinkles', which is paler and more lime-colored; *H.* 'Thai Brass', which has flatter and more pointed leaves.

Hosta 'Moon Waves' (Plater-Zyberk & Solberg 1994)

MEDIUM

Origin: *H.* 'August Moon' hybrid.

Clump Size & Habit: 24 in. wide × 16 in. high (60 × 40 cm). A dense mound.

Description: Leaf blade: 10 × 4¾ in. (25 × 12 cm); of good substance, chartreuse to golden yellow, waxy above and glaucous below, closely ribbed veins; edge intensely rippled, widely lanceolate with a twisted cuspidate tip, rounded to tapered open lobes. Petiole: chartreuse. Flower: funnel-shaped, near white on an upright, yellow, 30⅜ in. (76 cm) scape in high summer; fertility unknown.

Comments & Special Needs: Lutescent. Should tolerate morning sun with *H.* 'August Moon' as a parent.

Distinguishing Features: Exaggerated rippling almost distorts the leaf shape; however, it is an eye-catching hosta which needs careful placing. Would be set off well planted among ornamental grasses.

Similar: **H.* 'Ophir'.

Hosta 'Moon Waves'

Hosta 'Olive Oil'

Hosta 'Ogon Iwa'

Hosta 'Ogon Iwa' (Japan)

MEDIUM

Origin: Thought to be a seedling from *H. longipes* emanating from the Watanabe Nursery in the early 1990s. Previously known in the trade as *H. longipes* 'Aurea', an invalid epithet.

Clump Size & Habit: 36 in. wide × 15 in. high (90 × 38 cm). A rhizomatous mound.

Description: Leaf blade: 7½ × 3½ in. (19 × 9 cm); of average substance, golden yellow, matt above and shiny below, widely spaced veins; edge undulate to rippled, arching, widely oval with a cuspidate tip, heart-shaped open lobes. Petiole: intensely red-dotted, golden yellow. Flower: funnel-shaped, lavender on a leaning, leafy, 20 to 28 in. (50 to 70 cm) scape from late summer to early autumn; fertile.

Comments & Special Needs: Many natural sports of *H. longipes* with golden yellow leaves are still being found in the wild. A useful breeding plant since a high percentage of yellow-leaved seedlings arise when it is selfed. Plant be-

side rocks that are shaded from afternoon sun in a naturalistic setting for the best effect.

Hosta 'Olive Oil' (Dishon 1996)

LARGE

Origin: *H.* 'Yellow Splash' × *H. hypoleuca*.

Clump Size & Habit: 40¾ in. wide × 22¾ in. high (102 × 57 cm). An upright mound.

Description: Leaf blade: 11 × 7½ in. (28 × 19 cm); thick, lustrous chartreuse turning old-gold, closely ribbed veins, slightly dimpled, widely oval with a cuspidate tip, heart-shaped pinched lobes. Petiole: chartreuse. Flower: funnel-shaped, pale lavender with inner white striping on an upright, brown, leafy, 36 in. (90 cm) scape in high summer; fertile, green seedpods.

Comments & Special Needs: Lutescent. Site in morning sun followed by dappled to light shade. Moderate growth rate. Pest resistant.

Distinguishing Features: The glistening surface texture of the leaves.

Similar: *H.* 'Zounds'.

Hosta 'Ophir' (Fischer NR)

SMALL

Origin: Unknown.

Clump Size & Habit: 25⅛ in. wide × 12¾ in. high (63 × 32 cm). An upright mound of twisted leaves.

Description: Leaf blade: 7½ × 3⅛ in. (19 × 8 cm); thin, pale lemon-yellow, satiny above and glossy below, contrasting green veins; edge widely rippled to twisted, widely lanceolate with a cuspidate tip, tapered open lobes. Petiole: narrow, chartreuse, red-dotted toward the crown. Flower: funnel-shaped, lavender on an upright, leafy, chartreuse, 16 in. (40 cm) scape in mid- to late summer; fertility unknown.

Hosta 'Ophir'

Hosta 'Peedee Absinth'

Comments & Special Needs: Viridescent. Some morning sun in cooler climates only to maintain the yellow leaf color, otherwise the leaves will bleach. Lovely with *Heuchera* 'Cappuccino' and *Carex testacea*.

Distinguishing Features: Cherry-red petioles and mahogany streaking on lower half of the scape and at the joint of the scape bracts. Large bracts surrounding the flowers.

Similar: **H.* 'Moon Waves', which is lutescent and does not have purple dotting on the petioles.

Hosta 'Peedee Absinth' (Syre-Herz 1990)

MINIATURE–SMALL

Origin: *H.* 'Gold Drop' × *H. sieboldii* 'Subcrocea'.

Clump Size & Habit: 25⅛ in. wide × 8⅜ in. high (63 × 21 cm). A dense mound.

Description: Leaf blade: 3½ × 2⅜ in. (9 × 6 cm); thick, chartreuse turning old-gold, matt above and shiny below, slightly dimpled; edge slightly undulate, oval with a cuspidate tip, tapered pinched lobes. Petiole: chartreuse. Flower: funnel-shaped, lavender-striped near white on an upright, leafy, chartreuse, 10 in. (25 cm) scape in high summer; fertile.

Comments & Special Needs: Lutescent. Site in morning sun except in the hottest climates. An ideal hosta for the edge or front of the border; also suitable for growing in containers. Moderate growth rate. Pest resistant.

Similar: **H.* 'Gold Drop', which has smaller leaves with a smoother surface texture.

Hosta 'Peedee Dew Catcher' (Syre-Herz 1992)

MEDIUM–LARGE

Origin: *H.* 'City Lights' × *H.* 'Bold Ruffles'.

Clump Size & Habit: 40¾ in. wide × 20 in. high (102 × 50 cm). An overlapping mound.

Description: Leaf blade: 11 × 8⅜ in. (28 × 21 cm); thick, gray-green turning chartreuse then yellow, matt above and glaucous below, intensely seersuckered with some puckering, ribbed veins; edge almost flat, cupped or convex, nearly round with a mucronate tip, heart-shaped pinched to overlapping lobes. Petiole: gray-green turning chartreuse, appearing to pierce the blade. Flower: flaring, white on an upright, bare, pale green, 24 in. (60 cm) scape in early summer; fertile.

Comments & Special Needs: Lutescent. Morning sun to enhance the color of the leaves but careful placing in the garden is needed. Slow to moderate growth rate. Pest resistant.

Distinguishing Features: Early season gray-green leaf color that slowly turns yellow, given enough light. Racemes are only just above the leaf mound.

Hosta 'Piedmont Gold' (Payne 1982)

LARGE

Origin: Unknown.

Clump Size & Habit: 36 in. wide × 24 in. (90 × 60 cm) high. An overlapping mound.

Description: Leaf blade: 8 × 6 in. (20 × 15 cm); thick, chartreuse soon turning golden yellow, matt above and thinly glaucous below, prominently veined, dimpled when mature; edge slightly undulate, arching, convex, oblong to broadly oval with a cuspidate tip, heart-shaped pinched lobes. Petiole: deeply channeled chartreuse. Flower: funnel-shaped, near white on an upright or oblique, bare, gray-chartreuse, 30 in. (75 cm) scape in mid-summer; fertile.

Comments & Special Needs: Lutescent. Bright light but not direct sunlight will enhance the golden yellow leaf color; however, the color assumes a paler yellow hue in autumn. Becomes much larger given optimum growing conditions. Pest resistant. A classic hosta, the parent of many

Hosta 'Peedee Dew Catcher'

Hosta 'Piedmont Gold'

sports, and used as both a pod and pollen parent in hybridizing.

Distinguishing Features: Leaves of juvenile plants are smooth, only becoming ribbed and seersuckered as the plant matures.

Similar: *H*. 'Solar Flare'.

Sports: *H*. 'David Stone' has green-margined yellow leaves; *H*. 'Evening Magic', which suffers from the drawstring effect; *H*. 'Everglades', which is green-centered and gold-margined; *H*. 'Lakeside Symphony'; *H*. 'Moonshine', which is yellow-centered and green-margined; *H*. 'Satisfaction'; *H*. 'Summer Serenade'; *H*. 'Tyler's Treasure', which has gold-margined green leaves.

Hosta 'Prairie Fire' (Kuk 1994)

SMALL–MEDIUM

Origin: *H*. 'Gold Regal' × *H*. 'Tokudama' gold seedling.

Clump Size & Habit: 15 to 18 in. wide × 12 to 15 in. high (38 to 45 × 30 to 38 cm). A dense, semi-upright mound.

Description: Leaf blade: 7⅛ × 3½ in. (18 × 9 cm); thick, chartreuse turning rich, deep gold, matt above and glaucous below, prominently veined, seersuckered; edge distinctly rippled and twisted, oval with a cuspidate tip, rounded pinched lobes. Petiole: stout, deeply channeled chartreuse. Flower: funnel-shaped, long, near white from chartreuse buds on an upright, leafy, chartreuse, 20 in. (50 cm) scape in late summer; fertile.

Comments & Special Needs: Lutescent. Site in morning sun except in the hottest climates to enhance the fiery, deep golden color of the leaves which intensifies as the season progresses.

Similar: *H*. 'Alice Gladden'; *H*. 'Jimmy Crack Corn'; *H*. 'Moon Waves', which is a paler color.

Hosta 'Radiance' (Anderson 1980)

MEDIUM–LARGE

Origin: Unknown.

Clump Size & Habit: 30 in. wide × 24 to 30 in. high (75 × 60 to 75 cm). A diffuse mound.

Description: Leaf blade: 11 × 10 in. (28 × 25 cm); thick, yellow fading to chartreuse, matt above and glaucous below, intensely seersuckered with some puckering when mature; edge nearly flat to just undulate, folded or convex, nearly round with a mucronate tip, heart-shaped pinched to overlapping lobes. Petiole: yellow to chartreuse. Flower: funnel-shaped, pale lavender on an upright, bare, chartreuse, 34 in. (85 cm) scape in mid-summer; fertile.

Comments & Special Needs: Viridescent.

Distinguishing Features: A typical yellow-leaved *H*. 'Tokudama'.

Similar: *H*. 'Abiqua Recluse'; *H*. 'Golden Friendship'.

Hosta 'Raleigh Remembrance' (Zilis NR)

MEDIUM

Origin: *H*. 'Sum and Substance' × *H. plantaginea*.

Clump Size & Habit: 30 in. wide × 20 in. high (75 × 50 cm). An arching mound.

Description: Leaf blade: 9⅛ × 4 in. (23 × 10 cm); of average substance, glossy chartreuse turning old-gold, slightly dimpled, conspicuously ribbed veins; edge slightly undulate, arching, folded, oval with an acute tip, rounded open lobes. Petiole: narrow, chartreuse. Flower: funnel-shaped, lavender on an upright, bare, chartreuse, 30 in. (75 cm) scape in high summer; fertility unknown.

Comments & Special Needs: Lutescent. Morning sun in the hottest regions, followed by light shade; full sun else-

Hosta 'Prairie Fire'

Hosta 'Radiance'

where as long as there is sufficient moisture available. Moderate to fast growth.

Distinguishing Features: Flowers have not inherited the fragrance of the *H. plantaginea* parent.

Hosta 'Richland Gold' (Wade 1987)

MEDIUM

Origin: *H.* 'Gold Standard' sport.

Clump Size & Habit: 36 in. wide × 18 in. wide (90 × 45 cm). A dense mound.

Description: Leaf blade: 7½ × 4⅜ in. (19 × 11 cm); of good substance, chartreuse turning rich yellow, matt above and glaucous below, ribbed veins when mature, slight dimpling; edge slightly undulate, widely oval with a cuspidate tip, heart-shaped pinched to overlapping lobes. Petiole: chartreuse. Flower: see *H.* 'Fortunei Hyacinthina'.

Comments & Special Needs: Lutescent. Site in morning sun followed by dappled to light shade. Leaves are late to emerge. Plant size will exceed the given measurements if

Hosta 'Raleigh Remembrance'

grown in optimum conditions. Vigorous, a rapid increaser. Ideal at the edge of light woodland and suitable for container growing.

Sports: *H.* 'Zodiac'.

Hosta 'Rising Sun' (K. Vaughn 1988)

LARGE

Origin: *H.* 'Summer Fragrance' × *H.* 'Aztec Treasure' hybrid.

Clump Size & Habit: 30 to 34 in. wide × 28 in. high (75 to 85 × 70 cm). A moderately dense mound.

Description: Leaf blade: 10 × 5½ in. (25 × 14 cm); thick, glossy chartreuse to lemon-yellow, slightly dimpled when mature, closely ribbed veins; edge flat, arching to convex, oval with a cuspidate tip, heart-shaped open to pinched lobes. Petiole: chartreuse. Flower: funnel-shaped, lavender on an upright, leafy, chartreuse, 38 in. (95 cm) scape in late summer; fertility unknown.

Comments & Special Needs: Lutescent. Site in morning sun, then dappled to light shade. Moderate growth rate. Pest resistant.

Distinguishing Features: Flowers are clustered at the tip of the raceme.

Similar: *H.* 'Gold Regal'; *H.* 'High Noon'.

Hosta 'Royalty' (Anderson 1982)

MINIATURE

Origin: *H. capitata* hybrid.

Clump Size & Habit: 14 in. wide × 4 in. high (35 × 10 cm). A dense, symmetrical mound of attractively pointed leaves.

Description: Leaf blade: 2¾ × 1⅜ in. (7 × 3.5 cm); chartreuse to pale yellow, matt above and glaucous below; edge

Hosta 'Richland Gold' sporting from *H.* 'Gold Standard'

Hosta 'Rising Sun'

Hosta 'Royalty'

rippled, cupped, oval with a cuspidate tip, tapered open lobes. Petiole: shallow, pale chartreuse. Flower: bell-shaped, purple on an upright, thin, leafy, pale chartreuse, 14 in. (35 cm) scape in mid-summer; fertile.

Comments & Special Needs: Lutescent. Site in morning sun except in the hottest climates otherwise light shade will achieve the best leaf color.

Distinguishing Features: Leaves are exceptionally pointed; the very dense heads of flowers which are horizontally disposed.

Similar: *H.* 'Estrellita'; *H.* 'Yellow Submarine'; **H.* 'Yellow Waves'.

Hosta 'Sara' (Kuk 1994)

MEDIUM

Origin: *H.* 'Rippling Waves' hybrid.

Clump Size & Habit: 24 in. wide × 17⅜ in. high (60 × 43 cm). An upright mound.

Description: Leaf blade: 9⅛ × 7⅛ in. (23 × 18 cm); thick; chartreuse becoming rich, deep yellow with underlying hints of chartreuse, matt above and glaucous below, dimpled, prominent veins; edge slightly rippled, arching

Hosta 'Sara'

toward the cuspidate tip, oval with rounded to tapered pinched lobes. Petiole: chartreuse. Flower: bell-shaped, pale lavender on an upright, chartreuse, 25⅛ in. (63 cm) scape in mid-summer; fertile.

Comments & Special Needs: Lutescent. Site in morning sun to achieve the best leaf color, followed by dappled to light shade. Pest resistant.

Hosta 'Sea Bunny'

Hosta 'Sea Fire'

Hosta 'Sea Gulf Stream'

Hosta 'Sea Bunny' (M. Seaver 1986)

MEDIUM

Origin: Unknown.

Clump Size & Habit: 30 in. wide × 14 in. high (75 × 35 cm). A dome-shaped mound.

Description: Leaf blade: 10 × 5⅛ to 5½ in. (25 × 13 to 14 cm); thick, glossy, blue-tinted, iridescent golden yellow turning chartreuse-green by mid-summer; heavily seersuckered and puckered; edge slightly kinked, folded, widely oval with an acute tip, tapered pinched lobes. Petiole: chartreuse to olive-green. Flower: funnel-shaped, lavender-striped near white on an upright, green, 28 in. (70 cm) scape in high summer; fertility unknown.

Comments & Special Needs: Viridescent. Site in morning sun to achieve the best leaf color. Slow to moderate increase.

Distinguishing Features: This unusual multi-tone hosta has different leaf color combinations at different stages of the summer. Seersuckering is so intense that the leaf can become almost distorted.

Hosta 'Sea Fire' (M. Seaver NR)

MEDIUM

Origin: Unknown.

Clump Size & Habit: 45½ in. wide × 18 in. high (114 × 45 cm). An arching mound.

Description: Leaf blade: 10 × 8⅜ in. (25 × 21 cm); emerging fiery golden yellow from red shoots fading to light green by late summer, matt above and thinly glaucous below, dimpled; edge slightly rippled, widely oval to nearly round with a mucronate tip, heart-shaped pinched to overlapping lobes. Petiole: chartreuse with red dotting toward the base. Flower: funnel-shaped, pale lavender from purple buds on an upright, chartreuse, 24 to 38 in. (60 to 95 cm) scape in mid-summer; fertile.

Comments & Special Needs: Of average substance. Registered dimensions are easily exceeded in optimum growing conditions. Increases rapidly and is ideal ground cover in a lightly shaded woodland. Viridescent, but one of the brightest gold-leaved hostas in spring. Best known for its seedlings and sports, which includes 'Dawn's Early Light' which also has golden yellow leaves.

Distinguishing Features: Dramatic color contrasts among the leaves, flower buds, shoots and petioles.

Sports: *H.* 'Saint Elmo's Fire'.

Hosta 'Sea Gulf Stream' (Zilis & Seaver & Malloy 1999)

MEDIUM

Origin: Sport of *H.* 'Sea Gold Star'.

Clump Size & Habit: 28⅜ in. wide × 12¾ in. high (71 × 32 cm). A cascading mound.

Description: Leaf blade: 9⅛ × 6⅜ in. (23 × 16 cm); thick, vivid chartreuse turning yellow, matt above and thickly glaucous below, furrowed veining, dimpled to seersuckered; edge, saw-toothed, piecrusted and twisted, arching, folded, oval with a cuspidate tip, heart-shaped open to pinched lobes. Petiole: deeply channeled chartreuse. Flower: funnel-shaped, pale lavender to near white, subtended by purple-gray bracts on a narrow, arching, leafy, 22 to 24 in. (55 to 60 cm) scape in early summer; fertility unknown.

Comments & Special Needs: Lutescent. Site in morning sun to enhance the yellowness of the leaves. Lovely with blue-leaved *H.* 'Rock and Roll' to echo the blue midrib and veins which are noticeably blue early in the season.

Similar: *H.* 'Sea Gold Star', which has less rippled edges.

Hosta 'Shade Master' (Aden 1982)

MEDIUM–LARGE

Origin: *H.* 'White Vision' × *H.* 'Golden Rajah'.

Clump Size & Habit: 38⅜ in. wide × 22 in. high (96 × 55 cm). A layered mound.

Description: Leaf blade: 12 × 9 in. (30 × 22 cm); thick, glaucous light green turning rich, dark yellow, dimpled, closely ribbed veins; edge slightly rippled, folded, oval with a cuspidate tip, rounded overlapping lobes. Petiole: narrow, chartreuse. Flower: flared, pale lavender, densely packed on an upright, leafy, chartreuse, 30 in. (75 cm) scape in late summer; fertile.

Comments & Special Needs: Lutescent. Brightens up a shaded border but is equally good in some morning sun. Slow to increase at first. Pest resistant.

Similar: *H.* 'Gold Regal', both having exceptionally good flowers.

Sports: *H.* 'Summer Music'.

Hosta 'Shiny Penny' (Solberg 1997)

MINIATURE

Origin: *H.* 'Lemon Lime' × *H.* 'Shining Tot'.

Clump Size & Habit: 12 in. wide × 6 in. high (30 × 15 cm). A congested mound.

Description: Leaf blade: 3⅛ × 2 in. (8 × 5 cm); thick, glossy, bright yellow turning copper-yellow later, smooth, ribbed veins; edge rippled, elliptic to oval with slightly curved acute tip, tapered open lobes. Petiole: short, nearly flat, yellow. Flower: funnel-shaped, lavender on an upright chartreuse, leafy, 18 in. (45 cm) scape in late summer; fertile, chartreuse seedpods.

Comments & Special Needs: Site in morning sun to enhance the leaf color. A rapid increaser. Pest resistant.

Similar: *H.* 'Peedee Absinth', whose leaves do not assume a copper hue.

Sports: *H.* 'Cracker Crumbs', whose leaves are yellow with a green margin.

Hosta sieboldii 'Subcrocea' (AHS 1987)

SMALL–MEDIUM

Origin: Natural sport of *H. sieboldii*.

Clump Size & Habit: 25⅛ in. wide × 12 in. high (63 × 30 cm). A dense mound.

Description: Leaf blade: 6⅜ × 1⅜ in. (16 × 3.5 cm);

Hosta 'Shiny Penny'

Hosta 'Shade Master'

Hosta sieboldii 'Subcrocea'

chartreuse to golden yellow, smooth, closely ribbed veins; edge distinctly rippled, arching, folded, lanceolate with an acute tip, tapered open lobes. Petiole: shallow, yellow to chartreuse. Flower: see *H. sieboldii*.

Comments & Special Needs: Site in dappled to light shade in a moisture retentive soil. Leaf color depends on light levels, varying from chartreuse in full shade to parchment if exposed to strong sunlight. Viridescent. Substance is very thin. Vulnerable to pests.

Distinguishing Features: Leaf edges are more undulate than those of *H. sieboldii* 'Kabitan', which it closely resembles in shape. Flowers are only sparsely produced.

Similar: **H.* 'Royalty', which is a more muted yellow.

Hosta 'Solar Flare' (Gardenview Hort. Park 1981)
GIANT

Origin: Unknown, although it has many of the characteristics of *H. montana*.

Clump Size & Habit: 52¾ in. wide × 28⅜ in. high (132 × 71 cm). An arching mound.

Hosta 'Solar Flare'

Hosta 'Squash Casserole'

Description: Leaf blade: 14 × 10 in. (35 × 25 cm); thick, chartreuse turning golden yellow, thinly glaucous above early in the season and glaucous below, dimpled with some puckering at the midrib when mature, closely ribbed veins; edge attractively rippled, widely undulate and sometimes pinched along the midrib toward the mucronate tip, widely oval with heart-shaped open to pinched lobes. Petiole: stout, chartreuse. Flower: funnel-shaped, pale lavender on an upright, leafy, chartreuse, 36 in. (90 cm) scape in early summer; fertile.

Comments & Special Needs: Lutescent. Site in morning sun except in the hottest climates, followed by light shade. Leaves become flatter with the edges more widely undulate when grown in full shade. Midrib and veins usually remain green. Can easily exceed its given dimensions. Best in cooler climates. Pest resistant.

Distinguishing Features: Leaf is held horizontally to the petiole.

Similar: **H.* 'Alice Gladden'; **H.* 'Jimmy Crack Corn', whose leaves are more furrowed and have a more rippled edge; **H.* 'Piedmont Gold'.

Hosta 'Squash Casserole' (Avent 1995)
MEDIUM–LARGE

Origin: *H.* 'Hirao Elite' × *H.* 'August Moon'.

Clump Size & Habit: 46¾ in. wide × 20 in. high (117 × 50 cm). A dense, flattish mound.

Description: Leaf blade: 11 × 6⅜ in. (28 × 16 cm); of good substance, matt chartreuse-green turning old-gold, seersuckered, prominent veins; edge rippled, slightly undulate, widely oval with a cuspidate tip, rounded to heart-shaped open to pinched lobes. Petiole: stout, chartreuse. Flower: long, funnel-shaped, lavender on an arching or oblique, leafy, olive-green, 22 in. (55 cm) scape in high summer; fertile.

Comments & Special Needs: Although lutescent, *H.* 'Squash Casserole' remains a muted color even when exposed to sunlight. Ideal for Southern gardens, even in sun, if plenty of moisture is available.

Hosta 'Squire Rich' (Kuk's Forest 1988)
MEDIUM

Origin: Sport of *H.* 'Antoinette'.

Clump Size & Habit: 22¾ in. wide × 18 in. high (57 × 45 cm). A tiered, vase-shaped mound.

Description: Leaf blade: 9⅛ × 5½ in. (23 × 14 cm); of moderate substance, bright golden green, dull to satiny above and glossy below, some seersuckering and puckering; edge evenly rippled, widely oval with a cuspidate, sometimes pinched, tip, heart-shaped open to pinched lobes. Petiole: chartreuse. Flower: flared, lavender on an upright, leafy, dark green, 18 in. (45 cm) scape in late summer; fertile, with reddish seedpods.

Comments & Special Needs: Morning sun will produce the best color.

Distinguishing Features: Lutescence of the leaves is apparent in that the first leaves of the season will be golden yellow by mid-summer but the later ones will still be char-

treuse green, giving a two-tone effect. Dark olive-green scapes are a good contrast to the yellow leaves in late summer.

Similar: *H. 'Starboard Light'.

Hosta 'Starboard Light' (C. Seaver 1994)

LARGE

Origin: *H.* 'Komodo Dragon' hybrid.

Clump Size & Habit: 28 in. wide × 24 in. high (70 × 60 cm). An open, upright mound.

Hosta 'Squire Rich'

Hosta 'Starboard Light'

Hosta 'Sum and Substance'

Description: Leaf blade: 11 × 5⅛ in. (28 × 13 cm); of good substance, matt chartreuse turning rich, deep yellow, slightly dimpled, narrowly ribbed veins; edge rippled, folded, widely oval with a cuspidate tip, heart-shaped open lobes. Petiole: chartreuse. Flower: funnel-shaped, near white on an upright, leafy, chartreuse, 40 in. (100 cm) scape from mid- to late summer; fertile.

Comments & Special Needs: Lutescent, the midrib and veins usually remaining green. Site in morning sun, except in the hottest climates, where it is best suited to dappled shade. Pest resistant.

Distinguishing Features: The scape is bent near the tip.

Similar: *H. 'Gold Regal'; *H. 'Squire Rich'.

Hosta 'Sum and Substance' (Aden 1980)

GIANT

Origin: Unknown but thought to have H. 'Elatior' and H. *hypoleuca* in its parentage.

Clump Size & Habit: 60 in. wide × 36 in. high (150 × 90 cm). A spreading mound.

Description: Leaf blade: 18 × 15 in. (45 × 38 cm); thick, light green turning chartreuse to muted gold depending on light levels, shiny to waxy above and thinly glaucous below, barely dimpled, ribbed veins; edge slightly rippled, widely oval with a strongly cuspidate tip, slightly cupped or convex, heart-shaped overlapping lobes. Petiole: stout, shallow, pale green. Flower: funnel-shaped, pale lavender on a drooping, chartreuse, leafy, 44 in. (110 cm) scape in late summer; fertile.

Comments & Special Needs: Lutescent. Colors best in sun, which it will tolerate for most of the day in cooler climates. Morning sun with plenty of moisture in Southern gardens. Can suffer from stem blight. Rapidly exceeds its registered dimensions and can become one of the largest hostas of all. Thought to be triploid, and selfs very easily; it is a fine parent and has produced many sports. A classic hosta.

Distinguishing Features: Leaves emerge from mahogany-brown shoots. Huge leaves which can make a man's hand look small.

Sports: H. 'Beauty Substance', H. 'Bottom Line', H. 'David A. Haskell', the smaller *H. 'Eagle's Nest', *H. 'Lady Isobel Barnett', H. 'Lodestar', H. 'Sum It Up', H. 'Sum of All', H. 'Sum Total', H. 'Titanic', and H. 'Zebson' all have yellow-margined (with slight variations) green leaves; *H. 'Parhelion' and *H. 'Winter Snow' have chartreuse-yellow leaves margined white; H. 'Caliban' has crumpled, muted yellow leaves with pale green margins; H. 'Something

Good' and H. 'Variable Sum' have chartreuse-yellow leaves margined green; H. 'Domaine de Courson' has satiny dark green leaves with a blue cast; H. 'Green Gables' has glossy, pale green leaves; H. 'Vim and Vigor' has darker green leaves; H. 'Small Sum' has medium-sized, waxy, bright yellow leaves.

Hosta 'Sun Power' (Aden 1986)

LARGE

Origin: Unknown.

Clump Size & Habit: 36 in. wide × 24 in. high (90 × 60 cm). A dense upright mound.

Description: Leaf blade: 12 × 7 in. (30 × 17 cm); thick, chartreuse turning bright golden yellow, matt above and thinly glaucous below, prominently veined, slightly dimpled; edge widely undulate, oval with a cuspidate tip; heart-shaped pinched lobes. Petiole: chartreuse. Flower: funnel-shaped, lavender on an oblique, leafy, chartreuse, 36 in. (90 cm) scape from mid- to late summer; sterile.

Comments & Special Needs: Will become much larger given optimum growing conditions. Although lutescent, it achieves its best color early, which holds until the frosts. Site in morning sun even in the hottest climates with high humidity, provided there is always an abundant supply of moisture at the roots in high summer. Pest resistant. A classic hosta.

Distinguishing Features: In late summer the paler colored petiole seems to dramatically pierce the blade in contrast to the brassy golden color of the leaves.

Sports: *H. 'Abba Dabba Do'; H. 'Abba Dew' has yellow-margined, light green leaves; *H. 'Abba Windows'; *H. 'Paradise Power'.

Hosta 'Sun Power'

Hosta 'Super Bowl'

Hosta 'Sweet Sunshine'

Hosta 'Tangerine'

Hosta 'Super Bowl' (Aden NR)

LARGE

Origin: *H.* 'Tokudama' hybrid.

Clump Size & Habit: 22 in. wide × 18 in. high (55 × 45 cm). An upright mound.

Description: Leaf blade: 10¼ × 10¼ in. (26 × 26 cm); very thick, glaucous, chartreuse turning golden yellow, intensely seersuckered and puckered; edge nearly flat to just rippled, deeply cupped, nearly round with a mucronate tip, heart-shaped overlapping lobes. Petiole: chartreuse to yellow. Flower: bell-shaped, white on an upright, bare, chartreuse, 26 in. (65 cm) scape from mid- to late summer; fertile.

Comments & Special Needs: Lutescent. Site in morning sun except in the hottest climates. Will become much larger if given optimum growing conditions, although it is slow to increase. Pest resistant.

Distinguishing Features: Leaves are even more deeply cupped than similar hostas, sometimes as much as 3½ in. (9 cm), which causes the underside of the leaf to be visible.

Similar: *H.* 'Aspen Gold'; *H.* 'Midas Touch'.

Hosta 'Sweet Sunshine' (Solberg 1997)

SMALL–MEDIUM

Origin: *H.* 'Sweet Susan' × *H.* 'Tokudama Aureonebulosa'.

Clump Size & Habit: 24 in. wide × 14 in. high (60 × 35 cm). An upright mound.

Description: Leaf blade: 4¾ × 4⅜ in. (12 × 11 cm); of average substance, thick, satiny bright chartreuse barely turning yellow, seersuckered to puckered, prominently veined; edge flat, cupped, nearly round with a mucronate tip, heart-shaped overlapping lobes. Petiole: narrow, chartreuse. Flower: funnel-shaped, fragrant white on an upright, leafy, chartreuse, 22 in. (55 cm) scape from mid- to late summer; fertile.

Comments & Special Needs: Lutescent. Sun tolerant in the North but it needs good light in the South to encourage the production of the two to three flushes of leaves of which it is capable. Vigorous, a moderate increaser given plenty of moisture. Pest resistant.

Similar: *H.* 'Sunny Delight' is a sister seedling having oval leaves, which tolerates heat and sun even in the hottest climates.

Hosta 'Tangerine' (Elslager 1998)

SMALL–MEDIUM

Origin: *H.* 'Sea Sunrise' hybrid.

Clump Size & Habit: 21⅛ in. wide × 12 in. high (53 × 30 cm). An upright mound.

Description: Leaf blade: 8⅜ × 6⅜ in. (21 × 16 cm); thick, shiny chartreuse to rich, deep golden yellow, dimpled and puckered near the midrib, prominently veined; edge slightly rippled, nearly round with a mucronate tip, heart-shaped overlapping lobes. Petiole: glaucous yellow. Flower: funnel-shaped, purple-striped pale lavender on an upright, 16 in. (40 cm) scape in mid-summer; fertility uncertain, green seedpods.

Comments & Special Needs: Lutescent. Holds it color well but is best grown in high, filtered shade. Slow to increase. Pest resistant.

Hosta 'Tijuana Brass' (K. Vaughn 1988)

LARGE

Origin: Seedling of *H.* 'Golden Waffles' × *H.* 'Polly Bishop'.

Clump Size & Habit: 25⅛ to 28 in. wide × 20 in. high (63 to 70 × 50 cm). A dense, unruly mound.

Hosta 'Tijuana Brass'

Description: Leaf blade: 10 × 8⅜ in. (25 × 21 cm); thick, emerging chartreuse turning bright, brassy golden yellow with green undertones, shiny above and thinly glaucous below, intensely seersuckered and puckered; edge almost flat but sometimes has slight undulations, cupped or twisted, nearly round with a mucronate tip, heart-shaped overlapping lobes. Petiole: olive-green. Flower: flared, pale lavender on an upright or slightly oblique, leafy, olive-green, 32 in. (80 cm) scape in high summer; fertile.

Comments & Special Needs: Will easily exceed its registered dimensions.

Distinguishing Features: Probably has the most puckered and unruly leaves of any yellow-leaved hosta and will make a statement in any lightly shaded garden.

Similar: *H.* 'Aztec Treasure'.

Hosta 'Ultraviolet Light' (J. & J. Wilkins 1989)

MEDIUM

Origin: *H.* 'Gold Regal' hybrid.

Clump Size & Habit: 42 in. wide × 18 to 24 in. high (105 × 45 to 60 cm). A dense, tiered mound.

Description: Leaf blade: 8⅜ × 5⅛ in. (21 × 13 cm); of good substance, emerges rich golden yellow, turning char-

Hosta 'Ultraviolet Light'

treuse-yellow, satiny above and thinly glaucous below, prominently veined, some dimpling when mature; edge flat, slightly undulate, widely oval with a cuspidate tip, heart-shaped open lobes. Petiole: chartreuse, widening toward the blade. Flower: funnel-shaped, rich purple on an upright, leafy, chartreuse, 36 in. (90 cm) scape in late summer; fertile, producing many seedpods.

Comments & Special Needs: Viridescent. Light to full shade all day, except in cooler regions where two hours of morning sun will retain the golden color for longer. A superb hosta.

Distinguishing Features: Considerably smaller than *H.* 'Gold Regal' and a much brighter color.

Similar: **H.* 'Fort Knox', which is another hybrid from *H.* 'Gold Regal', being more dimpled and having more and larger bracts encircling the raceme.

Hosta 'Vanilla Cream' (Aden 1986)

SMALL

Origin: *H.* "Aden 456" × *H.* 'Little Aurora'.

Clump Size & Habit: 15 in. wide × 9⅛ in. high (38 × 23 cm). A somewhat rhizomatous mound.

Description: Leaf blade: 4⅜ × 4 in. (11 × 10 cm); of average substance, pale lemon-green becoming brighter yellow finally turning cream, matt above and thinly glaucous below, prominently veined, seersuckered; edge flat, convex or slightly cupped, nearly round with a mucronate tip, flat to heart-shaped open to pinched lobes. Petiole: pale green. Flower: funnel-shaped, lavender on an upright, bare, red-tinted, 12 in. (30 cm) scape in high summer; fertile.

Distinguishing Features: Lemon-green to pale yellow leaf color.

Comments & Special Needs: Lutescent. Site in morning sun followed by dappled shade gives the best leaf color. Lovely as a foreground to Japanese azaleas in early summer.

Similar: **H.* 'Eye Catcher'; **H.* 'Golden Teacup'; **H.* 'Little Aurora'; **H.* 'Maui Buttercups'.

Sports: *H.* 'Heart and Soul' emerges pale green to chartreuse becoming creamy white with a dark green margin; **H.* 'Ice Cream'; *H.* 'Ladybug' has brighter chartreuse coloring; **H.* 'Peppermint Cream'; *H.* 'Pistachio Cream' has dark green leaves; *H.* 'Wylde Green Cream'.

Hosta 'White Gold' (Fox NR)

MEDIUM

Origin: Selection of *H. fortunei* 'Albopicta Aurea'.

Clump Size & Habit: 40¾ in. wide × 18 in. high (102 × 45 cm). A dense mound.

Description: Leaf blade: 8⅜ × 5⅛ in. (21 × 13 cm); of average substance, palest chartreuse-white turning drab green from early summer depending upon the climate, matt above and glaucous below, dimpled when mature; edge slightly rippled, convex, widely oval with a cuspidate tip, heart-shaped overlapping lobes. Petiole: palest chartreuse. Flower: funnel-shaped, white on an upright, leafy, chartreuse, 28 in. (70 cm) scape in high summer; sterile.

Comments & Special Needs: Viridescent. Best in cooler gardens in which the pale color is maintained for longer. Site in good light to dappled shade among azaleas and rhododendrons. A moderate growth rate.

Similar: **H.* 'Fortunei Albopicta Aurea', whose leaves are a deeper color early in the season.

Hosta 'Vanilla Cream'

Hosta 'White Gold'

Hosta 'White Vision' (Aden 1978)

LARGE

Origin: *H.* 'Sun Glow' × *H.* 'Gold Cup'.

Clump Size & Habit: 32 in. wide × 24 in. high (80 × 60 cm). A billowing mound.

Description: Leaf blade: 10 × 8⅜ in. (25 × 21 cm); thick, glaucous chartreuse-yellow turning bright golden yellow and finally creamy yellow, intensely seersuckered; edge widely undulate, arched, widely oval to nearly round with a mucronate tip, heart-shaped pinched lobes. Petiole: stout, chartreuse. Flower: funnel-shaped, purple-striped pale lavender on an upright, bare, chartreuse, 30 in. (75 cm) scape in mid-summer; fertile, forming many seedpods.

Comments & Special Needs: Lutescent. A green cast on the midrib toward the petiole. Site in morning sun in cooler climates; light shade all day in the hottest regions. Easily exceeds its registered dimensions. Exceptionally pest resistant.

Similar: *H.* 'City Lights', which is now more popular. It is important, however, because it is the parent of many good yellow-leaved introductions.

Hosta 'Wind River Gold' (Janssen NR)

SMALL

Origin: Unknown.

Clump Size & Habit: 24 in. wide × 9⅛ in. high (60 × 23 cm). A spreading mound.

Description: Leaf blade: 5½ × 3⅛ in. (14 × 8 cm); thin, chartreuse turning muted golden yellow, matt above and shiny below, widely spaced veins; edge distinctly rippled and twisted, widely lanceolate with an acute tip, tapered open lobes. Petiole: pale chartreuse, purple-dotted toward the crown. Flower: funnel-shaped, lavender on an upright, leafy, chartreuse, 15 in. (38 cm) scape in late summer; fertile.

Comments & Special Needs: Lutescent, the color holding well until the frosts. Site in morning sun in cooler climates, otherwise dappled shade. A rapid increaser and a useful edging hosta. A good breeding plant.

Similar: **H.* 'Yellow Waves', which is smaller and has paler yellow leaves.

Hosta 'Yellow Eyes' (Ruh 1999)

MINIATURE

Origin: Sport of *H.* 'Green Eyes'.

Clump Size & Habit: 10 in. wide × 4 in. high (25 × 10 cm). A dense mound.

Hosta 'White Vision'

Hosta 'Wind River Gold'

Hosta 'Yellow Eyes'

Description: Leaf blade: 2⅜ × 1 in. (6 × 2.5 cm); thin, chartreuse to golden yellow, matt above and glossy below; edge rippled, twisted, lightly folded, lanceolate with an acute tip, tapered open to pinched lobes. Petiole: flattish, chartreuse. Flower: funnel-shaped, vivid purple on an upright, leafy, chartreuse, 13⅛ in. (33 cm) scape in late summer; fertile, reddish seedpods.

Comments & Special Needs: Lutescent. Site in morning sun in cooler climates, followed by dappled shade. Useful as an edging or foreground hosta. Moderate increaser.

Similar: *H. sieboldii 'Subcrocea'.

Hosta 'Yellow Waves' (Aden 1978)

MINIATURE

Origin: H. 'Ogon Koba' × H. 'Chartreuse Wiggles'.

Clump Size & Habit: 8⅜ in. wide × 4 in. high (21 × 10 cm). A low, dense mound.

Description: Leaf blade: 5⅛ × 1⅜ in. (13 × 3.5 cm); thin, bright pale yellow fading to chartreuse, matt above and shiny below, closely ribbed veins; edge distinctly rippled, arching toward the acute tip, folded, lanceolate with tapered open lobes. Petiole: long, arching, chartreuse, purple-dotted toward the crown. Flower: funnel-shaped, white to palest lavender on an upright, leafy, chartreuse, 10 in. (25 cm) scape in late summer; fertile.

Comments & Special Needs: Viridescent. Grow in good light to dappled shade. A useful edging hosta in light woodland.

Similar: *H. sieboldii 'Subcrocea', whose leaves are a brighter color.

Hosta 'Zitronenfalter' (Klose NR)

MEDIUM

Origin: Unknown.

Clump Size & Habit: 40 in. wide × 18 in. high (100 × 45 cm). A dense mound.

Description: Leaf blade: 8⅜ × 5⅛ in. (21 × 13 cm); of average substance, soft pale yellow, netted with green veins, turning drab green, matt above and glaucous below, dimpled when mature; edge slightly rippled, convex, widely oval with an acute tip, heart-shaped open lobes. Petiole: chartreuse. Flower: funnel-shaped lavender on an upright, leafy glaucous green 28 in. (70 cm) scape, purple-tinted towards the raceme, in high summer; fertility unknown.

Comments & Special Needs: Viridescent. Achieves the best leaf color when grown in good light or high, filtered shade. Best suited to cooler climates.

Hosta 'Yellow Waves'

Hosta 'Zitronenfalter'

Distinguishing Features: Unusual early season, icy lemon-green leaf color.

Similar: *H. 'Fortunei Albopicta Aurea'.

Hosta 'Zounds' (Aden 1978)

LARGE

Origin: H. 'Golden Waffles' × H. 'Golden Prayers'.

Clump Size & Habit: 30 in. wide × 20 in. high (75 × 50 cm). A dense mound.

Description: Leaf blade: 8⅜ to 10 × 8⅜ to 9⅛ in. (21 to 25 × 21 to 23 cm); thick, chartreuse turning metallic golden yellow, satiny above and thinly glaucous pale yellow below, strongly seersuckered to puckered when mature; edge almost flat to shallowly rippled, shallowly cupped or convex, nearly round with a mucronate tip, heart-shaped pinched to overlapping lobes. Petiole: stout, chartreuse.

Hosta 'Zounds'

Flower: funnel-shaped, pale lavender on an upright, chartreuse, leafy, 30 in. (75 cm) scape in mid- to high summer; fertile.

Comments & Special Needs: Lutescent. Site in good light or filtered to light shade, where it will glow like a beacon when surrounded by dark green leaved plants. Usually greatly exceeds the registered dimensions if given optimum growing conditions. Slow to moderate growth rate. Good pest resistance. A classic hosta.

Distinguishing Features: Strongly veined underside of the leaf.

Similar: *H.* 'Abiqua Zodiac'; *H.* 'City Lights'; *H.* 'Golden Rajah'; *H.* 'Golden Waffles'; *H.* 'Tijuana Brass'; *H.* 'White Vision'.

Sports: *H.* 'American Eagle'; *H.* 'Dick Ward' and *H.* 'Laura and Darrell' have yellow-margined, dark green leaves.

CHAPTER EIGHT

HOSTAS *with* GLAUCOUS BLUE, BLUE-GRAY, BLUE-GREEN & GRAY-GREEN LEAVES

HOSTAS WITH BLUE LEAVES HAVE LONG BEEN prized by gardeners and collectors, but the blueness is only skin deep. It is produced by an epidermal wax coating which can easily be rubbed away between finger and thumb or by rough handling in the garden, revealing the greenness of the leaf underneath. It can also melt away if the leaves are exposed to too much sun. The thicker the layer of wax, the bluer the leaf appears. The phenomenon is unusual in the plant world since hostas are shade tolerant, and most plants with a blue surface coating have it as protection against the heat of the sun. The underside of these leaves is also coated, but with a grayish white bloom that appears as a much lighter version of the upper surface. Some hostas have a thick, white, velvetlike surface on the underside of the leaf that developed through evolutionary processes over many centuries to protect the leaf from being scorched by heat radiating off the surface of the volcanic rocks on which they are growing.

Hostas with glaucous leaves perform best in temperate climates with high rainfall and a protracted spring season. Where springs are shorter, the year going straight from winter to summer, the blueness lasts for a shorter time. In the Midwest and the South, hostas with blue-toned leaves, even those in full shade, will all start to turn green as early as the end of May. The lack of frosts, high rainfall and temperate climate of the Pacific Northwest, particularly Washington and Oregon, provide hostas with their ideal growing conditions. There is just enough winter cold to initiate dormancy and just enough heat, together with the rainfall, to grow the biggest hostas in the world, apart from those in New Zealand. The inland Northwest is almost as good a growing region because of the slightly hotter summers, but more watering and soil amendment is needed to produce huge hostas.

Growing hostas with blue leaves in full, hot sun melts the coating, and the leaves soon turn a streaky gray-green. Some emerge less blue, more green or gray, and many turn green after mid-summer. I have placed the following hostas in this section of the directory in the color category which best represents them at mid-summer. I have not included those with a slight bluish cast early in the season (for example, some *H. nakaiana* seedlings) because I think they belong in the green category. I have also not mentioned the underside of the leaf in this section; it is always somewhat glaucous, unless it has exceptionally thick or white powdering.

Most of the bluest hostas are dark blue (such as *H.* 'Blue Wedgwood'), but there are a few striking light blue varieties. *Hosta* 'Camelot' is one such example. Some are borderline blue to blue-green, such as *H.* 'Blue Arrow', which I have placed in the blue-green section.

BLUE LEAVES

Listed below are those hostas which appear to have really blue leaves at mid-summer, not blue-green or blue-gray or green-gray. They are usually derived from the very blue *H.* 'Tokudama' or *H. sieboldiana* 'Elegans', which is a hybrid of *H. sieboldiana* × *H.* 'Tokudama'. Most will assume a blue-green tinge earlier or later in the growing season, but some will remain almost blue until autumn. This phenomenon, which depends on genetic make-up, light levels and degree of summer heat, will be discussed under the "Distinguishing Features" subheading.

Hosta 'Abiqua Blue Crinkles' (Walden-West & Purtymun 1999)

MEDIUM–LARGE

Origin: Unknown.

Clump Size & Habit: 36 in. wide × 24 in. high (90 × 60 cm). A dense mound.

Description: Leaf blade: 9⅛ × 6⅜ in. (23 × 16 cm); thick, intense pale blue, strongly seersuckered; edge flat, distinctly cupped; widely oval with a cuspidate tip, rounded to tapered open lobes. Petiole: wide, flattish, pale gray-blue, appearing to pierce the blade. Flower: bell-shaped, near white on an upright, leafy, glaucous gray, 30 to 32 in. (75 to 80 cm) scape from mid- to late summer; fertility unknown.

Comments & Special Needs: Given good light and high, filtered shade, it will remain blue well into late summer. Fast growing, which is unusual for this type of hosta, it can

Previous page: *Hosta* 'Osprey'

Hosta 'Abiqua Blue Crinkles'

Hosta 'Abiqua Drinking Gourd'

Hosta 'Am I Blue'

make clumps of up to 48 in. wide × 28 in. (120 × 70 cm) high in the Pacific Northwest. Pest resistant.

Similar: *H. 'Betcher's Blue', which has shallower cupping.

Hosta 'Abiqua Drinking Gourd' (Walden-West 1989)

MEDIUM–LARGE

Origin: *H*. 'Tokudama' × *H*. *sieboldiana* 'Elegans'.

Clump Size & Habit: 36 in. wide × 20 in. high (90 × 50 cm). An open mound of deeply cupped leaves.

Description: Leaf blade: 8⅜ × 8⅜ in. (21 × 21 cm); thick, rich dark blue, strongly seersuckered and puckered; edge flat, deeply cupped, nearly round with a mucronate tip, tapered overlapping lobes. Petiole: stout, gray-blue, appearing to pierce the blade. Flower: tubular, near white on an upright, leafy, gray-blue, 22 in. (55 cm) scape in midsummer; fertile.

Comments & Special Needs: Planting directly under a tree canopy should be avoided to prevent detritus falling into the leaves. Good light and protection from strong wind is advised.

Distinguishing Features: Depth of the leaf cupping can be up to 4 in. (10 cm). The powdery gray underside of the leaves is often visible because of the cupping.

Similar: *H. 'Blue Canoe'; H. 'Kayak'.

Hosta 'Am I Blue' (D. & J. Ward 1998)

GIANT

Origin: H. 'Reginald Kaye' hybrid.

Clump Size & Habit: 44¾ in. wide × 30 in. high (112 × 75 cm). A dense mound.

Description: Leaf blade: 13⅛ × 12 in. (33 × 30 cm); thick, intense blue, seersuckered, prominently veined; edge flat, slightly convex, nearly round with a mucronate tip, heart-shaped overlapping lobes. Petiole: oblique, glaucous blue-gray. Flower: small, bell-shaped, pale lavender on an upright, bare, glaucous blue-green, 27⅛ to 31⅛ in. (68 to 78 cm) scape in mid-season; fertility unknown.

Comments & Special Needs: Grow in light to full shade to maintain the wonderful leaf color. Slow to moderate growth. Pest resistant.

Similar: *H. 'Big Daddy'; H. 'Bressingham Blue'.

Hosta 'Azure Snow' (Ruh 1991)

MEDIUM–LARGE

Origin: H. hypoleuca hybrid.

Clump Size & Habit: 30 in. wide × 15 in. high (75 × 38 cm). A low, open mound.

Description: Leaf blade: 12¾ × 8⅜ in. (32 × 21 cm); thick, powdery turquoise to pale blue, powdery white below, widely spaced veins, dimpled; edge rippled, shallowly undulate, arching, oval to triangular with a cuspidate

---

*Indicates plants fully described elsewhere in this book.

Hosta 'Azure Snow'

Hosta 'Betcher's Blue'

Hosta 'Big Daddy'

tip; heart-shaped to rounded pinched lobes. Petiole: narrow, pale green. Flower: flared, lavender on an arching, leafy, mauve, 16¾ in. (42 cm) scape from mid- to late summer; fertile.

Comments & Special Needs: A moderate growth rate. Light to full shade all day.

Distinguishing Features: The only blue-leaved *H. hypoleuca* hybrid. Leaves have exceptionally thick, white undersides.

Similar: *H. 'Blue Betty Lou' also has this distinctive pale blue leaf with just a hint of turquoise; *H.* 'Maekawa', which is a selection of *H. hypoleuca*.

Hosta 'Betcher's Blue' (AHS 1986)

MEDIUM

Origin: *H.* 'Tokudama' hybrid.

Clump Size & Habit: 40¾ in. wide × 16 in. high (102 × 40 cm). A dense mound.

Description: Leaf blade: 9⅛ × 7½ in. (23 × 19 cm); thick, rich blue turning dark green later, shiny below, seersuckered; edge almost flat, cupped toward the edge, widely oval with a mucronate tip, heart-shaped pinched lobes. Petiole: shallow, pale green. Flower: funnel-shaped, pale lavender to near white on a pale green 16¾ in. (42 cm) scape in midsummer; fertility unknown, occasional seeds are produced.

Comments & Special Needs: Light shade all day to retain the blue color for as long as possible. Slow to increase. Pest resistant.

Distinguishing Features: Leaves are similar to those of *H.* 'Buckshaw Blue' and *H.* 'Tokudama' but even longer and more pointed, in outline resembling *H.* 'Tokudama Flavocircinalis'. Flowers are held just above the leaf mound.

Similar: *H. 'Buckshaw Blue'; *H.* 'Lee Armiger'; *H.* 'Tokudama'.

Hosta 'Big Daddy' (Aden 1978)

LARGE

Origin: Sport of a variegated *H.* "Robusta" seedling.

Clump Size & Habit: 40¾ in. wide × 26 in. high (102 × 65 cm). A dense mound.

Description: Leaf blade: 12 × 11½ in. (30 × 29 cm); very thick, rich blue turning green toward late summer, strongly seersuckered and puckered; edge almost flat, distinctly cupped, nearly round with a mucronate tip, heart-shaped folded to overlapping lobes. Petiole: stout, paler blue-green, appearing to pierce the blade. Flower: funnel-shaped, near white on an upright, bare, paler blue-green, 28 in. (70 cm) scape in mid-summer; fertile.

Comments & Special Needs: Will remain a chalky dark blue in a well-shaded situation for most of the season, becoming less blue in brighter light. Pest resistant. Very slow to increase, especially from a young tissue-cultured plant.

Distinguishing Features: Among the most distinctly cupped, larger, blue-leaved hostas.

Similar: *H. 'Aksarben'; *H.* 'Aqua Velva' is darker in

color; *H.* 'Bressingham Blue' is larger; *H.* 'Lakeside Blue Jeans' is less cupped.

Sports: *H.* 'Papa' has blue-margined leaves with golden yellow centers that hold for most of the summer; *H.* 'Sugar Daddy' has white-margined, blue leaves.

Hosta 'Blue Blush' [TF$_3$ × 1] (E. Smith & BHHS 1988)
SMALL

Origin: *H.* 'Tardiflora' × *H. sieboldiana* 'Elegans'.

Hosta 'Blue Blush'

Clump Size & Habit: 15 in. wide × 11 in. high (38 × 28 cm). An upright mound.

Description: Leaf blade: 6⅜ × 3⅛ in. (16 × 8 cm); thick, smooth, dark blue; edge flat to slightly undulate, slightly folded, twisted, widely lanceolate with an acute tip, tapered open lobes. Petiole: narrow, gray-blue. Flower: bell-shaped, rich lavender on an upright, bare, gray-blue, 14¼ in. (36 cm) scape in high summer; fertile.

Comments & Special Needs: Grow in high, filtered shade to medium shade. A good growth rate. Among the smaller in the Tardiana Group taking time to increase in size.

Similar: *H.* 'Hadspen Heron'; *H.* 'Sherborne Swift'.

Hosta 'Blue Danube' [TF$_2$ × 24](E. Smith & BHHS 1988)
MEDIUM

Origin: *H.* 'Tardiflora' × *H. sieboldiana* 'Elegans'.

Clump Size & Habit: 36 in. wide × 12 in. high (90 × 30 cm). A moderately dense mound.

Description: Leaf blade: 6⅜ × 5⅛ in. (16 × 13 cm); thick, intense dark blue, seersuckered; edge almost flat, shallowly cupped or convex, nearly round with a mucronate tip, heart-shaped open lobes. Petiole: pale green. Flower: funnel-shaped, pale lavender flowers on an upright, bare, mauve-gray, 18 in. (45 cm) scape in high summer; fertile.

Comments & Special Needs: Blue leaf color is retained

Hosta 'Blue Danube'

for longer if grown in dappled to light shade. Very slow to increase. Pest resistant.

Distinguishing Features: Resembles *H. sieboldiana* 'Elegans' in miniature.

Similar: *H.* 'Brother Ronald', which is more deeply cupped; *H.* 'Hadspen Blue', which is larger.

Hosta 'Blue Fan Dancer' (Aden 1976)

MEDIUM

Origin: Self of a *H.* 'Tokudama' hybrid.

Clump Size & Habit: 36 in. wide × 17⅜ in. high (90 × 43 cm). A layered mound.

Description: Leaf blade: 9⅛ × 6⅜ in. (23 × 16 cm); thick, rich blue, somewhat seersuckered; edge flat with an occasional wide undulation, flat with a slightly upturned edge widely oval to nearly round with a cuspidate tip, heart-shaped overlapping lobes. Petiole: stout, pale blue-green. Flower: funnel-shaped, near white on an upright, leafy, gray-blue, 18¾ in. (47 cm) scape in mid-summer; fertile.

Comments & Special Needs: Grow in dappled to light shade. Pest resistant. Faster growing than some of the *H.* 'Tokudama' hybrids.

Distinguishing Features: Rugose yet flat leaves arranged in layers.

Hosta 'Blue Ice' (R. Benedict 1987)

MINIATURE

Origin: *H.* 'Dorset Blue' × *H.* 'Blue Moon'.

Clump Size & Habit: 8⅜ to 10 in. wide × 4 to 6 in. high (21 to 25 × 10 to 15 cm). A low-growing, flattish mound.

Description: Leaf blade: 3½ × 3½ in. (9 × 9 cm); very thick, intense pale to mid-blue, pale glaucous gray below, dimpled to seersuckered; edge almost flat, folded to cupped,

heart-shaped to round with a cuspidate tip, heart-shaped open lobes. Petiole: short, flattish gray-blue. Flower: bell-shaped, near white to very pale lavender in dense clusters on an upright, bare, glaucous gray, 4 to 5⅛ in. (10 to 13 cm) scape in late summer; fertile.

Comments & Special Needs: Very slow to increase so worth exposing to morning sun as a young plant to boost its vigor even though it will temporarily lose its superb leaf color. Grow in a free-draining, moisture-retentive soil. Good in containers. Excellent pest resistance.

Similar: *H.* 'Blue Moon', which has a somewhat larger, darker blue leaf.

Hosta 'Blue Jay' (H. Benedict 1987)

SMALL

Origin: *H.* 'Dorset Blue' selfed.

Clump Size & Habit: 25⅛ in. wide × 10 in. high (63 × 25 cm). A compact mound.

Description: Leaf blade: 6 × 4 in. (15 × 10 cm); thick, in-

Hosta 'Blue Ice'

Hosta 'Blue Fan Dancer'

Hosta 'Blue Jay', flower.

tense dark blue turning dark green, dimpled; edge almost flat, folded to cupped, widely oval to nearly round with a mucronate tip, heart-shaped pinched to overlapping lobes. Petiole: narrow, blue-green. Flower: bell-shaped, white on an upright, bare, pale blue-green, 12 in. (30 cm) scape in high summer; fertile.

Comments & Special Needs: In essence a derivative of the Tardiana Group. Grow in dappled to medium shade. Slow growing. Pest resistant.

Similar: *H. 'Dorset Blue', which has rounder leaves.

Hosta 'Blue Mammoth' (Aden NR)

GIANT

Origin: H. sieboldiana 'Elegans' hybrid.

Clump Size & Habit: 48 in. wide × 34 in. high (120 × 85 cm). A widely layered mound.

Description: Leaf blade: 14 × 12 in. (35 × 30 cm); thick, light blue, intensely seersuckered and heavily puckered; edge almost flat to shallowly undulate; arching, pinched near the cuspidate tip, widely oval with heart-shaped pinched lobes. Petiole: stout, light blue-green. Flower: narrowly funnel-shaped, near white from lavender buds on an upright, bare, 32 in. (80 cm) scape in mid-summer; fertile.

Comments & Special Needs: Will tolerate about half a day's sun, but the blue coating will disappear much more quickly than it would in dappled sunlight to light shade. Pest resistant. Among the largest blue-leaved hostas and a paler color than most. Useful as a background specimen or in a light woodland setting.

Distinguishing Features: Flower scapes are taller than those of H. sieboldiana 'Elegans' and it is faster growing.

Similar: *H. 'Gray Cole'; H. 'Trail's End'; *H. sieboldiana 'Elegans'.

Sports: H. 'Bud Is Wiser' has a central variegation and is slow to increase; H. 'Cory's Blue', a natural sport, has irregular white margins.

Hosta 'Blue Mammoth'

Hosta 'Blue Moon'

Hosta 'Blue Rock'

Hosta 'Blue Wedgwood'

Hosta 'Blue Moon' [TF$_2$ × 2] (E. Smith & Aden 1976)

DWARF

Origin: *H.* 'Tardiflora' × *H. sieboldiana* 'Elegans'. Originally known as *H.* 'Halo' by Eric Smith.

Clump Size & Habit: 12 in. wide × 8⅜ in. high (30 × 21 cm). A neat, flattish mound.

Description: Leaf blade: 4⅜ × 4⅜ in. (11 × 11 cm); very thick, rich dark blue, some dimpling when mature; edge slightly undulate, cupped, widely oval to nearly round with a mucronate tip, heart-shaped open to folded lobes. Petiole: short, near horizontal, blue-gray. Flower: flared, near white to lavender-gray in a dense raceme on an upright, bare, blue-gray, 9 in. (22 cm) scape in mid- to high summer; fertile.

Comments & Special Needs: Grow in dappled to medium shade. Slow growing. Pest resistant. Often confused in the trade with the slightly larger *H.* 'Dorset Blue'.

Similar: **H.* 'Blue Ice'; *H.* 'Full Moon', which has larger, dark blue-green leaves; **H.* 'Kiwi Blue Baby', which is a slightly lighter blue.

Hosta 'Blue Rock' (Stone & Fisher 1986)

MEDIUM

Origin: *H. sieboldiana* 'Elegans' hybrid.

Clump Size & Habit: 36 in. wide × 20 in. high (90 × 50 cm). A tight mound.

Description: Leaf blade: 8 × 6 in. (20 × 15 cm); thick, rich blue, intensely seersuckered; edge flat, folded, heart-shaped to nearly round with a mucronate tip, heart-shaped overlapping lobes. Petiole: pale green appearing to pierce the blade. Flower: bell-shaped, white on an upright, bare, pale gray-blue, 26⅜ in. (66 cm) scape in mid-summer; fertile.

Comments & Special Needs: Light shade all day. Pest resistant.

Similar: **H.* 'Love Pat', whose leaves are more cupped and less folded.

Hosta 'Blue Wedgwood' [TF$_2$ × 9] (Smith-BHHS 1988)

MEDIUM

Origin: *H.* 'Tardiflora' × *H. sieboldiana* 'Elegans'.

Clump Size & Habit: 36 in. wide × 14 in. high (90 × 35 cm). A dense mound.

Description: Leaf blade: 6⅜ × 5½ in. (16 × 14 cm); thick, smooth, bright to deep powdery blue, strongly dimpled when mature; edge widely rippled, oval to wedge-shaped with a mucronate tip, kinked to flattish overlapping lobes. Petiole: burgundy-dotted, blue-green. Flower: bell-shaped, soft lavender on an upright, bare, 16 in. (40 cm) scape from mid- to high summer; fertile.

Comments & Special Needs: Light to full shade all day,

but even so the leaves will turn dark green early. Pest resistant.

Distinguishing Features: Has been confused in the trade with *H.* 'Blue Dimples', whose leaves are similar but more dimpled and not wedge-shaped.

Similar: *H.* 'Buffy'.

Hosta 'Brother Ronald' [TF$_2$ × 30] (Smith & BHHS 1988)
MEDIUM

Origin: *H.* 'Tardiflora' × *H. sieboldiana* 'Elegans'.

Clump Size & Habit: 20 in. wide × 15 in. high (50 × 38 cm). A dense mound.

Description: Leaf blade: 6⅜ × 4 in. (16 × 10 cm) ; thick, intense mid- to dark blue, slightly ribbed veining, dimpled; edge slightly undulate, cupped, widely oval with a mucronate tip, heart-shaped overlapping lobes. Petiole: pale blue green. Flower: bell-shaped, white in dense clusters on an upright, bare, glaucous gray-green, 18¾ in. (47 cm) scape in late summer; fertile.

Comments & Special Needs: A moderate increaser. Light to full shade.

Distinguishing Features: Among the bluest of the Tardiana Group. Rated one out of six on the Zilis blue-color scale (one being the bluest), but not the most shapely hosta in leaf or clump.

Hosta 'Buckshaw Blue' (Smith-AHS 1986)
MEDIUM

Origin: *H. sieboldiana* × *H.* 'Tokudama'.

Clump Size & Habit: 35½ in. wide × 14 in. high (89 × 35 cm). Outward-facing leaves giving a horizontal effect to the mound.

Description: Leaf blade: 5⅛ × 4½ in. (13 × 11.5 cm), thick, dark blue above and pale glaucous green below, heavily seersuckered, deeply impressed veins; edge almost flat, markedly cupped toward the lobes, nearly round with a mucronate tip, heart-shaped folded or overlapping lobes. Petiole: coarse, shallow, pale green, appearing to pierce the blade. Flower: bell-shaped, near white on an upright, bare, pale green, 18 in. (45 cm) scape in mid-summer; fertile.

Comments & Special Needs: The standard by which all blue-leaved hostas should be judged. Heavy, waxy coating on the leaves is retained until late summer in cooler climates, where it produces its best color if grown in full shade. Clear light gives the leaves a much lighter blue appearance. Should not be planted beneath a tree canopy because falling detritus can damage the attractive bloom on the leaves. Very slow to increase. Pest resistant.

Hosta 'Brother Ronald'

Hosta 'Buckshaw Blue'

Similar: *H.* 'Blue Velvet'; **H.* 'Moscow Blue'; **H.* 'Tokudama'.

Hosta 'Camelot' [TF$_2$ × 27] (E. Smith & BHHS 1988)
MEDIUM

Origin: *H.* 'Tardiflora' × *H. sieboldiana* 'Elegans'.

Clump Height & Habit: 34¾ in. wide × 16 in. high (87 × 40 cm).

Description: Leaf blade: 7⅛ × 5⅛ in. (18 × 13 cm); thick, intense light blue, seersuckered and puckered when mature; edge flat to slightly undulate, shallowly cupped or convex, heart-shaped to nearly round with a cuspidate tip, heart-shaped overlapping lobes. Petiole: long, light blue-green. Flower: bell-shaped, palest lavender on an upright, bare, blue-green, 18 in. (45 cm) scape in late summer; fertile.

Comments & Special Needs: Grow in dappled to light shade. Slow to moderate increase. Pest resistant.

Hosta 'Camelot'

Hosta 'Deep Blue Sea'

Distinguishing Features: The best of the lighter blue hostas in the Tardiana Group with a rounder, more pleasing leaf shape.

Similar: *H. 'Brother Ronald'; *H. 'Hadspen Blue'; H. 'Serena'; H. 'Sherborne Songbird'.

Hosta 'Deep Blue Sea' (C. Seaver 1994)

SMALL–MEDIUM

Origin: H. 'Blue Moon' hybrid.

Clump Size & Habit: 30 in. wide × 13⅛ in. high (75 × 33 cm). A stiff, open mound.

Description: Leaf blade: 8 × 7½ in. (20 × 19 cm); very thick, rich dark blue, intensely seersuckered and puckered; edge flat, distinctly cupped, nearly round with a mucronate to cuspidate tip, heart-shaped open lobes. Petiole: coarse, flattish, pale green, appearing to pierce the blade. Flower: bell-shaped, rich lavender in a dense raceme on an upright, bare, lilac-gray, 15 in. (38 cm) scape in high summer; fertile.

Comments & Special Needs: Grow in good light to dappled shade. Leaves unfurl light green soon becoming a superb blue and keeping their color for most of the summer.

Distinguishing Features: Exaggeratedly rugose to seersuckered toward central midrib, almost distorting the symmetry of the leaf. Lobes are sometimes twisted behind the petioles.

Similar: H. 'Willy Nilly', whose leaves are slightly less blue and somewhat twisted.

Hosta 'Dorset Blue' [TF$_2$ × 4] (E. Smith & Aden 1977)

SMALL

Origin: H. 'Tardiflora' × H. sieboldiana 'Elegans'.

Clump Size & Habit: 24 in. wide × 10 in. high (60 × 25 cm). An open mound.

Hosta 'Dorset Blue'

Description: Leaf blade: 4¾ × 4 in. (12 × 10 cm); thick, intense bright blue, seersuckered; edge slightly undulate, cupped, heart-shaped to nearly round with a mucronate or cuspidate tip, heart-shaped pinched lobes. Petiole: long, narrow, greenish blue. Flower: bell-shaped, grayish white in a dense raceme on an upright, bare, 14 in. (35 cm) scape in high to late summer; very fertile.

Comments & Special Needs: Grow in dappled shade. Pest resistant. Slow to increase. Much used in breeding for small, blue-leaved hostas.

Distinguishing Features: Slightly larger and bluer in leaf than H. 'Blue Moon' with an attractive silver overlay to the leaves, making this small member of the Tardiana Group a must-have for collectors of the bluest leaved hostas. Has been mistaken in the trade for H. 'Blue Moon'.

Similar: H. 'Blue Chip', which is a selfed H. 'Dorset Blue'.
Sports: *H. 'Dorset Clown'.

Hosta 'Dorset Charm'

Hosta 'Dorset Charm' [TF₁ × 1] (E. Smith & Ruh 1990)

SMALL–MEDIUM

Origin: *H.* 'Tardiflora' × *H. sieboldiana* 'Elegans'. Named for Eric Smith by Julie Morss.

Clump Size & Habit: 30 in. wide × 10 to 12 in. high (75 × 25 to 30 cm). A compact mound.

Description: Leaf blade: 5⅛ × 3⅛ in. (13 × 8 cm); very thick, dark blue, closely veined, dimpled; edge slightly rippled to widely undulate when mature, arching, widely oval with a cuspidate tip, rounded open to pinched lobes. Petiole: dark blue-green. Flower: bell-shaped, pale lavender on an upright, leafy, dark blue-green, 18 in. (45 cm) scape in late summer; fertile.

Comments & Special Needs: Grow in dappled to medium shade all day. Leaves are truly dark blue in cooler climates; in hotter climates it is considered to have dark blue-green leaves. Rated three out of six on the Zilis blue-color scale, one being the bluest. Although slow to establish, it can easily exceed its registered dimensions. A good breeding plant. Pest resistant.

Hosta 'Elvis Lives'

Hosta 'Elvis Lives' (Avent 1995)

MEDIUM

Origin: *H.* 'Peter Pan' × *H.* 'Green Fountain'.

Clump Size & Habit: 36 in. wide × 18 in. high (90 × 45 cm). A moderately dense mound.

Description: Leaf blade: 11 × 4⅜ in. (28 × 11 cm); of

good substance, smooth, rich powdery blue, widely spaced veins; edges distinctly rippled and twisted, arching toward the cuspidate tip, lanceolate to oval, rounded open lobes. Petiole: blue-green. Flower: long, tubular, lavender on an upright, bare, light green, 22 in. (55 cm) scape in early to mid-summer; fertile.

Comments & Special Needs: Grow in dappled to light shade. Blue suedelike upper surface of the leaf will be apparent for longer in cooler climates. A moderate increaser.

Similar: *H.* 'Venetian Blue'; **H.* 'Winfield Blue', which has bluer leaves for longer in the season.

Hosta 'Fragrant Blue' (Aden 1988)

MEDIUM

Origin: Unknown.

Clump Size & Habit: 36 in. wide × 15 in. high (90 × 38 cm). A dome-shaped mound.

Description: Leaf blade: 8⅜ × 6⅜ in. (21 × 16 cm); thick, smooth, powdery light blue, dimpled; edge almost flat, convex, widely oval with a cuspidate tip, heart-shaped open lobes. Petiole: blue-green. Flower: funnel-shaped, slightly fragrant, white from rich violet buds on an upright 30 in. (75 cm) scape in high summer; very fertile.

Comments & Special Needs: Grow in good light to dappled shade to maintain the waxy bloom on the leaf. Vigorous. Pest resistant. Among the few blue-leaved hostas with fragrant flowers, although the fragrance is only perceptible in hot climates.

Hosta 'Fragrant Blue'

Hosta 'Hadspen Blue'

Hosta 'Hadspen Blue' [TF$_2$ × 7] (E. Smith & Ruh 1976)

MEDIUM

Origin: *H.* 'Tardiflora' × *H. sieboldiana* 'Elegans'.

Clump Size & Habit: 34⅜ in. wide × 18⅜ in. high (86 × 46 cm). An open mound.

Description: Leaf blade: 7⅛ × 6½ in. (18 × 16.5 cm); thick, smooth rich blue, some dimpling when mature; edge almost flat, slightly cupped or convex, heart-shaped to nearly round with a mucronate tip, heart-shaped overlapping lobes. Petiole: stout, pale blue-gray. Flower: bell-shaped, lavender-gray to near white on an upright, bare, glaucous gray-blue, 18 in. (45 cm) scape in mid- to high summer; fertile.

Comments & Special Needs: Leaves do not form a symmetrical mound but the wonderful leaf color makes this a very worthwhile garden plant. Less shapely than the leaves of the illustrious *H.* 'Halcyon' but of a thicker substance and more glaucous with a suggestion of rugosity on the leaf surface. One of the most intense "blues" of the Tardiana Group, keeping its color for longer than most. Early to emerge. Slow to increase. Pest resistant.

Similar: *H.* 'Happiness'.

Sports: **H.* 'Aristocrat'; *H.* 'Honeysong Blue and Gold'; **H.* 'Kiwi Blue Marble'; *H.* 'Nobility', the reverse form of *H.* 'Aristocrat', not easy to grow.

Hosta 'Halcyon' [TF$_1$ × 7] (E. Smith & BHHS 1988)

MEDIUM

Origin: *H.* 'Tardiflora' × *H. sieboldiana* 'Elegans'.

Clump Size & Habit: 40¾ in. wide × 18 in. high (102 × 45 cm). A symmetrical mound.

Description: Leaf blade: 6⅜ × 4 in. (16 × 10 cm); thick, smooth to barely rugose, intense blue; edge almost flat, widely oval with a cuspidate tip, heart-shaped pinched to overlapping lobes. Petiole: flattish, blue-green, appearing to pierce the blade. Flower: bell-shaped, near white in a dense raceme on a thick, upright, bare, mauve-gray, 22⅜ in. (56 cm) scape in mid-summer; fertile, pale green seedpods.

Comments & Special Needs: A benchmark for all hostas in the Tardiana Group. However, the original *H.* 'Halcyon' is usually now only seen in older collections, since seed-raised strains and the advent of tissue have bastardized it.

Hosta 'Halcyon'

Holds its color well into late summer given good light to dappled shade. Juvenile leaves are conspicuously narrow, especially in micropropagated plants. A much used breeding plant. Superb in a container. Rated two out of six on the Zilis blue-color scale, one being the bluest. Winner of the 1987 Alex J. Summers Distinguished Merit Hosta Award.

Distinguishing Features: Attractive, small gray-green and mauve flower bracts.

Similar: *H. 'Devon Mist' has grayer leaves.

Sports: H. 'Canadian Shield' has dark green leaves; *H. 'Devon Green'; H. 'First Frost', which has white-margined leaves; *H. 'Goldbrook Glimmer'; *H. 'June'; H. 'Peridot', which has dark green leaves; H. 'Valerie's Vanity', which has dark green leaves.

Hosta 'Hillbilly Blues' (Avent 1999)

SMALL

Origin: H. 'Hirao Splendor' × 'Hadspen Blue'.

Clump Size & Habit: 36 in. wide × 10 in. high (90 × 25 cm). A low spreading mound.

Description: Leaf blade: 6⅜ × 4 in. (16 × 10 cm); of good substance, powdery blue, closely veined; edge flat, slightly convex, widely oval with a cuspidate tip, heart-shaped pinched lobes. Petiole: pale blue-green. Flower: tubular, pale lavender flowers on an oblique, glaucous blue-green, 15 in. (38 cm) scape in late summer; fertile.

Comments & Special Needs: Grow in light shade. Valuable for its late-flowering and blue leaves. Of moderate increase.

Hosta 'Kiwi Blue Baby' (Collier & Sligh 1999)

SMALL

Origin: H. 'Halcyon' selfed.

Clump Size & Habit: 19⅛ in. wide × 8 in. high (48 × 20 cm). A rounded, symmetrical mound.

Description: Leaf blade: 4 × 3⅛ in. (10 × 8 cm); thick; frosty to dark blue, prominently veined; edge nearly flat, flat to convex, widely oval with a cuspidate tip, heart-shaped pinched to overlapping lobes. Petiole: blue-green. Flower: bell-shaped, palest lavender on an upright, bare, blue-green, 10 in. (25 cm) scape in mid-summer; sterile.

Comments & Special Needs: Grow in good light or dappled to medium shade. Slow growing. Pest resistant.

Hosta 'Love Pat' (Aden 1978)

MEDIUM–LARGE

Origin: H. 'Blue Velvet' × H. 'Blue Vision'.

Clump Size & Habit: 40 in. wide × 20 in. high (100 × 50 cm). A dense mound.

Description: Leaf blade: 8⅜ × 8 in. (21 × 20 cm); thick, rich blue, intensely seersuckered; deeply cupped, nearly

Hosta 'Kiwi Blue Baby'

Hosta 'Hillbilly Blues'

Hosta 'Love Pat'

round with a mucronate tip, heart-shaped overlapping lobes. Petiole: stout, blue-green. Flower: A densely packed raceme of near bell-shaped, palest lavender to nearly white flowers on a leafy, grayish mauve, 22¾ in. (57 cm) scape, barely rising above the leaf mound in mid-summer; fertile.

Distinguishing Features: Upwardly poised, very cupped leaves, so the glaucous undersides of the leaves are often visible.

Comments & Special Needs: Good light to light shade all day but plant well away from a tree canopy. In the hottest climates it turns dark green after mid-summer. Slow to increase in its early years but in maturity much faster growing. Pest resistant.

Similar: *H. 'Blue Rock'; H. 'Blue Splendor', which is somewhat larger; *H. 'Rock and Roll', whose leaves are slightly grayer.

Sports: H. 'Love Burst' has streaked leaves.

Hosta 'Moscow Blue' (Arett 1986)

MEDIUM–LARGE

Origin: H. 'Tokudama' hybrid.

Clump Size & Habit: 40¾ in. wide × 20¾ in. high (102 × 52 cm). A dense mound.

Description: Leaf blade: 10 × 9⅛ in. (25 × 23 cm); thick, intense blue, dimpled to seersuckered, puckered when mature; edge almost flat, widely oval nearly round with a mucronate tip, heart-shaped overlapping lobes. Petiole: stout, light blue-green. Flower: bell-shaped white on an upright, bare, 26 in. (65 cm) scape from mid- to late summer; fertile.

Comments & Special Needs: Good light to light shade all day. Slow to increase. Pest resistant. Considered to be among the best of the many similar H. 'Tokudama' hybrids.

Similar: *H. 'Buckshaw Blue'; H. 'Groo Blue'.

Hosta 'Rock and Roll' (Kuk 1999)

LARGE

Origin: Unknown.

Clump Size & Habit: 40¾ in. wide × 26 in. high (102 × 65 cm). A dense mound.

Description: Leaf blade: 8⅜ to 10½ × 8⅜ to 11½ in. (21 to 27 × 21 to 29 cm); thick, rich blue, intensely seersuckered; edge almost flat, deeply cupped, nearly round with a mucronate tip, heart-shaped overlapping lobes. Petiole: pale blue-green. Flower: bell-shaped, near white on an upright, leafy, blue-green, 27⅛ in. (68 cm) scape in mid-summer; fertile, green seedpods.

Comments & Special Needs: Blue leaf color holds until the frosts in the North if grown in good light to light shade. Moderate growth rate. Pest resistant.

Distinguishing Features: Exceptionally powdery bloom on the upper leaf surface gives it an attractive pale blue coloring. Slow to increase. Pest resistant.

Similar: *H. 'Love Pat'; H. 'Skookumchuck'.

Hosta 'Samual Blue' (Krossa & Ruh 1981)

LARGE

Origin: Unknown.

Clump Size & Habit: 36 in. wide × 27⅛ in. high (90 × 68 cm). An upright mound.

Description: Leaf blade: 10¼ × 8½ in. (26 × 21.5 cm); thick, rich sapphire-blue, intensely seersuckered; edge slightly undulate, shallowly cupped, widely oval to nearly round with a mucronate tip, heart-shaped pinched lobes. Petiole: stout, light green, appearing to pierce the blade. Flower: funnel-shaped rich lavender on an upright, leafy, glaucous, light green, 28¾ in. (72 cm) scape in mid-season; fertile.

Hosta 'Moscow Blue'

Hosta 'Rock and Roll'

Hosta 'Samual Blue'

Comments & Special Needs: Very heavy bloom makes the leaf color exceptionally blue, so shade is essential. Slow to establish. Pest resistant. An older introduction but never bettered.

Similar: *H.* 'Blue Velvet'; *H.* 'Skookumchuck'.

Hosta 'Sea Blue Leather' (Seaver NR)

GIANT

Origin: Unknown.

Clump Size & Habit: 50¾ in. wide × 34 in. high (127 × 85 cm). An upright mound.

Description: Leaf blade: 14 × 12¾ in. (35 × 32 cm); very thick, leathery dark blue, seersuckered and puckered; edge almost flat, shallowly cupped or convex, widely oval to nearly round with a mucronate tip, heart-shaped overlapping lobes. Petiole: light blue-green. Flower: bell-shaped, white in a sparse raceme on an upright or oblique, 36 in. (90 cm) scape in mid-summer; fertile.

Comments & Special Needs: Grow in good light to light shade all day. Slow to increase. Pest resistant.

Distinguishing Features: Pruinose bloom soon fades from the upper leaf surface leaving a pronounced leathery texture.

Similar: *H.* 'Lakeside Sapphire Pleats'.

Hosta 'Sea Blue Leather'

Hosta 'Sea Sapphire' (M. Seaver NR)

MEDIUM–LARGE

Origin: Unknown.

Clump Size & Habit: 44 to 48 in. wide × 20 in. high (110 to 120 × 50 cm). A rounded mound.

Description: Leaf blade: 8 × 7⅛ in. (20 × 18 cm), very thick, powdery dark blue, lighter blue below, closely seersuckered; edge undulate, cupped or convex, widely oval to nearly round with a mucronate tip, heart-shaped pinched or

Hosta 'Sea Sapphire', a juvenile specimen

Hosta sieboldiana 'Elegans'

overlapping lobes. Petiole: flattish light blue-green. Flower: funnel-shaped, pale lavender in a dense raceme on an upright, bare, light green, 26 in. (65 cm) scape in mid-summer; fertile.

Comments & Special Needs: Good light to light shade all day to maintain the superb dark blue leaf color. Lovely with light green lacy ferns.

Similar: *H.* 'Blue Vision'; *H.* 'Lakeside Sapphire Pleats'; *H.* 'Sea Grotto'; *H.* 'Sea Hero'.

Hosta sieboldiana 'Elegans' (Ahrends & Hylander & AHS 2002)

LARGE

Origin: *H. sieboldiana* × *H.* 'Tokudama'.

Clump Size & Habit: 50¾ in. wide × 26 in. high (127 × 65 cm). A dense mound.

Description: Leaf blade: 14¼ × 10¼ in. (36 × 26 cm); very thick, rich medium blue, intensely seersuckered and puckered when mature; edge almost flat to slightly undulate, cupped or convex, widely oval to heart-shaped with a mucronate tip, heart-shaped overlapping lobes. Petiole: light green-blue. Flower: funnel-shaped, pale lavender-striped, near white in a dense raceme on an upright, bare, light blue-green, 27⅛ in. (68 cm) scape in mid- to high summer; very fertile.

Comments & Special Needs: Good light to light shade all day. Most effective, like all hostas of this type, in cooler gardens where the superb leaf color will be maintained for longer. Feed in early spring. Slow to establish. Pest resistant. Over the years this name has been applied to a variety of *H. sieboldiana* selections and it is likely that none of the plants in tissue culture under this name is the correct plant, which may now only be found in older collections.

Hosta 'Silver Bay'

Distinguishing Features: Flowers are bunched at the top of the scape that rises only just above the foliage mound.

Similar: *H.* 'Edina Heritage'; *H.* 'Helen Doriot', whose leaves are slightly smaller; *H.* 'Ryan's Big One', whose leaves are somewhat larger; **H. sieboldiana* 'Gray Cole'.

Sports: **H. sieboldiana* 'Borwick Beauty'; **H. sieboldiana* 'Frances Williams'; **H. sieboldiana* 'George Smith'; **H. sieboldiana* 'Great Expectations'; **H. sieboldiana* 'Northern Halo'; **H. sieboldiana* 'Northern Lights'; **H. sieboldiana* 'Northern Mist'.

Hosta 'Silver Bay' (Dean 1999)

MEDIUM

Origin: *H.* 'Silver Frost' × *H.* 'Blue Moon'.

Clump Size & Habit: 34⅜ in. wide × 13⅛ in. high (86 × 33 cm). A dense, flat-topped mound.

Description: Leaf blade: 6¾ × 6⅜ in. (17 × 16 cm); thick, intense silver-blue; seersuckered; edge slightly undulate, folded to slightly cupped, widely oval to nearly round with a mucronate tip, heart-shaped pinched to overlapping lobes. Petiole: light blue-green, appearing to pierce the blade. Flower: bell-shaped, pale lavender on an upright, bare, blue-green, 21⅛ to 23⅛ in. (53 to 58 cm) scape in high summer; fertile, light green seedpods.

Comments & Special Needs: Grow in good light to light shade. Of moderate increase. Pest resistant. Lovely grown with variegated dead nettle or yellow-leaved hostas.

Distinguishing Features: Among the best recently introduced blue-leaved hostas.

Hosta 'Tokudama' (Maekawa NR)

MEDIUM

Origin: Once considered a species but now thought to be of cultivated origin and first found in Japanese gardens.

Clump Size & Habit: 30 in. wide × 16 in. high (75 × 40 cm). Loosely mounding.

Description: Leaf blade: 8⅜ × 6½ in. (21 × 16.5 cm); thick, rich dark blue, closely seersuckered, closely veined; edge slightly undulate, shallowly cupped toward the edge, widely oval to nearly round with a mucronate tip, heart-shaped overlapping lobes. Petiole: flattish, light green, appearing to pierce the blade. Flower: narrowly funnel-shaped, near white in mid- to high summer; fertile.

Comments & Special Needs: Best planted out of direct sunlight but not under a tree canopy to avoid detritus falling into the leaves. Keeps its color for longer in shady sites. Very slow to increase. Pest resistant. Frequently produces sports and an excellent breeding plant.

Similar: *H.* 'Abiqua Blue Crinkles'; *H.* 'Betcher's Blue'; *H.* 'Buckshaw Blue', its well-known hybrid which has slightly longer leaves; *H.* 'I'm So Blue'; *H.* 'Moscow Blue'.

Sports: *H.* 'Tokudama Aureonebulosa', which has cloudy blue-streaked yellow leaves; *H.* 'Tokudama Flavocircinalis'.

Hosta 'True Blue' (Aden 1978)

LARGE

Origin: *H.* 'Chartreuse Wedge' × (*H. nigrescens* × *H.* 'Blue Vision').

Clump Size & Habit: 50¾ in. wide × 30 in. high (127 × 75 cm). An arching mound.

Description: Leaf blade: 12 × 10 in. (30 × 25 cm); thick intense light blue, glaucous gray-blue below, seersuckered; edge slightly undulate, arching, mostly convex, widely oval to heart-shaped with a cuspidate tip, heart-shaped pinched lobes. Petiole: wide, light green. Flower: widely funnel-shaped, near white in a dense raceme on an oblique, bare, blue-green, 32 in. (80 cm) scape in mid-summer; fertile.

Comments & Special Needs: Grow in good light to light

Hosta 'True Blue', a juvenile specimen

Hosta 'Winfield Blue'

Hosta 'Tokudama'

shade. Not suitable for container growing. Moderate growth rate. Pest resistant.

Distinguishing Features: The inner leaves are rounder, the outer leaves noticeably longer. Leaves arch downward from oblique petioles.

Similar: *H.* 'Perry's True Blue', which may be identical.

Hosta 'Winfield Blue' (Zilis & Falstad & Janssen NR)

SMALL

Origin: Formerly unnamed Tardiana Group seedling.

Clump Size & Habit: 45½ in. wide × 18 in. high (114 × 45 cm). An open mound.

Description: Leaf blade: 7½ × 5⅛ in. (19 × 13 cm); thick, powdery blue, slightly dimpled; edge distinctly rippled, slightly arching, oval with a cuspidate tip, tapered open lobes. Petiole: flattish, light blue. Flower: tubular, palest lavender on an upright, bare, light blue-green, 28 in. (70 cm) scape in high summer; fertile.

Comments & Special Needs: Outstanding blue leaf color holds late into the summer provided the plant is grown in light to full shade; the best results occurring in cooler climates.

Distinguishing Features: Among the bluest of all blue-leaved hostas and quite distinct.

Similar: *H.* 'Elvis Lives', whose leaves are not quite as blue later in the season.

BLUE-GRAY LEAVES

Hostas in this category are often as sophisticated as the purer blues and require careful placing in the garden. They are best used near the house, either as container specimens or planted to set off stonework or paving. Their grayish blue leaves are due either to the basic leaf color or sometimes to the denseness of a glaucous gray bloom on a blue leaf. The latter group of plants can quickly lose their bloom if exposed to hot sun, leaving a shiny or blotched surface on the leaves.

Hosta 'Babbling Brook' (K. Vaughn NR)

MEDIUM–LARGE

Origin: (*H.* 'Donahue Piecrust' × *H. pycnophylla*) × *H.* 'Regal Ruffles'.

Clump Size & Habit: 30 in. wide × 16 in. high (75 × 40 cm). A low, spreading mound.

Description: Leaf blade: 14 × 11 in. (35 × 28 cm); of good substance, gray-blue, later turning dark green, thickly glaucous below, widely spaced veins; edge distinctly rippled, widely oval with a cuspidate tip, heart-shaped pinched lobes. Petiole: pale green-gray. Flower: narrowly funnel-shaped, lavender on an upright then arching to horizontal, pale green-gray, 25⅛ in. (63 cm) scape in mid- to high summer; fertile.

Comments & Special Needs: Gray to silvery blue leaf color is retained for longer in cooler climates. Light to medium shade all day.

Distinguishing Features: When the raceme is heaviest, the scape arches down toward the ground in an unattractive manner.

Hosta 'Baby Bunting' (Savory 1982)

MINIATURE

Origin: Hybrid of *H.* 'Rough Waters'.

Clump Size & Habit: 12 in. wide × 8⅜ in. high (30 × 21 cm). A dense, rounded mound.

Hosta 'Babbling Brook'

Hosta 'Baby Bunting'

Hosta 'Blue Angel'

Description: Leaf blade: 3½ × 3½ in. (9 × 9 cm); thick, gray-blue, seersuckered, nearly round with a mucronate tip, deeply heart-shaped pinched lobes. Petiole: narrow, gray-green. Flower: bell-shaped, pale lavender on an oblique, bare, green, 18 in. (45 cm) scape in mid-summer; fertile.

Comments & Special Needs: Leaves turn green in very bright light and always become dark green by the end of the season. Among the smallest glaucous-leaved hostas to have distinctly corrugated leaves. The parent of several superb, even smaller-leaved sports. Grow in containers or as an edging plant in bright light to light shade. Water sparingly until the root system is established. Slow to increase. Pest resistant. Performs better in Northern gardens.

Similar: *H. 'Popo', which has smoother leaves; H. 'Tet-A-Poo'.

Sports: H. 'Cameo' has a wide yellow margin; H. 'Cherish' has yellow leaves with dark green margins; H. 'Hope' has a yellow-green margin; *H. 'Pandora's Box'.

Hosta 'Blue Angel' (Aden 1986)

GIANT

Origin: H. "Aden 365" × H. "Aden 361."

Clump Size & Habit: 71⅛ in. wide × 36 in. (178 × 90 cm). A graceful, cascading mound exhibiting characteristics from its H. montana heritage.

Description: Leaf blade: 16 × 12 in. (40 × 30 cm); thick, dark blue-gray to dark blue-green, slight dimpling when mature, prominent, closely ribbed veins; edges rippled, arching, convex, widely oval to wedge-shaped with a cuspidate tip, heart-shaped pinched lobes. Petiole: gray-green. Flower: open funnel-shaped, long lasting, palest lavender to near white in a dense raceme on a stout, upright, leafy, gray-green, 48 in. (120 cm) scape in mid-summer; fertile.

Comments & Special Needs: Grow in a few hours of

Hosta 'Blue Heaven'

morning sun in the North followed by light shade. Among the best large, blue-leaved hostas for Southern gardens. Can tolerate quite dry soil when fully established. If carefully sited, it almost gets into the bluest category at no. 6. A classic hosta.

Distinguishing Features: Among the largest blue-leaved hostas.

Sports: H. 'Angel Eyes' has dark blue margins with a viridescent white to light green center; H. 'Fallen Angel' emerges white with green speckling and turns green; *H. 'Guardian Angel'; H. 'Grey Ghost', whose leaves emerge ghostly, translucent white turning yellow and finally blue.

Hosta 'Blue Heaven' (Aden 1976)

MEDIUM

Origin: H. 'Blue Cadet' × H. "Aden 355."

Clump Size & Habit: 10 in. wide × 8 in. high (25 × 20 cm). An open mound.

Description: Leaf blade: 6⅜ × 3⅛ in. (16 × 8 cm); of average substance, silvery gray-blue, slightly dimpled, closely veined; edge flat to shallowly undulate, slightly folded, heart-shaped with a mucronate tip, heart-shaped pinched to overlapping lobes. Petiole: light gray-blue. Flower: bell-shaped, pale lavender on an upright, bare, light green-gray, 18 in. (45 cm) scape in mid-summer; fertile.

Comments & Special Needs: Grow in dappled to light shade. Moderately vigorous.

Distinguishing Features: Produces a multitude of scapes.

Hosta 'Bold Ruffles' (Arett 1975)

GIANT

Origin: Hybrid derivative of *H. sieboldiana* 'Elegans'.

Clump Size & Habit: 36 in. wide × 30 in. high (90 × 75 cm). A stiff, upright, somewhat unruly mound.

Description: Leaf blade: 15 × 12 in. (38 × 30 cm); very thick, blue-gray, seersuckered and crumpled; edge distinctly rippled especially on juvenile leaves, oval to nearly round with a mucronate to twisted tip, heart-shaped pinched to overlapping lobes. Petiole: coarse, wide, light gray-green. Flower: bell-shaped, near white on an upright, leafy, straight, 32 in. (80 cm) scape in mid-summer; fertile.

Comments & Special Needs: Loses its color during the second half of the season in hotter climates but will look good for longer if grown in out of direct sunlight. Will collect detritus if planted under a tree canopy, so careful siting is needed. Very slow to increase, therefore keep well fed and copiously watered; it will eventually well exceed its registered dimensions. Not suitable for container growing. Pest resistant.

Hosta 'Clarence' (Simpers & Soules 1996)

MEDIUM–LARGE

Origin: *H. sieboldiana* hybrid seedling.

Clump Size & Habit: 36 in. wide × 18 in. high (90 × 45 cm). An upright mound.

Description: Leaf blade: 9¾ × 8½ in. (24.5 × 21.5 cm); thick, blue-gray, seersuckered, with some puckering toward the tip; edge almost flat, shallowly cupped or convex, widely oval to nearly round with a mucronate tip, deeply heart-shaped open to pinched lobes. Petiole: nearly upright, pale green. Flower: flared, near white on an upright, bare, glaucous light green, 20 in. (50 cm) scape in mid-summer; fertility not known.

Comments & Special Needs: Grow in light to moderate shade. A moderate increaser. Pest resistant.

Distinguishing Features: Considered to be one of the best of this group.

Similar: *H.* 'Blue Plisse'.

Hosta 'Devon Blue' (A. & R. Bowden NR)

MEDIUM–LARGE

Origin: Tardiana Group seedling, not named by Eric Smith.

Hosta 'Clarence'

Hosta 'Bold Ruffles'

Hosta 'Devon Blue'

Clump Size & Habit: 40¾ in. wide × 20 in. high (102 × 50 cm). An arching mound.

Description: Leaf blade: 10 × 6⅜ in. (25 × 16 cm); thick, blue-gray, closely ribbed veins; edge undulate, arching toward the cuspidate tip, lanceolate to oval, rounded open lobes. Petiole: pale blue-green, appearing to pierce the blade. Flower: bell-shaped, palest lavender on an upright, bare, 30 in. (75 cm) scape in mid- to high summer; fertile.

Comments & Special Needs: Grow in dappled to full shade. Quickly turns green if exposed to sunlight. Vigorous. Pest resistant.

Similar: *H. 'Halcyon', which is smaller and has a better-defined leaf shape.

Hosta 'Devon Mist' (A. & R. Bowden NR)

MEDIUM

Origin: H. 'Buckshaw Blue' hybrid.

Clump Size & Habit: 28 in. wide × 15 in. high (70 × 38 cm). A congested mound.

Description: Leaf blade: 6⅜ × 4 in. (16 × 10 cm); thick, leathery, dark blue-gray turning green later, closely ribbed veins; edge rippled, widely oval to heart-shaped with a cus-

pidate tip, heart-shaped open lobes. Petiole: narrow, blue-green. Flower: bell-shaped, palest lavender, produced in profusion on an upright, bare, dark green, 20 in. (50 cm) scape in mid- to high summer; fertile.

Comments & Special Needs: Grow in good light to dappled shade. Slow to increase. Pest resistant.

Similar: *H. 'Blue Wedgwood', which has darker blue leaves.

Hosta 'Goldbrook Grayling' (S. Bond NR)

SMALL

Origin: H. 'Happiness' hybrid.

Clump Size & Habit: 18 in. wide × 8⅜ in. high (45 × 21 cm). A diffuse mound.

Description: Leaf blade: 5½ × 1½ in. (14 × 4 cm); thick, gray-blue; edge undulate to kinked, folded, lanceolate with an acute tip, tapered open lobes. Petiole; gray-green. Flower: bell-shaped, lilac-pink on an upright, bare, gray-green, 10 in. (25 cm) scape in late summer; fertility unknown.

Comments & Special Needs: Some morning sun in cooler climates. Of moderate increase. Pest resistant. Lovely in a container.

Hosta 'Devon Mist'

Distinguishing Features: Although it has many characteristics of Tardiana Group hosta, it is quite distinct in its gray leaves and pinkish flowers.

Hosta 'Great Plains' (Brincka & Petryszyn 1994)

LARGE–GIANT

Origin: *H.* 'Sagae' × *H.* 'Tokudama Flavocircinalis'.

Clump Size & Habit: 41½ in. wide × 25⅛ in. high (104 × 63 cm). A semi-upright mound.

Description: Leaf blade: 16 × 12 in. (40 × 30 cm); thick, gray-blue, furrowed veins; edge rippled to piecrusted, undulate, widely oval with a cuspidate tip, heart-shaped open lobes. Petiole: stout, light green. Flower: long, tubular, pale lavender in a dense raceme on an upright or oblique, leafy, blue-green, 41½ in. (104 cm) scape from mid- to high summer; fertile.

Comments & Special Needs: Grow in dappled to moderate shade. Upper leaf surface soon loses its waxy coating becoming satiny blue-green, finally dark green; the underside remains a light glaucous blue.

Similar: *H.* 'Grey Piecrust', which does not have the outstanding qualities of *H.* 'Great Plains'.

Hosta 'Krossa Regal' (Krossa 1980)

LARGE–GIANT

Origin: *H. nigrescens* hybrid.

Clump Size & Habit: 71⅛ in. wide × 32¾ in. high (178 × 82 cm). An upright and arching mound.

Description: Leaf blade: 11 × 7⅛ in. (28 × 18 cm); of good substance, smooth, soft gray-blue, widely veined; edge slightly undulate, slightly arching, oval with a cuspidate tip, rounded open lobes. Petiole: upright, gray-green. Flower: funnel-shaped, lavender on an upright, bare, light gray-green, 60 in. (150 cm) scape in mid- to high summer; sterile.

Comments & Special Needs: Dappled to light shade. Slug resistant. Clumps become more spreading with maturity. A hosta of great architectural merit as a specimen and good in a large container, which must be kept well-watered. Outstanding in leaf and flower. Winner of the 2001 Alex J. Summers Distinguished Merit Hosta Award.

Similar: * *H.* 'Pewter Frost'; *H.* 'Phoenix', which has a more refined leaf; *H.* 'Snowden'; *H.* 'Tenryu', which was collected from near the river Tenryu in Japan, and although closely related to *H. nigrescens*, it looks more like *H.* 'Krossa Regal'.

Sports: *H.* 'Regal Chameleon' has a viridescent, pale green, central variegation; *H.* 'Regal Splendor'; *H.* 'Regalia'; *H.* 'Tom Schmid'.

Hosta 'Goldbrook Grayling'

Hosta 'Great Plains'

Hosta 'Krossa Regal'

Hosta 'Metallic Sheen'

Hosta 'Mississippi Delta'

Hosta 'Metallic Sheen' (Zilis 1999)

LARGE–GIANT

Origin: *H.* 'Sum and Substance' × *H. sieboldiana* 'Elegans'.

Clump Size & Habit: 60 in. wide × 28 in. high (150 × 70 cm). An open mound.

Description: Leaf blade: 14 × 10 in. (35 × 25 cm); very thick, smooth, metallic gray-blue, turning dark green, seersuckered and puckered; edge almost flat, shallowly cupped or convex, widely oval to nearly round with a mucronate tip, heart-shaped open to overlapping lobes. Petiole: stout, light blue-gray to green, appearing to pierce the blade. Flower: funnel-shaped, glaucous pale lavender on an upright or leaning, leafy, 30 to 40 in. (75 to 100 cm) scape in late summer; fertile.

Comments & Special Needs: Some morning sun in cooler climates, otherwise light shade all day. Slow to moderate increase. Pest resistant.

Distinguishing Features: The huge leaves of the *H.* 'Sum and Substance' and the thickness and surface texture of the *H. sieboldiana* 'Elegans' parents make this an impressive hosta.

Hosta 'Mississippi Delta' (Petryszyn 1998)

GIANT

Origin: *H.* 'Sea Gold' × *H.* 'Golden Torch'.

Clump Size & Habit: 56¾ in. wide × 36 in. high (142 × 90 cm). Upright, outward-facing leaves in an open mound.

Description: Leaf blade: 12¾ × 12 in. (32 × 30 cm); very thick, rubbery, blue-gray, dimpled and puckered; edge slightly undulate, flat to shallowly cupped, nearly round with a mucronate tip, heart-shaped pinched to folded lobes. Petiole: stout, blue-green. Flower: long, tubular, near white in a dense raceme on an upright or oblique, light blue-

green, 40 in. (100 cm) scape in high summer; fertile, green seedpods.

Comments & Special Needs: Upper leaf surface soon loses its glaucous coating leaving a rubbery effect, but the best color is maintained if grown in light shade. Moderate growth rate. Pest resistant.

Distinguishing Features: Scape branching can occur in maturity.

Hosta 'Noah's Ark' (Hatfield NR)

MEDIUM

Origin: Unknown.

Clump Size & Habit: 44 in. wide × 20 in. high (110 × 50 cm). A dome-shaped mound.

Description: Leaf blade: 10 × 7½ in. (25 × 19 cm); thick, gray-blue to green, seersuckered, prominently veined; edge flat to occasionally undulate, folded, widely oval with a mucronate tip, heart-shaped pinched to overlapping lobes. Petiole: gray-green. Flower: bell-shaped, white on an upright, leafy, gray-green, 34 in. (85 cm) scape in high summer; sterile.

Comments & Special Needs: Good light to light shade all day. Slow to increase. Pest resistant. Ideal for woodland or landscape planting.

Hosta 'Osprey' [TF₂ × 14] (Smith & BHHS 1988)

MEDIUM

Origin: *H.* 'Tardiflora' × *H. sieboldiana* 'Elegans'.

Clump Size & Habit: 36 in. wide × 17⅜ in. high (90 × 43 cm). A compact mound.

Description: Leaf blade: 7⅛ × 5⅛ in. (18 × 13 cm); thick, light gray-blue with a hint of green, moderately seersuckered, widely spaced veins; folded to cupped, widely oval to nearly round with a mucronate tip, heart-shaped

Hosta 'Noah's Ark'

Hosta 'Pacific Blue Edger'

Hosta 'Osprey'

Hosta 'Pewter Frost'

overlapping lobes. Petiole: pale gray-green, appearing to pierce the blade. Flower: bell-shaped, white on a leafy, upright, pale gray-green, 24 in. (60 cm) scape in early to midsummer; fertile.

Comments & Special Needs: Will take two hours of morning sun in cooler climates, elsewhere prefers good light to light shade. Slow to increase. Pest resistant.

Hosta '**Pacific Blue Edger**' (Heims NR)

SMALL

Origin: Sport of *H.* 'Gold Edger'.

Clump Size & Habit: 12 in. wide ×7⅛ in. high (30 × 18 cm). A dense mound.

Description: Leaf blade: 5⅛ × 3⅛ in. (13 × 8 cm); of average substance, smooth blue-gray; edge undulate to kinked, folded, widely oval with an acute tip, heart-shaped pinched lobes. Petiole: narrow, blue-green. Flower: see *H.* 'Gold Edger'.

Comments & Special Needs: Grow in light to moderate shade. A rapid increaser, more so than its parent. Ideal as an edging plant.

Hosta '**Pewter Frost**' (Dishon 1996)

MEDIUM

Origin: *H. pycnophylla* × *H. montana*.

Clump Size & Habit: 40¾ in. wide × 13⅛ in. high (102 × 33 cm). An upright mound.

Description: Leaf blade: 10 × 7⅛ in. (25 × 18 cm); of moderate substance, intense blue-gray, prominently veined; edge slightly undulate, slightly arching, oval with a cuspidate tip, heart-shaped pinched lobes. Petiole: glaucous light green with scattered purple dotting. Flower: long, funnel-shaped, near white on an upright or oblique, leafy, glaucous light green, 33⅛ in. (83 cm) scape in high to late summer; fertile, green seedpods.

Comments & Special Needs: Grow in light shade. The

thick glaucous bloom soon disappears from the upper leaf surface, which is then very shiny, giving a gunmetal-like appearance. Moderate growth rate.

Hosta 'Pewterware' (Dean 1999)

SMALL

Origin: *H.* 'Urajiro Hachijo' × *H.* 'Blue Moon'.

Clump Size & Habit: 24 in. wide × 8 in. high (60 × 20 cm). A dense mound.

Description: Leaf blade: 5½ × 4⅜ in. (14 × 11 cm); thick, gray-blue; edge widely undulate, heart-shaped to almost round with a cuspidate tip, heart-shaped pinched lobes. Petiole: light gray-green. Flower: long, bell-shaped, lavender-striped, near white on an upright, glaucous light green, bare, 14 to 19⅛ in. (35 to 48 cm) scape in early autumn; fertility unknown, green seedpods.

Comments & Special Needs: Grow in dappled to full shade. Slow to increase. Pest resistant. A superb recent introduction.

Hosta 'Pewterware'

Hosta 'Popo'

Distinguishing Features: Leaves have a heavy glaucous bloom. Leaf substance is exceptionally heavy.

Hosta 'Popo' (O'Harra & Riehl 1993)

MINIATURE

Origin: Unknown.

Clump Size & Habit: 15 in. wide × 7 in. high (38 × 17.5 cm). A dense mound.

Description: Leaf blade: 2 × 1½ in. (5 × 4 cm); of good substance, light blue-gray, smooth; edge flat, slightly folded, widely oval with a cuspidate tip. Petiole: gray-green. Flower: funnel-shaped, pale lavender to near white on an upright, bare, light green, 12 in. (30 cm) scape in late summer; fertile.

Comments & Special Needs: Morning sun in cooler climates to boost the vigor, then dappled to light shade. Ideal for rock gardens, sinks and containers.

Similar: *H.* 'Peedee Graymulkin'.

Hosta 'Quilted Skies' (Soules 1985)

LARGE

Origin: *H. sieboldiana* 'Elegans' × *H.* 'Frances Williams'.

Clump Size & Habit: 48 in. wide × 26 in. high (120 × 65 cm). A billowing mound.

Description: Leaf blade: 12¾ × 10 in. (32 × 25 cm); thick, intense silvery blue-gray, deeply seersuckered and puckered; edge slightly undulate, shallowly cupped or convex, widely oval to nearly round with a cuspidate tip, deeply heart-shaped pinched lobes. Petiole: stout, pale blue green. Flower: bell-shaped palest lavender on an upright, bare, pale gray-green, 30 in. (75 cm) scape in mid- to high summer; fertile.

Hosta 'Quilted Skies'

Comments & Special Needs: Good light to light shade all day. Slow to establish and slow to take on its mature form but eventually the heavy leaves droop downward and fold lengthways as they do so. Pest resistant.

Hosta 'Sherborne Swift' [TF$_2$×26] (E. Smith & BHHS 1988)

SMALL–MEDIUM

Origin: *H.* 'Tardiflora' × *H. sieboldiana* 'Elegans'.

Clump Size & Habit: 30 in. wide × 8⅜ in. high (75 × 21 cm). A diffuse mound.

Description: Leaf blade: 5½ × 2⅜ in. (14 × 6 cm); thick blue-gray; edge almost flat with occasional kinks, arching toward the cuspidate tip, lanceolate with tapered open to pinched lobes. Petiole: narrow, gray-green. Flower: bell-shaped, near white in a dense raceme on an upright, leafy scape in mid-summer.

Comments & Special Needs: Light to full shade all day. Lovely with *Cimicifuga* 'Brunette'.

Distinguishing Features: Intensely gray-blue foliage.

Similar: *H.* 'Hadspen Hawk', whose leaves are a darker blue and smaller.

Hosta sieboldiana 'Gray Cole' (Kuk's Forest 1985)

GIANT

Origin: Early selected form of *H. sieboldiana* 'Elegans' but only registered in 1998.

Clump Size & Habit: 84¾ in. wide × 36 in. high (212 × 90 cm). A billowing mound.

Description: Leaf blade: 15 × 12¾ in. (38 × 32 cm);

Hosta sieboldiana 'Gray Cole'

Hosta 'Sherborne Swift'

thick, gray-blue turning gray-green, seersuckered and puckered; edge slightly undulate, shallowly cupped or slightly convex, widely oval to nearly round with a mucronate tip, raised heart-shaped overlapping lobes. Petiole: stout, gray-green, appearing to pierce the blade. Flower: funnel-shaped near white, on an upright, bare, glaucous green, 39⅛ in. (98 cm) scape in mid-summer; fertile.

Hosta 'Silberpfeil'

Comments & Special Needs: Will tolerate morning sun but the leaf will remain a better color if grown in dappled to full shade. Of moderate increase once established. Pest resistant.

Distinguishing Features: Bloom scape can be branched. Petaloid stamen double flowers are sometimes produced.

Similar: **H. sieboldiana* 'Elegans', which is slightly smaller.

Hosta 'Silberpfeil' (Klose NR)

SMALL–MEDIUM

Origin: *H.* 'Tardiflora' × *H. sieboldiana* 'Elegans'.

Clump Size & Habit: 25⅛ in. wide × 10 in. high (63 × 25 cm). An open mound.

Description: Leaf blade: 5⅛ × 1⅜ in. (13 × 3.5 cm); thick, pale silver-blue, closely veined; edge almost flat to widely undulate, slightly arching, lanceolate with an acute to cuspidate tip, tapered open lobes. Petiole: narrow, pale silver-blue, appearing to pierce the blade. Flower: bell-shaped, near white on an upright, bare, blue-gray, 12 in. (30 cm) scape in mid-summer; fertile.

Comments & Special Needs: *H.* 'Silberpfeil' was among

Hosta 'Something Blue'

a collection of unnumbered and unnamed Tardiana Group seedlings acquired by the German nurseryman and hosta collector, the late Heinz Klose.

Similar: *H.* 'Hadspen Hawk', whose leaves are a darker blue.

Hosta 'Something Blue' (Simpers & Ruh 1991)

MEDIUM–LARGE

Origin: *H.* 'Blue Beauty' × *H.* 'Blue Boy'.

Clump Size & Habit: 50¾ in. wide × 22 in. high (127 × 55 cm). An open mound.

Description: Leaf blade: 9⅛ × 8⅜ in. (23 × 21 cm); of good substance, blue-gray, deeply seersuckered and puckered; edge attractively rippled, folded to cupped, widely oval with a cuspidate to mucronate tip, heart-shaped folded lobes. Petiole: narrow, blue-green. Flower: tubular, rich lavender on an upright, bare, light blue-green, 26 in. (65 cm) scape in high summer; fertile.

Comments & Special Needs: Good light to light shade all day. Increases more rapidly than many similar blue-leaved hostas.

Distinguishing Features: Leaf color is an attractive blue-gray.

Similar: *H.* 'Blue Betty Lou'.

Hosta 'Tomoko' (Klose NR)

MEDIUM–LARGE

Origin: *H.* 'Tardiflora' × *H. sieboldiana* 'Elegans'. An unnumbered and unnamed Tardiana Group seedling, one of several given to the late Heinz Klose.

Clump Size & Habit: 32 in. wide × 20 in. high (80 × 50 cm). A dense mound.

Description: Leaf blade: 10 × 8⅜ in. (25 × 21 cm); thick, rich dark blue-gray, dimpled, closely veined; edge almost flat, convex, widely oval to nearly round with a mucronate tip, deeply heart-shaped pinched lobes. Petiole: blue-gray. Flower: bell-shaped, near white on an upright, bare, gray-blue, 22 in. (55 cm) scape in mid-summer; fertile.

Comments & Special Needs: Closely resembles its *H. sieboldiana* 'Elegans' parent but is somewhat smaller. Grow in dappled to light shade. Slow to establish. Pest resistant. Widely grown in European gardens.

Hosta 'Turning Point' (Lydell 2001)

SMALL–MEDIUM

Origin: *H.* "Minuta" streaked (thought to be a large form of *H. venusta*) seedling.

Clump Size & Habit: 30 in. wide × 12 in. high (75 × 30 cm). A dense mound.

Description: Leaf blade: 5⅛ × 1⅜ in. (13 × 3.5 cm); thick, smooth blue-gray; edge flat with an occasional kink; slightly folded, lanceolate with an acute tip, tapered open lobes. Petiole: narrow, blue-gray. Flower: bell-shaped, lavender on an upright, leafy, light purple, 24 to 30 in. (60 to 75 cm) scape from high summer to early autumn; fertile.

Comments & Special Needs: Grow in good light to dappled shade when the leaf color is long-lasting. Is sun tolerant in the North but the leaf surface will lose its pruinose coating. A moderate to good increaser.

Distinguishing Features: Leaves are upright then abruptly horizontal. Numerous flower scapes arise from the center of the mound and tower above the leaves.

Hosta 'Tomoko'

Hosta 'Turning Point'

BLUE-GREEN LEAVES

This category embraces all those hostas that are not quite blue enough to belong in the blue section and yet are definitely too blue to belong in the green section. Many leaves unfurl green, turn blue for a few weeks and finally take on greenish tints; others start blue but hold this for a very short time soon becoming greener.

Hosta 'Abiqua Trumpet' (Walden-West & Purtymun 1987)
SMALL

Origin: *H.* 'Tokudama' selection.

Clump Size & Habit: 21⅛ in. wide × 8⅜ in. high (53 × 21 cm). A flattish, dense mound.

Description: Leaf blade: 4 × 3⅛ in. (10 × 8 cm), thick, blue-green, dimpled to seersuckered; edge almost flat, folded to cupped, widely oval to nearly round with a mucronate tip at maturity, rounded open to pinched lobes. Petiole: narrow light green, appearing to pierce the blade. Flower: bell-shaped, pale lavender on an upright, leafy, glaucous green, 14 in. (35 cm) scape in late summer; fertile.

Comments & Special Needs: Some morning sun in cooler climates, otherwise light to medium shade. Floriferous. Vigorous, a moderately rapid increaser. Ideal in containers or as an edging plant. Pest resistant.

Distinguishing Features: Spoon-shaped leaves give *H.* 'Abiqua Trumpet' a pinwheel effect when seen from above. Leaves are bluer at the edges and greener toward the midrib.

Similar: *H.* 'Heart Throb' remains bluer-leaved for longer; *H.* 'Peter Pan' is slightly larger.

Hosta 'Andrew Jackson' (Sugita & Ruh & Zilis 2001)
LARGE–GIANT

Origin: Unknown. From Japanese seed.

Clump Size & Habit: 54 in. wide × 30⅜ in. high (135 × 76 cm). An upright mound.

Description: Leaf blade: 12¾ × 9¼ in. (32 × 23.5 cm); very thick, intense blue-green, seersuckered; edge distinctly rippled, undulate and slightly twisted, deeply folded, oval with a cuspidate tip, rounded pinched lobes. Petiole: glaucous pale blue appearing to pierce the blade. Flower: long, tubular, near white blushed lavender in a dense raceme on an upright, leafy, glaucous blue-green 31½ in. (79 cm) scape from early to mid-summer; fertility unknown.

Comments & Special Needs: Light to full shade. Pest resistant.

Distinguishing Features: Prominent white lines overlay the veins.

Hosta 'Abiqua Trumpet'

Hosta 'Andrew Jackson'

Hosta 'Bette Davis Eyes' (Vaughn 1987)

MEDIUM

Origin: Sibling to *H.* 'Summer Fragrance' × *H.* 'Christmas Tree'.

Clump Size & Habit: 24 in. wide × 12 in. high (60 × 30 cm). A dense mound.

Description: Leaf blade: 7½ to 9⅛ × 4⅜ in. (19 to 23 × 11 cm); thick, dark blue-green, strongly veined; edge distinctly rippled, arching, widely oval with a cuspidate tip, heart-shaped pinched to overlapping lobes. Petiole: blue-green. Flower: funnel-shaped, fragrant, near white, purple tipped on an oblique, leafy, dark green, 25⅛ in. (63 cm) scape from mid- to late summer; fertile.

Comments & Special Needs: Best in cooler climates and with plenty of moisture. Grow in light to medium shade to retain the blue sheen on the leaves. A moderate increaser. Pest resistant.

Distinguishing Features: Long-blooming, fragrant flowers.

Hosta 'Bette Davis Eyes'

Hosta 'Bigfoot' (Duback 1998)

LARGE–GIANT

Origin: Unknown.

Clump Size & Habit: 69⅛ in. wide × 30⅜ in. high (173 × 76 cm). A tiered mound.

Description: Leaf blade: 18¾ × 12 in. (47 × 30 cm); thick, mid-blue-green, dimpled, widely spaced, moderately prominent veins; edges slightly rippled, nearly flat, widely

Hosta 'Bigfoot'

oval with a cuspidate tip, heart-shaped overlapping lobes. Petiole: gray-green. Flower: large, tubular, near white on an upright, bare, glaucous green, 31⅛ in. (78 cm) scape in mid-summer; fertile.

Comments & Special Needs: Grow in a shaded area away from harsh winds to protect the slightly floppy leaves from damage. Slow to start then moderate growth. Pest resistant.

Distinguishing Features: The lack of cupping sets *H.* 'Bigfoot' apart from other similar hostas.

Hosta 'Big Mama' (Aden 1978)

LARGE

Origin: *H.* 'Blue Tiers' × *H.* 'Blue Angel'.

Clump Size & Habit: 60 in. wide × 26 in. high (150 × 65 cm). A mound of overlapping leaves.

Description: Leaf blade: 18 × 14 in. (45 × 35 cm); thick, dark blue-green, deeply ribbed veins, seersuckered and puckered; edge rippled, arching to convex, undulate near the cuspidate tip, widely oval with heart-shaped pinched lobes. Petiole: stout, pale blue-green. Flower: bell-shaped, palest lavender on an upright, bare, gray-green, 42⅜ in. (106 cm) scape from mid-summer; fertile.

Comments & Special Needs: Good light to full shade but can tolerate some morning sun in the North, although with more sun the blue leaf color will disappear. Very floriferous. A useful background hosta. Slow to get started. Pest resistant.

Distinguishing Features: Leaves are thicker and more rigid than those of *H.* 'Blue Angel'.

Hosta 'Blue Arrow' (Anderson 1982)

MEDIUM

Origin: Unknown.

Clump Size & Habit: 24 in. wide × 18 in. high (60 × 45 cm). A semi-upright and arching mound.

Description: Leaf blade: 8⅜ × 3½ in. (21 × 9 cm); of good substance, blue-green, pale glaucous green below, smooth, widely spaced veins; edge widely undulate and slightly upturned, widely lance-shaped with a cuspidate tip, heart-shaped open broad lobes. Petiole: pale green, appearing to pierce the blade. Flower: bell-shaped, near white on an upright, bare, 20 in. (40 cm) scape in high summer; very fertile.

Comments & Special Needs: Will tolerate some morning

Hosta 'Big Mama'

sun in cooler climates but the leaves remain bluer for longer in dappled to light shade. Pest resistant.

Distinguishing Features: Although not one of the Tardiana Group, it has similar characteristics.

Similar: Leaf blade is similarly shaped to that of *H.* 'Happiness' but is more undulate, turns green earlier and has a generally coarser appearance; **H.* 'Deane's Dream'; *H.*

'Hadspen Heron'; *H.* 'Happiness'; *H.* 'Kiwi Blue Heron'; **H.* 'Pineapple Poll'.

Hosta 'Blue Betty Lou' (Owens 1987)

LARGE

Origin: *H.* 'True Blue' × *H.* 'Gold Regal'.

Clump Size & Habit: 32 in. wide × 24 in. high (80 × 60 cm). A semi-upright habit with noticeable cupping.

Description: Leaf blade: 10½ × 9⅛ in. (27 × 23 cm), thick, light blue-green (almost turquoise), seersuckered, puckering from the midrib; edge shallowly undulate, deeply cupped, nearly round with a mucronate tip, kinked pinched lobes. Petiole: sturdy, turquoise. Flower: bell-shaped, lavender on an upright, bare, 32 in. (80 cm) scape in mid- to late summer; fertile.

Comments & Special Needs: Performs well in Southern gardens. Light to full shade all day. Lovely with *Heuchera* 'Velvet Night'. Slow to establish. Pest resistant.

Distinguishing Features: Among the most turquoise-hued hostas.

Similar: *H.* 'Blue Bayou', which is slightly greener.

Hosta 'Blue Arrow'

Hosta 'Blue Betty Lou'

Hosta 'Blue Blazes'

Hosta 'Blue Boy'

Hosta **'Blue Blazes'** (Vaughn 1988)

LARGE

Origin: *H.* 'Polly Bishop' × *H.* 'Blue Boy'.

Clump Size & Habit: 34¾ in. wide × 30 in. high (87 × 75 cm). An unruly mound.

Description: Leaf blade: 12¾ × 12⅜ in. (32 × 31 cm); thick, rich dark blue-green, intensely seersuckered and puckered; edge slightly undulate, cupped or convex, widely oval to nearly round with a mucronate tip, deeply heart-shaped overlapping lobes. Petiole: light blue-green, appearing to pierce the blade. Flower: bell-shaped, pale lavender to near white on a chunky, upright, bare, pale blue-green, 32 in. (80 cm) scape in mid-summer; fertile.

Comments & Special Needs: Grow in light to full shade. Much faster growing than most blue-leaved hostas. Pest resistant.

Distinguishing Features: Flower buds are level with the top of the foliage and large bracts cluster round the raceme. Leaf color remains an unusually rich, dark blue-green if grown in full shade all day.

Similar: *H.* 'Big Daddy'; *H.* 'Sea Grotto', both of which are bluer in color.

Sports: *H.* 'Blue Blazes Supreme', which has streaked leaves.

Hosta **'Blue Boy'** (Stone & AHS 1986)

MEDIUM

Origin: *H. nakaiana* × *H. sieboldiana* 'Elegans'.

Clump Size & Habit: 45½ in. wide × 15 in. high (114 × 38 cm). A dense mound.

Description: Leaf blade: 8⅜ × 5⅛ in. (21 × 13 cm); of average substance, soft blue soon turning green, smooth, prominently veined; edge slightly rippled, folded, widely oval with a cuspidate tip, heart-shaped pinched to overlapping lobes. Petiole: thin, light blue-green. Flower: funnel-shaped, pale lavender to near white in profusion on an upright, leafy, light green, 22 in. (55 cm) scape in mid-summer; fertile.

Comments & Special Needs: Grow in dappled shade. Vigorous, a rapid increaser. Good ground cover and a useful edging plant.

Similar: *H.* 'Fond Hope'; *H.* 'Goldbrook Genie'.

Hosta **'Blue Cadet'** (Aden 1974)

MEDIUM

Origin: Although registered as a seedling of *H.* 'Tokudama', it has many of the characteristics of *H. nakaiana*.

Clump Size & Habit: 30 in. wide × 15 in. high (75 × 38 cm). A neat, dense mound.

Description: Leaf blade: 5⅛ × 4 in. (13 × 10 cm); of average substance, blue-green, matt above and glaucous below, slight dimpling when mature; edge flat, folded, heart-shaped with a cuspidate tip, cupped and folded lobes. Petiole: narrow, light gray-green. Flower: funnel-shaped, rich lavender in a long, dense raceme on an upright, bare, light green, 22 in. (55 cm) scape from mid- to late summer; fertile.

Comments & Special Needs: Leaves will turn dark green by late summer even if grown in good light to light shade. Vigorous, a rapid increaser. Light shade all day.

Distinguishing Features: Magnificent display of flowers atop the symmetrical mound. Good autumn color.

Similar: *H.* 'Banyai's Dancing Girl'; *H.* 'Blue Boy'; *H.* 'Drummer Boy'; *H.* 'Goldbrook Genie'; *H.* 'My Blue Heaven'; *H.* 'Pacific Blue Edger'; *H.* 'Saint Fiacre'; *H.* 'Serendipity'.

Sports: *H.* 'Medal of Honour', which has a cream margin.

Hosta 'Blue Cadet'

Hosta 'Blue Canoe' (Black & Ruh 1999)

MEDIUM

Origin: Seedling from an open-pollinated pod on *H.* 'Frances Williams', probably crossed with *H.* 'Halcyon'.

Clump Size & Habit: 19⅛ in. wide × 16 in. high (48 × 40 cm). An upright mound.

Description: Leaf blade: 5½ × 3¼ in. (15 × 8.5 cm); thick, blue-green, dimpled, strongly veined; edge slightly undulate, lightly twisted, deeply folded and cupped, widely oval with a mucronate tip, rounded to kinked folded lobes. Petiole: light blue-green. Flower: funnel-shaped, near white subtended by long green bracts on an upright, leafy, light green, 22 in. (55 cm) scape in mid-summer; fertility unknown, blue seedpods.

Comments & Special Needs: Even in cooler climates the leaf turns green early in the season. Assumes chartreuse tints in hot climates. Grow in moderate shade with plenty of moisture. Moderate growth rate. Pest resistant.

Distinguishing Features: Leaf is longer than that of *H.* 'Abiqua Drinking Gourd' but does not hold the blue as well; *H.* 'Kayak', a sibling of *H.* 'Blue Canoe', has smaller, narrower leaves.

Hosta 'Blue Canoe', early in the summer

Hosta 'Blue Clown' (H. Benedict & Stratton 1996)

MINIATURE

Origin: Selfed *H.* 'Dorset Blue' seedling.

Clump Size & Habit: 15 in. wide × 10 in. high (38 × 25 cm). An unsymmetrical mound.

Description: Leaf blade: 2⅜ × 2 in. (6 × 5 cm); thick, blue-green, moderately seersuckered, closely ribbed veins;

Hosta 'Blue Clown'

Hosta 'Blue Diamond'

edge slightly rippled, slightly folded to cupped, widely oval with a mucronate tip, heart-shaped overlapping lobes. Petiole: light green. Flower: flared, white on an upright, bare, light green, 8⅜ in. (21 cm) scape in mid-summer; fertile.

Comments & Special Needs: Good light to light shade. Very slow to increase and best grown in a pot until it has established a root system. Pest resistant.

Similar: *H*. 'Blue Monday'; *H*. 'Blue Skies', which is slightly larger and keeps its color better in cooler gardens.

Hosta 'Blue Diamond' [TF₂ × 23] (E. Smith & BHHS 1988)

MEDIUM

Origin: *H*. 'Tardiflora' × *H. sieboldiana* 'Elegans'.

Clump Size & Habit: 17⅜ in. wide × 12 in. high (43 × 30 cm). A dense mound.

Description: Leaf blade: 7⅛ × 5⅛ in. (18 × 13 cm); thick, soft blue-green, dimpled when mature; edge slightly undulate, slightly arching, lanceolate to oval with a cuspidate tip, rounded open to pinched lobes. Petiole: light blue-green. Flower: bell-shaped, pale lavender on an upright, bare, light glaucous green, 18 in. (45 cm) scape in mid-summer; fertile.

Comments & Special Needs: Good light to light shade. Leaf color is much bluer in cooler climates. Moderate increase. Pest resistant.

Similar: *H*. 'Hadspen Heron', which has more rippled edges.

Hosta 'Blue Horizon' (Englerth 1985)

MEDIUM

Origin: *H*. 'Tokudama' hybrid.

Clump Size & Habit: 32⅜ in. wide × 17⅜ in. high (81 × 43 cm). An open mound.

Description: Leaf blade: 8⅜ × 7½ in. (21 × 19 cm); very

thick, rich blue-green, intensely seersuckered with some puckering; edge almost flat, mainly convex, nearly round with a mucronate tip, heart-shaped pinched to overlapping lobes. Petiole: light blue-green. Flower: bell-shaped, white on an upright, bare, light glaucous green, 18 in. (45 cm) scape in mid-summer; fertile.

Comments & Special Needs: Worth the trouble of placing carefully in light to moderate shade to retain the superb leaf color for as long as possible; avoid positions under trees or in drafts.

Similar: *H*. 'Blue Dome'; *H*. 'Blue Velvet'; *H*. 'Lady In Waiting', which is larger.

Hosta 'Blue Mouse Ears' (Deckert 2000)

MINIATURE

Origin: Unknown.

Clump Size & Habit: 11 in. wide × 6⅜ in. high (28 × 16 cm). An open, horizontal mound.

Description: Leaf blade: 2⅜ × 2 in. (6 × 5 cm); very thick, almost rubbery, rich blue-green, some dimpling; edge almost flat, shallowly cupped, oval when young, nearly round with a mucronate tip when mature, heart-shaped open lobes. Petiole: stout, shallow dark green. Flower: superb clusters of bell-shaped, rich violet-striped lavender on a thick, upright, leafy, pale green, 8⅜ in. (21 cm) scape in mid- to high summer; sterile.

Comments & Special Needs: Grow in some morning sun in the North or in good light to light shade. An excellent specimen for a rock garden, a gravel bed or a container. Moderate growth rate. Reasonably pest tolerant.

Distinguishing Features: Racemes are striking especially when in bud. Buds are held horizontally and swell up like mini-balloons before partially opening.

Similar: *H*. 'Baby Bunting'; *H*. 'Popo'.

Hosta 'Blue Horizon'

Hosta 'Blue Mouse Ears', a young plant

Hosta 'Blue Seer'

Hosta **'Blue Seer'** (Aden NR)

LARGE–GIANT

Origin: *H. sieboldiana* 'Elegans' hybrid.

Clump Size & Habit: 50¾ in. wide × 30 in. high (127 × 75 cm). An upright mound of horizontally poised leaves.

Description: Leaf blade: 14 × 13½ in. (35 × 34 cm); thick, light blue-green, intensely but shallowly seersuckered, puckered when mature; edge almost flat but sometimes with a kink at the lobes, shallowly cupped, nearly round with a mucronate tip, heart-shaped pinched to over-lapping lobes. Petiole: stout, upright, paler blue-green, appearing to pierce the blade. Flower: funnel-shaped, white on an upright, bare, blue-green, 34 in. (85 cm) scape in mid-summer; fertile.

Comments & Special Needs: Grow in light to full shade. Floriferous.

Distinguishing Features: Flowers are compacted on the scape.

Similar: *H.* 'Evelyn McCafferty', whose leaves are more deeply and widely seersuckered and more puckered.

Hosta 'Blue Troll'

Hosta 'Blue Umbrellas'

Hosta 'Brigadier'

Hosta **'Blue Troll'** (R. Savory 1973)

MEDIUM

Origin: Unknown.

Clump Size & Habit: 24 in. wide × 12 in. high (60 × 30 cm). A compact, layered mound.

Description: Leaf blade: 8⅜ × 5⅛ in. (21 × 13 cm); thick, blue-green, seersuckered; edge shallowly undulate and slightly furled, folded or convex, oval with an indistinct mucronate tip, heart-shaped pinched to overlapping lobes. Petiole: stout, light green, appearing to pierce the blade. Flower: bell-shaped, almost white on an upright, bare, glaucous green, 18 in. (45 cm) scape in high summer; fertile.

Comments & Special Needs: Will tolerate some morning sun in the North or light to moderate shade all day. Slow to establish. Pest resistant.

Distinguishing Features: Leaves are longer than most in this color and size; the glaucous bloom tends to disappear early from the edge of the leaf leaving the center a good blue.

Hosta **'Blue Umbrellas'** (Aden 1978)

GIANT

Origin: *H.* 'Tokudama' × *H. sieboldiana* 'Elegans'.

Clump Size & Habit: 54¾ in. wide × 36 in. high (137 × 91 cm). An upright, stiff, open mound.

Description: Leaf blade: 14 × 10 in. (36 × 25 cm); very thick, blue-green, turning dark green, seersuckered and puckered, widely spaced veins; edge flat, usually convex but sometimes cupped, almost round with a mucronate tip, heart-shaped folded to overlapping lobes. Petiole: pale blue-green, appearing to pierce the leaf blade. Flower: bell-shaped, almost white on an upright, bare, pale green, 36 in. (90 cm) scape in mid-summer; fertile.

Comments & Special Needs: Will tolerate some morning sun in cooler climates but the leaf color will remain bluer in light to moderate shade. Slow to increase. Pest resistant.

Distinguishing Features: Leaves, which soon turn shiny dark green, droop downward at the edges giving an umbrella-like appearance.

Similar: **H.* 'Millenium'; **H.* 'Placemat'; **H.* 'Sea Lotus Leaf'.

Sports: *H.* 'Parasol', whose leaves have golden yellow centers and blue-green margins.

Hosta **'Brigadier'** (Q & Z Nursery NR)

LARGE–GIANT

Origin: *H. sieboldiana* 'Elegans' × *H.* 'Hirao Supreme'.

Clump Size & Habit: 60 in. wide × 28 in. high (150 × 70 cm). An upright mound.

Description: Leaf blade: 13⅛ × 10 in. (33 × 25 cm); thick, smooth, blue-green; edge rippled when young then

Hosta 'Deane's Dream'

Hosta 'Devon Giant'

flatter at maturity, arching, folded, narrowly oval with a cuspidate tip, heart-shaped overlapping lobes. Petiole: stout, oblique, pale green. Flower: funnel-shaped, palest lavender on an upright or oblique, bare, pale green, 34¾ in. (87 cm) scape from mid- to late summer; fertile.

Comments & Special Needs: Light to moderate shade but the leaves will still turn green in hot climates. Good growth rate for a large blue-leaved hosta. Pest resistant.

Distinguishing Features: Some leaves display a subtle lighter color on the tips.

Hosta 'Deane's Dream' (Solberg 2000)

MEDIUM

Origin: *H.* 'Blue Arrow' × *H.* 'Sea Fire'.

Clump Size & Habit: 28 in. wide × 16 in. high (70 × 40 cm). An upright mound.

Description: Leaf blade: 9⅛ × 4 in. (23 × 10 cm); thick, aquamarine to turquoise; slightly rippled edges, folded, widely oval with a graceful cuspidate tip, tapered to heart-shaped open to pinched lobes. Petiole: narrow, bright purple. Flower: tubular, pale lavender on an upright, glaucous blue, 22 to 26 in. (55 to 65 cm) scape in late summer; fertile, green seedpods.

Comments & Special Needs: Moderate growth rate. Performs well in the Southern heat but needs light to full shade all day. Grow at eye level to feature the attractive mauve petioles, which are unusual in a hosta with this leaf color.

Distinguishing Features: The combination of attractive turquoise leaves with bright purple petioles that are more intensely purple-dotted than those of *H.* 'Venetian Blue'.

Similar: **H.* 'Blue Arrow'; *H.* 'Hadspen Heron'; **H.* 'Pineapple Poll'.

Hosta 'Devon Giant' (A. & R. Bowden NR)

GIANT

Origin: *H.* 'Hadspen Blue' hybrid.

Clump Size & Habit: 70 in. wide × 36 in. high (175 × 90 cm). A dense mound.

Description: Leaf blade: 18¾ × 18 in. (47 × 45 cm); thick, dark blue-green, seersuckered and puckered toward the midrib; edge almost flat to slightly undulate, almost round with a mucronate tip, deeply heart-shaped overlapping lobes. Petiole: stout, green. Flower: bell-shaped, near white to lavender on an upright, leafy, green, 38 in. (95 cm) scape in mid- to high summer; fertile.

Comments & Special Needs: Grow in light to moderate shade. A superb background specimen or for a woodland garden. Slow to establish but eventually will become one of the largest hostas. Pest resistant.

Hosta 'Evelyn McCafferty' (Arett 1975)

LARGE

Origin: *H.* 'Tokudama' hybrid.

Clump Size & Habit: 48 in. wide × 24 in. high (120 × 60 cm). A crumpled mound.

Description: Leaf blade: 12 × 11 in. (30 × 28 cm); very thick; light blue-green, exceptionally seersuckered, crumpled and puckered; edge almost flat, shallowly cupped, nearly round with a mucronate tip, heart-shaped overlapping lobes. Petiole: stout, light green. Flower: bell-shaped, white, subtended by distinctive blue-green bracts on an upright, leafy, 25⅛ in. (63 cm) scape in mid- to high summer; fertile.

Comments & Special Needs: Grow in light to moderate shade with an ample supply of moisture. A superb speci-

Hosta 'Evelyn McCafferty'

men hosta. Several seasons of growth are needed to produce the crumpled leaves for which it is prized.

Similar: **H.* 'Blue Seer'; *H.* 'Fantastic', whose leaves are more gray-green.

Hosta 'H. D. Thoreau' (Walden-West 1999)

GIANT

Origin: *H.* 'Sagae' × *H. hypoleuca*.

Clump Size & Habit: 84¾ in. wide × 38 in. high (212 × 95 cm). A monumentally large, upright mound.

Description: Leaf blade: 18 × 15 in. (45 × 38 cm); very thick, leathery, intense blue-green with a silvery cast, dimpled, widely spaced veins; edge slightly rippled, nearly convex, nearly round with a mucronate tip, heart-shaped overlapping lobes. Petiole: sturdy light green-blue. Flower: long, bell-shaped, light lavender on an upright, bare, glaucous green, 46¾ in. (117 cm) scape in high to late summer; fertile.

Comments & Special Needs: Grow in light to medium shade. Slow to increase. Pest resistant. Thought to be tetraploid.

Distinguishing Features: Leaves are almost rubbery. Very large, semi-double flowers have a glaucous bloom. An outstanding hosta.

Hosta 'Incredible Hulk' (Elslager 1998)

GIANT

Origin: Unknown.

Clump Size & Habit: 58 in. wide × 34⅜ in. high (145 × 86 cm). An upright mound.

Description: Leaf blade: 16 × 14 in. (40 × 35 cm); very thick, rich blue-green, intensely seersuckered to puckered; edge distinctly rippled, deeply cupped, almost round with a mucronate tip, heart-shaped overlapping lobes. Petiole: thick, glaucous green. Flower: tubular, near white, lavender-striped on an upright, leafy, 38 in. (96.5 cm) scape in high summer; fertile.

Comments & Special Needs: Light to full shade all day. Pest resistant.

Distinguishing Features: Underside of the leaf has a thick white pruinose coating.

Hosta 'H. D. Thoreau'

Hosta 'Kingfisher'

Hosta 'Incredible Hulk'

Hosta 'Lakeport Blue'

Hosta **'Kingfisher'** [TF₂ × 17] (E. Smith & BHHS 1988)

MEDIUM

Origin: *H.* 'Tardiflora' × *H. sieboldiana* 'Elegans'.

Clump Size & Habit: 30 in. wide × 12¾ in. high (75 × 32 cm). An open mound.

Description: Leaf blade: 7⅛ × 3½ in. (18 × 9 cm); thick, smooth, dark gray-blue becoming dark green, dimpled; edge widely undulate, folded to slightly cupped, widely oval with a cuspidate tip, heart-shaped open lobes. Petiole: dark purple-gray. Flower: funnel-shaped, pale lavender on an upright, bare, glaucous green, 14 in. (35 cm) scape in late summer; fertile.

Comments & Special Needs: Keep out of direct sunlight to retain the unusual glaucous, dark blue-green for as long as possible. Is prized for its late summer to autumn blooming flowers.

Distinguishing Feature: Distinct from other hostas of the Tardiana Group in that it dramatically changes color from dark blue-gray to very dark green early in the season.

Hosta **'Lakeport Blue'** (Tompkins 1984)

LARGE

Origin: *H. sieboldiana* hybrid.

Clump Size & Habit: 64 in. wide × 27⅛ in. high (160 × 68 cm). An upright mound.

Description: Leaf blade: 16 × 14 in. (40 × 35 cm); thick, intense blue-green, seersuckered; edge almost flat, deeply cupped, widely oval to nearly round with a mucronate tip, heart-shaped overlapping lobes. Petiole: stout, light blue-green. Flower: bell-shaped, white on a dense raceme, upright, bare, glaucous mauve-gray, 36 in. (90 cm) scape in late summer; fertile.

Comments & Special Needs: Performs well in hot, humid climates, the good blue-colored leaves holding far into summer. Light to full shade. Pest resistant.

Similar: *H.* 'Blue Ox', a seedling of *H.* 'Lakeport Blue', whose leaves are rounder and grayer in color.

Hosta 'Lakeside Blue Cherub'

Hosta 'Lakeside Blue Cherub' (Chastain 1991)

MINIATURE–SMALL

Origin: Sport of *H.* 'Honey Moon'.

Clump Size & Habit: 36 in. wide × 6⅜ in. high (90 × 16 cm). A neat, compact mound.

Description: Leaf blade: 3½ × 2¼ in. (9 × 6.5 cm); thick, leathery pale blue-green, dimpled, closely ribbed veins; edge slightly undulate, folded, widely oval to round with a mucronate tip, heart-shaped pinched lobes. Petiole: light green. Flower: see *H.* 'Honey Moon'.

Comments & Special Needs: Turquoise-hued leaves retain their attractive color in fairly low-light levels. Vigorous. An excellent edging hosta.

Hosta 'Metallica'

Hosta 'Metallica' (W. & E. Lachman 1991)

MEDIUM

Origin: *H.* 'Beatrice' hybrid × *H.* 'Blue Moon'.

Clump Size & Habit: 21⅛ in. wide × 16 in. high (53 × 40 cm). A dense mound.

Description: Leaf blade: 7½ × 4 in. (19 × 10 cm); of average to good substance, dark blue-green turning shiny dark green by high summer, slightly dimpled, closely ribbed veins; edge rippled, slightly twisted, folded, widely oval with a cuspidate tip, heart-shaped pinched to overlapping lobes. Petiole: light blue-green. Flower: widely funnel-shaped, rich lavender on an upright, leafy, blue-green, 25⅛ to 30 in. (63 to 75 cm) scape in high summer; fertility unknown.

Hosta 'Millenium'

Comments & Special Needs: Will easily exceed its registered dimensions.

Hosta 'Millenium' (J. & J. Wilkins 1995)

GIANT

Origin: *H.* 'Herb Benedict' × *H.* 'Sagae'.

Clump Size & Habit: 54 in. wide × 36 in. high (135 × 90 cm). An upright, open mound.

Description: Leaf blade: 16¾ × 14 in. (42 × 35 cm); thick, intense blue-green turning green, seersuckered, puckered and crimped, prominently veined; edge slightly undulate, shallowly cupped or convex, widely oval to nearly round with a mucronate tip, heart-shaped pinched to overlapping lobes. Petiole: stout, light green appearing to pierce the blade. Flower: long, tubular, white on an upright, bare, 44¾ to 50 in. (112 to 125 cm) thick scape in high summer; fertile.

Comments & Special Needs: Grow in cool, moist shade all day. Slow to increase. Pest resistant.

Similar: **H.* 'Metallic Sheen', which is slightly smaller and whose leaves are less blue.

Hosta 'Moongate Flying Saucer'

Hosta 'Moongate Flying Saucer' (Issacs & Solberg 1996)

SMALL–MEDIUM

Origin: *H.* 'Serendipity' × *H.* 'Blue Blazes'.

Clump Size & Habit: 22 in. wide × 11 in. high (55 × 28 cm). An open mound.

Description: Leaf blade: 5⅛ × 3⅛ in. (13 × 8 cm); thick, blue-green turning dark green, seersuckered; edge almost flat, folded to cupped, oval with a cuspidate tip, heart-shaped to round open lobes. Petiole: light green, appearing to pierce the blade. Flower: long, funnel-shaped, pale lavender on an upright, bare, glaucous light green, 22 in. (55 cm) scape in early summer; fertile.

Comments & Special Needs: Grow in good light to light shade to retain the blue color for as long as possible. A moderate increaser.

Hosta 'Mr. Big' (Walden-West NR)

GIANT

Origin: *H. montana* × *H. sieboldiana* 'Elegans'.

Clump Size & Habit: 80 in. wide × 40 in. high (200 × 100 cm). An open, layered, wide-spreading mound.

Description: Leaf blade: 22 × 20 in. (55 × 50 cm); very thick, light blue-green, puckered, crumpled and pleated when mature, widely spaced veins; edge nearly flat, convex, widely oval to nearly round with a mucronate tip, heart-shaped overlapping lobes. Petiole: stout, dark glau-

cous green. Flower: funnel-shaped, near white on an upright, leafy, glaucous green, 45 in. (112.5 cm) scape in mid-summer; fertility not known.

Comments & Special Needs: Underside of the leaf is pale glaucous blue making the upper surface appear bluer, the whole leaf becoming bluer with maturity. Very slow. Pest resistant.

Hosta 'Mr. Big'

Hosta nigrescens

Distinguishing Features: Uneven shirring along the veins is apparent in some leaves when mature. Among the largest hostas ever introduced, probably rivaling *H.* 'Sum and Substance' with individual leaves measuring 28 × 24 in. (70 × 60 cm).

Hosta nigrescens (Maekawa)

LARGE

Origin: Northern Honshu, Japan.

Clump Size & Habit: 62 in. wide × 30 in. high (155 × 75 cm). A semi-upright, vase-shaped mound.

Description: Leaf blade: 12 × 10 in. (30 × 25 cm); thick, emerging blue-green then turning dark green, intensely glaucous below, seersuckered; edge almost flat, deeply cupped, widely oval to nearly round with a mucronate tip, heart-shaped pinched lobes. Petiole: stout, ash-gray. Flower: small, funnel-shaped, purple-streaked pale lavender on an upright, glaucous gray, leafy, 44 in. (110 cm) scape in late summer; barely fertile.

Comments & Special Needs: Light to full shade all day. A moderate increaser. Pest resistant. Small hostas and other ground-covering plants can be grown at its feet.

Distinguishing Features: Shoots emerge darkly colored, almost black. Scapes tower above the foliage mound.

Similar: *H.* 'Kelly'; *H.* 'Naegato'.

Hosta 'Party Favour' (Solberg 2000)

MEDIUM

Origin: *H.* 'Donahue Piecrust' × *H.* 'Akebono'.

Clump Size & Habit: 28 in. wide × 14 in. high (70 × 35 cm). A flattish mound.

Description: Leaf blade: 6 × 3½ in. (15 × 8 cm); blue-green, conspicuously ribbed veins; edge serrated, evenly and closely rippled, undulate, flat to slightly arching, oval with a cuspidate tip, heart-shaped pinched lobes. Petiole: oblique, light green appearing to pierce the leaf blade. Flower: funnel-shaped, lavender on an upright, leafy, blackish, 26⅜ in. (66 cm) scape in mid-summer; fertile, green seedpods.

Comments & Special Needs: Of good substance and rapid growth.

Distinguishing Features: Has the piecrust ruffled edges of both parents and blackish scapes that gradually turn blue-green.

Hosta 'Reptilian' (Sawyer NR)

MEDIUM

Origin: Unknown.

Clump Size & Habit: 26 in. wide × 15 in. high (65 × 38 cm). An upright mound.

Description: Leaf blade: 7½ × 4 in. (19 × 10 cm); very thick, rubbery, light gray-blue with a green cast, seersuckered and puckered when mature; edge rippled to piecrusted, flat to slightly folded, oval with a cuspidate tip, heart-shaped open to pinched lobes. Petiole: flattish, red-dotted light green, appearing to pierce the blade. Flower: funnel-shaped, lavender on an upright or oblique, leafy, red-dotted, 18 in. (45 cm) scape in mid-season; fertility unknown.

Comments & Special Needs: Grow in good light to light shade. Of moderate increase. Pest resistant. Takes several seasons and good cultivation with plenty of moisture to achieve its full potential.

Distinguishing Features: The heavily textured surface of the leaves.

Hosta 'Party Favour'

Hosta 'Reptilian'

Hosta 'Rhapsody in Blue', a juvenile plant

Hosta 'Riptide'

Hosta 'Rhapsody in Blue' (Benedict & J. & J. Wilkins 1995)

MEDIUM

Origin: *H. rupifraga* hybrid.

Clump Size & Habit: 30 in. wide × 14 in. high (75 × 35 cm). An open mound.

Description: Leaf blade: 7½ × 7⅛ in. (19 × 18 cm); thick, leathery, intense dark blue-green, smooth, widely spaced veins; edge undulate, nearly round with an exaggeratedly mucronate tip, heart-shaped open lobes; Petiole: flattish light green. Flower: flared, white-striped, rich mauve surrounded by purple-tinted glossy green bracts on a thick, leafy, upright or oblique, purple-tinted, 22¾ in. (57 cm) scape in late summer to early autumn; fertile.

Comments & Special Needs: Light but full shade needed to retain the exquisite blue-green leaf color for as long as possible, although during hot summers the leaves will soon turn shiny dark green.

Similar: *H.* 'Maruba Iwa'; *H.* 'Moonlight Sonata', which is larger and has slightly fragrant, deep violet flowers; *H. rupifraga*.

Hosta 'Riptide' (Sellers 1987)

MEDIUM

Origin: Unknown.

Clump Size & Habit: 30 in. wide × 20 to 24 in. high (75 × 50 to 60 cm). An open mound.

Description: Leaf blade: 6⅜ × 5⅛ in. (16 × 13 cm); thick, blue-green, strongly veined, dimpled; edge rippled, arching, widely oval to almost round with a mucronate tip, heart-shaped folded lobes. Petiole: light glaucous green, intensely claret-dotted. Flower: bell-shaped pale lavender to near white on a thin, leaning, leafy, claret-dotted, pale green, 20 in. (50 cm) scape in late summer; fertile.

Hosta 'Ryan's Big One'

Comments & Special Needs: Light to full shade. Of moderate increase. Pest resistant.

Distinguishing Features: The underside of the leaves has a thick white coating.

Hosta 'Ryan's Big One' (Englerth 1982)

GIANT

Origin: Unknown.

Clump Size & Habit: 60 in. wide × 30¾ in. high (150 × 77 cm). A dense, overlapping mound.

Description: Leaf blade: 12¾ × 11 in. (32 × 28 cm); thick, intense blue-green, seersuckered and puckered; edge slightly undulate, convex, widely oval with a mucronate tip, heart-shaped overlapping lobes. Petiole: stout, light blue-green. Flower: funnel-shaped, near white on an upright, leafy, glaucous green, 50¼ in. (126 cm) scape from early to high summer; fertile.

Comments & Special Needs: Grow in light to medium shade with plenty of moisture to sustain the very large leaves. Slow to increase. Pest resistant. One of the best-known large, blue-leaved hostas by which all newer introductions are measured.

Similar: *H. sieboldiana* 'Elegans', whose leaves are slightly smaller.

Sports: *H.* 'Louise Ryan' is a chartreuse-margined sport that is late to color.

Hosta 'Salute' (R. & D. Benedict 1995)

MEDIUM

Origin: *H.* 'Dorset Blue' F_4 selfed.

Clump Size & Habit: 15 in. wide × 14 in. high (38 × 35 cm). A dense, semi-upright mound.

Description: Leaf blade: 8⅜ × 4 in. (21 × 10 cm); thick, smooth, intense blue-green, widely spaced veins; edge widely undulate to kinked, twisted, widely lanceolate with an acute to cuspidate tip, tapered open to pinched lobes. Petiole: blue-green. Flower: flared, near white on a drooping, leafy, glaucous green-blue, 24 in. (60 cm) scape from late summer to early autumn; fertile.

Comments & Special Needs: Light to full shade. A moderate increaser. Pest resistant.

Distinguishing Features: The contrasting, very pale, glaucous blue-gray leaf backs are often visible because of the upright poise of the leaves.

Similar: *H.* 'Blue Arrow'; *H.* 'Pineapple Poll'.

Hosta 'Sea Lotus Leaf' (M. Seaver 1885)

MEDIUM–LARGE

Origin: *H.* 'Wagon Wheels' hybrid.

Clump Size & Habit: 60 in. wide × 25⅛ in. high (150 × 63 cm). Stiff, oblique to upright mound, the leaves horizontal.

Description: Leaf blade: 9⅛ × 9⅛ in. (23 × 23 cm), very thick, blue-tinted green turning green, evenly seersuckered; edge flat, shallowly cupped, round with a mucronate tip, heart-shaped open to pinched lobes. Petiole: stout, shallow, light green. Flower: narrowly funnel-shaped, pale lavender on a leaning, leafy, light green, 24 in. (60 cm) scape in late summer; very fertile.

Comments & Special Needs: Grow in dappled to full shade. Slow to increase at first, vigorous when established. Pest resistant. A useful parent for cupped leaf seedlings.

Similar: *H.* 'Blue Umbrellas'; *H.* 'Roundabout'.

Hosta 'Salute'

Hosta 'Sea Lotus Leaf'

Hosta 'Serendipity' (Aden 1978)

MEDIUM

Origin: *H.* 'Blue Cadet' × *H.* 'Tokudama'.

Clump Size & Habit: 30 in. wide × 16¾ in. high (75 × 42 cm). A dense mound.

Description: Leaf blade: 5½ × 4 in. (14 × 10 cm); of average substance, smooth, intense light blue-green, slightly dimpled when mature; edge flat to slightly undulate, folded, widely oval to heart-shaped with a mucronate tip, heart-shaped open to pinched lobes. Petiole: long, narrow, light green. Flower: funnel-shaped, dark lavender, produced in abundance on a thin, upright, light green, 28 in. (70 cm) scape in high summer.

Comments & Special Needs: Leaf color can be almost turquoise if given the correct balance of good light and moderate shade. Flowers can be in bloom for up to four weeks, making an excellent display.

Hosta 'Serendipity'

Hosta 'Sherborne Songbird'

Hosta 'Silver Bowl'

Similar: *H. 'Blue Cadet'; H. nakaiana, which has greener leaves.

Hosta 'Sherborne Songbird' [TF$_2$ × 19] (Smith & BHHS 1988)

MEDIUM

Origin: H. 'Tardiflora' × H. sieboldiana 'Elegans'.

Clump Size & Habit: 32 in. wide × 18 in. high (80 × 45 cm). A dense mound.

Description: Leaf blade: 7½ × 4⅜ in. (19 × 11 cm); moderately thick, dark blue-green above and glaucous pale green below, dimpled, strongly veined when mature; edge undulate, widely oval with a cuspidate tip, heart-shaped open to pinched lobes. Petiole: shallow light green. Flower: funnel-shaped, pale lavender in a dense raceme on an upright, purple-tinged, gray-green, leafy, 18⅜ in. (46 cm) scape from mid- to late summer; fertile.

Comments & Special Needs: With high, filtered or dappled shade, it will retain the dark coloring until autumn. Of moderate increase. Pest resistant.

Distinguishing Features: Exceptionally dense, nearly one-sided flower truss. Similar to but having a wider leaf than the better-known H. 'Halcyon'.

Hosta 'Silver Bowl' (Fisher & AHS 1986)

LARGE

Origin: H. 'Tokudama' hybrid.

Clump Size & Habit: 60 in. wide × 20 in. high (150 × 50 cm). An open mound.

Description: Leaf blade: 12 × 10¼ in. (30 × 26 cm); thick, blue turning shiny dark green, seersuckered and puckered; edge almost flat, deeply cupped, widely oval to nearly round with a mucronate tip, pinched overlapping lobes. Petiole: stout, light green, appearing to pierce the blade. Flower: bell-shaped, lavender-striped white on an oblique, bare, glaucous green, 30 in. (75 cm) scape in midseason; fertile, many seedpods.

Comments & Special Needs: Grow in light to moderate shade. A superb hosta even when the blue coating has faded. Slow to increase. Pest resistant.

Similar: *H. 'Love Pat' and *H. 'Rock and Roll', which are slightly smaller and have bluer leaves.

Hosta 'Silvery Slugproof' (Grenfell 1996)

MEDIUM

Origin: H. 'Tardiflora' × H. sieboldiana 'Elegans'. An unnamed, unnumbered Tardiana Group seedling originally from Eric Smith.

Clump Size & Habit: 40¾ in. wide × 16 in. high (102 × 40 cm). A dense mound.

Description: Leaf blade: 7½ × 5⅛ in. (19 × 13 cm);

Hosta 'Silvery Slugproof'

Hosta 'Tet-A-Poo'

thick, smooth, silvery blue-green; edge undulate, flat to slightly folded, widely oval with an acute tip, heart-shaped pinched lobes. Petiole: gray-green, red-dotted. Flower: bell-shaped, pale lavender on an upright, leafy, gray-green, 22 in. (55 cm) scape in high summer; fertile.

Comments & Special Needs: Will tolerate some morning sun in cooler climates, otherwise light to moderate shade. Of moderate increase. Very pest resistant.

Distinguishing Features: Scapes are occasionally branched.

Hosta 'Tet-A-Poo' (Aden 1976)
DWARF

Origin: Unknown.

Clump Size & Habit: 12 in. wide × 3⅛ in. high (30 × 8 cm). A low-growing, dense mound.

Description: Leaf blade: 1½ × ⅜ in. (4 × 1 cm); of good substance, smooth blue-green; edge almost flat with occasional kinks, folded, oval with a cuspidate tip, tapered open to pinched lobes. Petiole: shallow, green-blue. Flower: funnel-shaped, near white on an upright, bare, light green, 3½ in. (9 cm) scape in mid-season; fertility unknown.

Comments & Special Needs: Grow in some morning sun in cooler climates. Ideal for sink and container growing. Establishes best in a pot until a root system is well established. Among the smallest hostas and now very rare.

Distinguishing Features: The blue-toned leaves are most unusual for a hosta of this size.

Similar: H. 'Tot Tot'.

Hosta 'Topaz' (Johnson NR)
MEDIUM

Origin: H. 'Neat Splash' × H. 'Dorset Blue'.

Hosta 'Topaz', a juvenile plant

Clump Size & Habit: 32¾ in. wide × 16 in. high (82 × 40 cm). A dense mound.

Description: Leaf blade: 6⅜ × 5⅛ in. (16 × 13 cm); rich, intense blue-green, dimpled; edge widely undulate, slightly folded, widely oval with a cuspidate tip, heart-shaped pinched lobes. Petiole: gray-green. Flower: funnel-shaped, lavender on an upright, leafy, glaucous blue-green, 16 to 18⅜ in. (40 to 46 cm) scape in high summer; fertile.

Comments & Special Needs: Light to moderate shade all day will preserve the waxy coating. Leaves are almost blue enough to be included in the bluest category. A rapid increaser.

Hosta 'Tutu' (Vaughn NR)
LARGE

Origin: H. 'Donahue Piecrust' × H. pycnophylla.

Clump Size & Habit: 46 in. wide × 16 in. high (115 × 40 cm). An open tiered mound.

Hosta 'Tutu'

Hosta 'Ulysses S. Grant'

Description: Leaf blade: 9⅛ × 7⅛ in. (23 × 18 cm); thick, dark blue-green, distinct widely spaced veins, dimpled and puckered; edge ruffled, flat, slightly folded to cupped, oval with a cuspidate tip, heart-shaped overlapping lobes. Petiole: narrow, purple-dotted light green, appearing to pierce the blade. Flower: funnel-shaped, lavender on an oblique, glaucous green, 43 in. (108 cm) scape in late summer; fertile.

Comments & Special Needs: Grow in light shade to retain the blue-toned leaf color. Use as a specimen or in a woodland setting with *Asplenium scolopendrium*, whose strap-shaped leaves have a contrasting shape but echo the ruffled edges of the hosta.

Distinguishing Features: Evenly piecrust margins of the leaves are intensely glaucous on the undersides. Scapes are weighed down by the dense racemes.

Similar: *H.* 'Blue Piecrust'.

Hosta 'Ulysses S. Grant' (Sugita & Zilis & Ruh 2001)

GIANT

Origin: From Japanese seed.

Clump Size & Habit: 65⅛ in. wide × 34¾ in. high (163 × 87 cm). An upright mound.

Description: Leaf blade: 13⅛ × 11½ in. (33 × 29 cm); thick, blue-green, moderately seersuckered; edge slightly rippled, somewhat twisted, folded, widely oval with a mucronate tip, heart-shaped folded lobes. Petiole: stout, blue-green. Flower: tubular, pale lavender on an upright, bare, glaucous blue-green, 50¼ in. (126 cm) scape in mid- to high season; fertility unknown.

Comments & Special Needs: Increases rapidly, an unusual trait for a hosta of *H. sieboldiana* ancestry, making it a valuable garden plant. Light to full shade. Pest resistant.

Distinguishing Features: The ripple-edge leaves and the dense raceme poised well above the raceme distinguish it from **H. sieboldiana* 'Elegans'.

Hosta 'Warwick Cup' (Jones 1993)

MEDIUM

Origin: *H.* 'Tokudama' seedling.

Clump Size & Habit: 48 in. wide × 21⅛ in. high (120 × 53 cm). An open mound.

Description: Leaf blade: 10 × 9⅛ in. (25 × 23 cm); thick, very dark blue green, deeply seersuckered, puckered when mature; edge almost flat, deeply cupped, near round with a mucronate tip, heart-shaped open to pinched lobes. Petiole: light green, appearing to pierce the blade. Flower: tubular, near white on an upright, bare, light green, 24 in. (60 cm) scape in mid-season, fertile.

Comments & Special Needs: Grow in light to moderate shade. Leaves are crumpled and unsymmetrical but a lovely shape and color. Slow to increase. Pest resistant.

Distinguishing Features: Leaves are greener than *H.* 'Buckshaw Blue'.

Similar: **H.* 'Buckshaw Blue'; **H.* 'Tokudama'.

Hosta 'Warwick Essence' (Jones 1993)

LARGE

Origin: *H.* 'Northern Halo' × *H. plantaginea*.

Clump Size & Habit: 54⅜ in. wide × 24 in. high (136 × 60 cm). An arching mound.

Description: Leaf blade: 12 × 10 in. (30 × 25 cm); thick, blue-green quickly becoming satiny, prominently veined, seersuckered; edge flat to shallowly undulate, slightly arching, oval with an acute tip, heart-shaped pinched lobes. Petiole: narrow, green-gray. Flower: funnel-shaped, white,

Hosta 'Warwick Cup'

Hosta 'Wheaton Blue'

strongly fragrant on a thin, upright, leafy, gray-green, 33⅛ in. (83 cm) scape in late summer; infertile.

Comments & Special Needs: Will tolerate morning sun in cooler climates as long as there is adequate moisture. Of moderate increase. Very fragrant, white flowers on a hosta of *H. sieboldiana* 'Elegans' parentage is most unusual.

Distinguishing Features: Exceptionally good flowers.

Hosta 'Wheaton Blue' (Zilis 1999)

MEDIUM–LARGE

Origin: Tissue-cultured sport of *H.* 'Paul's Glory'.

Clump Size & Habit: 36 in. wide × 18 to 24 in. high (90 × 45 to 60 cm). A dense mound.

Description: Leaf blade: 7½ × 5½ in. (19 × 14 cm); thick, blue-green, seersuckered and puckered when mature;

edge slightly undulate, convex, widely oval with a mucronate tip, heart-shaped pinched lobes. Petiole: oblique, light green, appearing to pierce the blade. Flower: see *H.* 'Paul's Glory'.

Comments & Special Needs: Although it performs well in high temperatures the best leaf color is achieved if grown in light to medium shade. A moderate increaser. Pest resistant.

Hosta 'Yankee Blue' (Baletewicz 1999)

LARGE

Origin: *H.* 'Blue Angel' × *H.* 'Elatior'.

Clump Size & Habit: 56 in. wide × 20 in. high (140 × 50 cm). A dome-shaped mound.

Description: Leaf blade: 10 × 6⅜ in. (25 × 16 cm); of good substance, rich blue-green, closely veined; edge flat with occasional kinks, slightly arching, widely lanceolate to oval with an acute tip, tapered open lobes. Petiole: light blue-green. Flower: long, tubular, near white on an upright, leafy, green, 20 to 24 in. (50 to 60 cm) scape in midto high summer; fertile, green seedpods.

Comments & Special Needs: Light to moderate shade all day. Vigorous, a rapid increaser for a blue-leaved hosta.

Hosta 'Yankee Blue'

GRAY-GREEN LEAVES

Unlike the blue-gray hostas, which have a thick glaucous bloom on their leaves, hostas in this category have a thin bloom. In some cases, the bloom disappears rapidly, even on plants growing in shade and their distinctive grayness gives way to green. There are, however, some outstandingly good gray-green-leafed hostas that look their best when grown in naturalistic plantings or on the waterside.

Hosta 'Abiqua Ground Cover' (Walden-West 1988)
MINIATURE

Origin: Unknown.

Clump Size & Habit: 12 in. wide × 9⅛ in. high (30 × 23 cm). A rhizomatous mound.

Description: Leaf blade: 2⅜ × 2 in. (6 × 5 cm); of average substance, smooth gray-green, widely spaced veins; edge slightly undulate, slightly folded, widely oval with a mucronate tip, heart-shaped pinched lobes. Petiole; light gray-green. Flower: bell-shaped lavender on an upright or oblique, leafy, glaucous gray-green, 15 in. (38 cm) scape in high summer; fertile.

Comments & Special Needs: Two hours of morning sun in cooler climates, otherwise good light or moderate shade all day. Vigorous, a rapid increaser. A superb hosta for ground cover purposes although not forming dense mounds.

Hosta 'Big John' (Owens 1986)
GIANT

Origin: *H. sieboldiana* 'Mira' hybrid.

Clump Size & Habit: 50¾ in. wide × 26 in. high (127 × 65 cm). A dense, overlapping mound.

Description: Leaf blade: 18 × 15 in. (45 × 38 cm); thick, dark bluish green soon becoming dark green, dimpled; edge flat to slightly ripped, arching, widely oval with a mucronate tip, heart-shaped overlapping lobes. Petiole: stout, glaucous light green. Flower: bell-shaped, white-striped pale lavender, level with or just above the leaf mound in dense clusters on an upright, bare, glaucous green, 32 in. (80 cm) scape in mid- to late season; fertile.

Comments & Special Needs: Rapidly exceeds its registered dimensions to become the largest hosta of all both in clump and individual leaf size.

Distinguishing Features: Most of the glaucous bloom on the upper leaf surface is toward the midrib. Underside of the leaf is gray-green, and the general effect of the leaves is gray-green.

Hosta 'Eric Smith' [TF$_2$ × 31] (Smith & Archibald 1987)
SMALL–MEDIUM

Origin: An Eric Smith seedling, probably not a *H.* 'Tardiana' hybrid, although given a number. Selected by Jim Archibald to honor Eric Smith.

Hosta 'Abiqua Ground Cover'

Hosta 'Big John'

Hosta 'Eric Smith'

Hosta 'Fortunei Hyacinthina'

Hosta 'Goblin'

Clump Size & Habit: 36 in. wide × 16 in. high (90 × 40 cm). A dense mound.

Description: Leaf blade: 5½ × 4⅜ in. (14 × 11 cm); of good substance, smooth, dark gray-green, slight dimpling; edge slightly undulate, heart-shaped with a mucronate tip, heart-shaped pinched lobes. Petiole: light green. Flower: bell-shaped, rich lavender in a dense raceme on an upright, leafy, light green, 30 in. (75 cm) scape in high season; fertile.

Comments & Special Needs: Grow in good light or moderate shade. Vigorous.

Distinguishing Features: Probably the greenest leaved of the numbered Tardiana Group hostas, now thought to have *H. nakaiana* and not *H. sieboldiana* 'Elegans' as a parent.

Hosta 'Fortunei Hyacinthina' (Hylander & AHS 1987)

MEDIUM–LARGE

Origin: Unknown but thought to have evolved in a European garden in the mid-nineteenth century.

Clump Size & Habit: 45½ in. wide × 20 in. high (114 × 50 cm). A dense mound.

Description: Leaf blade: 8⅜ × 6⅜ in. (21 × 16 cm); of good substance, dark gray-green turning green, thickly glaucous below, dimpled; edge slightly undulate with a distinct hyaline line, slightly cupped, widely oval with a cuspidate tip, heart-shaped pinched to overlapping lobes. Petiole: dark green. Flower: funnel-shaped, pinkish lavender, from rich violet buds, in a dense raceme on an upright, leafy, glaucous green, 28 in. (70 cm) scape, purple-tinted toward the raceme, in high summer; poor fertility.

Comments & Special Needs: Adaptable. Vigorous, a rapid increaser. Tolerates morning sun, which enhances the already excellent flowers but causes the slight blueness in the leaves to disappear. Is nowadays grown less for its garden value than its propensity to throw sports, the classic

being *H.* 'Gold Standard', the parent of a multitude of other sports.

Distinguishing Features: So named because of the resemblance of the flowers to those of a hyacinth. They are among the best in the genus.

Similar: *H.* 'Fortunei Rugosa', which has grayer, more deeply seersuckered leaves.

Sports: *H.* 'Arctic Rim' and *H.* 'Julia', whose dark gray-green leaves have creamy white margins; *H.* 'Gold Standard'; *H.* 'Heliarc'; *H.* 'Sheila West'; *H.* 'Thelma Pierson', whose leaves are bright yellow.

Hosta 'Goblin' (Lydell NR)

MEDIUM

Origin: *H.* 'Halcyon' hybrid.

Clump Size & Habit: 36 in. wide × 14 in. high (90 × 35 cm). A dense mound.

Description: Leaf blade: 7⅛ × 4⅜ in. (18 × 11 cm); thick, gray-green, dimpled; edge slightly rippled, folded, wedge-shaped to widely oval with a cuspidate tip, tapered

Hosta kikutii 'Leuconota'

Hosta 'Phantom', a juvenile plant

Hosta 'Pineapple Poll'

open lobes. Petiole: narrow, gray-green. Flowers: funnel-shaped, pale lavender on a thin, upright, leafy, green, 20 to 22 in. (50 to 55 cm) scape in early to mid-season; fertile.

Comments & Special Needs: Some morning sun in the North. Vigorous, a good performer.

Distinguishing Features: Scapes are leaning at the tips.

Hosta kikutii 'Leuconota' (Schmid 1991)
MEDIUM

Origin: Aichi and Shizuoka Prefectures, Japan. Formerly known as *H. kikutii* 'Pruinose'.

Clump Size & Habit: 34¾ in. wide × 15 in. high (87 × 38 cm). An arching mound.

Description: Leaf blade: 11 × 2⅜ in. (28 × 6 cm); of average substance, smooth, gray-green, deeply impressed veins; edge slightly undulate, arching, lanceolate with an acute tip, tapered open lobes. Petiole: glaucous light green. Flower: funnel-shaped, glaucous, near white in a dense raceme on a leaning, smooth, leafy, glaucous green, 16 in. (40 cm) scape in early autumn; fertile.

Comments & Special Needs: Grow in dappled to moderate shade. Vigorous, a good increaser.

Distinguishing Features: Leaves are coated in a thick white indumentum. Flower buds resemble a bird's head.

Hosta 'Phantom' (Solberg & Wilkins 1995)
MEDIUM

Origin: *H.* 'Riptide' hybrid.

Clump Size & Habit: 33⅛ in. wide × 18 in. high (83 × 45 cm). A moderately dense mound.

Description: Leaf blade: 10 × 7½ in. (25 × 19 cm); dark gray-green, glaucous light green below, ribbed veins, slight dimpling when mature; edge rippled to piecrusted, arching, oval with a cuspidate tip, round to heart-shaped open

to pinched lobes. Petiole: wide, red dotted and red backed. Flower: superb, near bell-shaped, lavender from a rich violet bud on an oblique to upright, leafy, glaucous mauve-purple, 32¾ in. (82 cm) scape in late summer; sterile.

Comments & Special Needs: Of good substance. Good light to dappled shade.

Distinguishing Features: Ghostly, gray-coated leaves, intensely red-dotted and red-backed petioles and thickly glaucous scapes all make it a distinct and extremely garden-worthy hosta. Best grown at eye level to appreciate its virtues.

Similar: **H. pycnophylla*, which has less obvious red-dotted petioles and scapes.

Hosta 'Pineapple Poll' (Smith & BHHS 1988)
MEDIUM

Origin: *H. sieboldiana* 'Elegans' × *H.* 'Lancifolia'.

Clump Size & Habit: 45½ in. wide × 18 in. high (114 × 45 cm). An open, rippling mound of upward and outward pointing leaves.

Description: Leaf blade: 9⅛ × 3½ in. (23 × 9 cm); thick,

smooth, green with a gray cast; edge conspicuously rippled, slightly twisted widely lanceolate with an acute tip, tapered open lobes. Petiole: flattish, light green. Flower: funnel-shaped, purple-striped near white on an upright, leafy, heavily glaucous green, 34¾ in. (87 cm) scape in late summer; fertile.

Comments & Special Needs: Grow in light to full shade. A rapid increaser

Distinguishing Features: Named for the apparent resemblance of the leaf mound to the tuft of leaves at the top of a pineapple.

Similar: *H. 'Blue Arrow'; H. 'Hadspen Heron'.

Hosta 'Prince of Wales' (Grenfell 2003)

GIANT

Origin: *H. sieboldiana* × *H. montana*.

Clump Size & Habit: 71⅛ in. wide × 36 in. high (178 × 90 cm). A stately, dense mound.

Description: Leaf blade: 20¾ × 14 in. (52 × 35 cm); thick, silvery gray-green with a slight blue cast in early season, seersuckered, strongly veined; edge slightly undulate,

slightly arching, elliptic to oval with a cuspidate tip, heart-shaped overlapping lobes. Petiole, oblique, stout grayish white. Flower: funnel-shaped, lavender gray in a heavy truss on an upright to leaning, swan-necked, leafy, glaucous gray-green, 35⅛ in. (88 cm) scape in mid-season; fertile, gray-brown seedpods.

Comments & Special Needs: Some morning sun in cooler climates otherwise light to moderate shade. A moderate increaser. Grow with purple-leaved *Heuchera* 'Purple Petticoats' at its feet for an outstanding contrast of foliage color.

Distinguishing Features: Long leaf blade and impressive flower scape weighed down by the long, heavy raceme.

Hosta 'Quilted Hearts' (Soules 1989)

LARGE

Origin: *H. sieboldiana* hybrid.

Clump Size & Habit: 46 in. wide × 20 in. high (115 × 50 cm). A dense mound.

Description: Leaf blade: 11½ × 9⅛ in. (29 × 23 cm); very thick, dark gray-green with a slight blue cast early in

Hosta 'Prince of Wales'

the season, matt above and thickly glaucous pale green below, intensely seersuckered; edge almost flat, slightly convex, nearly round with a mucronate tip, heart-shaped overlapping lobes. Petiole: stout, light green, appearing to pierce the blade. Flower: funnel-shaped, pink-tinted white on an upright, leafy, glaucous light green, 20 in. (50 cm) scape in late summer; fertile.

Comments & Special Needs: Light to moderate shade all day. Slow to establish but eventually makes an impressive clump. Pest resistant.

Distinguishing Features: Intensely seersuckered leaves are shirred along the veins giving a pebbled effect.

Similar: *H. 'Quilted Skies' is similar, but the leaves are longer, narrower and blue-gray with bell-shaped flowers.

Hosta 'Red October' (Herold NR)

SMALL–MEDIUM

Origin: Unknown.

Clump Size & Habit: 28 in. wide × 10 in. high (70 × 25 cm). An upright, open mound.

Description: Leaf blade: 8⅜ × 3½ in. (21 × 9 cm); thick, dark gray green, smooth, closely ribbed veins; edge rippled to kinked, arching, widely lanceolate with an acute tip, tapered open lobes. Petiole: gray-green streaked and speckled with red, the speckling extending 1 in. (2.5 cm) into the leaf blade. Flower: funnel-shaped, lavender in a dense raceme on an upright or slightly oblique, leafy, reddish, 24 in. (60 cm) scape in late autumn; fertility unknown.

Hosta 'Red October'

Hosta 'Quilted Hearts'

Comments & Special Needs: Among the best of the newer introductions with red petioles and scapes.

Distinguishing Features: Underside of the leaf is covered in a thick white coating.

Hosta sieboldiana (Hooker) (Engler 1888)

LARGE

Origin: Central and Northern Honshu, Japan.

Clump Size & Habit: 60 in. wide × 24 in. high (150 × 60 cm). A dense mound.

Description: Leaf blade: 17⅜ × 11 in. (43 × 28 cm); thick, green with a slight gray-blue cast early in the season, slightly dimpled, strongly veined; edge slightly undulate, widely oval with a cuspidate tip, heart-shaped pinched lobes. Petiole: stout, light green. Flower: funnel-shaped, lavender-striped near white on an upright, glaucous green, 24 to 25⅛ in. (60 to 63 cm) scape in mid-season; fertile, many seedpods.

Comments & Special Needs: Some morning sun in cooler climates. Of slow to moderate increase. Pest resistant.

Distinguishing Features: Is quite different from the *H. sieboldiana* grown in most gardens today, which are mostly forms of *H. sieboldiana* 'Elegans'. Many of its characteristics resemble *H. montana*, to which it is closely related.

Similar: *H. sieboldiana* 'Mira', which has larger, flatter leaves.

Hosta 'Snowden' (Smith & BHHS 1988)

LARGE–GIANT

Origin: *H. sieboldiana* × *H.* 'Fortunei Albopicta Aurea'.

Clump Size & Habit: 52¾ in. wide × 32 in. high (132 × 80 cm). An upright mound.

Description: Leaf blade: 14 × 10 in. (35 × 25 cm); thick, gray-green with a faint blue cast early in the season, dimpled, closely ribbed veins when mature; edge slightly undulate, flat to convex, oval with a cuspidate tip, heart-shaped pinched lobes. Petiole: gray-green. Flower: widely funnel-shaped, white on an upright, bare, 48 in. (120 cm) scape in mid- to high season; occasionally sets seed.

Comments & Special Needs: Grow in good light or moderate shade. Slow to establish but eventually forms a magnificent specimen which can be grown in a container if profusely watered.

Similar: **H.* 'Krossa Regal'; **H. sieboldiana* 'Mira'.

Hosta sieboldiana 'Mira'

Hosta 'Snowden'

CHAPTER NINE

HOSTAS *with* MARGINALLY VARIEGATED LEAVES

APART FROM SELECTED SEEDLINGS, most varigated, margined hostas are natural or tissue-cultured sports of hostas already in existence. The hostas described in this category have, or are likely to become, classic or popular hostas in their own right, a prime example being *Hosta* 'Frances Williams'. Less popular or little-known sports are referred back to the hosta from which they sported or mutated. The hostas I list include all those whose central leaf coloring is darker than the margin.

Hosta 'Abba Dabba Do' (Avent 1998)

LARGE

Origin: Sport of *H*. 'Sun Power'.

Clump Size & Habit: 71⅛ in. wide × 24 in. high (178 × 60 cm). An upright, rippling mound.

Description: Leaf blade: 12 × 6⅜ in. (30 × 16 cm); thick, leathery, olive-green, narrowly and irregularly margined yellow, matt above and thinly glaucous below, strongly veined, slightly dimpled; edge widely rippled, elliptic with a cuspidate tip, rounded open lobes. Petiole: light olive-green. Flower: see *H*. 'Sun Power'.

Comments & Special Needs: Performs well in sun even in hotter climates. Pest resistant. A moderate to good increaser.

Distinguishing Features: Leaves emerge green but quickly develop the attractive, bright yellow margin.

Sports: *H*. 'Abba Dew', which has much wider yellow margins; *H*. 'Zippity Do Dah'.

Hosta 'Abby' (Ruh 1990)

SMALL

Origin: One of the most popular sports of *H*. 'Gold Drop'.

Clump Height & Habit: 16¾ in. wide × 6½ in. high (42 × 16.5 cm). A ground-hugging, open mound.

Description: Leaf blade: 4 × 2⅜ in. (10 × 6 cm); of good substance, smooth, dark green with an irregular chartreuse to yellow margin, strongly veined; edge shallowly undulate, folded at the lobes, widely oval with a cuspidate tip, heart-shaped open to pinched lobes. Petiole: short, narrow almost imperceptibly outlined in cream. Flower: see *H*. 'Gold Drop'.

Comments & Special Needs: Light to full shade. Increases rapidly. A superb small hosta.

Sports: *H*. 'Amy Elizabeth', which is yellow with a green margin.

Hosta 'Abiqua Moonbeam' (Walden-West 1987)

MEDIUM–LARGE

Origin: Sport of *H*. 'August Moon'.

Clump Size & Habit: 32 in. wide × 26 in. high (80 × 65 cm). A dense mound.

Description: Leaf blade: 7½ × 6½ in. (19 × 16.5 cm); thick, glaucous green, widely and irregularly margined chartreuse turning yellow, dimpled; edge almost flat, widely oval with a cuspidate tip, heart-shaped overlapping lobes. Petiole: glaucous light green. Flower: see *H*. 'August Moon'.

Hosta 'Abba Dabba Do'

Hosta 'Abby'

---

*Indicates plants fully described elsewhere in this book.

Previous page: *Hosta* 'Antioch'

Comments & Special Needs: Grow in morning sun in cooler climates to promote the lutescent habit of the leaves, but the color will look richer if grown in shade. A moderate to fast increaser.

Distinguishing Features: Emerges yellow, the center gradually turning green.

Similar: *H.* 'August Beauty'; *H.* 'Carolina Moon' is more intensely seersuckered and puckered; *H.* 'Mayan Moon', which appears identical.

Sports: *H.* 'Gemini Moon' has wider margins.

Hosta 'Afternoon Delight' (Q & Z Nursery NR)
LARGE

Origin: Tissue-cultured sport of *H.* 'High Noon'.

Clump Size & Habit: 46¾ in. wide × 24 in. high (117 × 60 cm). An upright, spreading mound.

Description: Leaf blade: 12 × 8 in. (30 × 20 cm); thick, dark green, widely margined rich gold, matt above and

glaucous below, seersuckered; edge randomly undulate, mostly convex, broadly oval with a cuspidate tip, heart-shaped lobes open to pinched. Petiole: chartreuse, appearing to pierce the blade. Flower: funnel-shaped, pale lavender on an upright, bare, glaucous yellow, 32 in. (80 cm) scape in high season; fertile, long seedpods

Comments & Special Needs: Some morning sun will turn the leaf margins brighter gold. Slow to moderate increase. Reasonably pest resistant.

Similar: *H.* 'Tyler's Treasure'.

Hosta 'Alex Summers' (Santa Lucia 1989)
LARGE

Origin: Sport of *H.* 'Gold Regal'.

Clump Size & Height: 60 in. wide × 32 in. high (150 × 80 cm). A striking, vase-shaped mound.

Description: Leaf blade: 9¼ × 7½ in. (23.5 × 19 cm); thick, mid-green, very widely margined chartreuse turning

Hosta 'Abiqua Moonbeam'

Hosta 'Alex Summers'

Hosta 'Afternoon Delight' in foreground

Hosta 'Independence Day'

creamy yellow jetting toward the midrib, dimpled, closely veined when mature; edge slightly undulate, slightly dished, oval with a cuspidate tip, heart-shaped open to pinched lobes. Petiole: stout, oblique, glaucous green. Flower: see *H*. 'Gold Regal'.

Comments & Special Needs: Morning sun in the North will intensify the leaf color that will remain muted if planted in deep shade. Of moderate increase.

Similar: *H*. 'David Reath'; *H*. 'Independence Day', which has a narrower margin and is more muted in color.

Hosta 'Alligator Shoes' (Benedict & Hatfield NR)

MEDIUM

Origin: *H*. 'Dorothy Benedict' × *H. montana*.

Clump Size & Habit: 24 in. wide × 18 in. high (60 × 45 cm). A well-poised mound.

Description: Leaf blade: 7½ × 5⅛ in. (19 × 13 cm); thick, blue-green to olive-green irregularly and narrowly margined cream to white with random gray-green streaks jetting toward the midrib, matt above and glaucous below, closely seersuckered; edge unevenly rippled, arching, con-

vex, widely oval with a twisted cuspidate tip, heart-shaped open lobes. Petiole, shallow, gray-green. Flower: open, funnel-shaped, palest lavender on a leaning, leafy, green, 36 in. (90 cm) scape from mid- to late summer; fertile.

Comments & Special Needs: Grows better if exposed to morning sun and increases moderately well. Pest resistant.

Hosta 'Alligator Shoes'

Hosta 'Alvatine Taylor'

Distinguishing Features: The distinct, rough, pebbled texture of the leaf's surface gives this recent introduction a great personality.

Hosta 'Alvatine Taylor' (Fairway Enterprises 1990)

LARGE

Origin: Sport of *H.* 'Lady In Waiting'.

Clump Size & Habit: 48 in. wide × 30 in. high (120 × 75 cm). A colorful, dense mound.

Description: Leaf blade: 9 to 10 × 7⅛ to 8⅜ in. (22 to 25 × 18 × 21 cm); thick, glaucous blue-gray widely and irregularly margined muted golden yellow, prominently veined, seersuckered and puckered when mature; edge slightly undulate, widely oval with a cuspidate to mucronate tip, heart-shaped rounded to flat lobes. Petiole: stout, light green. Flower: funnel-shaped, white on an upright, leafy, glaucous green, 32 in. (80 cm) scape in high season; fertile.

Comments & Special Needs: Tolerates morning sun in the North. Slow to moderate increase. Pest resistant. Leaf surface develops an attractive sheen by the end of the summer. Winner of the 1998 Alex J. Summers Distinguished Merit Hosta Award.

Distinguishing Features: Differs from similar hostas in having a muted, golden yellow margin, longer leaves and an ability to withstand sun damage.

Similar: *H.* 'Abiqua Moonbeam'.

Sports: *H.* 'Doubloons'.

Hosta 'American Dream' (Wade 1999)

MEDIUM–LARGE

Origin: Sport of *H.* 'High Fat Cream'.

Clump Size & Habit: 40¾ in. wide × 24 in. high (102 × 60 cm). A dense, upright mound.

Description: Leaf blade: 10 × 7½ in. (25 × 19 cm); of good substance, chartreuse turning golden creamy yellow, widely and irregularly margined white, matt above and thinly glaucous below, seersuckered; edge slightly rippled, cupped or convex, widely oval with a mucronate tip, heart-shaped folded lobes. Petiole: chartreuse, outlined in cream. Flower: see *H.* 'High Fat Cream'.

Comments & Special Needs: Grows best in morning sun in the North and so placed the white margin does not burn. Slow to increase but a strong grower. A superb new hosta.

Distinguishing Features: The variegated margin can be up to 2¾ in. (7 cm) wide, which is wider than that of hostas with similar coloring.

Similar: *H.* 'Moon Glow', a seedling of *H.* 'August Moon',

among the first hostas with yellow and white variegation, although it has now been superseded; *H.* 'Sea Dream'; *H.* 'Sunshine Glory'; *H.* 'Zodiac'.

Hosta 'American Eagle' (Van Wade 1999)

LARGE

Origin: Natural sport of *H.* 'Zounds'.

Clump Size & Habit: 30 in. wide × 20 in. high (75 × 50 cm). An upright mound.

Description: Leaf blade: 9⅛ × 8½ in. (23 × 21.5 cm); thick, very dark green, widely and irregularly margined, golden yellow jetting toward the midrib, matt above and glaucous below, seersuckered; edge almost flat, shallowly dished, nearly round with a mucronate tip, heart-shaped pinched lobes. Petiole: dark green, finely outlined in creamy yellow. Flower: see *H.* 'Zounds'. An outstanding newer introduction.

Comments & Special Needs: Some morning sun in the North. Slow growing. Pest resistant.

Hosta 'American Dream'

Hosta 'American Eagle'

Distinguishing Features: The 2 in. (5 cm) margin is a striking contrast to the exceptionally dark green leaves.

Similar: *H.* 'Laura and Darrell'.

Hosta 'American Halo' (Van Wade 1999)

GIANT

Origin: Sport of *H.* 'Northern Halo', originally known as *H.* 'Northern Halo' ('Wade's Form').

Clump Size & Habit: 71⅛ in. wide × 22 in. high (178 × 55 cm). A dense mound.

Description: Leaf blade: 14 × 10 in. (35 × 25 cm); thick, glaucous, dark blue-green irregularly margined, yellow turning ivory-white, seersuckered, strongly veined; edge randomly undulate, widely oval with a mucronate tip, heart-shaped overlapping lobes. Petiole: stout, light green. Flower: broadly funnel-shaped, pure white on a bare, glaucous green, 22 to 24 in. (55 × 60 cm) scape in early to midsummer; fertile.

Comments & Special Needs: Tolerates morning sun in the North. Slow to establish but eventually becomes a huge mound. Pest resistant. Winner of the 2002 Alex J. Summers Distinguished Merit Hosta Award.

Similar: *H.* 'Barbara Ann'; *H.* 'Northern Halo', which is smaller with narrower margins.

Hosta 'Angel Feathers' (K. Vaughn NR)

MEDIUM

Origin: (*H.* 'William Lachman' × sibling) × self.

Clump Size & Habit: 34¾ in. wide × 16¾ in. high (87 × 42 cm). Dense, somewhat upright mound.

Description: Leaf blade: 7⅛ × 4⅜ in. (18 × 11 cm); thick, medium green, widely and irregularly margined, golden yellow to creamy white with feathering toward the midrib, satiny above and glaucous below, dimpled; edge widely rippled, triangular with a cuspidate tip, round to tapered pinched lobes. Petiole: green, outlined in creamy yellow. Flower: pale purple on an upright, leafy, 24 in. (60 cm) scape in mid-season; fertility unknown.

Comments & Special Needs: Grow in shade all day. A rapid increaser which makes a colorful, hosta with attractively shaped leaves.

Distinguishing Features: The leaf edge becomes flatter with maturity.

Hosta 'American Halo', escess sunlight having removed the glaucous bloom

Hosta '**Antioch**' (Tompkins & Hofer & Ruh 1979)

MEDIUM–LARGE

Origin: *H*. 'Fortunei' hybrid.

Clump Size & Habit: 49 in. wide × 22 in. high (122 × 55 cm). A dense mound.

Description: Leaf blade: 10 × 5½ in. (25 × 14 cm); of good substance, mid- to dark green, irregularly margined chartreuse, turning creamy yellow and finally white, with celadon streaking jetting toward the midrib, satiny above and thinly glaucous below, strongly veined; arching to the ground, convex, oval with a cuspidate tip, heart-shaped pinched lobes. Petiole: dark green, outlined in creamy white. Flower: narrowly funnel-shaped, lavender in a dense raceme on an upright, leafy, green, 28¾ in. (72 cm) scape in high season; low fertility.

Comments & Special Needs: Grow in light to moderate shade where it will be vigorous and increase rapidly. Well-nourished soil and plenty of moisture will increase the

amount of variegation. Emerges late. Winner of the 1984 Alex J. Summers Distinguished Merit Hosta Award.

Distinguishing Features: Differs from *H*. 'Fortunei Albomarginata' in its longer, more pointed leaves and wider variegation.

Similar: *H*. 'Kiwi Treasure Trove'; *H*. 'Moerheim'; *H. 'Rhapsody'; *H*. 'Shogun'; *H*. 'Silver Crown'; *H*. 'Spinners'.

Hosta '**Antoinette**' (Kuk 2000)

MEDIUM

Origin: Sport of *H*. 'Squire Rich'.

Clump Size & Habit: 24 in. wide × 20 in. high (60 × 50 cm). An upright mound.

Description: Leaf blade: 8½ × 7⅛ in. (21.5 × 18 cm); dark green, irregularly margined, green-gold with some jetting toward the midrib, satiny above and very glossy below, strongly veined; edge rippled, slightly convex, oval with a cuspidate tip, heart-shaped open lobes. Petiole: narrow, green, outlined in cream. Flower: see *H*. 'Squire Rich'.

Comments & Special Needs: Site in light shade all day. Leaves emerge lightish green, gradually darkening. Moderate growth rate.

Similar: *H. 'Queen Josephine', which has less rippled edges.

Hosta '**Aristocrat**' (Walters Gardens 1997)

MEDIUM

Origin: Tissue-cultured sport of *H*. 'Hadspen Blue'.

Clump Size & Habit: 16 in. wide × 12 in. high (40 × 30 cm). An open mound.

Description: Leaf blade: 7¾ × 5½ in. (19.5 × 14 cm); thick, glaucous, rich blue, widely and very irregularly margined, creamy white jetting toward the midrib, dimpled,

Hosta 'Angel Feathers'

Hosta 'Antioch'

Hosta 'Antoinette'

Hosta 'Aristocrat'

Hosta 'Austin Dickinson'

strongly veined; edge slightly rippled, slightly cupped, widely oval with a mucronate tip, heart-shaped overlapping lobes. Petiole: blue-green, outlined in cream. Flower: see *H.* 'Hadspen Blue'.

Comments & Special Needs: Site in morning sun in cooler climates to boost the vigor. Slow to increase but well worth the wait. Water sparingly until the root system is established. An ideal pot or container plant as well as a superb specimen plant for a smaller garden.

Distinguishing Features: Eventually has a wider margin than other hostas of this type and coloring.

Hosta '**Austin Dickinson**' (W. & E. Lachman 1992)
MEDIUM
Origin: *H.* 'Resonance' × *H. plantaginea*.

Clump Size & Habit: 49 in. wide × 18¾ in. high (122 × 47 cm). An upright mound.

Description: Leaf blade: 8⅜ × 6⅜ in. (21 × 16 cm); of average substance, medium green, widely and irregularly margined, chartreuse turning pure white with streaks jetting toward the midrib, matt above and shiny below, dimpled when mature, widely spaced veins; edge slightly rippled, folded, oval with a mucronate tip, heart-shaped open to pinched lobes. Petiole: dark green, outlined in cream. Flower: fragrant, flaring deep purple-striped lavender on an upright or oblique, leafy, mahogany-tinted, green, 28¾ in. (72 cm) scape in late summer, fertile.

Comments & Special Needs: Site in some morning sun in cooler climates. An abundant supply of moisture enables the already attractive leaf margin to widen further. A moderate to fast increaser.

Similar: *H.* 'Emily Dickinson', from which it differs in having flatter and wider leaf margins.

Hosta 'Beatrice'

Hosta '**Beatrice**' (F. Williams NR)
SMALL
Origin: *H. sieboldii* seedling.

Clump Size & Habit: 20 to 24 in. wide × 12 to 15 in. high (30 to 60 × 30 to 38 cm). An open mound.

Description: Leaf blade: 5⅛ × 1½ in. (13 × 3.5 cm); thin, smooth, olive-green, irregularly margined, pure white with streaks jetting toward the midrib, matt above and satiny below, closely ribbed veins; edge slightly rippled, arching, elliptic with an acute tip, tapered open lobes. Flower: funnel-shaped lavender on an upright, leafy, olive-green, 22⅜ in. (56 cm) scape in mid-season; fertile.

Comments & Special Needs: Site in some morning sun then light to moderate shade. It is prone to throw streaked sports. *Hosta* 'Beatrice Streaked' was the first streaked hosta to be introduced and is now among the best-known breeding plants. Sets seed readily.

Distinguishing Features: Variegation is extremely unsta-

Hosta 'Bobbie Sue', in deep shade

Hosta 'Bold Edger'

Hosta 'Bob Olson'

ble, producing leaves which can be streaked and mottled ivory-green.

Similar: *H. 'Bold Edger'.

Hosta 'Bobbie Sue' (Owens 1994)

MEDIUM–LARGE

Origin: Sport of H. 'Marbled White'.

Clump Size & Habit: 46 in. wide × 16 in. high (115 × 40 cm). A spreading mound.

Description: Leaf blade: 9¼ × 4 in. (23.5 × 10 cm); thick, dark olive-green, irregularly margined, creamy white with chartreuse transitional splashing, satiny above and glossy below, slightly dimpled when mature; edge randomly rippled, slightly undulate, oval with a cuspidate tip, rounded to tapered open lobes. Petiole: flat, olive-green, finely outlined in cream. Flower: tubular, 2¾ in. (7 cm) long, purple-striped rich lavender on an upright, leafy, green, 32 in. (80 cm) scape from mid-summer; fertile.

Comments & Special Needs: Site in shade in the hottest regions, elsewhere some morning sun is beneficial. Of moderate to fast increase. A superb new introduction.

Distinguishing Features: Leaves become flatter and wider with maturity.

Hosta 'Bob Olson' (H. & D. Benedict 1995)

SMALL

Origin: H. 'Yellow Splash' selfed.

Clump Size & Habit: 12 in. wide × 5⅛ in. high (30 × 13 cm). An upright mound.

Description: Leaf blade: 3⅛ × 2 in. (8 × 5 cm); of good substance, satiny, dark olive-green irregularly margined creamy white, moderately prominent veining; edge slightly rippled, slightly undulate, somewhat folded, lanceolate to elliptic with an acute tip, rounded open to pinched lobes. Petiole: dark green, outlined in creamy white. Flower: bell-shaped on an upright, leafy, purple-flecked green, 16 in. (40 cm) scape in late summer; fertility unknown.

Comments & Special Needs: Performs well in a sunny position for half a day except in the hottest regions. Fast growing.

Distinguishing Features: The conspicuously upright habit.

Hosta 'Bold Edger' (K. Vaughn 1983)

MEDIUM

Origin: H. 'Beatrice' × H. 'Frances Williams'.

Clump Size & Habit: 20 in. wide × 20 in. high (50 × 50 cm). A fairly dense, irregular mound.

Description: Leaf blade: 6⅜ × 4 in. (16 × 10 cm); of good substance, mid- to dark olive-green widely and irregularly margined, yellow turning white, matt above and glaucous below, prominently veined; edge shallowly rippled, widely undulate, arching to convex, widely oval with a cuspidate tip, heart-shaped open lobes. Petiole: dark green, outlined in cream. Flower: widely funnel-shaped, purple striped lavender on an upright, leafy, green, 30 in. (75 cm) scape in late summer; fertile.

Comments & Special Needs: Site in moderate shade. Increases rapidly.

Distinguishing Features: Clump habit does not live up to the very attractive individual leaves.

Similar: *H. 'Emily Dickinson'; *H. 'Queen Josephine'; *H. 'Tambourine'.

Hosta 'Bold Ribbons' (Aden 1976)

SMALL–MEDIUM

Origin: Unknown.

Clump Size & Habit: 33⅛ in. wide × 15 in. high (83 × 38 cm). A dense mound.

Description: Leaf blade: 6⅜ × 3½ in. (16 × 9 cm); thin, smooth dark green, irregularly margined, creamy white and splashed with some celadon streaking, satiny above and

glossy below; edge slightly undulate, arching, lanceolate with an acute tip, rounded pinched lobes. Petiole: dark green, outlined in cream. Flower: funnel-shaped, lavender on an upright, leafy, green, 28 in. (70 cm) scape in midsummer; fertility unknown.

Comments & Special Needs: Site in light to moderate shade. Vigorous, a rapid increaser, ideal for edging. Not suitable as a pot plant.

Distinguishing Features: Petioles ascend obliquely, the leaves arch downwards.

Similar: H. 'Neat Splash Rim'.

Hosta 'Border Bandit' (W. & E. Lachman 1992)

SMALL

Origin: H. 'Halcyon' hybrid.

Clump Size & Habit: 15 in. wide × 9⅛ in. high (38 × 23 cm). A compact mound.

Description: Leaf blade: 5½ × 3½ in. (14 × 9 cm); thick, blue-green, widely and irregularly margined, creamy white with much celadon streaking, glossy above and matt below; edge slightly rippled, kinked toward the base, con-

Hosta 'Bold Ribbons'

Hosta 'Border Bandit'

Hosta 'Brass Ring'

Hosta 'Brave Amherst'

vex, spear-shaped with a cuspidate tip, rounded open lobes. Petiole: dark green, finely outlined in cream. Flower: funnel-shaped, lavender on an upright, leafy, dark green, 18 in. (45 cm) scape in late summer; fertile.

Comments & Special Needs: Slow to increase at first but becomes a superb plant.

Distinguishing Features: The slight twist to the leaves gives this very attractive hosta a dramatic presence in the shaded border; also an ideal pot plant.

Hosta 'Brass Ring' (Lydell 2000)

MEDIUM–LARGE

Origin: *H.* 'Neat Splash' hybrid.

Clump Size & Habit: 40¾ in. wide × 20 in. high (102 × 50 cm). A horizontal mound.

Description: Leaf blade: 10 × 7⅛ in. (25 × 18 cm); thick, dark gray-green, widely and irregularly margined, golden yellow becoming ivory-white, very seersuckered and puckered, satiny above and glaucous below; edge slightly undulate, convex, widely oval with a cuspidate tip, heart-shaped folded lobes. Petiole: flattish green, outlined in cream. Flower: tubular, pale lavender on an upright, leafy, green, 22 to 26 in. (55 to 65 cm) scape in late summer; sterile.

Comments & Special Needs: Site in light to moderate shade and provide plenty of food and moisture. Average to good increase.

Distinguishing Features: A very showy margin, which is brassy yellow in spring, and leaves of heavy substance.

Hosta 'Brave Amherst' (W. & E. Lachman 1993)

MEDIUM

Origin: *H.* 'Christmas Tree' × *H.* 'Reversed'.

Clump Size & Habit: 25⅛ in. wide × 18 in. high (63 × 45 cm). A dense mound.

Description: Leaf blade: 9⅛ × 6½ in. (23 × 16.5 cm); very thick, light blue-green, narrowly and irregularly margined and streaked yellow turning cream, matt above and glaucous below, seersuckered, moderately prominent veins; edge slightly rippled, slightly cupped or convex, widely oval with a mucronate tip, heart-shaped overlapping lobes. Petiole: stout, glaucous green, outlined in cream. Flower: tubular, near white on an upright, leafy, glaucous green, 24 in. (60 cm) scape in early summer; fertile.

Comments & Special Needs: A better performer than *H.* 'Frances Williams' but very slow to establish. Light to full shade. A great improvement on similar hostas since the margins do not scorch. Pest resistant.

Distinguishing Features: Has longer, somewhat smaller leaves than the similar *H.* 'Aurora Borealis' or **H. sieboldiana* 'Frances Williams'.

Hosta 'Brim Cup'

Hosta 'Candy Cane', in deep shade

Hosta 'Brim Cup' (Aden 1986)

SMALL–MEDIUM

Origin: *H.* 'Wide Brim' hybrid.

Clump Size & Habit: 15 in. wide × 12 in. high (38 × 30 cm). An open mound.

Description: Leaf blade: 6⅜ × 5⅛ in. (16 × 13 cm); thick, dark green with a blue cast, widely and irregularly margined and splashed chartreuse turning yellow and finally creamy white jetting toward the midrib, matt above and glaucous below, seersuckered; edge slightly rippled, cupped, widely oval to nearly round with a mucronate tip, heart-shaped open to pinched lobes. Petiole: shallow, dark green outlined in cream. Flower: funnel-shaped, opening light blue turning white on an upright, bare, green, 18 in. (45 cm) scape in mid-summer; fertile.

Distinguishing Features: Particularly wide and well-defined variegation for a hosta of this size.

Comments & Special Needs: Site in two hours morning sun in Northern gardens. Slow to increase. Superb as a young plant but the edges can split or tear in maturity; nonetheless it remains popular, especially as a pot plant, because of the strikingly variegated leaves.

Hosta 'Candy Cane' (Fisher & Ruh 1995)

SMALL

Origin: Unknown but undoubtedly has *H. sieboldii* in its ancestry.

Clump Size & Habit: 14 in. wide × 7⅛ in. high (35 × 18 cm). A diffuse, cascading mound.

Description: Leaf blade: 6⅜ × 2⅜ in. (16 × 6 cm); of average to good substance, satiny, dark green irregularly and variably margined, golden yellow fading to cream, some dimpling on mature outer leaves; edges rippled, arching, lanceolate to oval with an acute tip, tapered open lobes.

Hosta 'Carnival', in deep shade

Petiole: flattish dark green, outlined in cream. Flower: tubular, dark purple-striped lavender on an upright, leafy, dark green, 12¾ to 16 in. (32 to 40 cm) scape in late summer; fertility unknown.

Comments & Special Needs: Site in light to moderate shade since the margin will turn white if exposed to direct sunlight. Vigorous, fast growing. Suitable for edging in light woodland. Not suitable as a pot plant.

Similar: *H.* 'Resonance'.

Hosta 'Carnival' (W. & E. Lachman 1986)

MEDIUM–LARGE

Origin: *H.* 'Beatrice' pod parent × *H.* 'Frances Williams'.

Clump Size & Habit: 40¾ in. wide × 16 to 18 in. high (102 × 40 to 45 cm). An open mound.

Description: Leaf blade: 9⅛ × 7½ in. (23 × 19 cm); thick, mid- to dark green-blue to green-gray, widely and irregularly margined, yellow to cream with celadon streaking and mottling jetting toward the midrib, matt above and

Hosta 'Carolina Sunshine'

Hosta 'Carrie Ann'

glaucous below, mature leaves intensely seersuckered; edge slightly rippled, convex, oval to heart-shaped with a mucronate tip, heart-shaped open lobes. Petiole: wide, green strongly outlined cream. Flower: long-lasting, funnel-shaped lavender on a stout, upright, leafy, glaucous gray-green, 30 in. (75 cm) scape in mid-summer; fertile.

Distinguishing Features: Wide margins are distinctly feathered with two-tone mottling. Flower scapes are poised well above the leaf mound and have very attractive large variegated bracts surrounding the purple flower buds.

Comments & Special Needs: Light to full shade. Leaves lose their intense color if exposed to too much sun. Slow to establish but eventually becomes a strikingly colorful mound.

Similar: *H.* 'Carousel', which is smaller with leaves that are not as shapely; *H.* 'Cavalcade', whose leaves do not have the mottling and streaking.

Hosta 'Carolina Sunshine' (Avent 1999)

MEDIUM

Origin: *H. tibae* hybrid.

Clump Size & Habit: 40¾ in. wide × 14 in. high (102 × 35 cm). A diffuse mound.

Description: Leaf blade: 9⅛ × 5⅛ in. (23 × 13 cm); thin to average substance, glossy, mid- to dark green widely and very irregularly margined and splashed butterscotch-yellow turning cream, widely spaced veins; edge conspicuously rippled, arching, elliptic with an acute tip, tapered pinched lobes. Petiole: narrow, dark green finely outlined in cream. Flower: tubular, lavender on an upright, leafy, green, 20 in. (50 cm) scape in late summer; fertile.

Comments & Special Needs: Very sun tolerant even in the South. A rapid increaser and easy to grow.

Hosta 'Carrie Ann' (Stone & Ruh 1988)

SMALL

Origin: Unknown but has the characteristics of *H. sieboldii* ancestry.

Clump Size & Habit: 24 in. wide × 9⅛ in. high (60 × 23 cm). An open mound.

Description: Leaf blade: 4⅜ × 2 in. (11 × 5 cm); of average substance, smooth, medium gray-green with a narrow, irregular, light yellow to white margin, strongly veined; edge widely rippled or kinked, slightly undulate, lanceolate with an acute tip, tapered open lobes. Petiole: green, outlined in white. Flower: funnel-shaped, white on an upright, leafy, green, 20 in. (50 cm) scape in late summer; fertility unknown.

Comments & Special Needs: Site in some morning sun in cooler climates to boost the rather poor vigor. Slow to increase but worth the wait since there are so few white-margined hostas with white flowers.

Distinguishing Features: The blade is set obliquely on the petiole and the white flowers have green tips

Similar: *H.* 'Emerald Isle' and *H.* 'Louisa', which are slightly smaller and have white flowers on upright, leafy, dark green, 34 in. (85 cm) scapes in mid- to high season; fertile.

Hosta 'Chantilly Lace' (W. & E. Lachman 1988)

SMALL

Origin: *H.* 'Calypso' × *H.* 'Halcyon'.

Clump Size & Habit: 40¾ in. wide × 16 in. high (102 × 40 cm). A dense, upright mound.

Description: Leaf blade: 6⅜ × 3⅛ in. (16 × 8 cm); of average substance, smooth, dark gray-green, randomly margined and streaked white, matt above and glaucous below; edge rippled or kinked, elliptic to oval with a cusp-

Hosta 'Chantilly Lace'

Hosta 'Christmas Pageant'

idate tip, rounded pinched lobes. Petiole: narrow, olive-green, finely outlined in white. Flower: large, flared, almost white on an upright, leafy, olive-green, 18⅜ in. (46 cm) scape from mid- to late summer; fertility unknown.

Comments & Special Needs: Site in light to moderate shade. Good growth rate.

Distinguishing Features: The leaf blade is held horizontally.

Similar: *H.* 'Everlasting Love'; *H.* 'Lacy Belle'; **H.* 'Torchlight'.

Hosta 'Christmas Pageant' (Pinterics 2000)

MEDIUM–LARGE

Origin: Sport of *H.* 'Christmas Tree'.

Clump Size & Habit: 36 in. wide × 20 in. high (90 × 50 cm). A dense mound.

Description: Leaf blade: 7½ × 5⅛ in. (19 × 13 cm); very thick, dark green, very widely and irregularly margined, cream turning white, some transitional celadon streaking jetting toward the midrib, matt above and glaucous below, intensely seersuckered; edge slightly undulate, convex, nearly round with a mucronate tip, heart-shaped pinched lobes. Petiole: shallow, green finely outlined in cream. Flower: see *H.* 'Christmas Tree'.

Comments Special Needs: Site in light to moderate shade all day. Moderate growth rate. Pest resistant. Leaf substance indicates it is possibly a tetraploid.

Distinguishing Features: The margins are wider and much more striking than those of its illustrious parent, *H.* 'Christmas Tree'. A superb new hosta.

Hosta 'Christmas Tree' (K. Vaughn & M. Seaver 1982)

MEDIUM–LARGE

Origin: *H.* 'Frances Williams' × *H.* 'Beatrice'.

Hosta 'Christmas Tree'

Clump Size & Habit: 36 in. wide × 20 in. high (90 × 50 cm). A somewhat unruly mound.

Description: Leaf blade: 8⅜ × 6⅜ in. (21 × 16 cm); very thick, olive-green to dark green with a slight blue cast early in the season, narrowly and irregularly margined cream turning white, some transitional celadon streaking jetting toward the midrib, matt above and glaucous below, intensely seersuckered when mature; edge slightly rippled, widely oval to nearly round with a mucronate tip, heart-shaped pinched lobes. Petiole: dark green, finely outlined in white. Flower: funnel-shaped, pale lavender on an upright, leafy, glaucous green, 18 in. (45 cm) scape in mid- to late summer; fertile, red seedpods.

Comments & Special Needs: Will tolerate two hours of morning sun in the North. A specimen that is also suitable for growing in a large container. Pest resistant.

Distinguishing Features: In full bloom, the outline is pyramidal, having a fancied resemblance to a Christmas tree.

Similar: *H.* 'Grand Master'; *H.* 'Van Wade'.

Sports: **H.* 'Christmas Gold'; **H.* 'Christmas Pageant'.

Hosta 'Citation'

Hosta 'Coquette'

Hosta 'Cordelia'

Hosta 'Citation' (Aden 1980)

MEDIUM

Origin: *H.* 'Vicki Aden' hybrid.

Clump Size & Habit: 30 in. wide × 15 in. high (75 × 38 cm). A near horizontal, dense mound.

Description: Leaf blade: 9⅛ × 7⅛ in. (23 × 18 cm); of good substance, smooth, chartreuse to golden yellow, widely and fairly evenly margined cream turning white, matt above and slightly glaucous below, conspicuously veined; edge widely rippled, widely oval with an acute tip, rounded open lobes. Petiole: chartreuse, outlined in white. Flower: funnel-shaped, pale lavender to near white on an upright, leafy, light green, 18 in. (45 cm) scape in late summer; fertile.

Comments & Special Needs: Some morning sun in Northern gardens will turn the chartreuse leaves yellow. For a more muted effect, site in light shade all day. A moderate increaser.

Distinguishing Features: Edges are markedly undulate in young plants but the leaves broaden and flatten considerably with maturity.

Sports: *H.* 'Excitation' has chartreuse leaves turning green.

Hosta 'Coquette' (R. Benedict 1987)

MEDIUM

Origin: *H.* 'Neat Splash' × seedling of *H.* 'Neat Splash' selfed.

Clump Size & Habit: 40¾ in. wide × 16⅜ in. (102 × 41 cm). An open mound.

Description: Leaf blade: 6½ × 4⅜in. (16.5 × 11 cm); of average substance, light, bright green, almost evenly and widely margined and streaked chartreuse to ivory-white, matt above and glossy below, dimpled when mature,

widely spaced veins; edge with slight wide undulations, oval with an obtuse tip, rounded open to pinched lobes. Petiole: wide, green outlined in white. Flower: narrowly funnel-shaped, rich purple from purple buds on an oblique, bare, green, 30 in. (75 cm) scape in late summer; fertile.

Comments Special Needs: Site in light to moderate shade. Of moderate increase.

Distinguishing Features: Conspicuously margined, paddlelike leaves.

Similar: **H.* 'Bold Edger'; **H.* 'Decorata'; **H.* 'Tea and Crumpets'.

Hosta 'Cordelia' (Kuk 1991)

MEDIUM

Origin: Open-pollinated seedling of *H.* 'Neat Splash'.

Clump Size & Habit: 36 in. wide × 14 in. (90 × 36 cm). A dense mound.

Description: Leaf blade: 6½ × 3⅛ in. (16.5 × 8 cm); of average substance, smooth, glossy dark green with fairly regular creamy yellow margins turning ivory-white jetting toward the midrib, widely spaced veins; edge slightly undulate, narrowly ovate with an acute tip, rounded, open to pinched lobes. Petiole: purple-dotted, dark green outlined in cream. Flower: funnel-shaped, vivid deep purple on an upright, leafy, green, 26 in. (65 cm) scape in late summer; fertile.

Comments & Special Needs: Site in light to moderate shade. A rapid grower with outstanding flowers. Ideal in light woodland or a border accompanied by ferns.

Similar: *H. 'Don Stevens'; *H. 'Queen Josephine'.

Hosta 'Crepe Soul' (Naylor Creek Nursery NR)

MINIATURE

Origin: Seedling from an open-pollinated streaked *H.* 'Crepe Suzette'.

Clump Size & Habit: 15 in. wide × 6¾ in. high (38 × 17 cm). An upright mound.

Description: Leaf blade: 4 × 1 in. (10 × 2.5 cm); thick, mid- to dark green widely margined, creamy white with transitional celadon streaking toward the midrib, matt to satiny above and glossy below, dimpled; edge deeply rippled, widely elliptic to oval with an obtuse tip, tapered open lobes. Petiole: short, flat, green widely outlined ivory-white. Flower: funnel-shaped, dark lavender on an upright, leafy, green, 10 in. (25 cm) scape in mid-summer; fertile.

Comments & Special Needs: Site in light to full shade. Ideal for a rock garden. Of moderate increase.

Distinguishing Features: The goffering or crimping on the blade margin continues down the petiole but is less marked as the leaf widens with maturity. The regular, wide, creamy white margin offers a striking effect.

Similar: Leaves are longer and narrower than those of *H.* 'Crepe Suzette'.

Hosta 'Crepe Suzette' (W. & E. Lachman 1986)

MINIATURE–SMALL

Origin: *H.* 'Flamboyant' hybrid.

Clump Size & Habit: 15 in. wide × 7⅛ in. high (38 × 18 cm). An open mound.

Description: Leaf blade: 5⅛ × 2 in. (13 × 5 cm); of moderate substance, dark green, widely margined crisp white, matt above and slightly shiny below, strongly veined; edge slightly undulate, oval with an obtuse tip, tapered open lobes. Petiole: flat, wide, dark green outlined in white. Flower: funnel-shaped, lavender on a leaning, leafy, dark green, 10 to 12 in. (25 to 30 cm) scape in late summer; fertile, dark green seed heads.

Comments & Special Needs: Site in light to moderate shade. Slow to increase.

Distinguishing Features: The margins on this distinctly oval-leaved hosta turn cream toward the end of the season and are exceptionally wide for a hosta of this size.

Similar: *H.* 'Cream Cheese', which is slightly smaller; *H.* 'Decorata'; *H.* 'Moon River'.

Hosta 'Crested Surf' (R. Benedict 1990)

SMALL

Origin: *H.* 'Neat Splash' selfed.

Clump Size & Habit: 30 in. wide × 10 in. high (75 × 25 cm). A dense mound of twisting leaves.

Description: Leaf blade: 5½ × 2⅜ in. (14 × 6 cm); thin, gold turning green, margined yellow to creamy white and transitionally splashed gray-green, satiny above and glaucous below; edge conspicuously rippled, arching, lanceolate to oval kinked toward the obtuse tip, tapered open to pinched lobes. Petiole: kinked, green outlined in white. Flower: funnel-shaped purple on an upright, leafy, 16 in.

Hosta 'Crepe Soul'

Hosta 'Crepe Suzette'

(40 cm) scape in late summer; fertile, reddish-purple seed-pods.

Comments & Special Needs: Site in light to moderate shade. A fast grower suitable for covering large areas. Needs dividing every four to five years in garden borders. Rippled petioles become less marked as the hosta matures.

Distinguishing Features: Attractive combinations of leaf color are at their best toward the end of the most active growth period because there are white-margined gold-and-green leaves at the same time.

Similar: *H.* 'Resonance', whose leaves are less rippled; *H.* 'Stiletto'; *H.* 'Suzanne', which has narrower leaves.

Hosta 'Crispula' (Maekawa & Schmid & AHS 2001)

LARGE

Origin: Of Japanese garden origin.

Clump Size & Habit: 36 in. wide × 20 in. high (90 × 50 cm). A dense, rippling mound.

Hosta 'Crested Surf'

Hosta 'Crispula'

Description: Leaf blade: 12 × 6 in. (30 × 15 cm); of good substance, dark green, irregularly margined pure white with some transitional celadon streaking, satiny above and shiny below, deeply depressed veins, some dimpling when mature; edge dramatically rippled, arching, oval with a distinctly twisted cuspidate tip, heart-shaped pinched lobes. Petiole: narrow dark green, finely outlined in white. Flower: funnel-shaped, palest lavender on a drooping, leafy, green, 24 to 36 in. (60 to 90 cm) scape in early summer; fertile.

Comments & Special Needs: Site in good light to moderate shade. Slow to establish and difficult to propagate. The "true" *H.* 'Crispula' is less often seen in cultivation since the 1960s and is used very little as a breeding plant; *H.* 'Rocky Mountain High' is one of the few exceptions. Prone to virus infection. Prone to virus infection. Forms many seedpods.

Distinguishing Features: The leaves have a 180° twist making this hosta quite distinct. Decorative, flowerlike bracts extend the length of the scape. Many seedpods are formed.

Similar: *H.* 'Enchantment'; **H. montana* 'Mountain Snow'; *H.* 'Snow Crust'; *H.* 'Spring Fling', which is larger and a superb new hosta; **H.* 'Zippity Do Dah'.

Sports: *H.* 'Crispula Viridis' with green leaves; *H.* 'Minuet', which is smaller.

Hosta 'Crusader' (W. & E. Lachman 1989)

MEDIUM

Origin: *H.* 'Halcyon' hybrid.

Clump Size & Habit: 36 in. wide × 18 in. high (90 × 45 cm). A dense mound.

Description: Leaf blade: 6⅜ × 5⅛ in. (16 × 13 cm);

Hosta 'Crusader'

thick, dark green with a blue cast early in the season, narrowly and irregularly margined creamy yellow turning white with some streaking, satiny above and thinly glaucous below, seersuckered when mature; edge undulate, shallowly cupped or convex, widely oval with a mucronate tip, rounded, pinched lobes. Petiole: slightly oblique, green outlined in creamy white. Flower: funnel-shaped pale lavender in a dense raceme on a slightly oblique, bare, glaucous, purple-tinted green, 28 in. (70 cm) scape in late summer; fertility unknown.

Comments & Special Needs: If exposed to strong sunlight the upper leaf surface develops a metallic sheen, but if grown in good light to moderate shade, the depth of color is better. Vigorous, a good increaser. An effective specimen for both leaves and flowers.

Similar: *H. 'Tambourine', which is larger.

Hosta 'Crystal Moon' (Tower 2002)

LARGE

Origin: *H.* 'August Moon' sport.

Clump Size & Habit: 30 in. wide × 18 in. high (75 × 45 cm). An open mound.

Description: Leaf blade: 8⅜ × 6⅜ in. (21 × 16 cm); of good substance, smooth, chartreuse to apple-green, irregularly margined, creamy white with many celadon streaks jetting toward the midrib, widely spaced veins; edge almost flat to slightly rippled, convex, heart-shaped to round with a mucronate tip, heart-shaped pinched lobes. Petiole: light green, outlined creamy white. Flower: long-tubed, widely funnel-shaped, fragrant pure white on an upright, bare, pale green, 28 in. (70 cm) scape in mid- to high summer; fertility unknown.

Comments & Special Needs: Morning sun in cooler climates. Vigorous, a moderate to rapid increaser. A superb new introduction.

Distinguishing Features: The flower, which has also mutated, is white, deliciously fragrant, and 2¾ in. (7 cm) in diameter across the mouth of the perianth.

Similar: *H.* 'Fragrant Bouquet', whose leaf substance is not as heavy and whose flowers are smaller.

Hosta 'Dark Star' (Herold 1999)

SMALL–MEDIUM

Origin: *H.* 'Swoosh' × *H.* 'Hadspen Heron'.

Clump Size & Habit: 24 in. wide × 12 in. high (60 × 30 cm). A rippling mound.

Description: Leaf blade: 7⅛ × 3½ in. (18 × 9 cm); of average substance, smooth, dark green with a blue cast, irregularly margined ivory with some transitional chartreuse streaking jetting toward the midrib, satiny above and glaucous below; edge widely rippled, arching, narrowly oval with an acute tip, rounded open lobes. Petiole: olive-green, finely outlined in ivory near the blade. Flower: tubular, lavender on an upright, glaucous, red-dotted green, 18 to 24 in. (45 to 60 cm) scape in mid-summer; fertile, green seedpods.

Comments & Special Needs: Site in light to full shade. A rapid increaser providing excellent ground cover but also good in containers.

Distinguishing Features: Leaves widen with maturity so that young plants and mature plants are hardly recognizable as the same hosta.

Similar: *H. kikutii* 'Kifukurin Hyuga'; *H.* 'Shelleys'.

Hosta 'Crystal Moon'

Hosta 'Dark Star'

Hosta 'Decorata'

Hosta 'Delta Dawn'

Hosta 'Decorata' (Bailey NR)

MEDIUM

Origin: Species of convenience originating in Japan.

Clump Size & Habit: 36 in. wide × 15 in. high (90 × 38 cm). A rhizomatous mound.

Description: Leaf blade: 6⅜ × 4 in. (16 × 10 cm); of average substance, smooth, olive to dark green, fairly evenly margined and streaked pure white, matt above and glossy below, widely spaced veins; edge undulate, oblong to oval with a sometimes recurved obtuse tip, rounded open to pinched lobes. Petiole: broadly winged, olive-green, outlined in white. Flower: narrowly bell-shaped, long, white-throated rich purple on an upright, leafy, green, 24 in. (60 cm) scape in mid-season; fertile, producing an abundance of seedpods.

Comments & Special Needs: Site in light to moderate shade. Although it can be difficult in a garden setting, it can be very effective if left alone to increase around trees or in light woodland.

Similar: *H.* 'Coquette', which has smaller, rounder leaves; *H.* 'Crepe Suzette'.

Hosta 'Delta Dawn' (K. Vaughn NR)

LARGE

Origin: *H.* 'Aztec Treasure' hybrid.

Clump Size & Habit: 30 in. wide × 20 in. high (75 × 50 cm). An open mound.

Description: Leaf blade: 12 × 9⅛ in. (30 × 23 cm); thick, olive-green turning chartreuse-yellow, widely and irregularly margined cream to ivory-white with some transitional chartreuse streaking jetting toward the midrib, matt above and glaucous below, seersuckered when mature; edge widely undulate, convex, widely oval with a recurved cuspidate tip, heart-shaped pinched lobes. Petiole: shallow,

Hosta 'Dew Drop'

chartreuse, finely outlined in cream. Flower: widely flared, pale lavender to near white from purple-gray bracts on an upright, leafy, mauve-green, 24 in. (60 cm) scape in early summer; fertility unknown.

Comments & Special Needs: Site in some morning sun to promote the best leaf color contrast. Some dimpling is apparent in young plants, becoming more seersuckered with maturity. Of moderate growth rate.

Distinguishing Features: Extra-wide ivory margins make a superb tonal contrast with the changing base color of the leaves. A spectacular hosta.

Similar: *H.* 'Joshua's Banner', whose base leaf color is brighter, is an equally lovely hosta.

Sports: *H.* 'Delta Dawn Supreme', a streaked form.

Hosta 'Dew Drop' (Walters Gardens 1988)

MINIATURE

Origin: Tissue-cultured sport of *H.* 'Gold Drop'.

Clump Size & Habit: 8⅜ in. wide × 6⅜ in. high (21 × 16 cm). A dense mound.

Description: Leaf blade: 3½ × 2⅜ in. (9 × 6 cm); thick, smooth, green, narrowly margined ivory-white with transitional celadon streaks jetting toward the midrib, matt above and thinly glaucous below, dimpled when mature, ribbed veins; edge almost flat, convex, oval to heart-shaped with a cuspidate tip, rounded open to pinched lobes. Petiole: narrow, green, finely outlined in ivory. Flower: see *H.* 'Gold Drop'.

Comments & Special Needs: Morning sun in all but the hottest climates. Moderate to good growth rate. Pest resistant. Ideal for containers or rock gardens.

Hosta 'Diamond Tiara' (T & Z Nursery & Zilis 1985)

SMALL

Origin: Tissue-cultured sport of *H.* 'Golden Tiara'.

Clump Size & Habit: 25⅛ in. wide × 14 in. high (63 × 35 cm). A spreading mound.

Description: Leaf blade: 4 × 3½ in. (11 × 9 cm); thin, mid- to dark green with irregular pure white margins sometimes jetting toward the midrib, matt above and shiny below, some dimpling when mature; edge slightly rippled, slightly folded, widely oval with a cuspidate tip, rounded open to pinched lobes. Petiole: green, outlined in pure white. Flower: see *H.* 'Golden Tiara'.

Comments & Special Needs: Site in good light to moderate shade. A moderate to rapid increaser. An ideal edging plant and also a good pot plant.

Similar: *H.* 'Touchstone' appears identical; *H.* 'Pearl Tiara', smaller and with a wider margin.

Sports: *H.* 'Pearl Tiara'.

Hosta 'Diana Remembered' (Kulpa 1997)

MEDIUM

Origin: Tissue-cultured sport of *H.* 'Seventh Heaven'.

Clump Size & Habit: 24 in. wide × 15 in. high (60 × 38 cm). An open mound.

Description: Leaf blade: 7⅛ × 6⅜ in. (18 × 16 cm); of good substance, blue-green widely and irregularly margined creamy white with transitional celadon streaking jetting toward the midrib, widely spaced veins, satiny above

Hosta 'Diamond Tiara'

and matt below, dimpled; edge slightly rippled, folded, widely oval with a mucronate tip, heart-shaped pinched lobes. Petiole: green, crisply outlined in white. Flower: fragrant, 3⅛ in. (8 cm) long, tubular, near white, waxy on a stout, upright, leafy, green, 22 in. (55 cm) scape in late summer; fertile.

Comments & Special Needs: Site in sun for most of the day in cool climates, morning sun only in hotter regions but plenty of moisture is essential. A rapid increaser. A superb hosta with many attributes.

Distinguishing Features: Large, striking, variegated bracts subtend the raceme.

Similar: *H. plantaginea* 'Ming Treasure'.

Sports: Sometimes produces sports with streaked leaves.

Hosta 'Dixie Chick' (Avent 1999)
MINIATURE
Origin: *H.* 'Masquerade' × *H.* 'Invincible'.

Hosta 'Diana Remembered'

Hosta 'Dixie Chick'

Clump Size & Habit: 10 in. wide × 4 in. high (25 × 10 cm). A spreading mound.

Description: Leaf blade: 3½ × 1½ in. (9 × 4 cm); leathery, smooth, medium green narrowly margined cream to ivory-white with some random streaking, glossy above and matt below; edge slightly rippled, widely lance-shaped with an acute tip, rounded open lobes. Petiole: green, finely outlined in white, appearing to pierce the blade. Flower: large, tubular, pale lavender on an upright, bare, green, 12 in. (30 cm) scape in late summer; infertile.

Comments & Special Needs: Site in morning sun in cooler climates. A rapid increaser that makes a useful edging plant or that contrasts well with larger hostas in a border.

Distinguishing Features: Green-speckled margins and a leaf tip that can be conspicuously curved.

Similar: *H.* 'Herbie', which does not have green-speckled margins.

Hosta 'Don Stevens' (M. Seaver NR)
MEDIUM
Origin: *H.* 'Neat Splash' hybrid.

Clump Size & Habit: 40¾ in. wide × 18 in. high (102 × 45 cm). A neat, tight mound.

Description: Leaf blade: 9⅛ × 6⅜ in. (23 × 16 cm); of average substance, dark green, widely and irregularly margined and streaked rich yellow turning white, glossy above and satiny below, dimpled; edge widely rippled and sometimes upturned when mature, widely oval with an acute to cuspidate tip, heart-shaped pinched lobes. Petiole: light olive-green outlined in cream, red dotted on the outer surface near the crown. Flower: trumpet-shaped, lavender on an upright, leafy, red-dotted, dark green, 31⅛ in. (78 cm) scape in late summer; fertility unknown.

Hosta 'Don Stevens'

Comments & Special Needs: Site in light to full shade. A moderate to good increaser.

Distinguishing Features: Juvenile leaves can be streaked before settling down to a marginal variegation. The margin can be ¾ in. (2 cm) wide in mature leaves.

Similar: *H. 'Queen Josephine', whose leaves are larger.

Sports: H. 'Don Juan' is white centered with a green margin; H. 'Don Quixote' has green margins and a streaked center.

Hosta 'Dress Blues' (Zumbar 1995)

MEDIUM

Origin: H. 'Breeder's Choice F_1' × H. 'Halcyon'.

Clump Size & Habit: 36 in. wide × 24 in. high (90 × 60 cm). An upright, open mound.

Description: Leaf blade: 7⅛ × 3½ in. (18 × 9 cm); thick, smooth, gray-tinted blue-green irregularly margined creamy yellow with some transitional celadon streaking jetting toward the midrib, matt to glaucous above and glaucous below, closely veined; edges slightly rippled, arching, lanceolate to oval with an acute tip, tapered pinched lobes. Petiole: flattish, gray-green outlined in ivory, purple dotted at the base. Flower: tubular, pale lavender on an upright, leafy, glaucous green, 34 in. (85 cm) scape in late summer; fertile.

Comments & Special Needs: Site in light to full shade. Increases rapidly but can revert to blue-green if not regularly divided.

Similar: *H. 'Chantilly Lace'.

Sports: H. 'Moonstruck' has white-centered blue leaves and is vigorous for this type of hosta.

Hosta 'Eagle's Nest' (Lydell 2000)

LARGE

Origin: Tissue-cultured sport of H. 'Sum and Substance'.

Clump Size & Habit: 30 in. wide × 18 in. high (75 × 45 cm). An impressive mound.

Description: Leaf blade: 12 × 10 in. (30 × 25 cm); very thick, bright chartreuse to mid-green, widely margined and streaked yellow to cream sometimes jetting toward the midrib, glossy above for part of the season and glaucous below, seersuckered and puckered; edge slightly undulate, deeply cupped, nearly round with a strongly cuspidate to mucronate tip, heart-shaped folded lobes. Petiole: short, thick, green, outlined in cream. Flower: see H. 'Sum and Substance'.

Comments & Special Needs: Site in morning sun in Northern gardens to achieve the brightest leaf color. Moderate growth rate. Pest resistant. Ideal for inclusion in a subtropical border, assorting well with Miscanthus sinensis 'Zebrinus' and the exotic spider daylily, Hemerocallis 'Yellow Angel'.

Distinguishing Feature: Differs from most other H. 'Sum and Substance' sports in that the leaves are smaller with distinct cupping and it is somewhat slower growing. Blooms are tightly clustered just above the foliage mound.

Similar: H. 'Lodestar', whose leaves have conspicuously rippled edges and even more exaggerated tips.

Hosta 'El Capitan' (W. & E. Lachman 1987)

LARGE

Origin: H. 'Beatrice' hybrid.

Clump Size & Habit: 42 in. wide × 24 in. high (105 × 60 cm). An open mound.

Description: Leaf blade: 10¼ × 9⅛ in. (26 × 23 cm); thick, dark sage-green, widely and irregularly margined and streaked creamy yellow, matt above and powdery below, seersuckered and puckered, prominently veined; edge slightly undulate, kinked at the lobes, slightly arching or

Hosta 'Dress Blues'

Hosta 'Eagle's Nest'

convex, oval to round with a mucronate tip, heart-shaped open to pinched lobes. Petiole: dark green, outlined in cream. Flower: bell-shaped rich mauve from gray-mauve buds on an upright, bare, 34⅜ in. (86 cm) scape from mid- to late summer; fertile.

Distinguishing Features: The transitional celadon streaking and misting sets this hosta apart from most others of its type.

Comments & Special Needs: Site in some morning sun except in the hottest climates, otherwise in light to full shade. Reasonably pest resistant. Increases rapidly. A border specimen or for background planting and lovely with blue-leaved hostas.

Similar: *H. 'Carnival'; *H. 'Standing Ovation'.

Hosta 'Electrum Stater' (Malloy 1997)
MEDIUM

Origin: Sport of H. 'Abiqua Recluse'.

Clump Size & Habit: 26 in. wide × 12 in. high (65 × 30 cm). A dense mound.

Hosta 'El Capitan'

Hosta 'Electrum Stater'

Description: Leaf blade: 7½ × 6½ in. (19 × 16.5 cm); thick, shiny chartreuse to bright golden yellow irregularly margined cream-yellow turning pure white with some transitional chartreuse streaks jetting toward the midrib, seersuckered and puckered; edge slightly rippled, cupped or convex, widely oval to nearly round with a mucronate tip, heart-shaped overlapping lobes. Petiole: chartreuse-yellow outlined in cream. Flower: see H. 'Abiqua Recluse'.

Comments & Special Needs: Takes sun all day except in the hottest regions, where two hours of morning sun is sufficient. A rapid increaser. Pest resistant.

Distinguishing Features: The three-tone effect of the leaves and margins at different stages of their color changes and the streaks jetting into the leaf center make this a most colorful hosta with many attributes.

Similar: H. 'Gaiety' is slightly smaller and needs shade; *H. 'Saint Elmo's Fire'; *H. 'Zodiac'.

Hosta 'Emily Dickinson' (W. & E. Lachman 1987)
MEDIUM

Origin: H. 'Neat Splash' × H. plantaginea.

Clump Size & Habit: 40¾ in. wide × 18 in. high (102 × 45 cm). A dense mound.

Description: Leaf blade: 6½ × 4 in. (16.5 × 10 cm); of average substance, smooth, medium green widely and irregularly margined yellow turning creamy white with streaks jetting toward the midrib, satiny above and shiny below; edge slightly undulate, oval with an occasionally kinked, acute tip and rounded pinched lobes. Petiole: green, finely outlined creamy white. Flower: funnel-shaped, rich lavender on an upright, leafy, green, 28 in. (70 cm) scape in late summer; fertility unknown.

Comments & Special Needs: Site in some morning sun in cooler climates if moisture is available. A rapid increaser.

Hosta 'Emily Dickinson'

Similar: *H. 'Austin Dickinson'; *H. 'Bold Edger'; H. 'Lacy Belle', which needs shade all day since it has bluer leaves; *H. 'Tambourine'.

Hosta 'Emma' (D. & J. Ward 1999)

SMALL–MEDIUM

Origin: H. 'Sum and Substance' hybrid.

Clump Size & Habit: 18 in. wide × 9⅛ in. high (45 × 23 cm). A dense mound.

Description: Leaf blade: 5⅛ × 3½ in. (13 × 9 cm); of good substance, medium green, widely margined creamy yellow to ivory-white with transitional celadon streaking jetting toward the midrib, satiny above and matt below, closely ribbed veins; edge rippled, arching, oval with a cuspidate tip, flat to rounded open to pinched lobes. Petiole: green, outlined in cream. Flower: tubular, near white on an upright or leaning, green, 14 to 15 in. (35 to 38 cm) scape in high summer; fertile, green seedpods.

Comments & Special Needs: Site in two hours of morning sun except in Southern gardens, then in moderate shade. A good increaser.

Hosta 'Eventide' (W. & E. Lachman 1992)

MEDIUM

Origin: H. 'Tokudama Aureonebulosa' hybrid.

Clump & Habit: 40¾ in. wide × 16¾ in. high (102 × 42 cm). A tiered mound.

Description: Leaf blade: 10 × 7⅛ in. (25 × 18 cm); thick, matt, rich olive-green, narrowly and irregularly margined

Hosta 'Emma'

Hosta 'Eventide'

white with some transitional celadon streaks jetting toward the midrib, prominently veined; edge conspicuously and evenly rippled, slightly arching, widely oval with a cuspidate tip, heart-shaped pinched lobes. Petiole: green, outlined in white. Flower: flaring, palest lavender to near white with contrasting mauve anthers on an upright, stout, leafy, green, 34 in. (85 cm) scape in mid- to late summer; fertile.

Comments & Special Needs: Site in light to full shade. Moderate to good increase. Pest resistant.

Distinguishing Features: An outstanding and unusual hosta with interesting leaf surface texture, white rippled edges and white flowers on scapes with white variegated leafy bracts.

Hosta 'Fool's Gold' (Europe, Bowden & Ruh 2002)

MEDIUM–LARGE

Origin: *H.* 'Fortunei' sport, originating in Europe, though its origin is now thought to be *H.* 'Fortunei Stenantha Variegata', now an invalid name.

Clump Size & Habit: 36 in. wide × 24¾ in. high (90 × 62 cm). A dense mound.

Description: Leaf blade: 8⅜ × 7½ in. (21 × 19 cm); of average substance, mid-green with a grayish cast irregularly margined muted yellow, matt above and glaucous below, strongly marked veins, dimpled when mature; edge slightly undulate, arching, oval with a cuspidate tip, heart-shaped open to overlapping lobes. Petiole: narrow, gray-green, finely outlined in cream. Flower: long, funnel-shaped, lavender on an upright, leafy, green, 40¾ in. (102 cm) scape in mid-summer; fertility unknown.

Comments & Special Needs: Tolerates some sun but the leaf color will fade; looks best grown in light to moderate shade. Vigorous. Its dimensions will increase if given optimum growing conditions.

Distinguishing Features: The muted butterscotch-khaki, margined leaves hold all season and provide a different emphasis in a border with its unusually contrasting variegation.

Similar: **H.* 'Brass Horn' is identical; *H.* 'Heliarc', although said to be a *H.* 'Fortunei Hyacinthina' sport, is remarkably similar; *H.* 'Fortunei Obscura Variegata' has darker, more seersuckered leaves.

Hosta 'Formal Attire' (K. Vaughn 1988)

LARGE

Origin: *H.* 'Breeder's Choice' × *H.* 'Frances Williams'.

Clump Size & Habit: 60 in. wide × 26 in. high (150 × 65 cm). An open mound.

Description: Leaf blade: 10 × 8⅜ in. (25 × 21 cm); of good substance, intense blue-green, widely and irregularly margined creamy yellow turning white with transitional celadon streaking, matt above and glaucous below, seersuckered, widely spaced veins; edge slightly rippled, convex, widely oval with a mucronate tip, heart-shaped pinched to overlapping lobes. Petiole: green, outlined in cream. Flower: widely funnel-shaped, pale lavender on an upright, leafy, green, 38 in. (95 cm) scape in high summer; fertility unknown.

Comments & Special Needs: Site in light to moderate shade as a specimen or in a large container. Of moderate to good increase. Is prized by flower arrangers for its contrasting leaf color and pebbled surface texture.

Similar: **H.* 'Robert Frost', whose leaves have more streaking; **H. sieboldiana* 'Northern Exposure', which has a smoother, less seersuckered leaf.

Hosta 'Fool's Gold'

Hosta 'Formal Attire'

Hosta 'Fortunei Albomarginata' (Hylander & AHS 1887)

MEDIUM–LARGE

Origin: Sport of *H.* 'Fortunei'.

Clump Size & Habit: 50¾ in. wide × 22 in. high (127 × 55 cm). A dense mound.

Description: Leaf blade: 10 × 6½ in. (25 × 16.5 cm); of good substance, smooth, dark green, irregularly margined white with streaks jetting toward the midrib, satiny above and thinly glaucous below, strongly marked veins; edge rippled and curved toward the tip, slightly arching, oval with a cuspidate tip, rounded pinched lobes. Petiole: dark green, outlined in white. Flower: Narrowly funnel-shaped, 2 in. (5 cm) long, pale lavender in a dense raceme on an upright, leafy, green, 32 in. (80 cm) scape in high summer; slight fertility.

Comments & Special Needs: Will only succeed if grown in shade all day with plenty of moisture at its roots even in cooler climates. Now surpassed in garden value by some of its selections and sports, which are less fussy about their cultural conditions. Has a tendency to throw sports with variable white margins.

Similar: *H.* 'Carol', whose leaves are cupped when mature; *H.* 'North Hills' is similar but smaller; *H.* 'Zager's White Edge'.

Sports: **H.* 'Francee'.

Hosta 'Fortunei Aureomarginata' (Hylander & AHS 1987)

MEDIUM–LARGE

Origin: Natural sport of *H.* 'Fortunei' origin.

Clump Size & Habit: 50¾ in. wide × 22¾ in. high (127 × 57 cm). A dense mound.

Description: Leaf blade: 8⅜ × 6⅜ in. (21 × 16 cm); of good substance, smooth, dark olive-green, irregularly margined and streaked rich golden yellow turning cream, satiny above and thinly glaucous below; almost flat, slightly convex, oval with a cuspidate tip, heart-shaped pinched lobes. Petiole: olive-green, outlined in creamy yellow. Flower: narrowly funnel-shaped, 2 in. (5 cm) long, pale lavender on an upright, leafy, green, 30 in. (75 cm) scape in high to late summer; marginally fertile.

Comments & Special Needs: Will tolerate plenty of sun, although the leaf color will fade somewhat. Vigorous, easy

Hosta 'Fortunei Albomarginata'

Hosta 'Fortunei Aureomarginata'

Hosta 'Fragrant Bouquet'

to cultivate. Ideal for covering large areas because it is inexpensive and has been superseded in many gardens by modern introductions; however, it is still considered a classic hosta. A favorite of flower arrangers.

Distinguishing Features: Flower bracts subtending the blooms are ornamental even after flowering is over.

Similar: *H.* 'Anne'; *H.* 'Ellerbroek'; *H.* 'Royal Flush'; **H.* 'Twilight'; *H.* 'Viette's Yellow Edge' is similar but has longer leaves.

Sports: **H.* 'Twilight'.

Hosta 'Fragrant Bouquet' (Aden 1982)

LARGE

Origin: *H.* 'Fascination' × *H.* 'Summer Fragrance'.

Clump Size & Habit: 26 in. wide × 18 in. high (65 × 45 cm). An open mound.

Description: Leaf blade: 8⅜ × 6⅜ in. (21 × 16 cm); of moderate substance, chartreuse to apple-green, widely margined yellow to creamy white, satiny above and thinly glaucous below, some dimpling when mature, conspicuously veined; edge widely undulate, convex, widely oval with a cuspidate tip, heart-shaped open to pinched lobes. Petiole: pale green, outlined in cream. Flower: large, very fragrant, widely funnel-shaped, near white flowers radially arranged, on an upright, pale green, 36 in. (90 cm) scape in late summer; occasional large, variegated bracts toward the raceme; usually sterile.

Comments & Special Needs: Site in full sun all day, except in the hottest climates, to produce the best leaf color and the most prolific display of flowers; moisture at the roots is essential. A rapid increaser. *Hosta* 'Fragrant Bouquet' was registered as being a streaked hosta but all those offered for sale have a marginal variegation. Named Hosta

Hosta 'Fragrant Dream'

of the Year by the American Hosta Growers Association in 1998.

Distinguishing Features: *H.* 'Fragrant Dream' has the same wonderful flowers of its parent but its leaves are much darker green and the margin is a brighter yellow.

Similar: **H.* 'Crystal Moon'; **H.* 'Sugar and Cream'; **H.* 'Sweetie'.

Sports: *H.* 'Color Parade' is unstable in its variegation; *H.* 'Fragrant Dream'; **H.* 'Guacamole'.

Hosta 'Francee' (Klopping & AHS 1986)

MEDIUM

Origin: Sport of *H.* 'Fortunei Albomarginata'.

Clump Size & Habit: 50¾ in. wide × 21⅛ in. high (127 × 53 cm). A dense mound.

Description: Leaf blade: 8⅜ × 5⅛ in. (21 × 13 cm); of average substance, rich dark green, crisply and narrowly margined white with some transitional celadon streaks,

Hosta 'Francee'

Hosta 'Fresh'

matt above and glaucous below, dimpled when mature; edge almost flat, widely oval with a cuspidate tip, heart-shaped open or folded lobes. Petiole: dark green, outlined in white. Flower: narrowly funnel-shaped, pale lavender on an upright, leafy, green, 28 in. (70 cm) scape in high to late summer; a few viable seeds.

Comments & Special Needs: Will tolerate morning sun in all but the hottest climates but the leaf color will fade to palest olive-green. Superb in a large container and also excellent for landscaping since it is a rapid increaser. A classic hosta.

Distinguishing Features: Distinctive, bright purple shoots of *H.* 'Francee' emerge very late in the season as they do with all hostas of the Fortunei Group. The narrowly funnel-shaped flowers do not always open at the tips of the scapes.

Similar: *H.* 'Carol' has a slightly wider margin and a more glaucous leaf surface; **H.* 'Fortunei Albomarginata'; *H.* 'North Hills'; *H.* 'Fringe Benefit' and *H.* 'Green Gold', which have yellow to cream margins; *H.* 'Rhino' has a thicker substance and a more defined margin; *H.* 'Zager's White Edge'.

Sports: *H.* 'Academy Fire' emerges with yellow leaves turning light green; **H.* 'Jade Beauty'; *H.* 'Minuteman'; *H.* 'Pathfinder' occasionally produces a misted effect in the center of the leaf; **H.* 'Patriot'; *H.* 'The Matrix' has a central variegation that emerges golden yellow, becoming white-flecked with green; *H.* 'Trailblazer', which displays a sharp contrast between the wide, creamy white margins and the dark green center.

Hosta 'Fresh' (Aden NR)

SMALL

Origin: Sport of *H.* 'Amy Aden'.

Clump Size & Habit: 20 in. wide × 8⅜ in. high (50 × 21 cm). An open mound.

Description: Leaf blade: 5⅛ × 2⅜ in. (13 × 6 cm); thin, smooth, chartreuse to yellow, narrowly margined ivory-white; edge slightly rippled, arching, widely lanceolate with an acute tip, rounded open to pinched lobes. Petiole: chartreuse, outlined in ivory. Flower: funnel-shaped, lavender on an upright, bare, pale green, 12 in. (30 cm) scape in late summer; fertility unknown.

Comments & Special Needs: Grow in shade accompanied by ferns with dark green leaves for foliage and color contrast. A low-key hosta but useful for lighting up dark areas. Not vigorous or a rapid grower.

Similar: *H.* 'Bizarre', which has dimpled mature leaves.

Hosta 'Frosted Jade' (Maroushek 1978)

LARGE–GIANT

Origin: *H. montana* hybrid.

Clump Size & Habit: 60 in. wide × 28 to 32 in. high (150 × 70 to 80 cm). An upright, arching mound.

Description: Leaf blade: 14 × 10 in. (35 × 25 cm); of good substance, dark sage-green, narrowly and irregularly margined pure white with some transitional celadon streaks jetting toward the midrib, matt above and thinly glaucous below, strongly veined; edge closely rippled, oval with a mucronate tip, heart-shaped pinched lobes. Petiole: deeply channeled green, outlined in white. Flower: funnel-shaped, near white in a dense raceme on a leaning leafy, green, 40 in. (100 cm) scape in mid-summer; fertile producing abundant seed.

Hosta 'Gay Blade'

Hosta 'Frosted Jade'

Hosta 'Ginko Craig'

Comments & Special Needs: Site in light to moderate shade as a specimen or at the edge of woodland.

Distinguishing Features: Slightly upturned leaf edges set it apart from similar hostas.

Similar: *H. montana* 'Mountain Snow'; *H. montana* 'Snow Crust'; *H. montana* 'Summer Snow' has evenly white margins and the leaves are a darker green; *H. montana* 'White On'.

Hosta 'Gay Blade' (W. & E. Lachman 1988)

MEDIUM

Origin: Seedling of *H.* 'Resonance' × *H.* 'Halcyon'.

Clump Size & Habit: 40¾ in. wide × 18 in. high (102 × 45 cm). A rippling mound.

Description: Leaf blade: 8⅜ × 2¾ in. (21 × 7 cm); of good substance, smooth, gray-green, irregularly margined ivory to pure white with streaks jetting toward the midrib, satiny above and glaucous below; edge widely rippled, undulate, elliptic with an acute tip, heart-shaped pinched

lobes. Petiole: oblique, gray-green, finely outlined in white. Flower: funnel-shaped, 2 in. (5 cm) long, lavender on an upright, leafy, purple-dotted gray-green, 28 in. (70 cm) scape in late summer; fertility unknown.

Comments & Special Needs: Light to full shade all day as the margins can burn if exposed to strong sunlight, even in cooler climates. Vigorous, easy to grow.

Distinguishing Features: Leaves last well into autumn.

Similar: *H.* 'Chantilly Lace', which has leaves of thinner substance.

Hosta 'Ginko Craig' (Craig & Summers & AHS 1986)

SMALL–MEDIUM

Origin: Imported from Japan, now considered to be identical to *H. helonioides* 'Albopicta'.

Clump Size & Habit: 44¾ in. wide × 14 in. high (112 × 35 cm). A dense, spreading mound.

Description: Leaf blade: 5⅛ × 2¼ in. (13 × 5.5 cm); thin, dark green, crisply margined pure white with some transitional celadon streaking, matt above and slightly shiny below, some dimpling when mature; edge rippled, arching, slightly convex, elliptic with an acute tip, tapered open lobes. Petiole: shallow, green, distinctly outlined in white. Flower: open funnel-shape, dark purple-striped purple on an upright, bare, green, 22 in. (55 cm) scape from late summer to early autumn; very fertile.

Comments & Special Needs: Site in light to moderate shade. The supreme edging hosta since it is vigorous and easy to grow. A very noticeable difference between the narrow, rippled, lanceolate, juvenile leaf blades and the mature elliptic to oval ones.

Similar: *H.* 'Allen P. McConnell'; *H.* 'Blade Runner'; *H.* 'Bunchoko'; *H.* 'Excalibur' is identical; *H.* 'Ground Master'; *H.* 'Jadette' has a creamier margin; *H.* 'Little Wonder'; *H.* 'Peedee Laughing River' has slightly wider and more rippled leaves; *H.* 'Princess of Karafuto' is virtually identical.

Sports: *H.* 'Hi Ho Silver'; *H.* 'Sarah Kennedy', which has significantly wider margins.

Hosta 'Ginsu Knife' (Solberg 2002)

MEDIUM

Origin: *H.* 'Irongate Supreme' × *H.* 'Green Fountain'.

Clump Size & Habit: 28 in. wide × 14 in. high (70 × 35 cm). A cascading mound.

Description: Leaf blade: 10 × 3½ in. (25 × 9 cm); of av-

Hosta 'Ginsu Knife'

Hosta 'Sarah Kennedy'

erage substance, shiny, olive-green, widely and irregularly yellow-margined fading to near white with transitional chartreuse streaking, ribbed veins; edge serrate, conspicuously undulate, arching with an acute twisted tip, elliptic, tapered open to slightly pinched lobes. Petiole: flat, olive-green, outlined and streaked cream and chartreuse, rippled. Flower: open, flared with reflexed petals, fragrant, white on an upright to arching, bare, green, 20 in. (40 cm) scape in late summer; fertility not established.

Comments & Special Needs: Site in morning sun in cooler regions, otherwise light shade. Dimensions are likely to increase in optimum growing conditions. Of average substance. Unstable variegation can produce streaking into the center of the blade and has now produced a streaked form. *Hosta* 'Ginsu Knife' is a superb, distinct new hosta.

Distinguishing Features: Dramatically arching, serrated leaves.

Sports: *H*. 'Ginsu Knife Streaked'.

Hosta 'Gloriosa' (Krossa & Summers & AHS 1986)

MEDIUM

Origin: No specific source cited but thought to belong with the *H*. 'Fortunei' assemblage.

Clump Size & Habit: 42 to 46⅜ in. wide × 18 in. high (105 to 116 × 45 cm). A dense mound.

Description: Leaf blade: 7⅛ × 4 in. (18 × 10 cm); of average substance, dark green, very narrowly and regularly margined pure white, matt above and thinly glaucous below, ribbed veins, dimpled when mature; edge almost flat, slightly cupped when mature, elliptic to oval with a cuspidate to mucronate tip, tapered open lobes. Petiole: olive-green, very finely outlined in white. Flower: funnel-shaped, pale lavender on an oblique, leafy, olive-green, 38 in. (95 cm) scape in late summer; sterile.

Comments & Special Needs: Site in light to moderate shade. Although the variegation is usually uniform, it occasionally throws white streaks toward the midrib. Vigorous, easy to grow.

Distinguishing Features: Leaves have a distinctly upturned stance when mature. The raceme is bunched toward the top of the scape.

Similar: *H*. 'Change of Tradition'.

Hosta 'Goddess of Athena' (Kuk 1987)

MEDIUM

Origin: Self pollinated seedling of *H*. 'Decorata'.

Clump Size & Habit: 30 in. wide × 16⅜ in. high (75 × 41 cm). A spreading mound.

Description: Leaf blade: 7⅛ × 4⅜ in. (18 × 11 cm); of good substance, dark green, consistently margined creamy yellow to ivory-white with occasional streaks, satiny above and glossy below, widely and conspicuously veined, slight dimpling toward the base; edge slightly undulate, oblong to oval with an obtuse tip, rounded open lobes. Petiole: narrow dark green, clearly outlined in cream. Flower: attractive, bell-shaped, rich purple on a leaning, bare, green scape up to 34¾ in. (87 cm) in late summer; fertile.

Comments & Special Needs: Site in light to moderate shade. Superb for woodland planting or ground cover as it increases fairly rapidly.

Distinguishing Features: Differs from *H*. 'Decorata' in having a creamier margin; is more rhizomatous than most hostas.

Similar: *H*. 'Bold Edger'; *H*. 'Decorata'; *H*. 'Queen Josephine'.

Sports: *H*. 'First Impressions' a streaked form; *H*. 'Green Smash', which has green leaves.

Hosta 'Gloriosa'

Hosta 'Goddess of Athena'

Hosta 'Golden Tiara'

Hosta '**Golden Tiara**' (Savory 1977)

SMALL–MEDIUM

Origin: Once thought to be an X-ray mutation of *H. nakaiana* but now considered to be of *H. capitata* origin. It is the mother plant of a number of similar sports.

Clump Size & Habit: 38¾ in. wide × 16 in. high (97 × 40 cm). A spreading mound.

Description: Leaf blade: 5⅛ × 4⅜ in. (13 × 11 cm); of moderate substance, mid-green, irregularly margined, chartreuse turning yellow then fading to cream with transitional chartreuse streaking, matt above and shiny below, some dimpling when mature; edge slightly rippled, widely oval with an acute to mucronate tip, heart-shaped open to pinched lobes. Petiole: olive-green, outlined in cream. Flower: widely funnel-shaped, rich lavender to purple in dense clusters on an upright, leafy, olive-green, 22 to 25⅛ in. (55 to 63 cm) scape in late summer; fertile, but few seedpods.

Comments & Special Needs: Site in good light to light shade. A rapid increaser and will exceed these dimensions given optimum growing conditions. Leaves are variable in shape, the outer ones being oval, the inner ones sometimes almost round. Flowers turn a deeper purple when exposed to sunlight. Among the most important hostas ever introduced. Lovely in a container. Winner of the 1994 Alex J. Summers Distinguished Merit Hosta Award.

Distinguishing Features: Some rebloom if spent scapes are removed.

Similar: *H.* 'Grand Tiara'.

Sports: *H.* 'Diamond Tiara'; *H.* 'Emerald Scepter'; *H.* 'Golden Scepter'; *H.* 'Jade Scepter'; *H.* 'Platinum Tiara'; *H.* 'Ribbon Tiara'; *H.* 'Royal Tiara'.

Hosta '**Grand Prize**' (Walters Gardens 1998)

SMALL–MEDIUM

Origin: Tissue-cultured sport of *H.* 'Grand Tiara'.

Clump Size & Habit: 36 in. high × 14 in. wide (90 × 35 cm). A dense mound.

Description: Leaf blade: 5⅛ × 4⅜ in. (13 × 11 cm); thick, mid-green, widely and irregularly margined bright golden yellow gradually turning ivory, matt above and shiny below, some dimpling when mature, widely spaced veins; edge almost flat, widely oval with a mucronate tip, heart-shaped pinched lobes. Petiole: green, outlined in yellow. Flower: see *H.* 'Golden Tiara'.

Comments & Special Needs: Site in morning sun to

Hosta 'Grand Tiara'

Hosta 'Grand Prize'

promote the best leaf color. A moderate to fast increaser, preferring a loose, friable soil. A border specimen and superb in containers. Polyploid. Pest resistant.

Similar: *H.* 'Grand Tiara', whose leaf margin is wider and not such a vivid color.

Hosta 'Grand Tiara' (A. Pollock 1991)

SMALL–MEDIUM

Origin: Polyploid tissue-cultured sport of *H.* 'Golden Tiara'.

Clump Size & Habit: 36 in. wide × 14 in. high (90 × 35 cm). A dense mound.

Description: Leaf blade: 5⅛ × 4⅜ in. (13 × 11 cm); thick, mid-green, very widely and irregularly margined chartreuse to yellow, later fading to ivory, matt above and shiny below, some dimpling when mature, widely spaced veins; edge almost flat, widely oval with a mucronate tip, heart-shaped pinched lobes. Petiole: green, outlined in chartreuse. Flower: see *H.* 'Golden Tiara'.

Comments & Special Needs: Morning sun essential to promote good leaf color. Vigorous, a rapid grower, preferring a loose, friable soil. Lovely with *Tricyrtis* 'Lightening Strike'. The first of the polyploid hostas of the Tiara Series, passing on leaves of thicker substance to its progeny.

Similar: *H.* 'Grand Prize'.

Sports: *H.* 'Amber Tiara'; *H.* 'Grand Gold' has golden yellow leaves; *H.* 'Crystal Tiara'; *H.* 'Gilded Tiara' has white-margined, golden yellow leaves; *H.* 'Gold Heart', which has the reverse variegation with more vivid coloring; *H.* 'Grand Prize'; *H.* 'Heavenly Tiara' is smaller than most of the hostas of the Tiara Series and has golden yellow leaves margined ivory white; *H.* 'Topaz Tiara'.

Hosta 'Hawkeye'

Hosta 'Heartbeat'

Hosta 'Heart's Content'

Hosta 'Hawkeye' (Maroushek 1999)

SMALL

Origin: Sport of *H.* 'Gold Edger'.

Clump Size & Habit: 25⅛ in. wide × 10 in. high (63 × 25 cm). An open mound with upward-facing leaves.

Description: Leaf blade: 3½ × 2⅜ in. (9 × 6 cm), thick, bright mid-green, widely and irregularly margined yellow, satiny above and matt below, slightly dimpled; edge flat, folded, nearly round with a mucronate tip, heart-shaped open lobes. Petiole: narrow, green, finely outlined in yellow. Flower: see details for *H.* 'Gold Edger'.

Comments & Special Needs: Site in morning sun except in Southern gardens. Seen at its best in containers or a rock garden. Of moderate increase.

Similar: *H.* 'Radiant Edger'; *H.* 'Timothy'.

Hosta 'Heartbeat' (Dean 1999)

SMALL–MEDIUM

Origin: *H.* 'Liberty Bell' × *H.* 'Dorset Clown'.

Clump Size & Habit: 31⅛ in. wide × 11 in. high (78 × 28 cm). A dense mound.

Description: Leaf blade: 6½ × 5⅛ in. (16.5 × 13 cm); thick, mid-green, irregularly margined cream to golden yellow, shiny above and glaucous below, dimpled, ribbed veins; edge slightly undulate, shallowly cupped or convex, widely oval with a cuspidate tip, heart-shaped overlapping lobes. Petiole: narrow, light green. Flower: bell-shaped, lavender on an upright, leafy, pale green, 20 in. (50 cm) scape in late summer; sterile.

Comments & Special Needs: Site in light to moderate shade. Of average growth. Grow in containers or the front of the border for a colorful effect and nicely textured leaves.

Hosta 'Heart's Content' (K. Vaughan NR)

LARGE

Origin: *H.* 'Breeder's Choice' × *H.* 'Polly Bishop'.

Clump Size & Habit: 46¾ in. wide × 22⅜ in. high (117 × 56 cm). An overlapping, compact mound.

Description: Leaf blade: 8½ × 6⅜ in. (21.5 × 16 cm); very thick, dark sage-green, widely and irregularly margined cream to white, a small amount of transitional celadon splashing, matt above and thinly glaucous below, some seersuckering; edge slightly undulate, mostly convex, widely oval with a mucronate tip, heart-shaped open lobes. Petiole: sage-green, outlined in cream. Flower: funnel-shaped pale lavender on an upright, leafy, green, 36 in. (90 cm) scape in high summer; fertile.

Comments Special Needs: Site in moderate shade in the South, high, filtered shade elsewhere. A superb container specimen if well watered or as a foil for purple-leaved shrubs.

Distinguishing Features: Very floriferous. The leafy bracts are variegated.

Hosta 'Heavenly Tiara'

Hosta 'Hi Ho Silver'

Similar: *H. 'Leola Fraim'; *H. 'Robert Frost', whose leaves are more streaked.

Hosta 'Heavenly Tiara' (Walters Gardens 1998)

SMALL

Origin: Tissue-cultured sport of H. 'Grand Tiara'.

Clump Habit & Size: 36 in. wide × 14 in. high (90 × 35 cm). A spreading mound.

Description: Leaf blade: 4 × 3½ in. (10 × 9 cm); thick, smooth. chartreuse to golden yellow, widely and irregularly margined cream with streaks jetting toward the midrib, dimpled when mature; edge flat, folded to cupped, oval with a mucronate tip, tapered open to pinched lobes. Petiole: narrow, chartreuse, finely outlined in cream. Flower: see H. 'Golden Tiara'.

Comments & Special Needs: Best grown in good light under a north wall. A much tougher hosta than its delicate coloring suggests. Moderate growth rate.

Distinguishing Features: Leaf color brightens by early summer and the margins turn ivory. Reverse variegation of *H. 'Crystal Tiara'.

Similar: *H. 'Olympic Edger'.

Hosta 'Hi Ho Silver' (Walters Gardens 1997)

SMALL–MEDIUM

Origin: Tissue-cultured sport of H. 'Ginko Craig'.

Clump Size & Habit: 16 in. wide × 12 in. high (40 × 30 cm). A dense, spreading mound.

Description: Leaf blade: 6⅜ × 2 in. (16 × 5 cm); of good substance, smooth, mid olive-green with a wide pure white margin with some transitional chartreuse streaking, matt above and shiny below; edge conspicuously rippled, slightly folded, linear to lanceolate with an acute tip, ta-

Hosta 'His Honor'

pered open lobes. Petiole: green-streaked creamy white. Flower: see H. 'Ginko Craig'.

Comments & Special Needs: Site in light to moderate shade. Plant as a contrast in front of large blue-leaved hostas. Moderate rate of growth.

Distinguishing Features: Maintains its smaller leaves, eventually having wider margins than its parent.

Similar: *H. 'Ginsu Knife'.

Hosta 'His Honor' (J. Wilkins 2000)

LARGE

Origin: Seedling of H. 'Herb Benedict'.

Clump Size & Habit: 49 in. wide × 24 in. high (122 × 60 cm). A dome-shaped mound.

Description: Leaf blade: 14 × 11½ in. (35 × 29 cm); average to good substance, mid-green, widely and irregularly margined chartreuse turning creamy white, satiny above and matt below; edge widely rippled when juvenile and almost flat when mature, slightly convex, widely oval with a mucronate tip, heart-shaped overlapping lobes. Petiole: green, outlined chartreuse. Flower: tubular, lavender-striped, near white on an upright, leafy, green, 36¾ to 42¾ in. (92 to 107 cm) scape in high summer; fertile with green seedpods.

Comments & Special Needs: Site in good light to light shade. Moderate growth rate.

Distinguishing Features: Muted chartreuse margins are an unusual feature.

Hosta 'Honeysong' (A. Summers NR)

MEDIUM–LARGE

Origin: Unknown. Named for Alex Summers's Honeysong Farm in Delaware.

Clump Size & Habit: 36 in. wide × 18 in. high (90 × 45 cm). A dense mound.

Description: Leaf blade: 8⅜ × 5½ in. (21 × 14 cm); of good substance, dark blue-green, widely and irregularly margined, creamy white with transitional celadon streaks jetting toward the midrib, matt to glaucous above and glaucous below, seersuckered; edge with occasional shallow undulations, slightly arching toward the tip, inner leaves cupped, widely oval with a cuspidate tip, heart-shaped pinched lobes. Petiole: dark green, outlined in cream. Flower: funnel-shaped, finely purple-striped pale lavender on an upright, bare, glaucous green, 20 in. (50 cm) scape in mid-summer; fertile.

Comments & Special Needs: Leaves color best in high, filtered shade. Vigorous, a rapid increaser. A superb specimen and lovely as a pot plant.

Similar: *H.* 'Mama Mia'; **H.* 'Wide Brim', which is almost identical.

Hosta 'Hot Diggity Dog' (Elslager 1998)

SMALL–MEDIUM

Origin: *H.* 'Sea Prize' hybrid.

Clump Size & Habit: 18 in. wide × 15 in. high (45 × 38 cm). An upright mound.

Description: Leaf blade: 7⅛ × 6⅜ in. (18 × 16 cm); thick, satiny rich chartreuse, widely and irregularly margined ivory turning golden yellow, intensely seersuckered; edge flat, cupped, nearly round with a mucronate tip, heart-shaped open to pinched lobes. Petiole: olive-green, outlined in ivory. Flower: funnel-shaped, white on an upright, leafy, ivory-green, 18 to 24 in. (45 to 60 cm) scape in mid- to high summer; fertile, green seedpods.

Comments & Special Needs: Site in morning sun in the North to promote the best leaf color, elsewhere shade all day. Slow to increase but a superb recent introduction.

Similar: **H.* 'June Moon'.

Hosta 'Ice Cream' (Rossing 1998)

SMALL

Origin: Tissue-cultured sport of *H.* 'Vanilla Cream'.

Clump Size & Habit: 12 in. wide × 9⅛ in. high (30 × 23 cm). A low, rhizomatous mound.

Description: Leaf blade: 3¼ × 3¼ in. (8.5 × 8.5 cm); thick, satiny, mid to dark olive-green, widely and irregularly margined muted golden yellow, slightly dimpled, widely spaced veins; edge almost flat, slightly convex, widely oval to round with a mucronate tip, heart-shaped open to pinched lobes. Petiole: short, shallowly channeled green, outlined creamy yellow. Flower: see *H.* 'Vanilla Cream'.

Comments & Special Needs: Site in morning sun to high, filtered shade in the North. Moderate rate of growth. Reasonably pest resistant.

Hosta 'Honeysong'

Hosta 'Hot Diggity Dog'

Hosta 'Iced Lemon' (A. & R. Bowden NR)

SMALL–MEDIUM

Origin: Sport of *H.* 'Lemon Delight'.

Clump Size & Habit: 18 in. wide × 12 in. high (45 × 30 cm). A tight mound.

Description: Leaf blade: 3 × 1 in. (7.5 × 2.5 cm); thin, chartreuse, narrowly and irregularly margined white with paler transitional streaking, matt above and shiny below, widely spaced veins; edge rippled, arching toward the tip, widely lanceolate with an acute tip, tapered open to pinched lobes. Petiole: green finely outlined in white. Flower: see *H.* 'Lemon Lime' of which *H.* 'Lemon Delight' is a sport.

Comments & Special Needs: A rapid increaser. Dimensions will quickly be exceeded. Leaves will color better with morning sun in the North.

Distinguishing Features: Scapes rise well above the leaf mound and may rebloom if cut down after the first flush of flowers.

Hosta 'Ice Cream'

Hosta 'Iced Lemon'

Hosta 'Indiana Knight' (Goodwin 1990)

MEDIUM–LARGE

Origin: Sport of *H.* 'August Moon'.

Clump Size & Habit: 40¾ in. wide × 18 in. high (102 × 45 cm). An open mound.

Description: Leaf blade: 7½ × 5½ in. (19 × 14 cm); thick, mid-green with irregular muted chartreuse margins strongly seersuckered; edge flat to slightly rippled, widely oval to nearly round with a mucronate tip, heart-shaped pinched lobes. Petiole: chartreuse, margined light yellow. Flower: see *H.* 'August Moon'.

Comments & Special Needs: Site in at least two hours of morning sun to boost the leaf color. Vigorous, easy to grow. Reasonably pest resistant.

Sports: *H.* 'Winter Lightening' is white-streaked with misty netting over cream, widely and irregularly margined golden yellow.

Hosta 'Iron Gate Glamour' (Sellers 1881)

LARGE

Origin: *H. plantaginea* hybrid.

Clump Size & Habit: 40¾ in. wide × 20 in. high (102 × 50 cm). A dense mound.

Description: Leaf blade: 9⅛ × 5½ in. (23 × 14 cm); of average substance, shiny dark olive-green, widely and irregularly margined yellow turning creamy white with streaks jetting toward the midrib, dimpled, strongly veined; edge widely rippled, arching, oval with an acute to cuspidate tip, heart-shaped pinched lobes. Petiole: dark green, outlined in yellow. Flower: funnel-shaped, pale lavender in a dense raceme on an upright, leafy, light green, 36 in. (90 cm) scape from late summer; fertile.

Comments & Special Needs: Site in morning sun. Flow-

Hosta 'Indiana Knight'

Hosta 'Iron Gate Glamour'

Hosta 'Jewel of the Nile'

Hosta 'Jack of Diamonds'

ers last until the first frosts in cooler regions, giving a welcome late autumn bonus, especially appreciated when grown in a container near the house. A rapid increaser. More stable than similar hostas.

Similar: *H.* 'Iron Gate Delight', whose variegation is more unstable.

Hosta 'Jack of Diamonds' (R. Savory 1985)

MEDIUM

Origin: *H. sieboldiana* × a seedling mutation.

Clump Size & Habit: 20 in. wide × 16 in. high (50 × 40 cm). A dense, overlapping mound.

Description: Leaf blade: 7½ × 6⅜ in. (19 × 16 cm); very thick, leathery, rich blue-green irregularly margined yellow turning cream, matt above and glaucous below, seersuckered ; edge slightly undulate, shallowly cupped or convex, widely oval with a mucronate tip, heart-shaped folded lobes. Petiole: light green, outlined in cream. Flower: funnel-shaped, near white in a dense raceme on an upright, leafy, glaucous gray, 16 to 17⅜ in. (40 to 43 cm) scape in early to mid-summer; fertile.

Comments & Special Needs: The golden yellow margin does not scorch but the best leaf color will be achieved by siting in high, filtered shade. Slow to increase. Pest resistant.

Distinguishing Features: Smaller, with flatter leaves than *H.* 'Frances Williams'.

Similar: *H.* 'Cartwheels'; *H.* 'Fleeta Brownell Woodroffe'; *H.* 'Kara'; *H.* 'Merry Sunshine'; *H.* 'Wagon Wheels'.

Hosta 'Jewel of the Nile' (Walek 2000)

MEDIUM–LARGE

Origin: Sport of *H.* 'Dee's Golden Jewel'.

Clump Size & Habit: 24 in. wide × 28⅜ in. high (60 × 71 cm). An upright mound.

Description: Leaf blade: 8⅜ × 6½ in. (21 × 16.5 cm); thick, blue-green irregularly margined golden yellow turning cream with streaks jetting toward the midrib, dimpled with slight puckering when mature; edge widely rippled, widely oval with a cuspidate tip, heart-shaped pinched lobes. Petiole: pink-tinted light green, outlined in yellow. Flower: see *H.* 'Dee's Golden Jewel'.

Comments & Special Needs: Tolerates plenty of sun, even in Southern gardens, but the hotter the sun the more the leaf color will fade. A moderate increaser. Pest resistant. A superb hosta for all climates.

Hosta 'June Moon' (Lachman 1991)

MEDIUM

Origin: Unknown.

Clump Size & Habit: 25⅛ in. wide × 18 in. high (63 × 45 cm). An upright mound.

Description: Leaf blade: 9½ × 8⅜ in. (24.5 × 21 cm); thick, acid lime-green to chartreuse-yellow, very widely margined ivory to white with some streaking, intensely seersuckered and puckered when mature; edge slightly rippled when young, widely oval to nearly round with a cuspidate to mucronate tip, heart-shaped overlapping, lobes. Petiole: light green, outlined in ivory. Flower: funnel-shaped, near white on an upright, bare, glaucous green, 18¾ in. (47 cm) scape in later summer; sterile.

Hosta 'June Moon'

Comments & Special Needs: Site in morning sun to promote the best leaf base color. Slow to moderate increase. Pest resistant.

Distinguishing Features: Puckering over seersuckering on the leaf surface almost amounts to distortion: it is leaf texture taken to extremes. This feature is not apparent in juvenile plants.

Similar: *H.* 'Electrum Stater', on which there are streaks jetting toward the midrib on most of the leaves.

Hosta kikutii 'Kifukurin Hyuga' (Japan)

MEDIUM–LARGE

Origin: Natural sport of *H. kikutii*.

Clump Size & Habit: 36 in. wide × 20 in. high (90 × 50 cm). A graceful open mound.

Description: Leaf blade: 9⅛ × 5⅛ to 6⅜ in. (23 × 13 × 16 cm); of average substance, shiny, mid- to dark green irregularly margined yellow turning cream, with some streaks jetting toward the midrib, prominently ribbed veins; edge rippled, arching, oval with a cuspidate tip, heart-shaped overlapping lobes. Petiole: narrow, green outlined in cream. Flower: see *H. kikutii*.

Comments & Special Needs: Tolerates some morning sun in most regions. Of moderate to good increase.

Hosta kikutii 'Kifukurin Hyuga'

Distinguishing Features: The heavily ribbed cascading leaves.

Similar: *H.* 'Shelley's', which flowers several weeks later, is now considered to be a natural sport of *H. kiyosumiensis*.

Hosta 'Kissing Cousin' (Elslager 1998)

MEDIUM

Origin: Sport of *H.* 'Wide Brim'.

Clump Size & Habit: 32 in. wide × 16 in. high (80 × 40 cm). A dense mound.

Description: Leaf blade: 6¼ × 4¼ in. (15 × 10 cm); of good substance, dark green with a slight blue cast, irregularly margined pale yellow turning ivory, closely ribbed veins, dimpled when mature; edge kinked, arching, widely oval, sometimes cupped, sometimes convex, with a cuspidate tip, heart-shaped open to pinched lobes. Petiole: dark green, outlined in cream. Flower: see *H.* 'Wide Brim'.

Comments & Special Needs: Light to full shade to retain the blue cast to the leaves. The unusual shape of the leaves makes it an interesting container specimen.

Distinguishing Features: Differs from *H.* 'Wide Brim' in having distinctly kinked leaf edges and a conspicuous tip.

Hosta 'Lady Isobel Barnett' (Grenfell 1996)

LARGE–GIANT

Origin: First registered sport of *H.* 'Sum and Substance'.

Clump Size & Habit: 60¾ in. wide × 30 in. high (152 × 75 cm). A dense mound.

Description: Leaf blade: 18 × 10 in. (45 × 25 cm); thick, light olive-green, irregularly margined golden yellow turning cream, satiny above and glaucous below; edge slightly undulate, widely oval to nearly round with a strongly cuspidate to mucronate tip, heart-shaped overlapping lobes.

Petiole: leaning, stout, light green, outlined in cream. Flower: see *H.* 'Sum and Substance'.

Comments & Special Needs: Grows equally well in sun or shade provided there is adequate moisture available. Of moderate to good increase. Pest resistant. Yellow margins of similar cultivars are said to be visible earlier in the new season's growth, but once they are all in full growth, there is virtually no difference in the width or the color of the margins. Lovely with orange daylilies but impressive as a specimen in a huge container.

Similar: *H.* 'Beauty Substance'; *H.* 'Bottom Line'; *H.* 'David A. Haskell'; *H.* 'Small Sum'; *H.* 'Something Good'; *H.* 'Sum It Up'; *H.* 'Sum of All'; *H.* 'Sum Total'; *H.* 'Titanic'; *H.* 'Vim and Vigor'.

Hosta 'Lakeside April Snow' (Chastain 1994)

LARGE

Origin: *H.* 'Fascination' × *H.* 'Lakeside Symphony'.

Hosta 'Lady Isobel Barnett'

Hosta 'Kissing Cousin'

Hosta 'Lakeside April Snow'

Clump Size & Habit: 36 in. wide × 26⅜ in. high (90 × 66 cm). A compact mound.

Description: Leaf blade: 8⅜ × 6⅜ in. (21 × 16 cm); of good substance, matt soft chartreuse-yellow widely and irregularly margined cream to white with some splashes jetting toward the midrib, dimpled; edge flat to slightly rippled, slightly convex, widely oval with a cuspidate tip, open to pinched heart-shaped lobes. Petiole: chartreuse, finely edged cream. Flower: tubular, near white on an upright, leafy, pale green, 27⅛ in. (68 cm) scape in early to midsummer. Fertility unknown.

Comments & Special Needs: The leaf has good substance.

Distinguishing Features: The 1 in. (2.5 cm) wide margin is in dramatic contrast with the light green leaf center.

Similar: *H.* 'Joshua's Banner'.

Hosta 'Lakeside Cha Cha' (Chastain 1994)

MEDIUM

Origin: *H.* 'Fascination' × *H. montana*.

Clump Size & Habit: 27⅛ in. wide × 14 in. high (68 × 35 cm). A semi-upright, open, tiered mound.

Description: Leaf blade: 8⅜ × 6⅜ in. (21 × 16 cm); thick, soft golden-chartreuse widely and irregularly margined creamy white, satiny above and glaucous below, dimpled, widely spaced veins; edge slightly rippled, moderately undulate, widely oval with a cuspidate tip, heart-shaped pinched lobes. Petiole: stout, chartreuse, outlined in cream. Flower: funnel-shaped, pale lavender on an upright, leafy, light green, 28 in. (70 cm) scape in mid- to late summer; sterile.

Comments & Special Needs: Site in morning sun in cooler regions. Lutescent. Leaves gradually assume a bright yellow glow, distinguishing them from *H.* 'Saint Elmo's Fire', which turns from a vivid yellow to a soft green, but the variegation can sometimes disappear.

Hosta 'Lakeside Explosion' (Chastain 1995)

MINIATURE

Origin: Unknown.

Clump Size & Habit: 11 in. wide × 5⅛ in. high (28 × 13 cm). An upward-facing mound.

Description: Leaf blade: 4⅜ × 1 in. (11 × 2.5 cm); of average substance, dark green irregularly margined pure white, satiny above and matt below; edge slightly rippled, lanceolate with an acute tip, tapered open lobes. Petiole: olive-green, outlined in ivory. Flower: tubular, deep purple on an upright, leafy, green, 12 in. (30 cm) scape in late summer; fertile.

Comments & Special Needs: Site in moderate shade all day. Vigorous, so ideal as a small edging plant, but needs to stay in a pot until the roots are well established.

Distinguishing Features: No distinction between the leaf blade and petiole.

Hosta 'Lakeside Kaleidoscope' (Chastain 1994)

SMALL

Origin: Unknown.

Clump Size & Habit: 15 in. wide × 8⅜ in. high (38 × 21 cm). A compact mound.

Description: Leaf blade: 6⅜ × 4 in. (16 × 10 cm); thick, shiny, blue-green, widely and irregularly margined creamy white with many transitional celadon streaks jetting toward the midrib, strongly veined; edge variably undulate, widely oval with a cuspidate tip, heart-shaped pinched lobes. Petiole: blue-green, outlined in creamy white. Flower: tubular,

Hosta 'Lakeside Cha Cha'

Hosta 'Lakeside Explosion'

Hosta 'Lakeside Kaleidoscope'

Hosta 'Lakeside Ninita'

near white on an upright, leafy, green-streaked, 24 in. (60 cm) scape in late summer; fertile.

Comments & Special Needs: Site in shade all day, though tolerant of most conditions. Vigorous and quickly forms clumps. Leaves markedly widen as the plant matures. An extremely attractive small hosta with striking color combinations.

Distinguishing Features: A very wide-feathered margin; sometimes over 50 percent of the leaf is variegated. A superb little hosta making a colorful contribution to the garden.

Hosta 'Lakeside Ninita' (Chastain 1993)

MINIATURE

Origin: *H*. 'Hydon Sunset' sport.

Clump Size & Habit: 12 in. wide × 4 in. high (30 × 10 cm). A dense mound.

Description: Leaf blade: 3⅛ × 2⅜ in. (8 × 6 cm), thin, golden-chartreuse irregularly margined creamy white, with streaks jetting toward the midrib, satiny above and matt below; edges undulate, oval with a cuspidate tip, flat to tapered open lobes. Petiole: short, light green, outlined in cream. Flower: tubular, lavender on an upright, leafy, light green, 15 in. (38 cm) scape in mid-summer; fertile.

Comments & Special Needs: Light to moderate shade all day. Vigorous, quickly forming clumps. Use for edging or pots.

Distinguishing Features: Leaves hold their color throughout the season.

Hosta 'Lakeside Zinger' (Chastain 1998)

SMALL

Origin: Unknown.

Hosta 'Lakeside Zinger'

Clump Size & Habit: 9⅛ in. wide × 6½ in. high (23 × 16.5 cm). A low-growing, dense mound.

Description: Leaf blade: 3⅛ × 1¾ in. (8 × 4.5 cm), thin, smooth, satiny olive-green irregularly margined pure white, with streaks jetting toward the midrib; edge randomly undulate, oval with a cuspidate tip, rounded open lobes. Petiole: shallow, green, clearly outlined in white. Flower: tubular, pale lavender on an upright, dark, leafy, green, 11 to 18 in. (28 to 45 cm) scape in mid-to high summer; fertile.

Comments & Special Needs: Site in good light to moderate shade. A rapid increaser, quickly forming a clump.

Distinguishing Features: Green dots on the leaf margin. Large conspicuous variegated flower bracts.

Hosta 'Leading Lady' (J. & J. Wilkins 1995)

LARGE

Origin: Sport of a *H*. 'William Lachman' seedling.

Clump Size & Habit: 40¾ in. wide × 22⅜ in. high (102 × 56 cm). An upright, moderately dense mound.

Description: Leaf blade: 14 × 10 in. (35 × 25 cm); thick, dark olive-green narrowly and irregularly margined rich golden yellow turning creamy white, satiny above and glaucous below, prominently veined, dimpled and puckered; edge widely undulate, convex toward the cuspidate tip, widely oval with heart-shaped pinched to overlapping

Hosta 'Leading Lady'

lobes. Petiole: narrow, pale green, finely outlined in cream. Flower: tubular, pale lavender on an upright, leafy, glaucous green, 38¾ in. (97 cm) scape in late summer; fertility unknown.

Comments & Special Needs: Site in light to full shade. Of moderate increase. A superb specimen hosta.

Similar: *H. 'Sagae', whose leaves have wider margins.

Hosta 'Leola Fraim' (W. & E. Lachman 1986)

MEDIUM

Origin: *H.* 'Swoosh' hybrid.

Clump Size & Habit: 16¾ in. wide × 10¼ in. high (42 × 26 cm). A symmetrical mound.

Description: Leaf blade: 8⅜ × 6⅜ in. (21 × 16 cm); of good substance, dark gray-green widely and irregularly margined white with some celadon splashing, matt above and glaucous below, seersuckered; edge slightly undulate, cupped or convex, widely oval with a mucronate tip, heart-shaped open to folded lobes. Petiole: flattish, gray-green, outlined in white. Flower: funnel-shaped lavender on an upright, bare, 28 in. (70 cm) scape in late summer; fertile.

Comments & Special Needs: Site in high, filtered shade.

Hosta 'Leola Fraim'

Lovely in a container and for flower arrangements. A moderate increaser.

Distinguishing Features: Is more seersuckered than *H.* 'Minuteman', *H.* 'Patriot' or *H.* 'Trailblazer'. On most leaves the margin is narrower toward the lobes.

Similar: *H.* 'Circle of Light' is about half the leaf size and can tolerate more sun, a full day's sun in northern Virginia in fact; *H.* 'Columbus Circle', which has a slightly narrower margin; **H.* 'Heart's Content'; **H.* 'Mildred Seaver'; **H.* 'Minuteman'; **H.* 'Patriot'; *H.* 'Trailblazer'.

Hosta 'Liberty' (Machen 2000)

LARGE–GIANT

Origin: Tissue-cultured sport of *H.* 'Sagae'.

Clump Size & Habit: 38¾ in. wide × 28 in. high (97 × 70 cm). An upright mound.

Description: Leaf blade: 12⅜ × 9⅛ in. (31 × 23 cm); of good substance, dark blue-green turning green, widely margined golden yellow turning ivory-cream jetting toward the midrib, matt to glaucous above and glaucous below; edge flat, folded, widely oval with a mucronate tip, heart-shaped open to overlapping lobes. Petiole: narrow, green, outlined in cream. Flower: see *H.* 'Sagae'.

Comments & Special Needs: Site in light to moderate shade as a specimen in the border, with plenty of moisture available to encourage the leaf to widen. Slower to increase than its parent and may need extra care to achieve its potential.

Distinguishing Features: The spectacular 2⅜ in. (6 cm) wide margin.

Similar: *H.* 'Ivory Coast', which has rippled edges.

Hosta 'Little Bo Peep' (Kuk 1991)

MINIATURE

Origin: *H.* 'Neat Splash' hybrid.

Clump Size & Habit: 8½ in. wide × 3½ in. high (21.5 × 9 cm). A dense mound.

Description: Leaf blade: 3½ × 1⅛ in. (9 × 3 cm); thin, glossy bright green widely and irregularly margined creamy white, prominently veined; edge with occasional undulations, arching, lanceolate with an acute tip, tapered pinched lobes. Petiole: green, outlined in creamy white. Flower: tubular, rich violet-purple on an upright, leafy, green, 8½ in. (21.5 cm) scape in late summer; fertile with maroon and green striped seedpods.

Comments & Special Needs: Site in light to moderate shade all day. A reasonably rapid increaser. Good in a pot or a sink garden, especially if contrasted with a hosta with heart-shaped leaves of a single color.

Similar: **H.* 'Neat Splash', which is more rhizomatous in habit; *H.* 'Striker'.

Hosta 'Little Bo Peep'

Hosta 'Liberty'

Hosta 'Little Doll'

Hosta 'Little Doll' (K. Vaughn NR)

SMALL–MEDIUM

Origin: *H*. 'Breeder's Choice' × *H*. 'Blue Shadows'.

Clump Size & Habit: 34 in. wide × 15 in. high (85 × 38 cm). An open mound.

Description: Leaf blade: 5½ × 5⅛ in. (14 × 13 cm); thick, blue-green to gray-green, widely and irregularly margined bright yellow turning white by summer, with celadon splashes jetting toward the midrib, matt above and glaucous below, dimpled to seersuckered; edge almost flat, nearly round with a mucronate tip, heart-shaped open to pinched lobes. Petiole: narrow, green, outlined in cream. Flower: flared, pale lavender on an upright, thin, leafy, glaucous mauve, 25⅛ in. (63 cm) scape in mid- to late summer. Fertility unknown.

Comments & Special Needs: Site in light to moderate shade. Moderate growth rate. Pest resistant. A superb specimen for a container, which will set off the beautifully shaped leaves with their striking, sometimes two-toned variegation.

Similar: **H*. 'Peace', which has slightly bluer leaves.

Hosta 'Lovelight' (W. & E. Lachman 1992)

MEDIUM

Origin: *H*. 'Flamboyant' × *H*. 'Banana Sundae'.

Clump Size & Habit: 27⅛ in. wide × 14 in. high (68 × 35 cm). A dense mound.

Description: Leaf blade: 7⅛ × 5⅛ in. (18 × 13 cm); of average substance, light green widely and irregularly margined golden yellow turning ivory with some streaking, glaucous above and matt below, dimpled; edge widely undulate, convex, widely oval with a cuspidate tip, heart-shaped pinched lobes. Petiole: light green, outlined in

ivory. Flower: flaring, pure white on an upright, leafy, light green, 36 in. (90 cm) scape in early summer; fertile.

Comments & Special Needs: Site in good light to moderate shade. A moderate to good increaser.

Distinguishing Features: The hosta with everything. Sinuous undulate leaves framed by a 1½ in. (4 cm) ivory margin echo the pure white flowers and are a lovely contrast to the light green base color. It deserves to be better known.

Hosta 'Mack the Knife' (Dishon 1996)

MINIATURE

Origin: *H*. 'Galaxy' × *H*. 'Hadspen Heron'.

Clump Size & Habit: 15 in. wide × 4¾ in. high (38 × 12 cm). An open mound.

Description: Leaf blade: 5 × 2¾ in. (12 × 2.6 cm) thick, dark green widely and irregularly margined deep golden yellow to almost orange, with paler streaks jetting toward the midrib, satiny above and matt below, slightly dimpled when mature; edge rippled, slightly convex, oval with a cuspidate tip, tapered open to pinched lobes. Petiole: shallow, dark green, outlined in yellow. Flower: funnel-shaped, pale lavender on an upright, bare, green, 13⅛ in. (33 cm) scape in high summer; fertility unknown.

Comments & Special Needs: Site in morning sun in cooler climates, otherwise light to moderate shade. Slow to increase. Best suited to containers or rock gardens.

Distinguishing Features: The orange-yellow margin color fades toward the end of the season.

Hosta 'Merry Sunshine' (Elslager 1998)

MEDIUM

Origin: *H*. 'Fascination' × *H. hypoleuca*.

Hosta 'Lovelight'

Hosta 'Mack The Knife'

Hosta 'Merry Sunshine'

Hosta 'Mike Shadrack'

Clump Size & Habit: 22 in. wide × 12¾ in. high (55 × 32 cm). An upright mound.

Description: Leaf blade: 8⅜ × 6½ in. (21 × 16.5 cm); thick, mid-green irregularly margined ivory with golden overtones, satiny above and thickly glaucous below, seersuckered; edge slightly undulate, slightly arching, widely oval with a mucronate tip, heart-shaped pinched or overlapping lobes. Petiole: green, outlined and streaked ivory. Flower: tubular, purple-striped pale lavender on an upright, leafy, 20 in. (50 cm) scape in early to mid-summer; fertility unknown, green seedpods.

Comments & Special Needs: Site in good light or high, filtered shade. Slow growing, but a newish hosta worth seeking out.

Distinguishing Features: The underside of the leaf is noticeably white.

Similar: *H.* 'June Moon'.

Hosta 'Mike Shadrack' (Kuk 2001)

MEDIUM

Origin: *H.* 'Great Expectations' × *H.* 'Rock and Roll'.

Clump Size & Habit: 24 wide × 18 in. high (60 × 45 cm). A vase-shaped mound.

Description: Leaf blade: 10 × 9⅛ in. (25 × 23 cm); thick, gray-green irregularly margined creamy yellow, with transitional celadon splashes jetting toward the midrib, matt above and glaucous below, seersuckered; edge almost flat, cupped or convex, widely oval to round with a mucronate tip, heart-shaped pinched lobes. Petiole: wide, gray-green, outlined in cream. Flower: widely flared, near white on a stout, upright, leafy, gray-green, 20 in. (50 cm) scape with variegated leaf and flower bracts in mid-summer; fertile, mid-green seedpods.

Comments & Special Needs: Site in good light or high, filtered shade. Moderate growth rate that is increased by copious watering. Pest resistant.

Distinguishing Features: Very showy variegated leaf and flower bracts enhance the already ornamental value of this great new introduction.

Hosta 'Mildred Seaver' (K. Vaughn 1881)

LARGE

Origin: *H.* 'Frances Williams' hybrid.

Clump Size & Habit: 50¾ in. wide × 20 in. high (127 × 50 cm). A dense mound.

Description: Leaf blade: 9⅛ × 8⅜ in. (23 × 21 cm); thick, mid- to dark green widely and irregularly margined bright golden yellow turning ivory-white with some transitional celadon splashes, matt above and thinly glaucous below, moderately seersuckered; edge slightly rippled, slightly arching, widely oval with a cuspidate tip, heart-shaped pinched lobes. Petiole: dark green, outlined in yellow. Flower: funnel-shaped, pale lavender on an upright, leafy, green, 22⅜ in. (56 cm) scape in mid- to late summer; fertile.

Comments & Special Needs: Easily exceeds the registered dimensions given optimum cultivation. Site in light to moderate shade. Of moderate to good increase.

Similar: *H.* 'Crusader'; *H.* 'Fringe Benefit'; *H.* 'Goldbrook Gratis', which has shinier leaves and more uniform margins; *H.* 'Leola Fraim'.

Hosta 'Millie's Memoirs' (Hansen & Shady Oaks Nursery 1999)

MEDIUM

Origin: Tissue-cultured sport of *H.* 'Aspen Gold'.

Hosta 'Mildred Seaver'

Clump Size & Habit: 36 to 40¾ in. wide × 18 to 20 in. high (90 to 102 × 45 to 50 cm). An open mound.

Description: Leaf blade: 9⅛ × 6¾ in. (23 × 17 cm); very thick, mid-green, very widely margined and splashed chartreuse to rich yellow jetting toward the midrib, matt above and glaucous below, intensely seersuckered; edge almost flat, deeply cupped, nearly round with a mucronate tip, heart-shaped overlapping lobes. Petiole: shallow, green, outlined in yellow. Flower: see *H.* 'Aspen Gold'.

Comments & Special Needs: Site in morning sun to turn the margins yellow. However, the more subtle late spring coloring of bluish green leaves with chartreuse margins can be maintained if grown in shade. Very slow to increase but easy to grow in all climates. Pest resistant.

Similar: *H.* 'Aardvark' has the reverse variegation in a muted color contrast; *H.* 'Tranquility'.

Hosta '**Mistress Mabel**' (Lachman 1995)

MEDIUM–LARGE

Origin: (*H.* 'Beatrice' F-6 seedling × *H.* 'Blue Moon') × *H. plantaginea*.

Hosta 'Millie's Memoirs'

Clump Size & Habit: 30 in. wide × 18 in. (75 × 45 cm). A compact mound.

Description: Leaf blade: 8½ × 5¾ in. (21.5 × 14.5 cm); of average substance, mid-green irregularly margined creamy white with many celadon streaks jetting toward the midrib, satiny above and glossy below, widely spaced veins, dimpled; edge rippled, folded, widely oval with a cuspi-

Hosta 'Mistress Mabel'

Hosta montana 'Aureomarginata'

date tip, heart-shaped pinched lobes. Petiole: mid-green, outlined in cream. Flower: tubular, fragrant, pale lavender on a curved, brown-tinted green, 22¾ in. (57 cm) scape in late summer; fertile.

Comments & Special Needs: Site in morning sun in cooler gardens with plenty of moisture available. Moderate growth rate.

Distinguishing Features: A tricolor leaf effect is visible in early summer as the early variegation turns white, a contrast to the yellow variegation on the newer leaves. Rebloom is possible in autumn provided the first spent blooms are cut off at ground level.

Hosta montana 'Aureomarginata' (AHS 1987)

LARGE

Origin: Natural sport of *H. montana*, originally found in Tokyo Prefecture.

Clump Size & Habit: 65⅛ in. wide × 27⅛ in. high (163 × 68 cm). A cascading mound.

Description: Leaf blade: 15 × 8⅜ in. (38 × 21 cm); of average substance, rich dark green, widely and irregularly margined golden yellow to creamy white, depending upon the light available, with light olive-green transitional streaks jetting toward the midrib, matt above and glossy below and rough to the touch, closely spaced veins; edge slightly undulate, arching, oval with a cuspidate tip, heart-shaped pinched to overlapping lobes. Petiole: wide, green, outlined in yellow. Flower: funnel-shaped, pale lavender in a dense raceme on a leaning, leafy, light green, 38⅜ in. (96 cm) scape in mid- to high summer; fertile, producing many seedpods.

Comments & Special Needs: Site in light to moderate shade. Of moderate increase. Although not one of the eas-

Hosta montana 'Mountain Snow'

iest hostas to grow, it is still one of the most outstandingly eye-catching variegated hostas ever introduced. Among the first to emerge in spring; the vulnerable new shoots may need pest protection. Late frosts can also scorch the leaves. Winner of the 1985 Alex J. Summers Distinguished Merit Hosta Award.

Sports: *H.* 'Ebb Tide', which is smaller.

Hosta montana 'Mountain Snow' (T & Z Nursery & Zilis 1988)

LARGE

Origin: Tissue-cultured sport from *H. montana* (Mt. Fuji strain).

Clump Size & Habit: 60 in. wide × 27⅛ in. high (150 × 68 cm). A dense mound.

Description: Leaf blade: 12 × 8⅜ in. (30 × 21 cm); of average substance, smooth, mid- to dark green, narrowly margined pure white, with many celadon streaks jetting to-

Hosta 'Moonlight'

Hosta 'Moon River'

ward the midrib, matt above and shiny below, closely ribbed veins; edge lightly rippled, arching to convex, oval with a cuspidate tip, heart-shaped pinched lobes. Petiole: stout, green, finely outlined in white. Flower: see *H. montana*.

Comments & Special Needs: Site in light to moderate shade as a specimen or in woodland. Of moderate to good increase. Emerges later than most of this species so is not troubled by late frosts. *Hosta* 'Mountain Snow' is prized for the delicate feathered margin in combination with its narrowly furrowed leaf.

Similar: **H.* 'Frosted Jade', which has less white streaking than *H. montana* 'Mountain Snow'; *H.* 'White On'.

Hosta 'Moonlight' (P. Banyai 1977)

LARGE

Origin: Sport of *H.* 'Gold Standard'.

Clump Size & Habit: 50¼ in. wide × 20 in. high (126 × 50 cm). A dense mound.

Description: Leaf blade: 9⅛ × 5⅛ in. (23 × 13 cm); of average substance, olive-green turning chartreuse-yellow irregularly margined pure white, strongly ribbed veins, dimpled when mature; edge slightly rippled, dished or slightly convex, widely oval with a cuspidate tip, heart-shaped open lobes. Petiole: chartreuse-green, outlined in white. Flower: see *H.* 'Fortunei Hyacinthina'.

Comments & Special Needs: Site carefully in good light to light shade since the changes of leaf color over the season are the main attraction. A rapid increaser.

Similar: *H.* 'Moon Glow', which will tolerate some sun; **H.* 'Patriot's Fire'.

Hosta 'Moon River' (W. & E. Lachman 1991)

MEDIUM

Origin: *H.* 'Crepe Suzette' × *H.* 'Blue Moon'.

Clump Size & Habit: 30 in. wide × 10 in. high (75 × 25 cm). A dense, rounded mound.

Description: Leaf blade: 4⅜ × 4 in. (11 × 10 cm); thick, glaucous, dark blue-green irregularly and widely margined yellow turning ivory-white with some streaks jetting toward the midrib, seersuckered; edge flat, shallowly cupped, almost round with a mucronate tip, heart-shaped pinched or overlapping lobes. Petiole: dark green, outlined in cream. Flower: flared lavender on an upright, leafy, 16 in. (40 cm) scape in mid- to late summer; sterile.

Comments & Special Needs: Site in good light to light shade. Slow to increase.

Similar: *H.* 'Cherub', which is slightly smaller and has narrower margins; **H.* 'Pilgrim'.

Hosta 'Olympic Edger' (Naylor Creek Nursery 1999)

SMALL

Origin: Sport of *H.* 'Gold Edger'.

Clump Size & Habit: 12 in. wide × 8⅜ in. high (30 × 21 cm). A diffuse, open mound.

Description: Leaf blade: 4 × 2¾ in. (10 × 7 cm); thick, smooth, apple-green to chartreuse narrowly and irregularly margined cream turning white with transitional yellow streaks jetting toward the midrib; edge almost flat, slightly folded, slightly arched at the tip, oval with tapered pinched lobes. Petiole: narrow, chartreuse. Flower: see *H.* 'Gold Edger'.

Comments & Special Needs: Site in morning sun, then high, filtered shade. A rapid increaser and a superb edging plant, lovely as a foreground to cerise Japanese azaleas.

Hosta 'Olympic Edger'

Hosta 'Opipara Bill Brincka'

Among the very few small yellow hostas that has thin white margins.

Similar: *H.* 'Gold Edger Surprise' has greener leaves with a thin white margin.

Hosta 'Opipara Bill Brincka' (Brincka 1988)

LARGE

Origin: Japan. A clone of *H.* 'Opipara'.

Clump Size & Habit: 60 in. wide × 28 in. high (150 × 70 cm). A rhizomatous, dense, unsymmetrical mound.

Description: Leaf blade: 10 × 8⅜ in. (25 × 21 cm); of good substance, waxy, bright olive-green widely and fairly evenly margined rich yellow turning ivory, slight dimpling when mature; edge undulate to twisted, arching, oval with a cuspidate tip, flat to tapered open lobes. Petiole: shallow, short, olive-green, outlined in cream. Flower: tubular, rich purple striped deep lavender on an upright, leafy, green, 30 in. (75 cm) scape in late summer; fertile.

Comments & Special Needs: Site in light to moderate shade. Flowers are held well above the leaf mound. A rapid increaser. Not suitable for container growing.

Distinguishing Features: *H.* 'Opipara Bill Brincka' is a virus-free clone of *H.* 'Opipara', registered to distinguish it from *H.* 'Opipara', which was originally thought to be virus-prone.

Similar: *H.* 'Opipara Koriyama' is smaller in leaf and stature.

Hosta 'Orange Crush' (Elslager 2000)

MEDIUM

Origin: *H.* 'Sea Prize' × *H.* 'Maekawa'.

Clump Size & Habit: 32¾ in. wide × 24 in. high (82 × 60 cm). An upright mound.

Hosta 'Opipara Koriyama'

Description: Leaf blade: 10¼ × 9⅛ in. (26 × 23 cm); thick, golden yellow widely and irregularly margined creamy white with some streaking or feathering, satiny above and glaucous below, heavily seersuckered; edge slightly rippled, cupped, nearly round with a mucronate tip, heart-shaped lobes. Petiole: narrow, chartreuse with a well-defined cream margin. Flower: tubular, striped pale lavender on an upright, leafy, glaucous green, 18 to 20 in. (45 to 50 cm) scape in late summer; fertile, green seedpods.

Comments & Special Needs: Some morning sun except in the hottest regions then good light to dappled shade. A rapid increaser. Reasonably pest resistant.

Distinguishing Features: Orange-yellow leaves with a noticeably lighter toned midrib rimmed by a 1½ in. (3 cm) margin that is widest toward the petiole. The leaf surface has an attractive pebbled and crumpled texture making this hosta an outstanding new introduction.

Hosta 'Orange Crush'

Hosta 'Parhelion'

Hosta 'Parhelion' (Walters Gardens 1997)

GIANT

Origin: Tissue-cultured sport of *H.* 'Sum and Substance'.

Clump Size & Habit: 60 in. wide × 36 in. high (150 × 90 cm). A dense mound.

Description: Leaf blade: 15 × 12 in. (38 × 30 cm); very thin, bright chartreuse to light green, narrowly and irregularly margined white, shiny above and thinly glaucous below, dimpled to seersuckered; edge gently rippled, shallowly cupped or convex, widely oval with a cuspidate tip, rounded open to pinched lobes. Petiole: narrow, chartreuse, finely outlined in white. Flower: see *H.* 'Sum and Substance'.

Comments & Special Needs: Site in morning sun in cooler climates, otherwise moderate shade. The margin sometimes disappears altogether in parts of the leaf edge. A rapid increaser but not as robust as other sports of *H.* 'Sum and Substance'.

Distinguishing Features: Quite distinct from all other sports of *H.* 'Sum and Substance' because of its thin, pale green leaves and narrow white margin.

Similar: *H.* 'Zebson' has more substance and the margin, from which there is streaking, is wider.

Hosta 'Parky's Prize' (Hawes & Summers 1999)

MEDIUM

Origin: Sport of *H.* 'Birchwood Parky's Gold'.

Clump Size & Habit: 45½ in. wide × 18 in. high (114 × 45 cm). A dense, compact mound.

Description: Leaf blade: 6⅜ × 5⅛ in. (16 × 13 cm); thin to average substance, dark green, crisply margined golden yellow, matt above and slightly glaucous below, dimpled; edge shallowly undulate, oval to round with a mucronate

Hosta 'Parky's Prize'

tip, flat open to pinched lobes. Flower: see 'Birchwood Parky's Gold'.

Comments & Special Needs: Tolerates morning sun in cooler climates although the leaf color will fade. A rich color is maintained in high, filtered light. A rapid increaser that makes a colorful edging plant. Also good in pots.

Distinguishing Features: The reverse-variegated form of *H.* 'Sweet Home Chicago'.

Hosta 'Patrician' (Skrocki & Avent 1991)

MEDIUM

Origin: Unknown but possibly a yellow-margined sport of *H.* 'Decorata'.

Clump Size & Habit: 24 in. wide × 10 in. high (60 × 25 cm). A dense mound.

Description: Leaf blade: 4 × 2 in. (10 × 5 cm); of average substance, matt to satiny, olive-green irregularly margined golden yellow with streaks jetting toward the midrib, dim-

Hosta 'Patrician'

Hosta 'Patriot'

pled when mature, widely ribbed veins; edge moderately rippled, widely oval with an obtuse tip, rounded pinched lobes. Petiole: shallow, green outlined in creamy yellow. Flower: tubular, lavender on an upright, leafy, green, 24 in. (60 cm) scape in late summer; fertile.

Comments & Special Needs: Bright yellow margins will fade if exposed to much direct sunlight. Ideal for landscaping or ground cover.

Similar: *H.* 'Opipara Koriyama'.

Hosta 'Patriot' (Machen 1991)

MEDIUM–LARGE

Origin: Sport of *H.* 'Francee'.

Clump Size & Habit: 50¾ in. wide × 20 in. high (127 × 50 cm). A dense mound.

Description: Leaf blade: 6½ × 5⅛ in. (16.5 × 13 cm); of good substance, dark green, widely and irregularly margined ivory turning white with some celadon streaks jetting toward the midrib, satiny above and glaucous below, dimpled; edge slightly rippled, widely oval with a cuspidate tip, rounded open to pinched lobes. Petiole: dark green, edged in white. Flower: see *H.* 'Francee'.

Comments & Special Needs: Site in good light to moderate shade. It emerges late from rich violet shoots. A moderate to fast increaser. Among the most popular variegated hostas ever introduced, superb in the border and in containers. Named Hosta of the Year by the American Hosta Growers Association in 1997.

Similar: *H.* 'Minuteman', whose leaves are slightly darker green and the margins a purer white, has exceptionally large flowers for a hosta of *H.* 'Fortunei' ancestry; it is slightly smaller at maturity.

Sports: **H.* 'Fire and Ice'; *H.* 'Loyalist'; **H.* 'Patriot's Fire'; *H.* 'Paul Revere'.

Hosta 'Patriot's Fire' (Summers & Walek 1996)

MEDIUM

Origin: Sport of *H.* 'Patriot'.

Clump Size & Habit: 36 in. wide × 20 in. high (90 × 50 cm). An upright mound.

Description: Leaf blade: 8⅜ × 4⅜ in. (21 × 11 cm); of average substance, golden yellow with a narrow, irregular pure white margin with some streaks jetting toward the midrib, matt to satiny above and slightly glaucous below,

Hosta 'Patriot's Fire'

moderately prominent veining, dimpled when mature; edge slightly undulate, cupped, oval with a cuspidate tip, rounded open to pinched lobes. Petiole: chartreuse outlined in white. Flower: see *H.* 'Francee'.

Comments & Special Needs: Site in good light to light shade. A rapid grower, frequently sports to other leaf patterns. Differs from the very similar *H.* 'Moonlight' in having smaller, more elongated leaves that change color earlier.

Distinguishing Features: The variegation is lutescent so there is a wide variation in the leaf coloring between the earlier emerging leaves and those that emerge later in the season.

Similar: **H.* 'Moonlight'.

Hosta 'Peace' (Aden 1987)
SMALL–MEDIUM
Origin: *H.* 'Love Pat' hybrid.
Clump Size & Habit: 9⅛ in. wide × 4⅜ in. high (23 × 11 cm). A neat overlapping mound.
Description: Leaf blade: 5½ × 3½ in. (14 × 9 cm); thick, dark blue-green, irregularly margined cream to white with transitional celadon streaks jetting toward the midrib, matt

above and a powdery bloom below, seersuckered; edge almost flat, slightly cupped, widely oval to nearly round with a mucronate tip, heart-shaped open to pinched lobes. Petiole: narrow, blue-green, outlined in cream. Flower: well-spaced, rich lavender poised at right angles on an upright, glaucous green, 12 in. (30 cm) scape in late summer; fertile.

Comments & Special Needs: Slow to increase but can eventually become larger than its registered dimensions given optimum growing conditions. Pest resistant. The center is bluer if grown in shade, but a magnificent display of flowers emerges if grown in some sun.

Distinguishing Features: Flower scapes stand well above the leaf mound for a hosta of this type, and the flowers are a deeper color.

Similar: **H.* 'Little Doll'.

Hosta 'Pilgrim' (Rasmussen & Malloy 1997)
SMALL
Origin: *H.* 'Flamboyant' seedling.
Clump Size & Habit: 20¾ in. wide × 8⅜ in. high (52 × 21 cm). A dense mound.

Hosta 'Peace'

Description: Leaf blade: 4 × 3⅛ in. (10 × 8 cm); of average substance, matt, gray-green to dark green, widely and irregularly margined golden yellow turning creamy white, ribbed veins; edge flat to occasionally kinked, widely oval with a cuspidate tip, flat to heart-shaped open to pinched lobes. Petiole: green, very finely outlined cream. Flower: tubular, lavender on an upright, bare, dark green, 20¾ in. (52 cm) scape in mid-summer; fertile, green seedpods.

Comments & Special Needs: Site in good light to moderate shade. Vigorous, a rapid increaser, easily exceeding its registered dimensions. An excellent front of the border specimen and good in containers.

Similar: *H.* 'Cherub'; **H.* 'Moon River'.

Sports: *H.* 'Pilgrim's Progress', which has an even more dramatic marginal contrast, having margins that can be up to 2 in. (5 cm) wide.

Hosta 'Pixie Vamp' (D. & J. Ward 1996)

SMALL

Origin: *H.* 'Pin Stripe' hybrid.

Clump Size & Habit: 12 in. wide × 6⅜ in. high (30 × 16 cm). A low-growing, dense mound.

Description: Leaf blade: 2⅜ × 2⅜ in. (6 × 6 cm); of average substance, smooth, dark green, widely and irregularly margined cream to white with many celadon streaks jetting toward the midrib, matt above and satiny below; edge slightly rippled, nearly round with a cuspidate tip, heart-shaped pinched lobes. Petiole: narrow, green, outlined in cream. Flower: funnel-shaped, deep purple from

Hosta 'Pixie Vamp'

Hosta 'Pilgrim'

Hosta 'Pizzazz'

Hosta 'Platinum Tiara'

purple buds on a thin, upright, leafy, mahogany, 12¾ in. (32 cm) scape in high summer; sterile.

Comments & Special Needs: Site in good light to moderate shade. Of slow to average increase. A superb front of the border hosta which deserves to be better known.

Distinguishing Feature: Near black scapes and dark purple buds contrast well with the wide light margins.

Hosta 'Pizzazz' (Aden 1986)

MEDIUM–LARGE

Origin: Unknown.

Clump Size & Habit: 49 in. wide × 21⅛ in. high (122 × 53 cm). An unruly mound.

Description: Leaf blade: 10 × 8⅜ in. (25 × 21 cm); thick, glaucous blue-green irregularly margined yellow turning creamy white with many celadon streaks jetting toward the midrib, seersuckered and puckered; edge rippled, distinctly cupped, nearly round with a mucronate tip, heart-shaped open to pinched lobes. Petiole: paler green, finely outlined in cream. Flower: bell-shaped, near white in a dense raceme on an upright, leafy, glaucous green 25⅛ in. (63 cm) scape from mid- to late summer; fertile.

Comments & Special Needs: Site in light to moderate shade. Slow to increase and not always easy to grow. Pest resistant.

Hosta 'Platinum Tiara' (Walters Gardens 1987)

SMALL–MEDIUM

Origin: Tissue-cultured sport of H. 'Golden Scepter'.

Clump Size & Habit: 36 in. wide × 16 in. high (90 × 40 cm). A dense, overlapping mound.

Description: Leaf blade: 4 × 3½ in. (10 × 9 cm); thin, smooth, chartreuse to golden yellow narrowly margined pure white with occasional streaks jetting toward the midrib, widely spaced veins; edge slightly rippled widely oval

with a cuspidate tip, rounded pinched lobes. Petiole: narrow, chartreuse, finely outlined in white. Flower: see H. 'Golden Tiara'.

Comments: Site in good light to promote the golden yellow base color. Slower growing than many of the other hostas of the Tiara Series making it an ideal pot plant. Winner of the 1989 Alex J. Summers Distinguished Merit Hosta Award.

Similar: *H. 'Olympic Edger'.

Hosta 'Prima Donna' (J. & J. Wilkins 1995)

LARGE

Origin: H. 'William Lachman' sport.

Clump Size & Habit: 56¾ in. wide × 21⅛ in. high (142 × 53 cm). A compact mound.

Description: Leaf blade: 14 × 10 in. (35 × 25 cm); of good substance, dark green with golden yellow margins turning cream, with occasional streaks jetting toward the midrib, satiny above and glaucous below, some puckering when mature, conspicuously veined; edge widely undulate, slightly folded, widely oval with a cuspidate tip, heart-shaped pinched lobes. Petiole: dark green, outlined in yellow. Flower: long, tubular, pale lavender on an upright, glaucous green, 45½ in. (114 cm) scape in late summer; sterile.

Comments & Special Needs: Site in moderate to full shade with plenty of space around it so that the undulating leaves can be fully appreciated. A rapid increaser.

Distinguishing Features: Flower bracts are tricolored cream, green and lavender.

Hosta pulchella 'Kifukurin Ubatake' (hort.)

MINIATURE

Origin: Natural sport of H. pulchella found on Kyushu Island, Miyazaki Prefecture, Japan.

Hosta 'Prima Donna'

Hosta pulchella 'Kifukurin Ubatake'

Hosta 'Queen Josephine'

Clump Size & Habit: 8⅜ to 12 in. wide × 5⅛ in. high (21 to 30 × 13 cm). Somewhat rhizomatous, making an open mound.

Description: Leaf blade: 2¾ × 1⅛ in. (7 × 3 cm); of moderate substance, smooth, light olive-green narrowly margined cream, glossy above and shiny white below; edge rippled, widely lanceolate with an acute tip, tapered open lobes. Petiole: short, lighter green. Flower: widely funnel-shaped, deep lavender on an oblique, purple-tinted, 5⅛ to 12 in. (13 to 30 cm) scape in mid- to late summer; fertile.

Comments & Special Needs: Site in good light to light shade. Best established in a pot before planting out. Ideal for rock gardens.

Hosta 'Queen Josephine' (Kuk 1991)

MEDIUM

Origin: Sport of *H*. 'Josephine'.

Clump Size & Habit: 34 in. wide × 16¾ in. high (85 × 42 cm). A vase-shaped mound.

Description: Leaf blade: 7⅛ × 5½ in. (18 × 14 cm); of

average substance, smooth, satiny dark green evenly and irregularly margined golden yellow turning creamy white, with streaks jetting toward the midrib, conspicuously veined; edge almost flat, oval with an obtuse tip, heart-shaped open to pinched lobes. Petiole: dark green, outlined in yellow. Flower: see *H.* 'Joseph'.

Comments & Special Needs: Site in morning sun in cooler climates, otherwise good light or moderate shade.

Similar: *H.* 'Abiqua Delight'; **H.* 'Antoinette'; **H.* 'Bold Edger'; **H.* 'Cordelia'; **H.* 'Don Stevens'; **H.* 'Emily Dickinson'; **H.* 'Goddess of Athena'.

Hosta 'Regal Splendor' (Walters Gardens 1987)

LARGE

Origin: Tissue-cultured sport of *H.* 'Krossa Regal'.

Clump Size & Habit: 36 in. wide × 34 in. high (90 × 85 cm). A vase-shaped mound.

Description: Leaf blade: 11 × 6¾ in. (28 × 17 cm); thick, glaucous gray-blue irregularly margined yellow to creamy white with some streaks jetting toward the midrib, closely ribbed veins; edge rippled, arching, folded, oval with a cuspidate tip, tapered to pinched lobes. Petiole: light green, outlined in cream. Flower: see *H.* 'Krossa Regal'.

Comments & Special Needs: Site in good light to light shade. Of moderate to good increase. Pest resistant. A striking specimen and superb in antique stone containers giving a quite regal appearance. Named Hosta of the Year by the American Hosta Growers Association in 2003.

Hosta 'Resonance' (Aden 1976)

MEDIUM

Origin: Unknown.

Clump Size & Habit: 30 in. wide × 9⅛ in. high (75 × 23 cm). A spreading mound.

Description: Leaf blade: 6⅜ × 2⅜ in. (16 × 6 cm); thin, dark green, irregularly margined yellow turning creamy white, matt above and shiny below; edge rippled, arching, widely lanceolate, acutely tipped, tapered open lobes. Petiole: dark green, outlined in yellow. Flower: funnel-shaped, lavender on an upright, light green, 20 in. (50 cm) scape in late summer; fertile.

Comments & Special Needs: Site in light to moderate shade. A rapid increaser, making useful ground cover. Not suitable as a pot plant. Very susceptible to pest damage. Much used as a breeding plant.

Similar: **H.* 'Austin Dickinson'; **H.* 'Candy Cane'; **H.*

Hosta 'Regal Splendor'

'Crested Surf'; *H. 'Gay Blade'; H. 'Ground Master', which seems identical; H. 'Suzanne'.

Hosta 'Rhapsody' (Hatfield NR)

MEDIUM–LARGE

Origin: H. 'Fool's Gold' sport.

Clump Size & Habit: 30 in. wide × 15 in. high (75 × 38 cm). A tiered mound.

Description: Leaf blade: 9⅛ × 6½ in. (23 × 16.5 cm); of good substance, sage-green irregularly margined and splashed pure white, matt above and glaucous below, strongly veined, dimpled, puckered; edge undulate, arching, oval with an acute tip, heart-shaped pinched lobes. Petiole: narrow, green, finely outlined in white. Flower: see H. 'Fool's Gold'.

Comments & Special Needs: Light to full shade all day. Like all H. 'Fortunei' hostas, it is a superb border plant and does well in containers.

Similar: H. 'Antioch', which has larger, darker green leaves.

Hosta 'Resonance'

Hosta 'Rhapsody'

Hosta 'Rhino' (Goodwin 2000)

MEDIUM

Origin: H. 'Splashed Leather' sport.

Clump Size & Habit: 30 in. wide × 18 in. high (75 × 45 cm). A dense mound.

Description: Leaf blade: 8⅜ × 4 in. (21 × 10 cm); very thick, mid-green, crisply margined pure white, glossy above and satiny below, dimpled to seersuckered, widely spaced veins; edge almost flat, arching toward the mucronate tip, nearly round with heart-shaped overlapping lobes. Petiole: green, outlined in white. Flower: tubular, lavender on an upright, leafy, 20 to 24 in. (50 to 60 cm) scape in late summer; fertile, green seedpods.

Comments & Special Needs: Very sun tolerant in the North but site in two hours of morning sun in the South. Vigorous, easy to grow. Pest resistant.

Distinguishing Features: The leathery, pebbly surface texture of the leaves has a fancied resemblance to a rhino's skin.

Similar: *H. 'Francee', whose leaves are smoother.

Hosta 'Robert Frost' (W. & E. Lachman 1988)

LARGE

Origin: H. 'Banana Sundae' × H. 'Frances Williams'.

Clump Size & Habit: 42 in. wide × 22¾ in. high (105 × 57 cm). An impressive mound.

Description: Leaf blade: 10 × 8⅜ in. (25 × 21 cm); thick, dark blue-green turning gray-green, widely and irregularly margined creamy white to white with celadon streaks jetting toward the midrib, thinly glaucous above and more glaucous below, dimpled; edge almost flat to slightly rippled, cupped or convex, widely oval with a mucronate tip,

Hosta 'Rhino'

Hosta 'Robert Frost'

Hosta 'Rocky Mountain High'

Hosta rohdeifolia 'Rohdeifolia'

heart-shaped open to pinched lobes. Petiole: flattish, green, outlined in cream. Flower: bell-shaped, near white from pale lavender buds on a thin, upright, leafy, green, 34¾ in. (87 cm) scape in late summer; fertility unknown.

Comments & Special Needs: Site in good light to light shade because the blue-green center of the leaf becomes a matt olive-green if exposed to sun. Of moderate increase. Pest resistant. A background plant where drama is needed.

Distinguishing Features: The striking effect of the wide and splashy creamy white margin outlining the darker center of the leaf.

Similar: *H.* 'Formal Attire'; *H.* 'Heart's Content'.

Hosta 'Rocky Mountain High' (Kuk 1991)

MEDIUM

Origin: *H.* 'Crispula' × *H. sieboldiana*.

Clump Size & Habit: 16 in. wide × 16 in. high (40 × 40 cm). An upright mound.

Description: Leaf blade: 8⅜ × 5½ in. (21 × 14 cm); thick, leathery mid-green irregularly margined chartreuse with streaks jetting toward the midrib, seersuckered to puckered, satiny above and glaucous below; edge closely rippled, arching, convex, widely oval to nearly round with a twisted tip, heart-shaped overlapping lobes. Petiole: stout, wide pale green, outlined in chartreuse. Flower: funnel-shaped, rich lavender on an upright, leafy, pale green, 28 in. (70 cm) scape in early summer; fertile.

Comments & Special Needs: Site in light to moderate shade. Of moderate increase but now known to exceed its registered dimensions. A superb plant and one of the few introductions involving *H.* 'Crispula'.

Distinguishing Features: Leaves with an attractively rippled, strongly pebbled appearance.

Hosta rohdeifolia 'Rohdeifolia' (Maekawa)

SMALL–MEDIUM

Origin: Natural sport of *H. rohdeifolia*, formerly known as *H. helonioides* 'Albopicta'.

Clump Size & Habit: 30 in. wide × 14 in. high (75 × 35 cm). An upright, spreading mound.

Description: Leaf blade: 6½ × 2⅜ in. (16.5 × 6 cm); of average substance, smooth, mid-green irregularly margined yellow turning white, matt above and shiny below; edge almost flat, slightly folded, elliptic with an obtuse tip, tapered open lobes. Petiole: flattish, green, outlined in creamy yellow. Flower: almost bell-shaped, purple striped lavender from a ball-like bud on an upright, leafy, 30 in. (75 cm) scape in late summer; fertile.

Comments & Special Needs: Site in good light to moderate shade. An excellent ground cover but not a rampant increaser.

Distinguishing Features: Leaves have a fancied resemblance to those of *Rohdea japonica* (Japanese name is *Omoto*).

Similar: *H. rectifolia* 'Chionea'.

Hosta 'Sagae'

Hosta 'Sagae' (Watanabe 1996)

LARGE–GIANT

Origin: Formerly known incorrectly as *H. fluctuans* 'Variegated'.

Clump Size & Habit: 71⅛ in. wide × 30 in. high (178 × 75 cm). An impressive mound.

Description: Leaf blade: 14 × 10¼ in. (35 × 26 cm); thick, smooth blue-tinted mid-green turning gray-green, widely and irregularly margined bright yellow turning creamy white by mid-summer with celadon streaks jetting toward the midrib, matt above and glaucous below, widely spaced veins; edge widely undulate, flat to slightly folded, widely oval with a cuspidate tip, heart-shaped open to pinched lobes. Petiole: narrow, green, barely outlined in cream. Flower: funnel-shaped, lavender in profusion on a thick, oblique, leafy, intensely glaucous, 49 in. (122 cm) scape in high to late summer; fertile.

Comments & Special Needs: Site in light to moderate shade. It emerges early and is slow to establish and to show its potential, but eventually makes a huge specimen. A superb, classic hosta. Named Hosta of the Year by the American Hosta Growers Association in 2000. Winner of the 1995 Alex J. Summers Distinguished Merit Hosta Award.

Similar: *H. 'Silk Kimono'; H. 'Victory'.

Sports: *H. 'Ivory Coast' and *H. 'Liberty', which both have wider and thus more dramatic variegation.

Hosta 'Satisfaction' (Wasitis 2000)

LARGE

Origin: Natural sport of *H. 'Piedmont Gold'.

Clump Size & Habit: 49 in. wide × 25⅛ to 30 in. high (122 × 63 to 75 cm). An arching mound.

Description: Leaf blade: 9⅛ × 7⅛ in. (23 × 18 cm); of good substance, satiny, very dark green, widely and irregularly margined rich gold with celadon streaks jetting toward the midrib, closely veined, seersuckered; edge rippled, slightly undulate, arching, widely oval with a cuspidate tip, heart-shaped pinched lobes. Petiole: long, dark green, outlined in yellow. Flower: see *H.* 'Piedmont Gold'.

Hosta 'Satisfaction'

Hosta 'Savannah'

Comments & Special Needs: The leaf base has a slightly blue tint early in the season if sited in good light to moderate shade. A moderate growth rate.

Distinguishing Features: A margin that covers nearly one-third of the leaf blade, up to nearly 2 in. (5 cm), making this a stunningly beautiful hosta.

Similar: *H.* 'Tyler's Treasure'.

Hosta 'Savannah' (Zilis 1999)

MEDIUM–LARGE

Origin: Unknown.

Clump Size & Habit: 60 in. wide × 25⅛ in. high (150 × 63 cm). A dense mound.

Description: Leaf blade: 11 × 7½ in. (28 × 19 cm); of average substance, smooth, olive-green irregularly margined creamy yellow turning white with some streaks jetting toward the midrib, matt above and glossy below; edge slightly rippled, arching toward the cuspidate tip, slightly folded, oval with rounded, pinched lobes. Petiole: narrow, olive-green, finely outlined in cream. Flower: funnel-shaped, somewhat fragrant, lavender on an oblique, leafy, olive-green, 36 in. (90 cm) from late summer to early autumn until the first frosts in cooler climates; fertility unknown.

Comments & Special Needs: Site in morning sun in Northern zones with adequate moisture available. A rapid increaser and therefore suitable for landscaping; also good in containers.

Similar: *H.* 'Edwin Bibby', a slightly streaked useful breeding plant; *H.* 'Summer Fragrance'.

Sports: *H.* 'Savannah Emerald' has green leaves; *H.* 'Savannah Supreme' has streaked leaves.

Hosta 'Scooter'

Hosta 'Scooter' (R. Benedict 1990)

SMALL

Origin: *H.* 'Yellow Splash' hybrid.

Clump Size & Habit: 16 in. wide × 8⅜ in. high (40 × 21 cm). A dense, arching mound.

Description: Leaf blade: 6⅜ × 4 in. (16 × 10 cm); of average substance, dark green widely and irregularly margined creamy white with celadon streaks jetting toward the midrib, matt above and shiny below, dimpled when mature; edge slightly rippled, arching, lanceolate to oval with an acute tip, heart-shaped open lobes. Petiole: very rippled when young, dark green, outlined in cream. Flowers: lavender on a 24 in. (60 cm) scape in late summer.

Comments & Special Needs: Site in light to moderate shade. Early to emerge. Makes excellent ground cover.

Similar: *H.* 'Ground Master' and **H.* 'Resonance', which both have slightly narrower leaves.

Hosta 'Sea Beacon'

Hosta 'Sea Dream'

Hosta 'Sergeant Pepper'

Hosta **'Sea Beacon'** (M. Seaver NR)

MEDIUM

Origin: Unknown.

Clump Size & Habit: 50¾ in. wide × 22 in. high (127 × 55 cm). A dense mound.

Description: Leaf blade: 8⅜ × 5⅛ in. (21 × 13 cm); of good substance, bright green, widely and irregularly margined creamy white to white, with conspicuous streaks jetting toward the midrib, matt above and shiny below, strongly veined, slightly dimpled; edge rippled, arching toward the cuspidate tip, widely oval with heart-shaped pinched lobes. Petiole: narrow, pale green finely outlined in white. Flower: funnel-shaped lavender on an upright, leafy, green, 30 in. (75 cm) scape in late summer; fertility unknown.

Comments & Special Needs: Site in light to moderate shade; lovely in association with blue-leaved hostas.

Hosta **'Sea Dream'** (M. Seaver 1984)

MEDIUM–LARGE

Origin: Open-pollinated *H.* 'Neat Splash' seedling.

Clump Size & Habit: 49 in. wide × 24 in. high (122 × 60 cm). An overlapping mound.

Description: Leaf blade: 9⅛ × 6⅜ in. (23 × 16 cm); of average substance, emerging green, soon turning yellow with a variable narrow ivory-white to pure white margin, matt above and shiny below, dimpled; edge shallowly undulate, arching toward the cuspidate tip, widely oval with heart-shaped open lobes. Petiole: narrow, pale green, very finely outlined in cream. Flowers: funnel-shaped pale lavender from darker buds on an upright, chartreuse, 30 in. (75 cm) scape in late summer; fertility unknown.

Comments & Special Needs: Viridescent. Site in morning sun in Northern zones to achieve the best leaf color, then good light to dappled shade. Thinnish leaves need protection from strong wind. A rapid increaser.

Distinguishing Features: Flowers are held well above the leaf mound.

Similar: **H.* 'Electrum Stater' has heavier substance; *H.* 'Golden Torch', which has thicker, more seersuckered leaves; **H.* 'Saint Elmo's Fire', which is more noticeably seersuckered; **H.* 'Zodiac'.

Sports: *H.* 'Winfield Gold', which has yellow leaves.

Hosta **'Sergeant Pepper'** (Wasitis 2001)

MEDIUM

Origin: Unknown.

Clump Size & Habit: 36 in. wide × 16 in. high (90 × 40 cm). An open mound.

Description: Leaf blade: 6⅜ × 5⅛ in. (16 × 13 cm); thick, matt, bright, pale green very widely and irregularly margined chartreuse turning golden yellow, seersuckered, strongly veined; edge rippled, widely oval with a cuspidate tip, heart-shaped pinched to overlapping lobes. Petiole: olive-green, widely outlined in creamy yellow. Flowers: tubular, lavender-tinted near white on an upright, leafy, green, 22 in. (55 cm) scape in mid-summer; fertility unknown.

Comments & Special Needs: Sun tolerant in most zones, except in the Deep South.

Distinguishing Features: There is more gold margin than green center to the leaf.

Hosta 'Shirley Vaughn' (K. Vaughn NR)

MEDIUM–LARGE

Origin: *H.* 'Breeder's Choice' × *H. pycnophylla*.

Clump Size & Habit: 60 in. wide × 26 in. high (150 × 65 cm). A dense mound.

Description: Leaf blade: 9⅛ × 7⅛ in. (23 × 18 cm); of good substance, smooth, shiny green widely and irregularly margined yellow turning ivory-white, widely spaced veins; edge shallowly undulate, slightly arching, widely oval with a cuspidate tip, tapered pinched lobes. Petiole: narrow, green, finely outlined in white. Flower: tubular, lavender on an upright, leafy, green, 32¾ in. (82 cm) scape in mid- to late summer; fertility unknown.

Comments & Special Needs: Site in good light to moderate shade. A moderate increaser. A worthwhile hosta that deserves to be better known.

Hosta sieboldiana 'Frances Williams' (Williams 1986)

GIANT

Origin: Sport of *H. sieboldiana* 'Elegans'.

Clump Size & Habit: 50¾ in. wide × 32 in. high (127 × 80 cm). A dense mound.

Description: Leaf blade: 12 × 11½ in. (30 × 29 cm); thick, glaucous, blue-green widely and irregularly margined yellow turning creamy beige, seersuckered, strongly veined; edge almost flat, slightly cupped, widely oval to nearly round with a mucronate tip, heart-shaped folded lobes. Petiole: stout, light green, outlined in creamy yellow. Flower: see *H. sieboldiana* 'Elegans'.

Comments & Special Needs: Site in light to moderate shade to prevent the edges scorching. Edges can scorch even in full shade in Southern zones. Impressive in a large container but it will need dividing every three years. Margins are chartreuse, the base color a darker blue if grown in low-light conditions. Slow to establish but nonetheless among the most popular hostas ever introduced. Breeding with *H.* 'Frances Williams' often produces streaked offspring. Winner of the 1986 Alex J. Summers Distinguished Merit Hosta Award.

Similar: *H.* 'Alvatine Taylor', whose longer leaves do not scorch; *H.* 'Aurora Borealis'; *H.* 'Eldorado'; *H.* 'Gilt Edge'; *H.* 'Golden Circles'; *H.* 'Olive Bailey Langdon', whose edges do not scorch; *H.* 'Samurai' appears to be slightly more vigorous, otherwise identical; *H.* 'Wagon Wheels' is similar but smaller and also can scorch at the edges.

Sports: *H.* 'DuPage Delight'; **H.* 'Queen of Islip'.

Hosta sieboldiana 'Northern Exposure' (Walters Gardens 1997)

GIANT

Origin: Tissue-cultured sport of *H. sieboldiana* 'Elegans'.

Clump Size & Habit: 70 in. wide × 36 in. high (175 × 90 cm). A dense mound.

Hosta 'Shirley Vaughn'

Hosta sieboldiana 'Frances Williams'

Description: Leaf blade: 12¾ × 11 in. (32 × 28 cm); thick, glaucous blue-green, widely and irregularly margined cream turning ivory-white, seersuckered; edge almost flat, flat to slightly folded or slightly convex, widely oval with a mucronate tip, heart-shaped overlapping lobes. Petiole: light, green, outlined in cream. Flower: see *H. sieboldiana* 'Elegans'.

Comments & Special Needs: Site in good light to high, filtered shade in cooler climates, otherwise shade all day. Slow to establish but well worth the wait. Pest resistant.

Similar: *H.* 'Frances Williams'; *H.* 'Northern Halo', which has many forms.

Hosta sieboldii 'Paxton's Original' (Paxton NR)
SMALL

Origin: Natural sport of the green-leaved population that is found on moors and meadowlands in many regions of Japan.

Clump Size & Habit: 30 in. wide × 12¾ in. high (75 × 32 cm). A dense, spreading mound.

Description: Leaf blade: 6½ × 2⅜ in. (16.5 × 6 cm); of average substance, smooth, olive-green, narrowly margined pure white with some celadon streaks jetting toward the midrib, widely spaced veins; edge flat to just rippled, flat to arching, elliptic with an obtuse tip, rounded pinched lobes. Petiole: green, finely outlined in white. Flower: widely funnel-shaped, purple-striped lilac on a thin, upright, leafy, 25⅛ in. (63 cm) scape in high to late summer; fertile.

Comments & Special Needs: Site in morning sun or good light to light shade. Easy to grow and eventually spreads into huge clumps. A superb parent for variegated seedlings. Less often seen in domestic gardens since the advent of showier variegated introductions.

Similar: *H.* 'Change of Tradition'; *H.* 'Cotillion'; *H.* 'Gaijin'; *H.* 'Gloriosa'; *H.* 'Silver Lance'.

Hosta 'Silk Kimono' (Gowen & Hansen & Benedict 1999)
LARGE

Origin: *H.* 'Dorothy Benedict' × *H. montana*.

Clump Size & Habit: 60 in. wide × 18 in. high (150 × 45 cm). An upright, tiered mound.

Description: Leaf blade: 12¾ × 9⅛ in. (32 × 23 cm); of good substance, smooth, matt, gray-green widely and irregularly margined creamy white with many celadon streaks jetting toward the midrib, widely spaced veins; edge rippled, undulate, widely oval with a cuspidate tip, heart-shaped pinched lobes. Petiole: sage-green, outlined in cream. Flower: tubular, purple-striped pale lavender on an upright, leafy, green, 36 in. (90 cm) scape in mid- to high summer; fertility unknown, green seedpods.

Comments & Special Needs: Site in light to moderate shade.

Hosta sieboldii 'Paxton's Original'

Hosta sieboldiana 'Northern Exposure'

Hosta 'Silk Kimono'

Distinguishing Features: Leaf tips arch down conspicuously.

Similar: *H. 'Sagae'.

Hosta 'Silverado' (Kuk's Forest 1987)

MEDIUM

Origin: Possible sport of H. 'Lancifolia'.

Clump Size & Habit: 33⅛ in. wide × 12 in. high (83 × 30 cm). An arching mound.

Description: Leaf blade: 6½ × 2 in. (16.5 × 5 cm); thin, mid-green narrowly margined chartreuse turning white, glossy above and shiny below, closely veined; edge rippled, arching, lanceolate with an acute tip, tapered open lobes. Petiole: narrow, green, finely outlined in cream. Flower: funnel-shaped purple on an upright, leafy, green, 24 in. (60 cm) scape in late summer to early autumn; fertility unknown.

Comments & Special Needs: Light to full shade. Lovely in a container.

Distinguishing Features: Flowering earlier than H. 'Lancifolia' and the color is a deeper purple.

Similar: H. 'Gaijin'; H. 'Silver Lance'; H. 'Silver Lining'.

Hosta 'Soft Shoulders' (Avent 1997)

SMALL–MEDIUM

Origin: H. 'Swoosh' × H. 'Tardiflora'.

Clump Size & Habit: 24 in. wide × 10 in. (60 × 25 cm) high. A compact, symmetrical mound.

Description: Leaf blade: 8⅜ × 4 in. (21 × 10 cm); of good substance, satiny mid- to dark green, widely margined golden yellow turning creamy white, prominently veined; edge rippled, slightly arching, widely lanceolate with an acute tip, rounded pinched lobes. Petiole: green,

finely outlined in white. Flower: bell-shaped, lavender on an upright, leafy, green, 22 to 25 in. (55 × 60 cm) scape in late summer; fertile.

Comments & Special Needs: Some morning sun except in Southern zones, then light to full shade if plenty of moisture is available. Grow with lacy ferns.

Hosta 'So Sweet' (Aden 1986)

MEDIUM

Origin: H. 'Fragrant Bouquet' hybrid.

Clump Size & Habit: 22 in. wide × 14 in. high (55 × 38 cm). An open mound.

Description: Leaf blade: 7⅛ × 4⅜ in. (18 × 11 cm); of average substance, mid- to dark green irregularly margined yellow turning creamy white, with light chartreuse streaks jetting toward the tip, satiny above and glossy below; edge slightly undulate to kinked, slightly arching, oval with an acute tip, tapered pinched lobes. Petiole: dark green, outlined in cream. Flower: open funnel-shaped, very fragrant pale lavender on an upright, leafy, green, 22 in. (55 cm) scape in late summer to early autumn; barely fertile.

Comments & Special Needs: Site in morning sun, then good light to light shade. Leaves are much narrower in juvenile plants. Increases rapidly and soon reaches maturity. Superb in containers, especially when sited near the house so that its fragrant flowers, which can last until the frosts in cooler climates, can be appreciated. Named Hosta of the Year by the American Hosta Growers Association in 1996.

Similar: *H. 'Bold Edger'.

Hosta 'Sparky' (Aden 1987)

MINIATURE

Origin: H. 'Amy Aden' × H. pulchella.

Hosta 'Silverado'

Hosta 'So Sweet'

Clump Size & Habit: 8⅜ in. wide × 4 in. high (21 × 10 cm). A congested mound.

Description: Leaf blade: 6⅜ × 1½ in. (16 × 3.5 cm); moderately thick, smooth, matt, mid to dark olive-green irregularly margined creamy yellow to white with some chartreuse streaks jetting toward the midrib; edge conspicuously rippled which distorts the lance-shaped blade, cuspidate tip, tapered open to pinched lobes. Petiole: flattish, clearly outlined in cream. Flower: funnel-shaped, pendulous, purple-striped white on an upright, bare, purple-dotted green 9⅛ in. (23 cm) scape in late summer; fertile.

Comments & Special Needs: Variegation is albescent. Light to moderate shade all day. Moderate to rapid growth rate. A delightful small edging hosta.

Hosta 'Standing Ovation' (Vaughn 1987)

LARGE

Origin: *H.* 'Goliath' hybrid.

Clump Size & Habit: 66 in. wide × 34 in. high (165 × 85 cm). A tiered mound.

Description: Leaf blade: 12 × 10¼ in. (30 × 26 cm); thick, dark green widely and fairly evenly margined golden yellow turning creamy white, matt above and glaucous below, cupped and convex; edge widely rippled, arching widely oval with a cuspidate tip, heart-shaped open lobes. Petiole: stout, dark green, outlined in yellow. Flower: funnel-shaped on an upright, leafy, green, 34 to 40 in. (85 to 100 cm) scape in mid-summer; very fertile.

Hosta 'Sparky'

Hosta 'Soft Shoulders'

Hosta 'Standing Ovation'

Hosta 'Stetson'

Comments & Special Needs: Site in good light to light shade. A better performer than many large hostas of *H. sieboldiana* ancestry in that the wide margin does not scorch.

Distinguishing Features: Scapes stand high above the leaf mound, an unusual characteristic in hostas of this parentage.

Similar: **H.* 'Carnival'; **H.* 'El Capitan'.

Hosta 'Stetson' (Falstad 1997)

MEDIUM

Origin: Tissue-cultured sport of *H.* 'Wide Brim'.

Clump Size & Habit: 25⅛ in. wide × 16 in. high (63 × 40 cm). An open mound.

Description: Leaf blade: 7½ × 6½ in. (19 × 16.5 cm); of good substance, glaucous dark green with a slight blue cast, widely and irregularly margined yellow turning creamy white with celadon streaks jetting toward the midrib; edge slightly undulate and conspicuously furled, widely oval with a cuspidate tip, heart-shaped overlapping lobes. Petiole: dark green, outlined in creamy white. Flower: see *H.* 'Wide Brim'.

Comments & Special Needs: Site in light to moderate shade but not under a tree canopy. A fairly rapid increaser best used as a feature plant in a large container.

Distinguishing Features: The edge is so markedly furled that the glaucous underside of the leaf offers another point of interest.

Sports: *H.* 'Cowrie' is said to have even more markedly upturned leaves.

Hosta 'Stiletto' (Aden 1987)

SMALL

Origin: *H.* 'Amy Aden' × *H. pulchella* 'Kifukurin Ubatake'.

Clump Size & Habit: 32 in. wide × 12 in. (80 × 30 cm) high. A low, cascading, dense mound.

Hosta 'Stiletto'

Description: Leaf blade: 5½ × 1½ in. (14 × 4 cm); thin, satiny, mid to dark olive-green narrowly margined yellow to creamy white, a hint of dimpling on mature leaves, prominently veined; edge distinctly rippled, slightly arching, lanceolate with an acute tip, no junction between the blade and the petiole. Petiole: ripple-edged, flattish, green, outlined in cream. Flower: slightly bell-shaped, purple-striped on an upright, thin, leafy, green, 25⅛ in. (63 cm) scape in mid- to late summer; fertile.

Comments & Special Needs: Good light to moderate shade all day. An excellent edging or ground cover hosta that increases rapidly. Needs dividing every four to five years to retain the rippled edges.

Distinguishing Features: The intense rippling becomes less marked as the hosta matures.

Similar: **H.* 'Crested Surf', which has wider leaves; **H.* 'Wiggle Worms', which has narrower leaves.

Sports: *H.* 'Boogie Woogie' is a streaked form.

Hosta 'Sugar and Cream' (Zilis 1984)

MEDIUM–LARGE

Origin: Tissue-cultured sport of *H*. 'Honeybells'.

Clump Size & Habit: 50¾ in. wide × 24 in. high (127 × 60 cm). A dense mound.

Description: Leaf blade: 11 × 5½ in. (28 × 14 cm); of average substance, olive-green irregularly margined creamy yellow turning white, satiny above and glossy below, widely spaced veins; edge rippled, arching downward toward the pinched tip, elliptic to oval with rounded lobes. Petiole: olive-green, finely outlined in cream. Flower: see *H*. 'Honeybells'.

Comments & Special Needs: Tolerates sun in most regions provided it is amply supplied with moisture, though the leaf color will fade considerably. In the South, morning sun only. Increases rapidly, covering large areas. A useful landscaping hosta that has been superseded by newer introductions for garden use. Sweetly fragrant flowers are a bonus.

Similar: *H*. 'Savannah'; *H*. 'Summer Fragrance', whose variegated margins are narrower and remain more yellow.

Hosta 'Sugar and Cream'

Hosta 'Sultana' (Zumbar 1988)

SMALL

Origin: Sport of *H*. 'Little Aurora'.

Clump Size & Habit: 30 in. wide × 16 in. high (75 × 40 cm). A compact mound.

Description: Leaf blade: 5½ × 4⅜ in. (14 × 11 cm); thick, dark green, widely margined rich yellow turning

Hosta 'Sultana'

creamy white, oval to heart-shaped closely seersuckered dark green leaves with very wide bright golden margins, satiny above and thinly glaucous below, seersuckered when mature; edge almost flat to slightly kinked, shallowly cupped or convex, widely oval with a cuspidate tip, heart-shaped pinched lobes. Petiole: narrow, outlined in yellow. Flower: see *H.* 'Little Aurora'.

Comments & Special Needs: Site in morning sun in Northern zones, otherwise light to moderate shade. Slow to moderate increase. Pest resistant. A most strikingly variegated small hosta suitable as a specimen plant for the border or a container.

Distinguishing Features: Scapes bear attractively variegated leafy bracts.

Hosta 'Summer Breeze' (Zilis-Diesen 1999)

MEDIUM–LARGE

Origin: Sport of *H.* 'Summer Music'.

Clump Size & Habit: 50¾ in. wide × 22 in. high (127 × 55 cm). An open mound.

Description: Leaf blade: 8½ × 7⅛ in. (21.5 × 18 cm); thin, dark green widely and irregularly margined and splashed chartreuse-yellow, matt above and satiny below, dimpled to moderately seersuckered; edge occasionally undulate, lightly wavy, widely oval with a mucronate tip, heart-shaped pinched lobes. Petiole: short, wide, green, outlined in chartreuse. Flower: see *H.* 'Summer Music'.

Comments & Special Needs: Light to moderate shade all day to produce the best leaf color. A moderately rapid increaser. Susceptible to pest damage.

Hosta 'Sundance' (Walters Gardens 1984)

MEDIUM

Origin: Tissue-cultured sport of *H.* 'Aoki'.

Clump Size & Habit: 36 in. wide × 22 in. high (90 × 55 cm). A dense mound.

Description: Leaf blade: 9⅛ × 5⅛ in. (23 × 13 cm); of good substance, gray-green, with blue overtones in early summer, irregularly margined creamy yellow turning ivory-white with some celadon streaks jetting toward the midrib, matt above and glaucous below, dimpled to seersuckered; edge slightly rippled, convex to arching, widely oval with a cuspidate tip, heart-shaped pinched to folded lobes. Petiole: dark green, outlined in cream. Flower: funnel-shaped, lavender-gray on an upright, leafy, green, 36 in. (90 cm) scape in high summer; fertility unknown.

Comments & Special Needs: Site in two hours of morning sun in Northern zones. Variegation will alter in color with different light levels, remaining more yellow in deeper shade.

Distinguishing Features: The variegated leafy bracts are conspicuously large.

Hosta 'Sunny Smiles' (Tompkins 2001)

MEDIUM

Origin: Unknown.

Clump Size & Habit: 50¾ in. wide × 18 in. high (127 × 45 cm). A compact mound.

Description: Leaf blade: 9⅛ × 8⅜ in. (23 × 21 cm); thick, satiny, light green to chartreuse-yellow widely and irregularly margined creamy yellow turning white, with streaks jetting toward the midrib, seersuckered, widely spaced veins; edge widely undulate, twisted at the cuspidate tip, widely undulate with rounded to heart-shaped open lobes. Petiole: light green, outlined in creamy white. Flower: widely bell-shaped, pale lavender on an upright, bare, chartreuse, 24 in. (60 cm) scape from mid- to late summer; fertility unknown.

Comments & Special Needs: Morning sun in Northern zones will give the brightest leaf color contrast. Of moderate increase.

Hosta 'Summer Breeze'

Hosta 'Sundance'

Similar: *H.* 'Shade Fanfare' has a smoother leaf surface and needs more shade; *H.* 'Verna Jean' is smaller.

Hosta 'Sweetie' (Aden 1988)

MEDIUM

Origin: *H.* 'Fragrant Bouquet' × *H.* 'Fragrant Candelabra'.

Size & Habit: 30 in. wide × 20 in. high (75 × 50 cm). An unruly mound.

Description: Leaf blade: 8⅜ × 5⅛ in. (21 × 13 cm); of average substance, yellow turning bright chartreuse, widely and irregularly margined ivory to white, satiny above and thinly glaucous below, ribbed veins, some dimpling when mature; edge conspicuously undulate, arching with a cuspidate tip, oval with heart-shaped overlapping lobes. Petiole: pale green, outlined in ivory. Flowers: funnel-shaped, white on an upright, leafy, green, 32 in. (80 cm) scape in late summer; fertile.

Comments & Special Needs: Viridescent. Leaves will stay yellow longer if grown in sun for most of the day. Vigorous. Moisture at the roots is essential especially in hotter climates.

Hosta 'Sunny Smiles'

Distinguishing Features: Leaves are longer and narrower than those of *H.* 'Fragrant Bouquet'.

Similar: *H.* 'Sugar and Cream', whose leaves are greener and less undulate.

Hosta 'Tambourine' (W. & E. Lachman 1987)

MEDIUM

Origin: (*H.* 'Resonance' × seedling) × *H.* 'Halcyon'.

Clump Size & Habit: 24 in. wide × 13⅛ in. high (60 × 33 cm). A dense mound.

Description: Leaf blade: 6⅜ × 5⅛ in. (16 × 13 cm); of good substance, mid-green widely and irregularly margined yellow turning ivory to pure white with chartreuse streaks jetting toward the midrib, satiny above and thinly glaucous below, dimpled, widely spaced veins; edge almost flat, widely oval with an acute tip, flat to heart-shaped pinched lobes. Petiole: narrow, dark green outlined in ivory, rosy mauve backed. Flower: funnel-shaped, lavender in a dense raceme on an upright, leafy, green, 20 in. (50 cm) scape in late summer; fertile.

Comments & Special Needs: Leaves will assume a blue-green overtone if grown in good light but not direct sun. Increases rapidly and will make good ground cover.

Distinguishing Features: The tightly packed leaf mound causes the edges to turn up.

Similar: *H.* 'Bold Edger'; *H.* 'Emily Dickinson'; *H.* 'Torchlight'.

Hosta 'Tea and Crumpets' (W. & E. Lachman NR)

SMALL

Origin: "*H.* 'Carnival' seedling" × *H.* 'Crepe Suzette' seedling.

Clump Size & Habit: 16 in. wide × 10 in. high (40 × 25 cm). An open mound.

Hosta 'Sweetie'

Hosta 'Tambourine'

Description: Leaf blade: 5⅛ × 4⅜ in. (13 × 11 cm); thick, dark sage-green, irregularly margined creamy white, matt above and glaucous below, seersuckered; edge almost flat, shallowly cupped, nearly round with flat open to pinched lobes. Petiole: shallow dark green, outlined in cream. Flower: tubular, dark lavender on a thick, upright, leafy, glaucous purple, 12 to 16 in. (30 to 40 cm) scape that has variegated leafy bracts from mid- to late summer; fertile.

Hosta 'Tea and Crumpets'

Comments & Special Needs: Site in good light to moderate shade. Suitable for the front of a border or in a container.

Distinguishing Features: Leaves are unusually spoon-shaped.

Similar: *H. 'Coquette'; H. 'Cream Cheese'; *H. 'Crepe Suzette'.

Sports: H. 'Champagne and Caviar'.

Hosta 'Thumbelina' (D. & J. Ward 1996)

MINIATURE–SMALL

Origin: Seedling of H. 'Pin Stripe Sister'.

Clump Size & Habit: 14 in. wide × 8⅜ in. high (35 × 21 cm). A small, tight mound.

Description: Leaf blade: 3⅛ × 2 in. (8 × 5 cm); of average substance, smooth, mid-green with an irregular creamy white margin with some streaks jetting toward the midrib, matt above and slightly shiny below; edge almost flat, oval with a cuspidate tip, rounded open lobes. Petiole: shallow, green, outlined in cream. Flower: tubular, pale lavender on an upright, green 3⅛ in. (8 cm) scape in mid-summer; fertility unknown.

Hosta 'Thumbelina'

Comments & Special Needs: Good light shade. Moderate growth rate. Best suited to rock gardens, gravel gardens or containers.

Hosta 'Thumbs Up' (Schwarz 1999)

MINIATURE

Origin: Sport of *H.* 'Achy Breaky Heart'.

Clump Size & Habit: 14 in. wide × 12 in. high ($35 × 30$ cm). An upright mound.

Description: Leaf blade: $4 × 3⅛$ in. ($10 × 8$ cm); of average substance, satiny, mid-green irregularly margined cream turning pure white with some streaks jetting toward the midrib, slight dimpling; edge flat, oval with a cuspidate tip, rounded pinched lobes. Petiole: short, green, outlined in white. Flower: tubular, lavender on an upright, bare, green, 16 to 20 in. (40 to 60 cm) scape in high summer; fertile, green seedpods.

Comments & Special Needs: Site in good light to moderate shade in a container, gravel or rock garden leaving plenty of space to emphasize the upright habit of the leaves. Of slow to moderate increase.

Hosta 'Tokudama Flavocircinalis' (Maekawa & AHS 1987)

MEDIUM

Origin: Natural sport of *H.* 'Tokudama'.

Clump Size & Habit: 49 in. wide × 16¾ in. high ($122 × 42$ cm). An open mound.

Description: Leaf blade: $7½ × 5½$ in. ($19 × 14$ cm); thick, glaucous blue with a wide irregular yellow to beige margin with streaks jetting toward the midrib, seersuckered; edge flat to slightly undulate, shallowly cupped, widely oval with a cuspidate tip, round pinched lobes. Pet-

iole: blue-green, outlined in yellow. Flower: see *H.* 'Tokudama'.

Comments & Special Needs: Site in light to moderate shade. Slow to increase. Pest resistant. A classic hosta which does not scorch at the margins.

Similar: *H.* 'Fleeta Brownell Woodroffe'; **H.* 'Jack of Diamonds'; *H.* 'Sunnybrook'.

Hosta 'Tom Schmid' (Schmid 1995)

MEDIUM–LARGE

Origin: Sport of *H.* 'Krossa Regal'.

Clump Size & Habit: 36 in. wide × 25⅛ in. high ($90 × 63$ cm). An upright mound.

Description: Leaf blade: $11½ × 7½$ in. ($29 × 19$ cm); thick, emerges gray-blue turning dark green by mid-summer widely and irregularly margined white, matt above and glaucous below, closely ribbed veins, dimpled; edge rippled, slightly folded, oval with a cuspidate tip, rounded

Hosta 'Tokudama Flavocircinalis'

Hosta 'Thumbs Up'

Hosta 'Tom Schmid'

pinched lobes. Petiole: stout, glaucous, pale green. Flower: see *H.* 'Krossa Regal'.

Comments & Special Needs: Site in good light to full shade all day. A moderate to rapid increaser. A border specimen and superb in a large container.

Similar: **H.* 'Regal Splendor', which has much wider margins.

Hosta 'Torchlight' (W. & E. Lachman 1990)

MEDIUM

Origin: *H.* 'Halcyon' hybrid.

Clump Size & Habit: 34 in. wide × 14 in. high (85 × 35 cm). An upright or vase-shaped mound.

Description: Leaf blade: 5½ × 4⅜ in. (14 × 11 cm); of good substance, dark olive-green, irregularly margined ivory turning white, with chartreuse streaks jetting toward the midrib, satiny above and shiny below, widely spaced veins, scarcely dimpled; edge widely rippled, slightly cupped, almost round with a cuspidate tip, heart-shaped open lobes. Petiole: narrow, olive-green outlined in ivory, red-streaked along the back and toward the base in the channeling. Flower: flared, funnel-shaped, rich lavender on an upright, leafy, dark green 22 in. (55 cm) scape in late summer; fertile, green seedpods.

Comments & Special Needs: A superb hosta needing light to full shade. Good growth rate. Plant as a specimen with contrasting foliage, such as ferns or grasses. Equally good in a container.

Distinguishing Feature: Burgundy-red petioles from the crown into the base of the leaf. Densely red-dotted scapes from the crown into the base of flower bud, white-margined, green, leafy bracts each containing a flower bud evenly spaced along the scape.

Similar: **H.* 'Chantilly Lace'; **H.* 'Tambourine' similar but larger.

Hosta 'Toy Soldier' (Solberg 2001)

SMALL

Origin: Tissue-cultured sport of *H.* 'Blue Cadet'.

Clump Size & Habit: 24 in. wide × 10 in. high (60 × 25 cm). A compact mound.

Description: Leaf blade: 4 × 3½ in. (10 × 9 cm); thick, glaucous blue-green irregularly margined chartreuse and creamy white, strongly marked veins, slight dimpling; edge randomly undulate, flat widely oval with a mucronate tip, heart-shaped open lobes. Petiole: narrow, blue-green, outlined in creamy chartreuse.

Comments & Special Needs: Site in light to moderate shade all day to preserve the subtle leaf coloring. A rapid increaser. Lovely with lacy ferns.

Distinguishing Features: A fascinating and quite distinct bicolored leaf margin, the outer margin chartreuse with white transitional feathering, the colors strengthening as the summer progresses.

Hosta 'Triumph' (Tower 2002)

LARGE–GIANT

Origin: *H.* 'Color Fantasy' hybrid.

Clump Size & Habit: 50¾ in. wide × 30 in. high (127 × 75 cm). A dense mound.

Description: Leaf blade: 15 × 12 in. (38 × 30 cm); of good substance, dark green widely and irregularly margined creamy white with transitional chartreuse streaks jetting toward the midrib, satiny above and glaucous below, some dimpling when mature; edge slightly undulate, widely oval with a cuspidate tip, heart-shaped pinched lobes. Petiole:

Hosta 'Torchlight'

Hosta 'Toy Soldier'

dark green, outlined in creamy white. Flower: funnel-shaped, pale lavender on an upright, leafy, green, 36 in. (90 cm) scape in high summer; fertility unknown.

Comments & Special Needs: Grow in good light to high, filtered shade with plenty of moisture to boost the already wide margins. A superb new introduction.

Distinguishing Features: Showy, wide leaf margins.

Hosta 'Twilight' (Van Eijk-Bos & Van Buren & Van Erven 1997)
MEDIUM

Origin: Tissue-cultured sport of *H.* 'Fortunei Aureomarginata'.

Clump Size & Habit: 32 in. wide × 20 in. high (80 × 50 cm). An open mound of elegantly poised leaves.

Description: Leaf blade: 10 × 7½ in. (25 × 19 cm); very thick, leathery, very dark green widely and irregularly margined creamy yellow with light olive-green streaks jetting toward the midrib, satiny above and matt below, strongly veined, slightly dimpled; edge slightly undulate, oval to

Hosta 'Triumph'

Hosta 'Twilight'

round with a cuspidate tip, rounded open to pinched lobes. Petiole: narrow, dark olive-green, finely outlined cream. Flower: see *H.* 'Fortunei Aureomarginata'.

Comments & Special Needs: Site in light to moderate shade. Of moderate to good increase. Pest resistant. Plant with *H.* 'Bowles Golden Grass', whose seeming fragility is a perfect foil for this bold hosta.

Distinguishing Features: Among the most striking green-leaved hostas with creamy yellow margins to be introduced. Exceptionally thick leaf substance. A tetraploid having higher fertility than the parent plant.

Similar: **H.* 'Fortunei Aureomarginata'; *H.* 'Anne', which is similar and possibly larger.

Sports: *H.* 'Morning Light'.

Hosta 'Unchained Melody' (J. & S. Wilkins 2002)
GIANT

Origin: *H.* 'Elatior' hybrid.

Clump Size & Habit: 60 in. wide × 29 in. high (150 × 74). A billowing mound.

Description: Leaf blade: 14 × 11½ in. (35 × 29 cm); of good substance, satiny sage-green irregularly margined greenish creamy white, dimpled; edge lightly rippled, shallowly cupped or convex, widely oval with a cuspidate tip, heart-shaped pinched lobes. Petiole: green, outlined in white. Flower: bell-shaped, near white on a thin, arching, leafy, light green, 36 to 42 in. (90 to 105 cm) scape in midsummer; fertile, green seedpods.

Comments & Special Needs: Site in light to moderate shade. Moderate growth rate. Pest resistant. A striking, recently introduced hosta which has a great future as a specimen plant.

Similar: *H.* 'Sagae'.

Hosta 'Unchained Melody'

Hosta 'Undulata Albomarginata'

Hosta 'Unforgettable'

Hosta 'Undulata Albomarginata' (AHS 1987)

MEDIUM–LARGE

Origin: Natural sport of *H.* 'Undulata'.

Clump Size & Habit: 36 in. wide × 18 in. high (90 × 45 cm). A dense mound.

Description: Leaf blade: 7⅛ × 4⅜ in. (18 × 11 cm); thin, mid-green irregularly margined ivory-white with transitional celadon splashing, matt above and glossy below, slightly dimpled when mature; edge slightly rippled, elliptic with a curved cuspidate tip, rounded pinched lobes. Petiole: green, outlined in ivory. Flower: see *H.* 'Undulata'.

Comments & Special Needs: Site in light to moderate shade. Vigorous. Adaptable to many situations, especially useful for covering large areas. Susceptible to pest damage.

Distinguishing Features: Often confused with *H.* 'Crispula', whose leaves are much more twisted and undulate.

Sports: *H.* 'Undulata Erromena', which has slightly wider, green leaves.

Hosta 'Unforgettable' (Kuk 1999)

MEDIUM–LARGE

Origin: Sport from the cross of *H.* 'Gold Regal' × 'Golden Medallion'.

Clump Size & Habit: 24 in. wide × 22 in. high (60 × 55 cm). An upright mound.

Description: Leaf blade: 8½ × 7⅛ in. (21.5 × 18 cm); thick, dark green widely margined and splashed chartreuse turning golden yellow with streaks jetting toward the midrib, satiny above and glaucous below, dimpled; edge slightly rippled, folded or convex, oval with a mucronate tip, rounded pinched lobes. Petiole: green, outlined in yellow. Flower: tubular, lavender on a stout, upright, green,

31½ in. (79 cm) scape in high summer; fertile, green seedpods.

Comments & Special Needs: Site in good light to light shade. A moderate growth rate. The contrast between the marginal variegation and the darker leaf blade is exceptionally striking. A superb introduction. Pest resistant.

Hosta ventricosa 'Aureomarginata' (Hensen & AHS 1987)

MEDIUM–LARGE

Origin: Natural sport of *H. ventricosa*.

Clump Size & Habit: 45½ in. wide × 22 in. high (114 × 55 cm). An overlapping mound.

Description: Leaf blade: 10 × 9⅛ in. (25 × 23 cm); thin, glossy, dark spinach green widely and irregularly margined yellow turning creamy white with streaks jetting toward the midrib, dimpled when mature; edge rippled, oval with a cuspidate tip, heart-shaped pinched to overlapping lobes. Petiole: dark green, outlined in yellow. Flower: see *H. ventricosa*.

Comments & Special Needs: Full shade all day. Of slow to moderate increase. Susceptible to pest damage.

Distinguishing Features: A classic hosta which has never been surpassed in beauty of leaf and flower.

Hosta 'Vera Verde' (Aden & Klehm Nursery 1990)

SMALL

Origin: Sport of *H. gracillima*.

Clump Size & Habit: 26 in. wide × 12¾ in. high (65 × 32 cm). A rhizomatous, diffuse mound.

Description: Leaf blade: 4 × 1½ in. (10 × 3.5 cm); leathery, satiny, mid-green narrowly margined creamy yellow to ivory-white; edge randomly rippled, linear to lanceolate

Hosta ventricosa 'Aureomarginata'

Hosta 'Vera Verde'

Hosta 'Veronica Lake'

with a curved acute tip, very tapered open lobes. Petiole: narrow, green. Flower: funnel-shaped lavender on an upright, bare, pale green, 28 in. (70 cm) scape in high to late summer; fertility unknown.

Comments & Special Needs: Site in good light to light shade. Vigorous. Will cover a large area quickly.

Distinguishing Features: Leaves flatten at the edge, and widen as the plant matures.

Similar: *H. gracillima* 'Kifukurin Ko Mame', which is smaller and has more pointed leaves.

Sports: *H.* 'Cheesecake' is an unstable, centrally variegated sport.

Hosta 'Veronica Lake' (Riehl 1993)

SMALL–MEDIUM

Origin: Sport of *H.* 'Pearl Lake'.

Clump Size & Habit: 42 in. wide × 18 in. high (105 × 45 cm). A dense mound.

Description: Leaf blade: 5⅛ × 4 in. (13 × 10 cm); of average substance, gray-green irregularly margined yellow turning cream, matt above and glaucous below, some dimpling when mature; edge occasionally kinked, slightly folded, widely oval with a mucronate tip, heart-shaped pinched lobes. Petiole: narrow, gray-green, outlined in cream. Flower: see *H.* 'Pearl Lake'.

Comments & Special Needs: Leaves fade to cream with an ivory margin if exposed to bright light or sunlight; the more subtle and attractive coloring is therefore achieved if grown in fairly low light or dappled shade. A foreground specimen and lovely in a pot. A rapid increaser.

Distinguishing Features: The overlapping dome-shaped mound with many scapes towering above.

Hosta 'Warwick Choice' (Jones 1993)

LARGE

Origin: *H.* 'William Lachman' selfed.

Clump Size & Habit: 49 in. wide × 22 in. high (122 × 55 cm). A symmetrical, dome-shaped mound.

Description: Leaf blade: 10 × 8⅜ in. (25 × 21 cm); thick, mid-green widely and irregularly margined bright golden yellow turning pure white, satiny above and matt below, ribbed veins; edge flat near the base and slightly rippled to-

Hosta 'Warwick Choice'

ward the cuspidate tip, widely oval with heart-shaped pinched to overlapping lobes. Petiole: dark green outlined in cream. Flower: tubular, near white on an upright, leafy, green, 38⅜ in. (96 cm) scape in mid-summer; fertile.

Comments & Special Needs: Site in light to moderate shade as a background specimen or in a shrub border. Of moderate increase.

Hosta 'Warwick Curtsey' (L. Jones NR)

SMALL

Origin: *H.* 'Dorothy Benedict' × *H. nakaiana*.

Clump Size & Habit: 37 in. wide × 15 in. high (92.5 × 38 cm). A neat mound.

Description: Leaf blade: 5⅛ × 4 in. (13 × 11 cm); of good substance, dark blue-green turning green, irregularly margined and splashed yellow turning cream, matt above and thinly glaucous below, dimpled when mature; edge nearly flat, flat to slightly convex, widely oval with a mucronate tip, heart-shaped open to pinched lobes. Petiole: thin, dark green outlined in cream. Flower: long, funnel-shaped, lavender on an upright, thin, leafy, dark green, 26 in. (65 cm) scape in mid-summer; fertility unknown.

Hosta 'Warwick Curtsey'

Comments & Special Needs: Site in good light to moderate shade. A rapid increaser producing well-proportioned clumps. A foreground specimen but also very effective in a large container.

Similar: *H.* 'Veronica Lake'.

Hosta 'Warwick Edge'

Hosta 'Warwick Sheen'

Hosta 'Warwick Edge' (L. Jones 1993)

SMALL–MEDIUM

Origin: *H.* 'William Lachman' × *H. nakaiana*.

Clump Size & Habit: 30 in. wide × 16 in. high (75 × 40 cm). A dense, neat mound.

Description: Leaf blade: 6⅜ × 5⅛ in. (16 × 13 cm); thick, matt blue-green irregularly margined pure white with some celadon streaks jetting toward the midrib, dimpled, moderately prominently veined; edge smooth, slightly folded, near round with a mucronate tip, flat open lobes. Petiole: narrow, green, finely outlined in white. Flower: tubular, purple on an upright green 14 in. (35 cm) scape in mid-summer; fertile.

Comments & Special Needs: Site in light to moderate shade all day. Vigorous. A superb foreground or container plant.

Hosta 'Warwick Sheen' (L. Jones NR)

MEDIUM

Origin: *H.* 'Christmas Tree' × *H.* 'Leather Sheen'.

Clump Size & Habit: 30 in. wide × 16 in. high (75 × 40 cm). Neat, open, nearly horizontal mound.

Description: Leaf blade: 5⅛ × 3½ in. (13 × 9 cm); thick, leathery, dark olive-green, almost evenly margined deep cream turning white with some celadon streaks jetting toward the midrib, satiny above and matt below, widely spaced veins, some dimpling when mature; edge slightly rippled, folded toward the base, oval with an acute tip, tapered open lobes. Petiole: flat, short, green, outlined in creamy white. Flower: bell-shaped, pale lavender on an upright, bare green 28 in. (70 cm) scape in high summer; fertility unknown.

Comments & Special Needs: Site in morning sun to light

Hosta 'Waving Winds'

shade in Northern zones. Vigorous, a rapid increaser. Pest resistant. Plant as a foreground specimen or in a gravel garden.

Distinguishing Features: Leaf surface has a rough but oily sheen, the outer leaves being more glossy and darker green.

Hosta 'Waving Winds' (W. & E. Lachman 1991)

MEDIUM

Origin: *H.* 'Galaxy' selfed.

Clump Size & Habit: 20 in. wide × 11 in. high (50 × 28 cm). An upright, unruly mound.

Description: Leaf blade: 6½ × 3½ in. (16.5 × 9 cm); thick, mid- to dark green, with a blue cast until mid-summer, irregularly margined and splashed yellow to ivory, matt above and thinly glaucous below, widely ribbed veins; edge widely undulate, slightly twisted, arching, lanceolate to elliptic with an acute tip, tapered pinched lobes. Petiole:

long, narrow, arching, dark green, outlined in cream. Flower: flared, lavender on an upright, leafy, green, 37½ in. (94 cm) scape in late summer; fertile.

Comments & Special Needs: Site in light to moderate shade. A rapid increaser and easy to propagate and cultivate.

Distinguishing Features: Leaves have a striking, restless habit.

Hosta 'Wide Brim' (Aden 1979)

MEDIUM

Origin: H. 'Bold One' × H. 'Bold Ribbons'.

Clump Size & Habit: 45½ in. wide × 18 in. high (114 × 45 cm). A dome-shaped mound.

Description: Leaf blade: 8⅜ × 6⅜ in. (21 × 16 cm); of good substance, dark green with a blue cast, widely and irregularly margined pale yellow to cream with streaks jetting toward the midrib, matt to glaucous above and thinly glaucous below, dimpled; flat to slightly folded, widely oval with a cuspidate tip, heart-shaped pinched lobes. Petiole: dark green, outlined in cream. Flower: funnel-shaped, violet-striped pale lavender in a dense raceme from attractive pale lavender-gray buds on an upright, bare, glaucous green, 24 in. (60 cm) scape in late summer; fertile.

Comments & Special Needs: Site in good light to high, filtered shade to retain the attractive leaf colors. A rapid increaser. Very popular with flower arrangers because of the pleasing outline, the rugosity, the distinctive wide margin and the contrasting dark base color. The leaf margin will reach up to 1½ in. (3.5 cm) if given optimum growing conditions. A classic hosta.

Similar: H. 'Jambeliah' in its margined form is larger and has more distinctly cupped leaves; H. 'Hilda Wassman', whose leaves have narrower margins; *H. 'Honeysong'; H. 'Mama Mia', which is slightly larger.

Sports: H. 'Cowrie', has narrowly variegated leaves with a very exaggerated brim; H. 'Java' is a shapely all-green form; *H. 'Kissing Cousins'; *H. 'Stetson'.

Hosta 'Wiggle Worms' (Draper NR)

SMALL

Origin: Unknown.

Clump Size & Habit: 10 in. wide × 7⅛ in. high (25 × 18 cm). A cascading mound.

Description: Leaf blade: 5⅛ × ¾ in. (13 × 2 cm); of average substance, smooth, matt, mid-green margined and streaked cream; edge conspicuously rippled, arching, strap-shaped with an acute tip. Petiole: flat, green, outlined in yellow, rippled along the edge, decurrent with the blade. Flower: funnel-shaped, lavender on an upright, bare 15 in. (38 cm) scape in high summer; fertility unknown.

Comments & Special Needs: Site in light to moderate shade. Grow as a foreground specimen or in a raised bed. A good breeding plant.

Distinguishing Features: The almost linear leaves make an unusual mound.

Similar: *H. 'Stiletto'; H. 'Sumi', which is smaller.

Hosta 'Winsome' (D. & J. Ward 1996)

MINIATURE–SMALL

Origin: Seedling of H. 'Pin Stripe Sister'.

Clump Size & Habit: 14 in. wide × 8⅜ in. high (35 × 21 cm). A very compact mound.

Description: Leaf blade: 3⅛ × 2 in. (8 × 5 cm); of average substance, matt, dark green, widely and irregularly margined creamy white with celadon streaks jetting toward

Hosta 'Wide Brim'

Hosta 'Wiggle Worms'

the midrib, prominently veined; edge slightly rippled, widely oval with a cuspidate tip, rounded open lobes. Petiole: shallow dark green, outlined in white. Flower: long, tubular, pale lavender on an upright dark green 16¾ in. (42 cm) scape with variegated leafy bracts in mid-summer; fertility unknown, clusters of long, green seedpods.

Comments & Special Needs: Site in light to moderate shade in a sink, trough or gravel garden. Suitable for small flower arrangements. A strong and vigorous grower with very large flowers for such a small hosta.

Hosta 'Wolverine' (J. & J. Wilkins 1995)

MEDIUM

Origin: Hybrid of a *H.* 'Dorset Blue' sport.

Clump Size & Habit: 38⅜ in. wide × 15 in. high (96 × 38 cm). A dense cascading mound.

Description: Leaf blade: 10¼ × 5½ in. (26 × 14 cm); of good substance, smooth, blue-tinted green, widely and ir-

Hosta 'Winsome'

Hosta 'Wolverine'

regularly margined and splashed cream to white with celadon streaks jetting toward the midrib, satiny above and glaucous below; edge slightly rippled, arching widely lanceolate with an acute tip, tapered open lobes. Petiole: flattish, green, faintly outlined cream. Flower: tubular, pale lavender on an upright, bare, green, 20 in. (50 cm) scape in late summer; fertility unknown.

Comments & Special Needs: Site in good light to moderate shade. Vigorous, a rapid increaser. Grow as a foreground specimen or in a tall terracotta chimney pot to accentuate the arching leaves.

Distinguishing Features: Unusual blue-green color in a leaf of this shape.

Sports: *H.* 'Curtain Call' has superb, rich, dark bluegreen leaves.

Hosta 'Yellow River' (Smith & Ruh 1993)

GIANT

Origin: Natural sport of *H. montana*.

Clump Size & Habit: 80 in. wide × 36 in. high (200 × 90 cm). An impressive, semi-upright mound.

Description: Leaf blade: 15 × 9 in. (38 × 22 cm); of good substance, matt, mid- to dark green widely and irregularly margined yellow turning creamy white with celadon splashes jetting toward the midrib, strongly veined, widely undulate or kinked, twisted and curved toward the cuspidate tip, widely oval with heart-shaped pinched to overlapping lobes. Petiole: stout, dark green, outlined in yellow. Flower: see *H. montana*.

Comments & Special Needs: Site in light to moderate shade. Ideal for a woodland planting with shrubs or as a specimen. A moderate to good increaser. Late to emerge.

Similar: *H.* 'Sagae', whose leaves are a more gray-green.

Hosta 'Yellow River'

Hosta 'Yellow Splash Rim'

Hosta 'Zippity Do Dah'

Hosta 'Yellow Splash Rim' (AHS 1986)

MEDIUM

Origin: Stable sport of *H.* 'Yellow Splash'.

Clump Size & Habit: 40¾ in. wide × 18 in. high (102 × 45 cm). A spreading mound.

Description: Leaf blade: 7½ × 3½ in. (19 × 9 cm); thin, smooth, mid-green widely and irregularly margined yellow turning ivory-white with streaks jetting toward the midrib, matt above and glossy below, conspicuously veined; edge occasionally kinked, slightly arching, elliptic with an acute tip, tapered pinched lobes. Petiole: red-dotted green outlined in ivory. Flower: funnel-shaped, rich lavender on an upright, bare, green, 28 in. (70 cm) scape in late summer; fertile.

Comments & Special Needs: Site in light to moderate shade. A rapid increaser covering large areas of ground. Not suitable as a pot plant.

Similar: *H.* 'Minnie Bell', which is slightly smaller.

Hosta 'Zippity Do Dah' (Walters Gardens 2000)

MEDIUM–LARGE

Origin: Tissue-cultured sport of *H.* 'Abba Dabba Do'.

Clump Size & Habit: 71⅛ in. wide × 24 in. high (178 × 60 cm). An upright mound.

Description: Leaf blade: 12 × 6⅜ in. (30 × 16 cm); of good substance, dark olive-green, evenly margined creamy white with occasional splashing, matt above and thinly glaucous below, closely veined; edge rippled, undulate and arching with a twisted tip, widely oval, heart-shaped open to pinched lobes. Petiole: dark olive-green. Flower: see *H.* 'Abba Dabba Do'.

Comments & Special Needs: Tolerates full sun in all but the hottest climates. Vigorous, easy to grow.

Similar: **H.* 'Crispula'.

Hosta 'Zodiac'

Hosta 'Zodiac' (Q & Z Nursery 2000)

LARGE

Origin: Sport of *H.* 'Richland Gold'.

Clump Size & Habit: 53½ in. wide × 18⅜ in. high (134 × 46 cm). An open mound.

Description: Leaf blade: 8⅜ × 5⅛ in. (21 × 13 cm); thick, chartreuse turning yellow irregularly margined creamy yellow turning white, matt above and glaucous below, seersuckered, strongly veined; edge slightly rippled, slightly convex, widely oval with a cuspidate tip, heart-shaped pinched lobes. Petiole: chartreuse. Flower: see *H.* 'Fortunei Hyacinthina'.

Comments & Special Needs: Some morning sun is needed to achieve the best leaf color. Vigorous, a moderate to rapid increaser. Lovely with *Heuchera* 'Amber Waves'.

Similar: **H.* 'Richland Gold'; **H.* 'Moonlight'.

CHAPTER TEN

HOSTAS *with* MEDIO-VARIEGATED LEAVES

MEDIO-VARIEGATED HOSTAS ARE those whose variegation is in the center rather than on the margin of the leaf. Since the 1990s they have become by far the most popular. However, they are usually not as vigorous as hostas with marginal variegation because so much of the central portion of the leaf blade lacks sufficient chlorophyll to enable the plants to thrive. A proportion of hostas with this type of variegation are placed in Chapter Ten, "Hostas for Connoisseurs," since they are more suited to regular tender loving care than to taking their chances with other garden plants, which is how most hostas can be grown.

Many blue-margined, medio-variegated hostas unfurl with only mid-green color and do not assume their expected variegation for several weeks. These include *Hosta* 'Paul's Glory', *H.* 'Inniswood' and *H.* 'Maui Rainforest'. By contrast, *H.* 'Great Expectations' does not have this trait and unfurls with its leaf colors sharply delineated. I describe the flowers of sports only if they differ from the parent plant or if the parent plant is not included. For example, *Hosta* 'High Noon', the parent of *H.* 'Five O'Clock Shadow', includes a description of the flowers because they are different from the parent flowers.

Hosta 'Abba Irresistible' (Aden NR)

MEDIUM

Origin: Unknown.

Clump Size & Habit: 22 in. wide × 12 in. high (55 × 30 cm). An upright mound.

Description: Leaf blade: 7½ × 5⅛ in. (19 × 13 cm); of average substance, matt, ivory-cream widely and irregularly margined dark olive-green with chartreuse streaks jetting toward the midrib, slightly dimpled; edge almost flat, folded, widely oval with a cuspidate tip, rounded pinched lobes. Petiole: ivory-white, finely outlined in dark green. Flower: funnel-shaped, lavender on an upright, leafy, ivory-white, 20 in. (50 cm) scape in mid- to high summer; fertility unknown.

Comments & Special Needs: Site in good light to light shade to make the most of the seasonal tonal changes in the leaf coloring. Leaves emerge with a pale chartreuse central variegation that lightens to give a more dramatic contrast. Scorching not found in cooler climates, the leaves remaining in good condition throughout the summer.

Hosta 'Ann Kulpa' (Kulpa 1999)

MEDIUM–LARGE

Origin: *H.* 'Pin Stripe Sister' hybrid.

Clump Size & Habit: 24 in. wide × 20 in. high (60 × 50 cm). A layered mound.

Description: Leaf blade: 8 × 6⅜ in. (20 × 16 cm); of good substance, satiny, yellow turning ivory-white with a very wide irregular light green turning dark green margin, with a blue cast in early summer and celadon streaks jetting toward the midrib, dimpled, strongly veined; edge flat to slightly undulate, folded, widely oval with a cuspidate tip, heart-shaped pinched lobes. Petiole: ivory-white, striped dark green. Flower: bell-shaped, lavender with translucent edges on an upright, leafy, ivory-white, 28 in. (70 cm) scape from mid- to high summer; sterile.

Comments & Special Needs: Site in morning sun in Northern zones. Vigorous, a moderate increaser. Will need frequent division to retain the centrally striped effect.

Hosta 'Abba Irresistible'

Hosta 'Ann Kulpa'

Previous page: *Hosta* 'Striptease'

Hosta 'Banana Boat' (W. & E. Lachman 1991)

SMALL–MEDIUM

Origin: H. 'Reversed' hybrid.

Clump Size & Habit: 20 in. wide × 9 in. high (50 × 22 cm). An upright mound.

Description: Leaf blade: 6⅜ × 4⅜ in. (16 × 11 cm); thick, leathery, ivory-white irregularly and widely margined dark green with conspicuous chartreuse streaks jetting toward the midrib, matt above and glaucous below, dimpled; edge flat, folded to slightly cupped, elliptic to narrowly oval with a cuspidate tip, kinked open to pinched lobes. Petiole: narrow, flattish, ivory, outlined in dark green. Flower: bell-shaped, violet, arranged sparsely on a slightly oblique, leafy, ivory, 12¾ in. (32 cm) scape in mid-summer; sterile.

Comments & Special Needs: Site in morning sun in Northern zones. Slow to increase. Needs careful placing so that it will get sufficient sun to provide vigor but not so much that it burns the leaf center. Slow to increase but it has a better constitution than many hostas of this type.

Distinguishing Features: Slightly inward-folding leaves create a "boat-shaped" outline. Attractively streaked and margined leaves and variegated leafy bracts add to the charms of this colorful hosta.

Hosta 'Brenda's Beauty' (Keller 1992)

MEDIUM

Origin: Sport of H. 'Gold Standard'.

Clump Size & Habit: 40¾ in. wide × 18 in. high (102 × 45 cm). An open mound.

Description: Leaf blade: 8 × 5⅛ in. (20 × 13 cm); of moderate substance, emerges pale chartreuse turning yellow and finally ivory, irregularly margined mid- to dark green with streaks jetting toward the midrib, matt above and glaucous below, slightly dimpled, strongly marked veins; edge undulate, slightly cupped, widely oval with a cuspidate tip, heart-shaped pinched lobes. Petiole: chartreuse to ivory, outlined in dark green. Flower: see H. 'Fortunei Hyacinthina'.

Comments & Special Needs: Site in good light to moderate shade in cooler climates, where the best leaf color is achieved, elsewhere shade all day. Vigorous, among the best of the many medio-variegated sports from H. 'Gold Standard'.

Distinguishing Features: Conspicuous netted veining is visible in the variegated portion of the leaf.

Similar: *H. 'Something Different', which has more contrasting leaf color and rippled leaf edges.

Hosta 'Bright Lights' (Aden & Klehm NR)

MEDIUM

Origin: Clone of H. 'Tokudama Aureonebulosa'.

Clump Size & Habit: 50¾ in. wide × 18¾ in. high (127 × 47 cm). An overlapping mound.

Description: Leaf blade: 9⅛ × 7⅛ in. (23 × 18 cm); thick, glaucous cloudy chartreuse to yellow, widely margined blue-green with streaks jetting toward the midrib, seersuckered; edge flat to occasionally kinked, folded, oval with a cuspidate tip, heart-shaped open to pinched lobes. Petiole: chartreuse. Flower: see H. 'Tokudama'.

Comments & Special Needs: Site in light to moderate shade so that the most subtle color contrast will be achieved. Leaves emerge blue slowly assuming the subtle variegation. Very slow to increase. Pest resistant.

Hosta 'Banana Boat'

Hosta 'Brenda's Beauty'

*Indicates plants fully described elsewhere in this book.

Hosta 'Bright Lights'

Hosta 'Cadillac'

Similar: *H.* 'Abiqua Hallucination', whose leaves are longer and larger; *H.* 'Blue Shadows', a selected form of *H.* 'Tokudama Aureonebulosa' in which the blue margin and streaking are much darker, almost navy blue, giving a greater contrast; *H.* 'Saybrook Surprise', which has somewhat rounder leaves.

Hosta 'Cadillac' (Skrocki & Avent 1998)

SMALL

Origin: Unknown.

Clump Size & Habit: 20 in. wide × 10 in. high (50 × 25 cm). A dense mound.

Description: Leaf blade: 6⅜ × 4⅜ in. (16 × 11 cm); thick, golden yellow, widely margined green with streaks jetting toward the midrib, intensely seersuckered; edge flat, slightly cupped, widely oval to nearly round with a mucronate tip, heart-shaped pinched lobes. Petiole: long, chartreuse. Flower: tubular, near white on an upright, bare, green, 16 to 20 in. (40 × 50 cm) scape in early to midsummer; fertile.

Comments & Special Needs: Lutescent. Site in light to moderate shade for the best color effect in the South; it tolerates morning sun in the North. Slow to increase. Pest resistant.

Hosta 'Captain Kirk' (Brill 1999)

MEDIUM

Origin: Sport of *H.* 'Gold Standard'.

Clump Size & Habit: 36 in. wide × 20 in. high (90 × 50 cm). An overlapping mound.

Description: Leaf blade: 9 × 7⅛ in. (22 × 18 cm); of good substance, emerging chartreuse turning first yellow then ivory, widely margined bright mid-green, matt above and glaucous below, dimpled, strongly veined; edge almost flat, slightly arching, slightly convex, widely oval with a

Hosta 'Captain Kirk'

cuspidate tip, heart-shaped pinched lobes. Petiole: flattish, cream, finely outlined in dark green. Flower: see *H.* 'Fortunei Hyacinthina'.

Comments & Special Needs: Some morning sun is beneficial but it needs careful placing in the garden. The margin can be up to 2¾ in. (7 cm) wide, and regular division is needed to keep the most pleasing proportion between the two portions of the leaf. Vigorous, a fairly rapid increaser.

Distinguishing Features: It differs from *H.* 'Gold Standard' in having thicker leaves and a narrower central variegation. It is said to hold its color better than its parent.

Hosta 'Cascades' (W. & E. Lachman 1993)

MEDIUM

Origin: *H.* 'Banana Sundae' × *H. sieboldiana* 'Frances Williams'.

Clump Size & Habit: 26 in. wide × 15 in. high (65 × 38 cm). An open, arching mound.

Hosta 'Cascades'

Description: Leaf blade: 11 × 4⅜ in. (28 × 11 cm); smooth, matt, ivory-white, widely margined dark green with some chartreuse streaks jetting toward the midrib; edge undulate, arching toward the sometimes curved acute tip, oval with rounded open to pinched lobes. Petiole: ivory-white, outlined in dark green. Flower: funnel-shaped white on a leaning, leafy, ivory-white, 36 in. (90 cm) scape in early summer; fertile.

Comments & Special Needs: Site in the center of a border of plain green- or blue-leaved hostas for maximum effect. Not always easy to grow, it needs the summer heat of a continental climate and regular feeding to attain its optimum size. Two hours of morning sun then light shade will produce the best results.

Distinguishing Features: The spectacular cascading habit shows off the color contrasts of the leaves.

Hosta 'Center of Attention' (Kulpa 1999)

MEDIUM

Origin: *H.* 'Sea Prize' hybrid.

Clump Size & Habit: 18 in. wide × 10 in. high (45 × 25 cm). An unsymmetrical, outward-facing clump.

Hosta 'Center of Attention'

Description: Leaf blade: 6⅜ × 5⅛ in. (16 × 13 cm), thick, glossy, golden yellow to ivory-white, very widely margined dark olive-green with many chartreuse streaks jetting toward the midrib, seersuckered, conspicuously veined; edge slightly undulate, slightly cupped, twisted in the juvenile stage, widely oval to nearly round with a mucronate tip, heart-shaped pinched lobes. Petiole: chartreuse to ivory, outlined in dark green. Flower: bell-shaped, lavender-striped on an upright, leafy, ivory-white, 18¾ in. (47 cm) scape in mid-summer; fertility unknown.

Comments & Special Needs: Site in morning sun except in the hottest climates. A smaller-leaved hosta than its parent. Vigorous, fast growing. Pest resistant.

Hosta 'Cherry Berry' (W. & E. Lachman 1991)
SMALL–MEDIUM

Origin: *H.* "Lachman 82-18-1" × *H.* "Lachman 81-9-2."

Clump Size & Habit: 14 in. wide × 10 in. high (35 × 25 cm). A diffuse, upright mound.

Description: Leaf blade: 6⅜ × 2⅜ in. (16 × 6 cm); thin, smooth, satiny, emerging yellow turning ivory-white, irregularly and widely margined dark olive-green with some chartreuse streaks jetting toward the midrib; edge with occasional shallow undulations, arching toward the tip, elliptic with an acute, sometimes curved or pinched tip, tapered open lobes. Petiole: flattish, pink-tinted ivory, widely outlined in dark olive-green. Flower: flared, violet, subtended by cream bracts on an upright, leafy, glossy, intense burgundy-red, 28 in. (70 cm) scape in high summer; fertility unknown, red seedpods.

Comments & Special Needs: Benefits from morning sun or very good light. Leaves will widen considerably in hot climates where it grows more vigorously. Very susceptible to pest damage.

Distinguishing Features: A tricolor effect is often visible on the leaves in early to mid-summer making it worthwhile to give this hosta special care. The burgundy-red scapes and red seedpods are other reasons to persevere.

Similar: *H.* 'Celebration', which does not have striking red petioles; *H.* 'Hot Lips';

H. 'Joyce Trott', which has wider leaves with more undulate edges; *H.* 'Xanadu' has slightly larger and wider leaves.

Sports: *H.* 'Maraschino Cherry'.

Hosta 'Chinese Sunrise' (Schaeffer & Summers & Ruh 1992)
SMALL–MEDIUM

Origin: Thought to be a sport of *H. cathayana*.

Clump Size & Habit: 28 in. wide × 14 in. high (70 cm). A dense, arching mound.

Description: Leaf blade: 6⅜ × 3⅛ in. (16 × 8 cm); thin, smooth, chartreuse-yellow fading to light olive-green, narrowly and irregularly margined dark olive-green, glossy above and satiny below, prominently veined; edge slightly undulate, lanceolate with an acute tip, tapered open lobes. Petiole: narrow, olive-green. Flower: bell-shaped, light purple in clusters on a thin, semi-oblique, very leafy, 28 in. (70 cm) scape in late summer; fertile.

Comments & Special Needs: One of the first hostas to emerge in spring. Site in morning sun to good light thus retaining the variegation for as long as possible. Best planted in clumps 12 in. (30 cm) apart as an edging plant, the leaves gradually changing color through the season. Also nice in pots.

Hosta 'Cracker Crumbs' (Solberg 2002)
SMALL

Origin: Sport of *H.* 'Shiny Penny'.

Clump Size & Habit: 12 in. wide × 6⅜ in. high (30 × 16 cm). A low-growing mound.

Description: Leaf blade: 3⅛ × 2 in. (8 × 5 cm); of good substance, smooth, glossy, copper-tinted golden yellow, irregularly margined dark green with streaks jetting toward the midrib, prominently veined; edge widely rippled, oval

Hosta 'Cherry Berry'

Hosta 'Chinese Sunrise'

with cuspidate tip, heart-shaped pinched lobes. Petiole: chartreuse. Flower: see *H.* 'Shiny Penny'.

Comments & Special Needs: Site in morning sun and apply plenty of water. A rapid increaser but ideal for sinks, troughs or gravel gardens.

Distinguishing Features: The contrasting dark green margins appear to have been painted onto the leaf.

Hosta 'Cupid's Arrow' (Walters Gardens 2000)

MEDIUM

Origin: Tissue-cultured sport of *H.* 'Candy Hearts'.

Clump Size & Habit: 18 in. wide × 10 in. high (45 × 25 cm). A dense mound.

Description: Leaf blade: 5⅛ × 4 in. (13 × 11 cm); of average substance, smooth, matt, ivory-white widely and irregularly margined dark green with some chartreuse streaks jetting toward the midrib; edge kinked, arching and twisted with a curved tip, widely oval with heart-shaped pinched

Hosta 'Cracker Crumbs'

Hosta 'Cupid's Arrow'

lobes. Petiole: white, outlined with fine green lines. Flower: see *H.* 'Candy Hearts'.

Comments & Special Needs: Very slow to increase. Requires careful cultivation. Site in good light to moderate shade.

Distinguishing Features: Leaves become much wider over the years but it was named when it was in its juvenile phase.

Similar: **H.* 'Undulata', which has longer leaves with narrower margins.

Hosta 'Delia' (Ford 1995)

MINIATURE–SMALL

Origin: Sport of *H.* 'Golden Prayers'.

Clump Size & Habit: 18 in. wide × 6⅜ in. high (45 × 16 cm). A compact mound.

Description: Leaf blade: 2¾ × 2 in. (7 × 5 cm); thick, light yellow irregularly margined mid-green with some streaks jetting toward the midrib, matt above and glaucous below, seersuckered, moderately prominent veins; edge flat to slightly rippled, folded, widely oval with a cuspidate tip, heart-shaped pinched lobes. Petiole: chartreuse to yellow. Flower: see *H.* 'Golden Prayers'.

Comments & Special Needs: Site in morning sun in cooler climates, otherwise light to moderate shade. Very slow to increase. Pest resistant.

Similar: *H.* 'Goldbrook Grace'.

Hosta 'Dick Ward' (Hatfield 1991)

MEDIUM–LARGE

Origin: Sport of *H.* 'Zounds'.

Clump Size & Habit: 40 in. wide × 18 in. high (100 × 45 cm). A dense mound

Hosta 'Delia'

Hosta 'Dick Ward'

Description: Leaf blade: 9⅛ × 9⅛ in. (23 × 23 cm); thick, glaucous, chartreuse-yellow turning golden yellow, irregularly margined dark green, seersuckered, edge wavy, cupped, widely oval to nearly round with a mucronate tip, heart-shaped overlapping lobes, lobes open to pinched. Petiole: chartreuse, margined dark green. Flower: see *H*. 'Zounds'.

Distinguishing Features: Becomes a brassy yellow if exposed to full sunlight.

Comments & Special Needs: Site in morning sun in Northern zones, then good light to moderate shade. Slow to establish but well worth the wait. Pest resistant.

Similar: *H*. 'Midwest Magic', which has a narrower, less intense dark green margin; *H. 'Paradigm'; *H. 'September Sun', which has slightly smaller leaves.

Hosta 'Dream Weaver' (Ruetenik & Walek 1996)

LARGE

Origin: Sport of *H*. 'Great Expectations'.

Clump Size & Habit: 36 in. wide × 18 in. high (90 × 45 cm). A dense mound over time.

Description: Leaf blade: 9⅛ × 8⅜ in. (23 × 21 cm);

Hosta 'Dream Weaver'

thick, chartreuse turning ivory-white, very widely margined dark blue-green with streaks jetting toward the midrib, matt above and glaucous below, seersuckered; edge slightly rippled, slightly cupped or convex, widely oval to nearly round with a mucronate tip, heart-shaped overlapping lobes. Petiole: ivory-green, outlined in dark green. Flower: see *H. sieboldiana* 'Elegans'.

Hosta 'Dylan's Dilly'

Hosta 'Emerald Crust'

Comments & Special Needs: The variegation is more albescent than lutescent. Lower light levels will produce a more pleasing leaf color. Great care over siting in the garden will be needed. Is an eye-catching specimen in the border. Growing in a container is also recommended since it needs regular division to retain the striking leaf pattern. Slow to increase. Pest resistant.

Distinguishing Features: 'H. 'Dream Weaver' has wider margins than H. 'Great Expectations' as well as a darker blue-green coloration and a much narrower central variegation. Needs dividing every nine months to keep the striking leaf pattern stable.

Similar: *H. 'Thunderbolt', which has the same "handprint" central variegation.

Hosta 'Dylan's Dilly' (Walden-West NR)

SMALL

Origin: Sport of a H. 'Fortunei'.

Clump Size & Habit: 20 in. wide × 15 in. high (50 × 38 cm). A wide, spreading mound.

Description: Leaf blade: 8⅜ × 5⅛ in. (21 × 13 cm); of good substance, pale chartreuse to cream, irregularly margined dark green with some streaks jetting toward the midrib, matt above and glaucous below; edge flat to slightly rippled, shallowly cupped, oval with a cuspidate tip, rounded open to pinched lobes. Petiole: chartreuse, finely outlined in dark green. Flower: funnel-shaped lavender on an upright, leafy, light green, 20 in. (50 cm) scape in mid- to high summer; sterile.

Comments & Special Needs: Some morning sun in cooler climates followed by good light results in the best leaf color, so it needs careful placing in the garden. Variegation is constant and stable. Vigorous, a moderately rapid increaser.

Distinguishing Features: Leaves are paler in color than those of H. 'Gold Standard' and the clump is tighter.

Similar: *H. 'Geneva Stark', which came from the same cross and has a very white central variegation.

Hosta 'Emerald Crust' (Zilis & T & Z Nursery 1988)

SMALL–MEDIUM

Origin: Uncertain.

Clump Size & Habit: 38 in. wide × 16¾ in. high (95 × 42 cm). An overlapping mound.

Description: Leaf blade: 11 × 6⅜ in. (28 × 16 cm); of average substance, chartreuse turning ivory-white, widely and irregularly margined dark green with streaks jetting toward the midrib, dimpled when mature, prominently veined; edge slightly rippled, slightly arching, oval with a cuspidate tip, heart-shaped pinched lobes. Petiole: ivory-white, outlined in dark green. Flower: funnel-shaped, pale lavender on an upright, leafy, ivory, 42 in. (105 cm) scape in high summer; fertility unknown.

Comments & Special Needs: Site in good light to moderate shade.

Similar: *H. 'White Christmas', which has more twisted leaves of less substance.

Hosta 'Emerald Tiara' (Walters Gardens 1988)

SMALL

Origin: Tissue-cultured sport of H. 'Golden Scepter'.

Clump Size & Habit: 34 in. wide × 14 in. high (85 × 35 cm). A dense, spreading mound.

Description: Leaf blade: 4⅜ × 3½ in. (11 × 9 cm); of average substance, smooth, muted gold irregularly margined rich dark green with some streaks jetting toward the midrib, widely spaced veins; edge flat to occasionally kinked, widely oval with a cuspidate tip, heart-shaped open

Hosta 'Emerald Tiara'

Hosta 'Fan Dance'

to pinched lobes. Petiole: chartreuse, outlined in dark green. Flower: see *H*. 'Golden Tiara'.

Comments & Special Needs: Site in some morning sun followed by good light to light shade. Leaf colors become more muted as the season progresses. More vigorous than its parent and easy to grow. A good foreground plant and also suitable for containers.

Similar: *H*. 'Emerald Scepter', which emerges with a gold center and gradually lightens to near white; is less vigorous and can scorch in sun more easily than other hostas of the Tiara Series; *H*. 'Stolen Kiss', once thought to be a sport of *H*. 'Cheatin Heart', now considered a tissue-cultured sport of *H*. 'Emerald Scepter', following a mix-up in a tissue culture laboratory.

Hosta 'Fan Dance' (R. Benedict 1987)

MEDIUM

Origin: Sport of *H*. 'Dorothy'.

Clump Size & Habit: 36 in. wide × 18 in. high (90 × 45 cm). A dense mound.

Description: Leaf blade: 7¼ × 5¼ in. (18.5 × 12.5 cm); thick, golden chartreuse to ivory-white narrowly and irregularly margined dark green, with some streaking jetting toward the midrib, matt above and glaucous below, strongly veined, dimpled when mature; edge slightly rippled, widely oval with a mucronate tip, heart-shaped pinched lobes. Petiole: narrow, ivory-chartreuse. Flower: funnel-shaped, purple-striped lavender held at right angles on an upright, bare, ivory-chartreuse, 25⅛ in. (63 cm) scape in high to late summer; sterile.

Comments & Special Needs: Strongly albescent. Site in good light to moderate shade. Slow to increase.

Distinguishing Features: In early summer, both gold and

Hosta 'Fascinator'

white centrally variegated leaves can appear together on the clump, creating an eye-catching tonal effect. Plant with hostas of dark green leaves to intensify the drama.

Similar: *H*. 'Janet', which often does poorly in the garden.

Hosta 'Fascinator' (J. Wilkins & Owens 1989)

MEDIUM

Origin: Sport of *H*. 'Golden Fascination'.

Clump Size & Habit: 32 in. wide × 14 in. high (80 × 35 cm). An open mound.

Description: Leaf blade: 7½ × 6⅜ in. (19 × 16 cm); thick, golden yellow turning ivory-white, widely and irregularly margined muted green, matt above and glaucous below, seersuckered, well-marked veins; edge almost flat, undulate and twisted in the juvenile stage, widely oval with a cuspidate tip, heart-shaped pinched lobes. Petiole: narrow, chartreuse. Flower: flared, lavender on an upright,

Hosta 'Fire and Ice'

Hosta 'Five O'Clock Shadow'

leafy, olive-green, 24 to 30 in. (60 to 75 cm) scape in late summer; fertile.

Comments & Special Needs: Albescent. Site in morning sun to light shade. Lights up a shaded shrub border. Slow to increase. Pest resistant.

Distinguishing Features: The 1 in. (2.5 cm) wide margin is not apparent when the leaf unfurls but gradually becomes visible.

Hosta 'Fire and Ice' (Hansen & Shady Oaks 1999)

MEDIUM

Origin: Reversed tissue-cultured sport of *H.* 'Patriot'.

Clump Size & Habit: 12 in. wide × 8 in. high (30 × 20 cm). A twisted-leaved, upright mound.

Description: Leaf blade: 6⅜ × 4 in. (16 × 10 cm); of good substance, smooth, creamy ivory to white, widely and irregularly margined dark green splashed several shades of green jetting toward the midrib, satiny above and shiny below; edge kinked, moderately folded to lightly twisted and curved at the acute tip, widely oval with rounded open lobes. Petiole: ivory-white, finely outlined olive-green. Flower: see *H.* 'Francee'.

Comments & Special Needs: Strong light in the morning, but hot afternoon sun should be avoided. Seemingly vigorous for a medio-variegated hosta.

Distinguishing Features: Scapes are white, as are the seedpods when they are produced. The clump is taller than most hostas of this type.

Similar: *H.* 'Flash of Light' has a more open habit and shows good vigor; *H.* 'Loyalist'; *H.* 'Paul Revere'.

Hosta 'Five O'Clock Shadow' (Solberg 2000)

LARGE

Origin: Sport of *H.* 'High Noon'.

Clump Size & Habit: 36 in. wide × 22 in. high (90 × 55 cm). An upright, spreading mound.

Description: Leaf blade: 10 × 8⅜ in. (25 × 21 cm); moderately thick, bright pale yellow, irregularly margined muted light green, satiny above and glaucous below, seersuckered to pebbled, strongly veined; edge shallowly undulate, slightly folded or slightly convex, widely oval with a cuspidate tip, heart-shaped pinched lobe. Petiole: narrow, chartreuse. Flower: funnel-shaped, near white on an upright or oblique, bare, glaucous yellow, 36 to 40 in. (90 to 100 cm) scape in early summer; fertile, green seedpods.

Comments & Special Needs: Site in morning sun to achieve the best leaf color. Moderate growth rate. Pest resistant.

Distinguishing Features: Very muted margin can attain a width of 1 in. (2.5 cm).

Similar: *H.* 'Rascal', which has larger leaves in a tighter clump.

Hosta 'Forncett Frances' (S. Bond NR)

LARGE

Origin: Sport of a *H.* 'Frances Williams' hybrid.

Clump Size & Habit: 40¾ in. wide × 24 in. high (102 × 60 cm). A dense mound.

Description: Leaf blade: 10 × 8⅜ in. (25 × 21 cm); thick, glaucous muted yellow, widely and irregularly margined and streaked dark blue-green, seersuckered; edge slightly undulate, convex, widely oval to nearly round with a mucronate tip, heart-shaped pinched lobes. Petiole: stout, pale green. Flower: funnel-shaped, white on an upright or

Hosta 'Forncett Frances'

Hosta 'Fortunei Albopicta'

Hosta 'Fuji Sunrise'

oblique, glaucous green, 28 in. (70 cm) scape in mid-summer; fertile.

Comments & Special Needs: Site in light to moderate shade all day. Slow to increase. Pest resistant.

Distinguishing Features: The muted central variegation is not present when the leaves unfurl, only gradually becoming apparent during the summer. This muted tone in a hosta of *H. sieboldiana* 'Elegans' ancestry appears to be unique.

Hosta 'Fortunei Albopicta' (Hylander & AHS 1987)

MEDIUM–LARGE

Origin: Natural *H.* 'Fortunei' sport.

Clump Size & Habit: 45⅛ in. wide × 22 in. high (113 × 55 cm). An overlapping mound.

Description: Leaf blade: 10 × 6⅜ in. (25 × 16 cm); of average substance, chartreuse to pale yellow, irregularly margined dark green with slight blue undertones, some pale chartreuse streaks jetting toward the midrib, matt above and glaucous below, moderately seersuckered when mature; edge slightly undulate, slightly folded or convex, widely oval with a cuspidate tip, heart-shaped pinched lobes. Petiole: chartreuse, outlined in dark green. Flower: funnel-shaped, purple-streaked lavender on an upright, leafy, glaucous green, 40¾ in. (102 cm) scape in mid- to high summer; barely fertile.

Comments & Special Needs: Viridescent. Variegation is maintained for longer if grown in light shade in a cooler climate. Exposure to full sun early in the season will bleach the central variegation to ivory-white. At its best soon after the leaves unfurl. Late to emerge. Vigorous, easy to grow.

Distinguishing Features: Veins appear like netting across the lighter portion of the leaf. By the end of the season the leaf blade is a dull, two-tone green.

Similar: *H.* 'Chelsea Babe', which is smaller in all its parts.

Sports: **H.* 'Fortunei Albopicta Aurea' is a viridescent yellow-leaved form.

Hosta 'Fuji Sunrise' (Heims NR)

MINIATURE

Origin: Unknown.

Clump Size & Habit: 6⅜ in. wide × 5⅛ in. high (16 × 13 cm). A diffuse mound.

Description: Leaf blade: 2¾ × ¾ in. (7 × 2 cm); thin, smooth, bright-chartreuse to golden yellow, narrowly and irregularly margined dark green, matt above and shiny below; edge rippled, slightly arching, slightly folded, lanceolate with a slightly curved, acute tip, tapered open lobes. Petiole: narrow, chartreuse, finely outlined in dark green. Flower: funnel-shaped, purple on a thin, upright, leafy, chartreuse, 10 in. (25 cm) scape in mid- to late summer; fertility unknown.

Comments & Special Needs: Site in light to moderate shade; the central variegation will bleach to ivory if exposed to full sunlight. Keep potted up until the root system is fully established, then plant in a rock or gravel garden or a larger container. Rapid growth rate.

Similar: *H. sieboldii 'Kabitan', which is larger; *H. 'Little Jim', which is similar in size and habit of growth.

Hosta 'Geneva Stark' (Walden-West & Hyslop 1999)

MEDIUM

Origin: Sport of H. 'Fortunei'.

Clump Size & Habit: 16 in. wide × 9⅛ in. high (40 × 23 cm). An upright mound.

Description: Leaf blade: 5⅛ × 2⅜ in. (13 × 6 cm); of moderate substance, glaucous white, irregularly margined dark green with two-tone green streaks jetting toward the midrib, dimpled; edge slightly rippled or kinked, twisted, widely lanceolate with an acute tip, rounded pinched lobes. Petiole: white, outlined, in dark green. Flower: tubular, pale lavender on an upright, leafy, glaucous ivory, 20 in. (50 cm) scape in mid- to late summer; fertility unknown.

Comments & Special Needs: Site in good light to moderate shade. Albescent. Emerges late.

Distinguishing Features: Its fast-growing habit (for a hosta) with white-centered leaves. A leaf center that is predominantly white.

Similar: *H. 'Morning Light'.

Hosta 'Gold Standard' (P. Banyai 1976)

MEDIUM–LARGE

Origin: Sport of H. 'Fortunei Hyacinthina Variegata'.

Hosta 'Geneva Stark'

Hosta 'Gold Standard'

Clump Size & Habit: 40¾ in. wide × 22 in. high (102 × 55 cm). A dense, overlapping mound.

Description: Leaf blade: 8⅜ × 5½ in. (21 × 14 cm); of good substance, chartreuse, turning yellow then ivory irregularly margined dark green with some streaks jetting toward the midrib, matt above and glaucous below, seersuckered; edge slightly rippled, slightly cupped, widely oval with a cuspidate tip, heart-shaped pinched to overlapping lobes. Petiole: chartreuse, outlined in dark green. Flower: see *H.* 'Fortunei Hyacinthina'.

Comments & Special Needs: Albescent. Is very sensitive to light levels so site in bright light to moderate shade, depending on summer heat and the leaf color required. Emerges late from purple shoots. Vigorous, easy to grow. A colorful specimen in the border and excellent in containers. Winner of the 1993 Alex J. Summers Distinguished Merit Hosta Award. Has probably produced more worthwhile sports than any other hosta. A classic.

Similar: *H.* 'Janet', which is less vigorous and not easy to grow.

Sports: *H.* 'Academy Muse' has green leaves with a subtle, darker green margin when grown in full shade. In partial sun the center lightens to gold with a green margin and green veins. *Hosta* 'Brenda's Beauty'; *H.* 'Captain Kirk'; *H.* 'Collector's Banner'; *H.* 'Darwin's Standard'; *H.* 'Gypsy Rose'; *H.* 'Kiwi Full Monty'; *H.* 'Paradise Standard'; *H.* 'Risky Business', whose dark green margined leaves have a chartreuse to ivory central variegation; *H.* 'Silver and Gold'; *H.* 'Something Different'; *H.* 'Striptease'.

Hosta 'Green with Envy' (Chrystal 2000)

DWARF
Origin: Natural sport of *H.* 'Dawn'.

Clump Size & Habit: 8 in. wide × 3⅛ in. high (20 × 8 cm). A dense mound.

Description: Leaf blade: 4 × 3⅛ in. (10 × 8 cm); thin, greenish white turning deep yellow, irregularly margined dark green with streaks jetting toward the midrib, matt above and satiny below, some dimpling when mature; edge slightly rippled, folded to slightly cupped, oval with a cuspidate tip, rounded open lobes. Petiole: narrow, chartreuse, finely outlined in dark green. Flower: bell-shaped, purple on an upright leafy, pale green, 12 to 15 in. (30 to 38 cm) scape in mid-summer; sterile.

Comments & Special Needs: Site in light to moderate shade. Vigorous and fast growing. Can be susceptible to pest damage.

Similar: *H.* 'Green Eyes', which has longer leaves; *H.* 'Twist of Lime' has a narrower leaf blade and is a more subdued color.

Hosta 'Guacamole' (Solberg 1994)

LARGE
Origin: Sport of *H.* 'Fragrant Bouquet'.

Clump Size & Habit: 50¾ in. wide × 24 in. high (127 × 60 cm). An overlapping mound.

Description: Leaf blade: 11 × 8⅜ in. (28 × 21 cm); of good substance, chartreuse turning old-gold, irregularly margined dark green with chartreuse streaks jetting toward the midrib, glossy above and thinly glaucous below, prominently veined; edge almost flat, slightly convex, widely oval with a mucronate tip, heart-shaped pinched to overlapping lobes. Petiole: chartreuse, faintly outlined in dark green. Flower: see *H.* 'Fragrant Bouquet'.

Comments & Special Needs: Site in full sun all day in cooler climates, sun in the morning only elsewhere. A rapid

Hosta 'Green with Envy'

Hosta 'Guacamole'

increaser. Named Hosta of the Year by the American Hosta Growers Association in 2002.

Distinguishing Features: Margin is barely visible in cooler climates even if exposed to sunlight.

Sports: *H.* 'Fried Green Tomatoes', which has dark green leaves; *H.* 'Stained Glass'.

Hosta 'Indian Feather' (Owens 1992)

MEDIUM

Origin: *H.* 'Yellow Splash' selfed.

Clump Size & Habit: 36 in. wide × 20 in. high (90 × 50 cm). A symmetrical mound.

Description: Leaf blade: 5⅛ × 2 in. (13 × 5 cm); thinnish, glossy, emerging deep cream turning ivory-white widely and irregularly margined and streaked dark green, ribbed veins; edge undulate, arching, widely oval when mature, with a cuspidate tip, heart-shaped pinched lobes. Petiole: ivory, outlined in dark green. Flower: tubular, white-striped lavender on an upright, leafy, ivory-green, 27⅛ in. (68 cm) scape in high summer; fertile.

Comments & Special Needs: Site in morning sun, especially in cooler climates, then light to moderate shade. Divide regularly to ensure that the dramatic balance between the dark margin and light center of the leaves is maintained. Very rare but deserves to be better known.

Similar: *H.* 'Gay Feather', which has narrower leaves and less feathered inner marginal streaking.

Hosta 'Inniswood' (Inniswood Metro Gardens 1993)

MEDIUM–LARGE

Origin: Natural sport of *H.* 'Sun Glow'.

Clump Size & Habit: 49 in. wide × 24 in. (122 × 60 cm) high. A dense mound.

Description: Leaf blade: 8½ × 6½ in. (21.5 × 16.5 cm); thick, rich golden yellow widely and irregularly margined dark green with some streaks jetting toward the midrib, matt above and glaucous below, heavily seersuckered; edge widely undulate, shallowly cupped or convex, widely oval to nearly round with a cuspidate tip, heart-shaped pinched to overlapping lobes. Petiole: stout, chartreuse, finely outlined in dark green. Flower: funnel-shaped, pale lavender on an upright, bare, glaucous chartreuse, 30 in. (75 cm) scape in mid-summer; fertile.

Comments & Special Needs: Site in light to moderate shade. Slow to increase. Pest resistant. Among the most popular hostas of its type.

Distinguishing Features: Leaves unfurl dark green, and the bright, golden yellow central variegation takes some weeks to develop.

Similar: *H.* 'Paradigm'; *H.* 'Paul's Glory', whose margins are blue-green.

Hosta 'Guacamole', flower.

Hosta 'Indian Feather'

Hosta 'Inniswood'

Hosta 'Island Charm'

Hosta 'Julie Morss'

Hosta 'Island Charm' (Rasmussen & Malloy 1997)

SMALL

Origin: Seedling of *H*. 'Flamboyant'.

Clump Size & Habit: 22 in. wide × 10 in. high (55 × 25 cm). An upright mound.

Description: Leaf blade: 4 × 3⅛ in. (10 × 8 cm); of average substance, smooth, matt ivory-cream, widely and irregularly margined in three shades of green, darkest at the edges with streaks jetting toward the midrib; edge flat, slightly cupped, widely oval with a cuspidate tip, heart-shaped open to pinched lobes. Petiole: narrow, ivory-white, finely outlined in dark green, purple-dotted at the base. Flower: flared, purple-streaked rich lavender on an upright, bare, pink, 16¾ in. (42 cm) scape; fertile, long, pink seedpods.

Comments & Special Needs: Site in morning sun in cooler climates to boost the vigor, otherwise light shade all day. Establishes best if started off in a pot until a proper root system has developed. Grow in shaded rock gardens, picking up the color of the petioles with *Heuchera* 'Cathedral Windows'.

Distinguishing Features: The flower buds are pink and the bracts are pink, margined green.

Similar: *H. sieboldii* 'Shiro Kabitan'.

Sports: *H*. 'Fantasy Island' has a wider green margin with many chartreuse streaks jetting toward the midrib. More vigorous and more suited to Southern gardens than its parent. *Hosta* 'Green Lama', has mid-green leaves, purple petioles and scapes, which are an unusual feature in a small hosta; *H*. 'Pink Panther' has wider green margins, more central green streaking, pink petioles and pink- and green-streaked seedpods.

Hosta 'Julie Morss' (Morss 1983)

MEDIUM–LARGE

Origin: Breeder states this is a *H*. 'Frances Williams' seedling, but other authorities have claimed it is a viridescent seedling of an unknown *H*. 'Fortunei'.

Clump Size & Habit: 44 in. wide × 20¾ in. high (110 × 52 cm). A dense mound.

Description: Leaf blade: 9⅛ × 7⅛ in. (23 × 18 cm); thick, chartreuse turning pale yellow, widely and irregularly margined mid-green with a blue cast, with celadon streaks jetting toward the midrib, matt above and glaucous below, dimpled; edge almost flat, slightly cupped, widely oval with a mucronate tip, heart-shaped pinched lobes. Petiole: pale yellow, outlined in green. Flower: bell-shaped, lavender-white on an upright, bare, glaucous yellow, 22¾ in. (57 cm) scape in high to late summer; fertile.

Comments & Special Needs: It colors best in cooler climates in somewhat low light or moderate shade all day. At its most colorful in early summer before the variegation fades. A slow to moderate increaser. Lovely planted among cerise and purple rhododendrons and azaleas.

Hosta 'June' (Neo Plants 1991)

MEDIUM

Origin: First tissue-cultured sport of *H*. 'Halcyon'.

Clump Size & Habit: 30 in. wide × 15 in. high (75 × 38 cm). A symmetrical, overlapping mound.

Description: Leaf blade: 6⅜ × 4 in. (16 × 10 cm); of good substance, smooth, chartreuse turning yellow, finally ivory, irregularly margined blue with streaks jetting toward the midrib, matt above and glaucous below; edge almost flat, slightly cupped, oval with a cuspidate tip, heart-shaped pinched lobes. Petiole: chartreuse-yellow. Flower: see *H*. 'Halcyon'.

Hosta 'June'

Hosta 'Katherine Lewis'

Hosta 'Kiwi Full Monty'

Comments & Special Needs: For the most subtle chartreuse and blue color, grow in light shade in a cool climate, but a stronger, harsher contrast will be achieved if it is exposed to morning sunlight. Indeed, the difference between plants grown in good light and plants grown in shade is so marked they look like different plants. A moderate to rapid increaser and easy to grow. A superb foreground specimen and lovely in a shiny blue ceramic pot. Named Hosta of the Year by the American Hosta Growers Association in 2001.

Similar: *H. 'Katherine Lewis'; *H. 'Paradise Joyce'; *H. 'Punky'.

Sports: H. 'Brazen Hussy' an extraordinarily brazen yellow with some thin, dark green streaking around the margin; H. 'Jitterbug' has very wide blue margins with transitional white flashing and is smaller than H. 'June'.

Hosta 'Katherine Lewis' (Lewis NR)
MEDIUM

Origin: H. 'Halcyon' seedling.

Clump Size & Habit: 30 in. wide × 16 in. high (75 × 38 cm). An overlapping mound.

Description: Leaf blade: 7⅛ × 5⅛ in. (18 × 13 cm); of good substance, smooth, old-gold to yellow turning ivory-white, irregularly and narrowly margined dark green with occasional streaks jetting toward the midrib, matt above and glaucous below, conspicuously veined; edge widely undulate, folded, oval with a cuspidate tip, heart-shaped pinched lobes. Petiole: chartreuse. Flower: widely funnel-shaped, lavender-gray on an upright, bare, glaucous yellow, 30 in. (75 cm) scape in mid-summer; fertility unknown.

Comments & Special Needs: Site in morning sun to achieve the brightest leaf coloring. A moderate to good increaser.

Distinguishing Feature: Striking tonal variation in the central variegation of the leaves can occur in mid-to late summer; the leaves are narrower than those of H. 'June'.

Similar: *H. 'June'; *H. 'Paradise Joyce'.

Hosta 'Kiwi Full Monty' (Sligh 2000)
MEDIUM

Origin: Sport of H. 'Gold Standard'.

Clump Size & Habit: 36 in. wide × 18 in. high (90 × 45 cm). An open mound.

Description: Leaf blade: 6⅜ × 3½ in. (16 × 9 cm); of good substance, glaucous, chartreuse turning creamy yellow to ivory, widely margined rich blue-green with occasional silver flecks at the junction between the center and the margin, slight dimpling; edge almost flat, folded, oval with a cuspidate tip, tapered open to pinched lobes. Petiole: narrow, chartreuse, outlined in dark blue-green. Flower: see H. 'Fortunei Hyacinthina'.

Comments & Special Needs: Site in good light to light

Hosta 'Gypsy Rose'

shade to maintain the rich but subtle variations in leaf color. Vigorous, a rapid increaser.

Distinguishing Features: The dark blue-green margins make this hosta stand out from similar introductions.

Similar: *H.* 'Gypsy Rose'; **H.* 'Striptease'.

Hosta 'Lakeside Love Affaire' (Chastain 1997)

LARGE

Origin: Unknown.

Clump Size & Habit: 36 in. wide × 18 in. high (90 × 45 cm). An upright, flaring mound.

Description: Leaf blade: 9⅛ × 7⅛ in. (23 × 18 cm); thick, white widely, margined dark green with lime-green streaks jetting toward the midrib, satiny above and matt below, prominent widely spaced veins; edge slightly rippled, widely oval with a cuspidate tip, heart-shaped open to pinched lobes. Petiole: white, sharply outlined in dark green. Flower: tubular, near white on an upright, bare, 22 in. (55 cm) light green scape from mid- to late summer; fertile, green seedpods.

Hosta 'Lakeside Love Affaire'

Comments & Special Needs: Site in light to moderate shade all day. Unusually large for a medio-variegated hosta. Lovely with the gray-leaved, shuttlecock ferns, *Otophorum okonum* or *Athyrium* 'Ghost'. A moderate increaser.

Distinguishing Feature: Great sculptural qualities as well as a striking tricolor effect on the leaves.

Hosta 'Lakeside Shore Master' (Chastain 1998)

MEDIUM

Origin: Unknown.

Clump Size & Habit: 30 in. wide × 14 in. high (75 × 35 cm). An open mound.

Description: Leaf blade: 10 × 8½ in. (25 × 21.5 cm); thick, ivory, rapidly turning light green to rich yellow very widely and irregularly margined dark blue-green with some streaks jetting toward the midrib, matt above and satiny below, intensely seersuckered; edge flat, slightly cupped, oval with a cuspidate tip, pinched to overlapping lobes. Petiole: chartreuse-yellow, outlined in dark green. Flower: funnel-shaped, pale lavender on an upright, leafy, chartreuse, 18 to 22 in. (45 to 55 cm) scape in high summer; fertile, dark green seedpods.

Comments & Special Needs: Site in good light to moderate shade. A rapid increaser. Pest resistant.

Distinguishing Features: A very colorful hosta with a pleasing leaf habit.

Hosta 'Lakeside Shore Master'

Hosta 'Lakeside Symphony' (Chastain 1988)

MEDIUM–LARGE

Origin: First known sport of *H.* 'Piedmont Gold'.

Clump Size & Habit: 60 in. wide × 25⅛ in. high (150 × 63 cm). A billowing mound.

Description: Leaf blade: 11 × 9⅛ in. (28 × 23 cm); of good substance, pale chartreuse turning yellow-gold widely and irregularly margined chartreuse with some old-gold streaks jetting toward the midrib, slightly dimpled, promi-

Hosta 'Lakeside Symphony'

nently veined; edge slightly undulate, convex, widely oval with a twisted and sometimes pinched, cuspidate tip, heart-shaped open to pinched lobes. Petiole: chartreuse to yellow. Flower: see *H*. 'Piedmont Gold'.

Comments & Special Needs: Site in good light to light shade. A moderate to rapid increaser. Among the first known hostas with this particular leaf color combination making an impressive specimen.

Similar: *H*. 'Rascal'.

Hosta 'Little Caesar' (Ward & Chrystal & S. Bond 2000)

MINIATURE

Origin: *H*. 'Breeder's Choice' seedling.

Clump Size & Habit: 12 in. wide × 5⅛ in. high (30 × 13 cm). An upright mound.

Description: Leaf blade: 3⅛ × 1½ in. (8 × 4 cm); of good substance, smooth, ivory-white irregularly margined mid-green, satiny above and glossy below; edge slightly rippled, undulate to twisted, folded, lanceolate with a cuspidate tip, wedge-shaped to tapered open lobes. Petiole: ivory, outlined in green. Flower: tubular, violet-striped lavender on an upright, leafy, light green, 8⅜ to 10 in. (21 to 25 cm) scape in mid- to high summer; fertility unknown.

Comments & Special Needs: Among the best of the smaller white-centered, green-margined hostas, it is a rapid increaser with unusually good substance.

Distinguishing Features: Leaves have a more pronounced twist when young.

Similar: *H*. 'Medusa', which has narrower leaves in a denser mound; *H*. 'Mountain Fog'; *H*. 'Surprised by Joy' has less twisted leaves and a creamier colored central variegation; a mini version of *H*. 'Whirlwind'.

Hosta 'Little Sunspot' (Briggs Nursery 1996)

SMALL

Origin: Sport of *H*. 'Little Aurora'.

Clump Size & Habit: 30 in. wide × 10 in. high (75 × 25 cm). A compact mound.

Description: Leaf blade: 5⅛ × 4 in. (13 × 10 cm); thick, rich yellow widely margined vivid dark green with subtle transitional dark to light chartreuse streaks, matt above and satiny below, seersuckered; edge slightly rippled, slightly cupped, widely oval to nearly round with a mucronate tip, heart-shaped pinched lobes. Petiole: chartreuse.

Comments & Special Needs: Site in morning sun in cooler regions when the leaf center will turn brilliant gold; shade all day in the hottest climates. Outstanding in leaf form and leaf color contrast.

Distinguishing Features: The marked contrast between the dark green margins and the bright golden leaves, which is less evident in *H*. 'Just So'.

Similar: *H*. 'Amy Elizabeth'; *H*. 'Just So' and *H*. 'Not So', in which the leaf color contrast is not so marked.

Hosta 'Lunar Orbit' (Lydell 1991)

MEDIUM

Origin: Sport of *H*. 'August Moon'.

Clump Size & Habit: 50¾ in. wide × 18 in. high (127 × 45 cm). An unruly mound.

Description: Leaf blade: 7⅛ × 5⅛ in. (18 × 13 cm); thick, leathery, butterscotch-yellow, irregularly margined dark green with streaks jetting toward the midrib, satiny above and glaucous below, dimpled to seersuckered, prominently veined; edge slightly undulate, shallowly cupped or convex widely oval to nearly round with a cuspidate tip, rounded open to folded lobes. Petiole: flattish,

Hosta 'Little Caesar'

Hosta 'Little Sunspot'

chartreuse, outlined in dark green. Flower: see *H.* 'August Moon'.

Comments & Special Needs: A very versatile hosta that will perform equally well in sun or shade. Excellent growth rate.

Distinguishing Features: The leaf center becomes deep gold in full sun, but given some shade the leaf will be chartreuse margined a rich, dark blue-green.

Similar: **H.* 'September Sun'.

Sports: *H.* 'Lunar Magic', which has wider, very dark green leaf margins.

Hosta 'Medusa' (Herold 1993)

MINIATURE

Origin: *H.* 'Neat Splash' × *H. gracillima*.

Clump Size & Habit: 12 in. wide × 6⅜ in. high (30 × 16 cm). An oblique to upward-facing mound.

Description: Leaf blade: 4⅜ × 1 in. (11 × 2.5 cm); thin, smooth, ivory to pale chartreuse, widely and irregularly margined and splashed emerald-green and olive-green, matt above and satiny below; edge slightly rippled, lance-olate with an acute to cuspidate tip, tapered open lobes. Petiole: rippled, shallow, widely outlined in two shades of green. Flower: tubular, deep lavender from green buds on an upright, leafy, chartreuse, 15 in. (38 cm) scape, purple-dotted at the base in late summer; fertile.

Comments & Special Needs: Site in good light to mod-

Hosta 'Medusa'

Hosta 'Lunar Orbit'

erate shade. Grow in a pot until the root system is well established before planting out. Best suited to a rock garden or small container with small, round-leaved hostas for contrast.

Distinguishing Features: Strongly undulate and twisted leaves cause the base of the blade to fold in the center. Variegated leafy bracts are clasped to the scapes. No distinct junction between leaf blade and petiole.

Hosta 'Moon Shadow' (Savory 1988)

SMALL

Origin: *H.* 'Butter Rim' hybrid.

Clump Size & Habit: 15 in. wide × 8⅜ in. high (38 × 21 cm). An arching mound.

Description: Leaf blade: 4 × 1½ in. (10 × 4 cm); thin, golden yellow widely and irregularly margined dark green, glossy above and satiny below, strongly veined, slightly dimpled; edge slightly rippled and kinked toward the ta-

Hosta 'Moon Shadow'

Hosta 'Morning Light'

pered open lobes, elliptic to lanceolate with an acute tip. Petiole: yellow, finely outlined in olive-green, narrowing toward the crown. Flower: see *H.* 'Butter Rim'.

Comments & Special Needs: Needs protection from pest damage.

Hosta 'Morning Light' (Van Eijk-Bos & Van Erven 2000)

MEDIUM

Origin: Reversed sport of *H.* 'Twilight'.

Clump Size & Habit: 28 in. wide × 18 in. high (70 × 45 cm). An upright mound.

Description: Leaf blade: 5½ × 3½ in. (14 × 9 cm); thick, rich ivory with occasional green flecks, widely and irregularly margined dark green with chartreuse to olive-green streaks, satiny above and matt below, strongly marked veins, some dimpling on mature leaves; edge flat to kinked, cupped, widely oval with a slightly twisted cuspidate tip, rounded pinched lobes. Petiole: narrow, ivory, outlined in dark green.

Comments & Special Needs: Site in some morning sun in cooler climates, followed by light to moderate shade. A moderate increaser.

Distinguishing Features: Leaves emerge pale chartreuse with light olive-green margins that darken later.

Similar: **H.* 'Geneva Stark', which has thinner leaves.

Hosta 'Night before Christmas' (Machen 1994)

MEDIUM–LARGE

Origin: Tissue-cultured sport of *H.* 'White Christmas'.

Clump Size & Habit: 30 in. wide × 18 in. high (75 × 45 cm). A moderately dense, semi-upright mound.

Description: Leaf blade: 8⅜ × 3⅛ in. (21 × 8 cm); of average substance, white, widely and irregularly margined dark

Hosta 'Night before Christmas'

olive-green with some streaks jetting toward the midrib, satiny above and shiny below, some dimpling when mature, widely spaced veins; edge slightly rippled, undulate to twisting, oval with a cuspidate tip, heart-shaped open to pinched lobes. Petiole: narrow, ivory, finely outlined in dark green.

Comments & Special Needs: Early to emerge. Site in bright light to moderate shade. Is larger and stronger than its parent and has less variegation because there is more chlorophyll in the leaves. Needs dividing every few years to keep the central white stripe at the most pleasing proportion to the dark green margin. Plant as a mid-ground specimen in a border with plain blue-leaved hostas.

Similar: *H. 'Undulata Univittata'.

Hosta 'Okaydokey' (H. Benedict NR)

MEDIUM

Origin: Sport of H. 'Aoki'.

Clump Size & Habit: 49 in. wide × 22 in. high (122 × 55 cm). A dense mound.

Description: Leaf blade: 9⅛ × 6⅜ in. (23 × 16 cm); of good substance, chartreuse turning yellow, narrowly and irregularly margined dark green with some streaks jetting toward the midrib, matt above and thinly glaucous below,

seersuckered, closely spaced veins; edge lightly rippled, widely oval with a cuspidate tip, heart-shaped pinched to overlapping lobes. Petiole: chartreuse, finely outlined in dark green. Flower: see H. 'Fortunei Hyacinthina'.

Comments & Special Needs: Needs careful placing in the garden to allow just enough sunlight to hold the leaf color yet prevent scorching.

Distinguishing Features: The dark green margin has a blue cast in early summer.

Similar: H. 'Janet'; *H. 'Stained Glass'.

Hosta 'Olive Branch' (Moldovan NR)

SMALL

Origin: Sport of H. 'Candy Hearts'.

Clump Size & Habit: 24 in. wide × 10 in. high (60 × 25 cm). An overlapping mound.

Description: Leaf blade: 3⅛ × 3⅛ in. (8 × 8 cm); thin, smooth, muted butterscotch-yellow, widely margined olive-green jetting toward the midrib, satiny above and glaucous below, widely spaced veins; edge rippled, flat, heart-shaped with a cuspidate tip, heart-shaped overlapping lobes. Petiole: narrow chartreuse, finely outlined olive-green. Flower: see H. 'Candy Hearts'.

Hosta 'Okaydokey'

Hosta 'Olive Branch'

Hosta 'On The Edge'

Comments & Special Needs: Site in bright light to moderate shade. A rapid increaser. Prone to pest damage.

Distinguishing Features: Probably the first hosta to have a muted butterscotch-yellow central variegation (at its best it is in the handprint pattern), but quite random in width so regular division is required.

Hosta 'On the Edge' (Scolnik NR)

MEDIUM

Origin: Tissue-cultured sport of *H.* 'Aspen Gold'.

Clump Size & Habit: 36 in. wide × 20 in. high (90 × 50 cm). An open mound.

Description: Leaf blade: 10 × 8⅜ in. (25 × 21 cm); thick, chartreuse turning bright yellow, narrowly and irregularly margined blue-green with streaks jetting toward the midrib, matt above and glaucous pale yellow below, intensely seersuckered and puckered; edge almost flat, deeply cupped, almost round with a mucronate tip, heart-shaped pinched to overlapping lobes. Petiole: pale yellow, finely outlined in green. Flower: see *H.* 'Aspen Gold'.

Comments & Special Needs: Variegation is lutescent. Site in morning sun to achieve the brightest leaf color. Very slow to increase. Pest resistant.

Distinguishing Features: Among the most deeply cupped and puckered hostas with this type of variegation.

Similar: *H.* 'Bright Lights', whose leaves are longer.

Hosta 'Paradigm' (Walden-West & Purtymun 1999)

LARGE

Origin: Sport of *H.* 'Abiqua Recluse', originally known as *H.* 'Abiqua Paradigm'.

Clump Size & Habit: 46¾ in. wide × 20 in. high (117 × 50 cm). A dense mound.

Hosta 'Paradigm'

Description: Leaf blade: 10½ × 9 in. (27 × 22 cm); thick, chartreuse-green turning yellow widely margined dark green jetting toward the midrib, satiny above and glaucous below, intensely seersuckered and puckered; edge almost flat to slightly rippled, folded to cupped, widely oval with a mucronate tip, heart-shaped pinched to overlapping lobes. Petiole: light green. Flower: see *H.* 'Abiqua Recluse'.

Comments & Special Needs: Lutescent. Tolerates two hours of morning sun in the North but the color is more likely to fade. A rapid increaser. Pest resistant.

Similar: *H.* 'Dick Ward'; *H.* 'Inniswood'; *H.* 'Paul's Glory'; *H.* 'September Sun'.

Hosta 'Paradise Beach' (Fransen NR)

SMALL–MEDIUM

Origin: Sport of *H.* 'Weihenstephan'.

Clump Size & Habit: 30 in. wide × 12¾ in. high (75 × 32 cm). An upright, spreading mound.

Hosta 'Paradise Beach'

Hosta 'Paradise Joyce'

Description: Leaf blade: 6⅜ × 3⅛ in. (16 × 8 cm); of thin to moderate substance, light yellow fading slightly through the summer, widely and irregularly margined mid-green with streaks jetting toward the midrib, matt above and satiny below, slightly dimpled when mature; edge flat to slightly rippled, slightly arching or twisted, elliptic to narrowly oval with an acute tip, rounded open to pinched lobes. Petiole: chartreuse, outlined in green. Flower: see *H. sieboldii* 'Alba'.

Comments & Special Needs: Site in light to moderate shade. A moderate to rapid increaser. May need protection from pest damage.

Distinguishing Features: Pure white flowers in late summer.

Hosta 'Paradise Joyce' (Fransen NR)

MEDIUM

Origin: Sport of *H.* 'Halcyon'.

Clump Size & Habit: 36 in. wide × 16 in. high (90 × 40 cm). An overlapping mound.

Description: Leaf blade: 6⅜ × 4 in. (16 × 10 cm); of good substance, smooth, medium yellow then ivory, irregularly margined blue with streaks jetting toward the midrib, matt above and glaucous below; edge almost flat, slightly cupped, oval with a cuspidate tip, heart-shaped pinched lobes. Petiole: chartreuse-yellow. Flower: see *H.* 'Halcyon'.

Comments & Special Needs: Grow in full sun in cooler climates when the leaf coloring will be much stronger, shade in Southern zones. A moderate to rapid increaser and easy to grow. A superb foreground specimen and lovely in containers.

Distinguishing Features: Differs from *H.* 'June' in that

Hosta 'Paradise Power'

the leaf emerges solid blue gradually turning cloudy chartreuse to brilliant yellow, finally bleaching to ivory-white. Also differs from *H.* 'Katherine Lewis' in remaining ivory-white until the leaves die down in autumn.

Similar: *H.* 'June'; *H.* 'Katherine Lewis'.

Hosta 'Paradise Power' (Fransen NR)

LARGE–GIANT

Origin: Sport of *H.* 'Sun Power'.

Clump Size & Habit: 71⅛ in. wide × 28 in. high (178 × 70 cm). A dense, upright mound.

Description: Leaf blade: 11 × 7½ in. (28 × 19 cm); thick, golden yellow irregularly margined dark green with narrow streaks jetting toward the midrib, matt above and thinly glaucous below, slight dimpling; edge widely undulate, oval with a cuspidate tip, heart-shaped pinched lobes. Petiole: chartreuse, finely outlined in dark green, appearing to pierce the blade.

Comments & Special Needs: Tolerates morning sun with abundant moisture at its roots except in the most Southern zones, where it needs light shade all day.

Distinguishing Features: The green margin is a much more vivid green than that of *H*. 'Lakeside Symphony'. A moderately fast increaser. Pest resistant.

Similar: *H. 'Lakeside Symphony', which is has a less striking contrast of colors.

Hosta 'Paul's Glory' (Ruh & Hofer 1987)

MEDIUM–LARGE

Origin: Natural sport of *H*. 'Perry's True Blue'.

Clump Size & Habit: 41½ in. wide × 24 in. high (104 × 60 cm). A dense mound.

Description: Leaf blade: 9⅛ × 7⅛ in. (23 × 18 cm); thick, chartreuse turning golden yellow, irregularly margined dark blue-green with some streaks, matt above and glaucous below, seersuckered; edge flat to slightly kinked, slightly folded or convex, widely oval with an cuspidate tip, heart-shaped pinched lobes. Petiole: narrow, chartreuse, outlined in dark green. Flower: funnel-shaped, pale lavender on an upright, bare, glaucous green, 40 in. (100 cm) scape in high summer; fertile.

Comments & Special Needs: *H*. 'Paul's Glory' performs well in high temperatures, keeping its leaf color better if sited in light shade. During the summer the center turns gold and the leaves turn dark green; the center will bleach to ivory-white if exposed to hot sun. Medium to fast growth rate but needs dividing every three to four years to retain the attractive variegation. Named Hosta of the Year by the American Hosta Growers Association in 1999. A colorful specimen or background hosta.

Distinguishing Features: Particularly vivid and dramatic leaf coloring, the margins being bluer than either *H. 'Inniswood' or *H. 'September Sun', which are similar.

Sports: *H*. 'American Glory Be', which has wider blue-green margins; *H. 'Chesterland Gold'; *H. 'Orange Marmalade', whose central variegation is orange-gold in early summer, gradually turning white.

Hosta 'Paul's Glory'

Hosta 'Peedee Gold Flash'

Hosta 'Peppermint Cream'

Hosta 'Peppermint Ice'

Hosta 'Peedee Gold Flash' (Syre-Herz 1987)

SMALL–MEDIUM

Origin: *H. sieboldii* 'Kabitan' hybrid.

Clump Size & Habit: 18 in. wide × 10 in. high (45 × 25 cm). An upright, spreading mound.

Description: Leaf blade: 6½ × 2⅜ in. (16.5 × 6 cm); thin, rich yellow to chartreuse, narrowly margined dark green with some chartreuse streaks jetting toward the midrib, matt above and satiny below, dimpled when mature, strongly marked veins; edges rippled, arching toward the acute to cuspidate tip, elliptic with tapered open lobes. Petiole: narrow, muted chartreuse, red-dotted at the base. Flower: funnel-shaped, purple-striped lavender on an upright, leafy, chartreuse, 12 in. (30 cm) scape in mid-summer; fertile.

Comments & Special Needs: Viridescent and needs good light to retain the leaf color but exposure to strong sun will bleach the leaf center ivory-white. A rapid increaser in optimum growing conditions, which are humid heat, shade and moisture at the roots. Performs best in a container in much cooler climates.

Similar: *H.* 'Lyme Regis', which has thicker leaves and white flowers; **H. sieboldii* 'Kabitan', which is less vigorous, especially in cooler climates.

Hosta 'Peppermint Cream' (Hatfield NR)

SMALL–MEDIUM

Origin: Natural sport of *H.* 'Vanilla Cream'.

Clump Size & Habit: 18 in. wide × 10 in. high (45 × 25 cm). A low-growing mound.

Description: Leaf blade: 3⅛ × 2½ in. (8 × 6.5 cm); of good substance, chartreuse turning yellow irregularly margined a shadowy mid-green, satiny above and glossy below,

some dimpling when mature, prominent veins; edge slightly rippled, convex, widely oval with a mucronate tip, heart-shaped pinched lobes. Petiole: chartreuse. Flower: see *H.* 'Vanilla Cream'.

Comments & Special Needs: Site in morning sun to bring out the contrast in variegation. Of moderate increase. Plant in front of dark, green-leaved hostas for the greatest foliage effect.

Hosta 'Peppermint Ice' (Belle Gardens 1994)

SMALL

Origin: *H.* 'William Lachman' × *H. montana*.

Clump Size & Habit: 22 in. wide × 8⅜ in. high (55 × 21 cm). A moderately dense, semi-upright mound.

Description: Leaf blade: 6⅜ × 3½ in. (16 × 9 cm); thick, ivory-white turning pure white, widely and irregularly margined dark green and streaked in several shades of green jetting toward the midrib, glossy above and satiny below, moderately prominently veined; edge almost flat, slightly folded or arching, widely oval with a cuspidate tip, heart-shaped open to pinched lobes. Petiole: ivory, outlined in green. Flower: funnel-shaped, rich lavender on an upright, leafy, ivory flushed burgundy, 20¾ in. (52 cm) scape in late summer; fertile.

Comments & Special Needs: Site in good light to moderate shade. A moderate increaser. Among the most colorful hostas of this type. Needs dividing every three to four years to retain the wide central variegation with the attractive streaking.

Distinguishing Features: The noticeably ivory-white scapes and the strongly white-margined leafy bracts.

Hosta 'Pete's Passion' (Ruh 1997)

MEDIUM

Origin: Reverse sport of *H.* 'Paul's Glory'.

Clump Size & Habit: 41½ in. wide × 24 in. high (104 × 60 cm). A tiered mound.

Description: Leaf blade: 11½ × 8⅜ in. (29 × 21 cm); thick, glaucous, chartreuse turning ivory, very widely and irregularly margined blue-green with streaks jetting toward the midrib, prominently veined, seersuckered; edge slightly rippled, widely oval with a mucronate tip, heart-shaped pinched to overlapping lobes. Petiole: stout, green, outlined in blue green. Flower: see *H.* 'Paul's Glory'.

Comments & Special Needs: Albescent. Tolerates morning sun but the color is richer if grown in good light to dappled shade. Increases rapidly. Pest resistant.

Similar: *H.* 'Peter Ruh', whose leaf margins are narrower.

Hosta 'Pineapple Upsidedown Cake' (Zilis & Q & Z Nursery 1999)

MEDIUM

Origin: Sport of *H.* 'Pineapple Poll'.

Clump Size & Habit: 50¾ in. wide × 18 in. high (127 × 45 cm). A rippled mound.

Description: Leaf blade: 9⅛ × 3½ in. (23 × 9 cm); of good substance, smooth, chartreuse to rich golden yellow developing a narrow and irregular dark green margin with some streaks jetting toward the midrib, matt above and glaucous below, closely veined; edge conspicuously rippled, slightly folded, elliptic with an acute tip, tapered open lobes. Petiole: narrow, chartreuse, finely outlined in dark green. Flower: funnel-shaped, lavender on an upright, leafy, gold, 24 to 36 in. (60 to 90 cm) scape in late summer; fertile.

Comments & Special Needs: Site in morning sun in cooler climates. Exposure to hot sun can bleach out the variegation. Less vigorous than the parent.

Hosta 'Pete's Passion'

Hosta 'Pineapple Upsidedown Cake'

Distinguishing Features: Slightly larger than *H.* 'Peedee Gold Flash' and *H. sieboldii* 'Kabitan' and with leaves of thicker substance.

Sports: *H.* 'Pineapple Juice' has yellow leaves that can bleach to white if exposed to hot sun.

Hosta 'Pinwheel' (R. Savory 1983)

SMALL

Origin: Sport of a *H. venusta* seedling.

Clump Size & Habit: 10 in. wide × 7⅛ in. high (25 × 18 cm). A low-growing mound.

Description: Leaf blade: 4 × 1½ in. (10 × 4 cm); of average substance, smooth, ivory-white irregularly margined mid-green, matt above and satiny below; edge almost flat, folded or twisted, widely oval with a cuspidate tip, rounded open lobes. Petiole: ivory, finely outlined in green. Flower: funnel-shaped, lavender on an upright, bare, ivory, 10 in. (25 cm) scape in mid-season; fertility unknown.

Comments & Special Needs: Site in light to moderate

Hosta 'Pinwheel'

Hosta 'Punky'

shade. Is best established in a pot before planting into a rock or sink garden or into a larger container. Of slow to moderate increase.

Distinguishing Features: The twisted leaves form a pinwheel pattern.

Hosta 'Punky' (Kuk & Ziarek 1999)

SMALL–MEDIUM

Origin: Sport of *H.* 'Blue Wedgwood'.

Clump Size & Habit: 24 in. wide × 12 in. high (60 × 30 cm). A dense mound.

Description: Leaf blade: 5½ × 3½ in. (14 × 9 cm); thick, glaucous, cream to golden yellow, narrowly and irregularly margined dark blue-green with streaks jetting toward the midrib, widely undulate to twisted, cupped, dimpled, oval with a flat base, cuspidate tip, open lobes. Petiole: chartreuse, outlined in dark green. Flower: see *H.* 'Blue Wedgwood'.

Distinguishing Features: A dramatic contrast between the dark margin and the bright, light center of the leaf when grown in full sun. The chartreuse petiole appears to penetrate the blade for about 1½ in. (3.5 cm).

Comments & Special Needs: Grows equally well in sun or shade in cooler climates, but morning sun only in hotter regions. Sun will bleach out the leaf color leaving a green skeleton of margin, midrib and veins. A moderate growth rate.

Similar: *H.* 'June'; *H.* 'Katherine Lewis'; *H.* 'Paradise Joyce'; *H.* 'Remember Me'.

Hosta 'Queen of Islip' (GoVery 1990)

LARGE

Origin: Sport of *H.* 'Frances Williams'.

Hosta 'Queen of Islip'

Clump Size & Habit: 40¾ in. wide × 27⅛ in. high (102 × 68 cm). A dense mound.

Description: Leaf blade: 10 × 9⅛ in. (25 × 23 cm); thick, glaucous chartreuse turning yellow and finally ivory-white, widely and irregularly margined dark blue with streaks jetting toward the midrib, seersuckered; edge almost flat, cupped or convex, nearly round with a mucronate tip, heart-shaped pinched or overlapping lobes. Petiole: stout, ivory, finely outlined in dark green. Flower: see *H. sieboldiana* 'Elegans'.

Comments & Special Needs: Variegation is albescent. Keep well shaded all day, especially in spring and early summer when the young leaves are particularly likely to scorch. Slow to increase. Pest resistant. Grow as a border specimen.

Similar: *H. sieboldiana* 'Borwick Beauty'.

Sports: *H.* 'Islip Gold'.

Hosta 'Regal Chameleon'

Hosta 'Remember Me'

Hosta 'Regal Chameleon' (Walters Gardens 2000)

LARGE

Origin: Tissue-cultured sport of *H.* 'Krossa Regal'.

Clump Size & Habit: 36 in. wide × 28 in. high (90 × 70 cm). An upright, vase-shaped mound.

Description: Leaf blade: 12 × 7⅛ in. (30 × 18 cm); thick, smooth, greenish white gradually turning green, irregularly margined and streaked dark blue-green, glaucous above and thickly glaucous below, conspicuously veined; edge widely rippled to twisted, folded, widely oval with a cuspidate tip, tapered pinched to overlapping lobes. Petiole: thickly glaucous, light blue-green. Flower: see *H.* 'Krossa Regal'.

Comments & Special Needs: Variegation is viridescent. Site in good light to moderate shade. Performs best in cooler climates and is at its peak in early summer; from then on the leaves fade to green. Best grown on a sheltered terrace in a large container to enjoy in May and June. Of moderate increase. Pest resistant.

Hosta 'Remember Me' (Van Eijk & Van Erven & Walters 2002)

MEDIUM

Origin: Pod parent is a *H.* 'June' hybrid; pollen parent is unknown.

Clump Size & Habit: 30 in. wide × 12 in. high (75 × 30 cm). A dense mound when mature.

Description: Leaf blade: 6⅜ × 4 in. (16 × 10 cm); thick, smooth, glaucous, bright ivory-white to creamy yellow, irregularly and narrowly margined mid-green with a blue undertone and some jetting toward the midrib; edge flat, widely oval with a cuspidate tip, heart-shaped pinched lobes. Petiole: narrow, cream outlined in dark blue-green.

Hosta 'Robert's Rapier'

Flower: tubular, lavender on an upright, bare, glaucous ivory, 15 in. (38 cm) scape in mid-summer; fertility unknown.

Comments & Special Needs: For the brightest effect, site in morning sun except in the hottest climates. Slower to increase than its parent. Good pest resistance. An outstanding new introduction best planted in masses or drifts at the front of the border.

Distinguishing Features: The contrast between the large light area and the narrow dark border will stand out in a garden setting.

Similar: *H.* 'Lakeside Cup Cake' has bluer margins and the leaves are rounder; *H.* 'Punky'.

Hosta 'Robert's Rapier' (Keller & White Oak Nursery 1996)

MEDIUM

Origin: Sport of *H.* 'White Christmas'.

Clump Size & Habit: 32 in. wide × 18 in. high (80 × 45 cm). An open mound.

Hosta 'September Sun'

Description: Leaf blade: 9⅛ × 5⅛ in. (23 × 13 cm); of average substance, smooth, a narrow flash of white, very widely and evenly margined dark green, matt above and thinly glaucous below, closely veined; edge slightly rippled, arching, oval with an acute tip, rounded open to pinched lobes. Petiole: white, widely outlined in dark green. Flower: see *H.* 'White Christmas'.

Comments & Special Needs: Site in light to moderate shade. A moderate increaser.

Divide the clump as soon as the white central streak starts to disappear.

Distinguishing Feature: The narrow central flash of white on the dark green leaf.

Similar: **H.* 'Undulata Univittata', which has a slightly wider central variegation.

Hosta 'September Sun' (Solberg 1985)

MEDIUM

Origin: First registered sport of *H.* 'August Moon'.

Clump Size & Habit: 50¼ in. wide × 24 in. high (126 × 60 cm). A dense mound.

Description: Leaf blade: 9¼ × 7½ in. (23.5 × 19 cm);

thick, golden yellow widely margined mid-green with occasional streaks jetting toward the midrib, matt above and glaucous below, seersuckered, conspicuously veined; edge slightly undulate, slightly cupped or convex, widely oval with a cuspidate tip, heart-shaped pinched lobes. Petiole: chartreuse, outlined in mid-green. Flower: see *H.* 'August Moon'.

Comments & Special Needs: Tolerates a considerable amount of sun, which makes the leaf coloring even brighter. Vigorous, a rapid increaser and easy to grow. Pest resistant. A forerunner of many similar hostas.

Similar: *H.* 'Lunar Magic'; **H.* 'Lunar Orbit'; **H.* 'Paradigm'; *H.* 'September Surprise'.

Sports: *H.* 'Hub City' has blue-green leaves.

Hosta 'Sheila West' (A. & R. Bowden NR)

MEDIUM–LARGE

Origin: Sport of *H.* 'Fortunei Hyacinthina'.

Clump Size & Habit: 45½ in. wide × 20 in. high (114 × 50 cm). A dense mound.

Description: Leaf blade: 8½ × 8⅜ in. (21.5 × 21 cm); of good substance, chartreuse turning soft yellow, irregularly margined and streaked dark green with a blue cast in early

Hosta 'Sheila West'

Hosta 'Shirley'

summer, matt above and glaucous below, dimpled when mature, widely spaced veins; edge almost flat, slightly convex, nearly round with a mucronate tip, heart-shaped pinched to overlapping lobes. Petiole: chartreuse, outlined in dark green. Flower: see *H.* 'Fortunei Hyacinthina'.

Comments & Special Needs: Site in good light to morning sun in cooler climates, then light to moderate shade. Emerges late. Vigorous, easy to grow.

Distinguishing Features: Differs from *H.* 'Phyllis Campbell' in its rounder leaf and in the variegation, which does not fade as the season progresses.

Similar: *H.* 'Phyllis Campbell', which has brighter central variegation early in the season, the leaf fading to two-tone green.

Hosta 'Shirley' (Van Wade 1998)

MEDIUM

Origin: Unknown.

Clump Size & Habit: 18 in. wide × 12 in. high (45 × 30 cm). An upright mound.

Description: Leaf blade: 7⅛ × 4⅜ in. (18 × 11 cm); of average substance, greenish white to golden yellow, widely and irregularly margined bright mid-green with some streaks jetting toward the midrib, matt above and satiny below, widely spaced veins, some dimpling when mature; edge rippled, slightly folded when young, convex when mature, widely oval with a cuspidate tip, heart-shaped pinched lobes. Petiole: chartreuse, finely outlined mid-green. Flower: bell-shaped, pale lavender on an upright, bare, pale green, 21⅛ to 27⅛ in. (53 to 68 cm) scape in mid-summer; fertile, green seedpods.

Comments & Special Needs: A very colorful hosta variegated in several shades of green, the colors deepening as the season progresses. Very sensitive to light levels, but

Hosta sieboldiana 'Borwick Beauty'

good light to dappled shade all day is recommended. Slow growing.

Distinguishing Features: Shallow, even ripples along the edge. The green margins are ¾ in. (2 cm) wide.

Similar: **H. ventricosa* 'Aureomaculata'.

Hosta sieboldiana 'Borwick Beauty' (G. & B. McBurnie & BHHS 1988)

LARGE

Origin: Natural sport of *H. sieboldiana* 'Elegans'.

Clump Size & Habit: 50¼ in. wide × 24 in. high (126 × 60 cm). An open mound.

Description: Leaf blade: 12 × 11 in. (30 × 28 cm), thick, glaucous, chartreuse, gradually turning white through yellow, widely and irregularly margined dark blue-green with celadon streaks jetting toward the midrib, conspicuously seersuckered; edge slightly undulate, cupped or convex, widely oval to nearly round with a mucronate tip, heart-shaped pinched or overlapping lobes. Petiole: stout ivory,

Hosta sieboldiana 'George Smith'

outlined in blue-green. Flower: see *H. sieboldiana* 'Elegans'.

Comments & Special Needs: The central variegation is lutescent or albescent. Exposure to sunlight, particularly in early summer, can cause the leaf center to scorch and eventually to melt out. Regular division is required to keep the variegation constant.

Similar: *H.* 'Color Glory', which is thought to be identical; *H.* 'DuPage Delight'; *H.* Queen of Islip', which can scorch badly at the edges; *H.* 'Kingswood Center'; *H.* 'Super Nova'.

Hosta sieboldiana 'George Smith' (G. Smith 1983)

LARGE

Origin: Natural sport of *H. sieboldiana* 'Elegans'.

Clump Size & Habit: 50¼ in. wide × 24 in. high (126 × 60 cm). An open mound.

Description: Leaf blade: 12 × 11 in. (30 × 28 cm); thick, glaucous, chartreuse to pale yellow, widely and irregularly margined dark blue-green with celadon streaks jetting toward the midrib, seersuckered; edge almost flat to slightly undulate, cupped or convex, widely oval to nearly round

with a mucronate tip, heart-shaped pinched to overlapping lobes. Petiole: stout, pale yellow, outlined in dark green. Flower: see *H. sieboldiana* 'Elegans'.

Comments & Special Needs: Central variegation is lutescent or albescent but the variegation is barely visible when the leaves emerge. Good light to moderate shade all day. Slow to increase. Pest resistant.

Similar: **H. sieboldiana* 'Borwick Beauty', whose variegation is more vivid earlier in the season.

Hosta sieboldiana 'Thunderbolt' (Hawksridge Farms NR)

MEDIUM–LARGE

Origin: Tissue-cultured sport of *H. sieboldiana* 'Elegans'.

Clump Size & Habit: 40¾ in. wide × 22 in. high (102 × 55 cm). A dense mound.

Description: Leaf blade: 9⅛ × 8⅜ in. (23 × 21 cm); very thick, glaucous, chartreuse-white turning cream to yellow, finally ivory-white, very widely and irregularly margined blue-green with streaks jetting toward the midrib, seersuckered; edge flat, cupped, widely oval to nearly round with a mucronate tip, heart-shaped overlapping lobes. Petiole: ivory, outlined in dark blue-green.

Hosta sieboldiana 'Thunderbolt'

Hosta 'Sitting Pretty'

Hosta 'Something Different'

Comments & Special Needs: The blue-green margins will remain much bluer and the central flash will remain more yellow if the plant is grown in light shade. Slow to increase. Pest resistant.

Similar: *H.* 'Dream Weaver', which has slightly greener margins and is less seersuckered.

Hosta 'Sitting Pretty' (Aden 1987)

MINIATURE

Origin: *H.* 'Reiko' × *H.* 'Amy Aden'.

Clump Size & Habit: 8⅜ in. wide × 4 in. high (21 × 10 cm). A flattish mound.

Description: Leaf blade: 7⅛ × 1½ in. (18 × 3.5 cm); thick, chartreuse turning ivory-white to yellow, irregularly margined dark and light olive-green, glossy above and matt below, dimpled when mature; edge almost flat, oval with a cuspidate tip, tapered pinched lobes. Petiole: narrow, chartreuse, attractively outlined dark green. Flower: funnel-shaped, bright purple on an upright, leafy, ivory to chartreuse, 12 in. (30 cm) scape in mid- to late summer; fertile.

Comments & Special Needs: Some morning sun in cooler gardens will intensify the leaf color.

Distinguishing Features: Flowers are disposed at 90° to the scape.

Sports: *H.* 'Junior Miss' has dark green leaves margined creamy yellow.

Hosta 'Something Different' (P. Banyai 1990)

MEDIUM

Origin: Sport of *H.* 'Gold Standard'.

Clump Size & Habit: 36 to 46⅜ in. wide × 16 to 18 in. high (90 to 116 × 40 to 45 cm). A dense mound.

Description: Leaf blade: 9⅛ × 5⅛ to 7⅛ in. (23 × 13 to 18 cm); of average substance, greenish white to bright chartreuse-yellow, irregularly margined dark green with a blue cast, some streaks jetting toward the midrib, matt above and thinly glaucous below, dimpled; edge rippled to twisted, oval with a cuspidate tip, heart-shaped open to pinched lobes. Petiole: chartreuse, outlined in dark green. Flower: see *H.* 'Fortunei Hyacinthina'.

Comments & Special Needs: Site in some morning sun in cooler climates. Variegation is more vivid early in the season, but careful placing in the garden may be necessary before the best coloring is achieved. Several seasons of growth is needed to achieve the mature leaf shape and color. Moderate growth rate.

Distinguishing Features: Leaves are tightly furled early in the season, becoming more lax. Quite distinct in leaf shape from *H.* 'Gold Standard'.

Similar: *H.* 'Brenda's Beauty'.

Hosta 'Spinning Wheel'

Hosta 'Spritzer'

Hosta 'Spinning Wheel' (M. Seaver NR)

LARGE

Origin: Sport of *H.* 'Golden Nugget'.

Clump Size & Habit: 50¾ in. wide × 20 in. high (127 × 50 cm). An open mound.

Description: Leaf blade: 11 × 10 in. (28 × 25 cm), thick, glaucous green, turning chartreuse to creamy yellow, irregularly margined and splashed blue-green, intensely seersuckered; edge almost flat, cupped or convex, nearly round with a mucronate tip, heart-shaped overlapping lobes. Petiole: flattish, chartreuse, outlined in blue-green. Flower: bell-shaped to flaring, near white on an upright, bare, glaucous mauve-gray, 18 in. (45 cm) scape in mid-summer; fertile.

Comments & Special Needs: Site in light to moderate shade. Slow growing. Pest resistant. Divide regularly to maintain the attractive variegation.

Similar: *H.* 'Aardvark'; *H.* 'Larry Englerth'; **H.* 'Lucy Vitols'.

Hosta 'Spritzer' (Aden 1986)

MEDIUM–LARGE

Origin: *H.* 'Green Fountain' hybrid.

Clump Size & Habit: 30 in. wide × 20 in. high (75 × 50 cm). An upright, arching mound.

Description: Leaf blade: 10 × 5⅛ in. (25 × 13 cm); thin, smooth, old-gold, widely and irregularly margined olive-green with many streaks jetting toward the midrib, shiny above and glossy below, prominently veined; edge rippled, arching and twisted and pinched toward the tip, narrowly oval with a cuspidate tip, rounded open lobes. Petiole: chartreuse, outlined in olive-green. Flower: funnel-shaped, pale lavender on a leaning, leafy, 30 in. (75 cm) scape from late summer to early autumn; fertile.

Hosta 'Stained Glass'

Comments & Special Needs: Site in light to moderate shade where the cascading mound can be best appreciated. *Hosta* 'Spritzer' is, in effect, the centrally variegated form of *H.* 'Green Fountain'; it increases rapidly but is well suited to container growing.

Distinguishing Features: The subtly variegated leaves on a cascading mound.

Hosta 'Stained Glass' (Hansen & Shady Oaks Nursery 1999)

MEDIUM

Origin: Tissue-cultured sport of *H.* 'Guacamole'.

Clump Size & Habit: 32 in. wide × 15 in. high (80 × 38 cm). A rounded, open mound.

Description: Leaf blade: 10¼ × 7⅛ in. (26 × 18 cm); of average substance, matt, golden yellow with a wide, irregular dark green margin, dimpled, strongly and widely veined; edge slightly undulate, convex, widely oval with a cuspidate tip, heart-shaped overlapping lobes. Petiole: chartreuse, finely outlined in dark green. Flower: see *H.* 'Guacamole'.

Comments & Special Needs: Vigorous. Somewhat sun tolerant with large, fragrant, pale lavender flowers. An all-around garden-worthy hosta.

Distinguishing Features: Differs from *H.* 'Guacamole' in its brighter golden yellow leaf and its vivid 2 in. (5 cm) wide margin.

Similar: *H. 'Okaydokey'.

Hosta 'Striptease'

Sports: *H.* 'Tortilla Chip', which has bright yellow leaves and fragrant, pale lavender flowers.

Hosta 'Striptease' (Thompson 1991)

MEDIUM

Origin: Sport of *H.* 'Gold Standard'.

Clump Size & Habit: 50¼ in. wide × 20 in. high (126 × 50 cm). A dense mound.

Description: Leaf blade: 8⅜ × 6⅜ in. (21 × 16 cm); of good substance, chartreuse turning yellow to ivory, widely margined dark green with a blue cast in early summer, with occasional silver-white flecks at the junction of the center and the margin, matt above and glaucous below, conspicuously veined; edge almost flat, slightly arching, oval with a cuspidate tip, heart-shaped to rounded, open to pinched lobes. Petiole: chartreuse, outlined in dark green. Flower: see *H.* 'Fortunei Hyacinthina'.

Comments & Special Needs: Careful siting in the garden is essential to achieve the most pleasing seasonal and light-level variations in leaf color. A moderate to fast increaser. Plant as a border specimen or in a large container.

Distinguishing Features: As originally registered, it has

Hosta 'Summer Joy'

only a few silver-white flecks, but later versions can have the flecking nearly all round the blade.

Similar: *H.* 'Gypsy Rose', which has smaller, more folded leaves with a brighter color contrast; **H.* 'Kiwi Full Monty', whose leaf margins are more blue than green.

Hosta 'Summer Joy' (Klehm 1998)

SMALL

Origin: Sport of *H.* 'Blue Moon'.

Clump Size & Habit: 20 in. wide × 10 in. high (50 × 25 cm). An upright mound.

Description: Leaf blade: 7⅛ × 6⅜ in. (18 × 16 cm); thick, chartreuse to ivory, widely and irregularly margined blue-green with celadon streaks jetting toward the midrib, satiny above and matt below, dimpled; edge slightly rippled, slightly cupped, oval with a cuspidate tip, heart-shaped overlapping lobes. Petiole: ivory, finely outlined in dark blue-green. Flower: see *H.* 'Blue Moon'.

Comments & Special Needs: Site in light to moderate shade, which will maintain the best leaf color. A slow to moderate increaser. Pest resistant. Is considerably larger than its parent, *H.* 'Blue Moon', and the scape somewhat taller, so its exact parentage may need investigating. Nonetheless, it is an attractive and colorful hosta.

Similar: *H.* 'Lakeside Cup Cake', which has slightly rounder leaves with a smoother surface.

Hosta 'Summer Music' (Klehm 1998)

MEDIUM

Origin: Sport of *H.* 'Shade Master'.

Clump Size & Habit: 21⅛ in. wide × 14 in. high (53 × 35 cm). An upright mound.

Description: Leaf blade: 7⅛ × 6⅜ in. (18 × 16 cm); thin, matt, chartreuse turning pure white widely and irregularly margined olive-green with chartreuse streaks jetting toward the midrib, dimpled to seersuckered, widely spaced veins; edge very slightly rippled, twisted, convex with the tip recurved, widely oval with heart-shaped overlapping lobes. Petiole: shallow, ivory, finely lined chartreuse with wider olive-green edges. Flower: see *H.* 'Shade Master'.

Comments & Special Needs: Site in good light to light shade all day, ensuring adequate moisture. A moderate to rapid increaser. Protect from pest damage.

Sports: *H.* 'Lakeside Meter Maid' has white leaves with wide, dark green margins; *H.* 'Last Dance' has chartreuse-green leaves with pale yellow margins.

Hosta 'Summer Serenade' (Klehm 1998)

LARGE

Origin: Sport of *H.* 'Piedmont Gold'.

Clump Size & Habit: 50¾ in. wide × 24 in. high (127 × 60 cm). An upright mound.

Description: Leaf blade: 10 × 9½ in. (25 × 24 cm); thick, chartreuse to yellow, irregularly margined dark olive-green with occasional streaks jetting toward the midrib, matt above and slightly glaucous below, smooth to seersuckered, ribbed veins; edge slightly rippled, slightly arching to convex, widely oval with a cuspidate tip, deeply heart-shaped lobes. Petiole: chartreuse, outlined in dark green. Flower: see *H.* 'Piedmont Gold'.

Comments & Special Needs: Site in morning sun except in the hottest climates. The color of the leaf center changes depending on the intensity of the light, being a deeper golden yellow in strong sunshine. A moderate increaser. Pest resistant. Among the best of the many sports of *H.* 'Piedmont Gold'. Fairly pest resistant.

Similar: *H.* 'David Stone'; *H.* 'Everglades'; **H.* 'Lakeside Symphony'.

Hosta 'Summer Music'

Hosta 'Summer Serenade'

Hosta 'Sweet Home Chicago'

Hosta 'Sweet Home Chicago' (Zilis NR)

MEDIUM

Origin: Tissue-cultured sport of *H.* 'Birchwood Parky's Gold'.

Clump Size & Habit: 45½ in. wide × 18 in. high (114 × 45 cm). A compact mound.

Description: Leaf blade: 6⅜ × 5⅛ in. (16 × 13 cm); of average substance, chartreuse to yellow, widely and irregularly margined mid-green, matt above and slightly glaucous below, dimpled; edge flat, widely oval to nearly round with a mucronate tip, flat open lobes. Petiole: chartreuse, outlined in dark green. Flower: see *H.* 'Birchwood Parky's Gold'.

Comments & Special Needs: Site in high, filtered light. Vigorous, a rapid increaser and easy to grow.

Distinguishing Features: The ⅜ in. (1 cm) wide green margin makes a dramatic contrast to the bright center of the leaf, the colors intensifying as the season progresses. Scapes have attractively variegated leafy bracts near the raceme.

Hosta 'Twist of Lime'

Hosta 'Twist of Lime' (Banyai & Solberg 1991)

SMALL

Origin: Sport of *H.* 'Lemon Lime'.

Clump Size & Habit: 30 in. wide × 12 in. high (75 × 30 cm). A dense mound.

Description: Leaf blade: 3½ × 1½ in. (9 × 4 cm); thin, smooth, chartreuse to lemon-yellow, narrowly and irregularly margined dark green with streaks jetting toward the midrib, matt above and satiny below; edge rippled, arching, folded, lanceolate with an acute tip, tapered open lobes. Petiole: chartreuse. Flower: see *H*. 'Lemon Lime'.

Comments & Special Needs: Site in light to moderate shade. Vigorous, a rapid increaser and easy to grow. An ideal edger or ground cover. Susceptible to pest damage.

Similar: *H*. 'Green Eyes'; **H. 'Green with Envy'.

Hosta 'Undulata' (Bailey/AHS 2001)

MEDIUM

Origin: Japanese gardens.

Clump Size & Habit: 30 in. wide × 12 in. high (75 × 30 cm). An unruly mound.

Description: Leaf blade: 6⅜ × 3⅛ in. (16 × 8 cm); thin, smooth, pure white, irregularly margined dark green with streaks jetting toward the midrib, matt above and satiny below; edge rippled and twisted, oval with a cuspidate tip, rounded open lobes. Petiole: ivory-white, outlined in dark green. Flower: narrowly funnel-shaped, pale lavender on an upright, leafy, ivory, 25⅛ in. (63 cm) scape in high summer; virtually sterile.

Comments & Special Needs: Site in good light to moderate shade. Leaves can scorch if exposed to strong sunlight when wet. Plenty of moisture and feeding are required because it lacks vigor and is slow to increase. Flower habit is poor since only a few flowers open consecutively and the scape begins to decline before flowering is over. Needs regular division to prevent the stronger, green-marginal portion of the leaf from taking over.

Distinguishing Features: The second flush of leaves is mottled green in the center. The variegated scape bracts can be almost the same size as the leaves.

Similar: *H*. 'Kiwi Spearmint', whose leaves are longer; *H*. 'White Christmas'.

Sports: **H. 'Undulata Albomarginata'; **H. 'Undulata Erromena'; *H*. 'Undulata Univittata', whose leaves have a narrower central variegation.

Hosta 'Undulata Univittata' (AHS 1987)

MEDIUM–LARGE

Origin: Natural sport of *H*. 'Undulata'.

Clump Size & Habit: 45½ in. wide × 18 in. high (114 × 45 cm). An open mound.

Description: Leaf blade: 7⅛ × 4 in. (18 × 10 cm); of average substance, pure white, very widely margined dark green with streaks jetting toward the midrib, matt above and satiny below, prominently veined; edge slightly rip-

Hosta 'Undulata'

Hosta 'Undulata Univittata'

pled, convex, widely oval with a cuspidate tip, heart-shaped open to pinched lobes. Petiole: ivory-white, outlined in dark green. Flower: see *H*. 'Undulata'.

Comments & Special Needs: Site in light to moderate shade. Feed and water copiously throughout the growing season. More vigorous than the parent plant. Divide regularly to prevent the variegation from disappearing.

Distinguishing Features: A much narrower variegation than its parent but the width of the central variegation is very variable.

Similar: **H. 'Robert's Rapier', which has an even narrower central flash.

Sports: *H*. 'White Ray' has a very narrow, white, central flash.

Hosta ventricosa 'Aureomaculata'

Hosta ventricosa **'Aureomaculata'** (Hensen & AHS 1987)

MEDIUM–LARGE

Origin: Natural sport of *H. ventricosa*.

Clump Size & Habit: 36 in. wide × 16 in. high (90 × 40 cm). A diffuse mound.

Description: Leaf blade: 9 × 8⅜ in. (24 × 21 cm); thin, chartreuse to yellow turning old-gold, widely and irregularly margined dark spinach-green with many streaks jetting toward the midrib, shiny above and glossy below, some dimpling when mature, widely spaced veins; edge slightly rippled, widely oval with a cuspidate tip, heart-shaped pinched lobes. Petiole: chartreuse-yellow, outlined in dark green. Flower: see *H. ventricosa*.

Comments & Special Needs: Site in moderate shade. Slow to increase but well worth the wait.

Distinguishing Features: Variegation gradually fades during the summer, more rapidly in hot climates.

Similar: *H.* 'Flame Stitch'; *H.* 'Shirley'; *H.* 'Stained Satin'.

Hosta **'Whirligig'** (Walden-West NR)

MEDIUM

Origin: *H.* 'Fortunei Albopicta' seedling.

Clump Size & Habit: 24 in. wide × 16 in. high (60 × 40 cm). An upright, twisting mound.

Description: Leaf blade: 6⅜ × 4 in. (16 × 10 cm); of average substance, pale yellow, turning chartreuse finally mid-green, widely and irregularly margined dark green with streaks jetting toward the midrib, matt above and glaucous below, slight dimpling; edge dramatically twisted from the base, oval with a cuspidate tip, kinked to heart-shaped pinched lobes. Petiole: ivory turning green. Flower: tubular, rich lavender on an upright, leafy, gray-green, 24 in. (60 cm) scape, which is purple toward the raceme, in mid- to high summer; fertility unknown.

Comments & Special Needs: Variegation is viridescent, but throughout the season there is always pale new growth giving a very colorful effect. Site in morning sun in cooler climates otherwise light to medium shade all day. Careful positioning is advised. A moderate to fast increaser.

Hosta 'Whirligig'

Hosta 'Whirlwind'

Distinguishing Features: The upward stance of the twisted folded leaves with their dramatic mid-summer variegation.

Similar: *H. 'Fortunei Albopicta', which is a larger plant.

Hosta 'Whirlwind' (Kulpa 1989)

MEDIUM

Origin: Possible sport of a H. 'Fortunei Hyacinthina'.

Clump Size & Habit: 40¾ in. wide × 18 in. high (102 × 45 cm). A twisted, upright mound.

Description: Leaf blade: 7⅛ × 5½ in. (18 × 14 cm); thick, pale chartreuse becoming ivory to bright yellow then fading to drab green, widely and irregularly margined dark olive-green with celadon streaks jetting toward the midrib, strongly veined, matt above and glaucous below, slightly dimpled, twisted, recurved at the exaggerated tip, kinked at flat open lobes. Petiole: flat toward the blade, which it appears to pierce. Flower: funnel-shaped, pale lavender on an upright, leafy, glaucous gray-green, 20 in. (50 cm) scape, which has occasional large variegated leafy bracts in late summer; fertility unknown.

Comments & Special Needs: Leaf color varies with temperature and the age of the plant. Some morning sun is beneficial. Vigorous and easy to grow. Makes superb ground cover.

Distinguishing Features: H. 'Whirlwind' is quite distinct among the centrally variegated hostas because of its broad, twisted leaves on long petioles and the conspicuous green veining on the leaf's surface.

Similar: *H. 'Whirlwind Tour', which is smaller and without the markedly twisted leaves.

Sports: H. 'Dust Devil' has dark green leaves with char-

Hosta 'Whirlwind Tour'

treuse margins that turn creamy white; H. 'Whirling Dervish' has green leaves with very wide yellow margins; *H. 'Whirlwind Tour'.

Hosta 'Whirlwind Tour' (Q. & Z. Nurseries NR)

SMALL

Origin: Tissue-cultured sport of H. 'Whirlwind'.

Clump Size & Habit: 44 in. wide × 10 in. high (110 × 45 cm). An upright mound.

Description: Leaf blade: 7⅛ × 5½ in. (18 × 14 cm); of average substance, olive-green, gradually becoming rich creamy yellow, irregularly margined and streaked several shades of green jetting toward the midrib, matt above and slightly shiny below, some dimpling when mature; edge almost flat, widely oval with a cuspidate tip, rounded pinched lobes. Petiole: narrow, pale green, finely outlined in dark green. Flower: see H. 'Whirlwind'.

Comments & Special Needs: Site in morning sun in cooler climates to produce brighter leaf centers and more turgid leaves. Vigorous and easy to grow.

Similar: *H.* 'Phyllis Campbell', whose leaves are more seersuckered.

Hosta 'Wylde Green Cream' (J. & E. Stratton 1996)

SMALL

Origin: Sport of *H.* 'Vanilla Cream'.

Clump Size & Habit: 16 in. wide × 8 in. high (40 × 20 cm). A compact mound.

Description: Leaf blade: 4 × 3½ in. (10 × 9 cm); thick, chartreuse to yellow, irregularly margined bright dark green with streaks jetting toward the midrib, matt above and thinly glaucous below, dimpled, prominently veined; edge slightly rippled, widely oval to nearly round with a mucronate tip, heart-shaped pinched lobes. Petiole: narrow, chartreuse, finely outlined in dark green. Flower: see *H.* 'Vanilla Cream'.

Comments & Special Needs: Site in morning sun then light to moderate shade. Slow to increase. Pest resistant.

Hosta 'Wylde Green Cream'

Distinguishing Features: An attractive contrast between the pale but bright center and the dark green, which resembles a hand-painted decoration.

Similar: *H.* 'Heart and Soul'; *H.* 'Peppermint Cream' has a much paler green margin; *H.* 'Rainforest Sunrise' appears virtually identical.

CHAPTER ELEVEN

HOSTAS *with* STREAKED, STIPPLED, FLECKED, MARBLED, MISTED *&* UNUSUALLY MARKED LEAVES

MANY HOSTAS WITH STREAKED, stippled, flecked, marbled, misted and unusually marked leaves are valued not only for their unusual leaf patterns but also as breeding plants. Hybridizers especially cherish streaked hostas for the variability of the seedlings they produce, many having marginal variegations. The odds of getting a variegated seedling from any other sort of hosta, by contrast, are infinitely remote. Streaked hostas themselves are not stable, and in some hostas no two leaves look the same. The streaking will often migrate to the margins or result in the leaves becoming a solid color. Quite often these reversions result in new and possibly very desirable plants.

Hostas with streaked leaves have a small but dedicated following; usually they are sought after only by those wishing to incorporate genes for variegation into their breeding programs, the streaked hostas being used as the pod parents (since variegation is almost always inherited from the female parent). Clumps of streaky-leaved hostas need to be divided every three to five years if this characteristic is to be retained. Unfortunately, it is all too easy to allow the clump to mutate to a centrally or marginally variegated hosta—or even to the original parent.

Fairly uniform streaking can, however, produce a most unusual and arresting effect in the garden border, especially when those specimens are grown among others with plain green, yellow or blue leaves. Most streaky-leaved hostas arise from parents that need dappled or full shade (for example, Hosta 'Neat Splash'), and are often not very vigorous and need constant attention. Streaky-leaved hostas that arise from H. plantaginea and its hybrids will tolerate a good deal of sun and are very valuable in an exotically themed garden. Flower arrangers prize streaky-leaved hostas when a uniformly streaked clump is not essential, such as when the instant visual appeal of bold streaking is of the essence.

Streaking is caused by colored plastids arising in the middle layer of the leaf, L2, and in the epidermal layer, L3, which determines the margin. The main area of the leaf blade is a mixture of L2 and L3. The relationship of these two parts of the leaf explains why streaky variegation often migrates to the margin of the leaf. Breeders find streaky hostas especially valuable because of the 50 percent chance of getting a variegated seedling. Streaky hostas are used as the pod parents, and the less fertile the pollen parent, the narrower is the line of breeding, thus making these seedlings the most valuable. The "snow flurry" or mottling effect can be achieved by selfing Hosta 'Frances Williams'. Other unusual types of marking in the center of a hosta leaf are caused by viral infection or a chromosome deficiency.

Many of the hostas I list here are only of interest to breeders and as such are rare and difficult to find. They may be obtained from specialist suppliers.

Hosta 'Allegan Fog' (Herrema 2000)

MEDIUM

Origin: Sport of H. 'Fortunei Albopicta Aurea'.

Clump Size & Habit: 18 in. wide × 13⅛ in. high (45 × 33 cm). A compact mound.

Description: Leaf blade: 4¾ × 3⅛ in. (11.5 × 8 cm); thin, greenish white becoming finely flecked dark green, irregularly margined dark green, matt above and glaucous below; edge slightly rippled, twisted, arching, widely lanceolate with a long, curved acute tip, tapered open lobes. Petiole: narrow, white, outlined in dark green. Flower: see H. 'Fortunei Albopicta'.

Comments & Special Needs: Viridescent. Site in light to moderate shade; careful positioning is important in achieving the best color effect. Surprisingly vigorous, a fairly rapid increaser.

Distinguishing Features: Central variegation is stippled and flecked olive- to dark green.

Similar: H. 'Alley Oop', which is smaller.

Hosta 'Allen C. Haskell' (M. Seaver NR)

MEDIUM

Origin: Unknown. Originally named H. 'Monet' on account of the many colors in the streaking.

Clump Size & Habit: 36 in. wide × 18 in. high (90 × 45 cm). A tight mound.

Description: Leaf blade: 7⅛ × 5⅛ in. (18 × 13 cm); thick, satiny, blue-green, streaked white, cream, golden yellow and celadon, seersuckered; edge almost flat, folded, widely oval with a mucronate tip, heart-shaped pinched lobes. Petiole: blue-green with some streaking. Flower: funnel-shaped, pale lavender on an upright, leafy, glaucous green, 26 to 28 in. (65 to 70 cm) scape in mid-summer; it seldom, if ever sets seed.

Comments & Special Needs: Site in light to moderate shade. Slow to increase. Variegation is unstable so division

---

Previous page: Hosta 'Sweet Standard'

Hosta 'Allegan Fog'

Hosta 'Artist's Palette'

Hosta 'Allen C. Haskell'

Hosta 'Blizzard'

of the clump is necessary as soon as the streaking starts reverting to only marginal variegation.

Hosta 'Artist's Palette' (Kuk 1986)

MINIATURE–SMALL

Origin: *H.* 'Neat Splash' hybrid.

Clump Size & Habit: 4 in. wide × 2¾ in. high (10 × 7 cm). An open mound.

Description: Leaf blade: 2¼ × ¾ in. (5.7 × 2 cm); thick, glossy, smooth, ivory, randomly streaked and misted deep cream, chartreuse and dark green, cleanly margined white; edge kinked, folded, lanceolate to triangular with an acute to cuspidate tip, tapered open lobes. Petiole: flattish, streaked and mottled, outlined in white. Flower: long, tubular, purple-striped lavender on an upright, leafy, streaky green, 14 in. (35 cm) scape in late summer; fertile, streaked seedpods.

Comments & Special Needs: Registered dimensions are easily exceeded under optimum growing conditions. A useful pod parent for variegated seedlings. Will quickly revert

to an attractive, white-margined form if not regularly divided. Very rare and expensive.

Distinguishing Features: Unstable variegation; one season it appears with a marginal variegation, the next with streaked leaves.

Sports: *H.* 'Margin of Error' has dark green leaves, crisply margined creamy white.

Hosta 'Blizzard' (Winterberry Farms NR)

GIANT

Origin: Sport of *H.* 'Winter Snow'.

Clump Size & Habit: 71⅛ in. wide × 30 in. high (178 × 75 cm). A dense mound.

Description: Leaf blade: 20 × 15 in. (50 × 38 cm); thick, smooth, mottled, streaked and striped cream, green and yellow, satiny above and glaucous below; edge slightly rippled and cupped, widely oval with a conspicuous cuspidate tip, heart-shaped pinched lobes. Petiole: streaked, cream. Flower: see *H.* 'Sum and Substance'.

Comments & Special Needs: Sun-tolerant for most of

the day, except in the hottest climates. The streaked variegation is fairly stable. Is fertile and yields streaked seedlings. The substance is extremely good for a streak-leaved hosta.

Sports: *H.* 'Winterberry Farm' is the stable, white-margined sport; **H.* 'Winter Snow' has less streaking.

Hosta 'Breeder's Choice' (K. Vaughan & Seaver 1987)

SMALL–MEDIUM

Origin: *H.* 'Frances Williams' × *H.* 'Beatrice'.

Clump Size & Habit: 16 in. wide × 8⅜ to 12 in. high (40 × 21 to 30 cm). A compact mound.

Description: Leaf blade: 5⅛ × 4⅜ in. (13 × 11 cm); thick, mid-green, mottled, striped and streaked creamy yellow turning white, matt above and glaucous below, seersuckered; edge widely undulate, slightly folded, elliptic to widely oval with a mucronate tip, tapered open lobes. Petiole: narrow, chartreuse. Flower: bell-shaped, pale lavender on an upright, bare, ivory, 25⅛ to 30 in. (63 to 75 cm) scape in high summer; fertile, with seedpods that are sometimes mottled, indicating a high probability of streaky seedlings.

Comments & Special Needs: Site in good light to moderate shade. Slow to moderate increase. Variegation will stabilize if the plant is not divided every few years. Among the most prolific of all streaked breeding hostas and the parent of many well-known introductions.

Hosta 'Christmas Tree Gala' (Powell 2000)

MEDIUM

Origin: Sport of *H.* 'Christmas Tree'.

Clump Size & Habit: 30 in. wide × 20 in. high (75 × 50 cm). A dense mound.

Description: Leaf blade: 6⅜ × 4 in. (16 × 10 cm); thick, matt, dark green with a blue cast, mottled, streaked and striped cream turning yellow, seersuckered and puckered; edge slightly rippled, slightly cupped or convex, widely oval to nearly round with a mucronate tip, heart-shaped overlapping lobes. Petiole: cream, outlined in green. Flower: see *H.* 'Christmas Tree'.

Comments & Special Needs: Site in some morning sun except in the hottest regions.

A slow to moderate increaser.

Distinguishing Features: Each leaf is different, giving a colorful display. More suitable as a garden plant than some streaky-leaved hostas. Is a well-regarded breeding plant for variegated seedlings.

Similar: *H.* 'Galaxy'.

---

*Indicates plants fully described elsewhere in this book.

Hosta 'Breeder's Choice'

Hosta 'Christmas Tree Gala'

Hosta 'Color Fantasy' (Aden 1980)

MEDIUM

Origin: Putative *H.* 'Gala' hybrid.

Clump Size & Habit: 18 in. wide × 10 in. high (45 × 25 cm). An open mound.

Description: Leaf blade: 6⅜ × 4 in. (16 × 10 cm); thick, blue-green, streaked and striped, chartreuse and ivory, matt above and glaucous below, dimpled; edge flat, mostly arching, widely oval with a cuspidate tip, heart-shaped pinched lobes. Petiole: ivory, outlined in blue-green. Flower: funnel-shaped, lavender on a thin, upright or oblique, leafy, pale green, 16 in. (40 cm) scape in late summer; barely fertile.

Comments & Special Needs: Site in some morning sun except in the hottest regions, then light shade. Among the first of the streaky-leaved hostas introduced.

Distinguishing Features: Some leaves are predominantly blue-green, others are more conspicuously streaked.

Hosta 'Color Fantasy'

Hosta 'Crown Prince'

Hosta 'Color Parade'

Hosta **'Color Parade'** (Q & Z Nurseries 2000)

MEDIUM–LARGE

Origin: Tissue-cultured sport of *H.* 'Fragrant Bouquet'.

Clump Size & Habit: 25⅛ in. wide × 18 in. high (63 × 45 cm). A symmetrical mound.

Description: Leaf blade: 8⅜ × 6⅜ in. (21 × 16 cm); of average substance, pale olive-green to chartreuse-yellow, streaked and mottled yellow-cream turning ivory, satiny above and shiny below, prominently veined; edge shallowly undulate, convex, widely oval with a cuspidate tip, heart-shaped pinched lobes. Petiole: ivory, outlined in chartreuse. Flower: see *H.* 'Fragrant Bouquet'.

Comments & Special Needs: Sun tolerant in most regions. Protect from late frost damage. A valuable plant for breeding streaked, sun-tolerant hostas with fragrant flowers.

Distinguishing Features: The streaked leaf center is usually bordered by a distinct pale olive-green to chartreuse-yellow margin.

Hosta **'Crown Prince'** (Ross & Ruh 1987)

SMALL

Origin: Unknown.

Clump Size & Habit: 18 in. wide × 10 in. high (45 × 30 cm). An open mound.

Description: Leaf blade: 4⅜ × 2⅜ in. (11 × 6 cm); thin, emerging satiny, bright golden yellow turning first muted yellow then cream with bright green streaks, dimpled to seersuckered; edge slightly rippled, oval with a cuspidate tip, tapered open lobes. Petiole: flattish, pale green. Flower: flared, intense violet on an upright, leafy, green, 10 to 18 in. (30 to 45 cm) scape in late summer; fertility unknown.

Comments & Special Needs: Site in morning sun in cooler climates. Grow among small boulders with pulmonarias and ferns. Moderate growth rate and easy to grow. A very underrated hosta.

Distinguishing Features: Leaf color changes throughout the season giving a tricolor effect and also a vivid contrast with the rich violet flowers.

Hosta **'Cynthia'** (Tompkins 1984)

LARGE–GIANT

Origin: *H. montana* seedling.

Clump Size & Habit: 60 in. wide × 36 in. high (150 × 90 cm). A dense mound.

Description: Leaf blade: 12¾ × 10 in. (32 × 25 cm); thick, mid- to dark green, streaked, blotched and mottled chartreuse to creamy yellow, matt above and glaucous below, seersuckered, prominently veined; edge piecrusted, slightly arching, widely oval with a cuspidate tip, heart-shaped pinched lobes. Petiole: light green, appearing to pierce the blade. Flower: funnel-shaped, pale lavender on

Hosta 'Cynthia'

Hosta 'Devon Cloud'

an upright, leafy, green 30 to 34 in. (75 to 85 cm) scape in early summer; fertility unknown.

Comments & Special Needs: Site in light to moderate shade. A rapid increaser.

Distinguishing Features: The variegation, which is random and unstable, fades during the summer.

Hosta 'Devon Cloud' (A. & R. Bowden NR)

MEDIUM

Origin: Sport of *H.* 'Invincible'.

Clump Size & Habit: 40¾ in. wide × 20 in. high (102 × 50 cm). An arching mound.

Description: Leaf blade: 8⅜ × 6⅜ in. (21 × 16 cm); thick, leathery, glossy olive-green, streaked and clouded yellow, widely spaced veins; edge rippled, folded, wedge-shaped with an acute tip, rounded pinched lobes. Petiole: olive-green. Flower: see *H.* 'Invincible'.

Comments & Special Needs: If an abundance of moisture is available, site in sun for most of the day. A moderate to rapid increaser and easy to grow.

Distinguishing Features: The variegation has a shadowy, muted effect.

Hosta 'Don Quixote' (M. Seaver NR)

SMALL–MEDIUM

Origin: Streaked-leaf form of *H.* 'Don Stevens'.

Clump Size & Habit: 40¾ in. wide × 15 to 18 in. high (102 × 38 to 45 cm). A dense mound.

Description: Leaf blade: 9½ × 6 in. (24 × 15 cm); of average substance, dark olive-green streaked and splashed rich yellow turning ivory-white, prominently veined; edge slightly rippled, oval with a cuspidate tip, tapered pinched lobes. Petiole: red-dotted olive-green, outlined in creamy yellow. Flower: see *H.* 'Don Stevens'.

Hosta 'Don Quixote'

Comments & Special Needs: Site in good light to moderate shade. A moderate increaser and good breeding plant.

Distinguishing Features: The streaking is usually in the center of the leaf, which is margined green.

Hosta 'Dorothy Benedict' (H. R. Benedict 1983)

MEDIUM–LARGE

Origin: *H.* 'Frances Williams' selfed seedling.

Clump Size & Habit: 50¾ in. wide × 25⅛ in. high (127 × 63 cm). An open mound.

Description: Leaf blade: 14 × 9½ in. (35 × 24 cm); thick, glaucous, blue with golden yellow stripes between the veins and some golden yellow mottling, heavily seersuckered and puckered; edge flat to slightly rippled, slightly cupped or convex, widely oval with a mucronate tip, heart-shaped pinched to overlapping lobes. Petiole: light blue-green. Flower: bell-shaped, purple-marked white in a dense raceme on an upright, leafy, glaucous green, 27⅛ to 28 in. (68 to 70 cm) scape in mid-summer; fertile.

Comments & Special Needs: Site in good light to moderate shade. Very slow and very rare. Although prized as a pod parent producing seedlings of good substance, it is among the most attractive of its type and makes a striking specimen in the garden.

Similar: *H*. 'Doctor Reath', whose variegation fades during the summer; *H*. 'Homestead'.

Hosta 'Dorothy Benedict'

Hosta 'Dorset Clown' (R. Benedict NR)

SMALL

Origin: *H*. 'Dorset Blue' Group seedling.

Clump Size & Habit: 12¾ in. wide × 10 in. high (32 × 25 cm). An open mound.

Description: Leaf blade: 5⅛ × 2¾ in. (13 × 7 cm); thick, smooth, green with a blue cast, striped and mottled cream; edge flat with occasional kinks, folded, widely oval with a cuspidate tip, rounded pinched lobes. Petiole: green, outlined in cream. Flower: funnel-shaped, lavender-gray on an upright, bare, glaucous green, 12 in. (30 cm) scape in mid- to high summer; fertile.

Comments & Special Needs: Site in light to moderate shade. Slow growing. Pest resistant. A much sought-after breeding plant.

Hosta 'Fascination' (Aden 1978)

MEDIUM

Origin: *H*. 'Flamboyant' × *H*. 'High Fat Cream'.

Clump Size & Habit: 20 in. wide × 16 in. high (50 × 40 cm). A dense mound.

Description: Leaf blade: 5⅛ × 4 in. (13 × 10 cm); of

Hosta 'Dorset Clown'

good substance, dark green streaked with chartreuse, yellow and white, matt above and glaucous below, dimpled; edge almost flat, convex, widely oval with a cuspidate tip, heart-shaped pinched lobes. Petiole: chartreuse, outlined in green. Flower: flared, palest lavender on an upright, leafy, chartreuse, 20 in. (50 cm) scape in mid-summer; fertile.

Comments & Special Needs: A rapid increaser but one that is difficult to maintain in its truly streaked form, the plant usually reverting to a marginal variegation if it is not frequently divided. A good breeding plant producing many variegated seedlings.

Distinguishing Features: Direct sun will bring out many shades of yellow in the overlapping layers of variegation.

Similar: *H.* 'Whoopee' also has the reputation of being an excellent breeder.

Hosta 'Fascination'

Hosta 'Foxy Doxy'

Hosta 'Galaxy'

Hosta 'Foxy Doxy' (Belle Gardens 1994)

MEDIUM

Origin: *H.* 'William Lachman' × *H. sieboldiana* 'Frances Williams'.

Clump Size & Habit: 28 in. wide × 16 in. high (70 × 40 cm). A moderately dense, semi-upright mound.

Description: Leaf blade: 6⅜ × 5½ in. (16 × 14 cm); thick, glaucous blue-green, narrowly streaked yellow and creamy white, seersuckered; edge flat, slightly cupped or convex, widely oval to nearly round with a mucronate tip, heart-shaped pinched to overlapping lobes. Petiole: cream, outlined in dark blue-green. Flower: tubular, lavender on an upright, bare glaucous blue, 21⅛ in. (53 cm) scape in high summer; fertile.

Comments & Special Needs: Site in light to moderate shade. Slow to increase.

Hosta 'Galaxy' (W. & E. Lachman 1987)

MEDIUM

Origin: *H.* 'Beatrice' seedling × *H.* 'Frances Williams' seedling.

Clump Size & Habit: 30 in. wide × 15 in. high (75 × 38 cm). An open mound.

Description: Leaf blade: 10 × 8⅜ in. (25 × 21 cm); thick, dark blue-green, intensely mottled and streaked yellow to cream, matt above and glaucous below, seersuckered to puckered; edge slightly rippled, cupped or convex, widely oval with a mucronate tip, heart-shaped pinched lobes. Petiole: green, outlined in cream. Flower: widely funnel-shaped, purple-striped lavender on a stout, upright or oblique, leafy, glaucous purple-dotted, 27⅛ in. (68 cm) scape in mid- to late summer; fertile.

Comments & Special Needs: Site in light to medium shade with plain blue or green hostas to illuminate a dark area. With yellow-leaved hostas it will produce a more jazzy effect. Easily reverts, so frequent division is necessary to retain the particularly attractive streaking and mottling.

Distinguishing Feature: While *H.* 'Galaxy' can have leaves with large areas of the base color, it usually has more mottling than most streaked hostas and stands out as being among the best. A well-known progeny is *H.* 'Cherry Berry'.

Similar: **H.* 'Christmas Tree Gala'.

Sports: *H.* 'Galaxy Light' is smaller.

Hosta 'Gertie' (Riehl NR)

SMALL

Origin: Sport of *H.* 'Veronica Lake'.

Clump Size & Habit: 36 in. wide × 16 in. high (90 × 40 cm). A dome-shaped mound.

Hosta 'Gertie'

Hosta 'Ghost Spirit'

Description: Leaf blade: 4⅜ × 3½ in. (11 × 9 cm); of average substance, smooth, dark gray-green, mottled and streaked cream, widely spaced veins; edge slightly rippled, slightly folded, widely oval with a cuspidate tip, heart-shaped open to pinched lobes. Petiole: pale chartreuse, outlined in green. Flower: see *H.* 'Pearl Lake'.

Comments & Special Needs: Site in light to moderate shade. A moderate increaser but not as vigorous as its parent.

Distinguishing Features: Very few streaky breeders of *H. nakaiana* ancestry exist. Has a fine display of flowers.

Hosta 'Ghost Spirit' (Isaacs 1999)

MEDIUM–LARGE

Origin: Sport of *H.* 'Valentine Lace'.

Clump Size & Habit: 42 in. wide × 20 in. high (105 × 50 cm). An open mound.

Description: Leaf blade: 8⅜ × 5⅛ in. (21 × 13 cm); thick, smooth, pure white, with streaking and misting in creamy white soon appearing, widely margined blue-gray, dimpled; edge rippled and twisted, folded, oval with a cuspidate tip, heart-shaped pinched lobes. Petiole: narrow, green streaked and flecked white. Flower: funnel-shaped, pale lavender on an upright, leafy, near black, 26 in. (65 cm) scape in early summer; fertility unknown.

Comments & Special Needs: The unusual color holds best in shade but the young leaves have the strongest variegation. Moderate growth rate.

Distinguishing Features: Many leaves form a 1 in. (2.5 cm), deeply contrasting margin encircling the white center. Variegation fades during the summer into a faint misting. An unusual, near black scape.

Hosta 'Goldbrook Glimmer' (S. Bond NR)

MEDIUM

Origin: Natural sport of H. 'Halcyon'. The first of many sports of H. 'Halcyon'.

Clump Size & Habit: 30 in. wide × 15 in. high (75 × 38 cm). A symmetrical, overlapping mound.

Description: Leaf blade: 6⅜ × 4 in. (16 × 10 cm); of good substance, smooth, muted chartreuse to old-gold, widely and irregularly margined rich blue, matt above and glaucous below; edge almost flat, slightly folded to cupped, oval with a cuspidate tip, heart-shaped pinched lobes. Petiole: chartreuse, outlined in blue. Flower: see H. 'Halcyon'.

Comments & Special Needs: Site in cool shade to retain the central glimmer for as long as possible; it disappears

Hosta 'Goldbrook Glimmer', the gold center fading

Hosta 'High Fat Cream'

soonest in hotter climates. A moderate to rapid increaser. A foreground specimen and lovely in a shiny, dark blue ceramic pot.

Hosta 'High Fat Cream' (Aden 1976)

MEDIUM

Origin: Unknown.

Clump Size & Habit: 25⅛ in. wide × 18 in. high (63 × 45 cm). An open mound.

Description: Leaf blade: 7⅛ × 5⅛ in. (18 × 13 cm); thick, light olive-green, streaked and mottled chartreuse, yellow, ivory and white, matt above and thinly glaucous below, dimpled to seersuckered; edge smooth, widely oval to nearly round with a mucronate tip, rounded pinched lobes. Petiole: white, outlined in chartreuse. Flower: bell-shaped to flared, lavender on an upright, leafy, chartreuse, 18¾ in. (47 cm) scape in late summer; fertile.

Comments & Special Needs: Site in some morning sun in cooler climates to maintain the attractive but very unstable variegation. Slow to increase. Was a very popular breeding plant but since the 1980s extremely rare.

Similar: H. 'Flamboyant'; H. 'Whoopee'.

Sports: *H. 'American Dream'; H. 'Golden Guernsey', which has brilliant, golden yellow leaves.

Hosta 'Iron Gate Delight' (Sellers 1981)

MEDIUM–LARGE

Origin: Sport of H. 'Iron Gate Bouquet'.

Clump Size & Habit: 36 in. wide × 16 in. high (90 × 40 cm). An open mound.

Description: Leaf blade: 6⅜ × 4 in. (16 × 10 cm); thin, smooth, shiny, light olive-green irregularly margined yellow to ivory-white, with many streaks jetting toward the midrib, widely spaced deeply impressed veins; edge slightly rippled, arching, widely oval with an acute to cuspidate tip, rounded pinched lobes. Petiole: shallow, the narrow variegation extending into the petiole for approximately 1 in. (2.5 cm). Flower: open funnel-shaped, fragrant, palest lavender on an upright, bare, 24 in. (60 cm) scape from mid- to late summer; fertile.

Comments & Special Needs: Morning sun in cooler climates but only two hours of sun in the hottest climates, then light shade. Apply plenty of water throughout the growing season. Vigorous and easy to grow. A mid-ground specimen and suitable as a pot plant.

Distinguishing Features: Although the streaking is random and variable, some marginal variegation is usually present.

Similar: H. 'Iron Gate Supreme' has better-shaped leaves but less streaking.

Hosta 'Kiwi Blue Marble' (Sligh NR)

MEDIUM

Origin: Sport of H. 'Hadspen Blue'.

Clump Size & Habit: 40¾ in. wide × 16 in. high (102 × 40 cm). A dense mound when mature.

Description: Leaf blade: 7⅛ × 6⅜ in. (18 × 16 cm); thick, glaucous, intense blue, marbled and streaked golden yellow fading to near white, seersuckered when mature; edge almost flat, folded to slightly cupped, widely oval with a cuspidate tip, heart-shaped pinched lobes. Petiole: glaucous blue. Flower: see H. 'Hadspen Blue'.

Comments & Special Needs: Site in light to moderate shade all day. Leaf color is at its most intense in early summer, gradually darkening to almost pure blue that then assumes a green tinge. Slow to increase. Pest resistant.

Similar: *H. 'Spilt Milk', which has slightly larger, rounder, greener leaves.

Hosta 'Iron Gate Delight'

Hosta 'Kiwi Blue Marble', in its juvenile form

Hosta 'Kiwi Forest'

Hosta 'Korean Snow'

Hosta 'Kiwi Forest' (Sligh 1999)

MEDIUM

Origin: *H.* 'Tokudama' hybrid.

Clump Size & Habit: 30 in. wide × 16 in. high (75 × 40 cm). An open mound.

Description: Leaf blade: 6½ × 5½ in. (16.5 × 14 cm); thick, light blue-green, mottled and streaked cream, mottling early in the season turning dark blue-green, matt above and glaucous below, seersuckered; edge flat, cupped, nearly round with a mucronate tip, heart-shaped pinched to overlapping lobes. Petiole: blue-green, outlined in cream. Flower: tubular, near white on an upright, bare, blue-green 20 in. (50 cm) scape in mid- to high summer; fertile.

Comments & Special Needs: Site in good light to moderate shade. If well watered, a second flush of mottled foliage will emerge, making a lovely contrast to the first flush as it slowly turns blue-green. Slow to increase.

Hosta 'Korean Snow' (Niche Gardens & Solberg 1999)

SMALL–MEDIUM

Origin: *H. yingeri* selection from a seedling crop.

Clump Size & Habit: 30 in. wide × 12 in. high (75 × 30 cm). An unruly mound.

Description: Leaf blade: 6⅜ × 3½ in. (16 × 9 cm); of good substance, glossy, mid-green, randomly streaked and flecked creamy white giving a misted effect early in the season, slightly dimpled when mature, widely spaced veins; edge almost flat, elliptic to oval with a cuspidate tip, rounded open lobes. Petiole: chartreuse, finely outlined in green. Flower: small, spiderlike, dark purple, widely spaced around the thin, upright, leafy, green 20 in. (50 cm) scape in late summer; fertile, green- and white-streaked seedpods, the speckling being a seed-transmitted trait.

Hosta 'Lakeside Knickknack'

Comments & Special Needs: Among the first hostas to emerge, which is when its coloring is most striking. Site in morning sun in Northern zones followed by good light to maintain the variegation. Of moderate increase.

Distinguishing Features: Has a unique streaked and speckled variegation which shows no sign of stabilizing, although some leaves are more green than white.

Hosta 'Lakeside Knickknack' (Chastain 1994)

MINIATURE

Origin: *H.* 'Hydon Sunset' hybrid.

Clump Size & Habit: 15 in. wide × 8⅜ in. high (38 × 21 cm). A compact mound.

Description: Leaf blade: 3½ × 2⅜ in. (9 × 6 cm); of average substance, yellow-streaked light olive-green and very irregularly margined darker olive-green, satiny above and matt below; edge slightly rippled, oval with an obtuse tip, rounded open lobes. Petiole: flattish yellow, outlined in olive-green. Flowers: tubular, near white on an upright, leafy, streaked, 17⅜ in. (43 cm) scape in high summer; fertile.

Comments & Special Needs: Site in light to moderate shade. Rapid growth rate. Good pod parent for variegated progeny.

Distinguishing Features: Flowers have a repeat blooming tendency, sometimes up to three periods each summer, setting seed each time.

Hosta 'Lakeside Party Dress' (Chastain 1997)

MEDIUM

Origin: *H.* 'Spritzer' hybrid.

Clump Size & Habit: 30 in. wide × 7½ in. high (75 × 19 cm). A low, spreading mound.

Description: Leaf blade: 8⅜ × 3½ in. (21 × 3.5 cm); of average substance, satiny, emerging chartreuse turning golden yellow and finally chartreuse, irregularly margined creamy white, closely furrowed, creamy white veins; edge conspicuously rippled, widely lanceolate with a cuspidate tip, tapered open lobes. Petiole: chartreuse, red-dotted at the base. Flower: funnel-shaped, lavender on an upright, bare, chartreuse, 25⅛ in. (63 cm) scape in late summer; fertility unknown.

Comments & Special Needs: Viridescent. Site in bright light to light shade. Rapid increaser.

Distinguishing Features: Veins that are, seemingly uniquely, the same color as the leaf margin.

Hosta 'Little Jim' (R. Benedict 1986)

MINIATURE

Origin: Sport of *H.* 'Saishu Jima'.

Clump Size & Habit: 6⅜ in. wide × 5⅛ in. high (16 × 13 cm). A low-growing mound.

Description: Leaf blade: 2¾ × ¾ in. (7 × 2 cm); of average substance, dark olive-green, randomly streaked and splashed yellow, cream and white, satiny above and shiny below, closely ribbed veins; edge rippled, slightly arching, lanceolate with an acute tip, tapered open lobes. Petiole: dark green, finely outlined in cream. Flower: funnel-shaped, white-striped lavender on an upright, bare, olive-green, 12 in. (30 cm) scape in late summer; fertile.

Comments & Special Needs: Site in light to moderate shade. Keep potted until the root system is fully established, then plant in a larger container, rock or gravel garden. An excellent breeding plant.

Hosta 'Marbled Cream' (Owens 1985)

SMALL–MEDIUM

Origin: *H.* 'Yellow Splash' hybrid.

Clump size & Habit: 22 in. wide × 7⅛ in. high (55 × 18 cm). A dense mound.

Description: Leaf blade: 7¾ × 4 in. (19.5 × 10 cm); of

Hosta 'Little Jim'

Hosta 'Lakeside Party Dress'

Hosta 'Marbled Cream'

average substance, dark green randomly marbled, striped and splashed cream and white, matt above and satiny below, dimpled when mature, closely ribbed veins; edge distinctly rippled, oval with a cuspidate tip, heart-shaped pinched lobes. Petiole: olive-green. Flower: funnel-shaped, lavender on an upright, leafy, olive-green, 30 in. (75 cm) scape in late summer; fertile.

Comments & Special Needs: Site in light to moderate shade. Of moderate increase. Forms an attractive garden specimen and breeds good variegated offspring.

Distinguishing Features: The streaks and stripes can run the entire length of the leaf blade.

Hosta 'Misty Regal' (J. & E. Stratton 1996)

MEDIUM–LARGE

Origin: Sport of *H.* 'Gold Regal'.

Clump Size & Habit: 41½ in. wide × 21⅛ in. high (104 × 53 cm). A semi-upright mound.

Description: Leaf blade: 13⅛ × 7½ in. (33 × 19 cm); thick, glaucous, streaky blue-tinted chartreuse to yellow turning old-gold, widely and irregularly margined dark blue-green, deeply impressed veins; edge almost flat, shallowly undulate, widely oval with a mucronate tip, rounded pinched lobes. Petiole: chartreuse. Flower: see *H.* 'Gold Regal'.

Comments & Special Needs: Some morning sun followed by good light to maintain the best color. Moderate growth rate. Pest resistant.

Distinguishing Features: Very subtle variegation.

Hosta 'Neat Splash' (Aden 1978)

MEDIUM

Origin: Registered as *H.* 'Yellow Splash' × *H.* "Robusta" seedling, but now thought to be of *H. sieboldii* ancestry.

Clump Size & Habit: 36 in. wide × 12 in. high (90 × 40 cm). A spreading mound.

Description: Leaf blade: 7⅛ × 2⅜ in. (18 × 6 cm); thin, dark olive-green irregularly margined creamy white, randomly streaked chartreuse and creamy white and mottled toward the midrib, satiny above and glossy below; edge slightly rippled, arching, widely oblong to elliptic with an acute tip, rounded to tapered open to pinched lobes. Petiole: flattish, green outlined in creamy white. Flower: semi-bell shaped, rich purple on an oblique, leafy, green, 25⅛ in. (63 cm) scape in late summer; fertile.

Comments & Special Needs: Site in light to moderate shade. A rapid increaser. Among the first streaked hostas used in breeding and an excellent parent for variegated offspring.

Hosta 'Misty Regal'

Hosta 'Neat Splash'

Distinguishing Features: Very unstable variegation, the leaves often having large patches of green with no streaking.

Similar: **H.* 'Beatrice'; **H.* 'Breeder's Choice'; **H.* 'Don Quixote'; *H.* 'Green Marmalade'; **H.* 'Splish Splash'.

Sport: *H.* 'Neat Splash Rim' has a creamy yellow margin; **H.* 'Swoosh', *H.* 'Yellow Splash'.

Hosta 'Pin Stripe Sister' (K. Vaughn NR)

LARGE

Origin: Unknown.

Clump Size & Habit: 36 in. wide × 22 in. high (90 × 55 cm). A dense mound.

Description: Leaf blade: 11 × 10 in. (24 × 25 cm); thick, dark green with a blue cast early in the season, randomly mottled, streaked and splashed yellow turning ivory-white, matt above and glaucous below, seersuckered, closely veined; edge slightly rippled, convex, widely oval with a mucronate tip, rounded open to pinched lobes. Petiole: flat-

Hosta 'Pin Stripe Sister'

tish, striped green and ivory. Flower: funnel-shaped, near white from violet buds on a stout, upright, bare, glaucous green, 30 in. (75 cm) scape in mid- to high summer; fertile.

Comments & Special Needs: Site in light to moderate shade with ferns and dark-leaved plants to act as a background contrast to the random and unstable variegation of the hosta leaves. Slow to increase. Among the best-known and most highly regarded breeding hostas ever introduced.

Similar: *H.* 'Pin Stripe', another important breeder.

Hosta 'Renaissance' (Minks 1983)

MEDIUM

Origin: Sport of *H.* 'Flamboyant'.

Clump Size & Habit: 25⅛ in. wide × 16 in. high (63 × 40 cm). A compact mound.

Description: Leaf blade: 8⅜ × 6⅜ in. (21 × 16 cm); of average substance, dark green, striped and streaked chartreuse, golden yellow and cream, matt above and satiny below, dimpled when mature; edge flat, slightly convex, widely oval with a mucronate tip, heart-shaped pinched lobes. Petiole: narrow, chartreuse, outlined in dark green.

Hosta 'Renaissance'

Flower: funnel-shaped, lavender on an upright, leafy, chartreuse, 20 in. (50 cm) scape in mid-summer; fertile.

Comments & Special Needs: Site in good light to moderate shade. A very colorful hosta that maintains its variegation if divided regularly.

Distinguishing Features: Its repeat blooming qualities.

Hosta 'Revolution'

Hosta 'Sea Lightening'

Hosta **'Revolution'** (Van Eijk-Bos & Walters Gardens 2000)

MEDIUM

Origin: Tissue-cultured sport of *H.* 'Loyalist'.

Clump Size & Habit: 40¾ in. wide × 20 in. high (102 × 50 cm). An upright mound.

Description: Leaf blade: 7½ × 4 in. (19 × 10 cm); of moderate substance, smooth, creamy ivory conspicuously flecked green, widely margined dark green with light olive-green splashes jetting toward the midrib, satiny above and glaucous below; edge widely undulate, variably oval or heart-shaped with a cuspidate tip rounded, open to pinched lobes. Petiole: ivory-white, finely outlined in dark green. Flower: see *H.* 'Francee'.

Comments & Special Needs: Grow in some morning sun except in the South, but careful siting is necessary to achieve the right balance of sun and shade.

Distinguishing Features: Differs from *H.* 'Loyalist' in having green flecks in the center of the leaf; *H.* 'Pathfinder', which has rounder leaves when mature, thicker substance and less green flecking, may prove the more consistently better grower of the two.

Hosta **'Sea Lightening'** (M. Seaver 1981)

SMALL–MEDIUM

Origin: *H.* 'Neat Splash' hybrid.

Clump Size & Habit: 30 in. wide × 16 in. high (75 × 40 cm). An open mound.

Description: Leaf blade: 8⅜ × 4 in. (21 × 10 cm); thin, dark green markedly streaked and mottled yellow, cream and white, matt above and shiny below, closely ribbed veins; edge almost flat, slightly arching, elliptic with an acute tip, rounded open lobes. Petiole: green or cream outlined in green. Flower: widely funnel-shaped, purple on an upright, leafy, ivory, 36 in. (90 cm) scape in late summer; fertile.

Comments & Special Needs: Site in some early morning sun followed by moderate shade. Moderate to rapid increaser. Prone to pest damage. Extremely rare but a good breeder. Often reverts to *H.* 'Sea Thunder', which is medio-variegated.

Distinguishing Features: Leaves sometimes have green margins enclosing the streaked portion of the leaf, which is more cream than green. Sometimes the background of the whole leaf is green with random, paler streaking.

Hosta **'Sea Prize'** (M. Seaver NR)

MEDIUM

Origin: Unknown.

Clump Size & Habit: 14 in. wide × 12 in. high (35 × 30 cm). An open mound.

Description: Leaf blade: 5⅛ × 4 in. (13 × 10 cm); of good substance, dark green with a blue cast early in the season, mottled and streaked creamy yellow, no two leaves being alike, matt above and glaucous below, dimpled, closely veined; edge almost flat, slightly folded or cupped, widely oval with a cuspidate tip, heart-shaped overlapping lobes. Petiole: narrow, green, outlined in cream. Flower: bell-shaped, lavender on an upright, bare, green, 24 in. (60 cm) scape in high summer; fertility depends on weather conditions, an excellent pod parent.

Comments & Special Needs: Known to do best in morning sun followed by light to moderate shade. Slow to moderate increase.

Distinguishing Features: Very unstable random variegation.

Hosta 'Sea Prize'

Hosta 'Sharmon'

Hosta 'Seventh Heaven'

Hosta 'Seventh Heaven' (Kulpa 1994)

MEDIUM–LARGE

Origin: *H.* 'Kevin Vaughn' × *H. plantaginea*.

Clump Size & Habit: 30 in. wide × 18 in. high (75 × 45 cm). A compact mound.

Description: Leaf blade: 7½ × 6⅜ in. (19 × 16 cm); of good substance, dark olive-green mottled and streaked chartreuse, cream and white, usually cream to white margined, satiny above and matt below, dimpled; edge randomly rippled, slightly folded, oval with an obtuse tip, rounded pinched lobes. Petiole: ivory, striped green. Flower: long, fragrant, flared white on a slightly oblique, green- and cream-striped, 20 in. (50 cm) scape in late summer; fertile.

Comments & Special Needs: Site in morning sun with plenty of food and moisture throughout the growing season.

Distinguishing Features: Superb, white fragrant 3⅛ in.

(8 cm) long flowers, which emphasize the whiteness in some of the leaf streaks.

Sports: *H.* 'Diana Remembered'.

Hosta 'Sharmon' (Donahue 1986)

MEDIUM–LARGE

Origin: *H.* 'Fortunei' sport.

Clump Size & Habit: 40¾ in. wide × 24 in. high (102 × 60 cm). A dense mound.

Description: Leaf blade: 8⅜ × 6⅜ in. (21 × 16 cm); of good substance, mid-green with a blue cast early in the season, streaked and striped cream that fades by mid-summer to two-tone green, matt above and glaucous below, dimpled when mature; edge almost flat with occasional kinks, slightly folded, widely oval with a cuspidate tip, heart-shaped pinched lobes. Petiole: ivory, outlined in green. Flower: funnel-shaped, lavender-gray on an oblique, leafy, glaucous green, 34 in. (85 cm) scape in mid-summer; fertility uncertain.

Comments & Special Needs: Site in good light to moderate shade. Best in cooler climates, where the central variegation is brighter for longer. Moderate to rapid increase.

Distinguishing Features: Central variegation is overlaid with fine, netted veins.

Similar: *H.* 'Phyllis Campbell'.

Hosta 'Splish Splash' (Aden 1980)

MEDIUM

Origin: *H.* 'Fascination' × *H.* 'Intrigue'.

Clump Size & Habit: 22⅜ in. wide × 12 in. high (56 × 30 cm). An upright mound.

Description: Leaf blade: 7⅛ × 4¾ in. (18 × 12 cm) thick, ivory very widely margined dark blue-green with pale

Hosta 'Splish Splash'

Hosta 'Subtlety'

olive-green and chartreuse streaking and splashing toward the midrib, matt above and glaucous below, dimpled; edge kinked toward the base, upright or arching, widely oval with a recurved tip, heart-shaped pinched lobes. Petiole: ivory outlined in dark green. Flowers: flared, white on an upright, leafy, light green 21 to 24 in. (52.5 to 60 cm) scape in mid-summer; fertile.

Comments & Special Needs: Site in light to moderate shade. Slow to moderate increase. A colorful garden specimen as well as a useful breeding plant. Light to full shade.

Hosta 'Subtlety' (Tower NR)
SMALL

Origin: Sport of *H*. 'Little Aurora'.

Clump Size & Habit: 30 in. wide × 9⅛ in. high (75 × 23 cm). A dense mound.

Description: Leaf blade: 4 × 3½ in. (10 × 9 cm); thick, golden yellow, irregularly flecked and misted green either side of the midrib, matt above and thinly glaucous below, seersuckered; edge flat with occasional kinks, cupped, widely oval with a mucronate tip, heart-shaped pinched to overlapping lobes. Petiole: narrow, chartreuse-yellow. Flower: see *H*. 'Little Aurora'.

Comments & Special Needs: Site in morning sun except in the hottest climates. Slow to increase and takes time to establish. Pest resistant.

Distinguishing Features: The narrow central marking distinguishes this sport of *H*. 'Little Aurora' from all others and is quite unique.

Hosta 'Sweet Standard' (Zilis 1984)
MEDIUM–LARGE

Origin: Tissue-cultured sport of *H*. 'Honeybells'.

Clump Size & Habit: 40¾ in. wide × 24 in. high (102 × 60 cm). A lax mound.

Description: Leaf blade: 10 × 6 in. (25 × 15 cm); thin, smooth, olive-green randomly streaked and splashed chartreuse and cream, satiny above and shiny below; edges rippled, slightly arching, widely oval, pinched at the cuspidate tip, rounded pinched lobes. Petiole: narrow, olive-green finely outlined in creamy white. Flower: see *H*. 'Honeybells'.

Comments & Special Needs: Valuable as a sun-tolerant streaked hosta. Streaking will turn white if exposed to hot sun. A rapid increaser that is easy to grow. Needs regular division.

Similar: *H*. 'Iron Gate Delight', which has less streaking; *H*. 'Iron Gate Supreme', which usually has a creamy white margin with streaking in the center.

Hosta 'Swoosh' (Aden 1978)
SMALL–MEDIUM

Origin: *H*. 'Yellow Splash' × 'Neat Splash'.

Clump Size & Habit: 20 in. wide × 12 in. high (50 × 30 cm). A dense, cascading mound.

Description: Leaf blade: 6⅜ × 4 in. (16 × 10 cm); thin, smooth, dark green striped and splashed chartreuse, yellow, cream and white, matt above and satiny below; edge almost flat, slightly folded, widely lanceolate to elliptic with an acute tip, tapered open lobes. Petiole: narrow, green, cream or striped, purple-dotted at the base. Flower: funnel-shaped, lavender on an oblique, bare, purple-dotted, green 25⅛ in. (63 cm) scape in mid- to late summer; fertile.

Comments & Special Needs: Site in light to moderate shade. Moderate to rapid increase. A rare, much-prized breeding plant.

Hosta 'Sweet Standard'

Hosta 'Swoosh'

Hosta 'Wahoo'

Distinguishing Features: Striping quickly reverts to a marginal variegation unless the plant is divided often.

Hosta **'Wahoo'** (Aden 1976)

MEDIUM

Origin: *H.* 'Tokudama Aureonebulosa' × *H.* 'Tokudama Flavocircinalis'.

Clump Size & Habit: 36 in. wide × 16¾ in. high (90 × 42 cm). A dense mound.

Description: Leaf blade: 7½ × 5½ in. (19 × 14 cm); thick, glaucous rich blue, splashed, streaked and mottled chartreuse, yellow, cream and white, dimpled to seersuckered; edge flat, convex, widely oval with a mucronate tip, heart-shaped pinched lobes. Petiole: cream or green striped, depending on whether the midrib is plain or variegated. Flower: see *H.* 'Tokudama'.

Comments & Special Needs: Site in light to moderate shade. Very slow to increase. Pest resistant. A rare and sought-after breeding plant.

Distinguishing Features: Extremely unstable variegation, the clump or individual leaves being either basically blue with central markings or mainly streaked with some blue.

Hosta 'White Feather' (Heemskerk NR)

MEDIUM

Origin: Sport of *H.* 'Undulata'.

Clump Size & Habit: 25⅛ in. wide × 14 in. high (63 × 35 cm). An open mound.

Description: Leaf blade: 6⅜ × 2⅜ in. (16 × 6 cm); thin, emerging from palest lavender shoots, pure white gradually becoming mottled and streaked light green, matt above and shiny below, prominently veined; edge slightly undulate, slightly folded, elliptic with an acute tip, tapered open to pinched lobes. Petiole: white, becoming streaked with green. Flower: see *H.* 'Undulata'.

Comments & Special Needs: Viridescent. Tolerates morning sun in cooler climates. Of slow to moderate increase and very vulnerable to pest damage. Dramatic and unusual as the white leaves are, it is also very effective as a streaky-leaved hosta.

Distinguishing Features: As the streaking develops, the outline of the veins appears as a ghostly impression.

Hosta 'White Wall Tires' (Avent 1995)

MEDIUM

Origin: *H.* 'Outhouse Delight' hybrid.

Clump Size & Habit: 44⅜ in. wide × 16 in. high (111 × 40 cm). A moderately dense mound.

Description: Leaf blade: 11 × 5⅛ in. (28 × 13 cm); of good substance, smooth, matt creamy white with green mottling gradually turning light green with darker green, prominent veins; edge slightly rippled, elliptic with a cuspidate tip, tapered open lobes. Petiole: creamy white mottled green. Flower: tubular, pale lavender on an upright, bare, ivory-green, 40 in. (100 cm) scape from mid- to late summer; sterile.

Comments & Special Needs: Viridescent. Site in morning sun in cooler climates, then light to moderate shade. Moderate increase.

Distinguishing Features: Differs from *H.* 'White Feather'

Hosta 'White Feather'

Hosta 'White Wall Tires'

in having longer leaves that do not emerge pure white but creamy white.

Similar: *H.* 'Mostly Ghostly'.

Hosta 'William Lachman' (Vaughn 1981)

MEDIUM

Origin: *H.* 'Breeder's Choice' × *H.* 'Frances Williams'.

Clump Size & Habit: 24 in. wide × 18 in. high (60 × 45 cm). An open mound.

Description: Leaf blade: 6⅜ × 5⅛ in. (16 × 13 cm); thick, glaucous green with a blue cast in spring, mottled and streaked yellow and white, barely dimpled; edge slightly rippled, slightly cupped when young, convex in maturity, oval with a mucronate tip, heart-shaped overlapping lobes. Petiole: streaked green and yellow. Flower: funnel-shaped, lavender on an oblique, leafy, glaucous green, 18¾ in. (47 cm) scape in mid-summer; fertile.

Hosta 'William Lachman'

Hosta 'Winter Snow'

Comments Special Needs: Site in light to moderate shade. Will revert very easily to a marginal variegation or a plain color. Needs dividing once large areas of solid color begin to appear. A wonderful breeding plant but too unstable to be a successful garden plant.

Distinguishing Features: An almost imperceptible narrow, irregular margin usually borders the leaf blade.

Hosta 'Winter Snow' (Pine Forest Gardens NR)

LARGE–GIANT

Origin: Sport of *H.* 'Sum and Substance'.

Clump Size & Habit: 60 in. wide × 36 in. high (150 × 90 cm). An open mound.

Description: Leaf blade: 16 × 14 in. (40 × 35 cm); of good substance, chartreuse to old-gold, misted, streaked and striped cream and white, irregularly margined pure white, satiny above and glaucous below, prominently veined; edge undulate, slightly folded to cupped, widely oval with a strongly cuspidate tip, heart-shaped pinched to overlapping lobes. Petiole: chartreuse, striped cream and green. Flower: see *H.* 'Sum and Substance'.

Comments & Special Needs: Site in morning sun with plenty of moisture at the roots. Vigorous, but takes several seasons to establish before assuming a good growth rate.

Distinguishing Features: Is unstable in that sometimes there is just marginal variegation while at other times the center of the leaf is wholly misted and streaked. A colorful addition to the many marginal sports of *H.* 'Sum and Substance'.

CHAPTER TWELVE

HOSTAS *for* CONNOISSEURS

S OME HOSTAS WILL ALWAYS REMAIN collector or connoisseur plants. The reasons for this are several: the hostas may be difficult to cultivate, difficult to propagate, or new to cultivation, either only just introduced from abroad or so new that they are not even on the market yet. In turn, any of these reasons could make these plants expensive, which is another factor that tends to keep them rare. Many medio-variegated and miniature hostas fall into the connoisseur category, and I have included only those that are the most difficult to cultivate and only if they have good garden value. Many of the hostas included in this chapter are *Hosta sieboldii* derivatives.

Hosta 'Abba Satellite' (Aden NR)

MEDIUM

Origin: Unknown.

Clump Size & Habit: 28 in. wide × 16 in. high (70 × 40 cm). An open mound.

Description: Leaf blade: 6⅜ × 4 in. (16 × 10 cm); of good substance, yellow with the narrowest possible dark green central flash, matt above and glaucous below, seersuckered; edge almost flat, slightly cupped, widely oval with a cuspidate tip, rounded open lobes. Petiole: dark green, outlined in yellow. Flower: no details available.

Comments & Special Needs: Site in bright morning light to moderate shade. Not available in the trade at the time of writing, but now that this variation has occurred once, it can occur again.

Distinguishing Features: A central green marking that runs from the base of the leaf blade, where it feathers outwards to the tip.

Hosta 'Abba Windows' (Aden NR)

MEDIUM–LARGE

Origin: Sport of *H.* 'Sun Power'.

Clump Size & Habit: 40¾ in. wide × 25⅛ in. high (102 × 63 cm). An upright mound.

Description: Leaf blade: 9⅛ × 6⅜ in. (23 × 16 cm); of good substance, chartreuse turning golden yellow with a crimped center, marbling in blue-gray and white, matt above and thinly glaucous below, dimpled, closely ribbed veining; edge widely rippled, arching, oval with a curved cuspidate tip, rounded open to pinched lobes. Petiole: yellow. Flower: see *H.* 'Sun Power'.

Comments & Special Needs: Not on the market at the time of writing, but if this form of variegation has occurred once, it can occur again.

Distinguishing Features: A central variegation that distorts and puckers the leaf blade.

Hosta 'Amber Maiden' (Walters Gardens 1988)

SMALL

Origin: Sport of *H.* 'Candy Hearts'.

Clump Size & Habit: 22 in. wide × 14 in. high (55 × 35 cm). A dense mound. Description: Leaf blade: 5⅛ × 4 in. (13 × 10 cm); thin, dark green with a gray cast early in the season, irregularly margined chartreuse turning yellow,

Hosta 'Abba Satellite'

Hosta 'Abba Windows'

Previous page: *Hosta* 'White Christmas'

Hosta 'Amber Maiden'

Hosta 'American Masterpiece'

Hosta 'Ani Machi'

with chartreuse streaks jetting toward the midrib, matt above and thinly glaucous below; edge almost flat, folded to slightly cupped, widely oval with a mucronate tip, heart-shaped pinched lobes. Petiole: gray-green, outlined in yellow. Flower: see *H.* 'Candy Hearts'.

Comments & Special Needs: Site in light to moderate shade. Slow growing and lacking in vigor. Flowers are sterile although its parent plant, *H.* 'Candy Hearts', is very fertile. Mostly grown as a collector's plant.

Hosta 'American Masterpiece' (Wade 1999)

LARGE

Origin: Natural sport of *H.* 'Northern Mist'.

Clump Size & Habit: 36 in. wide × 24 in. high (90 × 60 cm). An open mound.

Description: Leaf blade: 8⅜ × 7⅛ in. (21 × 18 cm); thick, glaucous ivory-white, very widely and irregularly margined dark blue-green with chartreuse streaks jetting toward the midrib, intensely seersuckered; edge shallowly undulate and twisted at the curved tip, heart-shaped overlapping lobes. Petiole: ivory, outlined in blue-green. Flower: see *H. sieboldiana* 'Elegans'.

Distinguishing Features: Embroidered, crimped puckering, particularly on the margins on mature plants. Some misting or speckling into the center of the leaf blade on young leaves.

Comments & Special Needs: Site in light shade. Makes a superb border specimen. Regular division needed to maintain the most pleasing variegational balance. Although very slow to increase shows potential vigor. Still very rare.

Distinguishing Features: Margin is at least 2¾ in. (7 cm) wide.

Similar: *H. sieboldiana* 'Northern Mystery'.

Hosta 'Ani Machi' (Japan, Ruh 2002)

MEDIUM

Origin: Thought to be *H. sieboldii* × *H. rectifolia* and well known in Japan but usually known in the United States as *H.* 'Geisha', although it is not the hosta registered in 1983 as *H.* 'Geisha'.

Clump Size & Habit: 36 in. wide × 18 in. high (90 × 45 cm). An upright, unruly mound.

Description: Leaf blade: 7½ × 3¼ in. (19 × 5.5 cm); of average substance, smooth, glossy golden yellow, widely and evenly margined dark olive-green with occasional streaks jetting toward the midrib; edge slightly rippled, elliptic to narrowly oval and twisted toward the recurved acute tip, tapered open lobes. Petiole: shallow, yellow, outlined in dark green. Flowers: bell-shaped, light violet on an upright, leafy, green, purple-dotted, 26 in. (65 cm), scape in late summer; fertile.

Comments & Special Needs: Viridescent. Leaf center turns pale green at or before flowering time. Site in light to moderate shade. Slow to increase and needs good cultivation and hot summers to maintain a steady growth rate.

Distinguishing Features: The graceful poise of the leaves emphasizes their dramatic coloring.

Similar: *H. 'Mary Marie Ann', which is slightly smaller.

Sports: H. 'Apple Court', whose smaller leaves have a white center.

Hosta 'Anne Arett' (Arett 1975)

SMALL–MEDIUM

Origin: *H. sieboldii* 'Subcrocea' sport.

Clump Size & Habit: 20 in. wide × 10 in. high (50 × 25 cm). A low, arching mound.

Description: Leaf blade: 5⅛ × 1⅛ in. (13 × 3 cm); very thin, smooth, golden yellow fading to chartreuse, narrowly margined white, satiny above and dull below; edge rippled, arching, lanceolate with an acute tip, tapered open lobes. Petiole: narrow, flattish chartreuse-yellow. Flower: see *H. sieboldii*.

---

*Indicates plants fully described elsewhere in this book.

Comments & Special Needs: Site in bright light to moderate shade because the leaves may scorch if exposed to strong sunlight. Susceptible to pest damage. Lacking in vigor and needs an abundance of food and moisture to maintain it in steady growth. Use as foreground plant in light woodland among primulas and *Adiantum pedatum*, the bird's foot fern. Among the earliest introductions with this coloring and now considered a collector's plant.

Distinguishing Features: Edge becomes less rippled with maturity.

Hosta 'Butter Rim' (Summers & AHS 1986)

SMALL–MEDIUM

Origin: Uncertain, although considered a *H. sieboldii* derivative.

Clump Size & Habit: 33⅛ in. wide × 12¾ in. high (83 × 32 cm). A low, arching mound.

Description: Leaf blade: 6⅜ × 2⅜ in. (16 × 6 cm); thin, smooth, satiny olive-green irregularly margined yellow with streaks jetting toward the midrib; edge rippled, arching narrowly oval with an acute to cuspidate tip, tapered

Hosta 'Anne Arett'

Hosta 'Butter Rim'

Hosta 'Calypso'

open lobes. Petiole: narrow, green, outlined in yellow. Flower: funnel-shaped, white on an upright, bare, green, 30 in. (75 cm) scape in high summer; fertile.

Comments & Special Needs: Site in light to moderate shade. Lacks vigor and succeeds best in a warm, humid climate. A highly prized margined hosta in its day, but now only of interest to collectors.

Sports: *H*. 'Moon Shadow' has a creamy white center and green-margined leaf.

Hosta 'Calypso' (W. & E. Lachman 1987)

SMALL

Origin: *H*. 'White Christmas' hybrid.

Clump Size & Habit: 18 in. wide × 10 in. high (45 × 25 cm). An upright mound.

Description: Leaf blade: 6⅜ × 2⅜ in. (16 × 6 cm); thin, smooth, chartreuse turning yellow then ivory-white, widely and irregularly margined dark green with streaks jetting toward the midrib, matt above and thinly glaucous below; edge flat with an occasional kink, arching, folded or convex, lanceolate with an acute tip, tapered open to pinched lobes. Petiole: ivory-white, striped dark green. Flower: funnel-shaped, lavender on an upright, bare, ivory-white, 15 in. (38 cm) scape in mid-summer; fertile.

Comments & Special Needs: Grows best in light to moderate shade in a hot climate; even so, it will not thrive as a garden plant and the leaves will probably scorch. Prized as a breeding plant, however.

Hosta 'Cat's Eyes' (Japan, Heims NR)

DWARF

Origin: Sport of *H. venusta*.

Clump Size & Habit: 6 in. wide × 2 in. high (15 × 5 cm). A low-growing, dense mound.

Hosta 'Cat's Eyes', in dense shade

Description: Leaf blade: 1½ × ⅜ in. (4 × 1 cm); thin, smooth, matt yellow turning ivory-white, irregularly margined dark olive-green with streaks jetting toward the midrib; edge flat with occasional kinks, folded, lanceolate with an acute tip, tapered open lobes. Petiole: narrow, ivory-white, edged dark green. Flower: see *H. venusta*.

Comments & Special Needs: Albescent. Site in good light to light shade with some morning sun in cooler climates. Until a root system is well established, keep in a pot and do not divide. A free-draining soil will boost turgidity and vigor but the growth rate will always be much slower than that of a green-leaved *H. venusta*. Is best suited to a trough, sink or rock garden in company with other miniature hostas and tiny ferns.

Distinguishing Features: A two-tone effect in the central variegation at mid-summer between the first flush of leaves that then assumes a yellow variegation; the new leaves emerge with ivory-white centers.

Hosta 'Celebration'

Hosta **'Celebration'** (Aden 1976)

SMALL–MEDIUM

Origin: Cross of unnamed seedlings. A semi-rhizomatous mound.

Clump Size & Habit: 32¾ in. wide × 16¾ in. high (82 × 42 cm). A low-growing, dense mound.

Description: Leaf blade: 7⅛ × 2⅜ in. (18 × 6 cm); thin, creamy yellow turning white, widely and irregularly margined mid- to dark green with chartreuse streaks jetting toward the midrib, conspicuously veined; edge slightly rippled, arching, lanceolate to elliptic with a curved acute tip, tapering open to pinched lobes. Petiole: short, flattish, cream outlined in green. Flower: narrowly funnel-shaped, deep purple striped rich purple on an upright, bare, cream, 30 in. (75 cm) scape in late summer; sterile.

Comments & Special Needs: The streaky variegation was unique at the time of this hosta's introduction and every effort was made to suit its demanding requirements. Now it is grown mainly by dedicated collectors. Its variegational instability makes it a useful plant for breeding variegated hostas. Difficult to site since it needs sun to maintain vigor, but sun can cause the variegated portions to melt out.

Similar: **H.* 'Cherry Berry'; *H.* 'Gay Feather', which is larger; *H.* 'Goody Goody'; *H.* 'Hot Lips'.

Hosta **'Change of Tradition'** (Zilis & Q & Z Nursery 1985)

SMALL–MEDIUM

Origin: *H.* 'Lancifolia' sport.

Clump Size & Habit: 30 in. wide × 16 in. high (75 × 40 cm). A dense mound.

Description: Leaf blade: 6⅜ × 2⅜ in. (16 × 6 cm); of average substance, smooth, green very narrowly margined pure white, matt above and shiny below; edge flat, arching, lanceolate with an acute tip, tapered open lobes. Petiole: green, finely outlined in white. Flower: see *H.* 'Lancifolia'.

Comments & Special Needs: Site in good light to moderate shade. Not as vigorous as its parent and needs plenty of food and water to thrive. Slow to make growth.

Hosta **'Chartreuse Wiggles'** (Aden 1976)

SMALL

Origin: *H.* 'Ogon Koba' hybrid.

Clump Size & Habit: 25⅛ in. wide × 10 in. high (63 × 25 cm). A dense, spreading mound.

Hosta 'Change of Tradition'

Description: Leaf blade: 5⅛ × 1 in. (13 × 2.5 cm); thin, satiny, smooth, bright chartreuse to golden yellow, closely ribbed veins; edge distinctly rippled, arching, elliptic with an acute tip, tapered open lobes. Petiole: flattish, chartreuse. Flower: bell-shaped, purple-striped lavender on a thin, upright, bare, pale chartreuse, 18 in. (45 cm) scape in late summer; fertile.

Comments & Special Needs: Thrives best in a hot climate where the humidity level is high and where sufficient moisture at the roots can boost its singular lack of vigor. It can be successful in cooler climates, when grown in a container, despite its somewhat rhizomatous habit. Protect from bright sunlight and strong winds. Creates a restless, sinuous effect when planted as a foreground specimen or edger accompanying larger hostas, either echoing almost linear leaves or contrasting round or heart-shaped leaves.

Similar: *H.* 'Chartreuse Waves' is wider; *H.* 'Lauren'; *H.* 'Sea Wiggles'; **H. sieboldii* 'Subcrocea' is a deeper yellow and has less marginal rippling; *H.* 'Yellow Submarine' is somewhat larger and easier to cultivate.

Hosta 'Chartreuse Wiggles'

Hosta 'Chelsea Babe' (BHHS 1988)

SMALL–MEDIUM

Origin: Unknown.

Clump Size & Habit: 25⅛ in. wide × 12 in. high (63 × 30 cm). A dense mound.

Description: Leaf blade: 5⅛ × 3⅛ in. (13 × 8 cm); of average substance, smooth, emerging pale yellow turning

Hosta 'Chelsea Babe'

Hosta 'Collector's Banner'

green, irregularly margined dark green with streaks jetting toward the midrib, matt above and thinly glaucous below; edge widely rippled, oval with a twisted cuspidate tip, rounded pinched lobes. Petiole: yellow turning green, outlined in darker green. Flower: funnel-shaped, lavender-gray on an upright, bare, glaucous green, 22 in. (55 cm) scape in mid- to high summer; fertility unknown.

Comments & Special Needs: The attractive central variegation is maintained for longer in cooler climates when sited in bright light to light shade. Heat will darken the variegation within a few weeks of the leaves emerging. Reasonably vigorous and easy to grow.

Distinguishing Features: Appears to be a smaller version of *H.* 'Fortunei Albopicta' but there are no grounds for this assumption. Originally distributed in the early 1970s by Eric Smith without a provenance.

Similar: **H.* 'Fortunei Albopicta'.

Hosta 'Collector's Banner' (Janssen NR)
MEDIUM–LARGE

Origin: Sport of *H.* 'Gold Standard'.

Clump Size & Habit: 36 in. wide × 20 in. high (90 × 50 cm). An unruly mound.

Description: Leaf blade: 8⅜ × 6⅜ in. (21 × 16 cm); of average substance, the center is a combination of differing shades of green, gold and cream with a wide, irregular margin that becomes golden-green, matt above and glaucous below, seersuckered; edge rippled, furled, oval with kinked, pinched lobes. Petiole: green, chartreuse- and cream-streaked.

Comments & Special Needs: Site in good light to moderate shade since careful positioning is needed to produce the best leaf color. Of moderate increase.

Distinguishing Features: Each leaf is unique, assuming a variety of colors and patterns that change throughout the summer. The margin has a slightly embroidered or bubbled surface.

Similar: **H.* 'Embroidery'; **H.* 'Emerald Necklace'.

Hosta 'Cross Stitch' (Ruh & Zumbar 1992)
LARGE

Origin: *H.* 'Hirao Supreme' selfed.

Clump Size & Habit: 37½ in. wide × 20⅜ in. high (94 × 51 cm). A cascading mound.

Description: Leaf blade: 14 × 10¼ in. (35 × 26 cm); of good substance, glossy rich olive-green, satiny above and glossy below; edge shallowly undulate, pinched along the midrib toward the cuspidate tip, widely oval, heart-shaped pinched lobes. Petiole: paler green. Flower: flaring, lavender on an upright, leafy, green, 34⅜ in. (86 cm) scape in late summer; fertile.

Comments & Special Needs: Site in light to moderate shade. Of moderate increase. Makes an interesting specimen whose leaves should be seen at close range.

Distinguishing Features: Veins have a gathered, stitch-like effect producing heavy seersuckering in the spaces in between.

Hosta densa (Maekawa)
MEDIUM

Origin: Southwest Honshu, Japan.

Clump Size & Habit: 22⅜ in. wide × 26⅜ in. high (56 × 66 cm). A spreading mound.

Description: Leaf blade: 9 × 5⅛ in. (22 × 13 cm); of good substance, matt dark green above and matt lighter green below, closely ribbed veins; edge shallowly and

Hosta 'Cross Stitch'

Hosta 'Embroidery'

Hosta densa

evenly rippled, slightly arching, elliptic to oval with a cuspidate tip, rounded pinched lobes. Petiole: upright, green, purple-dotted toward the crown. Flower: funnel-shaped, purple-tinted, near white on a thick, leaning, leafy, purple-dotted green, 24 in. (60 cm) scape in early autumn; fertile.

Comments & Special Needs: Site in light to moderate shade. Rarely grown in gardens. A collector's plant.

Distinguishing Features: Its name, *H. densa*, refers to the tightly packed raceme.

Similar: **H. montana*, which is larger.

Hosta 'Embroidery' (Aden NR)

MEDIUM

Origin: Sport induced by radiation.

Clump Size & Habit: 30 in. wide × 15 in. high (75 × 38 cm). An upright mound with outward-facing leaves.

Description: Leaf blade: 10 × 8⅜ in. (25 × 21 cm); of average substance, yellowish white turning chartreuse to light olive-green, satiny on top and slightly glaucous below, prominently but irregularly spaced veins, seersuckered and puckered, margined with a stitched effect, smooth, slightly darker green; edge randomly rippled, kinked and twisted at the cuspidate tip, widely oval with heart-shaped pinched lobes. Petiole: wide, light green with faint purple dots near the crown. Flower: funnel-shaped, near white faintly striped purple from purple tipped buds surrounded by prominent purple tipped flower bracts on a stout, oblique to drooping, leafy, green, 24 in. (60 cm) scape, purple-dotted near the crown; sterile.

Comments & Special Needs: Site in good light to moderate shade. A collector's plant which might best be grown with ferns or grasses rather than in a hosta border.

Distinguishing Features: The exaggerated stitched and crimped effect along the junction of the ¾ to 1 in. (2 to 2.5 cm) margin and the center of the leaf well justifies its name.

Similar: **H.* 'Collector's Banner'; **H.* 'Emerald Necklace'.

Sports: *H.* 'Green Velveteen', which has smooth leaves with distinctly rippled edges.

Hosta 'Emerald Necklace' (Kuk 1994)

MEDIUM

Origin: Sport of a *H.* 'Tardiflora' seedling.

Clump Size & Habit: 32⅜ in. wide × 16⅜ in. high (81 × 41 cm). A moderately dense, semi-upright mound.

Description: Leaf blade: 5½ × 3½ in. (14 × 9 cm); thick, chartreuse-white turning mid-green, widely and irregularly margined dark blue-green, satiny above and shinier below, closely veined; edge rippled, oval with an acute tip, conspicuously twisted, rounded pinched lobes. Petiole: nar-

Hosta 'Emerald Necklace'

Hosta 'Fair Maiden'

Hosta 'Flame Stitch'

row, chartreuse to green. Flower: funnel-shaped, violet-striped lavender on an upright, bare, olive-green, 30 in. (75 cm) scape in late summer; fertile.

Comments & Special Needs: Not a difficult hosta to cultivate when the right situation is found, but careful siting between too much sun and too much shade is necessary for the interesting color changes. Grow as a foreground specimen or on a raised bed for best effect.

Distinguishing Features: The conspicuously puckered margin and the leaf center with crimping at the junction between the two give an embroidered appearance to the leaf. At its best in mid-summer while the contrasting colors of the center and margin are at their height.

Similar: *H.* 'Collector's Banner'; *H.* 'Embroidery'.

Hosta 'Fair Maiden' (Walters Gardens 1993)

SMALL

Origin: Tissue-cultured sport of *H.* 'Amber Maiden'.

Clump Size & Habit: 18 in. wide × 14 in. high (45 × 38 cm). A compact mound.

Description: Leaf blade: 6⅜ × 5⅛ in. (16 × 13 cm); of average substance, smooth, dark green, irregularly margined yellow turning ivory, with streaks jetting toward the midrib, matt above and thinly glaucous below, widely spaced veins; edge almost flat, slightly cupped, widely oval with a distinct cuspidate tip, heart-shaped pinched lobes. Flower: see *H.* 'Candy Hearts'.

Comments & Special Needs: Site in good light to light shade. Very slow to increase and lacking in vigor, which is disappointing since it is such an attractive small hosta.

Hosta 'Flame Stitch' (Falstad 1991)

MEDIUM

Origin: Tissue-cultured sport of *H. ventricosa* 'Aureomarginata'.

Clump Size & Habit: 24 in. wide × 18 in. high (60 × 45 cm). An open mound.

Description: Leaf blade: 8½ × 6½ in. (21.5 × 16.5 cm); thin, emerging glossy chartreuse turning yellow then ivory-white, widely and irregularly margined dark spinach-green, with conspicuous streaks jetting toward the midrib, widely spaced veins; edge almost flat, widely oval with a twisted cuspidate tip, heart-shaped open to pinched lobes. Petiole: ivory outlined in dark green with an inner line of chartreuse. Flower: see *H. ventricosa*.

Comments & Special Needs: Very slow and can even dwindle, although a new flush of leaves appears in mid-summer. The white leaf centers can scorch unless it is carefully sited between good light and just enough shade. Water and feed copiously.

Distinguishing Features: The leaves are more conspicuously heart-shaped than most hostas with this leaf patterning. The heavily streaked margins are tritone green varying from very dark to pale chartreuse.

Similar: *H.* 'Stained Satin'.

Hosta 'Gene's Joy'

Hosta 'Gene's Joy' (Aden NR)

SMALL–MEDIUM

Origin: Sport of *H.* 'Gene Summers'.

Clump Size & Habit: 14 in. wide × 10 in. high (35 × 25 cm). A compact mound.

Description: Leaf blade: 5⅛ × 4 in. (13 × 10 cm); thick, greenish yellow turning white if grown in bright light, widely margined mid- to dark green with many streaks jetting toward the midrib, matt above and glaucous below, seersuckered; edge flat, slightly cupped, widely oval with a mucronate tip, heart-shaped pinched lobes. Petiole: pale green to ivory, outlined in green.

Comments & Special Needs: Albescent. If grown with optimum care and regular division, it can be stabilized to produce wide margins and a consistent ivory to green central variegation. Site in bright light to moderate shade, even in morning sun in the coolest climates. Apply plenty of food and moisture. Slow to increase.

Similar: *⁎H.* 'Reversed'.

Hosta 'Gene Summers'

Hosta 'Gene Summers' (Aden 1978)

MEDIUM

Origin: *H.* 'Flamboyant' × *H.* 'Intrigue'.

Clump Size & Habit: 24 in. wide × 14 in. high (60 × 35 cm). An open mound.

Description: Leaf blade: 8⅜ × 5⅛ in. (21 × 13 cm); of good substance, ivory-white, irregularly margined dark spinach-green with many streaks jetting toward the midrib, matt above and glaucous below, dimpled, prominently veined; edge almost flat to slightly rippled, oval with an acute tip, rounded pinched lobes. Petiole: ivory-white, outlined in dark green. Flower: funnel-shaped, lavender on an upright, leafy, ivory, 18 in. (45 cm) scape in late summer; fertile.

Comments & Special Needs: An early morning boost of sun in cooler climates will improve the vigor of this slow to increase but very beautiful hosta.

Distinguishing Features: The streaking in the center of the leaf is very unstable.

Hosta 'Gold Heart' (Heims NR)

SMALL–MEDIUM

Origin: Tissue-cultured sport of *H.* 'Grand Tiara'.

Clump Size & Habit: 30 in. wide × 12 in. high (75 × 30 cm). A compact mound.

Description: Leaf blade: 5⅛ × 4 in. (13 × 10 cm); thick, smooth, white turning ivory then yellow, widely and irregularly margined in chartreuse to light green with streaks jetting toward the midrib, matt above and satiny below; edge almost flat, slightly cupped, widely oval with a cuspidate tip, rounded pinched lobes. Petiole: white to ivory, outlined in light green. Flower: see *H.* 'Golden Tiara'.

Comments & Special Needs: Site in morning sun except in the South, followed by light shade. Claimed to be a vigorous and moderate to rapid increaser but not yet widely enough grown for those claims to be substantiated.

Distinguishing Features: Among the most eye-catching of all the sports in the Tiara Series.

Hosta 'Guardian Angel' (R. Thompson 1995)

LARGE–GIANT

Origin: Sport of *H.* 'Blue Angel'.

Clump Size & Habit: 36 in. wide × 24 in. high (90 × 60 cm). A moderately dense mound.

Description: Leaf blade: 16 × 10 in. (40 × 25 cm); thick, emerging greenish white turning light blue-green and finally mid-green, widely and irregularly margined dark blue-green, with streaks jetting toward the midrib, matt above and glaucous below, dimpled when mature, prominently veined; edge conspicuously rippled with a twisted tip when young, folded, widely oval with a cuspidate tip, heart-shaped overlapping lobes. Petiole: chartreuse-white. Flower: see *H.* 'Blue Angel'.

Comments & Special Needs: Viridescent.

Distinguishing Features: The twisted appearance of the leaf is more apparent in young plants before the leaf has flattened and expanded with maturity. The variegation is not visible on the second flush of leaves.

Similar: *H.* 'Angel Eyes'.

Hosta 'Hart's Tongue' (Kuk 1987)

SMALL–MEDIUM

Origin: Sport of *H. sieboldii* 'Kabitan'.

Clump Size & Habit: 12 in. wide × 9⅛ to 9½ in. high (30 × 23 to 24 cm). An upright, arching mound.

Description: Leaf blade: 4 × 1 in. (10 × 2.5 cm); of good substance, bright chartreuse turning olive-green by midsummer, satiny above and glaucous below, dimpled; edge conspicuously rippled running into the decurrent petioles, narrowly lanceolate with an acute tip, tapered open lobes. Petiole: flattish, olive-green. Flower: see *H. sieboldii*.

Comments & Special Needs: Viridescent. Site in light to

Hosta 'Gold Heart'

Hosta 'Guardian Angel', in its juvenile form

Hosta 'Hart's Tongue'

Hosta 'Hoosier Harmony'

moderate shade. Plant with the Hart's tongue fern to produce a copycat effect.

Distinguishing Features: *H*. 'Hart's Tongue' bears a striking resemblance to the Hart's tongue fern, *Asplenium scolopendrium*.

Hosta 'Hoosier Harmony' (Indianapolis Hosta Society 1995)

MEDIUM–LARGE

Origin: Sport of *H*. 'Royal Standard'.

Clump Size & Habit: 36 in. wide × 18 in. high (90 × 45 cm). A lax, diffuse mound.

Description: Leaf blade: 8⅜ × 6⅜ in. (21 × 16 cm); of average substance, smooth, chartreuse to old-gold irregularly margined dark green, with streaks jetting toward the midrib, satiny above and shiny below, prominently veined; shallowly undulate, slightly arching, folded, oval with an acute tip, tapered open lobes. Petiole: chartreuse, finely outlined in dark green. Flower: see *H*. 'Royal Standard'.

Comments & Special Needs: Lutescent. Site in morning sun, applying plentiful amounts of food and water. Requires heat and humidity to thrive.

Distinguishing Features: Large, white, fragrant flowers make it worth the trouble.

Similar: *H*. 'Chelsea Ore', which has chartreuse leaves narrowly margined in dark green and is even less vigorous. Best grown in a greenhouse in cooler climates.

Hosta 'Jim Wilkins' (R. H. & D. Benedict 1990)

SMALL

Origin: *H*. 'Dorothy Benedict' selfed.

Clump Size & Habit: 24 in. wide × 10 in. high (60 × 25 cm). An open mound.

Hosta 'Jim Wilkins'

Description: Leaf blade: 8⅜ × 6½ in. (21 × 16.5 cm); very thick, green-white or cream-white depending on light levels, widely and irregularly margined blue-green with many celadon streaks jetting toward the midrib, matt above and glaucous below, heavily seersuckered; edge flat, folded to slightly cupped, widely oval to nearly round with a mucronate tip, heart-shaped pinched to overlapping lobes. Petiole: ivory, outlined in dark green. Flower: funnel-shaped, white-striped purple on an upright, leafy, glaucous ivory, 14 in. (35 cm) scape in high summer; fertile.

Comments & Special Needs: Albescent central variegation. Site in light to moderate shade because the leaves are prone to scorch. Regular watering is also necessary to maintain the vigor. Slow to increase. Pest resistant.

Distinguishing Features: The random streaks in the center of the leaf contribute to the attractiveness of this rare hosta, which is well worth seeking out.

Hosta jonesii

Hosta kiyosumiensis "Aureomarginata"

Hosta jonesii (Chung)

SMALL

Origin: Several islands off the coast of Korea.

Clump Size & Habit: 18 in. wide × 8 in. high (45 × 20 cm). A diffuse, rhizomatous mound.

Description: Leaf blade: 8 × 4 in. (20 × 10 cm); mid-green, matt above and shiny, paler green below; edge lightly undulate to rippled, elliptic to oval and arching toward the tip, tapered open lobes. Petiole: tapered, very pale green, purple-dotted toward the crown, appearing to pierce the blade almost to the tip. Flower: near bell-shaped, white-striped purple on an oblique to upright, leafy, purple-dotted green, 24 in. (60 cm) scape in late summer; fertile.

Comments & Special Needs: In cultivation usually seen only in specialist collections. Site in moderate shade all day.

Distinguishing Features: Scape branching sometimes occurs.

Similar: Closely related to *H. tsushimensis*, which lacks purple dots on the scape, has larger flowers and is more vigorous.

Hosta kiyosumiensis "Aureomarginata" (Maekawa)

LARGE

Origin: Honshu, Japan.

Clump Size & Habit: 64 in. wide × 22 in. high (160 × 55 cm). An open mound.

Description: Leaf blade: 11 × 4¾ in. (28 × 12 cm); of average substance, mid-green, irregularly margined yellow turning green, with streaks jetting toward the midrib, matt above and shiny below, closely ribbed veins; edge rippled, slightly arching toward the long acute tip, narrowly oval, tapered pinched lobes. Petiole: oblique, flattish, pale green, red-dotted toward the crown. Flower: narrow, funnel-shaped, lavender on an upright, leafy, light green, 36 in. (90 cm) scape in high to late summer; fertile.

Comments & Special Needs: Light to moderate shade. Of slow to average increase. Rarely seen in gardens but a sought-after collector's plant.

Similar: *H. kikutii* 'Kifukurin Hyuga', which is earlier to emerge; *H.* 'Shelley's', which I originally incorrectly assigned to *H. kikutii*, is thought to be identical.

Hosta kiyosumiensis 'Nafuku' (Japan)

MEDIUM

Origin: Aichi Prefecture, Japan.

Clump Size & Habit: 30 in. wide × 12 in. high (75 × 30 cm). An overlapping mound.

Description: Leaf blade: 5¾ × 2⅜ in. (14.5 × 6 cm); of average substance, vivid chartreuse to golden yellow, narrowly and irregularly margined bright green with streaks jetting toward the midrib, matt above and satiny below, prominently veined; edge slightly rippled, arching, convex, oval with a recurved cuspidate tip, rounded open lobes. Petiole: yellow, finely outlined in green. Flower: see *H. kiyosumiensis* 'Aureomarginata'.

Comments & Special Needs: Site in morning sun or good light ensuring adequate moisture at the roots. Ideal at the waterside because it will tolerate its roots growing in running water. A very rare, collector's plant.

Similar: *H. montana* 'Choko Nishiki', which has larger leaves.

Hosta kiyosumiensis 'Nafuku'

Hosta 'Lemon Meringue'

Hosta 'Koryu'

Hosta 'Koryu' (Japan)

SMALL

Origin: Japanese garden origin, formerly known as *H.* 'Fused Veins'.

Clump Size & Habit: 15 in. wide × 7⅛ in. high (38 × 18 cm). A diffuse mound.

Description: Leaf blade: 5¼ × 1⅛ in. (13.5 × 3 cm); thick, smooth, leathery, shiny, light green with thick dark green margins "fused" onto the leaf surface; edge rippled and twisted, narrowly lanceolate with an acute tip, tapered open lobes. Petiole: light green. Flower: funnel-shaped, lavender with paler petal margins on an upright, bare, light green, 12 in. (30 cm) scape from late summer to early autumn.

Comments & Special Needs: Site in light to moderate shade in a raised bed or a container so that the unusual leaves can be enjoyed close up. Grown by serious hosta collectors rather than general gardeners.

Distinguishing Features: The swollen areas, which are a stable genetic trait, are more prominent in some leaves than others and give the leaf a somewhat contorted effect ("Koryu" means *swollen variegation*.) Flowers are disposed all round the scape.

Similar: *H.* 'Emerald Necklace'; *H.* 'Hamada Contorted', which may be identical.

Hosta 'Lemon Meringue' (Ruh 1991)

MEDIUM–LARGE

Origin: *H. hypoleuca* hybrid.

Clump Size & Habit: 27⅛ in. wide × 18¾ in. high (68 × 47 cm). A somewhat unruly mound.

Description: Leaf blade: 11½ × 10 in. (29 × 25 cm); thick, chartreuse to light yellow, glaucous above and powdery white below, dimpled to seersuckered; edge rippled, nearly round with a mucronate tip, heart-shaped open lobes. Petiole: chartreuse. Flower: funnel-shaped, palest lavender on an oblique, bare, glaucous chartreuse, 22 in. (55 cm) scape from mid- to late summer; fertile.

Comments & Special Needs: Site in morning sun in all but the hottest regions to boost the vigor. Very slow to increase. Pest resistant. A beautiful hosta that is well worth persevering with.

Distinguishing Features: Areas of puckering either side of the midrib as well as hints of chartreuse in the seersuckering.

Similar: *H.* 'Glory'.

Hosta 'Lucy Vitols' (M. Seaver 1989)

MEDIUM

Origin: Sport of *H.* 'Christmas Gold'.

Clump Size & Habit: 36 in. wide × 14 in. high (90 × 38 cm). A congested mound.

Hosta 'Lucy Vitols'

Hosta 'Mary Marie Ann'

Description: Leaf blade: $10 \times 9\frac{1}{8}$ in. (25×23 cm); very thick, chartreuse to golden yellow widely and irregularly margined rich blue-green with streaks jetting toward the midrib, matt above and glaucous below, intensely seersuckered; edge slightly rippled, shallowly cupped or convex, widely oval to round with a mucronate tip, heart-shaped pinched lobes. Petiole: chartreuse. Flower: see *H.* 'Christmas Gold'.

Comments & Special Needs: Morning sun except in the hottest regions. Very slow to establish and increase so a plentiful supply of water is important. Pest resistant.

Distinguishing Features: The crumpled and puckered mature leaves almost reach a state of distortion, a feature much prized by flower arrangers.

Similar: *H.* 'Spinning Wheel'.

Hosta 'Mary Marie Ann' (Englerth 1982)
SMALL

Origin: Sport of *H.* 'Aoki'.

Clump Size & Habit: 30 in. wide × 14 in. high (75×35 cm). An open, dome-shaped mound.

Description: Leaf blade: $6\frac{3}{8} \times 3\frac{1}{2}$ in. (16×9 cm); of average substance, creamy yellow turning ivory then chartreuse to light green, widely margined darker green, satiny above, thinly glaucous below; edge flat to kinked with ripples on the flat of the margin, narrowly oval with a curved, acute tip rounded pinched lobes. Petiole: long, dark green. Flower: see *H.* 'Fortunei Hyacinthina'.

Comments & Special Needs: Site in morning sun to maintain the yellow central variegation. The leaf blade will expand and exhibit its curious characteristics better in a hot, humid climate. Lovely in a round or oval, antique stone bowl.

Distinguishing Features: The leaf margin is seersuckered, growing at a different rate from the lighter center, causing the blade to twist and distort and the margin to pucker.

Similar: *H.* 'Emerald Necklace'.

Hosta 'Masquerade' (Grenfell NR)
MINIATURE

Origin: First known as *H. venusta* 'Variegated', but is a possible seedling of *H. sieboldii* × *H. venusta*.

Clump Size & Habit: 15 in. wide × $5\frac{1}{8}$ in. high (38×13 cm). A dense mound.

Description: Leaf blade: $3\frac{1}{2} \times 1\frac{1}{8}$ in. (9×3 cm); thin, smooth, pure white irregularly margined dark green with streaks jetting toward the midrib, matt above and satiny below; edge widely rippled or kinked, folded, elliptic with an acute tip, tapered pinched lobes. Petiole: ivory-white outlined in dark green. Flower: funnel-shaped, lavender, striped purple inside on a thin, upright, leafy, chartreuse, 12 in. (30 cm) scape in mid-summer; fertile.

Comments & Special Needs: Site in light to moderate shade. Variegation is likely to fade to green in hot climates and it will start to produce leaves with flecking in the central variegation. Its main disadvantage is the strong tendency to reversion, with larger green leaves or streaked green leaves marring the attractive clump. Grow in rock gardens, sinks or troughs, and do not divide until a root system is fully established.

Similar: *H.* 'Island Charm', which has slightly larger leaves; *H.* 'Pinwheel', whose leaves are flatter.

Sports: *H.* 'Venessa' is a green-leaved form; *H.* 'Little White Lines' has white-margined green leaves but, like its parent, is unstable and needs regular division.

Hosta 'Masquerade'

Hosta montana 'Choko Nishiki' (Maekawa)

LARGE

Origin: Natural sport of *H. montana*, which is found in the wild in Japan.

Clump Size & Habit: 49 in. wide × 22 in. high (122 × 55 cm). A tiered mound.

Description: Leaf blade: 13⅛ × 8½ in. (33 × 21.5 cm); of average substance, bright yellow, with a green cast in shade, widely and irregularly margined bright dark olive-green with light olive-green streaks jetting toward the midrib, matt above and glossy below, and furrowed veins that are rough to the touch; edge shallowly undulate with an acute, often twisted tip, heart-shaped open to pinched lobes. Petiole: chartreuse, clearly outlined in dark green. Flower: see *H. montana*.

Comment & Special Needs: Emerges much later than *H. montana* 'Aureomarginata', the leaves unfurling from red-tinted shoots. Except in Southern gardens, some morning sun helps boost the vigor, provided there is adequate moisture, but it will eventually turn the yellow center ivory-

Hosta montana 'Choko Nishiki'

white. Often appears to dwindle rather than increase but thrives best in hot, humid conditions.

Similar: *H. montana* 'Kinkaku', a natural sport of *H. montana*; *H.* 'On Stage', which is considered identical.

Sports: *H.* 'Back Light' has yellow leaves.

Hosta montana 'Emma Foster'

Hosta 'My Child Insook'

Hosta montana 'Emma Foster' (Foster 1985)

LARGE

Origin: *H. montana* 'Aureomarginata' sport.

Clump Size & Habit: 30 in. wide × 20 in. high (75 × 50 cm). An open mound.

Description: Leaf blade: 7⅛ × 5⅛ in. (18 × 13 cm); of good substance, chartreuse turning golden yellow, satiny above and glossy below, seersuckered when mature, prominently veined; edge widely rippled, arching, oval with a cuspidate tip, heart-shaped pinched lobes. Petiole, stout, chartreuse. Flower: see *H. montana*.

Comments & Special Needs: Lutescent. Site in good light to moderate shade. Not vigorous and does not attain the size of its parent.

Distinguishing Features: Midrib and veins remain green, giving a two-tone effect that is particularly noticeable in bright light.

Similar: *H.* 'Back Light', a new introduction that may prove more vigorous; *H.* 'Mountain Sunrise', which is more vigorous.

Hosta 'My Child Insook' (R. & D. Benedict 1995)

MEDIUM–LARGE

Origin: Sport of *H.* 'Outrageous', the mother plant being a seedling of *H.* 'Dorothy Benedict' × *H. montana* 'Aureomarginata'.

Clump Size & Habit: 30 in. wide × 28 in. high (75 × 70 cm). A semi-upright mound.

Description: Leaf blade: 10 × 8⅜ in. (25 × 21 cm); of good substance, smooth, shiny, ivory-white, widely and irregularly margined dark green with chartreuse streaks jetting toward the midrib, dimpled, prominently veined; edge nearly round, heart-shaped pinched lobes. Petiole: white, finely outlined in dark green. Flower: funnel-shaped, pale

Hosta okomotoi

lavender on an upright, pale green, 40¾ in. (102 cm) scape in late summer; sterile.

Comments & Special Needs: Site in light to moderate shade. Among the most beautiful of the centrally variegated hostas and, although a fairly rapid increaser, is still rare and seen only in the gardens of serious collectors.

Hosta okomotoi (Araki)

MEDIUM

Origin: Kyoto Prefecture, Japan.

Clump Size & Habit: 16 in. wide × 12 in. high (40 × 30 cm). A flattish mound.

Description: Leaf blade: 5 × 2¾ in. (12 × 7 cm); leathery, smooth, mid-green, paler, satiny green below, some puckering when mature; edge flat to undulate, nearly round with a cuspidate tip, heart-shaped open to pinched lobes. Petiole: green, purple-dotted toward the crown. Flower: funnel-shaped, white with purple-suffusions inside, oblique, leafy, purple-dotted, 18 in. (45 cm) scape in autumn; fertile.

Comments & Special Needs: In cultivation, usually seen only in specialist collections. Light shade. Pest resistant.

Distinguishing Features: Differs from *H. aequinoctiiantha* in having longer scapes and more widely spaced flowers.

Hosta 'Orphan Annie' (Hansen & Shady Oaks NR)

DWARF

Origin: Natural sport of *H. venusta*. Known in Japan as *Otome Giboshi Fukurin*.

Clump Size & Habit: 6⅜ in. wide × 3⅛ in. high (16 × 8 cm). An upright mound.

Description: Leaf blade: 2 × 1 in. (5 × 2.5 cm); dark olive-green regularly margined and streaked parchment-white, with streaks jetting toward the midrib, matt above and satiny below, smooth; edge flat, folded, widely elliptic with an acute tip, tapered open lobes. Petiole: narrow, olive-green finely outlined in parchment-white. Flower: see *H. venusta*.

Comments & Special Needs: Of average substance, but the turgid leaves have a very perky appearance. Site in good light to moderate shade. Grow in small containers or sink gardens, allowing the plant to develop a good root system before division. A superb, tiny, rapidly growing hosta introduced around 2000 to the West from a Japanese nursery.

Similar: A much better grower than the similar **H. venusta* 'Kinbotan'.

Hosta pachyscapa (Maekawa)

MEDIUM

Origin: Honshu Island, Japan.

Clump Size & Habit: 36 in. wide × 20 in. high. (90 × 50 cm). A spreading mound.

Description: Leaf blade: 8 × 6 in. (20 × 15 cm); of good substance, mid- to dark green, satiny above and shiny below, closely ribbed veins, slightly dimpled; edge slightly rippled, arching, oval to elliptic with an acute tip, rounded pinched lobes. Petiole: green, slightly purple-dotted toward the crown. Flower: funnel-shaped, purple-striped

Hosta 'Orphan Annie'

Hosta pachyscapa

pale lavender on an upward to leaning, leafy, green 28 to 50 in. (70 to 125 cm) scape with purple dots near the crown and at the tip in high to late summer; fertile.

Comments & Special Needs: Rarely seen in cultivation. Increases rapidly. Grow in light shade at the waterside.

Distinguishing Features: Named for its extraordinarily thick scape, which tends to droop toward the end of the flowering period

Similar: *H. kiyosumiensis*, which is larger.

Hosta 'Pandora's Box' (Hansen & Shady Oaks 1996)

DWARF–MINIATURE

Origin: Tissue-cultured sport of H. 'Baby Bunting'.

Clump Size & Habit: 10 in. wide × 4 in. high (25 × 10 cm). A loose, diffuse mound.

Description: Leaf blade: 2⅜ × 1½ in. (6 × 4 cm); thick, glaucous, palest chartreuse to creamy white irregularly margined dark gray-green with transitional chartreuse streaks jetting toward the midrib, dimpled; edge almost flat, cupped or convex, widely oval to nearly round with a mucronate tip, heart-shaped pinched to folded lobes. Petiole: creamy chartreuse, distinctly outlined in green. Flower: see H. 'Baby Bunting'.

Comments & Special Needs: Site in good light but in high shade to retain the attractive blue cast to the leaf margins. Establish in a container before planting out. Slow to increase; do not divide until the root system is fully developed. Reversion to a plain green leaf is all too common, so regular division is essential.

Distinguishing Features: Flower scape is pale pink.

Similar: H. 'Cameo', whose leaves are streaked blue-green, white, cream, chartreuse and gold; H. 'Cherish'; H. 'Hope' has smaller chartreuse to yellow margins with a bright chartreuse center.

Hosta 'Praying Hands' (G. Williams 1996)

MEDIUM

Origin: Unknown.

Clump Size & Habit: 16 in. wide × 14 in. high (40 × 38 cm). An upright mound.

Description: Leaf blade: 7⅛ × 2¼ in. (18 × 5.7 cm); of average substance, smooth, olive-green with a very narrow yellow-gold margin, satiny above and glossy below, prominent veining; edge rippled and almost decurrent with the petiole, furled, lanceolate with an acute tip. Petiole: narrow, dark green finely outlined in yellow, mahogany-purple at the base. Flower: bell-shaped, lavender on an upright, bare, green, 16 in. (40 cm) scape in late summer; sterile.

Comments & Special Needs: Site in light to moderate shade. Grow at eye level to get the best effect from the unusual leaf habit. Plant with a collection of ferns or small hostas with contrasting, heart-shaped leaves, though it is more of a collector's talking point.

Distinguishing Features: Leaves are folded and rolled tightly in an upward, outward stance.

Similar: *H. 'Tortifrons'.

Hosta pycnophylla (Maekawa)

MEDIUM

Origin: Oshima Island, Japan.

Clump Size & Habit: 60 in. wide × 18¾ in. high (150 × 47 cm). An open mound.

Description: Leaf blade: 9⅛ × 7¾ in. (23 × 19.5 cm); of good substance, smooth, glaucous gray-green, thickly white-coated below, widely spaced veins; edge conspicuously rippled, slightly arching, widely oval with a cuspidate tip, heart-shaped open lobes. Petiole: red-dotted green. Flower: funnel-shaped, purple-striped lavender on a recumbent, leafy, red-dotted, glaucous green, 30 in. (75 cm)

Hosta 'Pandora's Box'

Hosta 'Praying Hands'

scape from late summer to early autumn; fertile, producing many seedpods.

Comments & Special Needs: Grow in morning sun in the South. Tolerates afternoon sun in the North, provided it is adequately supplied with moisture. A superb parent for white-backed, ripple-edged hostas. Wild specimens are much smaller than those in cultivation, although it is not an easy hosta to grow, seeming to dwindle rather than increase.

Distinguishing Features: Heavy white coating on the underside of the leaf.

Similar: *H.* 'Paradise Red Delight' is an attractive selection with intensely red-dotted petioles.

Sports and forms: *H.* 'High Kicker' has much frillier edges and is very slow to establish. *Hosta pycnophylla* 'Ogon' is a natural sport from which the yellow-leaved *H.* 'Guilt by Association' was selfed.

Hosta pycnophylla

Hosta 'High Kicker'

Hosta 'Regalia' (K. Anderson 1992)

LARGE

Origin: Sport of *H.* 'Krossa Regal'.

Clump Size & Habit: 47½ in. wide × 24 in. high (119 × 60 cm). An upright mound.

Description: Leaf blade: 10 × 7½ in. (25 × 19 cm); thick, light blue-green, widely margined dark blue-green, matt above and glaucous below, prominently veined, some dimpling when mature; edge heavily and widely undulate to twisted, widely oval to nearly round with a mucronate tip, rounded open to pinched lobes. Petiole: stout, shallow, glaucous light green. Flower: see *H.* 'Krossa Regal'.

Comments & Special Needs: Site in light to moderate shade. The leaf color, especially the deeper-toned margin, will be bluer if grown in full shade. Slower to increase than its parent but this majestic yet understated hosta deserves wider recognition. Impressive in a large container. *Hosta* 'Regalia' will always remain a rare hosta as it does not come true from micropropagation and needs to be increased by division.

Distinguishing Features: The 1 in. (2.5 cm) wide heavily undulate margins.

Similar: **H.* 'Emerald Necklace' has similar coloring.

Hosta 'Reversed' (Aden 1978)

MEDIUM

Origin: Sport of *H.* 'Splish Splash.

Clump Size & Habit: 36 in. wide × 16 in. high (90 × 40 cm). A dense mound.

Description: Leaf blade: 8⅜ × 6⅜ in. (21 × 16 cm); thick, chartreuse-yellow to ivory-green, widely and irregularly margined dark green with a blue cast in shade, celadon (shade) or chartreuse (sun) streaks jetting toward the midrib, matt above and glaucous below, seersuckered; edge

Hosta 'Regalia'

Hosta 'Reversed'

Hosta 'Royal Tiara'

randomly undulate or kinked, folded to slightly cupped, widely oval with a cuspidate tip, heart-shaped pinched lobes. Petiole: chartreuse to ivory-green. Flower: funnel-shaped, palest lavender on an upright, bare, ivory-green, 24 in. (60 cm) scape in high summer; fertile.

Comments & Special Needs: Site in light to moderate shade and provide plenty of water if moisture is not readily available from high rainfall or constant summer humidity. Slow to increase in all climatic regions but bluer tones in the margin will be more apparent in cooler climates. Divide regularly to maintain the best balance between the margin and central variegation. Although a challenge to gardeners, it is a much-used breeding plant.

Distinguishing Features: Several forms have wider margins and more vigor.

Similar: *H.* 'Gene's Joy'; *H.* 'Lakeside Shore Master', a faster grower and the leaves more turgid.

Hosta 'Royal Tiara' (Zilis 1988)
SMALL

Origin: Now considered by the raiser to be a sport of *H.* 'Gold Edger' but was originally registered as a sport of *H.* 'Golden Tiara'.

Clump Size & Habit: 16¾ in. wide × 8⅜ in. high (42 × 21 cm). A diffuse, twisted mound.

Description: Leaf blade: 4 × 2⅜ in. (10 × 6 cm); of good substance, smooth, pure white, widely and irregularly margined chartreuse to light green with streaks jetting toward the midrib, matt above and glaucous below; edge widely undulate causing the blade to twist, oval with a cuspidate tip, tapered open to pinched lobes. Petiole: white, outlined in light green. Flower: see *H.* 'Gold Edger'.

Comments & Special Needs: Site in good light to mod-

erate shade. More vigorous than would be expected of a hosta with such twisted leaves.

Hosta 'Saint Elmo's Fire' (Solberg 1995)
MEDIUM

Origin: Sport of *H.* 'Sea Fire'.

Clump Size & Habit: 45½ in. wide × 18 in. high (114 × 45 cm). A moderately dense mound.

Description: Leaf blade: 7⅛ × 4 in. (18 × 10 cm); of good substance, emerges satiny, sharp acid-yellow from red shoots that turn green, narrowly and irregularly margined greenish cream initially then turning pure white with streaks jetting toward the midrib, matt above and glaucous below, seersuckered, moderately prominently veined; edge flat to slightly undulate, convex when mature, oval with a cuspidate tip, heart-shaped pinched lobes. Petiole: light green, margined creamy white. Flower: see *H.* 'Sea Fire'.

Comments & Special Needs: Viridescent. High temperatures can rapidly effect its ability to change color. Well worth the trouble of finding the most appropriate site with some morning sun followed by good light or dappled shade. An attractive hosta but not very vigorous and prone to the drawstring effect unless given plenty of water.

Distinguishing Features: *H.* 'Saint Elmo's Fire' exhibits both yellow and green leaves throughout the growing season, making a colorful display.

Similar: *H.* 'Electrum Stater'; *H.* 'Lakeside Cha Cha'; *H.* 'Sea Dream'; *H.* 'Zodiac'.

Hosta 'Sea Thunder' (M. Seaver NR)
MEDIUM–LARGE

Origin: Sport of *H.* 'Sea Lightening'.

Hosta 'Saint Elmo's Fire'

Hosta 'Shere Khan'

Hosta 'Sea Thunder'

Clump Size & Habit: 40¾ in. wide × 16 to 22 in. high (102 × 40 to 55 cm). A dense, slightly unruly mound.

Description: Leaf blade: 8½ × 4⅜ in. (21.5 × 11 cm); thin, ivory-cream widely and irregularly margined mid- to dark olive-green with chartreuse streaks jetting toward the midrib, satiny above and glossy below, dimpled when mature; edge slightly rippled or kinked, elliptic to oval with an acute, sometimes curved tip, rounded, pinched lobes. Petiole: wide, red-dotted, continuing the distinctive variegation. Flowers: see *H.* 'Sea Lightening'.

Comments & Special Needs: Leaves can rapidly revert to a streaky variegation or the green margins can almost take over, so regular dividing is essential to retain the striking variegation. Site in early morning sun in cooler regions, otherwise shade is essential. The pale leaf center can burn out in times of excessive heat, so careful placing in the garden is advised.

Distinguishing Features: *H.* 'Sea Thunder' has a much wider central variegation than *H.* 'Sea Lightening', which has just a pale central strip.

Similar: **H.* 'Sea Lightening'.

Hosta 'Shere Khan' (Zumbar 1995)

MINIATURE

Origin: Sport of *H.* 'Just So'.

Clump Size & Habit: 7⅛ in. wide × 5⅛ in. high (18 × 13 cm). A dense, semi-upright mound.

Description: Leaf blade: 2 × 1 in. (5 × 2.5 cm); thick, light green-gold, narrowly margined pure white with some streaks jetting toward the midrib, matt above and satiny below, prominently veined, seersuckered; edge slightly undulate, widely oval with a cuspidate tip, heart-shaped open to pinched lobes. Petiole: narrow, pale green finely outlined in white. Flower: see *H.* 'Little Aurora'.

Comments & Special Needs: Lutescent. If sited in morning sun, the center of the leaves will turn golden yellow. Moderate growth rate. Pest resistant. Very rare, but a gem for collectors of tiny hostas.

Hosta sieboldiana 'Great Expectations' (J. Bond & Aden 1988)

MEDIUM–LARGE

Origin: Natural sport of *H. sieboldiana* 'Elegans'.

Clump Size & Habit: 45½ in. wide × 25⅛ in. high (114 × 63 cm). A dense mound.

Description: Leaf blade: 11 × 9¼ in. (28 × 23.5 cm); thick chartreuse-yellow turning cream-yellow to ivory-white, widely and irregularly margined rich blue-green, matt above and glaucous below, seersuckered; edge almost flat, widely oval to nearly round with a mucronate tip,

Hosta sieboldiana 'Great Expectations'

heart-shaped pinched to overlapping lobes. Petiole: stout, creamy, outlined in dark blue-green. Flower: see *H. sieboldiana* 'Elegans'.

Comments & Special Needs: Site in two hours of sun followed by light to moderate shade depending on the temperature and on what is desired, a harsher green-yellow or a subtler blue-chartreuse. Subtler colors can be maintained only in cooler climates. In many regions growers find it lacks vigor; indeed, it can dwindle rather than increase in size. Only the arresting tonal variegations of the leaves keep this hosta in favor.

Similar: *H.* 'Great American Expectations', which has greener margins and is thought to be more vigorous.

Sports: **H.* 'Dream Weaver'; *H.* 'Great American Expectations'.

Hosta sieboldiana 'Jim Matthews' (Matthews/Sligh 1998)

MEDIUM–LARGE

Origin: *H. sieboldiana* × *H. sieboldiana*.

Clump Size & Habit: 38⅜ in. wide × 15¾ in. high (96 × 39 cm). An open mound.

Hosta sieboldiana 'Jim Matthews'

Description: Leaf blade: 10½ × 7½ in. (27 × 19 cm); very thick, glaucous, creamy yellow to ivory-white, very widely and irregularly margined dark blue-green with conspicuous chartreuse streaks jetting toward the midrib, prominent, narrowly spaced veins; edge lightly undulate, cupped toward the base, widely oval to round with a mucronate tip, heart-shaped overlapping lobes. Petiole: cream, outlined in blue-green. Flower: see *H. sieboldiana* 'Elegans'.

Comments & Special Needs: Leaf color is more attractive if not exposed to direct sunlight since it varies considerably with differing light intensities. Slow to increase.

Distinguishing Features: Thought to have a more subtle coloring than *H.* 'Great Expectations'. Is more vigorous.

Similar: *H.* 'Dream Weaver'; *H.* 'Great Expectations'; *H.* 'Thunderbolt'.

Hosta sieboldiana 'Northern Mist' (Walters Gardens NR)

MEDIUM–LARGE

Origin: Tissue-cultured sport of *H. sieboldiana* 'Elegans'.

Clump Size & Habit: 40¾ in. wide × 19⅛ in. high (102 × 48 cm). An open mound.

Description: Leaf blade: 10 × 9⅛ in. (25 × 23 cm); thick, creamy yellow turning near white, speckled and misted blue-green, widely and irregularly margined dark blue-green with streaks in two shades of blue-green jetting toward the midrib, matt above and glaucous below, intensely seersuckered; edge undulate and twisted, widely oval to nearly round, lifted at the heart-shaped pinched lobes. Petiole: stout, cream, finely outlined in dark blue-green; fertile and an excellent breeding plant.

Comments & Special Needs: Site in light to moderate shade. Very slow to establish and increase. Although the colors will be richer in cooler climates, the plant will be larger and more vigorous with moderate summer heat and humidity rather than intense heat.

Distinguishing Features: Leaves have a pebbled surface texture with the central variegation having conspicuous netted veining.

Similar: *H.* 'Northern Lights' is even less vigorous but equally attractive.

Sports: *H. sieboldiana* 'Northern Mystery', which is even more streaked and mottled as a young plant; *H.* 'American Masterpiece'.

Hosta sieboldii 'Kabitan' (Maekawa NR)

SMALL–MEDIUM

Origin: Natural sport of *H. sieboldii* found in both Japan and Europe.

Clump Size & Habit: 32 in. wide × 14 in. high (80 × 35 cm). An arching, rippled, somewhat rhizomatous mound.

Description: Leaf blade: 6⅜ × 1½ in. (16 × 4 cm) thin, chartreuse, turning rich golden yellow, narrowly and irregularly margined dark green, satiny above and shiny below, slightly dimpled when mature; edge rippled, arching, lanceolate with an acute tip, tapered open lobes. Peti-

Hosta sieboldiana 'Northern Mist'

Hosta sieboldii 'Kabitan'

ole: flat, chartreuse outlined in dark green. Flower: see *H. sieboldii*.

Comments & Special Needs: Site in good light to light shade. A hot, humid climate is needed to maintain its vigor, when it will increase rapidly, making it suitable as an underplanting to larger hostas or as an edging hosta. In cooler climates, where the leaves will be considerably smaller, it is best grown in a pot with plenty of food and water. Very susceptible to pest damage.

Distinguishing Features: The blade is almost decurrent with the petiole.

Similar: *H.* 'Green Eyes', a selfed *H. sieboldii* 'Kabitan', whose leaf centers are slightly paler, has sported to a yellow-leaved form; *H.* 'Yellow Eyes'; *H.* 'On the Marc'; *H.* 'Peedee Gold Flash'.

Sports: *H.* 'Green Kabitan'.

Hosta sieboldii 'Shiro Kabitan'

Hosta 'Silver Spray'

Hosta sieboldii 'Shiro Kabitan' (Japan)

SMALL

Origin: Natural sport of *H. sieboldii* originally known as *H. sieboldii* 'Haku Chu Han'.

Clump Size & Habit: 18 in. wide × 6⅜ in. high (45 × 16 cm). A low, dense mound.

Description: Leaf blade: 4⅜ × 1 in. (11 × 2.5 cm); thin, pure white turning pale green, irregularly margined dark green with many paler green streaks jetting toward the midrib, matt above and shiny below; edge randomly rippled, elliptic with a sometimes curved, acute tip and tapered open lobes. Petiole: narrow, ivory-green, outlined in dark green. Flower: see *H. sieboldii*.

Comments & Special Needs: A hot, humid climate is necessary to maintain its vigor, when it will increase rapidly, making a colorful underplanting to larger, blue-leaved hostas or as an edging hosta. Liable to revert back to a green-leaved form. Very susceptible to pest damage.

Distinguishing Features: The variegation tends to lose its crisp whiteness toward the end of summer.

Similar: *H.* 'Gay Feather', which has slightly larger leaves; **H.* 'Island Charm'; **H.* 'Masquerade'; *H.* 'Silver Streak', which has leaves that are more twisted.

Hosta 'Silver Spray' (Osbourne 1991)

LARGE

Origin: Unknown.

Clump Size & Habit: 36 in. wide × 21⅛ in. high (90 × 53 cm). An open mound.

Description: Leaf blade: 10 × 9⅛ in. (25 × 23 cm); thick, glaucous gray to gray-green, margined pure white, with occasional streaks jetting toward the midrib, seersuckered; edge rippled, shallowly cupped, widely oval to nearly round with a mucronate tip, heart-shaped open lobes. Petiole: stout, gray-green, outlined in white. Flower: funnel-shaped, slightly striped, pale violet on a thick, upright, bare, glaucous gray-green, 26 in. (65 cm) scape in high summer. Fertility unknown.

Comments & Special Needs: Site in light to moderate shade ensuring a plentiful supply of food and water to prevent or diminish the slight drawstring effect on the leaves. Very slow growing but the leaf color, especially in early summer, is so distinct that it is worth taking trouble to give it extra care and attention. Lovely with *Dicentra* 'Bacchanal'.

Similar: *H.* 'Barbara Ann', which has no hint of the drawstring effect.

Hosta 'Spilt Milk' (M. Seaver 1999)

MEDIUM

Origin: Of *H.* 'Tokudama' ancestry.

Clump Size & Habit: 36 in. wide × 20 in. high (90 × 50 cm). Of mounding habit.

Description: Leaf blade: 9⅛ × 7⅛ in. (23 × 18 cm); thick, glaucous blue-green speckled and narrowly streaked milky white through the blade, the base color becoming slightly more chartreuse toward the midrib, dimpled to crumpled; edge slightly rippled, slightly cupped or convex, widely oval to almost round with a mucronate tip, heart-shaped, overlapping lobes. Petiole: shallow, blue-green. Flower: tubular, near white on an upright, bare, glaucous green, 24 to 30 in. (60 to 75 cm) scape in mid-summer; fertile, green seedpods.

Comments & Special Needs: Site in light to moderate shade. Very slow to increase. Although this once rare hosta is now readily available through micro propagation, plants produced by this method vary considerably. It is therefore

Hosta 'Spilt Milk'

worth seeking out originator stock to acquire a specimen of *H*. 'Spilt Milk', which is identical to the first introduction.

Distinguishing Features: The flecking, misting and streaking are stable, making this hosta instantly recognizable.

Similar: *H. 'Kiwi Blue Marble', which has bluer leaves.

Hosta 'Tattoo' (Avent 1998)

SMALL

Origin: Sport of *H*. 'Little Aurora'.

Clump Size & Habit: 12 in. wide × 6⅜ in. high (30 × 16 cm). A compact mound.

Description: Leaf blade: 2⅜ × 2⅜ in. (6 × 6 cm); of good substance, bright golden yellow irregularly margined light green, each leaf is then "tattooed" with the outline of a dark green maple leaf in the center, matt above and glaucous below; edge almost flat to slightly rippled, almost round with a mucronate tip, heart-shaped pinched lobes. Petiole: narrow, chartreuse to yellow. Flower: see *H*. 'Little Aurora'.

Comments & Special Needs: *H*. 'Tattoo' is a quite distinct modern hosta and much prized by collectors, but it

Hosta 'Tattoo'

can dwindle rather than increase. Its introducer, Tony Avent of Plant Delights Nursery in North Carolina, advises that it be grown in a container until it has bulked up into a clump, ensuring that new roots are developing. Site in dappled morning sun but move to a different location if it is not thriving. Keep moist and well fed. Plant as a foreground specimen or in a container so that the unusual variegation can be seen close up.

Hosta 'Topaz Tiara'

Hosta 'Tortifrons'

Hosta **'Topaz Tiara'** (Walters Gardens 1998)

SMALL

Origin: Tissue-cultured sport of *H.* 'Grand Tiara'.

Clump Size & Habit: 16 in. wide × 8⅜ in. high (40 × 21 cm). A compact mound. Description: Leaf blade: 4 × 3½ in. (10 × 9 cm); thick, matt, chartreuse to muted golden yellow, widely and irregularly margined dark green, with streaks jetting toward the midrib; edge flat to slightly kinked, widely oval with a cuspidate tip, heart-shaped open to pinched lobes. Petiole: chartreuse, outlined in dark green. Flower: see *H.* 'Golden Tiara'.

Comments: Not necessarily an improvement but a must for collectors wishing to grow the complete range of the Tiara Series.

Similar: *H.* 'Emerald Tiara' but with a darker center, less contrast and of thicker substance.

Hosta **'Tortifrons'** (Maekawa NR)

SMALL

Origin: Found in Japanese gardens. A possible *H. longipes* sport.

Clump Size & Habit: 17⅜ in. wide × 8⅜ in. high (43 × 21 cm). An upright mound.

Description: Leaf blade: 5⅛ × 1 in. (13 × 2.5 cm); thick, uneven, leathery, dark olive-green, matt above and glossy below; edge rippled, decurrent with the narrow petiole, narrowly elliptic with an acute tip. Petiole: narrow, dark green. Flower: large, funnel-shaped, lavender with reflexed tips on an upright, bare, green, 15 in. (38 cm) scape in autumn; fertile.

Comments & Special Needs: Site in light to moderate shade in a container or on a raised bed. Slow to increase.

Cannot be successfully reproduced by micropropagation, so it remains a rarity.

Distinguishing Features: The narrow, distorted leaves are held erect and have a distinct twist. This twisting is caused by an aberration in the make-up of the skin cells.

Similar: **H.* 'Embroidery'; **H.* 'Emerald Necklace'; **H.* 'Koryu'; **H.* 'Praying Hands'.

Hosta tsushimensis **'Ogon'** (Japan)

MEDIUM

Origin: Natural sport of *H. tsushimensis*, found in cultivation.

Clump Size & Habit: 26 in. wide × 10 in. high (65 × 25 cm). A diffuse, pendulous mound.

Description: Leaf blade: 6⅜ × 3⅛ in. (16 × 8 cm); thin, chartreuse turning light yellow, matt above and shiny below, closely ribbed veins; edge slightly rippled, arching to pendulous, widely lanceolate with an acute tip, tapered pinched lobes. Petiole: long, narrow, chartreuse to yellow, burgundy-dotted toward the crown. Flower: large, widely funnel-shaped, reflexed, white-striped purple on an upright, sometimes branched, burgundy-dotted, green, 30 in. (75 cm) scape in late summer; fertile.

Comments & Special Needs: Lutescent. Tolerates sun in cooler climates. In the South, grow in high, filtered shade with a plentiful supply of moisture. Still rare in cultivation.

Similar: *H.* 'Whiskey Sour', which has red petioles and leaf tips, is similar to its *H. tsushimensis* 'Ogon' parent. The leaves are of the thicker substance and glossier texture than those of its other parent, *H. yingeri*.

Hosta tsushimensis 'Ogon'

Hosta 'White Christmas'

Hosta venusta 'Kinbotan'

Hosta venusta 'Kinbotan' (Japan)

DWARF

Origin: *H. venusta* seedling.

Clump Size & Habit: 8⅜ in. wide × 4 in. high (21 × 10 cm). A compact mound.

Description: Leaf blade: 2 × ¾ in. (5 × 2.5 cm); of average substance, smooth, mid-green, narrowly margined golden yellow turning almost light green with many streaks jetting toward the midrib; edge slightly undulate to kinked, folded, oval with a cuspidate tip, tapered open lobes. Petiole: narrow, green, outlined in yellow. Flower: funnel-shaped, rich lavender on an upright, bare, leafy, green 15 in. (38 cm) scape in mid- to high summer; fertile.

Comments & Special Needs: Site in good light to light shade. Keep in a pot until the root system is well established; after that it is best grown in a container, sink or trough with other tiny hostas. Slow to increase and not easy to maintain in vigorous growth.

Distinguishing Features: The scapes tower above the low-growing leaf mound.

Similar: *H.* 'Gaijin', which is slightly larger; *H.* 'Orphan Annie', which is more vigorous.

Hosta 'White Christmas' (Krossa 1996)

MEDIUM

Origin: Stable form of *H.* 'Fortunei Krossa's Variegated'.

Clump Size & Habit: 25⅛ in. wide × 15 in. high (63 × 38 cm). An open mound.

Description: Leaf blade: 8⅜ × 4 in. (21 × 10 cm); thin, ivory to pure white, narrowly and irregularly margined dark green with some streaks jetting toward the midrib, satiny above and shinier below; edge conspicuously twisted with a sometimes curved, cuspidate tip, oval with rounded open to pinched lobes. Petiole: narrow, ivory, finely lined and margined dark green. Flower: funnel-shaped, drooping, pale lavender on an upright, leafy, ivory, 25⅛ in. (63 cm) scape in mid-summer; sterile.

Comments & Special Needs: Early to emerge. Once though to be a sport of *H.* 'Undulata'. Careful siting is essential. Tolerates long periods of good light but not exposure to full sun. Succeeds best in cooler regions and requires expert cultivation.

Distinguishing Features: The raceme is often surrounded by attractive ivory bracts, finely margined dark green.

Similar: *H.* 'Emerald Crust'; *H.* 'Undulata', with which it is often confused.

Sports: *H.* 'Night before Christmas'; *H.* 'Robert's Rapier'.

HARDINESS ZONE MAPS

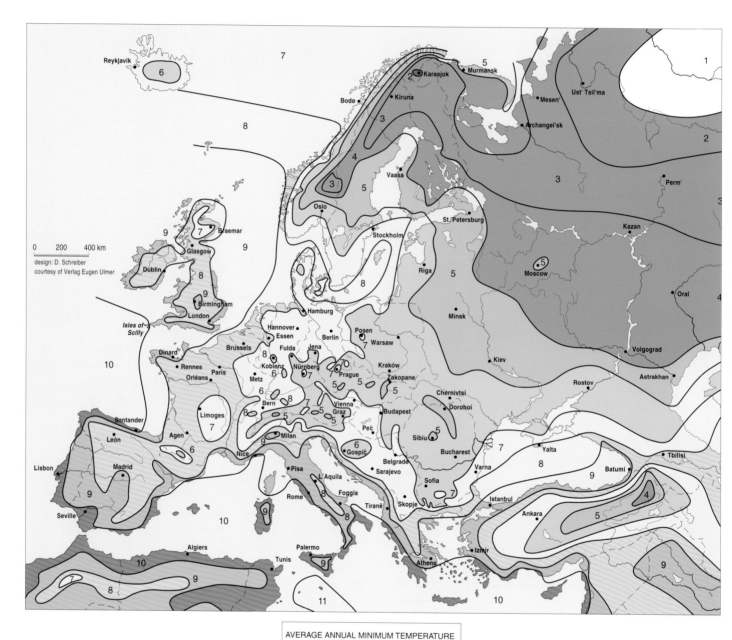

AVERAGE ANNUAL MINIMUM TEMPERATURE		
Temperature (°C)	Zone	Temperature (°F)
-45.6 and Below	1	Below -50
-45.5 to -40.0	2	-50 to -40
-40.0 to -34.5	3	-40 to -30
-34.4 to -28.9	4	-30 to -20
-28.8 to -23.4	5	-20 to -10
-23.3 to -17.8	6	-10 to 0
-17.7 to -12.3	7	0 to 10
-12.2 to -6.7	8	10 to 20
-6.6 to -1.2	9	20 to 30
-1.1 to 4.4	10	30 to 40
4.5 and Above	11	40 and Above

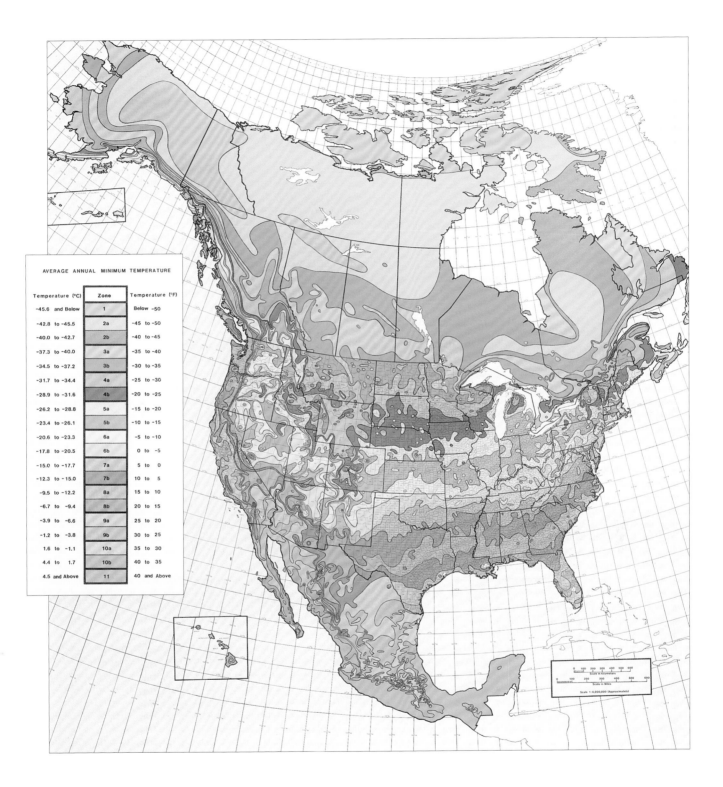

AVERAGE ANNUAL MINIMUM TEMPERATURE

Temperature (°C)	Zone	Temperature (°F)
-45.6 and Below	1	Below -50
-42.8 to -45.5	2a	-45 to -50
-40.0 to -42.7	2b	-40 to -45
-37.3 to -40.0	3a	-35 to -40
-34.5 to -37.2	3b	-30 to -35
-31.7 to -34.4	4a	-25 to -30
-28.9 to -31.6	4b	-20 to -25
-26.2 to -28.8	5a	-15 to -20
-23.4 to -26.1	5b	-10 to -15
-20.6 to -23.3	6a	-5 to -10
-17.8 to -20.5	6b	0 to -5
-15.0 to -17.7	7a	5 to 0
-12.3 to -15.0	7b	10 to 5
-9.5 to -12.2	8a	15 to 10
-6.7 to -9.4	8b	20 to 15
-3.9 to -6.6	9a	25 to 20
-1.2 to -3.8	9b	30 to 25
1.6 to -1.1	10a	35 to 30
4.4 to 1.7	10b	40 to 35
4.5 and Above	11	40 and Above

Scale in Kilometers

Scale in Miles

Scale 1:4,000,000 (Approximate)

The BEST HOSTAS *for* DIFFERENT PURPOSES

HOSTAS FOR FLOWER ARRANGEMENTS

H. 'Bold Ruffles'
H. 'Dragon Wings'
H. 'Fortunei Aureomarginata'
H. 'Frances Williams'
H. 'June'
H. 'June Moon'
H. 'Krossa Regal'
H. 'Lakeside Black Satin'
H. *longissima*
H. 'Minuteman'
H. 'Morning Light'
H. 'Niagara Falls'
H. 'Praying Hands'
H. *sieboldiana* 'Elegans'
H. 'Wide Brim'

HOSTAS WITH THICK SUBSTANCE

H. 'Aspen Gold'
H. 'Bubba'
H. 'Christmas Tree'
H. 'Grand Slam'
H. 'Green Sheen'
H. 'H. D. Thoreau'
H. *laevigata*
H. 'Lakeside Accolade'
H. 'Lakeside Looking Glass'
H. *longipes* 'Hypoglauca'
H. 'Potomac Pride'
H. 'Quilting Bee'
H. 'Rhapsody in Blue'
H. *rupifraga*
H. 'Sea Monster'
H. *yingeri*

HOSTAS WITH LEAVES OF PIECRUST EDGES

H. 'Betty'
H. 'Curls'

H. 'Cutting Edge'
H. 'Devon Discovery'
H. 'Elisabeth'
H. 'Ginsu Knife'
H. 'Grand Slam'
H. 'Jimmy Crack Corn'
H. 'Manhattan'
H. 'Moon Waves'
H. 'Niagara Falls'
H. 'Permanent Wave'
H. 'Quill'
H. 'Sparky'
H. 'Tutu'

HOSTAS WITH VERY WIDE MARGINS

H. 'Abiqua Moonbeam'
H. 'American Halo'
H. 'Captain Kirk'
H. 'Grand Tiara'
H. 'Liberty'
H. 'Little Bo Peep'
H. 'Lodestar'
H. 'Millie's Memoirs'
H. *montana* 'Aureomarginata'
H. 'Patriot'
H. 'Sergeant Pepper'
H. 'Sultana'
H. 'Twilight'
H. 'Wide Brim'

HOSTAS THAT ARE SUN TOLERANT

H. 'Abba Dabba Do'
H. 'August Moon'
H. 'Carolina Sunshine'
H. 'Circle of Light'
H. 'Dee's Golden Jewel'
H. 'Dixie Chick'
H. 'Eagle's Nest'

H. 'Fortunei Aureomarginata'
H. 'Fragrant Bouquet'
H. 'Guacamole'
H. 'Joshua's Banner'
H. 'Korean Snow'
H. *plantaginea*
H. 'Sum and Substance'

HOSTAS FOR SOUTHERN GARDENS (SHADE IS ESSENTIAL)

H. 'Alex Summers'
H. 'Alvatine Taylor'
H. 'Antioch'
H. 'Chelsea Ore'
H. 'Color Parade'
H. 'Daybreak'
H. 'Donahue Piecrust'
H. 'Frosted Jade'
H. 'Hadspen Samphire'
H. 'Heavenly Tiara'
H. 'June'
H. 'Krossa Regal'
H. 'Lakeside Shore Master'
H. 'Last Dance'
H. 'Little Sunspot'
H. 'Patriot'
H. 'Piedmont Gold'
H. *plantaginea*
H. 'Queen of Islip'
H. 'Saint Elmo's Fire'
H. 'Satisfaction'
H. 'So Sweet'
H. 'Sum and Substance'
H. 'Tambourine'

HOSTAS FOR BREEDING

H. 'Beatrice'
H. 'Breeder's Choice'
H. 'Color Parade'

H. 'Donahue Piecrust'
H. 'Dorothy Benedict'
H. 'Dorset Blue'
H. 'Dorset Clown'
H. 'Fascination'
H. 'Frances Williams'
H. 'Galaxy'
H. 'Gold Regal'
H. 'Halcyon'
H. 'High Fat Cream'
H. *laevigata*
H. *montana*
H. 'Neat Splash'
H. *pycnophylla*
H. *sieboldiana*
H. 'Splish Splash'
H. 'Sum and Substance'
H. *venusta*
H. 'Whoopie'
H. 'William Lachman'
H. *yingeri*

HOSTAS WITH OUTSTANDING FLOWERS

H. 'Blue Monday'
H. 'Carrie Ann'
H. 'Crystal Chimes'
H. 'Crystal Moon'
H. 'Diana Remembered'
H. 'Fall Bouquet'
H. 'Fragrant Dream'
H. 'Ginsu Knife'
H. 'Moonlight Sonata'
H. *plantaginea* and forms
H. 'Red October'
H. 'Rosedale Barnie'
H. 'Royal Standard'
H. 'Sweet Sunshine'
H. 'Tall Boy'
H. 'Temple Bells'

WHERE TO SEE HOSTAS

BELGIUM
Arboretum Kalmthout
Heuval 2, B2920 Kalmthout

CANADA
Trevor Cole
RR2
Kinburn, Ontario K0A 2H0
(by appointment only)

Dr. Phillip and Margaret Little
53 Roosevelt Avenue
Waterloo, Ontario N2L 2N3
(by appointment only)

Alex Waterhouse-Hayward
5909 Athlone
Vancouver, BC V6M 3A3
(by appointment only)

FRANCE
M. Thoby
Pépinière Botanique
Chateau de Gaujacq, 40330
    Gaujacq
(by appointment only)

Didier Willery
1 Petites Rues
62270 Boubers-sur-Canche
(by appointment only)

NETHERLANDS
Arboretum Trompenburg
Groene Wetering
46, 3062 PC Rotterdam

NEW ZEALAND
Barry Sligh
Taunton Gardens
Allandale, RD 1
Lyttleton (South Island)

UNITED KINGDOM
Dr. Gwen Black
The Beeches
42 The Green
Houghton, Carlisle CA3 0LL
(by appointment only)

Ann and Roger Bowden
Cleave House
Sticklepath
Okehampton, Devon EX20
    2NN
(by appointment only)

Paula Caiger
21 Brunswick Street
Walthamstow Village,
    London E17 9NB
(by appointment only)

Golden Acre Park
Leeds City Council
Bramhope
Leeds, Yorkshire LS16 5NZ

The Manor House
Heslington, York YO1 5ER
(by appointment only)

National Plant Collection of
    Hosta
Highgrove House
c/o NCCPG
The Stable Courtyard, Wisley
    Garden
Woking, Surrey GU23 6QP

National Plant Collection of
    Hosta
Una Dunnett
44 Windermere Drive
Warndon, Worcester WR4 9JA
(by appointment only)

John and Bee Newbold
Netherbury
36 Worgret Road
Wareham, Dorset BH20 4PN
(by appointment only)

The Savill Garden
Windsor Great Park, Wick
    Lane
Englefield Green, Surrey
    TW20 0UU

Tim Saville
12 Burnham Close
Cheadle Hulme, Cheshire
    SK8 6DN
(by appointment only)

Derrick and Denise Targett
The Old Rectory
Somerby, Lincolnshire DN38
    6EX
(by appointment only)

UNITED STATES
Steve and Helen Chamberlain
105 Academy Street
Manlius, New York 13104
(by appointment only)

David and Roberta Chopko
93 Intervale Road
Boonton, New Jersey 07005
(by appointment only)

Dubuque Arboretum and
    Botanical Gardens
3800 Arboretum Drive
Dubuque, Iowa 52001
www.dbq.com/arboretum

Longwood Gardens
Idea Garden
Kennett Square, Pennsylvania
    19348
www.longwood.gardens.org

Sandy and Larry Mackle
460 Goodhue
Bloomfield Hills, Michigan
    48304
(by appointment only)

Michigan State University
    Garden
Hidden Lake Gardens
6280 West Munger Road (M-
    50)
Tipton, Michigan 49287
www.cpp.mus.edu/hlg

Minnesota Landscape
  Arboretum
Hosta Glade
3675 Arboretum Drive
Chanhassen, Minnesota
  55317
www.arboretum.umn.edu

Pine Tree State Arboretum
153 Hospital Street
August, Maine 04330
www.communityforest.org

Warren and Ali Pollock
202 Hackney Circle
Surrey Park
Wilmington, Delaware 19803
(by appointment only)

Peter and Jean Ruh
9448 Mayfield Road
Chesterland, Ohio 44026

W. George Schmid
Hosta Hill
4417 Goodfellows Court
Tucker, Georgia 30084
(by appointment only)

The Scott Arboretum of
  Swarthmore College
Hosta Garden and Terry
  Shane Teaching Garden
500 College Avenue
Swarthmore, Pennsylvania
  19081
www.scottarboretum.org

Barbara and Robert Tiffany
27 Cafferty Road
Point Pleasant, Pennsylvania
  18950
(by appointment only)

Toledo Botanical Garden
5403 Elmer Drive
Toledo, Ohio 43615
www.toledogarden.org

Van and Shirley Wade
1288 Gatton Rocks Road
Bellville, Ohio 44813

Dr. James and Sandy Wilkins
7469 Hunters Ridge
Jackson, Michigan 49201
(by appointment only)

Toni Wright
3070 Hudson Way
Decatur, Georgia 30033
(by appointment only)

SOURCES *for* HOSTAS

NETHERLANDS
Marco Fransen Hostas
Hostakwekerij
Paradijsweg 5
2461 TK Ter Aar

UNITED KINGDOM
Ann and Roger Bowden
   Hostas
Sticklepath
Okehampton, Devon EX20
   2NL

Goldbrook Plants
Hoxne
Eye, Suffolk IP21 5AN

Merlin Hostas
Bicton
Shrewsbury, Shropshire SY3
   8EF

Mickfield Hostas
The Poplars
Mickfield
Stowmarket, Suffolk IP14
   5LH

Park Green Nurseries
Wetheringsett
Stowmarket, Suffolk IP14
   5QH

UNITED STATES
American Hostas and Daylilies
   and Other Perennials
Wade and Gatton Nurseries
1288 Gatton Rocks Road
Bellville, Ohio 44813

The Azalea Patch
2010 Mountain Road
Joppa, Maryland 21085

The Blueberry Patch
1285 West Hanley Road
Mansfield, Ohio 44904

Bridgewood Gardens
P.O. Box 391
Strasburg, Virginia 22657

Conner Nursery and Gardens
6605 North Smith Road
Edwards, Illinois 61528

Cooks Nursery
Eagle Bay Hosta Gardens
10749 Bennett Road
Dunkirk, New York 14048

Green Hill Farm
P.O. Box 16306
Chapel Hill, North Carolina
   27516

Hilltop Farm
315 N. State Highway F
Ash Grove, Missouri 65604

Homestead Division of
   Sunnybrook Farm
9448 Mayfield Road
Chesterland, Ohio 44026
Jim's Hostas
11676 Robin Hood Drive
Dubuque, Iowa 52001

Klehm Song Sparrow Peren-
   nial Farm
13101 East Rye Road
Avalon, Wisconsin 53505

Kuk's Forest Nursery
10174 Barr Road
Brecksville, Ohio 44141

Lakeside Acres
8119 Roy Lane
Ooletwah, Tennessee 37363

Naylor Creek Nursery
2610 West Valley Road
Chimacum, Washington
   98325

Pine Forest Gardens
556 Ellison Road
Tyrone, Georgia 30290

Plant Delights Nursery
9241 Sauls Road
Raleigh, North Carolina
   27603

Savory's Gardens
5300 Whiting Avenue
Edina, Minnesota 55439

Schmid Nursery and Gardens
847 Westwood Boulevard
Jackson, Michigan 49203

Silvers-Elbert Nursery
2024 McDaniel Mill Road
Conyers, Georgia 30094

Soules Garden
5809 Rahke Road
Indianapolis, Indiana 46217

Walden-West Hosta
5744 Crooked Finger Road
Scotts Mills, Oregon 97375

White Oak Nursery
6145 Oak Point Court
Peoria, Illinois 61614

Bill Zumbar
Adrian's Flowers of Fashion
   Nursery
855 Parkway Boulevard
Alliance, Ohio 44601

HOSTA SOCIETIES
& OTHER RESOURCES

The American Hosta Society
Sandie Markland, Membership Secretary
8702 Pinnacle Rock Ct.
Lorton, Virginia 22079
sam020857@msn.com
www.hosta.org

The British Hosta and Hemerocallis
    Society
Lynda Hinton, Hon., Membership
    Secretary
Toft Monks, The Hythe
Rodborough Common, Gloucestershire
    GL5 5BN
bhhs@classicfm.net
www.hostahem.org

The Dutch Hosta Society
Secretariaat, Nederlandse Hosta
Vereniging, Molenweg 45, 1619
EV Andijk
p.h.vriend@wxs.nl

Eureka Hosta/Iris Reference Guide
Ken Gregory
P.O. Box 7611
Asheville, North Carolina 28802
www.gardeneureka.com

The National Council for the Conserva-
    tion of Plants and Gardens
The Stable Courtyard, Wisley Garden
Woking, Surrey GU23 6QP

GLOSSARY

Acute Sharp pointed, as in *H. longissima*, *H.* 'Tardiflora'.

Albescent Becoming white.

Apomictic Of female flowers which form seed without having been pollinated or fertilized.

Bract A modified leaf usually at the base of a flower stem or sometimes forming part of the flower head itself.

Cordate Heart-shaped: strictly applied only to a pair of lobes at the base of the leaf but loosely used of hosta leaves (such as those of *H. sieboldiana*), which have the outline of a romanticized heart.

Cross A hybrid, or as a verb to create a hybrid.

Crown The upper part of the rootstock from which shoots grow and to which they die back in the fall.

Cuspidate Of a leaf tip, sometimes long and thin arising gradually from an oval leaf, as in *H. montana*.

Decurrent Running together, as when a leaf stalk and leaf blade merge into one another without obvious differentiation.

Dicotyledon A plant whose seedlings have two cotyledons or seed leaves, noticeably different from the normal leaves. One of the two great classes of flowering plants.

Diffuse Of a leaf mound that is wide-spreading but not dense.

Dimpled Of a leaf blade whose surface is pocked by small, round indentations.

Diploid A plant having the normal number of chromosomes for its species or variety.

Drawstring effect The puckering of the edge of a leaf caused by the center of the leaf growing faster than the margin, which causes the margin to look as though it has been pulled tight by a drawstring.

Fasciated A freak condition in which the stem of a plant becomes flattened, giving the impression that several stems have fused together. The flowers at the tip of such a shoot may also be abnormal.

Floriferous Free-flowering.

Furrowed Widely and deeply ribbed.

Glaucous Bluish green or bluish gray or covered with a bluish waxy coating.

Hybrid The offspring resulting from the mating of two genetically different parents.

Interface The junction between the inner and outer margin of a leaf.

Jetting Refers to a variegation that sends streaks of color, beginning at the leaf margin, toward the center of the leaf.

Lanceolate Lance-shaped.

Lutescent Becoming yellow.

Melting out Where the center of the leaves of some hostas, especially those with white centers, first shows signs of scorching but then disappears, as though it has melted away.

Monocotyledon A plant whose seedlings have a single cotyledon or seed leaf, usually similar to the adult leaf.

Mucronate Of a round leaf that is abruptly terminated by a short tip, as in *H.* 'Tokudama'.

Mutation A spontaneous, vegetative variation from the original type caused by accidental changes in the genetic make-up of the plant. Such mutations are usually deleterious to the plant, but when they are decorative, they may be maintained in cultivation by vegetative propagation.

Navel The apparent hole that appears when the lobes at the base of a hosta leaf overlap.

Oblique Of flower stems that lean away from the vertical.

Obtuse A leaf tip that is blunt-ended, as in *H.* 'Decorata'.

Ovate Egg-shaped. Of a leaf where the broadest part is nearest the base.

Pedicel The short stalk that connects a flower to a flower stem.

Polyploid Having more than the normal number of chromosomes for the species.

Pruinose The powdery, velvetlike, white substance that coats the underside of some leaves, such as those of *H. hypoleuca* and *H. pycnophylla*.

Puckering An exaggerated form of seersuckering, making folds in the leaf.

Raceme An elongated, unbranched flower head in which each flower is borne on an individual stalk or pedicel, with the youngest flowers at the apex.

Rhizomatous Having underground stems that last more than one season and that often grow horizontally, producing new plants at the ends furthest from the parent.

Rugose Wrinkled, a term usually applied to the surface of leaves.

Scape A flower stem that arises directly from ground level and bears no leaves. Used to refer to the flower stems of hostas which, though they may bear bracts, are without leaves.

Seersuckered Resembling seersuckered cloth, a lightweight cotton or linen fabric, and characterized by intense, even dimpling.

Sport A gardener's term for a mutation.

Stolon, stoloniferous A stolon is a horizontal stem produced either above or below ground, producing roots and new shoots at its tip.

Subtended Carried below: used of bracts on flower stems that are carried below the flower.

Tetraploid Having double the number of chromosomes of the typical plant.

Undulate Wavy, referring either to the whole leaf blade or to the margin. A margin can also be described as rippled or more closely piecrusted.

Viridescent Becoming green.

BIBLIOGRAPHY

Aden, P., ed. 1990. *The Hosta Book*. 2nd ed. Portland, Oregon: Timber Press.

Bond, S. 1992. *Hostas*. London: Ward Lock.

Brickell, C. D. 1968. "Notes from Wisley." *Journal of the Royal Horticultural Society* 93: 365–372.

Callaway, D. J., and M. Brett, eds. 2000. *Breeding Ornamental Plants*. Portland, Oregon: Timber Press.

Fox, R. 1997. *The Gardener's Book of Pests and Diseases*. London: Batsford.

Greenwood, P., A. Halstead, A. R. Chase, and D. Gilrein. 2000. *American Horticultural Society Pests and Diseases*. New York: Dorling Kindersley.

Grenfell, D. 1990. *Hosta: The Flowering Foliage Plant*. Portland, Oregon: Timber Press; London: Batsford.

Grenfell, D. 1993. *Hostas*. Pershore, Worcestershire, United Kingdom: The Hardy Plant Society.

Grenfell, D. 1996. *The Gardener's Guide to Growing Hostas*. Portland, Oregon: Timber Press; Newton Abbot, Devon: David and Charles.

Grenfell, D. 2002. *Hostas*. RHS Wisley Handbook. London: Cassell Illustrated.

Hillier Nurseries. 1988. *The Hilliers Manual of Trees and Shrubs*. Newton Abbot, Devon: David and Charles.

Huxley, A. 1981. *The Penguin Encyclopedia of Gardening*. London: Allen Lane.

Hylander, N. 1954. "The Genus *Hosta* in Swedish Gardens." *Acta Horti Bergiani* 1b (11): 350–366.

Kohlein, F. 1993. *Hosta [Funkien]*. Stuttgart: Ulmer.

Mikolajski, A. 1997. *Hostas*. The New Plant Library. New York and London: Lorenz Books.

Schmid, W. G. 1992, 1993. *The Genus Hosta—Giboshi Zoku*. Portland, Oregon: Timber Press; London: Batsford.

Stearn, W. T. 1996. *Botanical Latin*. Portland, Oregon: Timber Press.

Trehane, P., et al., eds. 1995. *International Code of Nomenclature for Cultivated Plants*. Wimborne, Dorset, United Kingdom: Quarterjack Press.

Wade, V. 2002. *The American Hosta Guide*. Bellville, Ohio: Wade and Gatton Nurseries.

Watanabe, K. 1985. *The Observation and Cultivation of Hosta*. Tokyo: New Science Company.

Westcott, C. 1973. *The Gardener's Bug Book*. New York: Doubleday.

Zilis, M. R. 2001. *The Hosta Handbook*. Rochelle, Illinois: Q & Z Nursery.

OTHER HELPFUL INFORMATION

The Hosta Journal. Published by the American Hosta Society.

British Hosta and Hemerocallis Society Bulletin. Published by the British Hosta and Hemerocallis Society.

The Hosta Finder. Published annually by Steve Greene of Sudbury, Massachusetts.

The Green Hill Gossip. Newsletter published by Robert Solberg of Green Hill Farm, Chapel Hill, North Carolina.

INDEX *of* HOSTA NAMES